Florida

D0068369

Fodor's Travel Publications,
New York & London

Fodor's Florida

Editors: Christopher Billy, Holly Hughes
Editorial Contributors: April Athey, Al Burt, Kathryn Kilgore, George Leposky, Rosalie Leposky, Honey Naylor, Karen Smith, Joice Veselka, David Wilkening, Fred Wright
Art Director: Fabrizio La Rocca
Cartographer: David Lindroth
Illustrator: Karl Tanner
Cover Photograph: Krist/Leo de Wys

Cover Design: Vignelli Associates

Special Sales

Fodor's Travel Publications are available at special discounts for bulk purchases (100 copies or more) for sales promotions or premiums. Special editions, including personalized covers, excerpts of existing guides, and corporate imprints, can be created in large quantities for special needs. For more information write to Special Marketing, Fodor's Travel Publications, 201 East 50th St., New York, NY 10022. Inquiries from the United Kingdom should be sent to Fodor's Travel Publications, 30–32 Bedford Square, London WC1B 3SG.

MANUFACTURED IN THE UNITED STATES OF AMERICA
10 9 8 7 6 5 4 3 2 1

Contents

Maps

Foreword

Florida is one of the world's most popular tourist destinations. Visitors from far and near are attracted to the state's sandy beaches, warm and sunny climate, and theme parks such as Disney World. Travelers find Florida rich in historic sites, vast stretches of wildlife preserves, fine restaurants and accommodations to suit every budget. Our Florida writers have put together information on the widest possible range of activities, and within that range present you with selections of events and places that will be safe, worthwhile, and of good value. The descriptions we provide are just enough for you to make your own informed choices from among our selections.

This is an exciting time for Fodor's, as we continue our ambitious program to rewrite, reformat, and redesign all 140 of our guides. Here are just a few of the new features:

★ Brand-new computer-generated maps locating all the top atattractions, hotels, restaurants, and shops

★ A unique system of numbers and legends to help readers move effortlessly between text and maps

★ A new star rating system for hotels and restaurants

★ Restaurant reviews by major food critics around the world

★ Stamped, self-addressed postcards, bound into every guide, give readers a chance to help evaluate hotels and restaurants

★ Complete page redesign for instant retrieval of information

★ FODOR'S CHOICE—Our favorite museums, beaches, cafés, romantic hideaways, festivals, and more

★ HIGHLIGHTS—An insider's look at the most important developments in tourism during the past year

★ TIME OUT—The best and most convenient lunch stops along exploring routes

★ Exclusive background essays create a powerful portrait of each destination

★ A mini-journal for travelers to keep track of their own itineraries and addresses

While every care has been taken to assure the accuracy of the information in this guide, the passage of time will always bring change, and, consequently, the publisher cannot accept responsibility for errors that may occur.

All prices and opening times quoted here are based on information available to us at press time. Hours and admission fees may change, however, and the prudent traveler will avoid inconvenience by calling ahead.

Fodor's wants to hear about your travel experiences, both pleasant and unpleasant. When a hotel or restaurant fails to live up to its billing, let us know, and we will investigate the complaint and revise our entries where the facts warrant it.

Send your letters to the editors of Fodor's Travel Publications, 201 E. 50th Street, New York, NY 10022.

Highlights '90 and Fodor's Choice

Highlights '90

The hotel boom continues throughout Florida. Palm Beach's latest and probably last hotel (due to strict zoning), the 169-room **Ocean Grand,** will open early in 1990 at 2800 S. Ocean Boulevard. The first hotel built under new zoning regulations along Fort Lauderdale Beach, unnamed at press time, is scheduled for completion in late summer. In Miami, the 40-room **Miami River Inn** expects to open its four historic structures along the river early in the year, and construction is just beginning on a 400-room hotel in the mixed-use **Brickell Gateway** development on Brickell Avenue between 14th Lane and 14th Terrace. Port Charlotte's 175-room **Ranger Inn** will open in late 1990; it's situated next to the Charlotte County Stadium where the Texas Rangers baseball club holds spring training. At Walt Disney World, Westin Hotels opened the 760-room **Walt Disney World Swan Resort** in late 1989. Following in 1990 will be the 1,510-room Sheraton-operated **Dolphin Hotel and Convention Center,** the 634-room **Disney Yacht Club Hotel,** and the 580-room **Disney Beach Club.**

Ft. Lauderdale's new **Performing Arts Center/Riverwalk,** which will include two theaters (one with 2,700 seats, the other with 600), will open in late 1990. By 1991 the new riverwalk with restaurants and shops will connect the theaters with Las Olas Boulevard. Across the state, the new $130 million, 14-acre **Tampa Convention Center** on the Hillsborough River in downtown Tampa opens in the fall of 1990. Historic Pensacola Village's new **Cultural Art Center** incorporates the old County Records Building and Jail, built in 1912. The Pensacola Little Theater will perform there, and 26,000 square feet of museum display space will accommodate local and traveling exhibitions. The first show, which opened in late 1989, honored Pensacola native Daniel "Chappie" James, Jr., who was the only black four-star general in the U.S. Air Force and the only man to hold that rank during the Vietnam era.

For the first time since Prohibition, Florida law now allows brew-pubs and microbreweries to produce beer for on-property consumption. In 1989 **McGuire's Irish Pub** in Pensacola and **Zum Alten Fritz,** a Miami restaurant, began offering free brewery tours. A brew-pub opening was planned in Tampa in late 1989, and other Florida brew-pubs expect to open early in 1990.

On the sports scene, 14,000 amateur Florida athletes will participate in 32 Olympic-style events during the **Sunshine State Games** in July 1990 in Miami's Arena, Knight Center, Orange Bowl Stadium, Tropical Park, and the North and South campuses of Miami-Dade Community College. **Homestead's** 186-acre baseball complex will open late in 1990 and will welcome a major-league team for spring training in 1991. The **Minnesota Twins** will hold spring training in 1991 in Lee County's new 7,500-seat stadium in Fort Myers. In 1991, Tampa Stadium will host the National Football League's **Silver Anniversary Super Bowl XXV** on January 27, at the height of Tampa's annual Gasparilla Festival.

In Central Florida's attractions belt, Metropolitan Life Insurance Company's **Life and Health Pavilion** was due to open late in 1989 in Epcot Center's Future World section at Walt Disney World. **Universal Studios Florida** plans to open in the spring of 1990, and Kennedy Space Center's **SPACE-PORT USA** is adding a new free 20-minute, 70mm film, *The Boy from Mars,* in its Galaxy Theater.

In early 1990 Henry Ford's winter home, **Mangoes**, in Fort Myers will be open to the public. Built in 1911, Mangoes is on the south (downriver) side of Thomas Edison's winter home and has been restored to its 1920s appearance.

By late 1990, Tampa's **Lowry Park Zoo** plans to complete a $7 million, 12-acre addition, including a new **"Florida at Night"** building featuring native nocturnal creatures, a manatee research center, and the 8-acre Lykes Florida Wildlife Center, where you'll be able to stroll among native plants and animals found from the Panhandle to the Keys.

The USS *Lexington,* an aircraft carrier based at Pensacola Naval Air Station for flight training, will dock most weekends at the Port of Pensacola and be open for free public tours through 1991. The enlarged **National Museum of Naval Aviation** on the Naval Air Station's grounds will be dedicated in October 1990, and President Bush is expected to attend. New displays in the museum include the only F-14 "Tomcat" on public view and four Blue Angel Sky Hawks suspended in a diamond formation in a new 7-story atrium.

Disney-MGM Studios and Universal Studios Florida

The silver screen has come to Central Florida. By mid-1990 you'll be able to explore the mystique and mechanics of the movies at two working studios just 12 miles apart from each other. One of these attractions, the **Disney-MGM Studios Theme Park** at Walt Disney World, opened to the public in 1989. The second, **Universal Studios Florida** in Orlando, is scheduled to open its doors to tourists in May 1990.

Both studios will produce feature films, TV shows, commercials, industrial films, and corporate audiovisual presentations. Independent filmmakers will be able to rent sound stages, office space, and post-production editing facilities at both complexes.

At both studios you can stroll along soundproofed corridors overlooking cavernous sound stages where movies and TV shows are produced. You may also be invited to join the audience for taping a TV show.

Back-lot tours promise to be popular attractions at both studios. Visitors get a chance to visit huge outdoor sets that simulate shooting locations and familiar scenes. The ride through the back lot at Disney-MGM traverses a New York cityscape and an "Anywhere U. S. A." avenue of suburban house facades (including the one where the "Golden Girls" live). Universal's back lot will offer some 50 different locations, including San Francisco's Fisherman's Wharf, 1930s Chicago, the New York waterfront, and the Bates Motel and house from *Psycho IV*.

"Thrill" rides are designed to showcase special-effects technology. In Disney-MGM's **Catastrophe Canyon** on the Backstage Studio Tour, your tram pauses at an oil field in a rocky canyon, where you are shaken and jostled by a violent earthquake. Oil tanks explode with a deafening roar, and you feel the heat. Finally, an intense thunderstorm and flash flood quench the fire. Universal is planning its own earthquake (this one in San Francisco), a ride on a pontoon boat that is attacked by the killer shark from *Jaws*, and a **Kongfrontation** experience during which the 37-foot-tall ape will pick up your Roosevelt Island tram car.

Both studios are also planning to offer strong doses of sci-fi space fantasy. Disney-MGM is collaborating with George Lucas of *Star Wars* on a **Star Tours** ride scheduled to open in the winter of 1990. With Steven Spielberg serving as creative consultant, Universal will employ similar technology to take you on a bike ride to **E. T.**'s home planet. Flight-simulator technology and Spielberg's touch also will be evident in Universal's ***Back to the Future*** time-travel ride in Doc Brown's gull-wing car.

Visitors can also gain insights into the art of animation. At Disney-MGM you can watch films and videos that explain the tools and techniques of animation art, stroll through an elevated corridor overlooking the animation studios to watch artists at work, see film clips of animated Disney classics, and emerge through a store selling pricey posters and pricier original drawings. Universal promises a more innovative approach to animation in **The Funtastic World of Hanna-Barbera**, where an adventure experience will give you the feeling of being inside a cartoon during a high-speed chase.

Hours: At either studio, plan to arrive when the park opens—9 *AM* for Disney-MGM, 9:30 *AM* for Universal—to beat the midday mob scene. Disney-MGM covers just 135 acres, which is a relatively small area for a theme park. Universal Studios will have about 200 acres.

After the crowds thin out about 4 *PM*, you can enjoy a pleasant evening at Disney-MGM until closing time, which ranges from 7 to 10 *PM*. Universal plans to close at 6 *PM* for most of the year, but will stay open as late as 9 *PM* in peak season.

Fodor's Choice

No two people will agree on what makes a perfect vacation, but it's fun and helpful to know what others think. We hope you'll have a chance to experience some of Fodor's Choices yourself while visiting Florida. For detailed information about each entry, refer to the appropriate chapter in this guidebook.

Sights

The Gulf of Mexico at sunset, particularly at Mallory Square in Key West, where sunset watching is an evening ritual

The boardwalk at Royal Palm Hammock in the Everglades

Art Deco District in Miami Beach

The main span of Sunshine Skyway Bridge, St. Petersburg

The eight-mile Palm Beach Bicycle Trail along Lake Worth

Gulf of Mexico beaches seen from a fixed-wing glider at Clearwater

White tigers at Busch Gardens, Tampa

Singing Apes of Borneo, Central Florida Zoo, Sanford

The view from the battlements at the Castillo de San Marcos, St. Augustine

San Agustin Antiguo, a restored Spanish colonial village in St. Augustine

Edison's Home, with adjoining museum displaying many of his inventions, Fort Myers

Hotels

Grand Bay Hotel, Coconut Grove *(Very Expensive)*

Indian River Plantation, Stuart *(Very Expensive)*

Marquesa Hotel, Key West *(Very Expensive)*

South Seas Plantation, Captiva Island *(Very Expensive)*

Amelia Island Plantation, Amelia Island *(Expensive–Very Expensive)*

Jacksonville Omni Hotel, Jacksonville *(Expensive–Very Expensive)*

Little Palm Island, Little Torch Key *(Very Expensive)*

Sandestin Beach Resort, Destin *(Expensive–Very Expensive)*

Bahia Mar Quality Royale Hotel and Yacht Center, Fort Lauderdale *(Expensive)*

Disney Inn, Walt Disney World *(Expensive)*

Grand Floridian Hotel, Walt Disney World *(Expensive)*

Pier House, Key West *(Expensive)*

Don CeSar Hotel, St. Petersburg Beach *(Moderate)*

Knights Inn Orlando Maingaite East, Walt Disney World *(Inexpensive)*

Snug Harbor, Amelia Island *(Inexpensive)*

Restaurants

Grand Cafe, Coconut Grove *(Very Expensive)*

Louie's Back Yard and Mira, Key West *(Very Expensive)*

Arthur's 27, atop Buena Vista Palace, Walt Disney World *(Expensive)*

Bern's Steak House, Tampa *(Expensive)*

Chef Allen, North Miami *(Expensive)*

Savannah Moon, Kendall suburb of Miami *(Expensive)*

Hy-Vong Vietnamese Cuisine, Little Havana section of Miami *(Moderate)*

Jamie's, Pensacola *(Moderate)*

Joe's Stone Crab House, Miami Beach *(Moderate)*

Harbor Docks, Destin *(Inexpensive–Moderate)*

Seagull, Fort Walton Beach *(Inexpensive–Moderate)*

Christini's Ristorante Italiano, Orlando *(Inexpensive)*

Homestead, Jacksonville *(Inexpensive)*

Numero Uno, Orlando *(Inexpensive)*

Oviedo Inn, Orlando *(Inexpensive)*

Wekiva Marina Restaurant, Longwood *(Inexpensive)*

Beaches

Crystal Beach Wayside Park

The Fort Pickens area of Gulf Islands National Seashore

John U. Lloyd Beach State Recreation Area, Dania

Pier Park, at the southern tip of Miami Beach and Lummus Park

Sarasota County beaches

Events

The ground shaking underfoot as a rocket soars spaceward from Cape Canaveral

King Orange Jamboree Parade preceding the Orange Bowl football game, Miami

Village Wine Festival, each February, Walt Disney World

Carnaval Miami, including the *Calle Oche* Open House, in the Little Havana district of Miami

Coconut Grove and Winter Park arts festivals

Sports

Fishing from the Redington Long Pier, or game fishing for the big ones off the Florida Keys

A jai-alai game at any of the many frontons throughout the state

Horse racing at Hialeah

The Orange Bowl Classic football game and its two attendant tennis tournaments, Miami

A round of golf at Key Biscayne Golf Course, which *Golf Digest* calls one of the best in the nation

Canoeing through a pristine forest at Wekiva Springs State Park, north of Orlando

After Hours

For local color, a drink at Captain Tony's, the original Sloppy Joe's, Hemingway's favorite bar in Key West

Comedy Corner, Palm Beach

Ragtime Tavern for Dixieland and classic jazz, Atlantic Beach

Tobacco Road bar and restaurant, Miami

Florida

ALABAMA

Pensacola

Perdido R.

Blackwater R.

De Funiak Springs

Fort Walton Beach

Panama City

Mariana

Chattahoochee

Quincy

Apalachicola R.

Tallahassee

Eastpoint

Gulf of Mexico

World Time Zones

Numbers below vertical bands relate each zone to Greenwich Mean Time (0 hrs.).
Local times may differ, as indicated by lightface numbers on the map.

Prime Meridian

Prime Meridian

-1 0 +1 +2 +3 +4 +5 +6 +7 +8 +9 +10
Greenwich
Mean Time

Introduction

by Kathryn Kilgore

A freelance journalist, Kathryn Kilgore has worked for The Village Voice *(New York City), and the* Montreal Gazette. *She recently completed her second novel. She has a house in Key West, where she lives and writes for part of each year.*

Florida casts no shadow. A snowbird (part-time resident) in jogging clothes makes this remark to me, the sunburned traveler, while I'm standing on the sunny steps of a small Florida library, holding 10 books on the history of Florida.

I study the snowbird's pale northern profile. He adjusts his sunglasses and continues: Cedar Key is nice; there are still Greek sponge divers at Tarpon Springs; the south edge of the Okefenokee Swamp is certainly worth a trip; don't forget all those empty county roads; and be sure to visit the Everglades. But it's not New England—he shakes his head. You can't feel the past, and you can't see it. The snowbird puts on his Walkman headphones and jogs away.

This traveler plans to drive all around the state, and she isn't ready to agree with this guy. Florida, after all, is bigger than New York State and New Jersey put together. She has just read that the "discovery" of Florida by Ponce de León in 1513 preceded the landing of the Mayflower by 107 years. St. Augustine is the oldest city in the United States. The Seminole Indians, whose ancestors refused to sign any treaty with the white man, still live as they wish in the Everglades and the Big Cypress Swamp. Miami is a glittering Spanish-speaking metropolis, a wide-open door to the Caribbean, Central America, and South America.

It is true, however, that hurricanes, mold, rot, ants, termites, floods, fires, and droughts have made a mess out of the monuments. The earliest architecture in North America has long since rotted away; the Indians left only shell mounds and pottery, and the Spanish left the mere foundations of forts. Although there were homesteads, of course, none has survived the intervening four centuries. As John Rothschild put it in his book *Up for Grabs*, "Historic St. Augustine inadvertently teaches Florida history: 450 years and no proof of occupancy." Still, there's got to be a shadow.

This traveler went to St. Augustine when she was young—in the back seat of her parents' station wagon. She remembers the narrow, peaceful streets of the little town, so different from industrial Jacksonville to its north. She climbed around the Spanish fort, the San Marcos, last rebuilt in 1672: the oldest building in America. She also saw Henry Flagler's fantastic hotels, built in the late 19th century for wealthy northern vacationers, which are among the oldest existing buildings in the state.

Yet in a way, that old snowbird had a point. Florida does feel as though it exists for a different, less serious purpose than does the rest of the country. It always has been a refuge for adventurers, entrepreneurs, and outcasts: conquistadores, both missionaries and gold hunters; escaped slaves and pirates; Seminoles from Georgia; cigar makers from Cuba, sponge divers from Greece; settlers from Minorca and Scandinavia; migrant laborers, refugees from Vietnam: *Marielitos*, who departed from Mariel, Cuba, in 1980, boat-people from Haiti, retirees, the rich, eccentrics from every-where, Mickey Mouse from Hollywood—and tourists.

It is also beautiful—a vast, wet, prickly state, empty of people in the center, with hundreds of lakes and huge cattle ranches and horse farms; with red-soil hills to the north, rockets to the east, castles at Orlando, and Confederate town squares near the Georgia border. Fantasy and fish, herons and gators thrive here; panthers still eke it out. The miles of swamps and plains, forests, and lakes outnumber the miles of crowded beaches. Often, even now, only the landscape survives for long, and that, too, floats, blows, or is dredged through changes, making it hard to place the past. The newspapers, even *The New York Times*, run their annual stories on how a hurricane could destroy Florida's high-rise-lined coast. The traveler already knows that this is a land that is still in control of those who live here.

A good way to begin to understand this land is to visit the Citrus Tower, "Florida's showplace for citrus," in Clermont. This traveler rode the elevator to the top of Citrus Tower, where she was supposed to "thrill to the panorama of 17 million citrus trees." What she actually saw were many, many acres of dead twisted branches, trunks, and empty fields, not a living orange tree in sight. This, Florida's finest citrus-growing country, was wiped out by the freeze of 1985 and then by citrus canker. This traveler was surprised, but the natives were sanguine: a killing freeze will occasionally happen. The last one was in 1895, and it resulted in the founding of that frost-free city, Miami. Every hundred years, someone informed the travel-er, it's time to move the trees.

Florida is mutable, whimsical, and at odds with itself, the traveler sees. As she begins to read.

On one side of Florida's history are the Indians and the Spanish, and later the Cubans and the Crackers (white farmers). The Spanish-Catholic and Cuban settlers looked to Havana and South America for support; they would have nothing to do with the northern colonies (Cuba is only 90 miles from Florida). The Indians and Crackers stuck to themselves.

On the other side of Florida's history are the slave owners, the hotel builders and land sellers, and the vacationers, all of whom came down from the North and divided the state between them: conquerers who fell for Florida's appeal as a fountain of youth—or at least as a place to begin again.

The poles of Florida now got switched; the northern part became "southern" as it filled with slave-operated plantations and joined the Confederate South. The swampy southern part of Florida gradually became "northern" (as well as Spanish and Caribbean), when pleasure-seeking invaders from the cold, northern states arrived, following the developers' dredges.

The glorification of Florida as the "Sunshine State," friend of the ill and the feeble—and the tourist—has been going on for a long while.

The early Cracker settlers found their country beautiful just as it was: a land of custard apple, moonvine, catfish, and moonshine. These Floridians developed their own attitude toward all the northern invaders. It was spread across the first state flag, which stated, "Let Us Alone."

The Sunshine State has 1,350 miles of coastline, on which the tourist loves to bake whenever possible. It has 10,000 miles of rivers and streams and 7,000 springs and lakes, including the 730-square-mile Lake Okeechobee. It has 12,000,000 residents, making it the fourth largest state in population. It has more than 40,000,000 tourists a year, and the recovering citrus industry produced, in 1988, 130 million boxes of oranges, 51 million boxes of grapefruit, and 799 million gallons of orange juice.

This traveler took off for a trip in her rental car. She explored the city of Miami, ate Cuban food on Calle Ocho, strolled down man-made Miami Beach, looking at the Art Deco hotels. She rode through the Everglades in an airboat driven by a Seminole. She went searching for bears and panthers in Big Cypress Swamp. She drove north through the sugarcane, past the migrant labor camps, the vast Lake Okeechobee. She fished and ate frog legs and then catfish. She drove past miles of cattle on the 35,000-acre Brighton Seminole Reservation. She then went to the west coast, to Sanibel and Captiva islands, walked the beaches, and picked her way among millions of shells. She cruised down to condominium-lined Marco Island, which had changed horribly since the days when her father had brought her there to fish. She struggled back up the coast, caught in a Winnebago spring-flow, and finally got to Sarasota. She visited Ringling's house and museum of Baroque art. She went on to Tampa and stopped among the old Ybor City cigar factories. She drove up to the sponging port in Tarpon Springs and walked through neighborhoods settled by Greeks.

She finally headed toward the quiet country of northern Florida. She went to tiny Cedar Key, with its wooden fishermen's cottages, and slept in a room right over the gulf. She went further off the track, driving small roads out along the bayous, finding fishing villages, where she ate delicious shrimp. She entered the Spanish-moss-covered woods and the empty pinelands. She drove on fine county roads, far from the highways, all the way up to pretty Talla-hassee.

Then she started back, following the Suwannee River. She meandered into the center of the state and cut through Marjorie Rawlings's rustic Cross Creek. She stopped at Ocala National Forest to swim in a spring and to camp. She dropped over to Lakeland to see all the buildings designed by Frank Lloyd Wright at Florida Southern College, then headed up across the state back to St. Augustine to see Ripley's Believe It or Not Museum. She dawdled down the east coast along the long white shore, passing John D. Rockefeller's last home at Ormond Beach. She studied the massive old rockets parked along Cape Canaveral. She saw fabulous Addison Mizner houses in Palm Beach. She cut back inland through the orange groves, up to Disney World and Epcot Center, which dip into the collective dream. She went back down the coast again and ambled along the boardwalk at Hollywood. She mailed postcards and set off for the Keys. She went deep-sea fishing and caught a tar-pon. As she drove back up to Miami, she began to think about Florida's shadow.

Florida raised itself slightly out of the ocean some 20 million years ago, a swampy newcomer to the conti-nent. It never experienced an ice age, but during the last one it became a popular migrating place, in spite of its rain. It did not take its final shape until 10,000 years ago.

Since the time it was first glimpsed by John Cabot, Florida has always been the object of some sort of land-claim frenzy.

In 1498, the mapmaker Cabot, out exploring for British King Henry VII, sailed down the coast from Labrador and discovered Florida, although it had already been claimed, unseen, by Christopher Columbus for Spain.

Ponce de León, representing Spain, got there second. He first saw La Florida on April 2, 1513, and landed a few days later at what is now St. Augustine. He was looking not for the fountain of youth but for the missing Bimini, where he was supposed to become governor. Finding nothing, he headed down the coast, past Los Martires (as he called the Florida Keys, which looked to him like kneeling martyrs), and up the west coast, stopping at present-day Fort Myers, where he encountered hostile Indians who shouted at him in Spanish. At this, he returned to Puerto Rico. He came back to conquer La Florida in 1521, bringing 200 settlers, including the first Catholic priests, who were supposed to reason with the heathens. The settlement near Charlotte Harbor was soon attacked by Apalachee or Calusa Indians. Ponce de León was wounded by an arrow, and the entire crew removed to Cuba, where he died.

Continuing the Spanish conquest, Pánfilo de Narváez ar-rived and landed in Tampa Bay in 1528. He immediately headed north, looking for the source of the Indian's gold, little suspecting that the gold he saw the Indians wearing around their necks was actually Spanish gold collected from shipwrecks.

Hernando de Soto came next. He landed at Tampa Bay in 1539 and quickly headed off in search of the same source of gold jewelry, going as far as North Carolina. He died after three years, still looking.

But then the Indians began to lose.

The Spaniard Pedro Menéndez de Aviles founded St. Augustine at long last in 1565. However, Jean Ribaut had established a French settlement at nearby Fort Caroline on the St. Johns River, and the Spanish knew this wouldn't do. Menéndez did not like those card-playing "Lutheran" French, whom he also considered pirates. Therefore, during a hurricane, he and his forces slaughtered them. All that survives of the French settlement are the journals and beautiful drawings of Native Americans done by Ribaut's mapmaker, Jacques le Moyne, who said of the Indians' costumes: "It is wonderful that men so savage should be capable of such tasteful inventions."

In a somewhat serendipitous revenge, England's Sir Francis Drake leveled St. Augustine in 1585. However, St. Augustine was rebuilt and survived (to become the town that Ralph Waldo Emerson, visiting in 1826, found to be full of "lazy desperadoes and land speculators" and that John J. Audubon called "the poorest hole in creation" in 1831).

Meanwhile, by 1560, the Indian population had withered away, as the native people were taken into slavery or died of smallpox, colds, diphtheria, or syphilis. In the 17th century, the total Indian population of 25,000, reduced by more than three-quarters, was tended to by Jesuits and Franciscans at some 50 monasteries.

The Spanish Cubans established "fishing ranchos" south in Calusa territory, and disease killed every Calusa. New British settlers arrived in the 17th century, seized native land, and drove the Timucuans and Apalachees south to their deaths.

By 1763 (when the British first took Florida from Spain in trade for Havana), the native Indians had all vanished. However, Creek Indians and Seminoles (a Creek name for wanderers or renegades), who had been crowded out of Georgia and the Carolinas, came down to replace the native Indians. They made their own land claims, which were soon challenged by the arriviste British/American settlers. Those competing claims eventually resulted in the first, second, and third Seminole wars, during the last of which Andrew Jackson crossed the border into Florida to (among other intentions) "punish" the Indians for living on land that was also claimed by white settlers.

Long before the wars, Florida's genetic pool began growing fast. The Creeks bred with Scots settlers to produce blue-eyed Creeks; the Seminoles kept black slaves and bred with them to produce black Seminoles. The result is that today you can't always guess the background of those you're talking to. In 1764, Londoner Denys Rolle started a colony near Palatka by importing vagrants, beggars, and debtors, who all abandoned him. A Scotsman named Dr. Andrew Turnbull started a colony at New Smyrna in 1768 by importing 1,255 starving Minorcans (and Greeks and Italians), all of whom fled to St. Augustine. The territory was a sort of renegade melting pot.

After Americans won its revolutionary war, Britain no longer wanted to bother with Florida and traded it back to Spain in 1783.

In 1821, Spain accepted the United State's offer to cancel a $5-million (somewhat bogus) debt in exchange for Florida, and Andrew Jackson again entered Pensacola, this time as governor. His stay was brief. In three months, he left what his wife Rachel called the "vast howling wilderness" and returned to Washington.

In 1830, Congress passed the Removal Law, which required all Indians in the East to be sent west to the Arkansas Territory. A delegation of Seminoles was tricked into signing this white man's treaty, which enraged the Indian Osceola, who pledged, "I will make the white man red with blood." This pledge was the beginning of the Second Seminole War, an affair that cost the white man $40,000 and some 1,500 lives. Osceola was defeated by an U.S. commander's treachery. He was captured during a false truce, and he died of malaria and grief in prison in Charleston, SC, an event that caused the white man to get much bad press in America.

Osceola's successor, Coacoochee, and his people, ragged and starving, soon requested a meeting with the white man. The Seminoles arrived at the parlay dressed in clothes they had stolen, which turned out to be an entire wardrobe of Shakespearean theater costumes. The American military negotiated with Hamlet, Richard III, Horatio, King Lear, and Caliban. Coacoochee said, "The red man's heart will always be free."

In 1842, 3,000 Seminoles were shipped along the "Trail of Tears," across the Mississippi. However, the fighting continued after 1855, when the last Seminole renegade leader, Billy Bowlegs, was caught and sent west. Three hundred of his Seminoles remained forever at large in the Florida swamps. Today their descendants raise cattle and fish, run bingo parlors, and sell trinkets and beads in south-central Florida. In 1976, the Seminoles accepted $16 million (or about 55 cents an acre) for their original 29 million acres of Florida.

Slaveholding Florida became a state in 1845, and five years later the population reached 87,445, of which 39,000 were black slaves who belonged to only 3,000 slave owners. The plantations produced cotton, turpentine, and lumber. The state's first senator, slave owner David Levy Yulee, whose grandfather was the grand vizier to the sultan of Morocco, built Florida's first cross-state railroad in the 1850s, from Fernandina to Cedar Key laying the tracks for the subsequent land boom.

Florida seceded from the Union in 1861 and became the third state to join the Confederacy. The Civil War cost Florida $20 million and 5,000 lives, and, worse, recovery took a century. The Ku Klux Klan emerged with a vengeance and became a powerful force. Blacks still drank at separate fountains, as they did elsewhere in the South, until the Civil Rights Act of 1964.

Events that tilted Florida toward the tourist market started quietly in the 19th century. In 1844, John Gorrie of Apalachicola invented an ice-making machine and the air conditioner, but nobody paid any attention to him, and his patents ran out. In 1873, Dr. John Wall discovered that mosquitoes carry yellow fever, but nobody paid any attention to him, either. In the 1880s, when the population of Florida reached 270,000, Hamilton Disston came down from Philadelphia, PA, bought four million acres, and began to drain the Caloosahatchee and Kissimmee valleys to make (and sell) a settlers' empire. A Chinese immigrant at Deland, named Lue Gim Gong, invented the frostproof orange, which prospered along the Indian River. In 1871, Gen. Henry Sanford, Lincoln's former ambassador to Belgium, started a citrus plantation and began to import and experiment with every kind of citrus then known. He also brought in an entire colony of Swedes to work the land.

Perhaps the biggest boost to Florida's image came in 1885, when the American Medical Association endorsed Pinellas Point at St. Petersburg as the healthiest spot in the United States. After that, the land race was on. The land boom that began at the turn of the century became madness by the mid-1920s, ebbed through the Great Depression and World War II, then took off again in the 1950s and 1960s. People were—and are—irrationally attracted to the sun.

Ailing 38-year-old Thomas Edison moved from Menlo Park, NJ, to Fort Myers in 1885. There, he built the first modern swimming pool in America, and his incandescent lights lit his estate and workshop 30 miles from the Seminoles who were hiding in Big Cypress Swamp.

The year 1885 also saw the influx of Cuban cigar makers into Tampa, attracted from Cuba and the Keys when Vincent Ybor, followed by others, built his Ybor cigar plant. Ybor spirited his workers away from the labor problems of Key West to this new tax haven after his Key West factory burned. Not much later, sponge divers also deserted Key West for the deep-water sponge beds off Tarpon Springs, in a move initiated by a Greek who recruited deep-water divers from his homeland until there was (and still is) a sizable Greek colony in that city.

After the cigar makers decided to come to Ybor City, the success of their business was guaranteed by Henry Plant, who constructed the Atlantic Coastline Railroad from Richmond, Virginia, to Tampa. Starting in 1884, Plant built the enormous Tampa Bay Hotel, which is modeled on the Alhambra in Grenada, Spain, and has 13 silver Moorish minarets. The guests traveled the long corridors of this hotel by riding in rickshas. The hotel, worth seeing, now houses a college.

Ybor City became deeply involved in Cuba's effort to free itself from Spain. Money and guns were run, and José Martí came from Cuba to Tampa to raise funds. In 1898, after the U.S.S. *Maine* was blown apart in Havana harbor and the United States entered the Spanish-American War, Plant arranged for Tampa to be the port of embarkation for the 30,000 American troops. The porch of the Tampa Bay Hotel was filled with reporters filing stories on their "rocking-chair war." Winston Churchill was there reporting, and Clara Barton came to set up a Red Cross hospital. Stephen Crane, Frederic Remington, and Richard Harding Davis spent time on this porch. Theodore Roosevelt and his Rough Riders shipped out of Tampa. The end of Spain in the New World was orchestrated from the very shore where Hernando de Soto, conquistador, first landed.

Meanwhile, Henry Morrison Flagler came to visit St. Augustine in income-tax-free Florida. Flagler, a retired Standard Oil baron, was annoyed with St. Augustine's reputation as a place for the sickly and bored by its lack of a decent hotel. In 1885, he started to build. He began with the immense and opulent poured-concrete Ponce de León Hotel, a Moorish-Renaissance monument for the very rich that is still in existence (though no longer a hotel), and followed up with the slightly more frugal Alcazar across the street. Flagler, of course, provided the transportation to his hotels, in the form of the Florida East Coast Railroad, which had an enormous impact on the state. He then continued down the coast, seeking warmth and constructing a series of fantastic hotels to popularize his railroad. Flagler set the tone for the "bastard-Spanish-Moorish-Romanesque-Gothic-Renaissance-bull-market-damn-the-expense"building style, which lasted through the land boom of the 1920s and peaked most elaborately in Addison Mizner's Palm Beach mansions, to which those with the socially necessary private railroad cars traveled. The St. Augustine hotels all closed after half a century when the tourists moved south. But Flagler was south before them, having bought the

Ormond Hotel in Ormond Beach in 1890. He built the Royal Poinciana Hotel at Palm Beach in 1893, the largest wooden hotel ever constructed, where Afromobiles (white wicker carts pulled by blacks—competition for Plant's rickshas) carried the guests about. Palm Beach wasn't even a town when the railroad came through, just a land spit covered by 20,000 coconut palms from a shipwreck.

At the persuasion of Julia Tuttle, who supposedly sent him an orange blossom during the freezing winter of 1894–95 (which had discouraged too many a fragile tourist), Flagler laid his railroad tracks down to the tiny settlement of Miami and incorporated it as a city. By 1896, he had built and opened the Royal Palm Hotel. From Miami, "America's sun porch," Flagler pushed on to Homestead and built the Overseas Railroad to Key West by 1912. (The Overseas Railroad blew away in the hurricane of 1935.) Flagler died in 1913, having been granted a free 2.4 million acres of Florida for his efforts.

In 1912, when millionaire Carl Fisher of Indianapolis came to Miami, all the hotels were on the Miami mainland. Because there was still not much to do, Fisher poked around Biscayne Bay and discovered a mangrove-covered barrier sandbar, where he soon bought land from Quaker avocado farmer John Collins. Fisher applied a dredge to it and came up with the tabula rasa that became Miami Beach, which he began to fill with imported birds, plants, polo fields, golf courses, tennis courts, grandstands, elephants, and picturesque architecture, including the Flamingo Hotel (Spanish-Moorish-Venetian-Arab style) and the Lincoln, Nautilus, King Cole, and Boulevard hotels.

"Carl discovered that sand could hold up a real estate sign, and that was all he wanted it for," said humorist Will Rogers. "Had there been no Carl Fisher, Florida would be known today as the Turpentine State."

In 1925 alone, 481 hotels and apartment buildings rose on Miami Beach. Fisher even built the Dixie Highway from Miami to Michigan. But his flashy bootleg resort was less stable than the competition at Palm Beach; after the land bust and the 1929 stock market crash, Al Capone and others of his ilk moved in. Fisher died broke and an alcoholic.

In 1916, John Deering's architect, the wacky Paul Chalfin, began work on the monstrously imposing Villa Vizcaya in Miami—a kind of Venetian palace with gardens and waterways and a village, furnished in the Medieval-Renaissance-Baroque-Rococo-Neoclassical style. After it was finished, Deering rattled around in Vizcaya alone or with his mother for 10 years until his death. The house and gardens, now restored, are open to the public, for whom there is ample room.

Addison Mizner came to Palm Beach in 1918 to rest his 300-pound frame. The flamboyant self-proclaimed architect, who frequently forgot to include a kitchen or stairs in his plans, soon began his first Palm Beach project, the Everglades Club, which the newspapers called "a little of Seville and the Alhambra, Madeira and Algiers, with Italian lagoon and terrace and garden."

In 1925, right in the middle of the land-sales boom (by which time 2.5 million suckers had rushed to buy their lots), Addison Mizner and his brother Wilson bought 17,500 acres of scrub, which they called Boca Raton. Addison built the Cloister Club and, with Wilson, went into the "surreal" real estate business, immediately selling $26 million of lots.

The scrupulous George Merrick created his beautifully designed Coral Gables (now part of Miami) out of his father's farm. In 1921, he began to sell lots in this, the country's first fully planned, city (with stucco gates and Chinese-and-French-style houses along Venetian canals in the Italian style, with roof tiles removed from houses in Cuba, imported, and reused). Merrick soon hired ex-Secretary of State William Jennings Bryan at $100,000 a year (along with 3,000 other salesmen) to stand by the Venetian pool and sell $150 million worth of property. Before the bust, Merrick had completed the Miami Biltmore Hotel and five international villages, each with houses in a different style: Dutch South African, Chinese, French City, French Country, and French Provincial. He had also established the University of Miami. (The Miami Biltmore reopened in 1987; this ghost-rich towering structure is well worth a visit.)

In the meantime, Florida natives—the white Crackers—farmed, fished, and harvested pines and turpentine to the north and inland. "Conchs" down in the Keys salvaged, caught turtles, rolled cigars, and went broke. Blacks worked at their tenant farms and went to juke joints to listen to music. Marjorie Kinnan Rawlings wrote *The Yearling* on her orange farm at Cross Creek (still there and still mysterious). Zora Neale Hurston of Eatonville, the first all-black community in the United States, wrote *Their Eyes Were Watching God*, about the 1928 hurricane that killed 2,000 people near Lake Okeechobee (there's a handsome WPA-built hurricane monument in Belle Glade). John Ringling, the circus king, set himself up at Sarasota, where he collected fine Baroque art and eventually built his Venetian ducal palazzo, Ca'd'Zan, and his art museum (well worth visiting) and where, in 1927, he first brought the "Greatest Show on Earth" to its new winter quarters.

The "Tin Can Tourists," back from World War I, arrived from the north in the early 1920s and hit the coasts in their new Fords. At first, they set up tent cities and ate out of cans, but before long they grew interested in owning a piece of the pie. Real estate scam artists, called "binder boys," flooded the state, buying up options on lots that they then resold over and over for a spiraling profit.

Things had gotten out of hand, but they didn't stop. The freeze of 1926 caused a temporary slowdown in the Florida land boom. The cold weather put a lot of people off, as did the crash of 1929, which wiped out the "paper" millionaires. The common people abandoned the small hurricane-swept lot that they'd been ill advised to buy in some impenetrable swamp and went back home. Ernest Hemingway, however, continued to fish off his royalties, down in Key West.

The WPA came to Florida and helped rescue the state from stagnation. Miami Beach's beautiful Streamline, Depression, and Tropical Deco hotels were built during the 1930s and managed to thrive. A steady migration of retirees to Florida also continued through the decade, because land was now cheap and the state still had no state income tax or inheritance tax. Later, many of the elderly ended up living in these same now-downgraded and run-down Art Deco hotels, only to be thrown out in the 1980s when some of the hotels were rescued but the tenants were not.

After World War II, business picked up a bit. By the 1950s, Florida was being redivided again, this time into lots with the kind of tract housing that had been tried successfully by visionaries such as William Levitt of Long Island, who came to Florida and started to build suburbs.

The subdividing continued briskly, and, by the 1960s, it was booming again, led by companies like the giant General Development Corporation, which offered roadless, serviceless land for $50 down, $10 a month, and by the treacherous Gulf American Corporation, which utilized the hard sell to force swamps on customers.

Now we're into visible history. This traveler believes she has glimpsed, but hasn't yet caught, the shadow. So what was she going to tell the snowbird?

She is on her way to meet the snowbird for cocktails. She crosses the bridge to Miami Beach and drives through the dusk down Collins Avenue, toward the Fontainebleau Hotel. That is the Fontainebleau ahead, isn't it? Yes, it is. No, it isn't!

It's even more startling and grandiose than the Fontainebleau she remembers. And it seems they've somehow slightly moved the Fontainebleau. Or else that gateway has distorted the view of the Fontainebleau? From the distance the tourist sees a beautiful Deco arch, beyond which is her destination. But as soon as she decides to drive through this gate, she sees she will crash right into . . . a solid wall. It's the Fontainebleau itself! And this thing before her, it's some sort of mural; it's a fake, a trompe l'oeil of the Fontainebleau Hotel! Painted by some type of trickster.

The traveler slows down. In her mind's eye, Florida's shadow rises over the flimsy suburbs of the 1950s and 1960s and the cement-slab condominiums of the 1970s, which now block the view of Florida's beaches, and farther over the alarm-controlled time-shares of the 1980s, where often nobody's home; and on again across those beautiful condominiums on wealthy Brickell Avenue in Miami—the colorful 21-story Atlantis, for instance, the one in the TV series "Miami Vice," the one with the hole in it, the one you can see best from the highway at high speeds. It's like Disney World escaped from Orlando and mutated. Like everything else here, it has the irresistibly playful spirit of a state that won't conform; it's fantastic. And, finally, she understands: that hole, that trompe l'oeil, this is the heart of Florida. Florida plays with shadows.

Conservationist Marjorie Stoneman Douglas wrote that she first saw Florida in 1915 as "lost in the light, as I was, streets, roofs, fringing round-leaved trees over wharves and houseboats, all silent, all asleep. Sea gulls floated in it, white shadows. It caught the pale breasts of pelicans on pilings in dancing nets. Bay or sky, it was all dazzling, diamond-edged."

Catch it if you can.

1 Essential Information

Before You Go

Visitor Information

Contact the **Florida Division of Tourism** for information on tourist attractions and answers to questions about traveling in the state.

In Florida: 126 Van Buren Street, Tallahassee 32301, tel. 904/487–1462 or 1463.

In Canada: 150 W. Bloor Street, Suite 310, Toronto, Ontario M5S 1M6 2X9, tel. 800/268–3791 or 416/928–3111.

In the United Kingdom: 18/24 Westbourne Grove, 1st floor, London W25RH, tel. 01/727–1661. British travelers can also get assistance from the **U.S. Travel and Tourism Administration** (22 Sackville St., London W1X 2EA, tel. 01/439–7433).

For additional information, contact the regional tourist bureaus and chambers of commerce in the areas you wish to visit (*see* individual chapters for listings).

Tour Groups

If you prefer to leave the driving to someone else, consider a package tour. Although you will have to march to the beat of a tour guide's drum rather than your own, you are likely to save money on airfare, hotels, and ground transportation. For the more experienced or adventurous traveler, a variety of special-interest and independent packages are available. Listed below is a sampling of available options. Check with your travel agent or the Florida Division of Tourism (904/487–1462) for additional resources.

When considering a tour, be sure to find out exactly what expenses are included (particularly tips, taxes, side trips, additional meals, and entertainment); ratings of all hotels on the itinerary and the facilities they offer; cancellation policies for you and for the tour operator; and, if you are traveling alone, the cost for a single supplement. Most tour operators request that bookings be made through a travel agent; there is no additional charge for doing so.

General-Interest Tours   **Cosmos/Globus Gateway** (150 S. Los Robles Ave., Suite 860, Pasadena, CA 91101, tel. 818/449–0919 or 800/556–5454) offers an Orlando/Bahamas tour. **American Express Vacations** (Box 5014, Atlanta, GA 30302, tel. 800/241–1700 or in GA 800/282–0800) offers packages to Orlando/Disney World and Miami/Key Biscayne. **Maupintour** (Box 807, Lawrence, KA 66044, tel. 913/843–1211 or 800/255–4266) sells sunny Florida packages during the winter months. **Domenico Tours** (751 Broadway, Bayonne, NJ 07002, tel. 800/554–TOUR) offers packages to Orlando, Miami Beach, Palm Beach, St. Petersburg, Ft. Lauderdale, and Miami Beach/Bahamas/Walt Disney World.

Special-Interest Tours   *Adventure*   **Sobek's International Explorers Society** (Box 1089, Angels Camp, CA 95222, tel. 209/736–4524) will take you canoeing through the Florida Everglades or island-hopping by sailboat off the gulf coast of Florida in their "Adventure Sail Escape."

Wilderness Southeast (711 Sandtown Rd., Savannah, GA 31410, tel. 912/897–5108) runs rugged trips through the Everglades and places like the Okefenokee Swamp in Georgia. Also available is a four-day trip through Central Florida, beginning with canoeing excursions in Ocala National Forest and ending with a snorkeling expedition on the Gulf Coast—this is the only location in the state where the tourist can legally swim with the manatees.

Nature Visit the loggerhead turtle on Sanibel Island, off Florida's gulf coast, with conservationists in an outing arranged by **Smithsonian Associates Travel Program** (1100 Jefferson Dr. SW, Washington, DC 20560, tel. 202/357–4700). You must pay a $20 fee to become a member of the Smithsonian to take any of the trips offered in the program.

Package Deals for Independent Travelers

American FlyAway Vacations (tel. 800/433–7300) offers city packages with discounts on hotels and car rentals. The airline offers a "Fly and Drive" package to the entire state as well as a number of three- and four-day trips to Orlando and its environs, including Sea World and Disney World. **Delta Air Lines** (tel. 800/872–7786) offers nine different packages in Florida, including trips to Disney World, Daytona, Ft. Lauderdale, Miami, Key West, Tampa, Orlando, Sarasota, Ft. Myers, and Marco Island. **American Express** has similar city packages, with half-day sightseeing tours, available from any American Express office.

Tips for British Travelers

Government Tourist Offices The **United States Travel and Tourism Administration** (22 Sackville St., London W1X 2EA, tel. 01/439–7433) will send brochures and give you advice on your trip to Florida.

Passports and Visas You will need a valid passport (£15) and a U.S. Visitors Visa that you can get either through your travel agent or by post from the **United States Embassy** (Visa and Immigration Dept., 5 Upper Grosvenor St., London W1A 2JB, tel. 01/499–3443). The embassy no longer accepts visa applications made by personal callers. No vaccinations are required.

Customs Visitors of 21 or over can take in 200 cigarettes or 50 cigars or three pounds of tobacco; one U.S. liter of alcohol; and duty-free gifts to a value of $100. Be careful not to try to take in meat or meat products, seeds, plants, fruits, etc. Avoid illegal drugs like the plague.

Returning to Britain you may bring home: (1) 200 cigarettes or 100 cigarillos or 50 cigars or 250 grams of tobacco; (2) two liters of table wine with additional allowances for (a) one liter of alcohol over 22% by volume (38.8° proof, most spirits), (b) two liters of alcohol under 22% by volume (fortified or sparkling wine), or (c) two more liters of table wine; and (3) 50 grams of perfume and ¼ liter of toilet water; and (4) other goods up to a value of £32.

Insurance We recommend that you insure yourself to cover health and motoring mishaps through **Europ Assistance** (252 High St., Croydon, Surrey CR0 1NF, tel. 01/680–1234).

It is also wise to take out insurance to cover loss of luggage (though check that this isn't already covered in any existing home-owner's policy). Trip-cancellation insurance is another wise buy. **The Association of British Insurers** (Aldermary House, Queen St., London EC4N 1TT, tel. 01/248–4477) will give comprehensive advice on all aspects of vacation insurance.

Tour Operators Numerous tour operators offer packages to Florida. Here we list just a few; contact your travel agent to find companies best suited to your needs and pocketbook.

Albany Travel (Manchester) Ltd. (190 Deansgate, Manchester M3 3WD, tel. 061/833–0202) offers an eight-day "Florida Resorts" tour featuring southern Florida and the Florida Keys. Prices start from £1,049 per person.

Jetlife Holidays (169–171 High St., Orpington, Kent BR6 0LW, tel. 0689/77061) has a wide range of vacations to various destinations in Florida.

Poundstretcher (Airlink House, Hazelwick Ave., Three Bridges, Sussex RH10 1YS, tel. 0293/548241) offers seven nights in Clearwater from £499 per person; seven nights in Fort Lauderdale from £599; and seven nights in Miami from £575. It also offers a wide range of fly-drive vacations, golf and tennis vacations, and cruises.

Speedbird (Alta House, 152 King St., London W6 0QU, tel. 01/741–8041) has excellent fly-drive offers and motor-camper vacations that are particularly flexible. Ask for the brochure.

Thomas Cook Select Holidays (Centurion House, Hertford, Herts. SG14 1BH, tel. 0992–554144) offers seven nights in Orlando starting at £426. Six-night stays at a Holiday Inn in Clearwater start at £473.

Airfares If you want to make your own way to Florida and need a reasonably priced ticket, try the small ads in the daily or Sunday newspapers or in magazines such as *Time Out*. You should be able to pick up something at rock-bottom prices. Be prepared to be flexible about your dates of travel and book as early as possible.

Also check out the APEX tickets offered by the major airlines, which are another good option. As we went to press, round-trip tickets to Orlando cost about £259; to Miami, £199. Be sure to ask if there are any hidden extras, since airport taxes and supplements can increase the price dramatically.

Car Rental There are offices of the major car rental companies in most large towns, and you can either make your arrangements before you leave or when you get to your destination.

Avis (Hayes Gate House, Uxbridge Rd., Hayes, Middlesex UB4 0JN, tel. 01/848–8733) offers seven days' rental of, say, a Chevrolet at about £92; extra days start at £23 per day.

Hertz (Radnor House, 1272 London Rd., London SW16 4XW, tel. 01/679–1799) offers an "Affordable America" program. At press time, seven days rental of a Ford Escort, for example, cost about $135; extra days run about $37 a day. Most rental offers include unlimited mileage, but don't forget to budget for the price of gas, local taxes, and collision insurance. Also check out the fly-drive offers from tour operators and airlines; some good bargains are usually available.

When to Go

Florida is a state for all seasons, although most visitors prefer October-April, particularly in southern Florida.

Winter is the height of the tourist season, when southern Florida is crowded with "snowbirds" fleeing the cold weather in the North. Hotels, bars, discos, restaurants, shops, and attractions are all crowded. Hollywood and Broadway celebrities appear in sophisticated supper clubs, and other performing artists hold the stage at ballets, operas, concerts, and theaters.

During the winter season, the Magic Kingdom at Disney World is more magical than ever, especially from mid-December through January 2, with daily parades and other extravaganzas. The crowds are overwhelming then, too. Winter fairs and festivals, art shows, parades, and fiestas take place in other parts of the state as well. In Tarpon Springs, youths dive for a golden cross during the Epiphany Festival on January 6. And in Tampa, the swashbuckling Gasparilla Festival attracts enormous crowds in mid-winter.

Summer in Florida, as smart budget-minded visitors have discovered, is often hot and very humid, but the season is made bearable along the coast by ocean breezes. Besides, many hotels lower their prices considerably during summer. In the Panhandle, though, summer is the peak season.

Families who want to explore Disney World-Epcot, Sea World, Busch Gardens, and other outstanding attractions will find some crowds in summer—but fewer during the week when children return to school in September.

For the college crowd, **spring** vacation is still the time to congregate in Florida, especially in the Fort Lauderdale and Daytona Beach areas.

For senior citizens, September-December are months for discounts to many attractions and hotels in Orlando and along the Pinellas Suncoast in the Tampa Bay area.

Climate What follows are average daily maximum and minimum temperatures for major cities in Florida.

Key West (The Keys)								
Jan.	76F	24C	**May**	85F	29C	**Sept.**	90F	32C
	65	18		74	23		77	25
Feb.	76F	24C	**June**	88F	31C	**Oct.**	83F	28C
	67	19		77	25		76	24
Mar.	79F	26C	**July**	90F	32C	**Nov.**	79F	26C
	68	20		79	26		70	21
Apr.	81F	27C	**Aug.**	90F	32C	**Dec.**	76F	24C
	72	22		79	26		67	19

Miami								
Jan.	74F	23C	**May**	83F	28C	**Sept.**	86F	30C
	63	17		72	22		76	24
Feb.	76F	24C	**June**	85F	29C	**Oct.**	83F	28C
	63	17		76	24		72	22
Mar.	77F	25C	**July**	88F	31C	**Nov.**	79F	26C
	65	18		76	24		67	19
Apr.	79F	26C	**Aug.**	88F	31C	**Dec.**	76F	24C
	68	20		77	25		63	17

Orlando	**Jan.**	70F	21C	**May**	88F	31C	**Sept.**	88F	31C
		49	9		67	19		74	23
	Feb.	72F	22C	**June**	90F	32C	**Oct.**	83F	28C
		54	12		72	22		67	19
	Mar.	76F	24C	**July**	90F	32C	**Nov.**	76F	24C
		56	13		74	23		58	14
	Apr.	81F	27C	**Aug.**	90F	32C	**Dec.**	70F	21C
		63	17		74	23		52	11

Current weather information for over 500 cities around the world may be obtained by calling **WeatherTrak** information service at 900/370–8728 or in TX, 900/575–8728. A taped message will tell you to dial the three-digit access code for the destination you're interested in. The code is either the area code (in the United States) or the first three letters of the foreign city. For a list of all access codes, send a stamped, addressed envelope to Cities, Box 7000, Dallas, TX 75209. For further information, phone 214/869–3035 or 800/247–3282.

Festivals and Seasonal Events

Top seasonal events in Florida include Speed Week's auto racing celebration in Daytona Beach in February; Miami Film Festival in February; Florida Derby Festival from March through April; Sunfest in Palm Beach in May; and Key West's celebration of Hemingway Days in July. For exact dates and details about the following events, contact the Florida Department of Commerce, Division of Tourism (126 Van Buren St., Tallahassee 32399, tel. 904/487–1462 or 1463).

Jan.: Hollywood Sun 'n Fun Festival includes celebrity entertainment and top-notch food (tel. 305/920–3330).

Early Jan.: Polo Season opens at the Palm Beach Polo and Country Club (13198 Forest Hill Blvd., West Palm Beach 33414, tel. 407/793–1440).

Jan. 6: Greek Epiphany Day includes religious celebrations, parades, music, dancing, and feasting at the St. Nicholas Greek Orthodox Cathedral (Box 248, Tarpon Springs 34689, tel. 813/937–3540).

Mid Jan.: Art Deco Weekend spotlights Miami Beach's historic district with an Art Deco street fair, a 1930s-style Moon Over Miami Ball, and live entertainment (661 Washington Ave., Bin L, Miami Beach 33119, tel. 305/672–2014).

Mid-Jan.: Taste of the Grove Food and Music Festival is a popular fund-raiser put on in Coconut Grove's Peacock Park by area restaurants (tel. 305/442–2001).

Late Jan.: South Florida Fair and Exposition takes place in West Palm Beach (General Office, 9067 Southern Blvd., West Palm Beach 33411, tel. 407/793–0333).

Late Jan. or early Feb.: Key Biscayne Art Festival is an annual juried show of 175 talented artists at the entrance to Cape Florida State Park (Richard Maloy, Key Biscayne Rotary Club, Box 490174, Key Biscayne 33149, tel. 305/361–0775).

Early Feb.–late Feb.: Speed Weeks is a three-week celebration of auto racing that culminates in the famous Daytona 500 in Daytona Beach (Daytona International Speedway, Drawer S, Daytona Beach 32015, tel. 904/253–6711).

Feb–Mar.: Winter Equestrian Festival includes more than 1,000 horses and three grand-prix equestrian events at the Palm

Beach Polo and Country Club in West Palm Beach (tel. 407/798–7000).

First weekend in Feb.: Sarasota Classic is a major event on the LPGA tour (Classic, Box 2199, Sarasota 33578).

Early Feb.: Scottish Festival and Games features a variety of events in Key Biscayne (tel. 305/757–6730).

Mid-Feb.: Florida State Fair includes carnival rides and 4-H competitions in Tampa (Box 11766, Tampa 33680, tel. 813/621–7821).

Mid-Feb.: Miami Film Festival is 10 days of international, domestic, and local films sponsored by the Film Society of America (7600 Red Rd., Penthouse Suite, Miami 33157, tel. 305/444–FILM).

Mid-Feb.: Florida Citrus Festival and Polk County Fair in Winter Haven showcases the citrus harvest with displays and entertainment (100 Cyprus Gardens Blvd., Winter Haven 33880, tel. 813/293–3175).

Mid-Feb.: Islamorada Sportfishing Festival features a weekend of fishing, arts and crafts, races, and prizes (tel. 305/664–4503).

Mid-Feb.: Coconut Grove Art Festival is the state's largest (tel. 305/447–0401).

Last full weekend in Feb.: Labelle Swamp Cabbage Festival is a salute to the state tree, the cabbage palm (tel. 813/675–0697).

Early Mar.–early Apr.: Florida Derby Festival is a series of cultural, social, artistic, and athletic events in Broward, Dade, and Palm Beach counties (Festival, Box 705, Hallandale 33008, tel. 305/454–8544).

First weekend in Mar.: Sanibel Shell Fair is the largest event of the year on Sanibel Island (tel. 813/472–2155).

Early Mar.: Carnaval Miami is a carnival celebration staged by the Little Havana Tourist Authority (970 S.W. First St., Miami 33130, tel. 305/324–7349).

Early Mar.: Cycle Week is a major motorcycle racing event at Daytona International Speedway that always takes place three weeks after the Daytona 500 (tel. 904/253–6711).

Mid-Mar. and early July: Arcadia All-Florida Championship Rodeo is professional rodeo at its best (Rodeo, Box 1266, Arcadia 33821, tel. 813/494–2014).

Mid-Mar.–Mid-Apr.: Springtime Tallahassee is a major cultural, sporting, and culinary event in the state capital (tel. 904/224–5012).

Late Mar.: Azalea Festival is a beauty pageant, arts and crafts show, and parade held in downtown Palatka and Riverfront Park (tel. 904/325–3815).

Late Mar.:Florida International Air Show at the Charlotte County Airport (Bill Graham, 1601 W. Marion Ave., Punta Gorda 33950, tel. 813/639–2788).

Late Mar.: Port Canaveral Seafood Festival requires hearty appetites at Cape Canaveral (tel. 407/459–2200).

Apr.: Arts in April presents a series of visual and performing arts events produced by local independent arts organizations (400 S. Orange Ave., Orlando 32801, tel. 407/849–2221).

Early Apr.: Spring Arts Festival attracts more than 300 artists and craftspeople from across the country to Gainesville (tel. 904/372–1976).

Early Apr.: Bounty of the Sea Seafood Festival in Miami includes a limbo contest, a chowder competition, an Underwater Film Festival, and more (International Oceanographic Foundation/

Planet Ocean, 3979 Rickenbacker Causeway, Miami 33149, tel. 305/361–5786).

Early Apr.–late May: Addison Mizner Festival in Boca Raton celebrates the 1920s in Palm Beach County (tel. 800/242–1774).

Palm Sunday: Blessing of the Fleet is held on the bay front in St. Augustine (tel. 904/829–5681).

Mid-Apr.–mid-May: Water Weeks in Panama City Beach is a spring festival of fishing tournaments, scuba treasure hunts, and sailing regattas (tel. 904/234–6575).

Easter Sunday: Easter Sunrise Service in Orlando is held at Sea World (tel. 407/351–3600).

Late Apr.: River Cities Festival is a three-day event in Miami Springs and Hialeah that focuses attention on the Miami River and the need to keep it clean (tel. 305/887–1515).

Late Apr.–early May: Sun 'n' Fun Festival includes a bathtub regatta, golf tournament, and nighttime parade in Clearwater.

Late Apr.–early May: Conch Republic Celebration in Key West honors the founding fathers of the Conch Republic, "the small island nation of Key West" (tel. 305/294–4440).

First weekend in May: Sunfest includes a wide variety of cultural and sporting events in West Palm Beach (tel. 407/659–5980).

Mid-May: Arabian Nights Festival in Opa-locka is a mix of contemporary and fantasy-inspired entertainment (tel. 305/686–4611).

Mid-May: Pompano Seafood Festival includes one of the nation's premier billfish tournaments, plus area restaurants that showcase their offerings (tel. 305/941–2940).

Early–mid-June: Billy Bowlegs Festival in Fort Walton Beach is a week of entertaining activities in memory of a pirate who ruled the area in the late 1700s (tel. 904/244–8191).

July 4: Firecracker Festival in Melbourne is one of the state's most colorful Independence Day celebrations.

Mid-July: Hemingway Days Festival in Key West includes plays, short-story competitions, and a Hemingway look-alike contest (tel. 305/294–4440).

Mid-July: The Greater Jacksonville King Fish Tournament offers a number of cash prizes (tel. 904/241–7127).

Month of Aug.: Boca Festival Days includes many educational, cultural, and recreational activities in Boca Raton (tel. 407/395–4433).

Mid-Aug.: Shark Tournament at Port of the Islands on Marco Islands awards prizes for the largest shark in three categories; at Port of the Islands Resort and Marina (Rte. 41, Marco Island 33937, tel. 800/237–4173 or in FL 800/282–3011).

Late Aug.: Worm Fiddler's Day is the biggest day of the year in Caryville (tel. 904/548–5116).

Labor Day Weekend: Florida Pro Surfing Event is held in Sebastian (tel. 407/984–4852).

Early Sept.: Anniversary of the Founding of St. Augustine is held on the grounds of the Mission of Nombre de Dios (tel. 904/829–5681).

Mid- to late Sept.: Festival Miami is three weeks of performing and visual arts sponsored by the University of Miami. (University of Miami School of Music, Box 248165, Coral Gables 33124, tel. 305/284–3941).

Late Sept.: Pensacola Seafood Festival means food and entertainment in Pensacola (tel. 904/433–6512).

Late Sept.: Miami Boat Show in the Grove draws up to 200,000 people to Coconut Grove in Miami (tel. 305/579–3310).

Oct.: Banyan Art Festival attracts craftspeople and artists to Coconut Grove (tel. 305/444–7270).

Mid-Oct.: Florida State Chili Cookoff Championship at Port of the Islands Resort in the Everglades means all the chili you can eat (25000 Tamiami Trail East, Naples 33961, tel. 800/237–4173 or in FL 800/282–3011).

Late Oct.: Fantasy Fest in Key West is an unrestrained Halloween costume party, parade, and town fair (tel. 305/294–4440).

Early Nov.: Light Up Orlando is a street celebration of bands, international foods, and the Queen Kumquat Sashay Parade.

Late Nov.: River Manatee Festival in Crystal River focuses on both the river and the endangered manatee (tel. 904/795–3149).

Early–late Dec.: Winterfest and Boat Show in Fort Lauderdale has a rodeo, shoreline competitions, a Fun Fest for children, and a boat parade and ends with a "Light Up Lauderdale" New Year's Eve bash (tel. 305/522–3983).

Mid-Dec.: Walt Disney World's Very Merry Christmas Parade in the Magic Kingdom (Walt Disney World, Box 10000, Lake Buena Vista 32830–1000).

Mid-Dec.: Christmas Regatta of Lights is a colorful display in St. Augustine (tel. 904/829–5681).

Late Dec.: Coconut Grove King Mango Strut is a parody of the Orange Bowl Parade (tel. 305/858–6253).

What to Pack

Pack light, because porters and luggage trolleys are hard to find. Luggage allowances on domestic flights vary slightly from airline to airline. Most allow three checked pieces and one carry-on. In all cases, check-in luggage cannot weigh more than 70 pounds each or be larger than 62 inches (length + width + height) and must fit under the seat or in the overhead luggage compartment.

The northern part of the state is much cooler in the winter than is the southern part. Winters are mild in the Orlando area, with daytime temperatures in the 70s and low 80s. But the temperature can dip to the 50s, even in the Keys, so take a sweater or jacket, just in case. Farther north, in the Panhandle area, winters are cool and there's often frost at night.

The Miami area and the Tampa/St. Petersburg area are warm year-round and often extremely humid during the summer months. Be prepared for sudden summer storms, but leave the plastic raincoats at home because they're uncomfortable in the high humidity.

Dress is casual throughout the state, with sundresses, jeans, or walking shorts appropriate during the day. A pair of comfortable walking shoes or sneakers is a must for Disney World. A few of the better restaurants request that men wear jackets and ties, but most do not. Be prepared for air-conditioning bordering on the glacial, especially in the Miami/Fort Lauderdale areas.

You can swim in Florida year-round. Be sure to take a sun hat and a good sunscreen because the sun can be fierce, even in the winter.

Cash Machines

Virtually all U.S. banks belong to a network of ATMs (automatic teller machines), which dispense cash 24 hours a day in cities throughout the country. There are some eight major networks in the United States, the largest of which are **Cirrus,** owned by MasterCard, and **Plus,** affiliated with Visa. Some banks belong to more than one network. These cards are not automatically issued; you have to ask for them. Cards issued by American Express, Visa, and MasterCard may also be used in the ATMs, but the fees are usually higher than the fees on bank cards, and there is a daily interest charge on the "loan," even if monthly bills are paid on time. Each network has a toll-free number you can call to locate machines in a given city. The Cirrus number is 800/424–7787; the Plus number is 800/843–7587. Check with your bank for fees and for the amount of cash you can withdraw per day.

Traveling with Film

If your camera is new, shoot and develop a few rolls before leaving home. Pack some lens tissue and an extra battery for your built-in light meter. Invest about $10 in a skylight filter and screw it onto the front of your lens; it will protect the lens and also reduce haze.

Film doesn't like hot weather. If you're driving in summer, don't store film in the glove compartment or on the shelf under the rear window. Put it behind the front seat on the floor, on the side opposite the exhaust pipe.

On a plane trip, never pack unprocessed film in check-in luggage; if your bags get X-rayed, say goodbye to your pictures. Always carry undeveloped film with you through security and ask to have it inspected by hand. (It helps to isolate your film in a plastic bag, ready for quick inspection.) Inspectors at American airports are required by law to honor requests for hand inspection.

The newer airport scanning machines used in all U.S. airports are safe for anything from five to 500 scans, depending on the speed of your film. The effects are cumulative; you can put the same roll of film through several scans without worry. After five scans, though, you're asking for trouble.

If your film gets fogged and you want an explanation, send it to the National Association of Photographic Manufacturers (600 Mamaroneck Ave., Harrison, NY 10528). It will try to determine what went wrong. The service is free.

Car Rentals

Florida is a car renter's bazaar, with more discount companies offering more bargains—and more fine print—than anywhere else in the nation. If you're planning to rent a car in Florida, shop around for the best combination rate for car and airfare. Jacksonville, for example, is often somewhat cheaper to fly into than Miami, but Miami's car-rental rate are usually lower than Jacksonville's. In major Florida cities, peak-season rates for a subcompact average around $110 a week, often with unlimited mileage. Some companies advertise peak-season promotional rates as low as $59 a week with unlimited mileage, but only a few cars are available at this rate, and you may have to pay twice as much if you keep the car less than seven days! Some of these companies require you to keep the car in the state and are quick to charge for an extra day when you return a vehicle late.

Avis (800/331–1212), **Budget** (tel. 800/527–0700), **Dollar** (tel. 800/421–6868), **Hertz** (tel. 800/654–3131), **National** (tel. 800/328–4567), **Sears** (tel. 800/527–0770), and **Thrifty** (tel. 800/367–2277) maintain airport and city locations throughout Florida. So do **Alamo** (tel. 800/327–9633) and **General** (tel. 800/327–7607), which offer some of the state's lowest rates. **Rent-A-Wreck** (tel. 800/221–8282) and **Ugly Duckling** (tel. 800/365–4357) rent used cars throughout the state, usually with more stringent mileage restrictions.

Besides the national rental companies, several regional and local firms offer good deals in major Florida cities. These include **Ajax** (tel. 800/352–2529), **Auto Host** (tel. 800/527–4678), **Payless** (tel. 800/237–2804), **Lindo's** (tel. 800/237–8396), **USA** (tel. 800/872–2277), and **Value** (tel. 800/327–2501). Ajax is a major budget renter in Jacksonville, with three beach offices. In Fort Lauderdale, local companies include **Aapex Thompson** (tel. 305/566–8663), and **Air and Sea** (tel. 305/764–1008). In Orlando, try **Buck An Hour** (tel. 407/273–4000) and **Wheels** (tel. 407/351–6461). Tampa–St. Petersburg companies include **A-Florida Rent-A-Heap** (tel. 813/581–4805) and **Phoenix** (tel. 813/360–6941). In Miami, **A-OK** (tel. 305/633–3313) and **Dolphin** (tel. 305/871–5553) are local budget companies, while **AutoExotica** (tel. 305/871–3686) and **Cars of the Rich and Famous** (tel. 305/945–2737) rent cars fit for a "Miami Vice" set. Down in Key West, try **Tropical Rent-a-Car** (tel. 305/294–8136).

It's always best to know a few essentials *before* you arrive at the car-rental counter. Find out what the collision damage waiver (CDW), usually an $8–$12 daily surcharge, covers and whether your corporate or personal insurance already covers damage to a rental car (if so, bring a photocopy of the benefits section along). More and more companies are now holding renters responsible for theft and vandalism damages if they don't buy the CDW; in response, some credit card and insurance companies are extending *their* coverage to rental cars. These include **Access America** (tel. 800/851–2800), **Chase Manhattan Bank Visa Cards** (tel. 800/645–7352), and **Dreyfus Consumer Bank Gold and Silver MasterCards** (tel. 800/847–9700). Find out, too, if you must pay for a full tank of gas whether you use it or not, and make sure you get a reservation number.

Traveling with Children

Publications *Family Travel Times,* an 8- to 12-page newsletter published 10 times a year by Travel with Your Children (80 Eighth Ave., New York, NY 10011, tel. 212/206–0688). The $35 subscription includes access to back issues and twice-weekly opportunities to call in for specific advice. Send $1 for a sample issue.

Great Vacations with Your Kids: The Complete Guide to Family Vacations in the U.S. by Dorothy Ann Jordon and Marjorie Adoff Cohen (E. P. Dutton, 2 Park Ave., New York, NY 10016; $9.95) details everything from city vacations to adventure vacations to child-care resources.

Bimonthly publications for parents that are filled with listings of events, resources, and advice are available free at such places as libraries, supermarkets, and museums: *Florida Parent* (4331 N. Federal Hwy., Ft. Lauderdale 33060, tel. 305/776–3305) covers Palm Beach, Broward, and Dade counties; *Tampa Bay Family Times* (Box 17481, Tampa 33682, tel. 813/877–0217) covers Hillsborough County. For a small fee, you can usually have an issue sent to you before your trip.

Hotels   Florida may have the highest concentration of hotels with organized children's programs in the United States. The following list gives examples of the kinds of services and activities offered by some of the major chains. It is by no means exhaustive. Be sure to ask about children's programs when you make a reservation.

Club Med (40 W. 57th St., New York, NY 10019, tel. 800/CLUB-MED) opened its new Sandpiper resort village in Port St. Lucie, including a "Baby Club" (4–23 months), "Mini Club" (2 years and up), and "Kids Club" (8 years and up). **Guest Quarters Suite Hotels** (Ft. Lauderdale and Tampa locations, tel. 800/424–2900) offers the luxury of two-room suites with kitchen facilities and children's menus in the restaurant. It also allows children under 18 to stay free in the same suite with their parents. Two **Sonesta International Hotels** (tel. 800/343–7170) have children's programs: Sonesta VillHotel Orlando and Sonesta Beach Hotel Key Biscayne. The **Hyatt Regency Grand Cypress** at Orlando (1 Grand Cypress Blvd., Orlando 32819, tel. 407/239–1234 or 800/228–9000) staffs a year-round child-care center for kids 3–12 and organizes summer activities for toddlers through teens. There's a Children's Creative Center at the **Delta Court of Flags** (5715 Major Blvd., Orlando 32819, tel. 407/351–3340). Also look for children's programs at **Marriott's Harbor Beach Resort** (3030 Holiday Dr., Ft. Lauderdale 33316, tel. 305/525–4000 or 800/228–9290); The **Stouffer Orlando Resort** (6677 Sea Harbor Dr., Orlando 32821, tel. 407/351–5555 or 800/468–3571); **Amelia Island Plantation Resort** (Rte. A1A, Amelia Island 32034, tel. 904/261–6161); **Holiday Inn Main Gate East** at Disney World (5678 Space Coast Hwy., Kissimmee 32741, tel. 407/396–4488 or 800/465–4329); and **Marriott's Marco Island Resort** (400 S. Collier Blvd., Marco Island 33937, tel. 813/394–2511 or 800/228–9290). Most **Days Inn** hotels (tel. 800/325–2525) charge only a nominal fee for children under 18 and allow kids 12 and under to eat free (many offer efficiency-type apartments, too).

Condo Rentals   See *The Condo Lux Vacationer's Guide to Condominium Rentals in the Southeast* by Jill Little (Vintage Books/Random House, New York; $9.95).

Home Exchange   See *Home Exchanging: A Complete Sourcebook for Travelers at Home or Abroad* by James Dearing (Globe Pequot Press, Box Q, Chester, CT 06412, tel. 800/243–0495 or in CT 800/962–0973; $9.95).

Getting There   On domestic flights, children under 2 who do not occupy a seat travel free. Various discounts apply to children 2–12. Reserve a seat behind the bulkhead of the plane, which offers more legroom and can usually fit a bassinet (supplied by the airline). At the same time, inquire about special children's meals or snacks, offered by most airlines. (See "TWYCH's Airline Guide," in the Feb. 1988 issue of *Family Travel Times,* for a rundown on the services offered by 46 airlines; an update is planned for February 1990.) Ask the airline in advance if you can bring aboard your child's car seat. (For the booklet "Child/Infant Safety Seats Acceptable for Use in Aircraft," write Community and Consumer Liaison Division, APA-400 Federal Aviation Administration, Washington, DC 20591, tel. 202/267–3479.)

Hints for Disabled Travelers

The Information Center for Individuals with Disabilities (Fort Point Place, 1st floor, 27–43 Wormwood St., Boston, MA 02117, tel. 617/727–5540) offers useful problem-solving assistance, including lists of travel agents that specialize in tours for the disabled.
Moss Rehabilitation Hospital Travel Information Service (12th St. and Taber Rd., Philadelphia, PA 19141, tel. 215/329–5715) provides information on tourist sights, transportation, and accommodations in destinations around the world. The fee is $5 for up to three destinations. Allow one month for delivery.
Mobility International (Box 3551, Eugene, OR 97403, tel. 503/343–1284) is a membership organization with a $20 annual fee offering information on accommodations, organized study, and so forth.
The Society for the Advancement of Travel for the Handicapped (26 Court St., Penthouse Suite, Brooklyn, NY 11242, tel. 718/858–5483) offers access information. Annual membership costs $40, or $25 for senior travelers and students. Send $1 and a stamped, self-addressed envelope.
The **National Park Service** provides a **Golden Access Passport** free of charge to those who are medically blind or have a permanent disability; the passport covers the entry fee for the holder and anyone accompanying the holder in the same private, noncommercial vehicle and a 50% discount on camping, boat launching, and parking. All charges are covered except lodging. Apply for the passport in person at any national recreation facility that charges an entrance fee; proof of disability is required. For additional information, write to the National Park Service (U.S. Dept. of Interior, 18th and C Sts. NW, Washington, DC 20240).
"Information/Referral Numbers for Physically Challenged Visitors" is a useful booklet available without charge from the Florida Bureau of Visitor Services (101 E. Gaines St., Fletcher Bldg., Room 422, Tallahassee 32399, tel. 904/488–7300).
Greyhound/Trailways (tel. 800/531–5332) will carry a disabled person and companion for the price of a single fare.
Amtrak (tel. 800/USA–RAIL) requests 72 hours' notice to provide redcap service, special seats, or wheelchair assistance at stations equipped to provide this service. All handicapped and elderly passengers are entitled to a 25% discount on regular, discounted coach fares. A special children's handicapped fare is also available, offering qualifying children ages 2–11 a 25% discount on their already discounted children's fare. It should be noted that there are exceptions to these discounts on certain prescribed days with various routes. Always check with Amtrak first. For a free copy of *Access Amtrak,* a guide to its services for elderly and handicapped travelers, write to Amtrak (National Railroad Corporation, 400 N Capitol St. NW, Washington, DC 20001).

Publications Twin Peaks Press (Box 129, Vancover, WA 98666, tel. 206/694–2462 or 800/637–2256 for orders only) specializes in books for the disabled:

Travel for the Disabled ($9.95) offers a comprehensive list of guidebooks and facilities geared to the disabled.

Directory of Travel Agencies for the Disabled ($12.95) lists more than 350 agencies throughout the world.

Wheelchair Vagabond ($9.95) helps independent travelers plan for extended trips in cars, vans, or campers. Twin Peaks also offers a "Traveling Nurse's Network," which provides registered nurses trained in all medical areas to accompany and assist disabled travelers.

The Itinerary (Box 1084, Bayonne, NJ 07002, tel. 201/858–3400) is a bimonthly travel magazine for the disabled. Call for a subscription ($10 for a year, $18 for two); it's not available in stores.

Access to the World: A Travel Guide for the Handicapped, by Louise Weiss, offers tips on travel and accessibility around the world. It is available from Henry Holt & Co. for $12.95 (tel. 800/247–3912, the order number is 0805 001417).

Access Travel, published in 1985 by the U.S. office of Consumer Affairs, is a free brochure that lists design features, facilities, and services for the handicapped at 519 airport terminals in 62 countries. Order publication 570V by writing S. James, Consumer Information Center-K, Box 100, Pueblo, CO 81002.

Access America: An Atlas and Guide to the National Parks for Visitors with Disabilities (published by Northern Cartographic, Box 133, Burlington, VT 05402, tel. 801/655–4321) contains detailed information about access for the 37 largest and most visited national parks in the United States. It costs $67.45 plus $5 shipping if ordered directly from the publisher.

Hints for Older Travelers

The **American Association of Retired Persons** (AARP, 1909 K St. NW, Washington, DC 20049, tel. 202/872–4700) has two programs for independent travelers: (1) the Purchase Privilege Program, which offers discounts on hotels, airfare, car rentals, and sightseeing, and (2) the AARP Motoring Plan, which offers emergency aid (road service) and trip-routing information for an annual fee of $33.95 per person or per married couple. The **AARP Travel Service** also arranges group tours in conjunction with two companies: Olson-Travelworld (100 N. Sepulvedo Blvd., El Segundo, CA 90245, tel. 800/227–7737) and RFD, Inc. (4401 West 110th St., Overland Park, KS 66211, tel. 800/448–7010). AARP members must be 50 or older. Annual dues are $5 per person or per married couple.

If you're planning to use an AARP or other senior-citizen identification card to obtain a reduced hotel rate, mention it at the time you make your reservation, not when you check out. At restaurants, show your card to the maître d' before you're seated, because discounts may be limited to certain set menus, days, or hours. When renting a car, remember that economy cars, priced at promotional rates, may cost less than cars that are available with your ID card.

Travel Industry and Disabled Exchange (TIDE, 5435 Donna Ave., Tarzana, CA 91356, tel. 818/343–6339) is an industry-based organization with a $15-per-person annual membership fee. Members receive a quarterly newsletter and information on travel agencies and tours.

National Council of Senior Citizens (925 15th St. NW, Washington, DC 20005, tel. 202/347–8800) is a nonprofit advocacy group with some 4,000 local clubs across the country. Annual membership is $10 per person or $14 per couple. Members receive a monthly newspaper with travel information and an ID for reduced rates on hotels and car rentals.

Mature Outlook (6001 N. Clark St., Chicago, IL 60660, tel. 800/336–6330), a subsidiary of Sears Roebuck & Co., is a travel club for people over 50, offering discounts at Holiday Inns and a bimonthly newsletter. Annual membership is $9.95 per person or per married couple. Instant membership is available at participating Holiday Inns.

Golden Age Passport is a free lifetime pass to all parks, monuments, and recreation areas run by the federal government. People over 62 should pick one up in person at any national park that charges admission. A driver's license or other proof of age is required.

September Days Club (tel. 800/241–5050) is run by the moderately priced **Days Inns of America.** The $12 annual membership fee for individuals or couples over 50 entitles them to reduced car rental rates and reductions of 15%–50% at 95% of the chain's more than 350 motels. Members also receive *Travel Holiday Magazine Quarterly* for updated information and travel articles.

Elderhostel (80 Boylston St., Suite 400, Boston, MA 02116, tel. 617/426–7788) is an innovative program for people age 60 or over (only one member of a traveling couple needs to qualify). Participants live on dorms on 1,200 campuses in the United States and around the world. Mornings are devoted to lectures and seminars, afternoons to sightseeing and field trips. The fee includes room, board, tuition (in the United States and Canada) and round-trip transportation (overseas). Special scholarships are available for those who qualify financially.

Publications "Travel Tips for Senior Citizens" (U.S. Dept. of State Publication 8970, revised Sept. 1987) is available for $1 from the Superintendent of Documents (U.S. Government Printing Office, Washington, DC 20402). *The Discount Guide for Travelers Over 55*, by Caroline and Walter Weintz, lists helpful addresses, package tours, reduced-rate car rentals, etc., in the United States and abroad. To order, send $7.95 plus $3 shipping and handling to NAL/Cash Sales (Bergenfield Order Dept., 120 Woodbine St., Bergenfield, NJ 07021, tel. 800/526–0275). *The Senior Citizen's Guide to Budget Travel in the United States and Canada* is available for $4.95 plus shipping from Pilot Books (103 Cooper St., Babylon, NY 11702, tel. 516/422–2225).

Although Florida probably attracts more elderly people than any other state, the state publishes no booklet addressed directly to senior citizens.

Senior-citizen discounts are common throughout Florida, but there are no set standards. Some discounts, like those for prescriptions at the Eckerd Drug chain, require that you fill out a card and register. The best bet is simply to ask whether there is a senior-citizen discount available on your purchase, meal, or hotel stay.

Further Reading

Suspense novels that are rich in details about Florida include Elmore Leonard's *La Brava*, John D. MacDonald's *The Empty Copper Sea*, and Joan Higgins's *A Little Death Music*. Pat Frank's *Alas Babylon* describes a fictional nuclear disaster in Florida.

Marjorie K. Rawlings's classic, *The Yearling*, poignantly portrays life in the brush country, and her *Cross Creek* re-creates the memorable people the author knew from 13 years of living at Cross Creek.

Look for *Snow White and Rose Red* and *Jack and the Beanstalk*, Ed McBain's novels about Matthew Hope, an attorney who practices law in a Florida gulf city. Pat Booth's novel *Palm Beach* describes the glittering Palm Beach scene of sun and sex.

Other recommended novels include Evelyn Mayerson's *No Enemy But Time; To Have and Have Not*, by Ernest Hemingway; *The Day of the Dolphin*, by Robert Merle; and *Their Eyes Were Watching God*, by Zora Neale Hurston, a tale of life in a black town in northern Florida.

Among the recommended nonfiction books are *Key West Writers and Their Homes*, Lynn Kaufelt's tour of homes of Hemingway, Wallace Stevens, Tennessee Williams, and others; *The Everglades: River of Grass*, by Marjory S. Douglas; *Florida*, by Gloria Jahoda, published as part of the Bicentennial observance; *Miami Alive*, by Ethel Blum; and *Florida's Sandy Beaches*, University Press of Florida.

Arriving and Departing

By Plane

Most major U.S. airlines schedule regular flights into Florida, and some, such as Delta, serve the Florida airports extensively.

Delta, Eastern, and Piedmont all have regular service into Jacksonville, Daytona Beach, Orlando, Melborne, West Palm Beach, Fort Lauderdale, Miami, Fort Myers, Tampa, Tallahassee, Gainesville, and Key West. Delta also flies into Sarasota, Naples, Pensacola, and Fort Pierce.

Other major airlines that serve the Florida airports include Continental, American, USAir, American Trans Air, Northwest, Pan Am, United, and TWA. Many foreign airlines also fly into some of the major airports in Florida; the smaller, out-of-the-way airports are usually accessible through the commuter flights of major domestic carriers.

Packages that combine airfare and vacation activities at special rates are often available through the airlines. For example, Delta (tel. 800/872–7786) and Pan Am (tel. 800/221–1111) both offer travel packages to Disney World in Orlando (*see* Package Deals for Independent Travelers).

When booking reservations, keep in mind the distinction between nonstop flights (no stops and no changes), direct flights (no changes of aircraft, but one or more stops), and connecting flights (one or more changes of planes at one or more stops). Connecting flights are often the least expensive, but they are the most time-consuming, and the biggest nuisance.

Smoking   If cigarette smoke bothers you, request a seat *far away from* the smoking section. Remember, FAA regulations require airlines to find seats for all nonsmokers.

Carry-on Luggage   Under new rules in effect since January 1988, passengers are usually limited to two carry-on bags. For bags stored under your seat, the maximum dimensions are 9″ × 14″ × 22″. For bags that can be hung in a closet, the maximum dimensions are 4″ × 23″ × 45″. For bags stored in an overhead bin, the maximum dimensions are 10″ × 14″ × 36″. Any item that exceeds the specified dimensions will generally be rejected as a carryon and handled as checked baggage. Keep in mind that an airline can adapt these rules to circumstances; on an especially crowded flight, don't be surprised if you are allowed only one carry-on bag.

In addition to the two carryons, passengers may also bring aboard: a handbag (pocketbook or purse), an overcoat or wrap, an umbrella, a camera, a reasonable amount of reading material, an infant bag, crutches, cane, braces, or other prosthetic device upon which the passenger is dependent, and an infant/child safety seat.

Note that these regulations are for U.S. airlines only. Foreign airlines generally allow one piece of carry-on luggage in tourist class, in addition to handbags and bags filled with duty-free goods. Passengers in first and business class are also allowed to carry on one garment bag. It is best to check with your airline ahead of time to find out what their exact rules are regarding carry-on luggage.

Checked Luggage   Luggage allowances vary slightly from airline to airline. Many carriers allow three checked pieces; some allow only two. It is best to check before you go. In all cases, check-in luggage cannot weigh more than 70 pounds per piece or be larger than 62 inches (length + width + height).

Lost Luggage   On domestic flights, airlines are responsible for lost or damaged property only up to $1,250 per passenger. If you're carrying valuables, either take them with you on the airplane or purchase additional insurance for lost luggage. Some airlines will issue additional luggage insurance when you check in, but many do not. Insurance for lost, damaged, or stolen luggage is available through travel agents or directly through various insurance companies. Two that issue luggage insurance are **Tele-Trip** (tel. 800/228–9792), a subsidiary of Mutual of Omaha, and **The Travelers Insurance Co.** (Ticket and Travel Dept., 1 Tower Sq., Hartford, CT 06183, tel. 800/243–3174 or 203/277–2318). Tele-Trip operates sales booths at airports, and it also issues insurance through travel agents. Tele-Trip will insure checked luggage for up to 180 days at $500–$3,000 valuation. For 1–3 days, the rate for a $500 valuation is $8.25; for 180 days, $100. The Travelers will insure checked or hand luggage at $500–$2,000 valuation per person, also for a maximum of 180 days. Rates for 1–5 days for $500 valuation are $10; for 180 days, $85.

Other companies with comprehensive policies include **Access America Inc.,** a subsidiary of Blue Cross-Blue Shield (Box 807, New York, NY 10163, tel. 800/851–2800); **Near, Inc.** (1900 N. MacArthur Blvd., Suite 210, Oklahoma City, OK 73127, tel. 800/654–6700); and **Travel Guard International** (*see* Health and Accident Insurance).

Before you go, itemize the contents of each bag in case you need to file an insurance claim. Be certain to put your home address on each piece of luggage, including carry-on bags. If your luggage is stolen and later recovered, the airline must deliver the luggage to your home free of charge.

By Car

Three major interstates lead to Florida from various parts of the country. I–95 begins in Maine, runs south through New England and the Mid-Atlantic states, and enters Florida just north of Jacksonville. It continues south past Daytona Beach, Vero Beach, Palm Beach, and Fort Lauderdale, eventually ending in Miami.

I–75 begins at the Canadian border in Michigan and runs south through Ohio, Kentucky, Tennessee, and Georgia before entering Florida. The interstate moves through the center of the state before veering west into Tampa. It follows the west coast south to Naples, then crosses the state and ends in Miami.

California and all the most southern states are connected to Florida by I–10. This interstate originates in Los Angeles and moves east through Arizona, New Mexico, Texas, Louisiana, Mississippi, and Alabama before entering Florida at Pensacola on the west coast. I–10 continues straight across the northern half of the state until it terminates in Jacksonville.

Speed Limits In Florida the speed limits are 55 mph on the state highways, 30 mph within city limits and residential areas, 55–65 mph on the interstates. These limits may vary, so be sure to watch road signs for any changes.

By Train

Amtrak (tel. 800/USA-RAIL) provides service to Orlando, Tampa, Miami, Tallahassee, Jacksonville, and several other major cities in Florida.

By Bus

Greyhound-Trailways passes through practically every major city in Florida, including Jacksonville, Daytona, Orlando, West Palm Beach, Fort Lauderdale, Miami, Sarasota, Tampa, Tallahassee, and Key West. For information about bus schedules and fares, contact your local Greyhound Information Center.

Staying in Florida

Tourist Information

The **Florida Division of Tourism** operates **welcome centers** on I–10, I–75, I–95, U.S. 231 (near Graceville), U.S. 1 and 301 (near Boulogne) and in the lobby of the new Capitol in Tallahassee

(Department of Commerce, 126 Van Buren St., Tallahassee 32399, tel. 904/487–1462).

Shopping

Malls in Florida are full of nationally franchised shops, major department-store chains, and one-of-a-kind shops catering to a mass audience. Small shops in out-of-the-way places, however, often have the best souvenirs and most special gift items.

Indian Artifacts Indian crafts are abundant, particularly in the southern part of the state, where you'll find billowing dresses and shirts, hand-sewn in striking colors and designs. At the Miccosukee Indian Village, 25 miles west of Miami on the Tamiami Trail (U.S. 41), as well as at the Seminole and Miccosukee reservations in the Everglades, you can also find handcrafted dolls, and beaded belts.

Seashells The best shelling in Florida is on the beaches of Sanibel Island off Fort Myers. Shell shops, selling mostly kitsch items, abound throughout Florida. The largest such establishment is The Shell Factory near Fort Myers (*see* Shopping in Chapter 10).

Citrus Fruit Orange juice—Florida's "liquid gold"—is a staple throughout the state. The welcome centers greet visitors with a fresh glass of it and many restaurants squeeze it for you while you watch. Fresh citrus is available most of the year, except in summer. Some groves still give free samples of juice and fruit slices, but many now charge a small fee for a taste.

Don't expect to roam the groves picking your own fruit. Public access was prohibited to limit the spread of a disastrous canker blight which threatened Florida's citrus industry in the mid-1980s.

Two kinds of citrus grow in Florida: the sweeter and more costly Indian River fruit from a thin ribbon of groves along the east coast, and the less-costly fruit from the interior. After killer freezes in 1984 and 1985 ruined many groves in the Orlando area, the interior growers began planting in warmer areas south and west of Lake Okeechobee.

Citrus is sold in quarter, half, three-quarter, and full bushels. Many shippers offer special gift packages with several varieties of fruit, jellies, and other food items. Some prices include U.S. postage, others may not. Shipping may exceed the cost of the fruit. If you have a choice of citrus packaged in boxes or bags, take the boxes. They are easier to label, are harder to squash, and travel better than the bags.

Malls and Boutiques The Greater Miami area has many look-alike shopping strips and malls with the same retail and discount shops. You'll find finer boutiques in specialty malls such as Mayfair Shops in the Grove (*see* Exploring Coral Gables/Coconut Grove/South Miami in Chapter 3) and the Bal Harbor Shops (9700 Collins Ave., Bal Harbour 33154, tel. 305/866–0311). The half mile of Flagler Street in the heart of downtown Miami is the nation's most important import-export center, where bargain items for international travelers include cameras, electronics, and jewelry (*see* Exploring Downtown Miami in Chapter 3).

Fort Lauderdale's finest shops cluster along six blocks of Las Olas Boulevard (*see* Exploring Fort Lauderdale in Chapter 5) and at the 150-store Galleria At Fort Lauderdale (2414 E. Sunrise Blvd., tel. 305/564–1015).

For the ultimate Florida shopping experience, stroll Palm Beach's Worth Avenue (*see* Shopping in Chapter 6). Here you'll find shops like Gucci and Ralph Lauren tucked between galleries selling ancient Chinese art or Oriental rugs, gourmet restaurants, one-of-a-kind jewelry stores, and chocolatiers.

South of Tampa Bay on Florida's west coast, St. Armand's Circle in Sarasota has many elegant clothing shops and fine restaurants (*see* Shopping in Chapter 10). North of Tampa Bay in Tarpon Springs, you'll enjoy exploring sponge shops and savoring Greek fare along Dodecanese Boulevard (*see* Shopping in Chapter 10).

Shops at the World Showcase in Epcot Center at Walt Disney World offer unusual lines of clothing, decorative items, gifts, and fine wines from many parts of the globe.

To shop and dine in a gracious 19th-century setting, visit the commercial heart of old Pensacola in the Palafox Historic District and the adjoining Seville Historic District centered around Seville Square. At the Quayside Thieves Market (712 S. Palafox St.), antiques shops, and a flea market occupy a historic 19th-century warehouse beside the port. Specialty shops in Pensacola's historic district offer art, Christmas decorations, cookware, fine gifts, linens, and out-of-print books (*see* Exploring North Florida in Chapter 11).

To travel even farther back in time, stroll the four-block pedestrian zone on Saint George Street in Old St. Augustine. Shoppers are serenaded by street musicians as they pause to window-wish or peer into dimly lit shops to watch craftsmen at work (*see* North St. Augustine in Chapter 11).

Antiques-lovers should explore Micanopy, south of Gainesville off I–75; the Antiques Mall in St. Augustine's Lightner Museum, on U.S. 1 north of Dania Beach Boulevard in Dania; and S.W. 28th Lane and Unity Boulevard in Miami (near the Coconut Grove Metrorail station).

Beaches

No point in Florida is more than 60 miles from saltwater. This long, lean peninsula is bordered by a 526-mile Atlantic coast from Fernandina Beach to Key West and a 792-mile coast along the Gulf of Mexico and Florida Bay from Pensacola to Key West. If you were to stretch Florida's convoluted coast in a straight line, it would extend for about 1,800 miles. What's more, if you add in the perimeter of every island surrounded by saltwater, Florida has about 8,500 miles of tidal shoreline— more than any other state except Alaska. Sand beaches comprise about 1,016 miles of Florida's coastline.

Visitors unaccustomed to strong subtropical sun run a risk of sunburn and heat prostration on Florida beaches, even in winter. The natives go to the beach early in the day or in the late afternoon. If they must be out in direct sun at midday, they limit their sun exposure and strenuous exercise and drink plenty of liquids.

The state owns all beaches below the mean high-tide line, even in front of hotels and private resorts, but gaining access to the public beach can be a problem along much of Florida's coastline. You must pay to enter and/or park at most state, county, and local beachfront parks. Where hotels dominate the beach frontage, public parking may be limited or nonexistent.

Along the Atlantic coast from the Georgia border south through the Daytona Beach area, the beaches are so broad and firm that you can drive on them. Some beachfront communities in this area charge for the privilege; others provide free beach access for vehicles.

From the Treasure Coast south, erosion has been gnawing away at the beaches. Major beach rehabilitation projects have been completed in Fort Lauderdale, the Sunny Isles area of north Dade County, Miami Beach, and Key Biscayne.

In the Florida Keys, coral reefs and prevailing currents prevent sand from building up to form beaches. The few Keys beaches are small, narrow, and generally have little or no sandy bottom.

On the Gulf Coast, Captiva Island is losing sand to neighboring Sanibel Island, where a stroll beside the water at sunrise or sunset can be a truly sensual experience. Currents bring all sorts of unusual shells onto Sanibel's beach, and scatter sharks' teeth across Venice and Caspersen beaches in south Sarasota County. Siesta Beach in Sarasota County claims to have Florida's softest white sand. At the north end of Longboat Key in Manatee County, accretion has built a magnificent beach in the vicinity of Beer Can Island. Much of that sand came from Coquina Beach and Bradenton Beach, county parks that remain popular with local residents despite their dwindling supply of sand. In Pinellas County, visit Caladesi Island State Park to experience what all the barrier islands used to look like.

In Florida's Panhandle, Gulf Island National Seashore administers 150 miles of beach frontage notable for their sugarlike sand and the impressive dune formations near Fort Walton Beach. Expect the beaches outside Panama City and Pensacola to be crowded on summer weekends.

Participant Sports

Bicycling   Bicycling is popular throughout Florida. The terrain is flat in the south and gently rolling along the central ridge and in much of the Panhandle. Most cities of any size have bike-rental shops, which are good sources of information on local bike paths.

Florida's Department of Transportation (DOT) publishes free bicycle trail guides, which you can request from the state bicycle-pedestrian coordinator. (605 Suwannee St., Mail Room Station 19, Tallahassee 32399-0450, tel. 904/488–4640). DOT also sells seven maps for bicycle trips of 35 to 300 miles. *Maps and Publications, 605 Suwannee St., Mail Room Station 12, Tallahassee 32399-0450, tel. 904/488–9220. Cost: $1 plus 6% sales tax per map.*

For information on local biking events and clubs, contact **Florida Bicycle Associations** (Box 16652, Tampa 33687-6652, tel. 800/ FOR BIKE). In Greater Miami, contact Dade County's bicycle-pedestrian coordinator (Office of the County Manager, Metro-

Dade Government Center, 111 N.W. 1st St., Suite 910, Miami 33128, tel. 305/375–4507).

Canoeing The best time to canoe in Florida is winter, the dry season, when you're less likely to get caught in a torrential downpour or be eaten alive by mosquitos.

The Everglades has areas suitable for flat-water wilderness canoeing that are comparable to spots in the Boundary Waters region of Minnesota. Other popular canoeing rivers include the Crystal, Peace, St. Johns, Suwannee, Wakulla, Wekiva, and Withlacoochee. A free guide issued by the Florida Department of Natural Resources (DNR), *Florida Recreational Trails System Canoe Trails,* describes nearly 950 miles of designated canoe trails along 36 Florida creeks, rivers, and springs (Office of Communications, Marjory Stoneman Douglas Building, 3900 Commonwealth Blvd., Tallahassee 32399, tel. 904/488–6327). Contact individual national forests, parks, monuments, reserves, and seashores for information on their canoe trails. Local chambers of commerce have information on canoe trails in county parks.

Two Florida canoe outfitter organizations publish free lists of canoe outfitters who organize canoe trips, rent canoes and canoeing equipment, and help shuttle canoeists' boats and cars. *Canoe Outpost System* is a brochure listing eight independent outfitters serving 11 Florida rivers (Rte. 7, Box 301, Arcadia 33821, tel. 813/494–1215). The **Florida Association of Canoe Liveries and Outfitters (FACLO)** publishes a free list of 26 canoe outfitters who organize trips on 28 creeks and rivers (Box 1764, Arcadia 33821).

Fishing When President Bush made his pre-inaugural bonefishing trip to Islamorada in 1989, he was following a time-honored angling tradition. Other celebrities who have come to Florida to cast a hook and line include President Theodore Roosevelt, British statesman Winston Churchill, and novelists Zane Grey and Ernest Hemingway.

In Atlantic and Gulf waters, fishing seasons and other regulations vary by location, and by the number and size of fish of various species that you may catch and retain. For a free copy of the annual *Florida Fishing Handbook,* write to the **Florida Game and Fresh Water Fish Commission** (620 Meridian St., Tallahassee 32399-1600, tel. 904/488–1960).

Opportunities for salt-water fishing abound from the Keys all the way up the Atlantic Coast to Georgia and up the Gulf Coast to Alabama. Many seaside communities have fishing piers that charge admission to fishermen (and usually a lower rate to watchers). These piers usually have a bait-and-tackle shop. Write the **Florida Sea Grant Extension Program** for a free list of Florida fishing piers (Rm. G-022, McCarty Hall, University of Florida, Gainesville 32611, tel. 904/392–1771).

Inland, there are more than 7,000 fresh-water lakes to choose from. The largest—448,000-acre **Lake Okeechobee,** the fourth-largest natural lake in the United States—is home to bass, bluegill, speckled perch, and succulent catfish (which the locals call "sharpies"). In addition to the state's many natural fresh-water rivers, South Florida also has an extensive system of flood-control canals. In 1989 scientists found high mercury levels in largemouth bass and warmouth caught in parts of the

Everglades in Palm Beach, Broward, and Dade counties, and warned against eating fish from those areas.

It's easy to find a boat-charter service that will take you out into deep water. Some of the best are found in the Panhandle, where small towns like Destin and Fort Walton Beach have huge fleets. The Keys, too, are dotted with charter services, and Key West has a sportfishing and shrimping fleet that you would expect to find in large cities. Depending on your taste, budget, and needs, you can charter anything from an old wooden craft to a luxurious, waterborne palace with state-of-the-art amenities.

Licenses are required for both freshwater and saltwater fishing. The fees for a saltwater fishing license are $30 for nonresidents and $12 for residents. Nonresidents can purchase freshwater fishing licenses good for 10 days ($15) or for one year ($30); residents pay $12 for an annual license. Combined annual freshwater fishing and hunting licenses are also available at $66 for nonresidents and $150 for residents.

Golf Except in the heart of the Everglades, you'll never be far from one of Florida's 930 golf courses. Palm Beach County, the state's leading golf locale with 130 golf courses, also hosts the home offices of the National Golf Foundation and the Professional Golfers Association of America.

Many of the best golf courses in Florida allow visitors to play without being members or hotel guests. Thus, you can pretend that you're playing in the annual Doral Ryder Open when you play the deadly 18th hole on the Blue Monster course at the Doral Resort and Country Club in Miami. Walt Disney World's popular Palm Course also is open to public play.

Especially in winter, you should reserve tee-off times in advance. Ask about golf reservations when you make your lodging reservations.

Hunting Hunters in Florida stalk a wide variety of resident game animals and birds, including deer, wild hog, wild turkey, bob white quail, ducks, and coots. A plain hunting license costs $11 for Florida residents, $50 for nonresidents.

Each year in June, the **Florida Game and Fresh Water Fish Commission** announces the dates and hours of the fall hunting seasons for public and private wildlife-management areas. Hunting seasons vary across the state. Where hunting is allowed, you need the landowner's written permission—and you must carry that letter with your hunting license in the field. Trespassing with a weapon is a felony. For a free copy of the annual *Florida Hunting Handbook,* contact the game commission (620 Meridian St., Tallahassee 32399–1600, tel. 904/ 488–1960).

Jogging, Running, and Walking All over Florida, you'll find joggers, runners, and walkers on bike paths and city streets—primarily in the early morning and after working hours in the evening. Some Florida hotels have set up their own running trails; others provide guests with information on measured trails in the vicinity. The first time you run in Florida, be prepared to go a shorter distance than normal because of higher heat and humidity.

Two major Florida festivals include important running races. Each year in January the **Capital Bank Orange Bowl 10K,** the state's best-known running event, brings world-class runners to Miami. In April, as part of the Florida Keys' annual Conch Republic Days, runners congregate near Marathon on one of the world's most spectacular courses for the **Seven Mile Bridge Run.**

Local running clubs all over the state sponsor weekly public events for joggers, runners, and walkers. For a list of local clubs and events throughout the state, call or send a self-addressed stamped envelope to the **Florida Athletics Congress** (1330 N.W. 6th St., Gainesville 32601, tel. 904/336–2120). For information about events in South Florida contact the 1,500-member **Miami Runners Club** (7920 S.W. 40th St., Miami 33155, tel. 305/227–1500).

Scuba Diving and Snorkling South Florida and the Keys attract most of the divers and snorkelers, but the more than 300 dive shops throughout the state schedule drift, reef, and wreck-diving trips for scuba divers all along Florida's Atlantic and Gulf coasts. The low-tech pleasures of snorkeling can be enjoyed all along the Overseas Highway in the Keys and elsewhere where shallow reefs hug the shore.

Inland in north and central Florida, divers explore more than 100 grottoes, rivers, sinkholes, and springs. In some locations, you can swim with manatees ("sea cows"), which migrate in from the sea to congregate around warm springs during the cool winter months. Ginnie Springs, near Bradford, is one of Florida's most famous springs (Rte. 1, Box 153, High Springs 32643, tel. 800/874–8571 or 904/454–2022). Crystal Lodge Resort Motel and Dive Center is a popular gateway to river-diving in the Crystal River in central Florida.

Contact the **Dive Industry Association** for a free directory of Florida dive shops. (Teall's Inc., 111 Saguaro La., Marathon 33050, tel. 305/743–3942).

Tennis Many Florida hotels have a resident tennis pro and offer special tennis packages with lessons. Many local park and recreation departments throughout Florida operate modern tennis centers like those at country clubs, and most such centers welcome nonresidents, for a fee. In the Miami area, you can play at the **Biltmore Tennis Center** in Coral Gables, home of the *Rolex/Orange Bowl International Tennis Championship* or Dade County's **International Tennis Center** on Key Biscayne, home of the *Lipton International Players Championships.*

For general information and schedules for amateur tournaments, contact the **Florida Tennis Association** (801 N.E. 167th St., Suite 301, North Miami Beach 33162, tel. 305/652–2866).

Parks and Nature Preserves

Although Florida is the fourth most-populous state in the nation, more than 5,550 square miles of undeveloped land—almost 10% of the state's total area—have been set aside in national forests, parks, monuments, reserves, and seashores; state forests and parks; county parks; and nature preserves owned and managed by private conservation groups.

On holidays and weekends, crowds flock to Florida's most popular parks—even some on islands that are accessible only by boat. Come early or risk being turned away. Write ahead to ask rangers in the parks, sanctuaries, and preserves about the best season to visit. In winter, northern migratory birds descend on the state. Many resident species breed in the warm summer months, but others (such as the wood stork) time their breeding cycle to the winter dry season. In summer, mosquitos are voracious and daily afternoon thundershowers add to the state's humidity, but this is when the sea turtles come ashore to lay their eggs and when you're most likely to see frigate birds and other tropical species.

Federal Parks The federal government maintains no centralized information service for its natural and historic sites in Florida. You must contact each site directly for information on current recreational facilities and hours. To obtain a copy of **Guide and Map of National Parks of U.S.**, which provides park addresses and facilities lists, write to *U.S. Government Printing Office, Washington, DC 20402. GPO No. 024005008527. Cost: $1.25 (no tax or postage).*

In 1908 the federal government declared the keys around what is now **Fort Jefferson National Monument** in the Dry Tortugas a wildlife sanctuary to protect the sooty tern. **Everglades National Park** was established in 1947. Other natural and historic sites in Florida under federal management include **Big Cypress National Preserve** and **Biscayne National Park** in the Everglades, **Canaveral National Seashore** in central Florida, **Castillo De San Marcos National Monument** in north Florida, **De Soto National Monument** in Bradenton, the 130-acre **Fort Caroline National Memorial** on the St. Johns River in Jacksonville *(tel. 904/641–7155)*, **Fort Matanzas National Monument** south of St. Augustine, and **Gulf Islands National Seashore** in north Florida.

The federal government operates three national forests in Florida. The **Apalachicola National Forest** encompasses 557,000 acres of pine and hardwoods in two ranger districts across the northern coastal plain (west: Apalachicola District Ranger, Box 579, Bristol 32321, tel. 904/643–2282; east: Wakulla District Ranger, Box 309, Crawfordville 32327, tel. 904/926–3561). The 336,000-acre **Ocala National Forest** includes the sandhills of the Big Scrub (*see* Exploring Central Florida in Chapter 9 and the essay in Chapter 2). Cypress swamps and numerous sinkhole lakes dot the 157,000-acre **Osceola National Forest** (District Ranger, Rte. 7, Box 95, Lake City 32055, tel. 904/752–2577).

Federal wildlife refuges in Florida include the **Great White Heron National Wildlife Refuge** and **National Key Deer Refuge** (in the Keys), **Loxahatchee National Wildlife Refuge** near Palm Beach, **J. N. "Ding" Darling National Wildlife Refuge** in southwest Florida, and **Merritt Island National Wildlife Refuge** (Refuge Manager, Box 6504, Titusville 32780, tel. 407/867–0667). The federal government also operates the **Key Largo National Marine Sanctuary** and **Looe Key National Marine Sanctuary**.

State Parks The **Florida Department of Natural Resources** is responsible for hundreds of historic buildings, landmarks, nature preserves, and an expanding state park system. When you request a free copy of the *Florida State Park Guide,* mention which parts of the state you plan to visit. For information on camping facilities at the state parks, ask for the free *Florida State Parks, Fees and Facilities* and *Florida State Parks Camping Reservation*

Procedures brochures (Marjory Stoneman Douglas Building, Room 613, 3900 Commonwealth Blvd., Tallahassee 32399, tel. 904/488–7326.)

Private Nature Preserves In 1905, Audubon Society warden Guy Bradley died while protecting the egrets nesting at Cuthbert Rookery, in what is now Everglades National Park. Private efforts to preserve Florida's fragile ecosystems continue today, as the **National Audubon Society** and the **Nature Conservancy** acquire and manage sensitive natural areas.

Wood storks nest at the National Audubon Society's **Corkscrew Swamp Sanctuary** near Naples. On Big Pine Key, Audubon has leased acreage without charge to the U.S. Fish and Wildlife Service in the **National Key Deer Refuge.** Audubon also controls more than 65 other Florida properties, including islands, prairies, forests, and swamps. Visitation at these sites is limited. For information, contact *National Audubon Society, Sanctuary Director* (Miles Wildlife Sanctuary, RR 1, Box 294, West Cornwall Road, Sharon CT 06069, tel. 203/364–0048).

Only three of the preserves managed by the Nature Conservancy are open to the public: **Blowing Rocks Preserve** *(see* the Treasure Coast section of Chapter 6), **Lignum Vitae Key** (*see* Chapter 7), and the 42-acre **Matanzas Pass Wilderness Preserve** on Estero Island (between Bay and School Streets east of the 3000 block of Estero Boulevard in Ft. Myers Beach).

Four other preserves are scheduled to be open for tours (by appointment only) by early 1990: the 150-acre **Spruce Creek Preserve** in Volusia County, **Apalachicola Bluffs & Ravines** in Liberty County, the 320-acre **Janet Butterfield Brooks Preserve** near Bristol in Hernando County, and the 970-acre **Cummer Sanctuary** in Levy County. For access to these tracts, information on self-guided tour information, and a guide to the Conservancy's holdings (scheduled for publication early in 1990), contact the *Florida Chapter* (The Nature Conservancy, 1353 Palmetto Ave., Winter Park 32789, tel. 407/628–5887). Visitors are welcome at the Winter Park office and at offices in Key West and Tallahassee. *Box 4958, 830 Fleming St., Key West 33041, tel. 305/745–2636; 515-A N. Adams St., Tallahassee 32301, tel. 904/222–0199. Open weekdays 9–5.*

Dining

Florida regional cuisine changes as you move across the state, based on who settled the area and who now operates the restaurants. Look for Minorcan cuisine in St. Augustine, and the traditional Miccosukee and Seminole Indian fried bread, catfish, and frog legs at tribe-owned restaurants in the Everglades. South Florida's diverse assortment of Latin American restaurants offer the distinctive national fare of Argentina, Brazil, Colombia, Cuba, El Salvador, Mexico, Nicaragua, and Puerto Rico as well as West Indian delicacies from the Bahamas, Haiti, and Jamaica.

The influence of earlier Latin settlements remains in Key West and Tampa's Ybor City.

All over Florida, Asian cuisine no longer means just Chinese. Indian, Japanese, Pakistani, Thai, and Vietnamese specialties are now available. Continental cuisine (French, German, Italian, Spanish, and Swiss) is also well represented all over Florida. Many of these restaurants have excellent wine lists. Bern's Steak House in Tampa has the largest wine list in the state—7,000 labels!

Although the better restaurants in all price categories pride themselves on using fresh seafood, in some cases the fish is imported from quite a long distance. Two South Florida seafood pioneers, Joe's Stone Crab Restaurant in Miami Beach and East Coast Fisheries in Miami, still have a steady local supply from their own fish houses in Marathon. In the Florida Keys, many small restaurants specialize in chowder, fritters, salads, and other dishes made with conch (a large shellfish, pronounced "konk").

Every Florida restaurant claims to make the best Key-lime pie. Pastry chefs and restaurant managers take the matter very seriously—they discuss the problems of getting good lime juice and maintaining top quality every day. Traditional Key-lime pie is yellow, not green, with an old-fashioned Graham cracker crust and meringue top. The filling should be tart, and chilled but not frozen. Some restaurants serve their Key-lime pie with a pastry crust; most substitute whipped cream for the more temperamental meringue. Each pie will be a little different. Try several, and make your own choice.

Ratings	Category	Cost*: Major City	Cost*: Other Areas
	Very Expensive	over $50	over $40
	Expensive	$30–$50	$25–$40
	Moderate	$15–$30	$10–$25
	Inexpensive	under $15	under $10

per person, excluding drinks, service, and 6% state sales tax

Lodging

Hotels and Motels All the major hotel and motel chains, including Days Inn, Econo Lodge, Hyatt, Hilton, Holiday Inn, Knight's Inn, Marriott, Motel 6, Peabody, Pickett, Quality Inns, Radisson, Ramada, Sheraton, Stouffer, and Westin are represented in Florida. Holiday Inn, Marriott, and Quality Inns operate under a variety of brand names offering varying levels of amenities and prices.

Although many hotels in Florida have affiliated with a chain to get business from its central reservation system, some fine hotels and resorts still remain independent. They include the Don Cesar Beach Resort on St. Petersburg Beach, Governors Inn in Tallahassee, and Pier House in Key West.

The Florida Hotel & Motel Association publishes an **Annual Travel Directory** which you can obtain without charge at Florida Welcome Centers or by contacting the **Florida Division of Tourism** (Department of Commerce, 126 Van Buren St., Tallahassee 32399, tel. 904/487–1462). You can also order it from the FH&MA if you send them a stamped, addressed No. 10 envelope and $1 for postage and handling (117 W. College Ave., Box

1529, Tallahassee 32301–1529, tel. 904/224–2888 or in FL, 800/
432–2004).

Ratings	Category	Cost*: Major City	Cost*: Other Areas
	Very Expensive	$150 peak season $100 off-peak	$100
	Expensive	$120–$150 peak season $80–$100 off-peak	$70–$100
	Moderate	$80–$120 peak season $50–$80 off-peak	$40–$70
	Inexpensive	under $80 peak season under $50 off-peak	under $40

**All prices are for a standard double room, excluding 6% state
sales tax and nominal (1%–3%) tourist tax.*

**Alternative
Lodgings**

Small inns and guest houses are becoming increasingly numerous and popular in Florida. Many offer the convenience of bed-
and-breakfast accommodations in a homelike setting; many, in
fact, are in private homes, and the owners treat you almost like
a member of the family. **Inn Route, Inc.** (225 W. 5th Ave.,
Mount Dora 32757, tel. 904/383–8397), a new statewide association of small, architecturally distinctive historic inns, planned
to publish a free brochure late in 1989. You can also order *Guide
to the Small and Historic Lodgings of Florida,* a paperback
book updated every two years (Pineapple Press Inc., Drawer
16008, Sarasota 34239, tel. 813/952–1085. Cost: $12.95 plus 6%
sales tax).

Bed-and-breakfast referral and reservation agencies in Florida
include: **A & A Bed & Breakfast of Florida, Inc.** (Box 1316, Winter Park 32790, tel. 407/628–3222), **Bed'n Breakfast—Central
Gulf Coast** (Box 9515, Pensacola 32513–9515, tel. 904/438–
7968), **Bed & Breakfast Co., Tropical Florida** (Box 262, Miami
33243, tel. 305/661–3270), **Bed & Breakfast East Coast** (Box
1373, Marathon 33050, tel. 305/743–4118), **Bed & Breakfast of
Volusia County** (Box 573, De Leon Springs 32028, tel. 904/985–
5068), **Suncoast Accommodations of Florida** (8690 Gulf Blvd.,
St. Petersburg Beach 33706, tel. 813/360–1753) and **Tallahassee
Bed & Breakfast, Inc.** (3023 Windy Hill Lane, Tallahassee
32308, tel. 904/385–3768).

**Camping and
RV Facilities**

Contact directly the national parks and forests you plan to visit
for information on camping facilities (*see* Federal Parks, above).
For information on camping facilities in state parks, contact the
Florida Department of Natural Resources (*see* State Parks,
above).

The free annual *Florida Camping Directory* lists 200 commercial campgrounds in Florida with 50,000 sites. It's available at
Florida Welcome Centers, from the Florida Division of Tourism, and from the **Florida Campground Association** (1638 N.
Plaza Dr., Tallahassee 32308–5323, tel. 904/656–8878).

**Vacation
Ownership Resorts**

Vacation ownership resorts sell hotel rooms, condominium
apartments, or villas in weekly, monthly, or quarterly incre-

ments. The weekly arrangement is most popular; it's often referred to as "interval ownership" or "time sharing." Of 1,100 vacation ownership resorts in the U.S., 300 are in Florida, with the heaviest concentration in the Disney World/Orlando area. Most vacation ownership resorts are affiliated with one of two major exchange organizations—**Interval International** *(6262 Sunset Dr., Penthouse One, South Miami, 33143, tel. 305/666–1861; 800–828–8200)* or **Resort Condominiums International** *(3502 Woodview Trace, Indianapolis, IN 46268–3131, tel. 317/876–8899, 800/338–7777).* As an owner, you can join your resort's exchange organization and swap your interval for another someplace else in any year when you want a change of scene. Even if you don't own an interval, you can rent at many vacation ownership resorts where unsold intervals remain and/or owners have placed their intervals in a rental program. For rental information, contact the exchange organizations (Interval International, tel. 800/722–1861; Resort Condominiums International, tel. 800/654–5000), the individual resort, or a local real estate broker in the area where you want to rent.

2 Portraits of Florida

In Search of the Real Florida

by April Athey

A freelance writer based in Tallahassee, April Athey has been writing about her home state for magazines and newspapers since 1977. Her work has appeared in many publications, including the New York Times, Chicago Tribune, Christian Science Monitor, Frequent Flyer, and Gulfshore Life.

It's hard to imagine a Florida without a magic kingdom, a spaceport to the stars, interstate highways, or high-rise beachfront hotels. But such a Florida exists, and today the state's natural and historical treasures are being imitated, refurbished, restored, and recognized for their lasting appeal.

Even the state's leader in family entertainment—Walt Disney World—is imitating and popularizing Old Florida with its new Grand Floridian Beach Resort, featuring gabled roofs and Victorian balustrades that were typical of Florida's turn-of-the-century beach resorts. Disney officials say the resort recalls the days when John D. Rockefeller, Thomas Edison, and even President Theodore Roosevelt led the annual winter pilgrimage to Florida's warm shores.

There are those who recall the day when Walt Disney World's fantasy lands and futuristic hotels opened in 1971, setting a technological standard in entertainment that may still be unrivaled. The owners of natural attractions like Silver Springs, Weeki Wachee, and Homosassa Springs struggled to keep the attention of technology-hungry Americans. The lush jungle-lined rivers, exotic wildlife, and crystal-clear spring waters somehow paled in contrast to the make-believe, never-a-dull-moment amusements for which the Disney corporation had become famous. The convenience of a one-stop, no-surprise vacation apparently made real wilderness cruises, beaches, wildlife, and historical attractions passé.

To see and appreciate the real thing, one had to leave the interstate highways and brave a few side roads. Because not many tourists cared to take the road less traveled, many owners of natural attractions were forced to expand their offerings with man-made amusements. If budgets weren't sweet enough to permit this sort of commercialization, the attractions (usually the lesser-known botanical gardens, great homes, and wildlife reserves) saw lean years.

Fortunately, the cycle is coming full circle. Technology-harassed Americans are now looking for the good old days, and Florida is obliging them.

Today, developers of new resorts are focusing attention on the Florida of the 19th century. New resorts not only imitate Old Florida architecture but also, through their landscaping, recall when the only silhouettes scraping Florida's sky were of stout cabbage palms, mossy oaks, towering cypress, and hardy evergreens.

Maintaining the ecological integrity of the land and its often-endangered inhabitants has become an increasing concern of developers. The Grand Cypress Resort in Orlando was designed to be complemented by a stand of native cypress, and the Registry Resort in Naples nestles at the edge of a 1,000-acre nature preserve, through which a $1-million boardwalk was built to provide access to the beach and protection for the delicate sand dunes.

St. Augustine is the oldest permanent European settlement in the United States—with an extensive historic district to prove it—and was the first Florida resort popularized by Henry Flagler when he brought his Florida East Coast Railroad and friends south for the winter. Key West was the last resort Flagler helped build. His Casa Marina hotel still stands, having been restored and expanded under management by Marriott. The island's "conch houses" also are being restored, and many have been converted into guest houses and restaurants. Flagler also put Palm Beach and its sister, West Palm Beach, on the map. Though his original wooden hotels burned to the ground, his private estate is now the Flagler Museum.

Sharing space with the glinting glass of skyscrapers are the castlelike villas and Old Florida-style homes of former Florida residents. You can tour Ca'd'Zan, the bay-side villa that John Ringling and his wife Mable built, which now is part of the Ringling Museums Complex in Sarasota. Like an oasis in the middle of Miami's asphalt-and-concrete desert, the palatial bay-front estate of John Deering, with its formal gardens and surrounding natural jungles (Vizcaya Museum and Gardens), may be toured daily. Visit Thomas Edison's Winter Home in Fort Myers, and dine out on Cabbage Key, the tiny island accessible by boat (offshore from Captiva)—the retreat of mystery writer Mary Roberts Rinehart. Ormond Beach has reminders of its heyday, when John D. Rockefeller and friends made the riverfront Ormond Hotel a world-renowned wintering spot. Rockefeller eventually built his winter home, The Casements, across the street from the hotel, and both still stand proudly by the shores of the Halifax River, just north of Daytona Beach. The Casements is now an art museum and site of an annual antique-auto show.

Fort Jefferson, the Civil War island fortress on which Samuel Mudd—the physician who treated Lincoln's assassin—was imprisoned, is only a seaplane flight away from tropical Key West. On Key West are the 19th-century fortifications —East and West Martello Towers—one now home to the city's historical museum, and the other the setting of the garden club. Recently excavated and open to the public on Key West is Fort Zachary Taylor. Living-history interpretations are conducted daily at Fort Clinch, a Civil War fortress in Fernandina Beach, and at Fort Foster in Hillsborough State Park, just west of Tampa. Speaking of

Tampa, the next time you order a rum and Coke, remember that the concoction was invented there by Teddy Roosevelt's Rough Riders.

In addition to the monuments of recent history, there are the archaeological reminders of Florida's first residents, the aboriginal Indians who greeted European explorers and expatriates. Several state parks preserve treasured archaeological sites, like Hontoon Island on the St. Johns River, Tomoka River State Park, near Daytona Beach (both sites of Timucuan Indian settlements), and Jonathan Dickinson State Park, near the Palm Beaches (site of a Quaker shipwreck and their subsequent imprisonment by Jaega Indians).

These and later Indians left their place names as a lasting legacy—names like Ichetucknee (now a tubing river north of Gainesville), Pensacola, Apalachicola, Tequesta, Kissimmee, Chassahowitzka (a national wildlife refuge near Homosassa Springs), Okeechobee (a 590-square-mile inland lake), Ocala, and Tallahassee (the state capital).

Victorian homes with gingerbread-trimmed wrap-around verandas, shaded by sloping tin roofs, are being restored and operated as bed-and-breakfast inns or chic restaurants. Check out K. C. Crump on the River in Homosassa Springs, near Ocala in Central Florida, a posh new restaurant in a restored, turn-of-the-century homestead. In Ocala, the newest B&B is the Seven Sisters Inn, which serves gourmet fare. Florida's B&Bs have increased from an estimated five in 1980 to more than 50 in 1988.

Main Street programs are flourishing throughout the state, revitalizing the business/entertainment districts of towns like Winter Park, Orlando, DeLand, and Quincy (in northwest Florida).

Historic hotels and inns, once threatened by wrecking crews, are living new lives. Check out the Heritage in St. Petersburg, a restored, 60-year-old hotel (the original Florida "cracker" home in the backyard now serves as an atrium-greenhouse bar); or book a weekend at Apalachicola's 100-year-old Gibson Inn.

Waterfront redevelopment projects like Miami's Bayside and Jacksonville Landing (Rouse Marketplace developments) are focusing fresh attention on the inlets and bays that once harbored renegade pirates and adventurous pioneers.

Quiet waterfront hamlets, built during the boom in steamboat travel—Sanford and Crescent City are good examples— are beginning to blossom again with the reemergence of riverboat cruising.

Wildlife and wilderness, once overlooked in favor of make-believe amusements, are once again attracting awed attention. In response, Silver Springs turned back the clock with a complete Victorian redesign.

Oddly enough, it may be easier to find an Old Florida vacation experience now than it was 20 years ago.

Though serving to popularize Old Florida, newcomers and their artful imitations are no substitutes for the real thing. The wilderness, wildlife, and historic homes and resorts are already here to enjoy.

Washed by both the Gulf of Mexico and the Atlantic Ocean, Florida seems to be more water than land. Underground freshwater rivers course through the limestone bedrock of its north and central highlands, often boiling to the surface and flowing overland to the sea. A bird's-eye view reveals a peninsula whose upper reaches are dotted and crisscrossed by hundreds of lakes and streams and whose ragged southern borders are home to a vast, shallow river of grass called the Everglades and a maze of mangrove clumps called the Ten Thousand Islands. From the town of Everglades City, on Florida's southwest tip, sightseeing boats meander through the maze of islands, and just off the Tamiami Trail (U.S. 41), on the north-central boundary of Everglades National Park, you can climb the observation deck at Shark Valley Overlook for a good look at the river of grass.

This view, perhaps more than anything, helps to remind people of what Floridians are trying to recapture.

The Florida Scrub

by Al Burt

A roving writer-columnist for The Miami Herald for the past 15 years, Al Burt specializes in Florida's history, natural habitat, and future. He has written two books on the state—Becalmed in the Mullet Latitudes and Florida: A Place in the Sun. In 1974, Burt left Miami's city life to make his base in his beloved Scrub Country, near Melrose in north Florida.

Understanding Florida requires at least some knowledge of the historic Scrub Country, the oldest, the driest, the harshest, and, in some ways, the most delicate part of the state. In water-loving Florida, the Scrub struggles to remain a desert outlaw.

If you have ever walked a beach and observed how the tides and the wind have rolled the sterile sands into a long, graceful dune on which grow a few scraggly, scratchy plants, you may have gotten some idea about Florida's unique Scrub Country and its peculiar beauty.

The Scrub, which once covered most of Florida with bone-dry sandhills, is the legitimate kin to a desert, and it's full of puzzles. The life forms there are persistent, thrifty, and fragile. Once, you could look across the low profile of its vegetation and see odd "islands" of fertility, little oases of tall trees and green life, while all around was the stunted, prickly, vulnerable Scrub growth. They were like oddly matched siblings of nature, growing up side by side, but, by freakish accident, one had been denied its vitamins.

The name came from an early and natural lack of appreciation. It was scrubby country, not like the scenic Florida of the travel books. Except in those "islands," it lacked the towering slash pines and the comfortable shade of large-crowned live oaks and the open landscapes beneath. The Scrub was a place unto itself, with few easy pleasures, and it was not good for conventional farming.

Loving the Scrub came easiest if you grew up with it, if it came naturally to you. Sometimes it became a fierce, protective thing, like a stubbornly loyal Cracker Mama who adored the scrawniest of her children most because it was the misfit.

Flooding rains leached quickly through Scrub sands and left them dry as ever. Rosemary bushes, prickly pears, saw palmettos, sandburs, gnarled dwarf oaks, and other scraggly little trees commonly grew there.

The deep sand made it difficult to walk with shoes on. The sands in summer burned the soles of bare feet with temperatures of 135–140 degrees. Everything in the Scrub seemed to scratch and claw at you, fighting for life.

Rattlesnakes loved it. Exotic little creatures (in addition to raccoons, bobcats, and deer), some of them now rare and endangered, made it home—scrub jays, lizards, skinks, gopher frogs and gopher tortoises, exotic mice, red widow spiders, and such.

For years, big patches of the Scrub Country, especially if they were inland and off the main tracks, lay abandoned. If they attracted anyone, it was likely to be the young, who sometimes found the sandhills great places for exploring or play, sliding down them, burrowing into them, and holding beer parties and buggy chases on the tricky sand.

The Scrub did not rebound easily from such use, but nobody cared. The track of a jeep across virgin scrub vegetation might take unaided nature years to erase. That was minor compared with what else happened in the history of the Scrub.

It began when Florida began. The Scrub probably was the first part of Florida to emerge from the ocean, geologists say. Its dunes or sandhills formed under pressures of wind and tides as the ocean levels rose and fell during the ice ages. Great, irregular ridges took shape, almost like terraces. Time altered them into graceful sandhills.

The original Scrub Country became the Central Highlands of Florida, which stretches from east of Gainesville in the north-central part of the state south for some 200 miles and flatten out into the prairies of Lake Okeechobee. In places, the elevation reaches 300 feet.

For Florida, those great sandhills became Sierra Citrus, center of one of its greatest trademark industries. The well-drained Scrub lands were easily cleared and were perfect for oranges—once the growers added fertilizers and artificial irrigation.

You can ride that ridge today in one of the state's most scenic inland drives and imagine the beginning. U.S. 27, a fine highway, rolls up and down those great sandhills, past a series of lakes, along the fringes of Disney World country, and through miles and miles of green and seasonally fragrant citrus groves. (Even though the freezes of recent winters blighted many of them, the scene remains impressive.)

Like smaller versions of the Central Highlands, lesser dunes trailed away to the ocean. All had similar characteristics, but closer to the coast there were subtle changes, particularly if they were close enough to get the windblown ocean spray.

The dunes and the life on them also differed in their northern stretches, where the climate was temperate and subject to more seasonal changes than in southern Florida. In the south, the influence of the Gulf Stream and the more prominent crosswinds from the gulf and the ocean produced an exotic subtropical climate.

Scrub Country was high ground. Water did not collect there, but in strategic or special places development did, especially along the coast. Around the turn of the century, Henry Flagler built his pioneering railroad partially on a

high dune ridge running down the east coast. Then he
opened up cities like Palm Beach, Miami, and eventually
Key West to tourists and development.

For the most part, the Scrub Country was an ugly duckling
among Florida real estate developers. Many wanted to use
it as raw material or take advantage of its special location,
but few perceived it as anything that was uniquely beautiful
or valuable in itself. As a result, 90% or more of this original
Florida scene no longer exists.

The sand, some of it as fine as sugar, was mined for construction materials. Great areas were leveled for shopping
centers and other development. Subdivisions turned dune
ripples into square blocks of cottages. Water was piped in,
and developers covered these desert sands with St. Augustine grass.

Except for exploiters, the Scrub Country had few advo-
cates. The most notable of them was the writer, Marjorie
Kinnan Rawlings, an easterner. Rawlings's work elevated
one area of the Scrub into legend.

I n 1928, Rawlings fled the rigors of newspaper life in
Rochester, NY, and settled in an old Cracker house by
an orange grove in an unlikely little village oasis called
Cross Creek. She sought inspiration in isolation and frontier surroundings. The creek (between Ocala and
Gainesville) was a lane of water connecting two large lakes
in north-central Florida.

Her love of the creek and its people expanded to the areas
nearby, which included a significant piece of Scrub Country
known locally as the Big Scrub. To enrich her knowledge of
it, she lived for a while with a family in the Scrub, hunted
there, and befriended the Crackers who chose it as a place
to live.

Rawlings's novels, particularly *The Yearling*, which won
the Pulitzer Prize and then was made into a popular movie,
realistically acknowledged but nevertheless romanticized
the Big Scrub. She depicted the impoverished Crackers as
primitives who lived by their own code—a code that she
clearly thought had a noble base.

Rawlings gave the Big Scrub and Florida's Scrub Country a
national identity. Within the past few years, her book of essays on Cross Creek and a short story entitled "Gal Young
'Un" also were made into well-received movies. Those films
renewed and enlarged Rawlings's loving images of the
Cross Creek area and the Big Scrub. Since then, the importance of the Scrub as a unique plant and animal habitat has
been recognized. Many scientists and conservationists have dedicated themselves to its study and preservation.

Rawlings's books became especially significant because the
largest remaining area of Scrub left in Florida, modified

though it may be, is the one she idealized. It lies in the central and western portions of the 380,000-acre Ocala National Forest (a multiple-use forest that permits hunting and camping) and still is called the Big Scrub.

The Big Scrub contains the world's largest stand of sand pines. Many of them occur naturally, but, because in some areas the pines were planted in rows so neat that the natural poetry of the forest is altered, some have criticized it as a sand-pine plantation. In either case, both the pines and the patches of dunes, as close as the road shoulders, are visible from the car during a drive through the forest. The area illustrates how sand pines and other scrub vegetation, over time, tend to close and fill in an area, giving it a canopy above and a soil below slowly being altered by collections of natural forest debris, especially leaves, fallen limbs, and root systems. This cycle can change the natural characteristics of the Scrubs, unless fire (the sand pine is highly flammable) or timbering activities interfere. Even so, the Scrub retains its mysteries. Even the foresters cannot always predict with certainty that the Scrub cycle will begin again after a fire.

Most of Florida's Scrub Country is now scattered in bits and pieces around the state. You have to search and guess and inquire locally. Aside from the Ocala forest, a visitor can see examples of it in the Jonathan Dickinson State Park, 13 miles south of Stuart on U.S. 1.

In that same area, you may see from the highway a typical patch of surviving Scrub—a high roadside dune topped by a windswept sand pine, so stressed that it seems picturesquely oriental. The same sand pine, seen in the Ocala Forest, may grow bushy and erect and look like an ideal Christmas tree.

Finding examples of the Scrub elsewhere becomes a matter of travel and identification, of looking for inland dunes left untouched by development. Where there is a low, sandy hill there could be scrub. You can find areas of it down the east coast, from St. Augustine to West Palm Beach, in northeast Florida near the coast and along Rte. A1A, and there are some that sweep back off the Panhandle beaches in northwest Florida. Little of the scrub, however—except that in public parks—has tourist convenience for study and enjoyment. Even in the state and national forests, the sandy footing, the heat, and the numerous insects discourage all but the most hardy explorers.

At least two large tracts are being maintained for scientific research. The University of Florida owns several thousand acres of Scrub east of Gainesville, and the Archbold Biological Station (established in 1941) has 3,800 acres of distinctive Scrub near Lake Placid on the southern slope of the Central Highlands. These are not open for public roaming, however.

One good thing to remember is that, globally, Florida lies in the zone of the great deserts, including the Sahara, so the Scrub is not out of character. Florida began with those ocean sands that bleached into dunes and sandhills and then into the variety that visitors enjoy today.

Remembering the past explains a lot about the true nature of Florida, no matter how wet it looks right now. The Scrub Country reminds us that the makings of a desert are still there, waiting.

Miami Beach Art Deco

by Hap Hatton

Born and raised in Florida, Hap Hatton now lives in New York City, where he is in charge of still photography for PBS station WNET 13. His previous books include The Tent Book *and* The Virgin Homeowner's Handbook.

By 1910 Miami Beach had failed first as a coconut plantation, then as an avocado farm. Now it was being tried as a residential development. It took 10 years to create the present landmass. Carl Fisher, the Hoosier millionaire who financed much of the dredging and land-clearing, envisioned the area as a playground for the wealthy. Interspersed between his opulent hotels were huge estates on lots running 400 feet in from Biscayne Bay. Meanwhile, the southern portion of the barrier island was developed by the Lummus brothers, who plotted smaller lots for a middle-class resort. Scarcely had the dredging begun than the Lummus brothers in 1912 opened the Ocean Beach Realty Company, the first real estate office on the beach. Steady growth was interrupted by World War I, but then Miami Beach took off—until the collapse of the Florida real estate boom and the ensuing Depression.

By 1936, assisted by an expanding tourist industry, south Florida had emerged from the Depression. Hundreds of small hotels and apartment buildings were constructed on the small Lummus lots at the rate of 100 a year until 1941, making Miami Beach one of the few cities in the United States to have a building boom during the Depression. Ernest Hemingway's brother Leicester, also a writer, explains the phenomenon:

During the Depression, people needed to let go. . . . They became wild on Miami Beach. . . . They didn't watch their nickels. . . . [Architects] were determined not to use any older styles like the Spanish. . . . They wanted something modern, so they smoothed out all the Spanish things. They smoothed everything until you got the feeling that life was smooth. The buildings made you feel all clean and new and excited and happy to be there.

The style that prevailed in South Miami Beach was a zesty, crowd-pleasing Art Deco built by a handful of architects and contractors. Many of the architects were not formally trained but freely adapted national design trends to this tropical setting, creating a uniformity in style and scale rarely found in an urban setting. Called Miami Beach Art Deco (the name Tropical Deco has also been applied to the style), this brand of Art Deco was both relatively inexpensive to construct and offered a slick, dramatic, fashionable appearance, while its strong visual tropical symbols—"Floridiana"—impressed upon visitors the unique charms of the area.

Florida didn't invent the decorative vegetative and animal motifs that dominated the more ornate Miami Beach Art Deco buildings, but it raised them to new stylistic heights with facade bas-reliefs of cast or dyed stone, etched windows, and decorative metalwork on doors and porches.

Flowers, especially voluptuous gladiolas, alluded to the fecund floral paradise. Nymphs and nudes hedonistically stressed sensuous youth and romance. Fountains as well as sunbursts and symbolic zigzag equivalents of rays conjured up the life-renewing natural properties of the climate. Animals such as peacocks, flamingos, greyhounds, herons, and pelicans were chosen for their romantic associations, arabesque shapes, and exaggerated proportions. Originally, most of the buildings were stark white, with trims of azure blue, ocean turquoise, blazing yellow, palm tree green, erotic pink, or purples and mauves that evoked tropical sunsets, bougainvillea, and feelings both sensuous and exotic.

The sense of place is strong among these Deco buildings, leaving no doubt that this is the tropics, far from the cold, gray, sooty, industrial North.

The variances in Miami Beach Art Deco reflected what was occurring economically and architecturally on the national scene. Among others, four prevalent Deco styles comprise Miami Beach Art Deco.

Art Deco. The earliest buildings adapted the original Art Deco style's sharply angular massing with shallow stepped-back facades. Ornate bas-relief panels often framed large central openings. The French love of luxurious, sensuous textures such as crystal, mother-of-pearl, and unusual woods translated into indigenous Florida oolitic limestone, etched glass, stucco, and terrazzo (a cast agglomerate of marble or granite particles in colored and polished cement).

Depression Moderne. By 1937 the mode had shifted to a deco with the more austere look of the reigning International Style. Art Moderne's vertical stucco bands, flat roof with stepped parapet, and facade symmetry were still there, but with an increased horizontal emphasis that would later become dominant in streamlining. Depression Moderne was also readapted for government buildings such as the Miami Beach Post Office, and called PWA Moderne for the Public Works Administration.

Streamlined Moderne. By 1939, a full-blown aerodynamic Moderne featured curved forms, applied racing stripes that accentuated horizontal emphasis, and "eyebrow" shading of the windows with cantilevered slabs to reduce the angle of penetration of the sun. The continuously wrapped stucco surfaces expressed concepts associated with travel and speed. Here the angularity of the originally imported Art Moderne was entirely replaced by soft flowing masses accented with horizontal lines and rows of windows. This phase combined smooth, sweeping curves with straight lines of the machine age in simple, definite, contrasting shapes. Combinations of Cubism's suggestion of dimensionality, Futurism's romance with speed, and Surrealist fantasy are cited as sources of inspiration. This streamlining restored the fun and humor drained by Depression Moderne.

Mannerism. A final development of Miami Beach streamlining was called Resort Mannerism or Mannerist Moderne (from Mannerism, a late 16th-century reaction against the High Renaissance characterized by a deliberate distortion of the existing artistic and architectural repertoire; it gave way to the Baroque, and today the term is associated with the exaggeration and/or distortion of existing themes). Resort Mannerism included Nautical Moderne, with its exaggerated and literal invocations of ships at sea with porthole windows, decklike balconies, and flagstaffs. This mature Moderne emphasized sinuous curves, stylized directional ornament, and bold projections, marking a conscious search by architects both here and in Europe for a unique form to express contemporary modernity. Never a pure style, it even incorporated highlights from the Spanish Mediterranean, such as sloping tile roofs or colored ceramic tiles. The late 1930s film influence brought soaring "trylons" or space-age needles to roofs and facades. This Flash Gordon touch turned the buildings visually into spaceships with Hollywood stage-set lobbies that were also referred to as Cinema Style and Hollywood Style.

Larger Deco hotels did make their appearance, but, by and large, the area known as Old Miami Beach consists of two- and three-story hostelries small in scale and rich in expression. Deco architecture prevailed here later than anywhere else in the country, until World War II abruptly terminated construction. By 1941, most hotels were occupied by the military in training for the war effort. After the war, the area began to decline as Miami Beach continued its development northward.

In 1979, one square mile of Miami Beach became this country's first 20th-century national historic district. It reflects a trend in architecture that took place between the two world wars, when more than 500 Art Deco structures went up in one small area. It is not only the largest and most cohesive concentration of Art Deco buildings in the world but the first historic district that has registered buildings less than 50 years old. It sits on one of the best pieces of real estate in Florida, perhaps on the entire East Coast.

The fight for preservation of these landmarks has raged for years between developers who want to erect more profitable high-rise condominiums and the local Miami Design Preservation League, founded by Barbara Baer Capitman. A former art historian and now president of the Art Deco

Society of Miami, she held her first organizational meeting in 1976 with six people and spoke of the area's potential as "capital of the Art Deco world." Capitman attracted 100 volunteers to survey and research the locality. Then the battle was launched that resulted in tax and zoning incentives for the owners of Deco buildings who preserve their original structures.

Developers fought back and, to block the legislation, lobbied successfully for an ordinance that required 100% owner approval for historic district designations (51% is standard). This ordinance was later struck down when, to avoid costly litigation, Miami Beach changed its ordinance to 51% approval. Some local businessmen see the preservation issue as one of property rights versus government coercion. A few, however, realize that the Art Deco district will yield them long-term beneficial results: It will create a desirable cultural center and provide a sense of identity vital to establishing Miami Beach as a unique city rather than a second-rate Las Vegas.

Because no corresponding local legislation had been passed to protect the district, its designation on the National Register of Historic Places did not prevent demolition of several landmark Art Deco hotels. The turning point came in July of 1986, when Richard Hoberman, president of the Miami Design Preservation League, orchestrated a campaign to secure designation of two key areas: a quarter-mile district covering Ocean Drive/Collins Avenue (from Fifth to Sixteenth streets) as well as Espanola Way, a six-block street that includes a 1920s Spanish theme village. Hoberman packed the city commission chambers with supporters wearing "Deco-pink" ribbons to witness the decisive 6–1 vote. Local designation means that a design review board must approve all renovation work for appropriateness, all new construction must be compatible with surrounding buildings, and—most important—there will be a six-month moratorium on demolition to allow time for other investors to step in. Now prospective developers need not fear that their preservation efforts will be invalidated by high rises, and successful rehabilitation within these two districts should help in the essential designation of additional areas. Things are looking good: Already one developer has turned a million-dollar profit in 10 months by restoring and reselling one of the district's Art Deco hotels. Seven years after federal recognition, the city fathers have finally understood the economic benefits of preservation.

The preservation movement on Miami Beach has generated admiration for Art Deco, and south Florida developers have invested millions of dollars building imitation Deco residential communities for those who want the look of Deco but wish to live outside the troubled inner-city area. These new homes have much of the generic look of huge housing developments, despite their attempt to blend International Style and Deco. They feature stepped walls and entrances, porthole windows, geometric shapes, and two-tone pastel colors. Builders toned down the bright Deco colors to Necco wafer hues of quiet pastels when a local homeowners' association complained of the bright aqua, peach, and intense pinks. This "switch rather than fight" approach is an attempt to sidestep the complex problems of gentrification. The buildings themselves mark a rejection of International Style anonymity, a recognition of the value of Art Deco, and a positive trend in Miami's search for its own architectural identity.

Meanwhile, in the Deco District the tax credits to be obtained by rehabilitating these architectural treasures have brought developers into the area, and dozens of hotels and apartment houses are being refurbished. The small hotels average 60 to 120 rooms, many having been converted to "pullmanettes" (rooms with kitchenettes). For the past quarter-century these have been popular with mostly Jewish and Eastern European retirees, and a decade ago more than half of the south Beach population was 65 or older. With retirement communities now proliferating in south Florida, for about a decade Miami Beach has ceased to be a destination point for the elderly, and now the percentage is less than one-quarter.

By its nature, rehabilitation means modernization and deviation from original design schemes, and nowhere is this more apparent than in color restoration. The original white with vivid color accents has been rejected in favor of a palette of Post-Modern cake-icing pastels now associated with the television series "Miami Vice." Leonard Horowitz, the designer who introduced these colors, rationalized that because the neighborhood had deteriorated and much of the original vegetation had died, there was justification for using a plethora of color. Finally, white is being reintroduced.

The buildings of the Miami Beach Historical District chronicle more than a decade of historic cultural change and served the emotional needs of the public in a time of national crisis. No orthodox academic style has accomplished this. Whatever their historical significance or their eventual evaluation as art, these Miami Art Deco habitations are built to the human scale where the desires of the people are met rather than dictated to by sociological or aesthetic theory. Such a value in buildings has generally been condescended to or given mere lip service by respected architects who consider the tastes of the public beneath contempt. Yet the art of living cannot be measured by formal architectural standards of purity or style, only by the pleasure of the time and place. Miami Beach Art Deco created this quality of life with consummate success.

Today, the buildings still hold magic for visitors and inhabitants. Although the romance is slightly tarnished by peeling facades, and idealistic dreams have succumbed to more jaded views, there is still a sense of desire and expectation in the air. There is a glamour about these buildings that invites thoughts of moonlit walks on sparkling beaches, movie-screen romances, dancing under starry skies. There is a sadness, too, of once-vital dreams lost, either demolished or covered over with gaudy wallpaper and wall-to-wall carpeting. But this special fantasy of Florida still twinkles seductively among the vast pile of urban mediocrity that threatens to engulf the Miami Beach Deco District.

3 Miami

Introduction

by George and Rosalie Leposky

A husband-wife team, George and Rosalie Leposky are veteran Florida travel writers. Their articles have appeared in some 100 newspapers and consumer magazines throughout North America. They also write for trade publications in the travel and hospitality field, including Hotel & Resort Industry *and* Lodging. *The Leposkys live in the Coconut Grove section of Miami.*

What they say about Miami is true. The city *is* different. Miami is different from what it once was and it's different from other cities. Once a sleepy southern resort town, Miami today is a burgeoning giant of international commerce and finance as well as a place to find pleasure and relaxation. Like all big cities, Miami inspires the first-time visitor with hopes and dreams. Also as in other cities, many of these hopes and dreams can be sidetracked by crime and violence.

Miami's natural difference can be detected when you fly into the city. Clinging to a thin ribbon of dry land between the marshy Everglades and the Atlantic Ocean, Miami remains vulnerable to its perennial mosquitoes, periodic flooding, and potential devastation by hurricanes. These perils give life in Miami a flavor of urgency, a compulsion to prosper and party before the dream ends.

Miami may be the wrong place for a city, but it's the right place for a crossroads. Long before Spain's gold-laden treasure ships passed offshore in the Gulf Stream, the Calusa Indians who lived here had begun to trade with their mainland neighbors to the north and their island brethren to the south. Repeating this prehistoric pattern, many U.S. and multinational companies now locate their Latin American headquarters in Greater Miami because no other city can match its airline connections to the Western Hemisphere.

That same ease of access, coupled with a congenial climate, attracts hordes of Latin tourists—especially in Miami's steamy summer months (South America's winter), when domestic visitors from the northern United States are less in evidence.

Access and climate also explain why Miami has become what *Newsweek* calls "America's Casablanca." Whenever a Latin American or Caribbean government erupts in revolution and economic chaos, the inevitable refugees flock inexorably to Miami (and open restaurants). Even without a revolution, Miami's cosmopolitan character and entrepreneurial spirit attract other immigrants from all over the world.

Today, more than 45% of Greater Miami's population is Hispanic—the majority from Cuba, with significant populations from Colombia, El Salvador, Nicaragua, and Panama. About 150,000 French- and Creole-speaking Haitians also live in Greater Miami, as do Brazilians, Germans, Greeks, Iranians, Israelis, Italians, Jamaicans, Lebanese, Malaysians, Russian Jews, Swedes, and more—a veritable Babel of tongues. Most either know or are trying to learn English. You can help them by speaking slowly and distinctly.

Try not to think of Miami as a "melting pot." Where ethnic and cultural diversity are the norm, there's less pressure to conform. Miamians practice matter-of-factly the customs they brought here—much to the consternation of other Miamians whose customs differ. The community wrestles constantly with these tensions and sensitivities.

As a big city, Miami has its share of crime, violence, and drug trafficking—but not the pervasive lawlessness portrayed on the "Miami Vice" TV show. You probably won't find the city's seamy underside unless you go looking for it.

What you will find just by coming to Miami is a multicultural metropolis that works and plays with vigor and that welcomes you to share its celebration of diversity.

Arriving and Departing by Plane

Airport **Miami International Airport (MIA),** six miles west of downtown Miami, is Greater Miami's only commercial airport. MIA has the nation's second-largest volume of international passenger and cargo traffic. MIA's busiest hours, when flight delays may occur, are 11 AM—8 PM.

MIA contains 108 aircraft gates along seven concourses. During 1990, expect to encounter renovation on concourse H.

When you fly out of MIA, plan to check in 55 minutes before departure for a domestic flight and 90 minutes before departure for an international flight. Services for international travelers include 24-hour multilingual information and paging phones and foreign currency conversion booths throughout the terminal. An information booth with multilingual staff and 24-hour currency exchange are at Concourse E.

Between the Airport and Center City By Bus **Metrobus.** The county's Metrobus system has one benefit—its modest cost—if you're willing to put up with the inconveniences of infrequent service, scruffy equipment, and the circuitous path that many routes follow. *Fare $1 (exact change), transfers 25 cents.*

Greyhound. You can take a Greyhound bus from the Metrobus depot at MIA to Homestead and the Florida Keys or to other Greyhound stations in Greater Miami *(see* By Bus).

By Taxi For trips originating at MIA or the Port of Miami, a $1 toll is added to the meter fare—except for the flat-fare trips described below. You'll pay a $12 flat fare between MIA and the Port of Miami, in either direction.

For taxi service from the airport to destinations in the immediate vicinity, ask a uniformed county taxi dispatcher to call an **ARTS (Airport Region Taxi Service)** cab for you. These special blue cabs will offer you a short-haul flat fare.

SuperShuttle vans transport passengers between MIA and local hotels, the Port of Miami, and even individual residences on a 24-hour basis. The company's service area extends from Palm Beach to Monroe County (including the Lower Keys). Drivers provide narration en route. It's best to make reservations 24 hours before departure, although the firm will try to arrange pick-ups within Dade County on as little as four hours' notice. *For information and reservations from inside MIA, tel. 305/ 871–8488. Reservations outside MIA, tel. 305/871–2000 (Dade and Monroe counties) or 305/674–1700 (Broward and Palm Beach counties). Pet transport fee: $5. Lower rate for 2nd passenger in same party for many destinations. Children under 3 ride free with parents. Credit cards: AE, MC, V.*

By Limousine **Bayshore Limousine** has chauffeur-driven four-door town cars and stretch limousines available on demand at MIA or through the 24-hour reservation service. It serves Miami, Fort Lauderdale, Palm Beach, and the Keys. *11485 S.W. 87th Ave., Miami, tel. 305/253–9046, 325–3851, or 858–5888. AE, MC, V.*

Arriving and Departing by Car, Train, and Bus

By Car The main highways into Greater Miami from the north are Florida's Turnpike (toll) and I–95. In Broward County (the next county north), you'll encounter major delays throughout 1990 from construction to widen the highway.

Delays on roads into Miami from other directions are most likely on weekends, when recreational traffic is the heaviest. From the northwest, take I–75 or U.S. 27 into town. From the Everglades to the west, use the Tamiami Trail (U.S. 41). From the south, use U.S. 1 and the Homestead Extension of Florida's Turnpike.

Rental Cars Six rental-car firms—**Avis Rent-a-Car, Budget Rent-a-Car, Dollar Rent-a-Car, Hertz Rent-a-Car, National Rent-a-Car,** and **Value Rent-a-Car**—have booths near the baggage claim area on MIA's lower level—a convenience when you arrive.

By Train **Amtrak's** two trains between Miami and New York City, the *Silver Meteor* and *Silver Star*, make different stops along the way. Each has a daily Miami arrival and departure.

Amtrak's "All Aboard" fare is the most economical way to travel to Florida, if you have time to meet the length-of-stay requirements. Trains run full all year, except in October and May. For the best fare, contact Amtrak as soon as you decide to take a trip. Ask for Amtrak's 1990 travel planner. *Amtrak Station, 8303 N.W. 37th Ave., Miami 33147. General office tel. 305/835–1200, passenger service tel. 305/835–1225. Advance reservations required. Reservations: Amtrak Customer Relations, 400 N. Capitol St., NW, Washington, DC 20001, tel. U.S. 800/USA-RAIL, Canada 800/4AMTRAK.*

Tri-Rail commuter trains connect Miami with Broward and Palm Beach weekdays. Call for schedule and details on weekly and monthly passes. *Tel. 305/728–8445 or 800/TRI-RAIL. Suite 801, 1 River Plaza, 305 S. Andrews Ave., Fort Lauderdale, FL 33301.*

By Bus **Greyhound/Trailways** buses (tel. 305/374–7222 or 305/373–6561) stop at seven bus stations in Greater Miami. No reservations.

Getting Around Miami

Greater Miami resembles Los Angeles in its urban sprawl and traffic congestion. You'll need a car to visit many of the attractions and points of interest listed in this book. Some are accessible via public transportation.

A department of county government, the Metro-Dade Transit Agency, runs the public transportation system. It consists of 450 Metrobuses on 67 routes, the 21-mile Metrorail elevated rapid transit system, and the 1.9-mile Metromover in downtown Miami. Free maps, schedules, and a First-Time Rider's Kit are available. *111 N.W. 1st St., Miami 33128. Maps by Mail, tel. 305/638–6137. Route information tel. 305/638–6700 daily 6 AM–11 PM. Fare $1, transfers 25 cents, exact change only.*

By Train Metrorail runs from downtown Miami north to Hialeah and south along U.S. 1 to Dadeland. *Service every 7 minutes in peak hours, 15–30 minutes other times. Weekdays 6AM–midnight, weekends 6:30 AM–6:30 PM. Runs until midnight for special events such as the Orange Bowl Parade. Fare: $1.*

Metromover's two loops circle downtown Miami, linking major hotels, office buildings, and shopping areas *(see* Exploring Downtown Miami*). Service every 90 seconds. Weekdays 6:30 AM–midnight, weekends 8:30 AM–midnight. Later for special events. Fare 25 cents.*

By Bus Metrobus stops are marked by blue-and-green signs with a bus logo and route information. The frequency of service varies widely. Obtain specific schedule information in advance for the routes you want to ride.

By Taxicab There are 1,709 taxicabs in Dade County. Fares are $1 for the first ⅛ mile, 20 cents for each additional 1/6 mile; waiting time 20 cents for the first 1 3/5 minutes, 20 cents for each additional 4/5 minute. No additional charge for extra passengers, luggage, or road and bridge tolls. Taxi companies with dispatch service are **Central Taxicab Service** (tel. 305/534–0694), **Diamond Cab Company** (tel. 305/545–7575), **Magic City Cab Company** (tel. 305/757–5523), **Metro Taxicab Company** (tel. 305/888–8888), **Society Cab Company** (tel. 305/757–5523), **Super Yellow Cab Company** (tel. 305/885–5555), **Tropical Taxicab Company** (tel. 305/945–1025), and **Yellow Cab Company** (tel. 305/444–4444).

By Car Finding your way around Greater Miami is easy if you know how the numbering system works. Miami is laid out on a grid with four quadrants—northeast, northwest, southeast, and southwest—which meet at Miami Avenue and Flagler Street. Miami Avenue separates east from west and Flagler Street separates north from south. *Avenues* and *courts* run north-south; *streets, terraces,* and *ways* run east-west. *Roads* run diagonally, northwest-southeast.

Many named streets also bear numbers. For example, Unity Boulevard is N.W. and S.W. 27th Avenue, LeJeune Road is N.W. and S.W. 42nd Avenue. However, named streets that depart markedly from the grid, such as Biscayne Boulevard and Brickell Avenue, have no corresponding numerical designations. Dade County and most other municipalities follow the Miami numbering system.

In Miami Beach, *avenues* run north-south; *streets,* east-west. Numbers rise along the beach from south to north and from the Atlantic Ocean in the east to Biscayne Bay in the west.

In Coral Gables, all streets bear names. Coral Gables uses the Miami numbering system for north-south addresses but begins counting east-west addresses westward from Douglas Road (S.W. 37th Ave.).

Hialeah has its own grid. Palm Avenue separates east from west; Hialeah Drive separates north from south. *Avenues* run north-south and *streets* east-west. Numbered streets and avenues are designated west, east, or southeast.

Important Addresses and Numbers

Information Centers
The Greater Miami Convention and Visitors Bureau plans to open tourist information centers in downtown Miami, Miami Beach, Homestead-Florida City, and Miami International Airport. Contact the bureau for locations and hours or to request information by mail.

Visitor Services, Greater Miami Convention and Visitors Bureau (701 Brickell Ave., Suite 2700, Miami 33131, tel. 305/539–3040).

Chambers of Commerce
Greater Miami has more than 20 local chambers of commerce, each promoting its individual community. Most maintain racks of brochures on tourist information in their offices and will send you information about their community.

Coconut Grove Chamber of Commerce (2820 McFarland Rd., Coconut Grove 33133, tel. 305/444–7270).
Coral Gables Chamber of Commerce (50 Aragon Ave., Coral Gables 33134, tel. 305/446–1657).
Gold Coast Chamber of Commerce (1100 Kane Concourse, Suite 210, Bay Harbor Islands 33154, tel. 305/866–6020). Serves the beach communities of Bal Harbour, Bay Harbor Islands, Golden Beach, North Bay Village, Sunny Isles, and Surfside.
Key Biscayne Chamber of Commerce (Key Biscayne Bank Bldg., 95 W. McIntyre St., Key Biscayne 33149, tel. 305/361–5207).
Miami Beach Chamber of Commerce (1920 Meridian Ave., Miami Beach 33139, tel. 305/672–1270).
South Miami Chamber of Commerce (6410 S.W. 80th St., South Miami 33143, tel. 305/661–1621).

Tickets
Ticketmaster. You can use this service to order tickets for performing arts and sports events by telephone. A service fee is added to the price of the ticket. *Tel. 800/446–3939 or tel. 305/654–3309 (Dade), 305/523–3309 (Broward), or 407/588–3309 (Palm Beach). MC, V.*

Emergencies
Dial 911 for **police** and **ambulance.** You can dial free from pay phones.

Telecommunication lines for the hearing impaired are used by hearing-impaired travelers with telecommunication devices (TDD) to reach TDD-equipped public services:

Fire/Police/Medical/Rescue (tel. 305/595–4749 TDD)
Operator and Directory Assistance (tel. 800/855–1155 TDD)
Deaf Services of Miami (4800 W. Flagler St., Room 213, Miami, tel. 305/444–2211 TDD or voice 305/444–2266). Operates daily 6 AM–midnight. Relays calls to help the hearing-impaired contact people who hear and speak normally.

Ambulance
Randle Eastern Ambulance Service Inc. Serves all of Greater Miami. Meets air ambulances and takes patients to hospitals. Services include advanced life-support systems. *35 S.W. 27th Ave., Miami 33135, tel. 305/642–6400. Open 24 hrs. AE, MC, V.*

Hospitals
The following hospitals have 24-hour emergency rooms:

Miami Beach: *Mt. Sinai Medical Center* (4300 Alton Rd., Miami Beach, tel. 305/674–2121; physician referral, tel. 674–2273). Just off Julia Tuttle Causeway (I–195).

St. Francis Hospital (250 W. 63rd St., Miami Beach, tel. 305/868–5000; physician referral, tel. 305/868–2728). Near Collins Ave. and north end of Alton Rd.

Central: *University of Miami/Jackson Memorial Medical Center.* Includes Jackson Memorial Hospital, a county hospital with Greater Miami's only trauma center. Near Dolphin Expressway. Metrorail stops a block away. *1611 N.W. 12th Ave., Miami, tel. 305/325–7429. Emergency room, tel. 305/549–6901. Interpreter service, tel. 305/549–6316. Patient relations, tel. 305/549–7341. Physician referral, tel. 305/547–5757.*
Mercy Hospital (3663 S. Miami Ave., Coconut Grove, tel. 305/854–4400; physician referral, tel. 305/285–2929). Greater Miami's only hospital with an emergency boat dock.
Miami Children's Hospital (6125 S.W. 31st St., tel. 305/666–6511; physician referral, ext. 2563).

South: *Baptist Hospital of Miami* (8900 N. Kendall Dr., Miami, tel. 305/596–1960; physician referral, tel. 305/596–6557).

24-Hour Pharmacies Of the 287 pharmacies in Greater Miami, only three are open 24 hours a day. Most pharmacies open at 8 or 9 AM and close between 9 PM and midnight. Many pharmacies offer local delivery service.

Eckerd Drugs. 1825 Miami Gardens Dr. N.E. (185th St.), North Miami Beach, tel. 305/932–5740 and 9031 S.W. 107th Ave., Miami, tel. 305/274–6776.

Walgreens. 5731 Bird Rd., Miami, tel. 305/666–0757.

Physician Referral Services **24-Hour Doctors House Calls.** Many Greater Miami hotels use this referral service, which will send a physician to you. Medical services available include general medicine, pediatrics, and geriatrics. In-office dental referrals. Translators available. *3801 N. University Dr., Suite 507, Sunrise, tel. 305/945–6325.*

East Coast District Dental Society. Office open weekdays 9 AM–4:30 PM for dental referral. Services include general dentistry, endodontics, periodontics, and oral surgery. *420 S. Dixie Hwy., Suite 2E, Coral Gables, tel. 305/667–3647.*

Guided Tours

Orientation Tours **Miami Vision** (2699 Collins Ave., Suite 113, Miami Beach, tel. 305/532–0040). Several packages combine city tours with attractions. Prices include admission to attractions. Both minivan and private-car tours are available. Well-informed, congenial guides speak English, French, German, Italian, Portuguese, and Spanish. Phone for hotel pickup time or ask your concierge.

Old Town Trolley of Miami. Narrated tours of Miami and Miami Beach leave Bayside Marketplace every half hour. *Box 12985, Miami 33101, tel. 305/374–8687. Miami tour: $11 adults, $4 children 3–15. Miami Beach: $7 adults, $4 children 3–15. No credit cards.*

Special-Interest Tours
Boat Tours ***Heritage of Miami II.*** Miami's official tall ship, an 85-foot steel traditional sailing schooner docks at Bayside Marina. Carries up to 49 passengers for day sailing, sleeps 16; children and cameras welcome. Ice and ice chest on board, soft drinks for sale; bring your own food. Standard Biscayne Bay day trip lasts two hours. Reservations recommended. *Dinner Key Marina, Mi-*

ami, tel. 305/858–6264. Sails daily, weather permitting. Cost: $20 adults, $15 seniors, $10 armed forces personnel and children under 12.

Island Queen. 90-passenger tour boat docks at the Hyatt Regency Hotel's patio dock, 400 S.E. 2nd Ave., Miami. Two-hour narrated tours of Port of Miami and Millionaires' Row. Transportation to and from Island Queen available from Miami Vision. *8265 S.W. 179th Ter., Miami 33157, tel. 305/379–5119. Tours daily. Cost: $9 adults, $4.50 children.*

Nikko Gold Coast Cruises. Three 150-passenger boats based at Haulover Park Marina specialize in water tours to major Greater Miami attractions. *10800 Collins Ave., Miami Beach, tel. 305/945–5461. Tours daily. Bayside Marketplace, $8 adults, $4.50 children under 12.*

History Tours **Art Deco District Tour.** Meet your guide at 10:30 AM Saturday at 661 Washington Avenue, the **Miami Design Preservation League's** Welcome Center, for a 90-minute tour. Wear comfortable shoes and bring a hat. Also available is the League's *Art Deco District Guide*, a book with 6 detailed walking or driving tours of the square-mile Art Deco District on Miami Beach. *Bin L, Miami Beach 33119, tel. 305/672–2014. Cost: $5.*

Historical Museum of Southern Florida. Guided tours available in English or Spanish. **Museum Tour** covers the exhibits, which survey 10,000 years of Miami-area history; includes 15-minute slide show. The **Curator's Cabinet Tour** combines the Museum Tour with a look behind the scenes at departments that visitors seldom see, including a research center with 500,000 photos and the cataloging and conservation departments. The museum also conducts tours throughout the Greater Miami area. *101 W. Flagler St., Miami, tel. 305/375–1492.*

Prof. Paul George. Explore Miami's history with a professional historian on a four-hour walking tour of downtown. Paul George is a history professor at Florida Atlantic University and the University of Miami and president of the Florida Historical Society. Tour begins on the north bank of Miami River behind the Hyatt Regency Hotel, 400 S.E. 2nd Ave. Wear comfortable walking shoes and a hat. Sat. 9 AM–1 PM by appointment. George also gives 3½-hour walking tours of historic Coconut Grove, Coral Gables, Little Havana, Miami's old city Cemetery, the Miami Beach Art Deco District, and downtown Fort Lauderdale. *1345 S.W. 14th St., Miami, tel. 305/858–6021. Cost: $8 adults, $6 children 7–14, under 7 free.*

Rickshaw Tours **Royal Rickshaw.** Look for rickshaws along Main Highway in Coconut Grove's Village Center (Box 0174 Coconut Grove 33233–0174, tel. 305/443–6571). Nightly 8 PM–2 AM in Coconut Grove. Rickshaw holds two adults. $3 per person for 10-minute ride through Coconut Grove, $6 per person for 20-minute lovers' moonlight ride down to Biscayne Bay. No credit cards.

Exploring Downtown Miami

Numbers in the margin correspond with points of interest on the Downtown Miami map.

Orientation From a distance you see downtown Miami's future—a 21st-century skyline already stroking the clouds with sleek fingers of steel and glass. By day, this icon of commerce and technology sparkles in the strong subtropical sun; at night, it basks in the man-made glow of floodlights.

On the streets downtown, you encounter a polyglot present. Staid-suited lawyers and bankers share the sidewalks with Hispanic merchants wearing open-neck, intricately embroidered shirts called *guayaberas*. Fruit merchants sell their wares from pushcarts. European youths with backpacks stroll the streets. Foreign businessmen haggle over prices in import-export shops. You hear Arabic, Chinese, Creole, French, German, Hebrew, Hindi, Japanese, Portuguese, Spanish, Swedish, Yiddish, and even a little English now and then.

With effort, you can find remnants of downtown Miami's past. Most of the city's "old" downtown buildings date from only the 1920s and 1930s—an incongruity if you're from someplace that counts its past in centuries. Remember that Miami is a young city, incorporated in 1896 with just 3,000 residents. A Junior League book, *Historic Downtown Miami*, locates and describes 27 elderly structures in and near downtown, including 21 you can see in a two-hour self-guided walking tour of slightly more than a mile.

Touring Downtown Miami Parking downtown is inconvenient and expensive. If you're staying elsewhere in the area, leave your car at an outlying Metrorail station and take the train downtown. Metromover, a separate light-rail mass-transit system, circles the heart of the city on twin elevated loops.

No part of downtown is more than two blocks from one of Metromover's nine stations. We've organized the downtown Miami tour around those stations, so you can ride Metromover directly to the attractions downtown that interest you most.

❶ ❷ When you get off the Metrorail train at **Government Center Station,** notice the **Dade County Courthouse** (73 W. Flagler St.). It's the building to the east with a pyramid at its peak, where turkey vultures roost in winter. Built in 1928, it was once the tallest building south of Washington, D.C.

❸ As you leave the Metrorail station, you'll enter **Metro-Dade Center,** the county government's 30-story office building. Designed by architect Hugh Stubbins, it opened in 1985.

❹ Across N.W. 1st Street from Metro-Dade Center stands the **Metro-Dade Cultural Center** (101 W. Flagler St.), opened in 1983. The 3.3-acre complex is a Mediterranean expression of architect Philip Johnson's postmodern style. An elevated plaza provides a serene haven from the city's pulsations and a superb setting for festivals and outdoor performances.

The Center for the Fine Arts is an art museum in the tradition of the European *kunsthalle* (exhibition gallery). With no permanent collection, it organizes and borrows temporary exhibitions on many artistic themes. Shows scheduled for 1990 include geometric abstract paintings since 1945 and "Soul and Form." *Tel. 305/375–1700. Open Tues.–Sat. 10–5, Thurs. 10–9, Sun. noon–5. Admission: $3 adults, $2.50 senior citizens, $2 children 6–12, under 6 free. Donations Tues.*

The Historical Museum of Southern Florida is a regional museum that interprets the human experience in southern Florida from prehistory to the present. Artifacts on permanent display include Tequesta and Seminole Indian ceramics, clothing, and tools; a 1920 streetcar; and an original edition of Audubon's *Birds of America. Tel. 305/375–1492. Open Mon.–Sat. 10–5,*

Downtown Miami

Bayfront Park, **12**

Bayfront Park
Station, **11**

Bayside Marketplace, **19**

CenTrust Tower, **8**

College Station, **17**

Dade County
Courthouse, **2**

Edcom Station, **21**

First St. Station, **15**

Ft. Dallas Park
Station, **5**

Freedom Tower, **22**

Government Center
Station, **1**

Gusman Center, **16**

HMS *Bounty*, **20**

Hotel Inter-Continental
Miami, **13**

James Knight Center, **9**

Metro-Dade Center, **3**

Metro-Dade Cultural
Center, **4**

Miami Arena, **25**

Miami Ave. Bridge, **6**

Miami Ave. Station, **10**

Miami-Dade
Community College, **18**

State/Plaza Station, **24**

Southeast Financial
Center, **14**

U.S. Courthouse, **23**

World Trade Center
Station, **7**

Thurs. 10–9, Sun. noon–5. Admission: $3 adults, $2 children 6–12, under 6 free. Donations Mon.

The Main Public Library has 700,000 volumes and a computerized card catalog. Inside the entrance, look up at the rotunda mural, where artist Edward Ruscha interpreted a quotation from Shakespeare: "Words without thought never to heaven go." You'll find art exhibits in the auditorium and second-floor lobby. *Tel. 305/375–BOOK. Open Mon.–Sat. 9–5, Thurs. 9–9, Sun. 1–5. Closed Sun. May–Sept.*

At Government Center Station, you can also transfer to Metromover's inner and outer loops through downtown. We've listed the stations and their attractions in sequence along the outer loop.

⑤
⑥ The first stop is **Ft. Dallas Park Station.** If you disembark here, you're a block from the **Miami Ave. Bridge,** one of 11 bridges on the river that open to let ships pass. From the bridge approach, watch freighters, tugboats, research vessels, and luxury yachts ply this busy waterway.

Time Out Stroll across the bridge to **Tobacco Road** for some liquid refreshment and a sandwich or snack. Built in 1912, this friendly neighborhood pub was a speakeasy during Prohibition. *626 S. Miami Ave., tel. 305/374–1198. Open weekdays 11:30 AM–5 AM, weekends 1 PM–5 AM. Lunch weekdays 11:30–2:30. Dinner served Sun.–Thurs. AE, DC.*

⑦
⑧ The next Metromover stop, **Knight Center Station,** nestles in a niche inside the **CenTrust Tower** (100 S.E. 1st St.), a wedge-shape 47-story skyscraper designed by I. M. Pei & Partners.
⑨ The building is brilliantly illuminated at night. Inside the CenTrust Tower, follow signs to the **James L. Knight International Center** (400 S.E. 2nd Ave., tel. 305/372–0929), a convention and concert hall adjoining the Hyatt Regency Hotel.

⑩ At the Knight Center Station, you can transfer to the inner loop and ride one stop to the **Miami Avenue Station,** a block south of **Flagler Street,** downtown Miami's commercial spine. Like most such thoroughfares, Flagler Street lost business in recent years to suburban malls—but unlike most, it found a new lease on life. Today, the half-mile of Flagler Street from Biscayne Boulevard to the Dade County Courthouse is the most important import-export center in the United States. Its stores and arcades supply much of the world with automotive parts, audio and video equipment, medical equipment and supplies, photographic equipment, clothing, and jewelry.

⑪
⑫ If you stay on the outer loop, you'll come next to **Bayfront Park Station**, opposite **Claude and Mildred Pepper Bayfront Park,** which extends from Biscayne Boulevard east to the edge of the bay. Japanese sculptor Isamu Noguchi redesigned the park just before his death in 1989; it now includes a memorial to the *Challenger* astronauts, an amphitheater, and a fountain honoring the late Florida Congressman Claude Pepper and his wife.
⑬
⑬ Just south of Bayfront Park, the lobby of the **Hotel Inter-Conti nental Miami** (100 Chopin Plaza) contains *The Spindle*, a huge sculpture by Henry Moore.

West of Bayfront Park Station stands the tallest building in
⑭ Florida, the 55-story **Southeast Financial Center** (200 S. Bis-

cayne Blvd.), with towering royal palms in its one-acre Palm Court plaza beneath a steel-and-glass space frame.

🕒 The next Metromover stop, **First Street Station,** places you a block north of Flagler Street and the **Gusman Center for the**
🕕 **Performing Arts,** an ornate former movie palace restored as a concert hall. Gusman Center resembles a Moorish courtyard with twinkling stars in the sky. Performances there include the Miami City Ballet, under the direction of Edward Villella, and the New World Symphony, a unique, advanced-training orchestra led by Michael Tilson Thomas. *Gusman Center: 174 E. Flagler St., Miami 33131. Box office tel. 305/372–0925; Ballet: 905 Lincoln Rd., Miami Beach, 33139, tel. 305/532–4880; Symphony: 555 Lincoln Rd., Miami Beach, 33139, tel. 305/371–3005.*

🕗 The **College/Bayside Station** Metromover stop serves the down-
🕘 town campus of **Miami-Dade Community College,** where you'll enjoy browsing through two fine galleries. The Francis Wolfson Art Gallery on the fifth floor houses traveling exhibitions of contemporary art. *300 N.E. 2nd Ave., tel. 305/347–3278. Weekdays 9–5:30. Free.* The Mitchell Wolfson, Jr., Collection of Decorative and Propaganda Arts on the third floor displays works from Mr. Wolfson's personal holdings. *Tel. 305/347–3429. Open weekdays 10–5. Admission free.*

🕙 College/Bayside Station is also the most convenient Metromover stop for **Bayside Marketplace,** a waterside mall built by The Rouse Company, between Bayfront Park and the entrance to the Port of Miami. Bayside's 235,000 square feet of retail space include 81 specialty shops, pushcarts in the mall's Pier 5 area, conventional restaurants, and a fast-food court with some 30 vendors. The mall adjoins the 208-slip Miamarina, where you can see luxurious yachts moored and ride in an authentic 36-foot-long Venetian gondola. *401 Biscayne Blvd., tel. 305/577–3344, for gondola rides 305/529–7178. Open Mon.–Sat. 10–10, Sun. noon–8.*

🕢 While you're at Bayside, tour the **H.M.S. *Bounty,*** a fully rigged reproduction of an 18th-century armed merchant ship. Built in Nova Scotia for the 1962 MGM film *Mutiny on the Bounty,* the ship has since participated in the Bicentennial tall-ships parade and Statue of Liberty celebration in New York Harbor. *Tel. 305/375–0486. Open Sun.–Thurs. noon–8, Fri. noon–10, Sat. 10–10. Admission: $3.50 adults, $2 seniors, $1.50 children 4–12, under 4 free. The **Bounty** may leave on tour June–Oct.*

🕑 🕢 As Metromover rounds the curve between College/Bayside Station and **College North Station,** look northeast to see **Freedom Tower** (600 Biscayne Blvd.), where the Cuban Refugee Center processed more than 500,000 Cubans who entered the United States to flee Fidel Castro's regime in the 1960s. Built in 1925 for the *Miami Daily News,* this imposing Spanish-baroque structure was inspired by the Giralda, an 800-year-old bell tower in Seville, Spain. After years as a derelict, Freedom Tower was renovated in 1988. To see it up close, walk north from College North Station to N.E. 6th Street, then two blocks east to Biscayne Boulevard.

🕦 A two-block walk south from College North Station will bring you to the **U.S. Courthouse,** a handsome keystone building erected in 1931 as Miami's main post office. Go to the second-floor central courtroom to see *Law Guides Florida Progress,* a huge depression-era mural by artist Denman Fink. *300 N.E. 1st Ave. Building open weekdays 8:30–5; during those hours, security guards will open courtroom on request. No cameras or tape recorders allowed in building.*

㉔
㉕ From **State Plaza/Arena Station,** walk two blocks north on N.W. 1st Avenue to the new **Miami Arena** (721 N.W. 1st Ave., tel. 305/374–6877), home of the Miami Heat, a National Basketball Association team. Other sports and entertainment events also take place there.

Just across the Miami River from downtown, a canyon of tall buildings lines **Brickell Avenue,** a southward extension of S.E. 2nd Avenue that begins in front of the Hyatt Regency Hotel (400 S.E. 2nd Ave.). For the best views, drive Brickell Avenue from north to south. You'll pass the largest concentration of international banking offices in the United States.

South of S.E. 15th Street, several architecturally interesting condominiums rise between Brickell Avenue and Biscayne Bay. Israeli artist Yacov Agam painted the rainbow-hued exterior of **Villa Regina** (1581 Brickell Ave.). Arquitectonica, a nationally prominent architectural firm based in Miami, designed three of these buildings: **The Palace** (1541 Brickell Ave.), **The Imperial** (1617 Brickell Ave.), and **The Atlantis** (2025 Brickell Ave.). The 20-story Atlantis, where a palm tree grows in a hole in the building between the 12th and 16th floors, forms a backdrop for the opening credits of the television show "Miami Vice."

At S.E. 25th Road, turn right, follow signs to **I–95,** and return to downtown Miami on one of the world's most scenic urban highways. I–95 parallels Brickell Avenue and soars 75 feet above the Miami River, offering a superb view of the downtown skyline. At night, the CenTrust Tower is awash with light, and, on the adjoining Metrorail bridge, a neon rainbow glows— Rockne Krebs's 3,600-foot-long light sculpture, *The Miami Line*. Just beyond the river, take the Biscayne Boulevard exit back to S.E. 2nd Avenue in front of the Hyatt Regency Hotel.

Exploring Miami Beach

Numbers in the margin correspond with points of interest on the Miami Beach map.

Orientation Most visitors to the Greater Miami area don't realize that Miami and Miami Beach are separate cities. Miami, on the mainland, is south Florida's commercial hub. Miami Beach, on 17 islands offshore in Biscayne Bay, is sometimes considered America's Riviera, luring refugees from winter to its warm sunshine, sandy beaches, and graceful palms.

In 1912, what would become Miami Beach was little more than a sandspit in the bay. Then Carl Graham Fisher, a millionaire promoter who built the Indianapolis Speedway, began to pour much of his fortune into developing the island city.

Ever since, Miami Beach has experienced successive waves of boom and bust—thriving in the early 1920s and the years just after World War II, but also enduring the devastating 1926 hurricane, the Great Depression, travel restrictions during World War II, and an invasion of criminals released from Cuba during the 1980 Mariel boatlift.

Today, a renaissance is under way as Miami Beach revels in the architectural heritage of its mile-square Art Deco District. About 650 significant buildings in the district are listed on the National Register of Historic Places.

The term "Art Deco" describes the modern architecture that emerged in the 1920s and 1930s. Its forms are eclectic, drawn from nature (including birds, butterflies, and flowers); from ancient Aztec, Mayan, Babylonian, Chaldean, Egyptian, and Hebrew designs; and from the streamlined, aerodynamic shapes of modern transportation and industrial machinery. For detailed information on touring the Art Deco District, contact the Miami Design Preservation League *(see* Guided Tours).

Driving Tour of Miami Beach   In our exploration, we direct you from the mainland to Miami Beach and through a cross section of the Art Deco District, and the elegant residential neighborhood surrounding the La Gorce Country Club.

From the mainland, cross the **MacArthur Causeway** (Rte. 41) to Miami Beach. To reach the causeway from downtown Miami, turn east off Biscayne Boulevard north of N.E. 11th Street. From I-95, turn east onto I-395. The eastbound Dolphin Expressway (Rte. 836) becomes I-395 east of the I-95 interchange. As you approach the MacArthur Causeway bridge across the Intracoastal Waterway, *The Miami Herald* building looms above Biscayne Bay on your left.

① Cross the bridge to **Watson Island,** created by dredging in 1931. Make the first left turn to the **Japanese Garden,** which has stone lanterns, a rock garden, and an eight-ton, eight-foot-tall statue of Hotei, Japanese god of prosperity. Industrialist Kiyoshi Ichimura gave the one-acre garden to the City of Miami in 1961 as an expression of friendship. It was restored in 1988.

East of Watson Island, the causeway leaves Miami and enters
② Miami Beach. On the left, you'll pass the bridge to **Palm and**
③ **Hibiscus islands** and then the bridge to **Star Island.** Past and present celebrities who have lived on these islands include Al Capone (93 Palm Ave., Palm Island), author Damon Runyon (271 Hibiscus Island), and TV star Don Johnson (8 Star Island).

East of Star Island, the causeway mounts a high bridge. Look
④ left to see an island with an obelisk, the **Flagler Memorial Monument**. The memorial honors Henry M. Flagler, who built the Florida East Coast Railroad to Miami, opening south Florida to tourism and commerce.

⑤ Just beyond the bridge, turn right onto Alton Road past the **Miami Beach Marina** (300 Alton Rd., tel. 305/673-6000), where dive boats depart for artificial reefs offshore in the Atlantic Ocean.

Continue to the foot of Alton Road, turn left on Biscayne
⑥ Street, then go right at Washington Avenue to enter **South Pointe Park** (1 Washington Ave.). From the 50-yard Sunshine Pier, which adjoins the mile-long jetty at the mouth of Government Cut, you can fish while watching huge ships pass. No bait or tackle is available in the park. Other facilities include two observation towers, and volleyball courts.

When you leave the park, take Washington Avenue north. On the northwest corner of Washington Avenue and 5th Street, Cassius Clay (now Muhammad Ali) prepared for his champion-

Art Deco District, **8**
Bass Museum of Art, **15**
Espanola Way, **9**
Fifth Street Gym, **7**
Flagler Memorial, **4**
Fontainebleau
Hilton, **16**
Hibiscus Island, **3**
Hotel National, **14**
Jackie Gleason
Theater, **13**
La Gorce Country
Club, **17**
Lincoln Rd. Arts
District, **10**
Miami Beach City
Hall, **11**
Miami Beach Marina, **5**
Palm Island, **2**
South Pointe Park, **6**
Stephen Muss
Convention Center, **12**
Watson Island, **1**

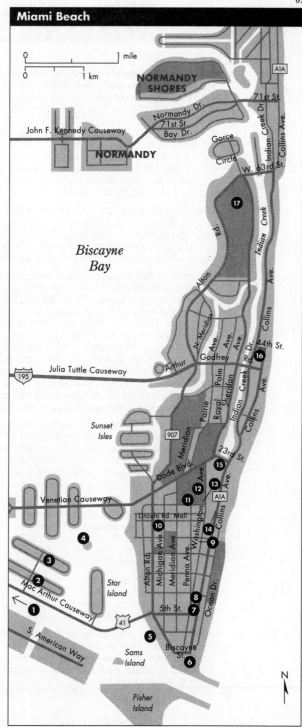

ship bouts in the **Fifth Street Gym.** You can visit to watch young boxers train. *501 Washington Ave., tel. 674–8481. Open Mon.– Sat. 8–7, Sun. 8–2. Admission: $1 to look, $3 to train.*

Time Out A block east on 5th Street and a block north on Collins Avenue, Albert Starr's **Nature's Garden Bakery** makes delicious kosher special-diet breads and cakes. Try the millet cookies and the apple strudel without salt, sweetener, eggs, or yeast. *600 Collins Ave., tel. 305/534–1877. Closed Fri. afternoon and Sat.*

Return to 5th Street, go a block east to Ocean Drive, and turn **❽** left. A block north at 6th Street, the **Art Deco District** begins. Take Ocean Drive north past a line of pastel-hued Art-Deco hotels on your left and palm-fringed Lummus Park and the beach on your right. Turn left on 15th Street, and left again at the next corner onto Collins Avenue.

Now drive along the Art Deco District's two main commercial streets. Take Collins Avenue south, turn right at 5th Street, and right again at the next corner onto **Washington Avenue,** an intriguing mixture of delicatessens, produce markets, and stores selling Jewish religious books and artifacts.

Go north on Washington Avenue and you'll come to the **Art Deco District Welcome Center** (661 Washington Ave., tel. 305/ 672–2014, open weekdays 10–6, Sat. 10–1; for more informa- tion, *see* Guided Tours). Continuing on Washington Avenue, go **❾** past 14th Street to **Espanola Way,** a narrow street of Mediterranean-revival buildings constructed in 1925 and fre- quented through the years by artists and writers. In the 1930s, Cuban bandleader Desi Arnaz performed in the Village Tav- ern, now part of the **Clay Hotel & International Youth Hostel** (406 Espanola Way, tel. 305/534–2988). The hostel caters to young visitors from all over the world who seek secure, inex- pensive lodgings within walking distance of the beach.

Turn left onto Espanola Way, go five blocks to Jefferson Ave- nue, and turn right. Three blocks north of Espanola Way is **Lincoln Road Mall,** a landscaped shopping thoroughfare known during its heyday in the 1950s as "Fifth Avenue of the South." Trams shuttle shoppers along the mall, which is closed to all other vehicular traffic between Washington Avenue and Alton Road.

Park in the municipal lot a half-block north of the mall to stroll **❿** through the **Lincoln Road Arts District,** where three blocks of storefronts on Lincoln Road from Meridian Avenue to Lenox Avenue have been transformed into galleries, studios, class- rooms, and art-related boutiques and cafes.

The arts district also includes the 500-seat **Colony Theater** (1040 Lincoln Rd., tel. 305/673–7486), a former movie house. Now it's a city-owned performing arts center featuring dance, drama, music, and experimental cinema.

From the parking lot, go to the first main street north of Lin- coln Road Mall and turn right. You're on 17th Street, recently renamed **Hank Meyer Boulevard** for the local publicist who en- couraged comedian Jackie Gleason to broadcast his TV show from Miami Beach in the 1950s. Two blocks east on your left, **⓫** beside the entrance to **Miami Beach City Hall** (1700 Convention

Center Dr., tel. 305/673–7030), stands *Red Sea Road*, a huge red sculpture by Barbara Neijna.

⑫ Also to your left is the **Stephen Muss Convention Center** (1901 Convention Center Dr., tel. 305/673–7311), doubled in size in 1988 to 1.1 million square feet of exhibit space.

⑬ Continuing two more blocks east, admire another large sculpture, *Mermaid*, by Roy Lichtenstein, in front of **Jackie Gleason Theater of the Performing Arts** (1700 Washington Ave., tel. 305/673–8300), where Gleason's TV show once originated. Now the 3,000-seat theater hosts touring Broadway shows and classical concert performers. Near the sculpture, stars appearing in the theater since 1984 have left their footprints and signatures in concrete. This **Walk of the Stars** includes George Abbott, Julie Andrews, Leslie Caron, Carol Channing, and Edward Villella.

Go two more blocks east on Hank Meyer Boulevard to Collins Avenue, toward three of the largest Art Deco hotels, built in the 1940s with streamlined tower forms reflecting the 20th century's transportation revolution:

⑭ The round dome atop the tower of the 11-story **Hotel National** (1677 Collins Ave., tel. 305/532–2311) resembles a balloon. The tower at the 12-story **Delano Hotel** (1685 Collins Ave., tel. 305/ 538–7881) sports fins suggesting the wings of an airplane or a Buck Rogers spaceship. The 11-story **Ritz Plaza** (1701 Collins Ave., tel. 305/531–6881) rises to a cylindrical tower resembling a submarine periscope.

⑮ Turn left on Collins Avenue. At 21st Street, turn left beside the Miami Beach Public Library in Collins Park, go two blocks to Park Avenue, and turn right. You're approaching the **Bass Museum of Art,** with a diverse collection of European art, including *The Holy Family*, a painting by Peter Paul Rubens; *The Tournament*, a 16th-century Flemish tapestry; and works by Albrecht Dürer and Henri de Toulouse-Lautrec. Park behind the museum and walk around to the entrance past massive tropical baobab trees. *2121 Park Ave., tel. 305/673–7530. Open Tues.–Sat. 10–5, Sun. 1–5. Admission: $2 adult, $1 students with ID, children 16 and under free. Donations Tues.*

⑯ Return on 21st Street or 22nd Street to Collins Avenue and turn left. As you drive north, a triumphal archway looms ahead, framing a majestic white building set in lush vegetation beside a waterfall and tropical lagoon. This vista is an illusion—a 13,000-square-foot outdoor mural on an exterior wall of the **Fontainebleau Hilton Resort and Spa** (4441 Collins Ave., tel. 305/538–2000). Artist Richard Haas designed the mural to illustrate how the hotel and its rock-grotto swimming pool would look behind the wall. Locals call the 1,206-room hotel "Big Blue." It's the giant of Miami Beach, with 190,000 square feet of meeting and exhibit space.

⑰ Go left on 65th Street, turn left again at the next corner onto Indian Creek Drive, and right at 63rd Street, which leads into Alton Road, a winding, landscaped boulevard of gracious homes styled along Art Deco lines. You'll pass the **La Gorce Country Club** (5685 Alton Rd. tel. 305/866–4421), which developer Carl Fisher built and named for his friend Oliver La Gorce, then president of the National Geographic Society.

To return to the mainland on the MacArthur Causeway, stay on Alton Road south to 5th Street, then turn right.

Exploring Little Havana

Numbers in the margin correspond with points of interest on the Miami, Coral Gables, and Key Biscayne map.

Orientation Thirty years ago, the tidal wave of Cubans fleeing the Castro regime flooded an elderly neighborhood just west of downtown Miami with refugees. This area became known as Little Havana. Today, with a half-million Cubans widely dispersed throughout Greater Miami, Little Havana remains a magnet for Cubans and Anglos alike. They come to experience the flavor of traditional Cuban culture.

That culture, of course, functions in Spanish. Many Little Havana residents and shopkeepers speak almost no English. If you don't speak Spanish, point and smile to communicate.

Touring Little Havana Begin this tour in downtown Miami, westbound on Flagler Street. Cross the Miami River to Little Havana, and park near Flagler Street and Ronald Reagan Avenue (S.W. 12th Ave.) to explore a thriving commercial district.

❶ Continue west on Flagler Street to Teddy Roosevelt Avenue (S.W. 17th Ave.) and pause at **Plaza de la Cubanidad,** on the southwest corner. Red-brick sidewalks surround a fountain and monument with a quotation from José Martí, a leader in Cuba's struggle for independence from Spain: *"Las palmas son novias que esperan."* (The palm trees are girlfriends who will wait.)

❷ Turn left at Douglas Road (S.W. 37th Ave.), drive south to **Calle Ocho** (S.W. 8th St.), and turn left again. You are now on the main commercial thoroughfare of Little Havana.

Time Out For a total sensory experience, have a snack or meal at **Versailles,** a popular Cuban restaurant. Etched-glass mirrors lining its walls amplify bright lights and the roar of rapid-fire Spanish. Most of the servers don't speak English; you order by pointing to a number on the menu (choice of English or Spanish menus). Specialties include *palomilla,* a flat beefsteak; *vieja ropa* (literally, old clothes), a shredded-beef dish in tomato sauce; and *arroz con pollo,* chicken and yellow rice. *3555 S.W. 8th St., tel. 305/445–7614. Open Sun.–Thurs. 8 AM–2 AM, Fri. 8 AM–3:30 AM, Sat. 8 AM–4:30 AM. AE, CB, DC, MC, V.*

East of Unity Boulevard (S.W. 27th Ave.), Calle Ocho becomes a one-way street eastbound through the heart of Little Havana, where every block deserves exploration. If your time is limited, we suggest the three-block stretch from S.W. 14th Avenue to S.W. 11th Avenue. Parking is more ample west of Ronald Reagan Avenue (S.W. 12th Ave.).

❸ At Calle Ocho and Memorial Boulevard (S.W. 13th Ave.) stands the **Brigade 2506 Memorial,** commemorating the victims of the unsuccessful 1961 Bay of Pigs invasion of Cuba by an exile force. An eternal flame burns atop a simple stone monument with the inscription: *"Cuba—A Los Martires de La Brigada de Asalto Abril 17 de 1961."* The monument also bears a shield with the Brigade 2506 emblem, a Cuban flag superimposed on a cross. Walk a block south on Memorial Boulevard from the Brigade 2506 Memorial to see other monuments relevant to Cuban history, including a statue of José Martí.

❹ When you return to your car, drive five blocks south on Ronald Reagan Avenue to the **Cuban Museum of Art and Culture.** Created by Cuban exiles to preserve and interpret the cultural heritage of their homeland, the museum has expanded its focus to embrace the entire Hispanic art community. It has a small permanent collection and mounts temporary exhibitions. *1300 S.W. 12th Ave., tel. 305/858–8006. Open weekdays 10–5, weekends 1–5. Admission: donation requested.*

To return to downtown Miami, take Ronald Reagan Avenue back north to S.W. 8th Street, turn right, go east to Miami Avenue or Brickell Avenue, turn left, and go north across the Miami River.

Exploring Coral Gables/Coconut Grove/ South Miami

Orientation This tour directs you through three separate communities, each unique in character. Two of them, Coral Gables and South Miami, are independent suburbs. The third, Coconut Grove, was annexed to the City of Miami in 1925 but still retains a distinctive personality.

Coral Gables, a planned community of broad boulevards and Spanish Mediterranean architecture, justifiably calls itself "The City Beautiful." Developer George E. Merrick began selling Coral Gables lots in 1921 and incorporated the city in 1925. He named most of the streets for Spanish explorers, cities, and provinces. Street names are at ground level beside each intersection on whitewashed concrete cornerstones.

The 1926 hurricane and the Great Depression prevented Merrick from fulfilling many aspects of his plan. The city languished until after World War II but then grew rapidly. Today, Coral Gables has a population of about 43,000. In its bustling downtown, many multinational companies maintain headquarters or regional offices.

A pioneer farming community that grew into a suburb, South Miami today retains small-town charm. Its main attraction for visitors is an architecturally impressive mall, The Bakery Centre, constructed on the former site of Holsum Bakery. Samples of the old bakery's architectural ornamentation are on display.

Coconut Grove is south Florida's oldest settlement, inhabited as early as 1834 and established by 1873, two decades before Miami. Its early settlers included Bahamian blacks, "conchs" from Key West, and New England intellectuals. They built a community that attracted artists, writers, and scientists to establish winter homes. By the end of World War I, more people listed in *Who's Who* gave addresses in Coconut Grove than anyplace else.

To this day, Coconut Grove reflects the pioneers' eclectic origins. Posh estates mingle with rustic cottages, modest frame homes, and starkly modern dwellings—often on the same block. To keep Coconut Grove a village in a jungle, residents lavish affection on exotic plantings while battling to protect remaining native vegetation.

Miami, Coral Gables, and Key Biscayne

ATLANTIC

Bill Baggs Cape Florida
State Recreation Area

Crandon
Park

KEY
BISCAYNE

Biscayne

Isle

Matheson
Hammock
Park

Crandon Park
Marina, 38

CORAL
GABLES

Coral Gables

Waterway

Sunset Dr.

Red Rd.

Old Cutler Rd.

The Bakery Centre, 17
The Barnacle, 23
Biltmore Country
Club, 14
Biltmore Hotel, 13
Brigade 2506
Memorial, 3
Calle Ocho, 2

Cape Florida
Lighthouse, 41
Caribbean
Marketplace, 42
Cartagena Plaza, 20
Coconut Grove
Exhibition Center, 2
Coconut Grove Farmers
Market, 24

Coconut Grove
Playhouse, 22
Colonnade Building, 7
Coral Gables City
Hall, 8
Coral Gables House, 10
Coral Way, 5

Cuban Museum, 4
DeSoto Plaza, 11
Dinner Key Marina, 26
Ermita de la
Caridad, 30
Fairchild Garden, 19
Five Points, 6
Granada Golf Course, 9
Hobie Island, 33

Kennedy Park, 29
Key Biscayne Golf
Course, 39
Lowe Art Museum, 16
Mayfair Shops in the
Grove, 25
Metro Zoo, 43
Miami City Hall, 28

Miami Marine
Stadium, 34
Miami Museum of
Science and
Planetarium, 31
Miami Seaquarium, 36
Monkey Jungle, 44
Nixon's home, 40

Parrot Jungle, 18
Planet Ocean, 35
Plaza de la Cubanidad, 1
Plymouth Church, 21
University of Miami, 15
Venetian Pool, 12
Virginia Key Beach, 37
Vizcaya Museum, 32

3 miles

3 km

The historic center of the Village of Coconut Grove went through a hippy period in the 1960s, laid-back funkiness in the 1970s, and a teenybopper invasion in the early 1980s. Today, the tone is increasingly upscale, mellow, and sophisticated—a congenial mix of art-cinema and legitimate theaters, galleries, boutiques, elegant restaurants, and bars and sidewalk cafes where the literati hang out.

Two Junior League books, *Historic Coral Gables* and *Historic Coconut Grove*, give directions for self-guided walking tours.

Driving Tour of Coral Gables/ Coconut Grove/ South Miami
❺
❻
This tour begins in downtown Miami. Go south on S.E. 2nd Avenue, which becomes Brickell Avenue and crosses the Miami River. Half a mile south of the river, turn right onto **Coral Way,** which at this point is S.W. 13th Street. Within half a mile, Coral Way doglegs left under I-95 and becomes S.W. 3rd Avenue. It continues another mile to a complex intersection, **Five Points,** and doglegs right to become S.W. 22nd Avenue.

Along the S.W. 3rd Avenue and S.W. 22nd Avenue segments of Coral Way, banyan trees planted in the median strip in 1929 arch over the roadway. The banyans end at the Miami/Coral Gables boundary, where **Miracle Mile** begins. This four-block stretch of Coral Way, from Douglas Road (37th Ave.) to Le Jeune Road (42nd Ave.) in the heart of downtown Coral Gables, is really a half-mile long. To stroll the full mile, walk up one side and down the other. Miracle Mile's 160 shops range from chain restaurants and shoe stores to posh boutiques and beauty salons. The stores are numbered from 1 to 399. As you go west, numbers and quality both increase. Request a complete directory from the Miracle Mile Merchants' Association (220 Miracle Mile, Suite 218, Coral Gables, tel. 305/445-0591).

❼ **The Colonnade Building** (133–169 Miracle Mile, Coral Gables) on Miracle Mile once housed George Merrick's sales office. Its rotunda bears an ornamental frieze and a Spanish-tile roof 75 feet above street level. The Colonnade Building has been restored and connected to the new 13-story Colonnade Hotel and an office building that echoes the rotunda's roofline.

❽ The ornate Spanish Renaissance structure facing Miracle Mile just west of Le Jeune Road is **Coral Gables City Hall,** opened in 1928. It has a three-tier tower topped with a clock and a 500-pound bell. Inside the bell tower, a mural by artist Denman Fink depicts the four seasons. *405 Biltmore Way, Coral Gables, tel. 305/442-6400. Open weekdays 8–5.*

❾ Follow Coral Way west of Le Jeune Road to the right of City Hall. You'll pass the **Granada Golf Course** (2001 Granada Blvd., Coral Gables, tel. 305/442-6484), one of two public courses in Coral Gables.

❿ One block west of the golf course, turn right on Toledo Street to park behind **Coral Gables House,** George Merrick's boyhood home. The city acquired the dwelling in 1976 and restored its 1920s appearance. It contains many Merrick family furnishings and artifacts. *907 Coral Way, Coral Gables, tel. 305/442-6593. Open Sun. and Wed. 1–4. Admission: $1 adults, 50 cents children.*

⓫ Return to Coral Way, turn right, then left at the first stoplight. Now you're southbound on Granada Boulevard, approaching **De Soto Plaza and Fountain,** a classical column on a pedestal with water flowing from the mouths of four sculptured faces. The closed eyes of the face looking west symbolize the day's end. Denman Fink designed the fountain in the early 1920s.

Follow the traffic circle almost completely around the fountain to northeast-bound De Soto Boulevard. On your right in the next block is **Venetian Pool,** a unique municipal swimming pool transformed from a rock quarry. *2701 De Soto Blvd., Coral Gables, tel. 305/442–6483. Summer hours: weekdays 11–7:30, weekends 10–4:30; winter hours: Tues.–Fri. 11–4, weekends 10–4:30. Admission (nonresident): $2.85 adults, $1.14 children under 13. Free parking across De Soto Blvd.*

From the pool, go around the block with right turns onto Almeria Avenue, Toledo Street, and Sevilla Avenue. You'll return to the De Soto Fountain and take De Soto Boulevard southeast to emerge in front of **The Biltmore Hotel** (1200 Anastasia Ave., Coral Gables, tel. 305/445–1926). Like the Freedom Tower in downtown Miami, the Biltmore's 26-story tower is a replica of the Giralda Tower in Seville, Spain.

The opulent Biltmore opened in January 1926 as the centerpiece of George Merrick's planned city. It suffered financially during the Great Depression, became a veterans' hospital during World War II, and stood vacant from 1968 to 1986. After extensive restoration and renovation, it has reopened as a 279-unit hotel.

Go inside the Biltmore to admire the lobby's vaulted ceiling and gargoyles, the two ballrooms' impressive chandeliers and intricately painted ceilings, and the open courtyard's fountain and gracious proportions. A second-floor promenade overlooks the 18-hole Biltmore Golf Course, now a public course known for its scenic and competitive layout, and the largest hotel pool in the United States, with a capacity of 1.25 million gallons.

Just west of The Biltmore Hotel stands a separate building, **The Biltmore Country Club,** which the city restored in the late 1970s. It's a richly ornamented beaux arts-style structure with a superb colonnade and courtyard. On its ground floor are facilities for golfers. In the former club lounge, Le Biltmore Restaurant occupies a lofty room paneled with veneer from 60 species of trees.

From the hotel, turn right on Anastasia Avenue, go east to Granada Boulevard, and turn right. Continue south on Granada Boulevard over a bridge across the **Coral Gables Waterway,** which connects the grounds of The Biltmore Hotel with Biscayne Bay. In the hotel's heyday, Venetian gondolas plied the waterway, bringing guests to a bayside beach.

At Ponce de León Boulevard, turn right. On your left is Metrorail's Stonehenge-like concrete structure, and on your right, the **University of Miami**'s 260-acre main campus. With nearly 20,000 students, UM is the largest private university in the Southeast.

Turn right at the first stoplight to enter the campus and park in the lot on your right designated for visitors to UM's **Lowe Art Museum.** The Lowe's permanent collection of 8,000 works includes Renaissance and Baroque art, American paintings, Latin American art, and Navajo and Pueblo Indian textiles and baskets. The museum also hosts traveling exhibitions. *1301*

Stanford Dr., Coral Gables, tel. 305/284-3535 for recorded information, 305/284-3536 for museum office. Open all year Sun. and Tues.-Fri. noon-5, Sat. 10-5. Admission: $2 adults, $1 students and seniors, children under 16 free.

Now exit the UM campus on Stanford Drive, pass under Metrorail, and cross Dixie Highway. Just beyond the Burger King on your right, bear right onto Maynada Street. Turn right at the next stoplight onto **Sunset Drive.** Fine old homes and mature trees line this officially designated "historic and scenic road" that leads to and through downtown South Miami.

On the northwest corner of Sunset Drive and Red Road (57th Ave.), note the pink building with a mural on which an alligator seems ready to devour a horrified man. This trompe l'oeil fantasy, *South Florida Cascade,* by illusionary artist Richard Haas, 🔟 highlights the main entrance to **The Bakery Centre.** *5701 Sunset Dr., South Miami, tel. 305/662-4155.*

On the third level of The Bakery Centre, the **Miami Youth Museum** features cultural arts exhibits, hands-on displays, and activities to enhance a child's creativity and inspire interest in artistic careers. *5701 Sunset Dr., South Miami, tel. 305/661-ARTS. Open weekdays 10-5, weekends noon-5. Admission: $3 adults, children under 2 free.*

Go south on Red Road and turn right just before Killian Drive 🔟 (S.W. 112th St.) into the grounds of **Parrot Jungle,** where more than 1,100 exotic birds are on display. Many of the parrots, macaws, and cockatoos fly free, but they'll come to you for seeds that you can purchase from old-fashioned gumball machines. Attend a trained-bird show, watch baby birds in training, and pose for photos with colorful macaws perched on your arms. The "jungle" is a natural hammock surrounding a sinkhole. Stroll among orchids and other flowering plants nestled among ferns, bald-cypress trees, and massive live oaks. Also see the cactus garden and Flamingo Lake, with a breeding population of 75 Caribbean flamingos. Opened in 1936, Parrot Jungle is one of Greater Miami's oldest and most popular commercial tourist attractions. *11000 S.W. 57th Ave., Miami, tel. 305/666-7834. Open daily 9:30-5. Admission: $9.75 adults, $4 children 3-12.*

From Parrot Jungle, take Red Road ⅓ mile south and turn left at Old Cutler Road, which curves north along the uplands of 🔟 South Florida's coastal ridge. Visit 83-acre **Fairchild Tropical Garden,** the largest tropical botanical garden in the continental United States. *10901 Old Cutler Rd., Coral Gables, tel. 305/667-1651. Open daily except Christmas 9:30-4:30. Admission: $4 adults, children under 12 free with parents. Hourly tram rides, $1 adults, 50 cents children 12 & under.*

North of the garden, Old Cutler Road traverses Dade County's oldest and most scenic park, **Matheson Hammock Park.** The Civilian Conservation Corps developed the 100-acre tracts of upland and mangrove swamp in the 1930s on land donated by a local pioneer, Commodore J. W. Matheson. The park's most popular feature is a bathing beach, where the tide flushes a saltwater "atoll" pool through four gates. *9601 Old Cutler Rd., Coral Gables, tel. 305/666-6979. Park open 6 AM-sundown. Pool lifeguards on duty winter 7:30 AM-6 PM, summer 7:30 AM-7 PM. Parking fee for beach and marina $2 per car, $5 per car with trailer. Limited upland parking free.*

⓴ Continue north on Old Cutler Road to **Cartagena Plaza,** cross the Le Jeune Road bridge over the waterway, and turn right at the first stoplight onto Ingraham Highway. Four blocks later, you're back in the City of Miami, at the south end of Coconut Grove. Follow Ingraham Highway to Douglas Road and turn right at the next stoplight onto Main Highway. You're following old pioneer trails that today remain narrow roads shaded by a canopy of towering trees.

One block past the stoplight at Royal Palm Avenue, turn left

㉑ onto Devon Road in front of **Plymouth Congregational Church.** Opened in 1917, this handsome coral-rock structure resembles a Mexican mission church. The front door, of hand-carved walnut and oak with original wrought-iron fittings, came from an early 17th-century monastery in the Pyrenees. A hole in the lower right side of the door gives the church cat access to mice. *3429 Devon Rd., Coconut Grove, tel. 305/444–6521. Ask at the office to go inside the church, weekdays 9–4:30. Services Sun. 10 AM.*

When you leave the church, go around the block opposite the church. Turn left from Devon Road onto Hibiscus Street, left again onto Royal Palm Avenue, and left at the stoplight onto Main Highway.

You're now headed for the historic **Village of Coconut Grove,** a trendy commercial district with red-brick sidewalks and more than 300 restaurants, stores, and art galleries.

Parking can be a problem in the village—especially on weekend evenings, when police direct traffic and prohibit turns at some intersections to prevent gridlock. Be prepared to walk several blocks from the periphery into the heart of the Grove.

As you enter the village center, note the apricot-hued Spanish

㉒ rococo **Coconut Grove Playhouse** to your left. Built in 1926 as a movie theater, it became a legitimate theater in 1956 and is now owned by the State of Florida. The playhouse presents Broadway-bound plays and musical reviews and experimental productions in its 1,100-seat main theater and 100-seat cabaret-style Encore Room. *3500 Main Hwy., Coconut Grove, tel. 305/442–4000 to box office; tel. 305/442–2662 to administrative office. Parking lot: $2 during the day, $4 at night.*

Benches and a shelter opposite the playhouse mark the en-

㉓ trance to **The Barnacle,** a pioneer residence that is now a state historic site. Commodore Ralph Munroe built The Barnacle in 1891. Its broad, sloping roof and deeply recessed verandas channel sea breezes into the house. A central stairwell and rooftop vent allow hot air to escape. Many furnishings are original. While living at The Barnacle, Munroe built shoal-draft sailboats. One such craft, the ketch *Micco*, is on display. *3485 Main Hwy., Coconut Grove, tel. 305/448–9445. Open for tours only Thurs.–Mon. 9, 10:30, 1, and 2:30; closed Tues. and Wed. Admission: $1 adults, 50 cents children under 12. Reservations for groups of 8 or more; others meet ranger at entrance gate.*

Time Out   Turn left at the next street, Commodore Plaza, and pause. **To Market/To Market,** a French gourmet cafe, features 16 kinds of muffins and a superb Greek-style salad bulging with brine-soaked olives and feta cheese. Other fare includes quiches, pâtés, sandwiches, cheeses, French pastries, American-style breakfasts, wine, beer, and soft drinks. On weekend mornings, locals bicycle in for a croissant-and-eggs brunch and a chat with the neighbors. *3195 Commodore Plaza, Coconut Grove, tel. 305/446–6090. Open Sun.–Thurs. 7 AM–10PM, Fri. and Sat. 7 AM–midnight. Inside and outdoors service and carryouts available. AE, CB, DC, MC, V.*

(24) If your timing is right, visit the **Coconut Grove Farmers Market,** a laid-back, Brigadoon-like happening that appears as if by magic each Saturday on a vacant lot. To get there from Commodore Plaza, go north to Grand Ave., cross McDonald Ave. (S.W. 32nd Ave.), and go a block west to Margaret Street. Vendors set up outdoor stands to offer home-grown tropical fruits and vegetables (including organic produce), honey, seafoods, macrobiotic foods, and ethnic fare from the Caribbean, the Middle East, and Southeast Asia. Nonfood items for sale include plants, handicrafts, candles, jewelry, and homemade clothing. A masseur plies his trade, musicians play, and the Hare Krishnas come to chant. People-watching is half the fun. Open Saturday 8–3.

(25) Now return to the heart of the village center. Then take Grand Avenue a block east to Virginia Street and enter **Mayfair Shops in the Grove,** an exclusive open-air mall with a small branch of high-fashion Burdines department store and 74 other upscale shops. The 181 rooms of Mayfair House, a luxury hotel, surround the mall's southern section. As you stroll through Mayfair, admire its fountains, copper sculptures, and lavish Romanesque ornamentation formed in concrete. The design recalls a classic building in Chicago, The Rookery—with good reason. Frank Lloyd Wright, who remodeled The Rookery in 1905, taught Mayfair's architect, Kenneth Treister. *2911 Grand Ave., Coconut Grove, tel. 305/448–1700. Open Mon., Thurs., and Fri. 10–9; Tues., Wed., and Sat. 10–7; Sun. noon–5:30.*

(26) Leaving the village center, take McFarlane Road east from its intersection with Grand Avenue and Main Highway. Peacock Park, site of the first hotel in Coconut Grove, is on your right. Ahead, seabirds soar and sailboats ride at anchor in **Dinner Key Marina** (3400 Pan American Dr., Coconut Grove, tel. 305/579–6980), named for a small island where early settlers held picnics. With 575 moorings, it's Greater Miami's largest marina.

(27) McFarlane Road turns left onto South Bayshore Drive. Turn right at the first stoplight onto Unity Boulevard (S.W. 27th Ave.), and go east into a parking lot that serves the marina and the 105,000-square-foot **Coconut Grove Exhibition Center** (3360 Pan American Dr., Coconut Grove, tel. 305/579–3310), where antique, boat, and home-furnishings shows are held.

(28) At the northeast corner of the lot is **Miami City Hall,** which was built in 1934 as the terminal for the Pan American Airways seaplane base at Dinner Key. The building retains its nautical-style art-deco trim. *3500 Pan American Dr., Coconut Grove, tel. 305/579–6325. Open weekdays 8–5.*

(29) From City Hall, drive west on Pan American Drive toward South Bayshore Drive, with its pyramidlike Grand Bay Hotel. Turn right on South Bayshore Drive, and go north past **Kennedy Park.** Leave your car in the park's lot north of Kirk Street and walk toward the water. From a footbridge over the mouth of a small tidal creek, you'll enjoy an unobstructed view across Biscayne Bay to Key Biscayne. Film crews use the park often to make commercials and Italian westerns.

Continue north on South Bayshore Drive to Fair Isle Street and turn right. You're approaching **Grove Isle,** a 26-acre island with a 49-room hotel, high-rise apartments, and a private club. Developer Martin C. Margulies displays selections from his extensive private art collection in the lobbies. Along a walk beside the bay stand massive sculptures by modern luminaries, including Alexander Calder, Jean Dubuffet, Willem de Kooning, Alexander Liberman, and Isamu Noguchi. *4 Grove Isle Dr., Coconut Grove, tel. 305/250-4000. Phone the club's membership office, weekdays 9-5, and mention Fodor's Florida 1990 to obtain a free guest pass.*

Return to South Bayshore Drive, turn right, and go north past the entrance to Mercy Hospital, where South Bayshore Drive becomes South Miami Avenue. At the next stoplight beyond the hospital, turn right on a private road that goes past St. Kieran's Church to **Ermita de La Caridad**—Our Lady of Charity Shrine—a conical building 90 feet high and 80 feet wide overlooking the bay so worshipers face toward Cuba. A mural above the shrine's altar depicts the history of Cuba. *3609 S. Miami Ave., Coconut Grove, tel. 305/854-2404. Open daily 9-9.*

Return to South Miami Avenue, turn right, go about three-tenths of a mile, and turn left to the **Miami Museum of Science and Space Transit Planetarium.** This is a participatory museum, chock-full of sound, gravity, and electricity displays for children and adults alike to manipulate and marvel at. A wildlife center behind the museum houses native Florida snakes, turtles and tortoises, birds of prey, and large wading birds. *3280 S. Miami Ave., Miami, tel. 305/854-4247; 24-hour Cosmic Hotline for planetarium show times and prices, 305/854-2222. Open daily 10-6. Admission to museum: $4 adults, $2.50 children; to planetarium shows $5 adults, $2.50 children and seniors; to laser light shows $6 adults, $3 children and seniors.*

Across South Miami Avenue is the entrance to **Vizcaya Museum and Gardens,** an estate with an Italian Renaissance-style villa built in 1912-16 as the winter residence of Chicago industrialist James Deering. The house and gardens overlook Biscayne Bay on a 30-acre tract that includes a native hammock and more than 10 acres of formal gardens and fountains. You can leave your car in the Museum of Science lot and walk across the street or drive across and park in Vizcaya's own lot.

The house contains 34 rooms of antique furniture, plus paintings, sculpture, and other decorative arts. These objects date from the 15th through the 19th centuries, representing the Renaissance, Baroque, Rococo, and Neoclassic styles. *3251 S. Miami Ave., Miami, tel. 305/579-2813 (recording) or 305/579-2808. House open 9:30-4:30; ticket booth open to 4:30, garden to 5:30. Admission: $6.50 adults, $4.50 children 5-18. Guided tours available, group tours by appointment.*

As you leave Vizcaya, turn north (left from the Museum of Science lot, right from the Vizcaya lot) onto South Miami Avenue.

You may follow South Miami Avenue all the way downtown or turn right at the first stoplight onto Federal Highway, which runs into Brickell Avenue one long block north, in front of the entrance to the Rickenbacker Causeway to Key Biscayne.

Exploring Virginia Key and Key Biscayne

Orientation Government Cut and the Port of Miami separate the dense urban fabric of Miami Beach from Greater Miami's playground islands, Virginia Key and Key Biscayne. Parks occupy much of both keys, providing congenial upland with facilities for basking on the beach, golf, tennis, softball, and picnicking—plus uninviting but ecologically valuable stretches of dense mangrove swamp. Also on the keys are several marinas, an assortment of water-oriented tourist attractions, and the laidback village where Richard Nixon set up his presidential vacation compound.

Driving Tour of Virginia Key and Key Biscayne To reach Virginia Key and Key Biscayne, take the **Rickenbacker Causeway** across Biscayne Bay from the mainland at Brickell Avenue and S.W. 26th Road, about two miles south of downtown Miami. A fitness pathway for biking and jogging parallels the causeway. *Toll: $1 per car, bicycles and pedestrians free.*

㉝ About 200 feet east of the toll gate (just across the first low bridge), you can rent windsurfing equipment on **Hobie Island.** *Sailboards Miami, Box 16, Key Biscayne, tel. 305/361–SAIL, open daily 9:30–dusk. Cost: $12/hour; $39 for 2-hr windsurfing lesson.*

The **Old Rickenbacker Causeway Bridge,** built in 1947, is now a fishing pier. The west stub begins about a mile from the toll gate. Park near its entrance and walk past fishermen tending their lines to the gap where the center draw span across the Intracoastal Waterway was removed. There you can watch boat traffic pass through the channel, pelicans and other seabirds soar and dive, and porpoises cavort in the bay.

The new high-level **William M. Powell Bridge** rises 75 feet above the water to eliminate the need for a draw span. The panoramic view from the top encompasses the bay, keys, port, and downtown skyscrapers, with Miami Beach and the Atlantic Ocean in the distance. The speed limit is 45 mph, and you can't stop on the bridge, so park in the fishing pier lot and walk up.

㉞ Next along the causeway stands the 6,538-seat **Miami Marine Stadium** (3601 Rickenbacker Causeway, Miami, tel. 305/361–6732), where summer pops concerts take place and name entertainers perform throughout the year. You can join the audience on land in the stadium or on a boat anchored just offshore. Fourth of July concertgoers enjoy a spectacular fireworks display that is visible for miles up and down the bay.

㉟ Adjoining the stadium is **Planet Ocean,** the world's largest marine science museum. Most of its displays invite your participation. Touch an iceberg; walk through the eye of a hurricane; and measure yourself against the smallest sailing vessel ever to cross the Atlantic, *April Fool*—an inch under six feet long. *3979 Rickenbacker Causeway, Miami, tel. 305/361–5786; recorded program information, 305/361–9455. Open daily 10–6. Admission: $7.50 adults, $6 senior citizens, $4 children 6–12.*

36 Down the causeway from Planet Ocean at the **Miami Seaquarium,** Lolita, a killer whale, cavorts in a huge tank. She performs three times a day, as do sea lions and dolphins in separate shows. Exhibits include a shark pool, 250,000-gallon tropical reef aquarium, and manatees. *4400 Rickenbacker Causeway, Miami, tel. 305/361–5705; recorded program information, 305/361–5703. Open daily 9:30–6:30. Admission: $13.95 adults, $11.95 senior citizens, $9.95 children 4–12.*

37 Opposite the causeway from the Seaquarium, a road leads north to **Virginia Key Beach,** a City of Miami park, with a two-mile stretch of ocean frontage, shelters, barbecue grills, ball fields, nature trails, and a fishing area. Ask for directions at the entrance gate. Cost is $2 per car.

38 From Virginia Key, the causeway crosses **Bear Cut** to the north end of Key Biscayne, where it becomes Crandon Boulevard. The **Crandon Park Marina,** behind Sundays on the Bay Restaurant, sells bait and tackle. *4000 Crandon Blvd., Key Biscayne, tel. 361–1161. Open 7–6.*

Beyond the marina, Crandon Blvd. bisects 1,211-acre **Crandon Park.** Turnouts on your left lead to four parking lots, adjacent picnic areas, ball fields, and 3.3 miles of beach. *Open all year 8 AM–sunset. Parking: $2 per car.*

39 On your right are entrances to the **Key Biscayne Golf Course,** and the **International Tennis Center.**

40 From the traffic circle at the south end of Crandon Park, Crandon Boulevard continues for two miles through the developed portion of Key Biscayne. You'll come back that way, but first detour to the site of **President Nixon's home** (485 W. Matheson Dr.). Turn right at the first stoplight onto Harbor Drive, go about a mile, and turn right at Matheson Drive. A later owner enlarged and totally changed Nixon's home.

Emerging from West Matheson Drive, turn right onto Harbor Drive and go about a mile south to Mashta Drive, and follow Mashta Drive east past Harbor Drive to Crandon Boulevard, and turn right.

You are approaching the entrance to **Bill Baggs Cape Florida State Recreation Area,** named for a crusading newspaper editor whose efforts prompted the state to create this 406-acre park. The park includes 1¼ miles of beach and a seawall along Biscayne Bay where fishermen catch bonefish, grouper, jack, snapper, and snook. There is a nature trail with native plants now rare on Key Biscayne.

41 Also in the park is the oldest structure in south Florida, the **Cape Florida Lighthouse,** erected in 1825 to help ships avoid the shallows and reefs offshore. In 1836 a band of Seminole Indians attacked the lighthouse and killed the keeper's helper. You can climb the 122 steps to the top of the 95-foot-tall lighthouse and visit a keeper's dwelling reconstructed and furnished as it might have appeared in the early 1900s, when Key Biscayne was a coconut plantation with just a handful of residents. *1200 S. Crandon Blvd., Key Biscayne, tel. 305/361–5811. Park open all year 8–sunset. Lighthouse tours daily except Tues. at 10:30, 1, 2:30, and 3:30. Admission to park: $1 per vehicle with* *driver, 50 cents per passenger, children under 6 free; to light-house and keeper's residence: $1 per person.*

When you leave Cape Florida, follow Crandon Boulevard back to Crandon Park through Key Biscayne's commercial center, a mixture of posh shops and stores catering to the needs of the neighborhood. On your way back to the mainland, pause as you approach the Powell Bridge to admire the downtown Miami skyline. At night, the brightly lit Centrust Building looks from this angle like a clipper ship running under full sail before the breeze.

Exploring Little Haiti

Of the nearly 150,000 Haitians who have settled in Greater Miami, some 60,000 live in Little Haiti, a 200-block area on Miami's northeast side. More than 350 small Haitian businesses operate in Little Haiti.

For many Haitians, English is a third language. French is Haiti's official language, but much day-to-day conversation takes place in Creole, a French-based patois. Smiling and pointing will bridge any language barriers you may encounter.

This tour takes you through the Miami Design District on the margin of Little Haiti, then along two main thoroughfares which form the spine of the Haitian community. The tour begins in downtown Miami. Take Biscayne Boulevard north to N.E. 36th Street, turn left, go about four-tenths of a mile west to North Miami Avenue. Turn right, and go north through the **Miami Design District,** where about 225 wholesale stores, showrooms, and galleries feature interior furnishings and decorative arts.

Little Haiti begins immediately north of the Design District in an area with some of Miami's oldest dwellings, dating from the dawn of the 20th Century through the 1920s land-boom era. Drive the side streets to see elegant Mediterranean-style homes, and bungalows with distinctive coral rock trim.

Return to North Miami Avenue and go north. A half-block east on 54th Street is the tiny storefront office of the **Haitian Refugee Center,** a focal point of political activity in the Haitian community. *32 N.E. 54th St., tel. 305/757–8538.*

Continue north on North Miami Avenue past the former Cuban consulate, a pretentious Caribbean-Colonial mansion that is now a Haitian physician's clinic.

North of 85th Street, cross the Little River Canal into **El Portal,** a tiny suburban village of modest homes where more than a quarter of the property is now Haitian-owned. Turn right on N.E. 87th Street and right again on N.E. 2nd Avenue. You are now southbound on Little Haiti's main commercial thoroughfare.

Time Out Stop for Haitian breads and cakes made with coconut and other tropical ingredients at **Baptiste Bakery.** *7488 N.E. 2nd Ave., tel. 756–1119. Open 8–8.*

Along N.E. 2nd Avenue between 79th Street and 45th Street, a riot of color assails your eyes. Merchants have painted their buildings in vivid yellows, greens, reds, pinks, purples, and blues that Haitians find congenial and mellow.

42 Look for the **Caribbean Marketplace,** which the Haitian Task Force (an economic development organization) expects to open by early 1990. Its 32 merchants will sell tropical fruits and vegetables, handmade baskets, and Haitian art and craft items. *5927 N.E. 2nd Ave., Miami, tel. Haitian Task Force, 305/751–9783, for marketplace phone number.*

This concludes the Little Haiti tour. To return to downtown Miami, take N.E. 2nd Avenue south to N.E. 35th Street, turn left, go east one block to Biscayne Boulevard, and turn right to go south.

Exploring South Dade

This tour directs you to major attractions in the suburbs southwest of Dade County's urban core. A Junior League book, *Historic South Dade*, locates and describes 40 historic structures and attractions in a South Dade County driving tour.

From downtown Miami, take the Dolphin Expressway (Rte. 836) west to the Palmetto Expressway (Rte. 826) southbound. Bear left south of Bird Road (S.W. 40th St.) onto the Don Shula Expressway (Rte. 874). Exit westbound onto Killian Drive (S.W. 104th St.) and go west to Lindgren Road (S.W. 137th Ave.). Turn left and go south to S.W. 128th Street, the entrance to the Tamiami Airport and **Weeks Air Museum,** where aircraft on display include a World War I-vintage Sopwith Camel (of Snoopy fame), and a B–17 Flying Fortress bomber and P–51 Mustang from World War II. *14710 S.W. 128th St., tel. 305/233–5197. Open: Wed.–Sun. 10–5. Admission: $4 adults, $2 children 12 and under and seniors.*

43 Continue south on Lindgren Road to Coral Reef Drive (S.W. 152nd St.). Turn left and go east to **Metro Zoo** and the **Gold Coast Railroad Museum.**

Metro Zoo covers 290 acres and is cageless; animals roam free on islands surrounded by moats. In "Wings of Asia," a 1.5-acre aviary, hundreds of exotic birds from southeast Asia fly through a rain forest beneath a protective net enclosure. The zoo has 3 miles of walkways, a monorail with 4 stations, and an open-air amphitheater for concerts. Paws, a petting zoo for children, opened in 1989. *12400 Coral Reef Dr. (S.W. 152nd St.), tel. 305/251–0400 for recorded information. Gates open daily 10–4. Park closes at 5:30. Admission: $6 adults, $3 children 3–12, under 3 free. Monorail tickets (unlimited use on day of purchase) $3 adults, $2 children. AE, MC; no credit cards at monorail and snack bar.*

The railroad museum's collection includes a 1949 Silver Crescent dome car; and the *Ferdinand Magellan*, the only Pullman car ever constructed specifically for U.S. presidents, used by Roosevelt, Truman, Eisenhower, and Reagan. *12450 Coral Reef Dr. (S.W. 152nd St.), tel. 305/253–0063. Open weekdays 10–3, weekends 10–5. Train rides weekends, holidays. Phone for details.*

Return to Coral Reef Drive, turn right (east) to the Homestead Extension of Florida's Turnpike, take the turnpike south, exit at Hainlin Mill Drive (S.W. 216th St.), and turn right. Cross

South Dixie Hwy. (U.S. 1), go three miles west, and turn right into **Monkey Jungle,** home to more than 4,000 monkeys representing 50 species—including orangutans from Borneo and Sumatra, golden lion tamarins from Brazil, and brown lemurs from Madagascar. Performing monkey shows begin at 10 AM and run continuously at 45-minute intervals. The walkways of this 30-acre attraction are caged; the monkeys roam free. *14805 Hainlin Mill Dr. (S.W. 216 St.), tel. 305/235–1611. Open daily 9:30–5. Admission: $7.50 adults, $6.50 seniors, $4 children 5– 12. AE, MC.*

Continue west on Hainlin Mill Drive to Newton Road (S.W. 157th Ave.), turn left and go south to **Orchid Jungle,** where you can stroll under live-oak trees to see orchids, ferns, bromeliads, and anthuriums, and peer through the windows of an orchid-cloning laboratory. *26715 SW 157th Ave., Homestead, tel. 305/ 247–4824, FL 800/344–2457, or US 800/327–2832. Open daily 8:30–5:30. Admission: $5 adults, $4 seniors, $4 children 13–17, $1.50 children 6–12.*

Continue south on Newton Road to South Dixie Hwy. (U.S. 1), and turn left. Almost immediately, you'll find **Coral Castel of Florida** on your right. It was built by Edward Leedskalnin, a Latvian immigrant, between 1920 and 1940. The 3-acre castle has a 9-ton gate a child can open, an accurate working sundial, and a telescope of coral rock aimed at the north star, Polaris. *28655 South Dixie Hwy., Homestead, tel. 305/248–6344. Open daily 9–9. Admission: $7.25 adults, $4.50 children 6–12. MC, V.*

Leaving Coral Castle, take South Dixie Highway to Biscayne Drive (S.W. 288th St.) and go east to the turnpike. Take the turnpike back to the Don Shula Expressway (Rte. 874), which leads to the Palmetto Expressway (Rte. 826), which leads in turn to the Dolphin Expressway (Rte. 836).

Miami for Free

Concerts **PACE** (Performing Arts for Community and Education, tel. 305/681–1470) supports free concerts in parks and cultural and religious institutions throughout the Greater Miami Area.

University of Miami School of Music (tel. 305/284–6477) offers many free concerts on the Coral Gables campus.

Museums Some museums are free all the time. Others have donation days, when you may pay as much or as little as you wish. *(See* Exploring and Historical Buildings and Sites for free-admission policies at major museums.)

Views Ride an elevator to the 18th floor of the new Metro-Dade Center to enjoy spectacular views east to Miami Beach and Biscayne Bay and west to the Orange Bowl and Miami International Airport. Open Mon.–Fri. 8–5 *(see* Exploring Downtown Miami).

What to See and Do with Children

Greater Miami is a family-oriented vacation destination. Most of the major hotels can provide access to baby-sitting for young children. Although the area lacks major theme parks, families stay occupied with visits to the beach, zoo, and museums. Activities for teenagers are most prevalent on the beaches during spring break but occur throughout the year.

Family Activities **Dade County Youth Fair.** For 18 days at the end of March each year, Greater Miami's only amusement park comes to life at the Dade County Youth Fair in 260-acre Tamiami Park. The fairgrounds features a mile-long midway with over 80 amusement and thrill rides. The world's largest youth fair displays 50,000 student exhibits in 30 categories, including science projects and farm animals and equipment. Professional entertainers perform daily on seven stages. If you buy something at a local Publix supermarket, you'll get a gate pass good for free admission on Thursdays. *10901 Coral Way, Miami, tel. 305/223–7060. Open weekdays 4–11, weekends, 10 AM–11 PM. Admission: $4 adults, $3 children 6–12.*

Shopping

Except in the heart of the Everglades, visitors to the Greater Miami area are never more than 15 minutes away from a major shopping area. Downtown Miami long ago ceased to be the community's central shopping hub. Today Dade County has more than a dozen major malls, an international free zone, and hundreds of miles of commercial streets lined with storefronts and small neighborhood shopping centers. Many of these local shopping areas have an ethnic flavor, catering primarily to one of Greater Miami's immigrant cultures.

In the Latin neighborhoods, children's stores sell *vestidos* (party dresses) made of organza and lace. Men's stores sell the *guayabera*, a pleated, embroidered shirt that replaces the tie and jacket in much of the tropics. Traditional bridal shops display formal dresses that Latin families buy or rent for a daughter's *quince*, a lavish 15th-birthday celebration.

No standard store hours exist in Greater Miami. Phone ahead. When you shop, expect to pay Florida's 6% sales tax unless you have the store ship your goods out of Florida.

Shopping Districts Greater Miami is the fashion marketplace for the southeastern
Fashion District United States, the Caribbean, and Latin America. Many of the 500 garment manufacturers in Miami and Hialeah sell their clothing locally, in more than 30 factory outlets and discount fashion stores in the Miami Fashion District, east of I-95 along 5th Avenue from 29th Street to 25th Street. Most stores in the district are open 9–5 Monday–Saturday and accept credit cards.

Miami Free Zone The Miami Free Zone (MFZ) is an international wholesale trade center where the U.S. Customs Service supervises the exhibition and sales space. You can buy goods duty-free for export or pay duty on goods released for domestic use. More than 140 companies sell products from 75 countries, including aviation equipment, chemicals, clothing, computers, cosmetics, electronics, liquor, and perfumes. The 54-acre MFZ is five minutes west of Miami International Airport off the Dolphin Expressway (Rte. 836), and about 20 minutes from the Port of Miami. *Miami Free Zone, 2305 N.W. 107th Ave., tel. 305/591–4300. Open weekdays 9–5.*

Cauley Square A tearoom and craft, antiques, and clothing shops now occupy this complex of clapboard, coral-rock, and stucco buildings erected 1907–20 for railroad workers who built and maintained the line to Key West. Turn right off U.S. 1 at S.W. 224th Street. *22400 Old Dixie Hwy., Goulds, tel. 305/258–3543. Open Mon.–Sat. 10–4:30.*

Books Greater Miami's best English-language bookstore, **Books & Books, Inc.,** specializes in books on the arts, architecture, Floridiana, and contemporary and classical literature. Collectors enjoy browsing through the rare book room upstairs, which doubles as a photography gallery. Frequent poetry readings and book signings. *296 Aragon Ave., Coral Gables, tel. 305/442–4408, and 933 Lincoln Rd. (Sterling Bldg.), Miami Beach, tel. 305/532–3222. Open weekdays 10–8, Sat. 10–7, Sun. noon–5. AE, MC, V.*

Children's Books and Toys The friendly staff at **A Likely Story** will help you choose books and educational toys that are appropriate to your child's interests and stage of development. *5740 Sunset Dr., South Miami, tel. 305/667–3730. Open Mon.–Sat. 10–5. MC, V.*

Wine The largest retail collection of fine wines in Florida is at *Foremost Sunset Corners,* home of the Miami chapter of *Les Amis du Vin.* Catalog available. *8701 Sunset Dr., Miami 33173, tel. 305/271–8492. Open Mon.–Sat. 8 AM–9:45 PM. MC, V.*

Beaches

Miami Beach From Haulover Cut to Government Cut, a broad sandy beach extends for 10 continuous miles. Amazingly, it's a man-made beach—a marvel of modern engineering to repair the ravages of nature.

Along this stretch, erosion had all but eliminated the beach by the mid-1970s. Waves threatened to undermine the seawalls of hotels and apartment towers. From 1977 to 1981, the U.S. Army Corps of Engineers spent $51.5 million to pump tons of sand from offshore, restoring the beach to a 300-foot width. Between 21st and 46th streets, Miami Beach built boardwalks and protective walk-overs atop a sand dune landscaped with sea oats, sea grape, and other native plants whose roots keep the sand from blowing away.

The new beach lures residents and visitors alike to swim and stroll. More than 7 million people visit the 7.1 miles of beaches within the Miami Beach city limits annually. The other 2.9 miles are in Surfside and Bal Harbour. Here's a guide to where kindred spirits gather:

The best windsurfing on Miami Beach occurs at First Street, just north of the Government Cut jetty, and at 21st Street. You can also windsurf at Penrod's windsurfing area in Lummus Park at 10th Street and in the vicinity of 3rd, 14th, and 21st streets. Lifeguards discourage windsurfing from 79th Street to 87th Street.

From 1st Street to 14th Street, senior citizens predominate early in the day. Later, a younger crowd appears, including family groups who flock to the new children's play areas in Lummus Park, between Ocean Drive and the beach at 5th and 14th streets.

The beaches opposite the Art Deco District, between 6th Street and 21st Street, attract a diverse clientele of locals and tourists from Europe and Asia. In this area, in an effort to satisfy foreign visitors, city officials don't enforce the law against female bathers going topless as long as everyone on the beach behaves with decorum. Topless bathing also occurs from 35th to 42nd streets. Gays tend to gather at 21st Street.

University of Miami students like the stretch of beach along Millionaires' Row, around 46th Street, where the big hotels have outdoor concession stands on the beach.

If you like a quiet beach experience, go to 35th, 53rd, or 64th streets. Tired young professionals there seek solitude to read a book. Paradoxically, young mothers like to bring their children to these beaches. The two groups coexist nicely.

French-Canadians frequent the 72nd Street beach.

High-schools groups gather at 1st, 10th, 14th, and 85th streets for pickup games of volleyball and football.

During the winter, the wealthy condominium crowd clusters on the beach from 96th Street to 103rd Street in Bal Harbour.

City of Miami Beach beaches open daily with lifeguards, winter 8–5, summer 9–6. Bal Harbour and Surfside have no lifeguards, beaches open daily 24 hours. Beaches free in all three communities; metered parking nearby.

County Park Beaches Metropolitan Dade County operates beaches at several of its major parks. Each county park operates on its own schedule that varies from day to day and season to season. Phone the park you want to visit for current hours and information on special events.

Crandon Park. Atlantic Ocean beach, popular with young Hispanics and with family groups of all ethnic backgrounds. *4000 Crandon Park Blvd., Key Biscayne, tel. 305/361–5421. Open daily winter 8–5, summer 8–7. Admission: $2 per car.*
Haulover Beach Park. Atlantic Ocean beach. A good place to be alone. Lightly used compared to other public beaches, except on weekends and in the peak tourist season, when it attracts a diverse crowd. *10800 Collins Ave., Miami, tel. 305/947–3525. Open daily winter 9–5, summer 9–7. Admission: $2 per car.*

Cape Florida **Bill Baggs Cape Florida State Recreation Area** (*see* Exploring Virginia Key and Key Biscayne).

Sports and Fitness

Miami's subtropical climate is paradise for active people, a place where refugees from the frozen north can enjoy warm-weather outdoor sports, such as boating, swimming, and golf, all year long. During Miami's hot, humid summers, people avoid the sun's strongest rays by playing early or late in the day. We've listed below some of the most popular individual and group sports activities.

Spa The **Doral Saturnia International Spa Resort** opened in 1988 on the grounds of the Doral Resort and Country Club. Formal Italian gardens contain the spa pool and a special waterfall under which guests can enjoy natural hydromassage from the gentle pounding of falling water. The spa's 100-foot-high atrium accommodates a 5,000-pound bronze staircase railing created in 1920 by French architect Alexandre Gustave Eiffel and fabricated by artist Edgar Brandt for Paris's Bon Marché department store. The spa combines mud baths and other European pampering techniques with state-of-the-art American fitness and exercise programs. A one-day sampler is available. *8755 N.W. 36th St., Miami 33178, tel. 305/593–6030. 48 suites. Facilities: 4 exercise studios (2 with spring-loaded floors), 3 outdoor heated swimming pools, David fitness equipment, beauty salon, 2 restaurants. AE, CB, DC, MC, V.*

Water Sports
Marinas

Listed below are the major marinas in Greater Miami. The dock masters at these marinas can provide information on other marine services you may need. Also ask the dockmasters for *Teall's Tides and Guides, Miami-Dade County,* and other local nautical publications.

The U.S. Customs Service requires boats of less than five tons that enter the country along Florida's Atlantic Coast south of Sebastian Inlet to report to designated marinas and call U.S. Customs on a direct phone line. The phones, located outside marina buildings, are accessible 24 hours a day. U.S. Customs phones in Greater Miami are at Haulover Marina and Watson Island Marina (both listed below).

Dinner Key Marina. Operated by City of Miami. Facilities include dockage with space for transients and a boat ramp. *3400 Pan American Dr., Coconut Grove, tel. 305/579–6980. Open daily 7 AM–11 PM.*

Haulover Park Marina. Operated by county lessee. Facilities include a bait-and-tackle shop, marine gas station, and boat launch. *10800 Collins Ave., Miami Beach, tel. 305/944–9647. Open daily 7 AM–5 PM.*

Watson Island Marina. City of Miami marina. Facilities include bait and tackle, boat ramp, and fuel. When the marina is busy, it stays open until all boaters are helped. *1050 MacArthur Causeway, Miami, tel. 305/371–2378. Open Mon.–Thurs. 7 AM– 7:30 PM, Fri.–Sun. 7 AM–11 PM.*

Sailing

Dinner Key and the Coconut Grove waterfront remain the center of sailing in Greater Miami, although sailboat moorings and rentals are located along other parts of the bay and up the Miami River.

Windsurfing and Jet Skis

Penrod's. Plans to rent jet skis, Hobie Cats, Windsurfers, and surfboards. *1001 Ocean Dr., Miami Beach, tel. 305/534–0687 or 305/538–1111. Open daily 10–sunset.*

Sailboards Miami. *(See* Exploring Virginia Key and Key Biscayne.)

Diving

Summer diving conditions in greater Miami equal or exceed the best of those in the Caribbean. Winter diving can be adversely affected when cold fronts come through. Dive-boat schedules vary with the season and with local weather conditions.

Fowey, Triumph, Long, and Emerald Reefs all are shallow 10– 15-foot dives that are good for snorkelers and beginning divers. These reefs are on the edge of the continental shelf, a quarter of a mile from depths greater than 100 feet. You can also paddle around the tangled prop roots of the mangrove trees that line Florida's coastline, peering at the fish, crabs, and other onshore creatures that hide there.

Dive Boats and Instruction. Look for instructors who are affiliated with PADI (Professional Association of Dive Instructors) or NAUI (National Association of Underwater Instructors).

Divers Paradise Corp (4000 Crandon Blvd., Key Biscayne, tel. 305/361–DIVE). Complete dive shop and diving charter service, including equipment rental and scuba instruction. PADI affiliation.

Omega Diving International. Private instruction throughout Greater Miami. Equipment consultation and specialty courses, including instructor training and underwater photography. PADI affiliation. *8420 S.W. 133 Ave., Miami, tel. 305/385–0779 or 800/255–1966. Open daily 8–6.*

Diver's Dream. This all-purpose dive shop is located right on the Miami Beach marina. *1290 5th St., Miami Beach 33139, tel. 305/534–7710. Open Mon.–Sat. 10 AM–7 PM. Beach store open weekdays 9 AM–7 PM, weekends 7 AM–6 PM.*

Tennis Greater Miami has more than 60 private and public tennis centers, of which 11 are open to the public. All public tennis courts charge nonresidents an hourly fee.

Florida Tennis Association (801 N.E. 167th St., Suite 301, North Miami Beach 33162, tel. 305/652–2866). Contact for amateur tournament information.

Coral Gables **Biltmore Tennis Center.** Ten well-maintained hard courts. Site of annual Orange Bowl Junior International Tennis Tournament for children 18 and under in December. *1210 Anastasia Ave., tel. 305/442–6565. Open weekdays 8 AM–10 PM, weekends 8–8. Nonresident day rate $3.04, night rate $4.33 per person per hour.*

Miami Beach **Flamingo Tennis Center.** Has 20 well-maintained clay courts. Site of the Rolex-Orange Bowl Junior International Tennis Tournament for teenagers 18 and under. *1000 12th St., tel. 305/673–7761. Open weekdays 8 AM–9 PM, weekends 8–6. Cost: day $2.12, night $2.65 per person per hour.*

Metropolitan Dade County **International Tennis Center.** Has 17 Laykold Cushion Plus hard courts, four lighted. Reservations necessary for night play. Closed to public play for about two weeks before and after the annual Lipton International Players Championships in March. *7300 Crandon Blvd., Key Biscayne, tel. 305/361–8633. Open daily 9 AM–9 PM. Cost: weekdays $3, weeknights $4, weekend days $4, weekend nights $5 per person per hour.*

Spectator Sports

Greater Miami offers a broad variety of spectator sports events, including such popular pastimes as football and baseball, and more specialized events, such as boat racing and rugby. However, the community lacks a central clearinghouse for sports information and ticket sales.

You can find daily listings of local sports events on page 3 of *The Miami Herald* sports section. The weekend section on Friday carries detailed schedules and coverage of spectator sports. The *Herald* provides a recorded "sports line" message with a brief selection of major sports scores (tel. 305/376–3505).

Orange Bowl Festival. The activities of the annual Orange Bowl and Junior Orange Festival take place early November-late February. Best-known for its *King Orange Jamboree Parade* and the *Federal Express/Orange Bowl Football Classic*, the festival also includes two tennis tournaments: the *Rolex/Orange Bowl International Tennis Championships* for top amateur national and international tennis players 16 and under, and an international tennis tournament for players 14 and under.

Other Orange Bowl sports events include a regatta series for university and professional sailors, a 5-km run in Coral Gables, the *Orange Bowl 10-km Race* on the 6.2-mile Grand Prix course, the annual *American Savings/Orange Bowl Marathon*, which draws over 2,500 runners, soccer games, bowling events, and a sports competition for physically disabled athletes. For tickets and a calendar of events: **Tickets, Orange Bowl Committee** (Box 350748, Miami 33135, tel. 305/642–5211).

Auto Racing   **Hialeah Speedway.** The Greater Miami area's only independent raceway holds stock-car races on a ⅓-mile asphalt speedway in a 5,000-seat stadium. Four divisions of stock cars run weekly. The Marion Edwards, Jr., Memorial Race for late-model stock cars is in November. Located on U.S. 27, ¼ mile east of Palmetto Expressway (Rte. 826). *3300 W. Okeechobee Rd., Hialeah, tel. 305/821–6644. Open every Sat. late Jan.–early Dec. Gates open 6 PM, racing 7:45–11. Admission: $7 adults, $1 children 6–12.*

Grand Prix of Miami. Held in February for the Camel GT Championship on a 1.9-mile, E-shape track in downtown Miami, south of MacArthur Causeway and east of Biscayne Boulevard. Drivers race three hours; the winner completes the most laps. Sanctioned by International Motor Sports Association (IMSA). *Miami Motor Sports, Inc., 7254 S.W. 48th St., Miami 33155, tel. 305/662–5660. Tickets available from Miami Motor Sports, Inc., tel. 305/665–RACE or 800/233–RACE or Ticketmaster* (see *Important Addresses and Numbers*).

Baseball   **University of Miami Hurricanes.** The baseball Hurricanes play home games in the 5,000-seat Mark Light Stadium, at 1 Hurricane Drive on UM's Coral Gables campus. The Hurricanes were the 1982 and 1985 NCAA baseball champions. *University of Miami Athletic Department, Box 248167, Coral Gables 33124, tel. 305/284–2655 or 800/GO-CANES. Open weekdays 8–6, Sat. 10–2. Season: 48 home games Feb.–May, day games 2 PM, night games 7:30. AE, CB, DC, MC, V.*

Basketball   **Miami Heat.** Second 41 home game season November–May for Miami's National Basketball Association Team. *Tickets: Miami Arena, Miami 33136–4102, tel. 305/577–HEAT or Ticketmaster* (see *Important Addresses and Numbers*). **University of Miami Hurricanes.** Games are held in the Miami arena. *University of Miami Athletic Department, Box 248167, Coral Gables 33124, tel. 305/284–2655, 800/GO-CANES. Open weekdays 8–6, Sat. 10–2. Game time 7:30. AE, CB, DC, MC, V.*

Dog Racing   The Biscayne Kennel Club, the Flagler Dog Track in Greater Miami, and Hollywood Greyhound Park in Ft. Lauderdale divide the annual racing calendar. Check with the individual tracks for dates. **Biscayne Kennel Club.** Greyhounds chase a mechanical rabbit around illuminated fountains in the track's infield. Near I-95 at N.W. 115th Street. *320 N.W. 115th St., Miami Shores, tel. 305/754–3484. Season: Nov.–Dec. and May –June. Admission: reserved seats $1, grandstand $1, clubhouse $2. Parking 50 cents–$2.*

Flagler Dog Track. Inner-city track in the middle of Little Havana, five minutes east of Miami International Airport off Dolphin Expressway (Rte. 836) and Douglas Road (N.W. 37th Ave.). *401 N.W. 38th Ct., Miami, tel. 305/649–3000. Open Sept.*

5–Oct. 30. General admission $1, clubhouse $2, parking 50 cents–$2.

Football   **Miami Dolphins.** Owner Joe Robbie enjoys a reputation for doing things his own way. In 1987, he moved the Dolphins from the Orange Bowl near downtown Miami into his own privately financed $100-million Joe Robbie Stadium. Robbie also intends to use the stadium for baseball.

The new 74,914-seat stadium has a grass playing-field surface, with built-in drainage under the sod to carry off rainwater quickly. Stadium tours include the field, team locker rooms, sky boxes, executive suites, and football press boxes. *Tel. 305/ 623–6471. Tours daily, except event days, 11 AM, 1, 3, and 5 PM. Admission: $4.*

Joe Robbie Stadium is on a 160-acre site, 16 miles northwest of downtown Miami, one mile south of the Dade-Broward County line, accessible from I-95 and Florida's Turnpike. On game days, the Metro-Dade Transit Authority runs buses to the stadium. Bus information, tel. 305/638–6700.

Dolphins tickets: *Miami Dolphins, Joe Robbie Stadium, 2269 N.W. 199th St., Miami 33056, tel. 305/620–2578. Open weekdays 10–6. Also available through Ticketmaster (see Important Addresses and Numbers).*

University of Miami Hurricanes. The Hurricanes, winners of the 1987 national college football championship, play home games in the Orange Bowl, near the Dolphin Expressway (Rte. 836) just west of downtown Miami. *1400 N.W. 4th St., tel. 305/ 579–6971. Game time 7:30 PM (unless changed for the convenience of the TV networks). Schedule and tickets: University of Miami Athletic Department, Box 248167, Coral Gables 33124, tel. 305/284–2655 or 800/GO-CANES. Open weekdays 8–6.*

Horse Racing   **Calder Race Course.** Opened in 1971, Calder is Florida's largest glass-enclosed, air-conditioned sports facility. This means that Calder actually has two racing seasons, one in fall or winter, another in spring or summer. Contact the track for this year's dates. In April, Calder holds the Tropical Park Derby for three-year-olds, the last major race in Florida before the Kentucky Derby. On the Dade-Broward County line near I-95 and the Hallandale Beach Boulevard exit., ¾ mile from Joe Robbie Stadium. *21001 N.W. 27th Ave., Miami, tel. 305/625–1311. Gates open 11 AM, post time 1 PM, races end about 5 PM. General admission $2, clubhouse $4, programs 50 cents, parking $1–$3.*

Hialeah Park. A superb setting for Thoroughbred racing, Hialeah's 228 acres of meticulously landscaped grounds surround paddocks and a clubhouse built in a classic French Mediterranean style. Since it opened in 1925, Hialeah Park has survived hurricanes, economic reverses, and changing trends in racing without losing its air of elegant informality.

During the racing season, the gates open early Sunday mornings for breakfast at Hialeah Park. Admission is free. You can watch the horses work out, explore Hialeah's gardens, munch on breakfast fare of tolerable palatability, and admire the park's breeding flock of 600 Cuban flamingos.

When racing is not in session, Hialeah Park opens daily for free tours 10–4:30. Metrorail's Hialeah Station is on the grounds of

Hialeah Park. *2200 E. 4th Ave., Hialeah, tel. 305/885–8000. Admission: grandstand $2, clubhouse $4, parking $1.50–$4 during racing season.*

Jai Alai **Miami Jai-Alai Fronton.** This game, invented in the Basque region of northern Spain, is the world's fastest. Jai-alai balls, called *pelotas*, have been clocked at speeds exceeding 170 mph. The game is played in a 176-foot-long court called a *fronton.* Players climb the walls to catch the ball in a *cesta*—a woven basket—with an attached glove. You bet on a team to win or on the order in which teams will finish. Built in 1926, Miami Jai-Alai is the oldest fronton in America. Each evening, it presents 13 games—some singles, some doubles. Located a mile east of Miami International Airport. *3500 N.W. 37th Ave., Miami, tel. 305/633–6400. Open nightly late Nov.–early Sept. except Sun., 7:15–midnight. Matinees Mon., Wed., and Sat. noon–5. Admission: $1, clubhouse $5. Dinner available.*

Rugby Without a large corporate organization, a regular office staff, or even a permanent home field, local rugby players have organized themselves into two regular teams. Although one team is called the *University of Miami Rugby Team*, it is not part of the university. The other is the *Miami Tridents.* Weekly throughout the year, a local rugby team plays a visiting team from a 16-team Florida league, from the Caribbean, or from a foreign ship in port. Both local teams participate each August in an annual tournament. Games Saturday 2 PM. *Holy Rosary Church, 9500 S.W. 184th St., Perrine. Spectators welcome. Free. For game information, call Bruce Swidarski, 8550 S.W. 126th Terr., Miami 33156, tel. 305/251–3305 (nights).*

Soccer **Miami Sharks.** This American Soccer League team played its first season in spring 1988. The Sharks' 1990 season includes at least 10 regular-season home games and five international exhibition games, all in the stadium at Milander Park (4800 Palm Ave., Hialeah). *Tickets: 240 E. 1st Ave., Suite 208, Hialeah 33010, tel. 305/888–0838 or Ticketmaster (see Important Addresses and Numbers).*

Tennis **Lipton International Players Championship (LIPC).** Shearson Lehman Brothers sponsors this two-week spring tournament at the 64-acre International Tennis Center of Key Biscayne. The tournament follows the Grand Slam format of the Australian, United States and French Opens and Wimbledon. The two main professional tennis organizations—Association of Tennis Professionals and Women's International Tennis Association—helped create this tournament and own part of it. *7300 Crandon Blvd., Key Biscayne, tel. for tickets 305/361–5252 or Ticketmaster (see Important Addresses and Numbers).*

Triathlon **Bud Light U.S. Triathlon Series.** Opens the triathlon season in May in Miami, with 1,500 participants in a 1.5-km swim, a 40-km bicycle ride, and a 10-km run. Swimmers swim .9 miles in 75-degree water in Biscayne Bay near Bicentennial Park. The 24.8-mile bike course goes from the Grand Prix course in downtown Miami to Key Biscayne and back. The 6.2-mile run loops around the Japanese Garden on Watson Island along the MacArthur Causeway. Contact CAT Sports, Inc. (5966 La Place Court, Suite 100, Carlsbad, CA 92008, tel. 619/438–8080), producer of the event.

Dining

by Rosalie Leposky You can eat your way around the world in Greater Miami, enjoying just about any kind of cuisine imaginable in every price category. The rich mix of nationalities here encourages individual restaurateurs and chefs to retain their culinary roots. Thus, Miami offers not just Latin fare but dishes distinctive to Spain, Cuba, Nicaragua, and other Hispanic countries; not just Oriental fare but specialties of China, India, Thailand, Vietnam, and other Asian cultures.

And don't neglect American fare just because it's not "foreign." Miami today is a center for innovation in regional cuisine and in combinations reflecting the diversity of domestic climates and cultures.

The most highly recommended restaurants in each price category are indicated by a star ★.

Category	Cost*
Very Expensive	over $55
Expensive	$35–$55
Moderate	$15–$35
Inexpensive	under $15

per person, excluding drinks, service, and 6% sales tax.

The following credit card abbreviations are used: AE, American Express; CB, Carte Blanche; DC, Diners Club; MC, MasterCard; V, Visa.

American
Coral Gables

Aragon Cafe. If George Merrick, the founder of Coral Gables, entered the bar of Aragon Cafe, he would see on display some of his mother's hand-painted china and silver and portraits of his sisters and wife on the dining room walls. In this new restaurant designed to look old and classy, subdued lighting emanates from gaslight-style chandeliers and etched-glass wall lights. The menu emphasizes fresh fish and reflects Merrick's desire to recreate the best of the Mediterranean in a Florida setting. Specialties include seafood minestrone made with shrimp, scallops, clams, new potatoes, carrots, and kidney and green beans; grilled goat cheese in banana leaves; grilled Florida dolphin with native starfruit sauce; and tuna steak au poivre in a mushroom-based sauce of peppercorns and cream. Dessert offerings include a white chocolate terrine with pistachio sauce. *180 Aragon Ave. in the Colonnade Hotel, Coral Gables 33134, tel. 305/448–9966. Reservations advised. Jacket required. No lunch Sat., no dinner Sun. Free valet parking. AE, DC, MC, V. Expensive.*

Downtown Miami
★

The Pavillon Grill. By day a private club, the Pavillon Grill becomes a gourmet restaurant at night. The mahogany, jade marble, and leather appointments of its salon and dining room exude the conservative classiness of an English private club. A harpist plays. The attentive staff serves regional American fare, including items that are low in calories, cholesterol, and sodium for diners who are on restricted diets. Specialties include marinated confit of duck and red Hawaiian papaya, grilled wild mushrooms, Pacific salmon pillows, cherry smoked lamb chops. The menu changes often. *100 Chopin Plaza, tel. 305/577–1000, ext. 4494 or 4462. Jacket and tie. Reservations required. AE, CB, DC, MC, V. Closed Sun. Very Expensive.*

Kendall
(S.W. Suburb)

Savannah Moon. Though you drive up to a typical shopping center, Savannah Moon's door leads to the foyer of a Southern mansion, complete with formal staircase. In the second-floor dining room, bentwood chairs, hanging plants, shuttered windows, sheer curtains, and original Audubon engravings suggest a tidewater inn. Evening and late-night entertainment —mellow blues, conservative jazz—makes the place popular with suburban professionals. This restaurant gives a nouvelle-cuisine twist to traditional Low Country coastal fare. Specialties include jambalaya (red rice with Creole sauce, chicken, shrimp, escargot, and Texas sausage); lamb with Southern Comfort sauce; and a dessert cart groaning with delights such as Kirsch-toasted almond cake, and southern bread pudding with nuts and raisins. *13505 South Dixie Hwy., tel. 305/238–8868. Jacket and tie. Reservations required on weekends, advised other times. AE, CB, DC, MC, V. No lunch on weekends. Expensive.*

Shorty's Bar-B-Q. Shorty Allen opened his barbecue restaurant in 1951 in a log cabin. Parents bring their teenage children to show them where mom and dad ate on their honeymoon. Huge fans circulate fresh air through the single screened dining room, where you dine family style at long picnic tables. The walls display an assortment of cowboy hats, horns, saddles, an ox yoke, and heads of boar and caribou. Specialties include barbecued pork ribs, chicken, and pork steak slow cooked over hickory logs and drenched in Shorty's own warm, spicy sauce, and side orders of tangy baked beans with big chunks of pork, corn on the cob, and coleslaw. *9200 South Dixie Hwy., tel. 305/665–5732. A second location opened in 1989 at 5989 South University Dr., Davie, tel. 305/680–9900. Dress: informal. Reservations not accepted. No credit cards. Closed Thanksgiving and Christmas. Inexpensive.*

North Miami Beach
★

Chef Allen's. In an art-deco world of glass block, neon trim, and fresh flowers, your gaze nonetheless remains riveted on the kitchen. Chef Allen Susser designed it with a picture window, 25 feet wide, so you can watch him create new American masterpieces almost too pretty to eat. Specialties include mesquite-grilled rare tuna with glazed onions and cranberry chutney; and lamb medallions with pine nuts and wilted spinach garnished with goat cheese. Desserts include white-chocolate macadamia nut torte, chocolate pizza, and a sugar junkie's delight—scoops of chocolate, raspberry, caramel, and pistachio ice cream floating in caramel sauce. Fine wines by the glass from a wine bar. *19088 N.E. 29th Ave., tel. 305/935–2900. Dress: informal weekdays, tie and jacket weekends. Reservations accepted. AE, MC, V. Closed for lunch weekends. Expensive.*

★

Max's Place. Owner/chef Mark Militello cooks *nouvelle* American regional fare in a special oak-burning oven imported from Genoa, behind a display case where you can admire the evening's selections of fish and meat awaiting preparation. The menu changes nightly, based on the availability of fresh ingredients. Typical selections include sea scallops and asparagus sautéed in butter and chardonnay with fresh basil, oregano, and thyme; wild mushrooms (shittake, tree oyster, chanterelles, angel trumpets, and brown hedgehog) roasted in the oak oven and served with grilled olive and walnut bread; whole yellowtail snapper with oriental ginger, black bean sauce, and a garnish of edible pansies; and cobia filet sautéed in brown butter mixed with orange segments, fresh mint, and bourbon. Desserts include chocolate espresso torte with a hazelnut crust and a warm apple tart with homemade vanilla and caramel sauce. *2286 N.E. 123rd St., North Miami 33181, tel. 305/893–6888. Reservations advised. Jacket and tie required. Closed Christmas. No lunch weekends. AE, DC, MC, V. Very Expensive.*

Chinese
Key Biscayne

Two Dragons. Robert Chow and his staff run this place like a small family restaurant, serving a Chinese cuisine with all ingredients fresh and prepared to order. Specialties include a Cantonese seafood nest (shrimp, scallops, and crabmeat with Chinese vegetables in a nest of crisp noodles), an orange beef Mandarin, and Szechuan eggplant with a spicy garlic-mustard sauce guaranteed to clear the sinuses. Dine in an intimate pagodalike booth behind hanging curtains of wooden beads or at an open table overlooking an outdoor Oriental garden. A Japanese steak house—the "second dragon"—serves Teppanyaki-style cuisine at six cooking tables in a separate room. *Sonesta Beach Hotel, 350 Ocean Dr., tel. 305/361–2021. Dress: semiformal. Dinner only. Reservations advised. AE, CB, DC, MC, V. Closed 2 weeks in Aug. or Sept. Moderate.*

South Miami

Tiger Tiger Teahouse. Design awards have been bestowed on Tiger Tiger's contemporary Chinese decor, with its embroidered silk panels depicting fierce tigers and its elegant rosewood chairs with jade cushions. Specialties include Peking duck (available without advance notice), lean and succulent beneath crisp orange-glazed skin, wrapped with plum sauce in wheat pancakes; hot, spicy Szechuan beef, marinated in sherry and spices, then stir-fried with Chinese vegetables; honey-garlic chicken; and creamy-smooth litchi ice cream. *The Bakery Center, 5785 Sunset Dr., tel. 305/665–5660. Dress: casual. Closed for lunch Sun. Reservations accepted. AE, CB, DC, MC, V. Closed Thanksgiving. Moderate.*

Continental
Coconut Grove
★

Grand Cafe. Understated elegance at all hours is the Grand Cafe's hallmark—a bilevel room with pink tablecloths and floral bouquets, sunbathed by day, dim and intimate after dark. Japanese-born, French-trained executive chef Katsuo Sugiura creates "international" cuisine, combining ingredients from all over the world in pleasing presentations that intrigue the palate. Specialties include black linguini (colored with squid ink); fresh smoked salmon; a superbly rich she-crab soup with roe, sherry, and cayenne pepper; "boned" Maine lobster presented in the shape of a lobster, with artichokes and a cream sauce of vermouth and saffron. Dessert specialties include a white-chocolate and pistachio mousse, with blackberry sauce and Beaujolais essence. The menu changes frequently. *2669 S. Bayshore Dr., tel. 305/858–9600. Jacket preferred. Reservations advised. AE, CB, DC, MC, V. Very Expensive.*

Kaleidoscope Restaurant. The tropical ambience here extends to a choice of indoor or outdoor seating—all in air-conditioned comfort, because fans blow cold air around a glass-roofed terrace overlooking a landscaped courtyard. Specialties include veal Oscar, and the chef's own fresh apple strudel. *3112 Com-*

Miami Area Dining

ATLANTIC

5 miles

5 km

Bill Baggs Cape Florida State Recreation Area

Causeway

29

28

Crandon Park

KEY BISCAYNE

Biscayne

S. Dixie Hwy.

13

10 **14** **15**

9

8

953

6

5

CORAL GABLES

S.W. 57th Ave.

Old Cutler Rd.

Red Rd.

Matheson Hammock Park

Bird Rd.

S.W. 72nd St.

986

973

Galloway Rd.

Sunset Dr.

Kendall Dr.

S.W. 152nd St.

S.W. 184th St.

Old Cutler Rd.

S. Dixie Hwy.

Howard Dr.

4

3

976

874

S.W. 87th

S.W. 40th St.

Florida's Turnpike

94

060

992

Don Shula Expwy.

N.

Eureka Dr.

Acapulco, **17**
Aragon Cafe, **8**
Biscayne Wine Merchants and Bistro, **30**
Cafe Chauveron, **36**
Cafe des Arts, **15, 34**
Casa Juancho, **18**

Chef Allen's, **38**
Chez Moy, **21**
Dominique's, **35**
East Coast Fisheries, **20**
La Fenice, **9**
Le Festival, **7**
The Fish Market, **25**

Grand Cafe, **13**
Granny Feelgood's, **22**
House of India, **11**
Hy-Vong Vietnamese Cuisine, **12**
Isla Canarias, **16**
Joe's Stone Crab Restaurant, **32**

Kaleidoscope Restaurant, **14**
La Paloma, **27**
La Parrilla, **2**
LB's Restaurant, **6**
Los Rancheros, **1**
Macrobatic Fdn. of Florida, **10**

Masa San, **39**
Max's Place, **26**
Mykonos, **19**
The Pavillon Grill, **23**
Pineapples, **33**
Savannah Moon, **3**

Shorty's Bar-B-Q, **4**
Sundays on the Bay, **29, 37**
Las Tapas, **24**
Tiger Tiger Teahouse, **5**
Tokyo Rose Bar & Grill, **31**
Two Dragons, **28**

modore Plaza, tel. 305/446–5010. Dress: casual. Reservations advised. AE, CB, DC, MC, V. Moderate.

North Miami **Biscayne Wine Merchants and Bistro.** In this 35-seat retail beer and wine store with a deli counter, strangers often become friends while sharing tables and sampling the merchandise. Owners Jan Sitko and Esther Flores stock over 300 wines (sold by the glass or bottle) and over 60 brands of beer. The menu changes daily but always includes bean and cream soups. Typical fare may include chicken Crustaces (a chicken breast stuffed with leeks, dill, and crab with a light dill sauce) and daily fresh fish specials such as amberjack, dolphin, shark, snapper, swordtail, and wahoo. Sitko and Flores like to create new dishes with fresh herbs, spices, fruits, and vegetables. One favorite is a tangy-sweet sauce with jalapeno and citrus. *12953 Biscayne Blvd., North Miami, tel. 305/899–1997. No Reservations. Dress: informal. Closed Thanksgiving, Christmas, and New Year's Day. No lunch weekends. AE, MC, V. Moderate.*

La Paloma. This fine Swiss Continental restaurant offers a total sensory experience: fine food, impeccable service, and the ambience of an art museum. In sideboards and cases throughout, owners Werner and Maria Staub display ornate European antiques that they have spent decades collecting. The treasures include Bacarrat crystal, Limoges china, Meissen porcelains, and Sevres clocks. The staff speak Spanish, French, German, Portuguese, or Arabic. Specialties include fresh local fish and seafood; Norwegian salmon Caroline (poached, served on a bed of spinach with hollandaise sauce); Wiener schnitzel; lamb chops à la *diable* (coated with bread crumbs, mustard, garlic, and herbs) passion-fruit sorbet; and kiwi soufflé with raspberry sauce. *10999 Biscayne Blvd., tel. 305/891–0505. Jackets requested. Reservations advised. AE, MC, V. Closed Mon. and July and part of Aug. Expensive.*

Cuban **Islas Canarias.** A gathering place for Cuban poets, pop music *Little Havana* stars, and media personalities. Wall murals depict a Canary Islands street scene and an indigenous dragon tree *(Dracaena draco)*. The menu includes such Canary Islands dishes as baked lamb, ham hocks with boiled potatoes, and *tortilla Española* (a Spanish omelet with onions and chorizo sausage), as well as Cuban standards, including palomilla steak, and fried kingfish. Don't miss the three superb varieties of homemade chips— potato, malanga, and plantain. Islas Canarias has another location in Westchester. *285 N.W. Unity Blvd. (N.W. 27th Ave.), tel. 305/649–0440. Dress: informal. Reservations not accepted. No credit cards. Inexpensive.*

Family Style **LB's Restaurant.** Town and gown meet at this sprout-laden ha- *Coral Gables* ven a half-block from the University of Miami's baseball stadium. Kitschy food-related posters plaster the walls. Relaxed atmosphere, low prices, no waiters. You order at the counter and pick up your food when called. Vegetarians thrive on LB's salads and daily meatless entrees, such as lasagna and moussaka. Famous for Saturday night lobster. (If you plan to come after 8, call ahead to reserve a lobster.) Other specialties include barbecued baby-back ribs, lime chicken, croissant sandwiches, and carrot cake. *5813 Ponce de León Blvd., tel. 305/661–7091. Dress: informal. Reservations not accepted. No credit cards. Closed Sun. Inexpensive.*

French
Coral Gables

Le Festival. The modest canopied entrance to this classical French restaurant understates the elegance within. Decor includes etched-glass filigree mirrors and light pink walls. Specialties include appetizers of salmon mousse, baked oysters with garlic butter, and lobster in champagne sauce en croute; rack of lamb (for two), and medallions of veal with two sauces—a pungent, creamy lime sauce and a dark port-wine sauce with mushrooms. Entrées come with real french-fried potatoes. Don't pass up dessert here; the mousses and soufflés are positively decadent. *2120 Salzedo St., tel. 305/442–8545. Jacket and tie. Reservations required for dinner, and for lunch parties of 5 or more. AE, MC, V. Closed Sat. noon, all day Sun., and Sept.–Oct. Expensive.*

Miami Beach
★

Cafe Chauveron. André Chauveron traces his cafe's roots to Cafe Chambord, which his father began in New York in 1935 on the block where the Citicorp Building now stands. A Florida institution since 1972, Cafe Chauveron serves classical French cuisine in rooms decorated with original paintings and wood paneling. The atmosphere is hushed, the service superb. Mounted pheasants guard the wine cabinet. Specialties include wild duck and pheasant pâté, filet of sole *bonne femme*, frogs' legs Provençale, sautéed veal chop Bercy (white wine and shallots) with braised endive, and dessert soufflés flambéed at tableside. *9561 E. Bay Harbor Dr., tel. 305/866–8779. Jacket and tie. Reservations required. AE, CB, DC, MC, V. Closed Aug.–Sept. Very Expensive.*

Cafe des Arts. Enjoy French-provincial cuisine in an art-deco setting amid tropical plants, antiques, and an art gallery that changes every six to eight weeks. Indoor and outdoor seating. Specialties include smoked-salmon pasta with artichokes, mushrooms, and brie sauce; roast duck in grape sauce; and quail salad. *918 Ocean Dr., tel. 305/534–6267. In 1989, a second location was opened at 3138 Commodore Plaza, Coconut Grove, tel. 305/446–3634. Dress: casual. Reservations advised. AE, MC, V. Closed 2 weeks in Aug. Moderate.*

★

Dominique's. Woodwork and mirrors from a Vanderbilt home and other demolished New York mansions create an intimate setting for a unique nouvelle-cuisine dining experience. Specialties include exotic appetizers, such as buffalo sausage, sautéed alligator tail, and rattlesnake-meat salad; rack of lamb (which accounts for 35% of the restaurant's total sales) and fresh seafood; and an extensive wine list. The restaurant also serves brunch on Sunday. *Alexander Hotel, 5225 Collins Ave., tel. 305/865–6500. Jacket required. Reservations advised. AE, CB, DC, MC, V. Very Expensive.*

Greek
Southwest Miami

Mykonos. A family restaurant serving typical Greek fare in a Spartan setting—a single 74-seat room adorned with Greek travel posters. Specialties include gyro; moussaka; marinated lamb and chicken; kalamari (squid) and octopus sautéed in wine and onions; and sumptuous Greek salads thick with feta cheese and briny olives. *1201 Coral Way, tel. 305/856–3140. Dress: informal. Reservations accepted for dinner. AE. Closed Sun. at noon, Christmas, and New Year's Day. Inexpensive.*

Haitian
Little Haiti

Chez Moy. Seating is outside on a shaded patio or in a pleasant room with oak tables and high-backed chairs. Specialties include *grillot* (pork boiled, then fried with spices); fried or boiled fish; stewed goat; and conch with garlic and hot pepper. Try a tropical fruit drink, such as sweet sop (also called *anon* or

cachiman) or sour sop (also called *guanabana* or *corrosol)*
blended with milk and sugar, and sweet potato pie for dessert.
*1 N.W. 54th St., tel. 305/756–7540. Dress: informal. No reser-
vations. No smoking allowed inside. MC, V. Moderate.*

Indian   **House of India.** The haunting strains of sitar music lull diners at
Coral Gables   this popular spot in Coral Gables. Specialties include hot coco-
★   nut soup with cardamon, milk, rose water, and sugar; curried
goat; and authentic chicken tandoori, cooked in a clay oven. The
weekday luncheon buffet is a good bargain. *22 Merrick Way,
tel. 305/444–2348. Dress: casual. Weekend reservations accepted. AE, MC, V. Closed for Sun. lunch, Labor Day, Christmas. Moderate.*

Italian   **La Fenice.** The restaurant is named for the Venice opera house
Coral Gables   that rose, phoenixlike, from the ashes of an earlier structure
after an 1831 fire; and it is decorated with paintings of St.
Mark's Square in Venice, ornate mahogany chairs from Padua,
a four-tier fountain, and stained-glass windows. Specialties include rigatoni in creamy vodka sauce topped with caviar; veal
scallopini sautéed with Gorgonzola cheese, cream sauce, and
mushrooms; and poached salmon with a sauce of sweet red peppers pureed with lemon juice. *2728 Ponce de León Blvd., tel.
305/445–6603. Jacket and tie. Reservations advised. AE, MC,
V. Closed Sat.–Sun. noon. Moderate.*

Japanese   **Tokyo Rose Bar & Grill.** Starkly modern decor—neon lights
North Miami   against a minimalist black-and-white backdrop—complements
the menu concept of contemporary Japanese fare. While nib-
bling on a bowl of boiled soybeans, you choose from an extensive
à la carte menu or a selection of daily Japanese- and American-
style specials. Typical offerings include California Naki, a nori
roll with crab, avocado, and cucumber served with *wasabi*
(horseradish) and ginger; Kamikaza salad, a conch salad with
cucumber and a spicy Korean-style hot pepper dressing; Ginza
strip, rare sirloin marinated in vinegar and sesame; Kaizoku, a
pasta dish with calamari, scallops, and shrimp in white wine
sauce; Tokyo's salmon, prepared with Japanese mayo, flying
fish eggs *(masago)*, onions, and lemon butter; and fresh Japanese desserts with coconut-flour crust. Owner Masa Yamazaki
plans to open a Japanese bakery next door to Tokyo Rose in
1989. *13400 Biscayne Blvd., North Miami 33181, tel. 305/945–
7782. Dress: neat but casual. Reservations advised. No lunch.
Live jazz by Kenny Millions Tues.–Sat. AE, DC, MC, V. Moderate.*

Masa-San. Owner Masa Yamazaki, a Tokyo native who came to
the University of Miami in 1971 to study marketing, opened this
traditional Japanese restaurant in 1980. It's in a Japanese-style
building with a high wood ceiling, rice-paper windows, a tropical fish aquarium, and an 18-seat sushi bar. All sushi is made to
order, depending on what Japanese and local fish are available.
Try cobia (a species of sea catfish) in sashimi and sushi. Specialties include smoked freshwater eel sushi; *wakame* (Japanese
seaweed) with dried squid, herring eggs, ginger, and cucumber; *koba* (seaweed) with ponzu sauce (soy sauce, vinegar,
sweet cooking wine, anon juice, sesame seeds, and scallions);
Chinese shark's-fin soup garnished with whole hard-boiled
quail eggs; *harumaki*, a Japanese-style eggroll containing
bean sprouts, broccoli, cabbage, carrots, celery, and onions;
komochi-age, deep fried mushroom with seafood stuffing; tem-
pura with a light, crisp batter; and teriyaki. *19355 N.W. 2nd*

Ave. (US 441), Miami 33169, tel. 305/651–7782. Dress: neat but casual. Reservations advised. No lunch weekends. Closed July 4 and Thanksgiving. AE, DC, MC, V. Moderate.

Mexican
Little Havana

Acapulco. Authentic Mexican cuisine in an intimate 70-seat room with adobe walls, wooden beams, tabletops of Mexican tiles, and sombreros and serapes on the walls. As soon as you sit down, a waiter descends on you with a free, ample supply of *totopos,* homemade corn chips served hot and crunchy, salt free, with a fiery *pico de gallo* sauce. Specialties include a rich, chunky guacamole; *carnitas asadas* (marinated pork chunks in lemon and butter sauce); *mole poblano* (chicken in chocolate sauce); shrimp and rice in a cherry wine sauce; and combination platters of tacos, burritos, and enchiladas. *727 N.W. Unity Blvd. (N.W. 27th Ave.), tel. 305/642–6961. Dress: informal. Weekend reservations required. AE, CB, DC, MC, V. Inexpensive.*

Natural
Coconut Grove

Macrobiotic Foundation of Florida. All-natural meals are prepared fresh daily with organic vegetables, seeds, grains, and fruits to balance acid and alkaline, Yin and Yang. Even if you don't share this philosophy, the people are nice and the food is tasty. Meals are served boardinghouse style at long tables in a former church parish house. Specialties include miso soup, whole grains, pasta primavera and *arame* (an edible seaweed). International Night, on Friday, features cuisine of a different country each week. *3291 Franklin Ave., tel. 305/448–6625. Dress: informal. Reservations required. No smoking allowed. Sunday brunch. MC, V. Closed for lunch Sat. and dinner Mon., Wed., and Sun. Moderate.*

Downtown Miami

Granny Feelgood's. "Granny" is a shrewd gentleman named Irving Field, who caters to health-conscious lawyers, office workers, and cruise-ship crews at five locations. Specialties include chicken salad with raisins, apples, and cinnamon; spinach fettuccine with pine nuts; grilled tofu; apple crumb cake; and carrot cake. *190 S.E. 1st Ave., tel. 305/358–6233. Dress: casual. No reservations. No smoking in restaurant. AE, MC, V. Closed Sun. Inexpensive.*

Miami Beach

Pineapples. Art-deco pink pervades this health-food store and restaurant. Specialties include Chinese egg rolls; lasagna filled with tofu and mushrooms; spinach fettuccine with feta cheese, fresh garlic, walnuts, and cream sauce; and salads with a full-flavored Italian-style dressing. *530 Arthur Godfrey Rd., tel. 305/538–0350. Dress: casual. No reservations. No smoking in restaurant. AE, MC, V. Moderate.*

Nicaraguan
Little Managua

La Parrilla. Ten miles west of downtown Miami, about 50,000 Nicaraguans have moved into the Fontainebleau Park subdivision and the tiny suburban town of Sweetwater. Typical of their fare are the beef and fish at La Parilla (Spanish for "the grille"), where hanging plants and sloping barrel-tile roofs above the booths create a rural ambience. An adjoining bar is popular with Nicaraguan *contras.* Specialties include *gallos pintos* (red beans and rice); *chicharron* (fried pork with yucca); and *pargo a la Tipitapa,* baby red snapper fried and served whole in Creole sauce with onions and peppers. *9611 W. Flagler St., tel. 305/553–4419. Dress: informal. Reservations accepted. AE, CB, DC, MC, V. Moderate.*

Los Ranchos. Julio Somoza, owner of Los Ranchos and nephew of Nicaragua's late president, Anastasio Somoza, fled to south

Florida in 1979. Somoza sustains a tradition begun 30 years ago in Managua, when the original Los Ranchos instilled in Nicaraguan palates a love of Argentine-style beef—lean, grass-fed tenderloin with *chimichurri*, a green sauce of chopped parsley, garlic, oil, vinegar, and other spices. Nicaragua's own sauces are a tomato-based marinara and the fiery *cebollitas encurtidas*, with slices of jalapeño pepper and onion pickled in vinegar. Specialties include *chorizo* (sausage); *cuajada con maduro* (skim cheese with fried bananas); and shrimp sautéed in butter and topped with a creamy jalapeño sauce. *125 S.W. 107th Ave., tel. 305/221-9367. Also at Bayside Marketplace. Dress: informal. Reservations advised, especially on weekends. AE, CB, DC, MC, V. Closed Good Friday, Christmas, New Year's Day. Moderate.*

Seafood
Downtown Miami

East Coast Fisheries. This family-owned restaurant and retail fish market on the Miami River features fresh Florida seafood from its own 38-boat fleet in the Keys. From tables along the second-floor balcony railing, watch the cooks prepare your dinner in the open kitchen below. Specialties include a complimentary fish-pâté appetizer, blackened pompano with owner David Swartz's personal herb-and-spice recipe, lightly breaded fried grouper, and a homemade Key-lime pie so rich it tastes like ice cream. *360 W. Flagler St., tel. 305/373-5515. Dress: informal. Beer and wine only. AE, MC, V. Inexpensive.*

The Fish Market. Tucked away in a corner of the Omni International Hotel's lobby, this fine restaurant boasts waiters fluent in French, German, and Spanish and a kitchen staff fluent in seafood's complexities. The menu changes with availability of fresh fish, fruits, and vegetables. Typical menu items include smoked salmon and dolphin mousse; seafood ravioli filled with shrimp, lobster, and scallop puree in a sauce made with ginger, white wine, and cream; and seafood sausage made from ground grouper, scallops gelatin, and cream served with brandied lobster sauce over Julienne carrots and celery. Daily seafood specials may include bluefish, dolphin, lemon sole, marlin, pompano, puppy shark, redfish, sea bass, sea trout, and tuna. Desserts include chocolate Key lime pie with a Graham-cracker crust and pistachio chocolate terrine with orange cream sauce. *Biscayne Blvd. at 16th St., Miami 33132, tel. 305/374-0000. Reservations accepted. Jacket required. Closed Sun. Free valet parking. AE, DC, MC, V. Expensive.*

Key Biscayne

Sundays on the Bay. Two locations overlook the water—the Crandon Park Marina at Key Biscayne and the Intracoastal Waterway at Haulover. Both have inside dining and outdoor decks, bars, live bands nightly playing reggae and top 40 hits, and an energetic young serving staff. Specialties from an extensive seafood menu include conch fritters, conch chowder (tomato-based, served with sherry and Tabasco sauce), and baked grouper topped with crabmeat and shrimp scampi. *Key Biscayne: 5420 Crandon Blvd., tel. 305/361-6777; Haulover Beach Park: 10880 Collins Ave., tel. 305/945-5115. Dress: informal. Reservations accepted; advised for Sun. brunch. AE, CB, DC, MC, V. Moderate.*

Miami Beach
★

Joe's Stone Crab Restaurant. A south Florida tradition since 1913, Joe's is a family restaurant in its fourth generation. You go to wait, people watch, and finally settle down to an ample à la carte menu. Joe's serves about a ton of stone crab claws a day, with drawn butter, lemon wedges, and a piquant mustard sauce (recipe available). Popular side orders include a vinegary coleslaw, salad with a brisk house vinaigrette dressing, creamed garlic spinach, french-fried onion rings and eggplant, and hash brown potatoes. Save room for dessert—a slice of Key-lime pie with graham cracker crust and real whipped cream or apple pie with a crumb-pecan topping. *227 Biscayne St., tel. 305/673-0365. Dress: informal, but no T-shirts, tank tops, or shorts. No reservations; to minimize the wait, come for lunch before 11:30, for dinner before 5 or after 9. AE, CB, DC, MC, V. Closed May 15–Oct. 15. Moderate.*

Spanish
Downtown Miami

Las Tapas. *Tapas*—"little dishes"—come in appetizer-size portions to give you a variety of tastes during a single meal. Specialties include *la tostada* (smoked salmon on melba toast, topped with a dollop of sour cream, across which are laid baby eels, black caviar, capers, and chopped onion) and *samfaina con lomo* (eggplant, zucchini, green pepper, onions, tomato, and garlic sautéed with two thin, delicately flavored slices of fresh boneless pork loin). Also available are soups, salads, sandwiches, and standard dinners. *Bayside Marketplace, 401 Biscayne Blvd., tel. 305/372-2737. Dress: casual. Reservations for large parties only. AE, CB, DC, MC, V. Moderate.*

Little Havana
★

Casa Juancho. A meeting place for the movers and shakers of Miami's Cuban community, Casa Juancho serves a cross section of Spanish regional cuisines. The interior recalls old Castile: brown brick, rough-hewn dark timbers, and walls adorned with colorful Talavera platters. Strolling Spanish balladeers will serenade you. Specialties include *cochinillo Segoviano* (roast suckling pig), and *parrillada de mariscos* (fish, shrimps, squid, and scallops grilled in a light garlic sauce) from the Pontevedra region of northwest Spain. For dessert, the *crema Catalana* has a delectable crust of burnt caramel atop a rich pastry custard. The wine list includes fine labels from Spain's Rioja region. *2436 S.W. 8th St., tel. 305/642-2452. Dress: semiformal. Reservations advised; not accepted after 8 PM Fri. and Sat. AE, CB, DC, MC, V. Closed Christmas Eve. Expensive.*

Vietnamese
Little Havana
★

Hy-Vong Vietnamese Cuisine. Chef and part owner Tung Nguyen's magic has poured forth from the tiny kitchen of this 36-seat restaurant since 1980. Now the word is out, so come before 7 PM to avoid a long wait. Specialties include spring rolls, a Vietnamese version of an egg roll, with ground pork, cellophane noodles, and black mushrooms wrapped in homemade rice paper; a whole fish panfried with *nuoc man* (a garlic-lime fish sauce); and thinly sliced pork, barbecued with sesame seeds and fish sauce, served with bean sprouts, rice noodles, and slivers of carrots, almonds, and peanuts. *3458 S.W. 8th St., tel. 305/446-3674. Dress casual. Reservations accepted for 5 or more. No smoking. No credit cards. Closed Mon., American and Vietnamese/Chinese New Years, and 2 weeks in Aug. Moderate.*

Lodging

Few urban areas can match Greater Miami's diversity of hotel accommodations. The area has hundreds of hotels and motels with lodgings in all price categories, from $8 for a night in a dormitory-style hostel bed to $2,000 for a night in the luxurious presidential suite atop a posh downtown hotel.

As recently as the 1960s, many hotels in Greater Miami opened only in the winter to accommodate Yankee "snowbirds." Now most stay open all year. In summer, they cater to business travelers and to vacationers from the American South and Latin America who find Miami quite congenial despite the heat, humidity, and intense thunderstorms almost every afternoon.

Although some hotels (especially on the mainland) have adopted year-round rates, many still adjust their rates to reflect the ebb and flow of seasonal demand. The peak occurs in winter, with only a slight dip in summer when families with schoolchildren take vacations. You'll find the best values between Easter and Memorial Day (a delightful time in Miami but a difficult time for many people to travel), and in September and October (the height of hurricane season).

The list that follows is a representative selection of the best hotels and motels, organized geographically.

The rate categories in the list are based on the all-year or peak-season price; off-peak rates may be a category or two lower.

The most highly recommended places in each price category are indicated by a star ★.

Category	Cost*
Very Expensive	over $120
Expensive	$90–$120
Moderate	$50–$90
Inexpensive	under $50

All prices are for a standard double room, excluding 6% state sales tax and nominal tourist tax.

The following credit card abbreviations are used: AE, American Express; CB, Carte Blanche; DC, Diners Club; MC, MasterCard; V, Visa.

Coconut Grove **Doubletree Hotel at Coconut Grove.** This high rise with a bay view was built in 1970 and renovated in 1988. Rooms are large, most with balcony, comfortable chairs, armoires, original artwork. Choice of a mauve or turquoise color scheme. Best rooms are on upper floors with bay views. Homemade chocolate-chip cookies are offered to arriving guests. *2649 S. Bayshore Dr., Coconut Grove, 33133, tel. 305/858–2500 or 800/528–0444. 190 rooms with bath, including 32 nonsmoker rooms, and 3 rooms for handicapped guests. Facilities: outdoor freshwater pool, 2 tennis courts, restaurant, bar. Guests have access to Casablanca, a private club on the top floor. AE, CB, DC, MC, V. Expensive.*

★ **Grand Bay Hotel.** This modern high rise overlooks Biscayne

Bay; rooms have traditional furnishings and original art. The building's stairstep facade, like a Mayan pyramid, gives each room facing the bay a private terrace. Best views, at the northeast corner, include downtown Miami. The staff pays meticulous attention to guests' desires. Only slightly more special than most rooms is 814, Luciano Pavarotti's two-level suite with a baby-grand piano, circular staircase, and canopied king-size bed. You can rent it when he's not there. *2669 S. Bayshore Dr., Coconut Grove 33133, tel. 305/858–9600. 181 rooms with bath, including 48 suites, 20 nonsmoker rooms. Facilities: outdoor pool, hot tub, health club, saunas, masseur, afternoon tea in lobby, gourmet restaurant and lounge, poolside bar. AE, CB, DC, MC, V. Very Expensive.*

★ **Grove Isle.** This luxurious mid-rise urban resort sits on a 26-acre island and adjoins the equally posh condominium apartment towers and private club. Developer Martin Margulies displays selections from his extensive private art collection on the premises *(see* Exploring). The oversized rooms have patios, bay views, ceiling fans, and tropical decor with area rugs and Spanish tiles. The rooms with the most light and best bay view are 201–205. *4 Grove Isle Dr., Coconut Grove 33133, tel. 305/858–8300 or 800/858–8300. 49 rooms with bath, including 9 suites. Facilities: outdoor freshwater swimming pool and whirlpool; 12 tennis courts; 85-slip marina; 40-ft. sailboat that guests can charter; health spa with saunas and steam rooms, Nautilus equipment, masseur and masseuse, running track around the island; in-room refreshment bar and coffee maker; free cable TV; free movies in room; complimentary Continental breakfast; restaurant with indoor and outdoor seating. AE, CB, DC, MC, V. Very Expensive.*

Mayfair House. This European-style luxury hotel sits within an exclusive open-air shopping mall *(see* Exploring). Public areas have Tiffany windows, polished mahogany, marble walls and floors, and imported ceramics and crystal. A glassed-in elevator whisks you to the corridor on your floor—a balcony overlooking the mall's central fountains and walkways. In all suites, outdoor terraces face the street, screened from view by vegetation and wood latticework. Each has a Japanese hot tub on the balcony or a Roman tub in the bathroom. Otherwise, each suite is unique in size and furnishings. Sunset (Room 505) is one of 48 suites with antique pianos. Some aspects of the building's design are quirky; you can get lost looking for the ballroom or restaurant, and, in many rooms, you must stand in the bathtub to turn on the water. The worst suite for sleeping is Featherfern (Room 356), from which you can hear the band one floor below in the club. *3000 Florida Ave., Coconut Grove 33133, tel. 305/441–0000 or 800/433–4555. 181 suites, including 22 nonsmoker suites. Facilities: rooftop recreation area with sauna in a barrel, small outdoor freshwater swimming pool, and snack bar; preferred shopper card for discounts in mall shops; complimentary airport limousine service. AE, CB, DC, MC, V. Very Expensive.*

Coral Gables **The Biltmore Hotel.** A historic high rise built in 1926, the Biltmore was restored and renovated in 1986 and reopened as a luxury hotel, but the luxury exists primarily in the historic, restored public spaces *(see* Exploring). The rooms have high-quality furnishings befitting their price tag, but they are nondescript, lacking the boom-time ambience you might expect from such a legendary property. The service can be uneven.

Miami Area Lodging

O C E A N

MIAMI BEACH

101

ATLANTIC

Venetian Causeway
MacArthur Causeway
Biscayne Bay
Virginia Key
Rickenbacker Causeway
Crandon Park
Biscayne Bay
KEY BISCAYNE
Bill Baggs Cape Florida State Recreation Area

MIAMI

N.W. 7th St.
W. Flagler St.
S.W. 8th St.
S.W. 22nd St.
S. Dixie Hwy.
Tamiami Trail
Miracle Mile
CORAL GABLES
Old Cutler Rd.
Matheson Hammock Park
Red Rd.
S.W. 57th Ave.
Coral Way
Bird Rd.
S.W. 72nd St.
N. Kendall Dr.
Dolphin Expwy.
W. Flagler St.
S.W. 24th St.
S.W. 40th St.
S.W. 87th Ave.
Sunset Dr.
Rd.

5 miles
5 km

Alexander Hotel, **22**
Art Deco Hotels, **20**
The Biltmore Hotel, **4**
Cavalier Hotel, **21**
The Colonade Hotel, **5**
Dadeland Marriott, **2**

Doral Hotel & Country Club, **1**
Doubletree Hotel at Coconut Grove, **9**
Fontainebleau Hilton, **23**
Grand Bay Hotel, Grove Isle, **11**

Holiday Inn North Miami, **16**
Hotel Place St. Michel, **6**
Hyatt Regency Coral Gables, **7**
Hyatt Regency Miami, **12**

Inter-Continental Miami, **14**
Marina Park Hotel, **13**
Mayfair House, **10**
Miami Lakes Inn, **3**
Omni International Hotel, **15**

Pan American Ocean Hotel, **25**
Sheraton Royal Biscayne Beach, **18**
Sonesta Beach Hotel, **19**
Surfside Beach Hotel, **24**
Turnberry Isle Yacht Club, **17**

Without telling guests in the tower suites, the management often turns off the tower elevators to discourage sightseers from going up there. Upper-floor rooms facing north and east toward the airport, downtown Miami, and Biscayne Bay have the most spectacular views but more airplane noise. *1200 Anastasia Ave., Coral Gables 33134, tel. 305/445-1926 or 800/445-2586. 275 rooms with bath, including 45 suites. Facilities: 18-hole championship golf course, 10 lighted tennis courts, health spa with sauna, swimming pool, restaurant, coffee shop, and lounge. AE, CB, DC, MC, V. Very Expensive.*

★ **The Colonnade Hotel.** The twin 13-story towers of this $65-million hotel, office, and shopping complex dominate the heart of Coral Gables, echoing architecturally the adjoining two-story Corinthian-style rotunda on Miracle Mile from which 1920s developer George Merrick sold lots in his fledgling city. Merrick's family provided old photos, paintings, and other heirlooms that are on display throughout the hotel. The oversize rooms come in 26 different floor plans, each with a sitting area, built-in armoires, and traditional furnishings of mahogany. The hospitality bars have marble counters and gold-plated faucets with 1920s-style ceramic handles. The pool is on a 10th-floor terrace, which offers a magnificent view south toward Biscayne Bay. *180 Aragon Ave., Coral Gables 33134, tel. 305/441-2600 or 800/533-1337. 157 rooms, including 17 suites, 18 nonsmoker rooms, and 4 rooms for handicapped guests. Facilities: outdoor heated pool with 2 saunas, Nautilus exercise equipment, 24-hr room service, 2 restaurants. AE, DC, MC, V. Very Expensive.*

★ **Hotel Place St. Michel.** Historic low-rise urban hotel built in 1926 and restored 1981-86. Art-nouveau chandeliers suspended from vaulted ceilings grace the public areas of this intimate jewel in the heart of downtown Coral Gables. Paddle fans circulate the air, filled with the scent of fresh flowers. Each room has its own dimension, personality, and imported antiques from England, Scotland, and France. *162 Alcazar Ave., Coral Gables 33134, tel. 305/444-1666. 28 rooms with bath, including 3 suites. Facilities: welcome basket of fruit and cheese in every room, Continental breakfast, restaurant, lounge, French snack shop. AE, CB, DC, MC, V. Moderate.*

★ **Hyatt Regency Coral Gables.** This urban high rise caters to business travelers. Opened in 1987, the hotel is part of a megastructure that includes two office towers. The entire structure follows the area tradition of Spanish Mediterranean architecture, with tile roofs, white-frame casement windows, and pink-stucco exterior. The hotel's interior decor of pastel hues and antique-style furnishings gives a comfortable, residential feel to the rooms and public areas. The best rooms face the pool; the worst face north toward the airport. *500 Alhambra Plaza, Coral Gables 33134, tel. 305/441-1234. 242 rooms with bath, including 50 suites, 45 nonsmoker rooms. Facilities: 2,900-sq.-ft. ballroom, restaurant, lounge, rooftop swimming pool, outdoor whirlpool, health club with Nautilus equipment and Life Cycles, and sauna and steam rooms. AE, CB, DC, MC, V. Very Expensive.*

Downtown Miami
★ **Hotel Inter-Continental Miami.** Stand on the fifth-floor recreation plaza and gaze up at this granite 34-story monolith that appears to be arching over you. This optical illusion aside, the Inter-Continental deals in congenial realities. The grain in the lobby's marble floor matches that in *The Spindle*, a massive

centerpiece sculpture by Henry Moore. With all that marble, the lobby could easily look like a mausoleum—and did before the addition of palm trees, colorful umbrellas, and wicker chairs and tables. Atop a five-story atrium, a skylight lets the afternoon sun pour in. The triangular hotel tower offers bay, port, and city views that improve with height. *100 Chopin Plaza, Miami 33131, tel. 305/577–1000 or 800/327–0200. 645 rooms with bath, including 34 suites, 48 nonsmoker rooms; corner rooms have extra-wide doors for handicapped guests. Facilities: out-door heated freshwater swimming pool beside the bay, 2 lighted clay tennis courts, 2 indoor racquetball courts, ¼-mile jogging track with rubber surface, in-room minibar, restaurants, nightclub, and lounge. AE, CB, DC, MC, V. Very Expensive.*

Hyatt Regency Miami. This centrally located, 24-story convention hotel adjoins the James L. Knight International Center (*see* Exploring). It nestles beside the Brickell Avenue Bridge on the north bank of the Miami River. From its lower lobby, you can watch tugboats, freighters, and pleasure craft ply the river. The best rooms are on the upper floors, facing east toward Biscayne Bay. A $7-million renovation of the hotel's public area has continued into 1989. Room renovations began in late 1988. *400 S.E. 2nd Ave., Miami 33131, tel. 305/358–1234 or 800/228–9000. 615 rooms with bath, 25 suites, 43 nonsmoker rooms, 19 rooms for handicapped guests. Facilities: outdoor freshwater swimming pool; health club with sauna; in-room safe; in-house pay-TV movies, 2 restaurants, and a lounge. AE, CB, DC, MC, V. Very Expensive.*

Marina Park Hotel. Centrally located mid rise owned by a French chain. A stark exterior hides the hotel's warm Gallic personality. Rooms have an attractive pastel color scheme with rattan and wicker furnishings, soft mattresses, and trilingual TV. The best views are from east rooms that overlook Bayside and the Port of Miami. *340 Biscayne Blvd., Miami 33132, tel. 305/371–4400 or 800/327–6565. 200 rooms with bath, including 25 suites, 100 newly remodeled. Facilities: pool, restaurant, bar. AE, CB, DC, MC, V. Moderate.*

Omni International Hotel. A 20-story hotel built in 1977, the Omni stands atop a 10.5-acre shopping and entertainment complex that includes Jordan Marsh and J. C. Penney department stores, 120 specialty shops, the Children's Workshop child-care center, and a hand-made Italian wood carousel. The lowest hotel floor is five stories up; rooms on upper floors have spectacular views of downtown Miami and Biscayne Bay. A $1.25 million room renovation in 1987 eschewed tropical-chic in favor of more traditional decor, with a blue-and-tan color scheme and mahogany furniture in many rooms. *1601 Biscayne Blvd., Miami 33132, tel. 305/374–0000 or 800/THE-OMNI. 535 rooms, including 50 suites, 25 nonsmokers rooms, and 1 room for handicapped guests. Facilities: outdoor heated pool on a terrace 5 stories above the street, lobby bar, terrace café, restaurant (The Fish Market), access to nearby health club and spa. AE, DC, MC, V. Very Expensive.*

Kendall **Dadeland Marriott.** Catering to business travelers, this 24-story hotel is part of a megastructure that includes the Datran Center office building and the southernmost Metrorail station, Dadeland South. Within walking distance of Dadeland Mall, the hotel has a four-story atrium overlooking the Datran Center's lobby and its extensive sculpture collection. The hotel's contemporary decor, in corals and light greens, incorporates Asian accents. All rooms have desks and good reading lights. The best rooms face the city on the upper floors; 717 and 719 have glass doors opening to the pool. The worst room, 805, overlooks the roof of the exercise room. *9090 Dadeland Blvd., Miami 33156, tel. 305/663–1035 or 800/228–9290. 303 rooms with bath, including 2 suites, nonsmoker floor with 15 rooms, 4 rooms for handicapped guests. Facilities: outdoor heated freshwater swimming pool, Jacuzzi, whirlpool, sauna, exercise room, restaurant, lounge, complimentary airport transportation. AE, MC, V. Expensive.*

Key Biscayne **Sheraton Royal Biscayne Beach Resort and Racquet Club.** Art-deco pinks, wicker furniture, and chattering macaws and cockatoos in the lobby set the tone for this three-story beachfront resort set amid the waving fronds of coconut palms. Built in 1952 and restored in 1985, this laid-back place has managed to keep its casual demeanor even after starring as a "Miami Vice" set. All rooms have garden and bay views; most have terraces. *555 Ocean Dr., Key Biscayne 33149, tel. 305/361–5775. 192 rooms with bath, including 4 suites with ocean view, 15 suites with kitchenette, 15 nonsmoker rooms. Facilities: a ¼-mile of ocean beachfront; 2 outdoor freshwater heated swimming pools; children's wading pool and playground; 10 tennis courts (4 lighted); sailboats, Windsurfers, Hobie Cats, aquabikes, snorkeling kits, and bicycles for rent; pay-TV movies, unisex beauty salon; restaurants and lounge. AE, CB, DC, MC, V. Expensive.*

★ **Sonesta Beach Hotel & Tennis Club.** Built in 1969, this eight-story beachfront resort underwent a $5-million renovation in 1985. Tropical hues focus attention on museum-quality modern art by prominent painters and sculptors. Don't miss Andy Warhol's five drawings of rock star Mick Jagger in the hotel's disco bar, Desires. The best rooms face the ocean on the eighth floor, a "club floor" with a small lobby and bar where breakfast is served. *350 Ocean Dr., Key Biscayne 33149, tel. 305/361–2021 or 800/343–7170. 315 rooms with bath, including 12 suites and 15 villas (3-, 4-, and 5-bedroom homes with full kitchens and screened-in swimming pools). Facilities: 750 feet of oceanfront beach; outdoor freshwater heated Olympic-size swimming pool and whirlpool; 10 tennis courts (3 lighted); health center with Jacuzzi, dry and hot steam rooms, aerobic dance floor, weight room, massage room, and tanning room; gift shops; restaurants, snack bar, deli, disco lounge. AE, CB, DC, MC, V. Very Expensive.*

Miami Beach **Alexander Hotel.** Newly remodeled throughout, with antique ★ furnishings and original art in every suite, this 16-story hotel offers ocean and bay views from every room. Rooms facing south have the best views. A computer keeps track of the mattresses, so you can request the degree of firmness you prefer. *5225 Collins Ave., Miami Beach 33140, tel. 305/865–6500. 212 suites, each with two baths. Facilities: ocean beach, 2 outdoor heated freshwater pools, 4 poolside Jacuzzis, cabanas, Sunfishes and catamarans for rent, Dominique's gourmet restaurant, and coffee shop. AE, DC, MC, V. Expensive.*

Art Deco Hotels. A trio of restored three-story hotels facing the beach are under common ownership and management. The **Hotel Cardozo** dates from 1939, the **Hotel Carlyle** from 1941, and the **Hotel Leslie** from 1937. All three are attractively decorated in art-deco pinks, whites, and grays. Many contain original walnut furniture, restored and refinished. Rooms are comfortable but small; inspect your room before registering to assure that it meets your needs. Air-conditioning has been installed, but most of the time you won't need it—especially in rooms facing the water, where a sea breeze usually blows. *1244 Ocean Dr., Miami Beach 33139, tel. 305/534–2135 or 800/338–9076. 168 rooms with bath, including 15 suites. Facilities: restaurants and bars with live entertainment in the Carlyle and Cardozo. AE, CB, DC, MC, V. Moderate.*

Fontainebleau Hilton Resort and Spa. The Miami area's foremost convention hotel boasts an opulent lobby with massive chandeliers, a sweeping staircase, and new meeting rooms in art-deco hues. However, many guest rooms need refurbishing. Upper-floor rooms in the Chateau Building have the best views. *4441 Collins Ave., Miami Beach 33140, tel. 305/538–2000. 1,206 rooms with bath, including 60 suites, 55 nonsmoker rooms. Facilities: ocean beach with 30 cabanas, windsurfing, parasailing, Hobie Cats, volleyball, basketball, 2 outdoor pools (one fresh, one salt), 3 whirlpool baths, 7 lighted tennis courts, health club with exercise classes, saunas, marina, free children's activities, 12 restaurants and lounges, Tropigala night club. AE, CB, DC, MC, V. Expensive.*

★ **Hotel Cavalier.** Rooms in this three-story beachfront hotel have period maple furnishings, new baths, and air-conditioning. The Cavalier is popular with the film and fashion industry; many guests are artists, models, photographers, and writers. The best rooms face the ocean; the worst are on the ground floor, rear south, where the garbage truck goes by in the morning. *1320 Ocean Dr., Miami Beach 33139, tel. 305/531–6424 or 800/338–9076. 44 rooms with bath, including 2 suites. Facilities: bottled water and flowers in all rooms, Continental breakfast in lobby each morning, airport pickup available. AE, CB, MC, V. Expensive.*

★ **Pan American Ocean Hotel, A Radisson Resort.** This beach hotel sits back from Collins Avenue behind a refreshing garden of coconut palms and seasonal flowers. It first opened in 1954, but a complete renovation took place in 1988–89. The best view faces the ocean from rooms 330, 332, and 333 on the third floor of the north wing. Street noise makes west-facing rooms the least desirable. *17875 Collins Ave., Miami Beach 33160, tel. 305/932–1100. 146 rooms, including 4 suites, 5 nonsmokers rooms; 3 rooms for handicapped guests available part of the year. Facilities: 400 ft of Atlantic Ocean beach, outdoor heated pool, 4 hard-surface tennis courts, tennis pro and pro shop, 2 shuffleboard courts, 9-hole putting green, beauty salon, coffee shop, pool gazebo bar, terrace lounge and restaurant, ping-pong room, video game room, card room, free shuttle service to Bal Harbor and Aventura shopping malls, coin-operated laundry room, refrigerators in all rooms. AE, CB, DC, MC, V. Very Expensive.*

Surfside Beach Hotel. If you like classic American cars of the 1950s, you'll love this 10-story Quality Inn franchise. Built in 1951, it was restored in 1986 and transformed into a museum for owner Michael Dezer's collection of cars and automotive memorabilia. The lobby display includes a turquoise 1955 Ford Thunderbird hardtop, a 1957 Studebaker Golden Hawk, a red 1950 Willys Jeepster, and their ancestor—a 1931 Ford Model A roadster. Every room is named after a car. *8701 Collins Ave., Miami Beach 33154, tel. 305/865–6661 or 800/228–5151. 220 rooms with bath, including 36 nonsmoker rooms. Facilities:*

300 feet of ocean beach frontage, outdoor freshwater swimming pool with mosaic of pink 1959 Cadillac El Dorado convertible on the bottom, American Classics restaurant, Chevy's dance club, lobby bar, gift shop. AE, CB, DC, MC, V. Moderate.

North Dade   **Holiday Inn North Miami—Golden Glades.** Mid-rise suburban hotel at major highway interchange; two miles from the beach, from Calder Race Course, and from Joe Robbie Stadium (where the Miami Dolphins football team plays home games). A 1987 renovation gave public areas modern furnishings and mauve, peach, and purple wallpaper. Rooms have a green-and-white color scheme with oak furniture. Local police patrol the premises nightly. Restaurant offers Weight Watchers menu. *148 N.W. 167th St., Miami 33169, tel. 305/949–1441 or 800/HOLIDAY. 163 rooms with bath, including 18 nonsmoker rooms, 12 lady executive rooms, 1 room for handicapped guests. Facilities: outdoor freshwater swimming pool, children's pool, outdoor exercise area for aerobics, in-room refreshment center, restaurant, and lounge. AE, CB, DC, MC, V. Moderate.*

Miami Lakes Inn, Athletic Club, Golf Resort. This low-rise suburban resort is part of a planned town being developed by Florida Senator Bob Graham's family about 14 miles northwest of downtown Miami. The golf resort opened in 1962 and added two wings in 1978. Its decor is English-traditional throughout, rich in leather and wood. All rooms have balconies. The inn opened in 1983 with a typically Florida-tropic look—light pastel hues and furniture of wicker and light wood. In both locations, the best rooms are near the lobby for convenient access; the worst are near the elevators. *Main St., Miami Lakes 33014, tel. 305/821–1150. 310 rooms with bath, including 32 suites. Facilities: 2 outdoor freshwater swimming pools; 9 lighted tennis courts; golf (18-hole par-72 course, lighted 18-hole par-54 executive course, golf school); saunas, steamrooms, and whirlpool baths; 8 indoor racquetball courts; Nautilus fitness center; full-size gym for volleyball and basketball; aerobics classes; restaurants and lounges; shopping discount at Main St. shops. AE, CB, DC, MC, V. Very Expensive.*

★ **Turnberry Isle Yacht and Country Club.** Part of an upscale condominium community on a 300-acre bayfront site 12 miles north of downtown Miami. Celebrities who live here include tennis stars Jimmy Connors, Vitas Gerulitis, and John McEnroe. Choose from the European-style Marina Hotel or the Country Club Inn beside the golf course. Rooms are oversize, with light woods and earth-tone colors at the inn, a nautical-blue motif at the hotel, large curving terraces, Jacuzzis, honor bar, and in-room safes. *19735 Turnberry Way, North Miami Beach 33163, tel. 305/932–6200. 250 rooms with bath, including 47 suites. (By spring 1990, 2 new 5-story minitowers and 24 tennis villas will be open, bringing the total room count to 370.) Facilities: Ocean Club with 250 feet of private beach frontage, diving gear, Windsurfers and Hobie Cats for rent, and complimentary shuttle service to the hotel; 2 outdoor freshwater swimming pools; 24 tennis courts, 18 with lights; 2 18-hole golf courses; helipad; marina with moorings for 125 boats up to 150 ft.; full-service spa with physician, nutritionist, saunas, steamrooms, whirlpools, facials, herbal wraps, Nautilus exercise equipment, indoor racquetball courts, and jogging course; 5 private restaurants, lounge, nightly entertainment. AE, CB, DC, MC, V. Very Expensive.*

West Dade **Doral Resort & Country Club.** Millions of airline passengers annually peer down upon this 2,400-acre jewel of an inland golf and tennis resort while fastening their seat belts. It's seven miles west of Miami International Airport and consists of eight separate three- and four-story lodges nestled beside the golf links. A renovation completed in 1988 gave the resort a tropical theme, with light pastels, wicker, and teak furniture. All guest rooms have minibars; most have private balconies or terraces with views of the golf courses or tennis courts. This is the site of the Doral Ryder Open Tournament, played on the Doral "Blue Monster" golf course. *4400 N.W. 87th Ave., Miami 33178, tel. 305/592–2000. 650 rooms with bath, including 56 suites. Facilities: 5 18-hole golf courses, and a 9-hole, par-3 executive course; pro shop and boutique; 15 tennis courts; Olympic-size heated outdoor freshwater swimming pool; 24-stall equestrian center, offers riding instruction; 3-mi jogging and bike path; bicycle rentals; lake fishing; restaurant and lounge; transportation to beach. AE, CB, DC, MC, V. Very Expensive.*

The Arts

Performing arts aficionados in Greater Miami will tell you they survive quite nicely despite the area's historic inability to support a professional symphony orchestra. In recent years, this community has begun to write a new chapter in its performing arts history.

The New World Symphony, a unique advanced-training orchestra, marks its third season in 1990. The fledgling Miami City Ballet has risen rapidly to international prominence in its four-year existence. The opera company ranks with the nation's best, and a venerable chamber music series brings renowned ensembles to perform here. Several churches and synagogues also run classical music series with international performers.

In theater, Miami offers English-speaking audiences an assortment of professional, collegiate, and amateur productions of musicals, comedy, and drama. Spanish theater also is active.

In the cinema world, the Miami Film Festival attracts more than 45,000 people annually to screenings of new films from all over the world—including some made here.

Arts Information. Greater Miami's English-language daily newspaper, *The Miami Herald*, publishes information on the performing arts in its Weekend Section on Friday and the Lively Arts Section on Sunday. The *Herald* is notorious for its inaccurate listings of the location and time of arts events. Phone ahead to confirm details before you go.

If you read Spanish, check *El Nuevo Herald* (a Spanish version of *The Miami Herald*) or *Diario Las Americas* (the area's largest independent Spanish-language paper) for information on the Spanish theater and a smattering of general performing arts news.

Other good sources of information on the performing arts are the calendar in *Miami Today*, a free weekly newspaper available each Thursday in downtown Miami, Coconut Grove, and Coral Gables; and *New Times*, a free weekly distributed throughout Dade County each Wednesday.

Arts. Miami's official guide to the arts is a pocket»size monthly publication covering music of all kinds, from the classics to rock and art gallery openings, theater, and major cultural events in Greater Miami, Broward, and Palm Beach. Editor Margo Morrison tries to be encylopedic and does a good job. Sold at newsstands all over Greater Miami. *Tel. 305/854–1790. 9–5. Annual subscription $15, individual copy $2. No credit cards.*

WTMI (93.1 FM) provides concert information on its Cultural Arts Line (tel. 305/550–9393).

Ballet **Miami City Ballet.** Florida's first major fully professional resident ballet company. Edward Villella, the artistic director, was principal dancer of the New York City Ballet under George Balanchine. Now the Miami City Ballet re-creates the Balanchine repertoire and has begun to introduce new works of its own. Miami City Ballet performances are at Gusman Center for the Performing Arts. Demonstrations of works in progress are at the 450-seat Colony Theater on Miami Beach. Villella narrates the children's and works-in-progress programs. *905 Lincoln Rd., Miami Beach 33139, tel. 305/532–7713. Season: Oct.–May. AE, MC, V. Ticketmaster (*see *Important Addresses and Numbers).*

Cinema **The Miami Film Festival.** During eight days in February, new films from all over the world are screened in the Gusman Center for the Performing Arts. Tickets and schedule: *444 Brickell Ave., Miami 33131, tel. 305/377–3456. AE, MC, V. Ticketmaster (*see *Important Addresses and Numbers).*

Concerts **Concert Association of Greater Miami.** A not-for-profit organization, directed by Judith Drucker, this is the South's largest presenter of classical artists. Ticket and program information: *555 Hank Meyer Blvd. (17th St.), Miami Beach 33139, tel. 305/ 532–3491. AE, CB, DC, MC, V.*
Friends of Chamber Music (44 W. Flagler St., Miami 33130, tel. 305/372–2975) presents an annual series of chamber concerts by internationally known guest ensembles, such as the Beaux Arts Trio, I Musici, and the Julliard String Quartet.

Drama **Check** *Miami's Guide to the Arts* for a complete English-language theater schedule. Traveling companies come and go; amateur groups form, perform, and disband. Listed below are the more enduring groups of Greater Miami's drama scene.
Coconut Grove Playhouse. Arnold Mittelman, artistic director, stages Broadway-bound plays and musical reviews and experimental productions. *3500 Main Hwy., Coconut Grove 33133, tel. 305/442–4000. AE, MC, V.*
Ruth Forman Theater. Six Actors Equity productions are staged here throughout the year. Each production lasts five weeks. *At Barry University, 11300 N.E. 2nd Ave., Miami Shores 33161. Oct.–May. MC, V. Write for details.*
Ring Theater. The University of Miami's Department of Theatre Arts presents four complete plays a year in this 311-seat hall. *University of Miami, 1312 Miller Dr., Coral Gables 33124, tel. 305/284–3355. No credit cards.*

Opera **Greater Miami Opera.** Miami's resident opera company has the seventh-largest operating budget of any American opera organization. It presents two complete casts for five operas in the Dade County Auditorium. The International Series brings such luminaries as Placido Domingo and Luciano Pavarotti; the National Series features rising young singers in the principal roles, with the same sets and chorus, but with more modest ticket prices. All operas are sung in their original language, with titles in English projected onto a screen above the stage. *1200 Coral Way, Miami 33145, tel. 305/854-7890. AE, MC, V. Ticketmaster (see Important Addresses and Numbers).*

Symphony
New World Symphony. Although Greater Miami still has no resident symphony orchestra, the New World Symphony, conducted by Michael Tilson Thomas, helps to fill the void. It's a unique phenomenon, a national advanced training orchestra for musicians aged 21–30 who have finished their academic studies and need performing experience in a professional setting before moving on to a permanent job. *541 Lincoln Rd., Miami Beach 33139, box office tel. 305/673-3331, main office 305/673-3330. AE, CB, DC, MC, V. Season: Oct.-Apr. Ticketmaster (see Important Addresses and Numbers).*

Theaters
Greater Miami lacks a modern performing arts center. Every auditorium and theater in town suffers from a shortage of space on and off the stage, and some have acoustical problems.

Dade County Auditorium (2901 W. Flagler St., Miami 33135, tel. 305/545-3395) satisfies patrons with 2,497 comfortable seats, good sight lines, and acceptable acoustics. Performers grumble at its shortcomings. The lack of a proper orchestra pit frustrates the Greater Miami Opera Association, and storage space is so minimal that the opera company must keep its paraphernalia outside the hall in trailers between performances.

Jackie Gleason Theater of the Performing Arts (1700 Washington Ave., Miami Beach 33119, tel. 305/673-8300), with 3,000 seats, has visibility and acoustics problems. Many top performers reportedly won't play there; many patrons are outspoken about not attending.

Gusman Center for the Performing Arts (174 E. Flagler St., Miami 33131, (tel. 305/372-0925). In downtown Miami, the center has 1,700 seats made for sardines—and the best acoustics in town. An ornate former movie palace, the hall resembles a Moorish courtyard. Lights twinkle, starlike, from the ceiling. Musicians dread Gusman because they must carry everything they need in and out for each performance.

Gusman Concert Hall (1314 Miller Dr., Coral Gables 33124, tel. 305/284-2438). This 600-seat hall on the University of Miami's Coral Gables campus has good acoustics, an orange and purple color scheme, and plenty of room for UM's basketball players to stretch their legs. Parking is a problem when school is in session.

Hirschfeld Theatre. Situated in the Castle Hotel and Resort, this 840-seat restored former cabaret once hosted Jackie Gleason and Rowan and Martin. Nine musicals are produced annually. *5445 Collins Ave., Miami Beach 33140, tel. 305/865-PLAY. AE, DC, MC, V.*

Spanish Theater
Spanish theater prospers, although many companies have short lives. About 20 Spanish companies perform light comedy, puppetry, vaudeville, and political satire. To locate them, read the Spanish newspapers. When you phone, be prepared for a conversation in Spanish. Most of the box-office personnel don't speak English.

Teatro Avanite (232 Minorca Ave). Three to six productions are staged annually in the 220-seat Minorca Playhouse. A Hispanic theater festival is held each May. *Box 453005, Miami, 33245, tel. 305/858-4155.*

Prometo. Has produced three to four bilingual Spanish-English plays a year for 15 years. *Miami-Dade Community College, New World Center Campus, 300 N.E. 2nd Ave., Miami, tel. 305/347–3263.*

Teatro de Bellas Artes. A 255-seat theater on Calle Ocho, Little Havana's main commercial street, presents eight Spanish plays and musicals a year. *Dramas Fri.–Sat. 9 PM and Sun. 3 PM. Musical comedy Sat. midnight and Sun. 9 PM. Recitals Sun. 6 PM. 2173 S.W. 8th St., Miami, tel. 305/325–0515. No credit cards.*

Nightlife

Greater Miami has no concentration of night spots like Bourbon Street in New Orleans or Rush Street in Chicago, but nightlife thrives throughout the Miami area in scattered locations, including Miami Beach, Little Haiti, Little Havana, Coconut Grove, the fringes of downtown Miami, and south-suburban Kendall. Individual clubs offer jazz, various forms of rock-and-roll, and top 40 sounds on different nights of the week. Some clubs refuse entrance to anyone under 21; others set the age limit at 25.

For current information, see the Weekend Section in the Friday edition of *The Miami Herald;* the calendar in *Miami Today,* a free weekly newspaper available each Thursday in downtown Miami, Coconut Grove, and Coral Gables; and *New Times,* a free weekly distributed throughout Dade County each Wednesday.

Love 94 (WLVE, 93.9 FM) sponsors a concert line with information on touring groups of all kinds, except classical (tel. 305/654–9436). Blues Hot Line lists local blues clubs and bars (tel. 305/666–6656). Jazz Hot Line lists local jazz programs (tel. 305/382–3938).

On Miami Beach, where the sounds of jazz and reggae spill into the streets, fashion models and photographers frequent the lobby bars of small art-deco hotels.

Throughout the Greater Miami area, bars and cocktail lounges in larger hotels operate discos nightly, with live entertainment on weekends. Many hotels extend their bars into open-air courtyards, where patrons dine and dance under the stars throughout the year.

Bars **Churchill's Hideaway.** This enclave of Anglicism in Little Haiti is popular with cruise-line employees and international sports fans. Its satellite dish picks up BBC news programs, and a Sharp Six System VHS plays foreign-format tapes of international soccer and rugby games. Four English beers on tap, 40 kinds of imported bottled beers. Four dart boards. The outdoor bar in back came from an old Playboy Club on Biscayne Boulevard. Entertainment on weekends. *5501 N.E. 2nd Ave., Miami, tel. 305/757–1807. Open 10 AM–2 AM Mon.–Thurs. and Sun., to 3 AM Fri.–Sat. No credit cards.*

Hungry Sailor. This small English-style pub is decorated with nautical charts, marine flags, and flotsam and jetsam. Five English ales and beers are on tap. There's traditional English food, and live entertainment nightly: folk, jazz, or reggae. *3064½ Grand Ave., Coconut Grove, tel. 305/444–9359. Open 11:30 AM–2:30 AM. AE, CB, DC, MC, V.*

Stuart's Bar-Lounge. Named for its owner and located in the Hotel Place St. Michel, Stuart's is an original Coral Gables hostelry built in 1926. *Esquire* called Stuart's one of the best new bars of 1987. It is decorated with beveled mirrors, mahogany paneling, French posters, pictures of old Coral Gables, and art-nouveau lighting. Live jazz on weekends. *162 Alcazar Ave., Coral Gables, tel. 305/444-1666. Open 5 PM–12:30 AM Mon.– Sat., 6 PM–12:30 AM Sun. AE, CB, DC, MC, V.*

Taurus Steak House. The bar, built in 1922 of native cypress, nightly draws an over-30 singles crowd that drifts outside to a patio. A band plays on weekends. Lunch and dinner. *3540 Main Hwy., Coconut Grove, tel. 305/448-0633. Open daily 5 PM– midnight. AE, CB, DC, MC, V.*

Tobacco Road. This bar, opened in 1912, holds Miami's oldest liquor license. Upstairs, in space occupied by a speakeasy during Prohibition, local and national blues bands perform Friday and Saturday and in scheduled weeknight concerts. The bar draws a diverse clientele from all over south Florida. *626 S. Miami Ave., Miami, tel. 305/374-1198. Open weekdays 11:30 AM–5 AM, weekends 1 PM–5 AM. Lunch served Mon.–Fri. Dinner served Sun.–Thurs. AE, DC.*

Tropics International Restaurant. Reggae is featured in art deco surroundings in the lobby of the Edison Hotel, built in 1936. Dinner. *960 Ocean Dr., Miami Beach, tel. 305/531-5335. Open daily 5 PM–3 AM. AE, MC, V.*

Comedy Clubs

Coconuts Comedy Clubs. This 1980s version of vaudeville comedy thrives with humor that's adult, but not obscene. Two acts per show; new performers each week. *Dadeland Marriott Hotel, 9090 S. Dadeland Blvd., Kendall, tel. 305/670-2022. Shows Wed., Thurs., and Sun. 9 PM; Fri. 9 and 11 PM; Sat. 8 PM, 10 PM, and midnight. Also at Howard Johnson, 16500 N.W. 2nd Ave., North Miami Beach, tel. 305/948-6887. Thurs. and Sun. 9 PM, Fri. 9 and 11 PM, Sat. 9 and 11 PM. Both suggest reservations. Cover and drink minimum. AE, MC, V.*

Disco/Rock Clubs

Stringfellows. Opened in May 1989, Peter Stringfellow's Coconut Grove club has been attracting guests from international artistic, business, and social circles, many of whom are already familiar with Stringfellow's other clubs in London and New York. Guests enter through green glass doors decorated with an etched-glass butterfly crest and ascend to the club's second-floor restaurant and nightclub. The restaurant, decorated with art-deco furnishings, pink tablecloths, and fresh orchids, features well-prepared international cuisine. A dinner-hour trio plays jazz. The nightclub, which opens at 11:30, features rock music pumped through a state-of-the-art sound system and a sophisticated light system capable of producing hundreds of variations. *3390 Mary St., Miami 33143, tel. 305/446-7555. Reservations advised. Club cover charge: $10 Sun.–Thurs., $15 Fri., $20 Sat. Closed Christmas. A-la-carte menu served 8 PM–2:30 AM, late-night supper from 2:30–4 AM. Club open 11:30 PM–5 AM. AE, DC, MC, V.*

Club Oz. This is a haven for south-suburban yuppies. The theme changes nightly, with many special events. Wood dance floor. *19995 S. Dixie Hwy., Miami, tel. 305/238-3700. Open Wed.–Sat. 9 PM–5 AM. AE, MC, V.*

Stefano's of Key Biscayne. Live band performs nightly, 7–11 PM. Then this northern Italian restaurant becomes a disco. Wood dance floor. *24 Crandon Blvd., Key Biscayne, tel. 305/361-7007. Open 5 PM–5 AM nightly. AE, CB, DC, MC, V.*

Club Nu. The decor at this club changes every three–four months. A large New York–style nightclub with separate champagne room and dining area, this spot attracts a fashion-conscious under-30 crowd, many in bizarre garb. Large terraz-zo dance floor. *245 22nd St., Miami Beach 33139, tel. 305/672–0068. Open Wed.–Sun. 9 PM–5 AM.*

Folk Music **Our Place Natural Foods Eatery.** On weekends, this small South Beach vegetarian restaurant becomes Greater Miami's only smoke-free live folk music club. Features local and national art-ists. Last Saturday of each month is "open mike" night. Full menu all night. *830 Washington Ave., Miami Beach, tel. 305/ 674–1322. Open 8 PM Fri.–Sat. till the musicians quit. No cred-it cards.*

Nightclubs **Les Violins Supper Club.** This standby has been owned for 25 years by the Cachaidora-Currais family, who ran a club and restaurant in Havana. The club's ceiling rises 10 feet during two nightly Las Vegas–style reviews, reminiscent of old Busby Berkeley movies. Live dance band. Wood dance floor. Dinner. *1751 Biscayne Blvd., Miami, tel. 305/371–8668. Open 7 PM. Closes Tues.–Thurs. and Sun. 1 AM, Fri. 2 AM, Sat. 3 AM. Closed Mon. Reservations suggested. AE, CB, DC, MC, V.*
Club Tropigala at La Ronde in the Fontainebleau Hilton Hotel. A seven-level round room decorated with orchids, banana leaves, and philodendrons to resemble a tropical jungle, this club is operated by owners of Les Violins. Two bands play Latin music for dancing on wood floor. Two live costumed shows nightly. Dinner. Long wait for valet parking. *4441 Collins Ave., Miami Beach, tel. 305/672–7469. Open Weds.–Sun. 7 PM–4 AM. Reservations advised. AE, CB, DC, MC, V.*

4 The Everglades

Introduction

by George and Rosalie Leposky

Greater Miami is the only metropolitan area in the United States with two national parks in its backyard: Everglades and Biscayne. Both have image problems.

Because Everglades is famous, people come expecting a spectacle like the mountainous western parks. What they see is a wide expanse of saw grass that at first glance looks frustratingly like a midwestern wheat field. In sea-girded Biscayne, you need a boat and snorkel or scuba gear.

At least these parks are easy to reach. You can drive to either one from downtown Miami in an hour, and their main entrances are just 21 miles apart. Between them sits Homestead, a bustling agricultural city of 25,000.

The creation of Everglades National Park in 1947 made many people in Homestead unhappy. The farmers wanted to plow much of the land that came under the park service's protection.

Today, Homestead is beginning to view the park with a less-jaundiced eye and transforming itself into a tourist center. New motels, shopping centers, and restaurants have opened; old ones are sprucing up. City officials have created a historic district downtown to promote restoration of Homestead's commercial heart. It's all an effort to house, feed, and amuse many of the million visitors who will explore the Everglades in 1990—and the 30,000 hardy souls who will discover Biscayne.

If you intend to spend just one day at Everglades National Park, take the 38-mile main park road from the Main Visitor Center to Flamingo to see a cross section of the park's ecosystems: hardwood hammock (tree islands), freshwater prairie, pineland, freshwater slough, cypress, coastal prairie, mangrove, and marine/estuarine.

At Shark Valley, on the park's northern edge, a 14-mile tram ride takes you to an observation tower overlooking the "river of grass" (*see* Guided Tours).

The Gulf Coast and Key Largo ranger stations and the Flamingo Visitor Center offer access to the mangroves and marine habitats—Gulf Coast in the Ten Thousand Islands region along the Gulf of Mexico near Everglades City; Flamingo and Key Largo in Florida Bay. You can take tour boat rides from Everglades City and Flamingo through this ecosystem (*see* Guided Tours) and hire a fishing guide to show you where the big ones bite (*see* Participant Sports).

Biscayne National Park encompasses almost 274 square miles, of which 96% are under water. Biscayne includes 18 miles of inhospitable mangrove shoreline on the mainland and 45 mangrove-fringed barrier islands seven miles to the east across Biscayne Bay. The bay is a lobster sanctuary and a nursery for fish, sponges, and crabs. Manatees and sea turtles also frequent its warm, shallow waters.

The islands (called keys) are fossilized coral reefs that emerged from the sea when glaciers trapped much of the world's water supply during the Ice Age. Today, a tropical hardwood forest grows in the crevices of these rocky keys.

East of the keys, coral reefs three miles seaward attract divers and snorkelers (*see* Participant Sports). Biscayne is the only national park in the continental United States with living coral reefs and is the nation's largest marine park.

The park boundary encompasses the continental shelf to a depth of 60 feet. East of that boundary, the shelf falls rapidly away to a depth of 400 feet at the edge of the Gulf Stream.

Getting Around

By Plane *Commercial Flights.* **Miami International Airport** (MIA) is the closest commercial airport to Everglades National Park and Biscayne National Park. It's 34 miles from Homestead and 83 miles from the Flamingo resort in Everglades National Park.

By Car From the north, the main highways to Homestead-Florida City are U.S. 1, the Homestead Extension of the Florida Turnpike, and Krome Avenue (Rte. 997).

From Miami to Biscayne National Park, take the turnpike extension to the Tallahassee Road (S.W. 137th Ave.) exit, turn left, and go south. Turn left at North Canal Drive (S.W. 328th St.), go east, and follow signs to park headquarters at Convoy Point. The park is about 30 miles from downtown Miami.

From Homestead to Biscayne National Park, take U.S. 1 or Krome Avenue (Rte. 997) to Lucy Street (S.E. 8th St.). Turn east. Lucy Street becomes North Canal Drive (S.W. 328th St.). Follow signs about eight miles to the park headquarters.

From Homestead to Everglades National Park's Main Visitor Center and Flamingo, take U.S. 1 or Krome Avenue (Rte. 997) south to Florida City. Turn right (west) onto Rte. 9336. Follow signs to the park entrance. The Main Visitor Center is 11 miles from Homestead; Flamingo is 49 miles from Homestead.

To reach the north end of Everglades National Park, take U.S. 41 (the Tamiami Trail) west from Miami. It's 40 miles to the Shark Valley Information Center and 83 miles to the Gulf Coast Ranger Station at Everglades City.

To reach the south end of Everglades National Park in the Florida Keys, take U.S. 1 south from Homestead. It's 27 miles to the Key Largo Ranger Station (between Mile Markers 98 and 99 on the Overseas Hwy.).

Rental Cars **Homestead Freedom Rent-a-Car** (tel. 305/248–8352 or 305/257–2525). Rental cars also available at MIA (*see* Miami Arriving and Departing).

By Bus **Metrobus** Route 1A runs from Homestead to MIA only during peak weekday hours: 6:30–9 AM and 4–6:30 PM. **Greyhound/Trailways** operates two trips daily north and south from MIA (*see* Miami Arriving and Departing).

By Taxi **Homestead Cab Company.** Service in Homestead-Florida City area. Full service to and from Flamingo and the tour boats in Biscayne National Park. Service from Homestead to MIA; *416 N.E. 1st Rd., Homestead, tel. 305/247–7777. Open 24 hours daily except 6 AM Sun.–5 AM Mon. No credit cards.*

By Boat **U.S. Customs.** The nearest U.S. Customs phones to the two national parks are at **Watson Island Marina** (1050 MacArthur Causeway, Miami, tel. 305/371–2378), about 25 nautical miles to Biscayne National Park headquarters, 50 nautical miles to Flamingo; and **Tavernier Creek Marina** (Mile Marker 90–½,

U.S. 1, Tavernier, tel. 305/252–0194 from Miami, 305/852–5854 from the Keys), about 48 nautical miles to Biscayne National Park headquarters, 25 nautical miles to Flamingo.

Scenic Drives **Main road to Flamingo in Everglades National Park.** It's 38 road miles from the Main Visitor Center to Flamingo, across six distinct ecosystems (with access from the road to two others). Highlights of the trip include a dwarf cypress forest, the ecotone (transition zone) between sawgrass and mangrove forest, and a wealth of wading birds at Mrazek and Coot Bay Ponds. Boardwalks and trails along the main road and several short spurs allow you to see the Everglades without getting your feet wet. Well-written interpretive signs en route will help you understand this diverse wilderness.

Tamiami Trail. U.S. 41 from Miami to the Gulf Coast crosses the Everglades and the Big Cypress National Preserve. Highlights of the trip include sweeping views across the sawgrass to the Shark River Slough, a visit to the Miccosukee Indian Reservation, and the Big Cypress National Preserve's variegated pattern of wet prairies, ponds, marshes, sloughs, and strands. It's 83 miles to the Gulf Coast Ranger Station at Everglades City.

Guided Tours

Tours of Everglades National Park and Biscayne National Park typically focus on native wildlife, plants, and park history. Concessionaires operate the Everglades tram tours and the boat cruises in both parks.

In addition, the National Park Service organizes a variety of free programs at Everglades National Park. Ask a ranger for the daily schedule.

Orientation Tours **All Florida Adventure Tours.** All-day narrated 250-mile tour of south Florida wetlands, through the Big Cypress National Preserve to Everglades City and Chokoloskee Island, and Corkscrew. *11137 North Kendall Dr., D105, Miami 33176, tel. 305/270–0219. Tours Tues. and Sat. Cost: $69.50 adults, $49.50 children. No credit cards.*

Miami Vision. Miccosukee Indian Village, lunch, and airboat ride. Minivan and private car tours. Well-informed, congenial guides speak English, Spanish, French, German, Italian, and Portuguese. *2699 Collins Ave., Suite 113, Miami Beach, tel. 305/532–0040. Cost: $49 adults, $39 children. MC, V.*

Safari Sightseeing Tours. Everglades tour includes airboat ride, Indian village, Shark Valley, and lunch. *6547 S.W. 116th Pl., Miami, tel. 305/226–6923 (day) or 305/223–3804 (night). Tours Wed., Sat., Sun. 8:30–5. Cost: $29.50 adults, $14.75 children under 12, includes transportation and admissions (but not lunch). No credit cards.*

Special-Interest Tours
Airboat Rides **Buffalo Tiger's Florida Everglades Airboat Ride.** The former chairman of the Miccosukee tribe will take you on a 30-minute airboat ride through the Everglades, with a stop at an old Indian camp. Opportunities to watch birds, turtles, and alligators. *Tour location: 29701 S.W. 8th St., 12 mi west of Krome Ave., 20 mi west of the Miami city limits (Rte. 997), tel. 305/559–5250. Open daily 9–6. Cost: $6 adults, $4 children under 10. No credit cards.*

Coopertown Airboat Ride. Chuck Norris filmed *Invasion U.S.A.* here. A 30-minute airboat ride through the Everglades sawgrass to visit two hammocks (subtropical hardwood forests) and alligator holes. Bird-watching opportunities. *Tour location: S.W. 8th St., 5 mi west of Krome Ave., 15 mi west of Miami city limits, tel. 305/226-6048. Open daily 8 AM-dusk. Cost: $7 per person. No credit cards.*

Everglades Air Boat Tours. A four-mile, 30-minute tour of the River of Grass leaves every half hour. *Tour location: 40351 S.W. 192nd Ave., tel. 305/AIRBOAT. Open daily 9–5. Cost: $7.50 adults, $6.50 senior citizens, $3.50 children 4–12, under 4 free. No credit cards.*

Boat Tours **Biscayne National Park Tour Boats.** You'll ride to Biscayne National Park's living coral reefs 10 miles offshore on a 53-foot glass-bottom boat. A separate tour to Elliott Key visitor center, on a barrier island seven miles offshore across Biscayne Bay, is conducted only in winter when mosquitoes are less active. *Tour location: East end of North Canal Dr. (S.W. 328th St.), Homestead, tel. 305/247-2400. Office open daily 8:30–5:30. Phone for daily schedule. Reservations required. AE, MC, V.*

Back Country Tour. A two-hour cruise from Flamingo Lodge Marina & Outpost Resort aboard a 40-passenger pontoon boat covers 12–15 miles through tropical estuaries fringed with impenetrable mangrove forests. You may see manatees, dolphins, sharks, alligators, and many species of bird life, including bald eagles. *Tour location: Flamingo Marina, Flamingo, tel. 305/253-2241 or 813/695-3101. Cruises daily. Phone for schedule. Reservations accepted. AE, DC, MC, V.*

Everglades National Park Boat Tours. Sammy Hamilton operates three separate 14-mile tours through the Ten Thousand Islands region along the Gulf of Mexico on the western margin of the park. *Tour location: At Everglades National Park's Gulf Coast Ranger Station on Rte. 29, about 3 mi south of U.S. 41 (Tamiami Trail), tel. 813/695-2591 or in FL 800/445-7724. Office open daily 8:30–4:30. Phone for schedule. No credit cards.*

Florida Bay Cruise. A 90-minute tour of Florida Bay from Flamingo Lodge Marina & Outpost Resort aboard *Pelican*, a 42-passenger pontoon boat. The tour offers a close look at bird life on rookery islands in the bay and on sandbars during low tide. In winter, you're likely to see white pelicans; in summer, magnificent frigatebirds. Also offers Backcountry and Sunset tours. *Tour location: Flamingo Marina, Flamingo, tel. 305/253-2241 or 813/695-3101. Cruises daily. Phone for schedule. Reservations accepted. AE, DC, MC, V.*

Florida Boat Tours. Back-country tours outside Everglades National Park in Everglades City area. Runs three 24-passenger airboats for 30-minute rides, 48-passenger pontoon boat for one-hour cruise. Boats are Coast Guard approved. *Tel. 813/695-4400 or in FL 800/282-9194. Phone for schedule. MC, V.*

Tram Tours **Wilderness Tram Tour.** Snake Bight is an indentation in the Florida Bay shoreline near Flamingo. You can go there aboard a 48-passenger screened tram on this two-hour tour through a mangrove forest and a coastal prairie to a 100-yard boardwalk over the mud flats at the edge of the bight. It's a good birding spot. Tram operates subject to mosquito, weather, and trail conditions. Driver has insect repellent on board. *Departs from Flamingo Lodge, tel. 305/253–2241 or 813/695–3101. Phone for schedule. Reservations accepted. AE, CB, DC, MC, V.*

Shark Valley Tram Tours. The trams take a new 15-mile loop road, which is two feet higher, has 200 culverts, and is considerably less flood prone when the summer rains come. Propane-powered trams travel into the interior, stopping at a 50-foot observation tower on the site of an oil well drilled in the 1940s. From atop the tower, you'll view the Everglades' vast "river of grass" sweeping south toward the Gulf of Mexico. The trams are covered but have open sides, so carry rain gear. *Tour location: Shark Valley entrance to Everglades National Park, 40 mi west of Miami off U.S. 41 (Tamiami Trail), tel. 305/221–8455. Open daily all year 9–4. Cost: $5 adults, $2.50 children, $4.50 senior citizens. Reservations recommended Dec.–Mar. No credit cards.*

Personal Guides **Flamingo Lodge Marina & Outpost Resort.** Captains of charter fishing boats are available to give individual tours out of Flamingo. Make reservations several weeks in advance through the marina store. *TW Services Inc., Everglades National Park, Box 428, Flamingo 33030, tel. 305/253–2241 or 813/695–3101. Nov. 1–Apr. 30 (except Christmas week). Cost: $215 a day, $140 a half day per person. AE, CB, DC, MC, V (see* Miami Guided Tours).

Important Addresses and Numbers

Tourist Information **South Dade Visitors Information Center.** *100 U.S. 1, Florida City 33034, tel. 305/245–9180. Open daily 8–5:30.*

Greater Homestead-Florida City Chamber of Commerce (650 U.S. 1, Homestead 33030, tel. 305/247–2332).

Emergencies Homestead, Florida City, and unincorporated Dade County use the same emergency number, 911. You can dial free from pay phones.

In the national parks, the rangers perform police, fire, and medical-emergency functions. Look for the rangers at park visitor centers and information stations, or phone the park switchboards: *Biscayne* (tel. 305/247–2044); *Everglades* (tel. 305/247–6211).

Hospitals **James Archer Smith Hospital.** 24-hour emergency room. *160 N.W. 13th St., Homestead, tel. 305/248–3232. Physician referral service, tel. 305/248–DOCS.*

Marine Phone Numbers **Biscayne National Park** (tel. 305/247–2044). Rangers staff Elliott Key Visitor Center and Adams Key Information Center around the clock and can call the mainland on ship-to-shore radio. Park headquarters on Convoy Point open daily 8–5.

Florida Marine Patrol. Law-enforcement arm of the Florida Department of Natural Resources. Boating emergencies: *24-hour tel. 305/325–3346.* Natural resource violations, including marine fishery laws, mangrove cuttings, manatee reports, filling of wetlands. 24-hour Resource Alert Hot Line: *tel. 800/342–1821, nonemergencies 305/325–3346.*

National Weather Service. National Hurricane Center office in Coral Gables supplies local forecasts. *Open Mon.–Fri. 7:30–5,* *tel. 305/665–0429. For 24-hr phone weather recording, tel. 305/661–5065.*

U.S. Coast Guard **Miami Beach Coast Guard Base** (tel. 305/535–4314 or 305/535–4315, VHF-FM Channel 16). Local marine emergencies, search-and-rescue, and reporting of navigation hazards.

Exploring Biscayne National Park

Numbers in the margin correspond with points of interest on the Everglades and Biscayne National Parks map.

Because 96% of Biscayne National Park's acreage is under water, you must take a boat ride to visit most of it and snorkel or scuba dive to appreciate it fully. If you don't have your own boat, a concessionaire will take you to the coral reefs 10 miles offshore. These dome-shape patch reefs—some the size of a student's desk, others as broad as a large parking lot—rely on the delicate balance of temperature, depth, light, and water quality that the park was created to maintain.

A diverse population of colorful fish flits through the reefs: angelfish, gobies, grunts, parrot fish, pork fish, wrasses, and many more.

From December through April, when the mosquito population is relatively quiescent, you can comfortably explore several of the mangrove-fringed barrier islands seven miles offshore. Tropical hardwood forests cloak the upper reaches of these fossilized coral reefs.

The list below describes the facilities at each of Biscayne National Park's visitor service areas, and also at the Metro-Dade County parks within the national park's boundaries.

❶ **Adams Key Information Station.** Boat dock, picnic area, rest rooms, short nature trail. Ranger station has ship-to-shore radio contact with mainland. Day use only.

❷ **Boca Chita Key.** Mark C. Honeywell, former president of Minneapolis' Honeywell Co., bought this island in 1937 and built the ornamental lighthouse, rainwater catchment cisterns, a wall, and other buildings of coral rock. There is a boat dock, picnic area, and rest rooms. Lighthouse open on occasion; ask rangers.

❸ **Convoy Point Information Station.** Park headquarters. Small visitor center and outdoor kiosk with bulletin boards. Launching ramp for canoes and small boats. Boardwalk over shallow water near shore to jetty and path along jetty. Picnic area. Dock where you board tour boats to reefs and Elliott Key. *At east end of North Canal Dr. (S.W. 328th St.), Homestead, tel. 305/247–2044. Open Dec.–Apr. weekdays 8–5, weekends 9–5:30; May–Nov. weekdays 10–4, weekends 10–6. Admission free.*

❹ **Elliott Key Visitor Center.** Indoor exhibit area on second floor displays coral, sponges, and sea-turtle shells on a "touching table" that children especially enjoy. A screened enclosure under the exhibit area houses picnic tables, bulletin boards, and a slide show. *Open Sat.–Sun. and holidays only 10–4.*

Sands Key. Back-country camping allowed; no facilities.

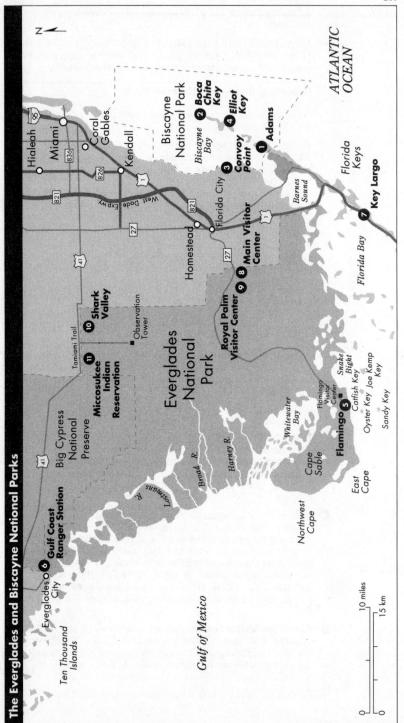

The Everglades and Biscayne National Parks

ATLANTIC OCEAN

Hialeah

Miami

Coral Gables

Kendall

Biscayne National Park

Biscayne Bay

2 Boca Chita Key

4 Elliot Key

1 Adams

3 Convoy Point

Barnes Sound

Florida Keys

Florida City

Homestead

Main Visitor Center

7 Key Largo

West Dade Expwy.

Everglades National Park

Florida Bay

Royal Palm Visitor Center

8

9

Shark Valley

10

Observation Tower

Tamiami Trail

Miccosukee Indian Reservation

11

Big Cypress National Preserve

Snake Bight

Flamingo Visitor Center

5 Flamingo

Catfish Key

Joe Kemp Key

Oyster Key

Sandy Key

Whitewater Bay

Cape Sable

East Cape

Northwest Cape

Broad R.

Harney R.

Lostmans R.

Gulf Coast Ranger Station

6

Everglades City

Ten Thousand Islands

Gulf of Mexico

10 miles

15 km

Exploring the Everglades

Winter is the best time to visit Everglades National Park. Temperatures and mosquito activity are moderate. Low water levels concentrate the resident wildlife around sloughs that retain water all year. Migratory birds swell the avian population.

Winter is also the busiest time in the park. Make reservations and expect crowds at Flamingo, the Main Visitor Center, and Royal Palm—the most popular visitor service areas.

In spring the weather turns increasingly hot and dry. After Easter, fewer visitors come, and tours and facilities are less crowded. Migratory birds depart, and you must look harder to see wildlife. Be especially careful with campfires and matches; this is when the wildfire-prone saw-grass prairies and pinelands are most vulnerable.

Summer brings intense sun and billowing clouds that unleash torrents of rain on the Everglades. Thunderstorms roll in almost every afternoon, bringing the park 90% of its annual 60-inch rainfall from June through October. Water levels rise. Wildlife disperses. Mosquitoes hatch, swarm, and descend on you in voracious clouds. It's a good time to stay away, although some brave souls do come to explore. Europeans constitute 80% of the summer visitors.

Summer in south Florida lingers until mid-October, when the first cold front sweeps through. The rains cease, water levels start to fall, and the ground begins to dry out. Wildlife moves toward the sloughs. Flocks of migratory birds and tourists swoop in, as the cycle of seasons builds once more to the winter peak activity.

Whenever you come, we urge you to experience the real Everglades by getting your feet wet—but most people who visit the park won't do that. Boat tours at Everglades City and Flamingo, a tram ride at Shark Valley, and boardwalks at several locations along the main park road allow you to see the Everglades with dry feet.

The list below describes the facilities at each of the park's visitor service areas.

⑤ Flamingo. Museum, lodge, restaurant, lounge, gift shop, marina, and campground. *Mailing address: Box 279, Homestead 33030, tel. 305/247-6211 (Park Service), tel. 305/253-2241 (Everglades Lodge). Visitor center open daily 8–5.*

⑥ Gulf Coast Ranger Station. Visitor center, where back-country campers pick up required free permits; exhibits; gift shop. *Follow Everglades National Park signs from Tamiami Trail (U.S. 41) south on Rte. 29, tel. 813/695-3311. Open daily winter 8–5, reduced hours in summer. Admission free.*

⑦ Key Largo Ranger Station. No exhibits. *98710 Overseas Hwy., Key Largo, tel. 305/852-5119. Not always staffed; phone ahead. Admission free.*

⑧ Main Visitor Center. Exhibits, film, bookstore, park headquarters. *11 mi west of Homestead on Rte. 9336, tel. 305/247-6211.*

Visitor Center open 8–5. Park open 24 hrs. Admission: $5 per car (good for 7 days); $3 per person on foot, bicycle, or motorcycle; senior citizens over 62 free.

❾ Royal Palm Visitor Center. Anhinga Trail boardwalk, Gumbo Limbo Trail through hammock, museum, bookstore, vending machines. *Tel. 305/247–6211. Open 8–4:30, with a half hour off for lunch.*

❿ Shark Valley. Tram tour, ¼-mile boardwalk, hiking trails, rotating exhibits, bookstore. *Box 42, Ochopee 33943, tel. 305/221–8776. Open daily 8:30–6. Admission: $3 per car, $1 per person on foot, bicycle, or motorcycle (good for 7 days); senior citizens over 62 free. Show Shark Valley admission receipt at Main Visitor Center and pay only the difference there.*

⓫ Miccosukee Indian Village. Near the Shark Valley entrance to Everglades National Park, the Miccosukee tribe operates an Indian village as a tourist attraction. You can watch Indian families cooking and making clothes, dolls, beadwork, and baskets. You'll also see an alligator-wrestling demonstration. The village has a boardwalk and a museum. *On Tamiami Trail (U.S. 41) 40 mi west of Miami. Mailing address: Box 440021, Miami 33144, tel. 305/223–8380. Open daily 9–5. Admission: $5 adults, $3.50 children. Airboat rides: $6 for 30-min trip to another Indian camp on an island in the heart of the Everglades.*

Shopping

Biscayne National Park   **Biscayne National Park Tour Boats.** T-shirts, snorkeling and diving gear, snacks, and information on Biscayne National Park are available at park headquarters north of the canal. A dive shop van with air compressor is parked south of the canal at Homestead Bayfront Park. *Tel. 305/247–2400. Open daily. Office open 8:30–5:30. AE, MC, V.*

Everglades National Park   **Flamingo Lodge Marina & Outpost Resort.** The gift shop sells mosquito repellent, Everglades guides, popular novels, T-shirts, souvenirs, and artwork (*see* Participant Sports). *Tel. 305/253–2241 or 813/695–3101. Open daily Nov.–Apr. 8–5. AE, CB, DC, MC, V.*

Florida City   **Robert is Here.** A remarkable fruit stand. Robert grows and sells (in season) any tropical fruit that will grow near Everglades National Park. *19200 Palm Dr. (S.W. 344th St.), tel. 305/246–1592. Open daily 8–7. No credit cards.*

Homestead   Homestead's main shopping streets are Homestead Boulevard (U.S. 1), Krome Avenue (Rte. 997), and Campbell Drive (S.W. 312th St., N.E. 8th St.). Shopping centers with major department stores are 10–20 miles north of Homestead along South Dixie Highway (U.S. 1).

Participant Sports

Most of the sports and recreational opportunities in Everglades National Park and Biscayne National Park are related in some way to water or nature study, or both. Even on land, be prepared to get your feet wet on the region's marshy hiking trails. In summer, save your outdoor activities for early or late in the day to avoid the sun's strongest rays and use a sunscreen. Carry mosquito repellent at any time of year.

Water Sports
Boating   Carry aboard the proper *NOAA Nautical Charts* before you
cast off to explore the waters of the parks. The charts cost
$12.50 each. They are sold at many marine stores in south Flor-
ida, at the Convoy Point Visitor Center in Biscayne National
Park, and in Flamingo Marina.

Waterway Guide (southern regional edition) is an annual publication of *Boating Industry Magazine*, which many boaters use
as a guide to these waters. Bookstores all over south Florida
sell it, or you can order it directly from the publisher. *Circula-
tion Department*, Waterway Guide, *850 Third Ave., New York,
NY 10022, tel. 800/233–3359 or 212/715–2600 in NY. Cost:
$18.95 plus $3 shipping and handling.*

Canoeing   The subtropical wilderness of southern Florida is a mecca for
flat-water paddlers. In winter, you'll find the best canoeing
that the two parks can offer. Temperatures are moderate, rainfall is minimal, and the mosquitoes are tolerable.

Before you paddle into the back country and camp overnight,
get a required free permit from the rangers in the park where
you plan to canoe (at Convoy Point, Elliott Key, and Adams Key
for Biscayne; at Everglades City or Flamingo for Everglades.
The Biscayne permit isn't valid for Everglades, and vice versa).

You don't need a permit for day-trips, but tell someone where
you're going and when you expect to return. Getting lost out
there is easy, and spending the night without proper gear can
be unpleasant, if not dangerous.

At Biscayne, you can explore five creeks through the mangrove
wilderness within 1½ miles of park headquarters at Convoy
Point.

Everglades has six well-marked canoe trails in the Flamingo
area, including the southern end of the 100-mile Wilderness
Waterway from Flamingo to Everglades City. North American
Canoe Tours in Everglades City runs a seven-hour shuttle
service to haul people, cars, and canoes 151 road-miles between
Everglades City and Flamingo.

The vendors listed below all rent aluminum canoes. Most have
17-foot Grummans. Bring your own cushions.

Biscayne National Park Tour Boats. At Convoy Point in Biscayne National Park. *Tel. 305/247–2400. Office open daily 8:30–
5:30. Cost: $5 per hr, $17.50 for 4 hrs, $22.50 per day. No
launch fee. AE, MC, V.*

Everglades National Park Boat Tours. Gulf Coast Ranger Station in Everglades City. *Tel. 813/695–2591, in FL 800/445–
7724. Open daily 8:30–4:30. Cost: $10 per half day, $15 per day;
Flamingo-Everglades City shuttle: $100. No credit cards.*

North America Canoe Tours at Glades Haven. This outfitter
rents canoes and runs guided Everglades trips approved by the
National Park Service. *800 S.E. Copeland Ave., Box 443,
Everglades City 33929, tel. 813/695–2746. Open daily 7 AM–9
PM; guided trips Nov. 1–Mar. 31. Canoes $18 the first day, $15
per day thereafter. No children under age 8 on guided tours. No
pets in park campsites. Reservations required. MC, V.*

Marinas   Listed below are the major marinas serving the two parks. The
dock masters at these marinas can provide information on other
marine services you may need.

Black Point Marina. A new 155-acre Metro-Dade County Park with a hurricane-safe harbor basin, five miles north of Homestead Bayfront Park. Facilities include storage racks for 300 boats, 178 wet slips, 10 ramps, fuel, a bait-and-tackle shop, canoe-launching ramp, power-boat rentals, and police station. Shrimp fleet docks at the park. At east end of Coconut Palm Drive (S.W. 248th St.). From Florida's Turnpike, exit at S.W. 112th Avenue, go two blocks north, and turn east on Coconut Palm Drive. *24775 S.W. 87th Ave., Naranja, tel. 305/258-4092. Open daily 6 AM-9 PM. AE, MC, V.*

Marine Management. At Black Point Marina. Rents 18–25-foot Well Craft. *Tel. 305/258-3500. Open daily Oct.–Mar. 8–5, Apr.–Sept. daily except Christmas. MC, V.*

Pirate's Spa Marina. Just west of Black Point Park entrance. Shrimp boats dock along canal. Facilities include boat hoist, wet and dry storage, fuel, bait and tackle, and boat rental. *8701 Coconut Palm Dr. (S.W. 248th St.), Naranja, tel. 305/257-5100. Open weekdays 7 AM–sundown, weekends open 6 AM. No credit cards.*

Flamingo Lodge Marina & Outpost Resort. Fifty-slip marina rents 40 canoes, 10 power skiffs, 5 houseboats, and several private boats available for charter. There are two ramps, one for Florida Bay, the other for Whitewater Bay and the back country. The hoist across the plug dam separating Florida Bay from the Buttonwood Canal can take boats up to 26 feet long. A small marina store sells food, camping supplies, bait and tackle, and automobile and boat fuel. *Tel. 305/253-2241 from Miami, 813/695-3101 from Gulf Coast. Open winter 6 AM–7 PM, summer 7–6. AE, DC, MC, V.*

Homestead Bait and Tackle. Facilities include dock and wet slips, fuel, bait and tackle, ice, boat hoist, and ramp. The marina is near Homestead Bayfront Park's tidal swimming area and concessions. *North Canal Dr., Homestead, tel. 305/245-2273. Open daily weekdays 7–5, weekends 7–6. MC, V.*

Diving
Dive Boats and Instruction

Biscayne National Park Tour Boats. This is the official concessionaire for Biscayne National Park. The center provides equipment for dive trips and sells equipment. Snorkeling and scuba trips include about 2½ hours on the reefs. *Reef Rover V*, an aluminum dive boat, carries up to 49 passengers. The resort course and private instruction lead to full certification. *Office and dive boat at Convoy Point. Mailing address: Box 1270, Homestead 33030, tel. 305/247-2400. Open daily 8:30–5:30. Snorkeling and scuba trips Tues. and Sat. 1–5; group charters any day. Cost: $19.52 snorkeling, $24.50 scuba. Reservations required. Children welcome. AE, MC, V.*

Pirate's Cove Dive Center. This is the last dive store north of the Keys, and it rents, sells, and repairs diving equipment. Staff teaches all sport-diving classes, including resort course, deep diver, and underwater photography. The center does not have a boat; instead they use dive boats at Homestead Bayfront Park. PADI affiliation. *116 N. Homestead Blvd., Homestead 33030, tel. 305/248-1808. Open all year weekdays 9–6:30, Sat. 8–6, Sun. 8–4. Open to 7:30 May–Sept., around the clock during annual 4-day sport divers' lobster season (in July or Aug.). AE, DC, MC, V.*

Fishing

The rangers in the two parks enforce all state fishing laws and a few of their own. Ask at each park's visitor centers for that park's specific regulations.

Swimming **Homestead Bayfront Park.** This saltwater atoll pool, adjacent to Biscayne Bay, which is flushed by tidal action, is popular with local family groups and teenagers. *N. Canal Dr., Homestead, tel. 305/247–1543. Open daily, 7 AM to sundown. Admission: $2 per car.*

Elliott Key. Boaters like to anchor off Elliott Key's 30-foot-wide sandy beach, the only beach in Biscayne National Park. It's about a mile north of the harbor on the west (bay) side of the key.

Bicycling and **Biscayne National Park.** Elliott Key's resident rangers lead in-
Hiking formal nature walks on a 1½-mile nature trail.

You can also walk the length of the seven-mile key along a rough path that developers bulldozed before the park was created.

Everglades National Park. Shark Valley's concessionaire has rental bicycles. You may ride or hike along the Loop Road, a 14-mile round-trip. Yield right of way to trams. *Shark Valley Tram Tours, Miami 33144, tel. 305/221–8455. Rentals daily 8:30–3, return bicycles by 4. Cost: $1.50 per hr. No reservations. No credit cards.*

Ask the rangers for *Foot and Canoe Trails of the Flamingo Area,* a leaflet that also lists bike trails. Inquire about water levels and insect conditions before you go. Get a free back-country permit if you plan to camp overnight.

Dining

Although the two parks are wilderness areas, there are restaurants within a short drive of all park entrances: between Miami and Shark Valley along the Tamiami Trail (U.S. 41), in the Homestead-Florida City area, in Everglades City, and in the Keys along the Overseas Highway (U.S. 1). The only food service in either park is at Flamingo in the Everglades.

The list below is a selection of independent restaurants on the Tamiami Trail, in the Homestead-Florida City area, and at Flamingo. Many of these establishments will pack picnic fare that you can take to the parks. (You can also find fast-food establishments with carryout service on the Tamiami Trail and in Homestead-Florida City.) The most highly recommended restaurants are indicated with a star ★.

Category	Cost*
Very Expensive	over $60
Expensive	$40–$60
Moderate	$20–$40
Inexpensive	under $20

per person without sales tax (6% in Florida), service, or drinks

The following credit card abbreviations are used: AE, American Express; CB, Carte Blanche; DC, Diners Club; MC, MasterCard; V, Visa.

Flamingo
American

Flamingo Restaurant. The view from this three-tier dining room on the second floor of the Flamingo Visitor Center will knock your socks off. Picture windows overlook Florida Bay, giving you a bird's-eye view (almost) of soaring eagles, gulls, pelicans, terns, and vultures. Try to dine at low tide when f-locks of birds gather on a sandbar just offshore. Specialties include a flavorful, mildly spiced conch chowder; teriyaki chicken breast; and pork loin roasted Cuban-style with garlic and lime. The tastiest choices, however, are the seafood. If marlin is on the dinner menu, order it fried so that the moisture and flavor of the dark, chewy meat are retained. *Picnic baskets available. Will cook fish you catch if you clean it at the marina. At Flamingo Visitor Center in Everglades National Park, Flamingo, tel. 305/253–2241 from Miami, 813/695–3101 from Gulf Coast. Dress: informal. Reservations required for dinner. AE, MC, V. Closed early May–mid-Oct. (The snack bar at the marina store stays open all year.) Moderate.*

Florida City
Mixed Menu
★

Richard Accursio's Capri Restaurant and **King Richard's Room.** This is where locals dine out—business groups at lunch, the Rotary Club each Wednesday at noon, and families at night. Specialties include pizza with light, crunchy crusts and ample toppings; mild, meaty conch chowder; mussels in garlic-cream or marinara sauce; Caesar salad with lots of cheese and anchovies; antipasto with a homemade, vinegary Italian dressing; pasta shells stuffed with rigatoni cheese, in tomato sauce; yellowtail snapper Française; and Key-lime pie with plenty of real Key lime juice. *935 N. Krome Ave., Florida City, tel. 305/247–1542. Dress: Capri informal, jacket and tie in King Richard's. Reservations advised. AE, MC, V. Closed Sun. except Mother's Day and Christmas. Inexpensive.*

Seafood
★

Captain Bob's. The Greek family who owns this restaurant has a list of more than 800 ways to prepare seafood. Specialties include snapper wrapped in phyllo dough in dill volute sauce; sea trout senator, with sliced almonds, mushrooms, scallions, and sherry-lemon butter sauce; and blackened wahoo. Save room for the Key-lime pie. *326 S.E. 1st Ave., Florida City, tel. 305/247–8988. Dress: informal. Reservations accepted. AE, CB, DC, MC, V. Inexpensive.*

Homestead
American

Downtown Bar and Outdoor Cafe. A south Florida interpretation of a New Orleans courtyard restaurant, complete with a wrought-iron gate and live entertainment. Specialties include Buffalo chicken wings (hot or mild) with celery and bleu-cheese dip; blackened or grilled dolphin or grouper from the Keys; raspberry nut cake; and refreshingly tart lemonade. *28 S. Krome Ave., Homestead, tel. 305/245–8266. Dress: informal. Reservations accepted. AE, MC, V. Closed Easter, Thanksgiving, Christmas. Inexpensive.*

Potlikker's. This southern country-style restaurant takes its name from the broth—*pot liquor*—left over from the boiling of greens. Live plants dangle from open rafters in the lofty pine-lined dining room. Specialties include fried Okeechobee catfish (all you can eat on Mondays), with Cajun spicing in a cornmeal-matzo-meal breading; roast turkey with homemade dressing, and at least 11 different vegetables to serve with lunch and dinner entrées. For dessert, try sweet potato pie. The Key-lime pie here is four inches tall and frozen; it tastes great if you dawdle over dessert while it thaws. *591 Washington Ave.,*

Homestead, tel. 305/248–0835. Dress: informal. No reservations. MC, V. Inexpensive.

Mexican **El Toro Taco.** The Hernandez family came to the United States from San Luis Potosí, Mexico, to pick crops. They opened this Homestead-area institution in 1971. They make salt-free tortillas and nacho chips with corn from Texas that they cook and grind themselves. The cilantro-dominated salsa is mild for American tastes; if you like more fire on your tongue, ask for a side dish of minced jalapeño peppers to mix in. Specialties include chile rellenos (green peppers stuffed with meaty chunks of ground beef and topped with three kinds of cheese), and chicken *fajitas* (chunks of chicken marinated in vinegar and spices, charbroiled with onions and peppers, and served with tortillas and salsa). Bring your own beer and wine; the staff will keep it cold for you and supply lemon for your Corona beer. *1 S. Krome Ave., Homestead, tel. 305/245–5576. Dress: informal. No reservations. No credit cards. Closed Christmas Day and Dec. 26. Inexpensive.*

Seafood **The Seafood Feast Restaurant.** Bob and Julie Cisco gave up a steak-house franchise to open this all-you-can-eat seafood buffet. It features shrimp, crabs' legs, frogs' legs, several choices of fish, salads, breads, and desserts. Specialties include Cajun-style crawfish from Louisiana, garlic crabs, steamed mussels, and oysters on the half shell (on request). *27835 S. Dixie Hwy., Naranja (3½ mi northeast of downtown Homestead), tel. 305/246–1445. Dress: informal. Reservations not accepted. No alcohol on premises. AE, MC, V. Moderate.*

Tamiami Trail **The Pit Bar-B-Q.** This place will overwork your salivary glands
American with its intense aroma of barbecue and blackjack oak smoke. You order at the counter, then come when called to pick up your food. Specialties include barbecued chicken and ribs with a tangy sauce, french fries, coleslaw, and fried biscuit, and catfish, frogs' legs, and shrimp breaded and deep-fried in vegetable oil. *16400 S.W. 8th St., Miami, tel. 305/226–2272. Dress: informal. No reservations. MC, V. Closed Christmas Day. Inexpensive.*

American Indian **Miccosukee Restaurant.** Murals with Indian themes depict women cooking and men engaged in a powwow. Specialties include catfish and frogs' legs breaded and deep-fried in peanut oil, Indian fry bread (a flour-and-water dough deep-fried in peanut oil), pumpkin bread, Indian burger (ground beef browned, rolled in fry bread dough, and deep-fried), and Indian taco (fry bread with chili, lettuce, tomato, and shredded cheddar cheese on top). *On Tamiami Trail, near the Shark Valley entrance to Everglades National Park, tel. 305/223–8380, ext. 332. Dress: informal. No reservations. AE, CB, DC, MC, V. Inexpensive.*

Floridian **Coopertown Restaurant.** A rustic 30-seat restaurant full of Floridiana, including alligator skulls, stuffed alligator heads, alligator accessories (belts, key chains, and the like). Specialties include alligator and frogs' legs, breaded and deep-fried in vegetable oil, available for breakfast, lunch, or dinner. *22700 S.W. 8th St., Miami, tel. 305/226–6048. Dress: informal. No reservations. No credit cards. Inexpensive.*

Lodging

Many visitors to the two parks stay in the big-city portion of Greater Miami and spend a day visiting one or both of the parks. For serious outdoors people, such a schedule consumes too much time in traffic and leaves too little time for nature-study and recreation.

At Shark Valley, due west of Miami, you have no choice. Only the Miccosukee Indians live there; there is no motel.

Southwest of Miami, Homestead has become a bedroom community for both parks. You'll find well-kept older properties and shiny new ones, chain motels, and independents. Prices tend to be somewhat lower than in the Miami area.

Hotel and motel accommodations are available on the Gulf coast at Everglades City and Naples.

The list below is a representative selection of hotels and motels in the Homestead area. Also included are the only lodgings inside either park. The rate categories in the list are based on the all-year or peak-season price; off-peak rates may be a category or two lower.

Category	Cost*
Very Expensive	over $120
Expensive	$90–$120
Moderate	$50–$90
Inexpensive	under $50

per room, double occupancy, without 6% state sales tax and modest resort tax

The following credit card abbreviations are used. AE, American Express; CB, Carte Blanche; DC, Diners Club; MC, MasterCard; V, Visa.

Flamingo Lodge Marina & Outpost Resort. This rustic low-rise wilderness resort, the only lodging inside Everglades National Park, is a strip of tentative civilization 300 yards wide and 1½ miles long. Accommodations are basic but attractive and well kept. An amiable staff with a sense of humor helps you become accustomed to alligators bellowing in the sewage-treatment pond down the road, raccoons roaming the pool enclosure at night, and the flock of ibis grazing on the lawn. The rooms have wood-paneled walls, contemporary furniture, floral bedspreads, and art prints of flamingos and egrets on the walls. Most bathrooms are near the door, so you won't track mud all over the room. Television reception varies with wind conditions and vultures perching on the antenna, but you don't come here to watch TV. All motel rooms overlook Florida Bay. The cottages are in a wooded area on the margin of a coastal prairie. Ask about reserving tours, skiffs, and canoes when you make reservations. *Box 428, Flamingo 33030, tel. 305/253–2241 from Miami, 813/695–3101 from Gulf Coast. 121 units with bath, including 102 motel rooms, 2 2-bath suites for up to 8 people, 17 kitchenette cottages (2 for handicapped guests). Facilities: screened outdoor freshwater swimming pool, restaurant,* *lounge, marina, marina store with snack bar, gift shop, coin laundry. AE, CB, DC, MC, V. Lodge, marina, and marina store open all year; restaurant, lounge, and gift shop closed May 1–Oct. 31. Moderate.*

Greenstone Motel. Centrally located low-rise motel, in downtown Homestead's Historic District, this place was built in 1960 and remodeled in 1987. Rooms decorated in earth tones, with photos of waves and seagulls over the beds, which are medium firm. The best rooms face south, overlooking a vest-pocket park with benches and shrubbery. The second floor balcony in front is a good vantage point to see the magnolia design in the pavement on the street below. *304 N. Krome Ave., Homestead 33030, tel. 305/247–8334. 24 rooms. Facilities: free HBO, coffee bar in lobby. AE, CB, DC, MC, V. Moderate.*

Holiday Inn. Low-rise motel on a commercial strip. The best rooms look out on the landscaped pool and adjoining Banana Bar. Rooms have contemporary walnut furnishings and firm, bouncy mattresses. *990 N. Homestead Blvd., Homestead 33030, tel. 305/247–7020 or 800/HOLIDAY. 139 rooms with bath. Facilities: outdoor freshwater swimming pool, restaurant and lounge with entertainment Wed.–Sat., poolside bar, radio and cable TV, massage shower heads. AE, CB, DC, MC, V. Moderate.*

Knights Inn. This low-rise motel opened in 1987 on a commercial strip next door to a McDonald's. Beds are a foot longer than normal, and the mattresses are firm. The inn is decorated in English half-timber style, inside and out. *401 U.S. 1, Florida City 33034, tel. 305/245–2800. 100 rooms, 11 fully equipped kitchenettes, 27 for handicapped guests. Facilities: outdoor freshwater swimming pool, free HBO and TV movies, free ice, free local phone calls, coffee bar in lobby, security at night. AE, CB, DC, MC, V. Moderate.*

Park Royal Inn. This low-rise motel on a commercial strip has rooms with rough wood walls, flower bedspreads, blue or gray carpet, gray chairs and dressers, and lamps with a shell or pelican design. No closet, very small clothes rack. *100 U.S. 1, Florida City 33034, tel. 305/247–3200 or 800/521–6004. 163-unit motel, including 1 efficiency apartment, 7 rooms for handicapped guests. Facilities: outdoor freshwater swimming pool, minirefrigerator in each room, color TV, phone. AE, CB, DC, MC, V. Moderate.*

Camping
Biscayne National Park

You can camp on designated keys seven miles offshore at primitive sites or in the back country. Carry all your food, water, and supplies onto the keys, and carry all trash off when you leave. Bring plenty of insect repellent. *Free. No reservations. No ferry or marina services. For back-country camping, obtain a required free permit from rangers at Adams Key, Convoy Point, or Elliott Key.*

Everglades National Park

All campgrounds are primitive, with no water or electricity. Come early to get a good site, especially in winter. Bring plenty of insect repellent. *Open all year. Check-out time 10 AM. Admission: $7 per site in winter, free in summer. Stay limited to 14 days Nov. 1–Apr. 30. Register at campground.*

Long Pine Key. 108 campsites, drinking water, sewage dump station.

Flamingo. 235 drive-in sites, 60 walk-in sites, drinking water, cold-water showers, and sewage dump station.

Back country. 34 designated sites, most with chickees (raised wood platforms with thatch roofs). All have chemical toilets. Carry all your food, water, and supplies in; carry out all trash. Get free permit from rangers at Everglades City or Flamingo. Permits issued for a specific site. Capacity and length of stay limited.

5 Fort Lauderdale

Introduction

If you think of Fort Lauderdale only as a spring-break mecca for collegians seeking sun, suds, and surf, your knowledge is both fragmentary and out of date. The 1960 film, *Where the Boys Are*, attracted hordes of young people to the city's beaches for more than two decades, but now the center of spring-break activity has shifted north to Daytona Beach.

Fort Lauderdale today emphasizes year-round family tourism focused on a wide assortment of sports and recreational activities, an extensive cultural calendar, artistic and historic attractions, and fine shopping and dining opportunities.

Sandwiched between Miami to the south and Palm Beach to the north along southeast Florida's Gold Coast, Fort Lauderdale is the county seat of Broward County. The county encompasses 1,197 square miles—17 square miles less than the state of Rhode Island. Broward County has 23 miles of Atlantic Ocean beach frontage, and it extends 50 miles inland to the west. A coastal ridge rising in places to 25 feet above sea level separates the coastal lowlands from the interior lowlands of the Everglades.

Broward County is named for Napolean Bonaparte Broward, Florida's governor 1905–09. His drainage schemes around the turn of the century opened much of the marshy Everglades region for farming, ranching, and settlement. In fact, the first successful efforts at large-scale Everglades drainage took place within Broward County's boundaries.

Fort Lauderdale's first known white settler, Charles Lewis, established a plantation along the New River in 1793. The city is named for a fort which Major William Lauderdale built at the river's mouth in 1838 during the Seminole Indian wars.

The area was still a remote frontier when Frank Stranahan arrived in 1892 to operate an overnight camp on the river. Stranahan began trading with the Indians in 1901 and built a store, which later became his residence. It's now a museum.

Fort Lauderdale incorporated in 1911 with just 175 residents, but it grew rapidly during the Florida boom of the 1920s. Today the city's population of 160,000 remains relatively stable, while suburban areas bulge with growth. Broward County's population is expected to exceed 1.35 million by 1990—more than double its 1970 population of 620,000. The county has become a haven for retirees; more than a third of the new arrivals are over the age of 55.

New homes, offices and shopping centers have filled in the gaps between older communities along the coastal ridge. Now they're marching west along I-75, I-595, and the Sawgrass Expressway, transforming the Everglades. Meanwhile, Fort Lauderdale is building skyscrapers downtown to cement its position as the county's financial and commercial hub.

Broward County is developing a concentration of clean high-technology industries, including computer manufacturing, data processing, and electronics. Port Everglades, a major deep-water seaport, handles refined petroleum products and general cargo. A cruise terminal at Port Everglades caters to luxury liners, leaving the mass-market cruise business to the Port of Miami.

To accommodate the traffic that comes with all this growth, the Florida Department of Transportation is expanding Broward County's road system. During 1990, construction on I–95 and I–595 threatens to create gridlock during rush hours. Tri-Rail, a tri-county commuter train running through Broward County from Miami to West Palm Beach, will take some cars off the highways, but you should still expect traffic delays and allow extra time to move around the county.

Even when you're stuck in traffic, you can still enjoy Broward County's near-ideal weather. The average temperature is 75 degrees (winter average 66 degrees, summer average 84 degrees). Rainfall averages 65 inches a year, with 60% of the total occurring in afternoon thunderstorms June–October. The warm, relatively dry winters help to give the county about 3,000 hours of sunshine a year.

Arriving and Departing by Plane

Airport **Fort Lauderdale-Hollywood International Airport (FLHIA),** four miles south of downtown Fort Lauderdale, is Broward County's major airline terminal. To get there off I–95, take the I–595 east exit to U.S. 1 and follow the signs to the airport entrance.

Between the Airport and Center City Broward Transit's bus route No. 1 operates between the airport and its main terminal at N.W. 1st Street and 1st Avenue in the center of Fort Lauderdale. The fare is 75 cents. Limousine service is available from *Yellow Airport Limousine Service* (tel. 305/527–8690) to all parts of Broward County. Fares range from $6 to $13 or more per person, depending on distance. Fares to most Fort Lauderdale beach hotels are in the $6–$8 range. Pickup points are at each of the new terminals.

Arriving and Departing by Car, Train, and Bus

By Car The access highways to Broward County from the north or south are Florida's Turnpike, I–95, U.S. 1, and U.S. 441; for a more scenic—and slower—drive, Rte. A1A, which generally parallels the beach area. The primary access road to Broward County from the west is Rte. 84.

By Train **Amtrak** provides daily service to Broward County, with stops at Hollywood, Fort Lauderdale, and Deerfield Beach. *Fort Lauderdale station, 200 S.W. 21st Terr., tel. 305/463–8251; reservations, tel. 800/872–7245.*
Tri-Rail, which connects Broward, Dade, and Palm Beach counties, has six stations in Broward. All stations are west of I–95; the location of the FLHIA station may change in 1990. *Tel. 305/728–8445 or 800/TRI-RAIL (in Dade, Broward, and Palm Beach counties).*

By Bus **Greyhound** Bus Lines (513 N.E. 3rd St., Ft. Lauderdale, tel. 305/764–6551 or 800/872–6242).

Getting Around

By Car In 1988 the Florida Department of Transportation (FDOT) began to build the last stage of the I–595/Port Everglades Expressway Project, which runs east-west through the middle of Broward County. By 1991, 15 interchanges will be improved and local roads will be linked to I–595, which follows the Rte. 84 corridor from I–75 east to the port.

At the same time, I–95 is being widened, disrupting north-south traffic for 46 miles from Yamato Road, in southern Palm Beach County, through Broward County to Rte. 836, in northern Dade County.

If you're driving into Florida, stop at a visitor center near the state line for a traveler advisory card on the current status of I–95 construction. Ask for current information on travel time and alternative routes.

FDOT officials urge you to take Florida's Turnpike or the Sawgrass Expressway through Broward County to avoid I–95. A new interchange at S.W. 10th Street in Deerfield Beach connects the Sawgrass Expressway directly to I–95. Other alternatives include crowded local roads such as A1A, U.S. 1, U.S. 441, and University Drive (Rte. 817).

Listen to radio traffic reports on the status of I–95 construction. Your hotel clerk should know which stations have them.

Try to avoid driving anywhere in Broward County—and especially on I–95—in the morning and evening rush hours (7–9 AM and 3–6 PM). Allow plenty of time to get where you're going, be patient, and stay calm. South Florida drivers can be among the world's worst.

FDOT has set up a consumer service organization to issue free publications and to provide traffic reports by phone. *Gold Coast Commuter Services, 6261 N.W. 6th Way, Suite 100, Fort Lauderdale, tel. 305/771–9500 or in FL 800/234–7433. Open 8–5.*

By Bus **Broward County Mass Transit** serves the entire county. The fare is 75 cents plus 10 cents for a transfer, with some bus routes starting as early as 5 AM; most end at 10 PM. Call for route information (tel. 305/357–8400). There are also special seven-day tourist passes for $8 that are good for unlimited use on all county buses. These are available at most major hotels.

By Taxi It's difficult to hail a taxi on the street; sometimes you can pick one up at a major hotel. Otherwise, phone ahead. Fares are not cheap; meters run at the rate of $2.20 for the first mile and $1.50 for each additional mile. The major company serving the area is **Yellow Cab** (tel. 305/565–5400).

By Water Taxi **Water Taxi** (tel. 305/565–5507) provides service along the Intracoastal Waterway between Port Everglades and Commercial Boulevard 10 AM–3 AM. The boats stop at 20 restaurants, hotels, and nightclubs; the fare is $2.50 one way.

Important Addresses and Numbers

Tourist Information The main office of the Greater Fort Lauderdale Convention & Visitors Bureau (tel. 305/765–4466) is at 500 E. Broward Boulevard, Suite 104. The office is open weekdays 8:30–5. A new information booth—the first of four—has been established at the Delta Terminal of the Fort Lauderdale International Airport and is open daily 10–10. Other communities in Broward County also have individual chambers of commerce, including Dania (Box 838, Dania 33004, tel. 305/927–3377), Hollywood (330 N. Federal Hwy., Hollywood 33020, tel. 305/776–1000), Oakland Park–Wilton Manors (181 N.E. 32nd Ct., Oakland Park 33334, tel. 305/564–8300), and Pompano Beach (2200 E. Atlantic Blvd., Pompano Beach 33062, tel. 305/941–2940).

Tickets Call **Ticketmaster** to order tickets for performing arts and sports events (tel. 800/446–3939 or tel. 305/523–3309).

Emergencies Dial 911 for **police** and **ambulance** in an emergency.

Poison Control (tel. 800/282–3171).

Hospitals. The following hospitals have a 24-hour emergency room: **Holy Cross Hospital** (4725 N. Federal Hwy., Fort Lauderdale, tel. 305/771–8000; physician referral, tel. 305/776–3223) and **Broward General Medical Center** (1 Corporate Plaza, Fort Lauderdale, tel. 305/355–4400; physician referral, tel. 305/466–2411).

24-Hour Pharmacies. Eckerd Drug (1385 S.E. 17th St., Fort Lauderdale, tel. 305/525–8173; and 154 University Dr., Pembroke Pines, tel. 305/432–5510). **Walgreens** (2855 Stirling Rd., Fort Lauderdale, tel. 305/981–1104; 71 S.E. 17th St., Fort Lauderdale, tel. 305/467–5448; and 289 S. Federal Hwy., Deerfield Beach, tel. 305/481–2993.)

24-Hour Doctors House Calls. Many Broward hotels use this referral service, which will send a physician to you. Medical services available include general medicine, pediatrics, and geriatrics. In-office dental referrals and translators are available. *3801 N. University Dr., Suite 507, Sunrise 33321, tel. 305/522–1522. MC, V.*

Telecommunications for the Hearing-Impaired. United Hearing and Deaf Services (4850 W. Oakland Park Blvd., Suite 207, Lauderdale Lakes, tel. 305/731–7208).

Guided Tours

The Voyager Sightseeing Train offers nine different tram tours, including a city tour of Fort Lauderdale. *600 Seabreeze Blvd., Fort Lauderdale, tel. 305/463–0401 (Broward County), tel. 305/944–4669 (Dade County).*

The *Jungle Queen,* built to resemble an old-time steamboat, travels day and night up the New River through the heart of Fort Lauderdale. Dinner cruises are available. The same company sends boats to Miami's Bayside Marketplace. All cruises leave from the Bahia Mar dock on Rte. A1A (*see* Hotels, below). *Tel. 305/462–5596 (Broward County), 305/947–6597 (Dade County).*

The *Paddlewheel Queen,* a flat-bottom luncheon and sightseeing cruise boat, visits major spots along Fort Lauderdale's Intracoastal Waterway. Four sailings daily. *2950 N.E. 30th St., a block south of Oakland Park Boulevard bridge, two blocks west of Rte. A1A, tel. 305/564–7659. AE, MC, V.*

Exploring Fort Lauderdale

Numbers in the margin correspond with points of interest on the Fort Lauderdale Area map.

Central Fort Lauderdale is diverse, picturesque, and surprisingly compact. Within a few blocks you'll find modern high-rise office buildings; a historic district with museums, restaurants and antique shops; a scenic riverfront drive; upscale shopping; and the only tunnel in Florida—all within two miles of the beach.

This tour begins on the beach at Las Olas Boulevard and Rte. A1A. Go north on Rte. A1A along **the beach,** with hotels, restaurants and shops on your left, the ocean on your right. Turn

❶ left at Sunrise Boulevard, then right into **Hugh Taylor Birch State Recreation Area.** Amid the 180-acre park's tropical greenery, you can stroll along a nature trail, picnic, and canoe. *3109 E. Sunrise Blvd., tel. 305/564–4521; concessions tel. 305/563–1714. Open 8–sundown. Admission: $1 per car and driver, 50¢ per passenger; (out of state): $2 per car and driver, $1 per passenger.*

Leaving the park, go south on Birch Road to Las Olas Boulevard, turn right, and cross the Intracoastal Waterway. You're

❷ now westbound through **The Isles,** Fort Lauderdale's most expensive and prestigious neighborhood, where the homes line a series of canals with large yachts beside the seawalls. When you reach the mainland, Las Olas becomes an upscale shopping street with Spanish-Colonial buildings housing high-fashion boutiques, jewelry shops, and art galleries. The heart of the **Las Olas Shopping District** is from S.E. 12th Avenue to S.E. 6th Avenue.

❸ Turn left on S.E. 6th Avenue, and visit **Stranahan House,** home of pioneer businessman Frank Stranahan. He arrived in 1892 and began trading with the Seminole Indians. In 1901 he built this building as a store, and later made it his home. Now it's a museum with many of the Stranahans' furnishings on display. *1 Stranahan Pl. (S.E. 6th Ave.), tel. 305/524–4736. Open Wed., Fri., Sat. 10–4. Admission: $3, $2 children under 12.*

Return to Las Olas Boulevard, go to S.W. 1st Avenue, and turn left beside the *News & Sun-Sentinel* building. Go a block south to New River Drive, where you can park and stroll a portion of

❹ the palm-lined **River Walk,** a linear park with walkways and sidewalk cafes along both banks of the New River. As part of a $44-million redevelopment program, Fort Lauderdale is improving and extending the River Walk. Unlike the Miami River, which carries a heavy load of commercial shipping, New River traffic is primarily recreational yachts and tour boats. This portion of New River Drive returns you to Las Olas Boulevard at S.W. 5th Avenue.

Turn left, and go to the **Museum of Art,** which features a major collection of works from the CoBrA (Copenhagen, Brussels, and Amsterdam) movement, plus American Indian, Pre-Columbian, West African, and Oceanic ethnographic art. Edward Larabee Barnes designed the museum building, which opened in 1986. *1 E. Las Olas Blvd., tel. 305/525–5500. Open Tues. 11–9, Wed.–Sat. 10–5, Sun. noon–5. Admission: $3.25*

Fort Lauderdale Area

Brooks Memorial
Causeway, **7**

Broward County
Museum of
Archaeology, **5**

Dania Jai-Alai
Palace, **12**

Davie, **18**

Flamingo Gardens, **19**

Gulfstream Park, **17**

Hillsboro Lighthouse, **11**

Hollywood Dog
Track, **16**

Hugh Taylor Birch State
Recreation Area, **1**

The Isles, **2**

Ocean World, **6**

Pompano Harness
Track, **9**

Quiet Waters Park, **10**

River Walk, **4**

Seminole Okalee Indian
Village, **15**

Six Flags Atlantis, **13**

Stranahan House, **3**

Swimming Hall of
Fame Museum, **8**

Topeekeegee Yugnee
Park, **14**

adults, $2.75 seniors, $1.25 students, free under 12. Free 1-hour highlight tours Tues. noon and 6:30 PM, Wed.–Sat. noon, Sun. 2 PM. Parking nearby in municipal garage.

⑤ Go west on Las Olas Boulevard to S.W. 1st Avenue, and stop at the **Broward County Museum of Archaeology.** Featured here are a 2,000-year-old skeleton of a Tequesta Indian girl, remains of Ice Age mammals, a diorama of Indian life, and information on archaeological techniques. Special shows display artifacts of African, pre-Columbian, and other cultures. *203 S.W. 1st Ave., tel. 305/525–8778. Open Tues.–Sat. 10–4, Sun. 1–4. Admission: $1 adults, 50¢ children and seniors.*

Take S.W. 1st Avenue north to S.W. 2nd Street, turn left, cross the Florida East Coast Railway tracks, and turn left onto S.W. 2nd Avenue. You're now in **Himmarshee Village,** an eight-square-block historic district. Park and walk to explore several fascinating museums.

The **Fort Lauderdale Historical Society Museum** surveys the city's history from the Seminole Indian era to World War II. A model in the lobby depicts old Fort Lauderdale. The building also houses a research library and a bookstore. *219 S.W. 2nd Ave., tel. 305/463–4431. Open Tues.–Sat. 10–4, Sun. 1–4. Admission by donation.*

The **Discovery Center** includes a science museum in the three-story **New River Inn,** Fort Lauderdale's first hotel, and a pioneer residence museum in the restored **King-Cromartie House.** The Discovery Center Museum is a child-oriented place with hands-on exhibits that explore optical illusions and bend rays of light, an insect zoo, a glass-front beehive, a loom, a computer center, and a small planetarium. *229 and 231 S.W. 2nd Ave., tel. 305/462–4115. Open Tues.–Fri. 2–5, Sat. and school holidays 10–5, Sun. 1–5. Admission (includes both museums): $3, under 3 free.*

A brick drive between the King-Cromartie House and the New River Inn brings you one block west to S.W. 3rd Avenue. On your left is the **Bryan House,** a 1904 dwelling which is now a restaurant.

Go north on S.W. 3rd Avenue past an assortment of antique shops and restaurants in some old commercial buildings that are also part of the Himmarshee Village historic district. At Broward Boulevard, turn right and go east to Federal Highway (U.S. 1). Turn right and go south through the **Henry E. Kinney Tunnel,** named for a founder of Fort Lauderdale; it dips beneath Las Olas Boulevard and the New River.

⑥ Continue south on Federal Highway to S.W. 17th Street, then turn left. About a mile east is the entrance to **Ocean World.** Continuous shows daily feature trained dolphins and sea lions. Display tanks hold sharks, sea turtles, alligators, and river otters. You can feed and pet a dolphin here. *1701 S.E. 17th St., tel. 305/525–6611. Open 10–6, last show starts 4:15. Admission: $8.95 adults, $6.95 children 4–12, under 4 free. Boat tour admission: $5 adults, $4 children 4–12, under 4 free.*

⑦ Go east on S.E. 17th Street across the **Brooks Memorial Causeway** over the Intracoastal Waterway, and bear left onto Seabreeze Boulevard (Rte. A1A). You'll pass through a neighborhood of older homes set in lush vegetation before emerging at the south end of Fort Lauderdale's beachfront strip. On your left at **Bahia Mar Resort & Yachting Center,** novelist John McDonald's fictional hero, Travis McGee, is honored with a plaque at the marina where he allegedly docked his houseboat (*see* Lodging). *801 Seabreeze Blvd., tel. 305/764–2233 or 800/ 327–8154.*

8 Three blocks north, visit the **Swimming Hall of Fame Museum,** featuring photos, medals, and other souvenirs from major swimming events around the world. Included are memorabilia from Johnny Weissmuller, Mark Spitz, and other swimming champions. An Olympic-size pool hosts special events and is open to the public for swimming at other times. *501 Seabreeze Blvd., museum tel. 305/462–6536, pool tel. 305/523–0994. Open Mon.–Sat. 10–5, Sun. 11–4. Museum admission: $4 adults, $2 children 6–21 and seniors, $10 family. Pool admissions: $3 nonresident adults, $1.50 nonresident students.*

This concludes the central Fort Lauderdale tour. To return to the starting point, continue north on Seabreeze Boulevard to Las Olas Boulevard.

Exploring North Beach

The northeast section of Broward County includes the communities of Pompano Beach, Sea Ranch Lakes, Lighthouse Point, Deerfield Beach, and Hillsboro Beach.

9 Exit I–95 at Atlantic Boulevard and go west to Power Line Road, which will lead you to the popular **Pompano Harness Track.** The Top 'O The Park restaurant overlooks the finish line. Post time: 7:30; call for dates, tel. 305/972–2000.

10 A unique water skiing cableway is at **Quiet Water Park,** just south of the racetrack, on Power Line Road. **Ski Rixen** offers lessons for beginners, plus skis and life vests. A cable pulls the skiers. If you're skilled enough, there are all sorts of variations to the two-hand, two-ski way of skimming across the water. *Tel. 305/421–3133. Open weekdays 10–sunset, weekends 9:30– sunset. Admission: weekdays free, weekends 50 cents. Children under 5 free at all times.*

11 Take Hillsboro Boulevard east to Rte. A1A, turn right, and go south to Hillsboro Beach and the **Hillsboro Lighthouse,** a major historic landmark since 1907 and one of the most powerful lighthouses in the United States. It marks the eastern tip of the Hillsboro inlet, which provides easy access to the ocean from the Intracoastal Waterway.

Exploring Southern Broward

In southern Broward County, an exploration can include native Indian crafts and lifestyles, high-stakes pari-mutuel wagering, and a unique natural park, all within the same driving loop.

12 Start with the **Dania Jai-Alai Palace** (301 E. Dania Beach Blvd., Dania, tel. 305/428–7766), offering one of the fastest games on the planet from early November through April.

13 Take Dania Beach Boulevard west to U.S. 1, turn left, go south to Sterling Road, turn right, and go west to **Atlantis,** one of the world's largest water-theme parks. It has 2 million gallons of water in 45 pools and water slides up to 7 stories high, plus seven amusement rides, and water ski and diving shows. Highlights include a wave pool and an activity pool with trollies, slides, and rope ladders. Riders on Thunderball, the steepest water slide, reach speeds near 40 mph. The park sets minimum and maximum height requirements for participants in some activities. *2700 Stirling Rd., Box 2128, Hollywood, tel. 305/926–1000. Summer hours 10 AM–10 PM; phone for hours at other times of year. Admission: $11.95 adults, $4.95 seniors over 55, $9.95 children 3–11.*

⑭ Take Dania Beach Boulevard west to I–95, and go south to the Sheridan Street exit, then west to **Topeekeegee Yugnee Park.** Rentals include sailboats, Windsurfers, paddleboats, and canoes. *Open daily 8–8. Admission weekends and holidays: $1 car and driver, 50 cents each passenger, children under 5 free, tel. 305/961–4430.*

⑮ Take Sheridan Street west to U.S. 441/Rte. 7, turn right, and go north through the **Seminole Okalee Indian Village,** a reservation of the never-conquered Seminole Indian tribe. The Indians sell native arts and crafts and run a high-stakes bingo parlor (4150 N. Rte. 7, tel. 305/961–5140 or 305/961–3220). Three bingo games daily; call recording for information. Continue north to **Anhinga Indian Museum and Art Gallery,** where Joe Dan and Virginia Osceola display a collection of artifacts from the Seminoles and other American Indian tribes. They also sell contemporary Indian art and craft objects. *5791 S. Rte. 7, tel. 305/581–8411. Open daily 9–6. V.*

⑯ Take U.S. 441/Rte. 7 south to Pembroke Road and go east to Federal Highway to the **Hollywood Dog Track** (831 S. Federal Highway, Hallandale, tel. 305/454–7000). Call for race dates.

⑰ Take Federal Highway south to **Gulfstream Park Race Track** (901 S. Federal Hwy., tel. 305/454–7000), home of the Florida Derby, one of the southeast's foremost horse racing events. Call for race dates.

Exploring Inland

Between the coastal cities and the watery wilderness of the Everglades, urban sprawl is rapidly devouring Broward County's citrus groves and cow pastures. If you go inland, you can still find vestiges of the county's agricultural past.

⑱ The **Davie Rodeo Complex** at Orange Drive and Davie Road (6591 S.W. 45th St., Davie 33314, tel. 305/797–1166) holds rodeos in March and December. Just north on Davie Road is the **Buehler Planetarium,** where star-studded skies are on view regardless of the weather. *On the Central Campus of Broward Community College, 3501 S.W. Davie Rd., tel. 305/475–6680 (recording) or 305/475–6681. Main feature Sat. 3 and 8:30, family show Fri. 7, Sat. 1:30. Admission: $2.50 adults, $1.50 children and seniors. Reservations required.*

Take Davie Road south past Orange Drive, cross the South New River Canal, and turn right on Griffin Road. Go west to **Spykes Grove & Tropical Gardens,** where the entire family can hop aboard a tractor-pulled tram for a 15-minute tour of working citrus groves. *7250 Griffin Rd., tel. 305/583–1987. Tours hourly. Admission free. Open daily Oct.–June 9–5:30.*

⑲ Head west on Griffin Road and turn right onto Flamingo Road to **Flamingo Gardens.** There are crocodiles, alligators, monkeys, pink flamingoes, and other exotic birds, along with a petting zoo, a mini botanical garden, 60 acres of orange groves, antique car and historical museums, and a tram ride. *3750 Flamingo Rd., tel. 305/473-2955. Open daily 9-5:30. Admission: $6.50 adults, $3.25 children 4-14.*

Return to Griffin Road and go west until the road ends at the edge of the Everglades. There you'll find **Everglades Holiday Park and Campground,** which offers a 45-minute narrated airboat tour and an alligator-wrestling show featuring Seminole Indians. The park has a 100-space campground that accommodates recreational vehicles and tents. *21940 Griffin. Rd., Ft. Lauderdale 33332, tel. 305/434-8111 (Broward County), 305/621-2009 (Miami). Tour: $11 adults, $5.50 children. MC, V.*

Fort Lauderdale for Free

Manatees During the winter, manatees frolic in the warm-water discharge from Florida Power & Light Company's Port Everglades power plant. The massive marine mammals, which may be 15 feet long and weigh three-quarters of a ton, are susceptible to cold and congregate around the outfall when the temperature in local waters falls below 68 degrees.

An observation deck at the plant's intake pipe is open to the public, without charge, at all times. There you may see angelfish, reef fish, and sea turtles as well as manatees. Take Rte. 84 east to its end inside the port, turn right at Eisenhower Boulevard, and look on your right near some railroad tracks for the observation deck and a nearby parking area.

One weekend a year, usually in late January, FP&L invites the public onto the plant grounds for a closer look at the manatees. Hourly viewings, film showings. *For schedule information, phone the Broward Parks & Recreation Division's recorded special-events number, tel. 305/563-PARK, or the administrative office, tel. 305/357-8100.*

What to See and Do with Children

Butterfly World. This attraction in Tradewinds Park South is a screened-in tropical rainforest on 2.8 acres of land, where thousands of caterpillars pupate and emerge as butterflies. Up to 150 species flit through the shrubbery. Many are so tame they will land on you. Best time to go is in the afternoon; school groups fill the place in the mornings. *3600 W. Sample Rd., Coconut Creek, tel. 305/977-4400. Open Mon.-Sat 9-5, Sun. 1-5. Admission: $6 adults, $4 children 3-12 and senior citizens.*

Shopping

Shopping Districts **Major malls:** *Galleria Mall* on Sunrise Boulevard, just west of the Intracoastal Waterway, occupies more than one million square feet and includes Neiman-Marcus, Lord & Taylor, Saks Fifth Avenue, and Brooks Brothers (open 10-9 Mon.-Sat., noon-5:30 Sun.). *Oceanwalk* in the Hollywood Beach Hotel (101 N. Ocean Dr., Hollywood) is in a seashore environment with shops, restaurants, food, and entertainment. The building is a historic landmark.
Antiques: More than 75 dealers line U.S. 1 (Federal Hwy.) in

Dania, a half mile south of the Fort Lauderdale International
Airport and a half mile north of Hollywood. Open 10–5 every
day but Sunday. Exit Griffin Road East off I–95.
Boutiques and Specialty Shops: *Las Olas Boulevard.* From S.E.
5th Avenue to a block east of the Himmarshee Canal. A tree-
lined boulevard with a divided grassy median and bricked
crosswalks, with some of the finest shops in Fort Lauderdale.

Beaches

The Fort Lauderdale area boasts an average temperature of
75.5 degrees and 25 miles of oceanfront beach. Parking is readily available, often at parking meters. At the southern end of
Broward County, **John U. Lloyd Beach State Recreation Area**
(6503 N. Ocean Dr., Dania) offers a beach for swimmers and
sunners, but also 251 acres of mangroves, picnic facilities, fishing, and canoeing. *Open 8 AM–sunset. Park tel. 305/923–2833.
Admission: nonresident $2 car and driver, $1 per passenger.
Concessions tel. 305/922–7320. Open: weekdays 9–3, weekends
9–4. Canoes not rented at low tide.*

Throughout Broward County, each municipality along the Atlantic has its own public beach area. Hollywood also has a 2.5-
mile boardwalk, edged with shops and eateries. Dania, Pompano Beach, Deerfield Beach, and Lauderdale-by-the-Sea have
fishing piers in addition to the beaches. The most crowded portion of beach in this area is along the **Fort Lauderdale "Strip,"**
which runs from Las Olas Boulevard north to Sunrise Boulevard.

In past years, there have been some serious oil spills and
dumpages by freighters and tankers at sea, and the gunk has
washed ashore in globules and become mixed with the beach
sand. The problem has been somewhat eased, but some hotels
still include a tar-removal packet with the toilet amenities. If
you're concerned, ask at the desk of your hotel or motel.

Participant Sports

Biking Bicycling is popular throughout Greater Fort Lauderdale.
Young children should ride accompanied by their parents because of heavy traffic and older drivers who have difficulty in
seeing children on low bicycles. Some south Florida auto drivers resent bike riders. Ride defensively to avoid being pushed
off the road.

Diving Good diving can be enjoyed within 20 minutes of shore along
Broward County's 25-mile coast. Among the most popular of
the county's 80 dive sites is the two-mile-wide, 23-mile-long
Fort Lauderdale Reef.

South of Port Everglades Inlet, experienced divers can explore
Barracuda and Hammerhead reefs. North of the port, three
parallel coral reefs extend most of the way to the Palm Beach
County line. The reef closest to shore comes within 100 yards of
the beach a block north of Commercial Boulevard; the most dis-
tant is in 100 feet of water about a mile offshore. Snorkelers and
beginning divers should stay on the first reef.

Dive Boats and All **Force E** stores rent scuba and snorkeling equipment. In-
Instruction struction is available at all skill levels. Dive boat charters are
available. *2700 E. Atlantic Blvd., Pompano Beach, tel. 407/943–*

3488 or 800/527–8660 (answered by West Palm Beach store). Open winter weekdays 10–8:30, Sat. 8–7, Sun. 8–5; summer weekdays 8 AM–9 PM, Sat. 8–2, Sun. 8–5. 2104 W. Oakland Park Blvd., Oakland Park, tel. 305/735–6227. Hours same as Pompano Beach store.

Spas If you watch "Lifestyles of the Rich and Famous" on TV, you'll recognize the names of Greater Fort Lauderdale's two world-famous spas, the Bonaventure Resort & Spa and Palm-Aire Spa Resort. At each resort, women comprise 75%–80% of the spa clientele.

Both resorts offer single-day spa privileges to non-guests. Price and availability of services vary with seasonal demand; resort guests have priority. At each resort, day users may receive a body massage, exercise class, facials, herbal wrap, spa-cuisine lunch, and other spa facilities and services.

Bring your own sneakers and socks. The spa provides everything else you'll need. Each spa will help you design a personal exercise-and-diet program tied to your lifestyle at home. If you already have an exercise program, bring it with you. If you have a medical problem, bring a letter from your doctor.

Bonaventure Resort & Spa (250 Racquet Club Rd., Fort Lauderdale, tel. 305/389–3300) is part of a hotel and convention complex near the Sawgrass Expressway interchange with I–595 in western Broward County. Free caffeine-free herbal teas served in the morning, fresh fruit in the afternoon. Staff nutritionist follows American Heart Association and American Cancer Society guidelines, and can accommodate macrobotic and vegetarian diets. Full-service beauty salon open to the public.

Palm-Aire Spa Resort (2501 Palm-Aire Drive N., Pompano Beach, tel. 305/968–2700 or 800/327–4960). This health, fitness and stress-reduction spa offers exercise activities, personal treatments, and calorie-controlled meals. Fifteen minutes from downtown Fort Lauderdale.

Spectator Sports

Baseball The New York Yankees hold spring training in 7,000-seat Lockhart Stadium (5301 N.W. 12th Ave., Fort Lauderdale, tel. 305/776–1921).

Rugby The Fort Lauderdale Knights play rough and ready on the green at Holiday Park. *Off of Federal Hwy., 2 blocks south of Sunrise Blvd., Fort Lauderdale, tel. 305/561–5263 for a recorded message. Games Sat. 2 PM Sept.–Apr. Admission free.*

Dining

The list below is a representative selection of independent restaurants in Fort Lauderdale and Broward County, organized geographically, and by type of cuisine within each region of the county. Unless otherwise noted, they serve lunch and dinner.

The most highly recommended restaurants are indicated by a star ★.

The following credit card abbreviations are used: AE, American Express; CB, Carte Blanche; DC, Diners Club; MC, MasterCard; and V, Visa.

Category	Cost*
Very Expensive	over $55
Expensive	$35–$55
Moderate	$15–$35
Inexpensive	under $15

per person, excluding drinks, service, and 6% sales tax

American   **Boodles.** In Sheraton Design Center Hotel, you may dine on a "porch" with a fountain, overlooking the lobby; or in a wine room, an intimate "plum room," or the main dining room. Specialties include a spicy-sweet alligator chili; Boodles's house salad of field greens with goat cheese, sun-dried tomatoes, and vinaigrette dressing; and mesquite-grilled salmon with basil Key-lime butter. *1825 Griffin Rd., tel. 305/920–3500. Dress: informal. Reservations accepted. Nonsmoking seating available. AE, CB, DC, MC, V. Expensive.*

★   **Cafe Max.** As you enter Cafe Max, you're greeted by the aroma of fragrant spices issuing from the open theater kitchen. The decor includes art deco-style black wood chairs, original art work, and cut flowers. Booth seating is best; the tables are quite close together. Owner-Chef Oliver Saucy combines the best of new American cuisine with traditional *escoffier* cooking. Specialties include Anaheim chili peppers stuffed with Monterey Jack cheese; mushroom duxelles served with goat-cheese sauce; duck and smoked mozzarella ravioli with sun-dried tomatoes and basil butter; soft-shell crab with fresh tomato-jicama relish; and grilled veal chops. Daily chocolate dessert specials include hazelnut chocolate capuccino torte and white-chocolate mousse pie with fresh raspberries. Other desserts include fresh fruit sorbets and homemade ice cream served with sauce *Anglais* and fresh raspberries. *2601 E. Atlantic Blvd., Pompano Beach, tel. 305/782–0606. Jacket preferred. Dinner only. Reservations advised. AE, DC, MC, V. Expensive.*

The Garden. Coral-rock walls, earth-tone rattan furnishings, and terraced seating gives this restaurant in the Bonaventure Resort and Spa an inviting, outdoorsy appearance. It's a relaxed family restaurant, catering primarily to a resort clientele but welcoming others as well. Specialties include seafood salad appetizer (shrimp, crab, scallops) served with mustard sauce on a bed of greens, veal Milanese (medallion of veal sautéed in egg batter, with a sauce containing tomatoes, ham, mushrooms, dill pickles, and cream), and tall cheesecake (chocolate, marble, blueberry, strawberry, and plain). *250 Racquet Club Rd., tel. 305/389–3300 or 800/327–8090. Dress: informal. Reservations not accepted. AE, DC, MC, V. Moderate.*

Shorty's Bar-B-Q. A clone of the original Shorty's on U.S. 1 in Miami, opened at the request of a loyal Broward following. The food's the same, and the decor resembles the original log cabin with long wooden tables—but the new building is air-conditioned! *5989 S. University Dr., Davie 33028, tel. 305/680–9900. Reservations not accepted. Dress: informal. Closed Christmas and Thanksgiving. No credit cards. Inexpensive.*

Continental   **Down Under.** When Al Kocab and Leonce Picot opened Down Under in 1968, the Australian government sent them a boomer-

Fort Lauderdale Area Dining and Lodging

Lodging

Bahia Mar Resort & Yachting Center, **11**
Bonaventure Resort and Spa, **6**
Casa Alhambra, **10**
De Vito by the Sea, **17**
Fort Lauderdale Marriott Hotel & Marina, **12**
Marriott's Harbor Beach Resort, **14**

Palm-Aire Spa/Resort, **2**
Pier 66 Hotel and Marina, **13**
Riverside Hotel, **8**
Royce Resort Hotel, **4**
Sheraton Design Center Hotel, **15**
Westin Cyprus Creek, **3**

Dining

Boodles, **15**
Cafe Max, **1**
Casa Vecchia, **9**
Down Under, **5**
The Garden, **6**
Renaissance, **6**
Shirttail Charlie's, **7**
Shorty's Bar-B-Q, **16**
Spa Restaurant, **6**

ang as a gift. The name actually describes the restaurant's location, below a bridge approach at the edge of the Intracoastal Waterway. The two-story structure was built to look old, with walls of antique brick deliberately laid off-plumb. Specialties include fresh Belon oysters and littleneck clams from Maine; Florida blue crab cakes; Brutus salad (Down Under's version of Caesar salad); fresh Idaho trout lightly sautéed and topped with Florida blue crab and Hollandaise sauce; and Florida lobster and stone crab in season. Desserts include Key-lime pie with meringue, crème brûlée, and pecan squares. *3000 E. Oakland Park Blvd., tel. 305/563–4123. Jackets preferred. Reservations advised. AE, CB, MC, V. Expensive.*

Italian **Casa Vecchia.** This old house (*casa vecchia*) stands beside the
★ Intracoastal Waterway, surrounded by a formal garden where you can watch boats cruise past. The garden also grows herbs which flavor the restaurant's fare. Casa Vecchia was built in the late 1930s. Diners are encouraged to roam through the building to admire antique furnishings and original statuary and paintings. Spanish tiles decorated Casa Vecchia's walls and many tabletops. Specialties include canneloni, fettuccine funghi (mushroom-flavored noodles tossed with butter, basil, and porcini), and *granchio* Casa Vecchia (Maryland lump crabmeat served with scallions, a splash of cognac, and red linguine). Desserts include full-flavored sorbets of fresh seasonal fruit prepared on the premises and poached pear with mascarpone cheese. *209 N. Birch Rd., tel. 305/463–7575. Jacket preferred. Reservations advised. AE, CB, MC, V. Expensive.*

Natural **Spa Restaurant.** In the Bonaventure Resort and Spa, this 70-seat restaurant caters primarily to spa guests. Menus state the number of calories in each item. Tropical pastels and white rattan furniture seem to match the healthful, low-calorie natural fare prepared in a separate kitchen by chefs attuned to special dietary needs. Specialties include cream of cauliflower soup, a broad variety of salads, medallions of turkey Santa Barbara with a tangy-sweet apricot-lingonberry sauce, peach cobbler topped with granola, and strawberry-rhubarb crustless pie. *250 Racquet Club Rd., tel. 305/389–3300 or 800/327–8090. Dress: informal. Breakfast, lunch, dinner. Reservations advised. Nonsmoking seating available. Closed last 2 weeks in Aug. AE, DC, MC, V. Moderate.*

Seafood **Shirttail Charlie's.** You can watch the world go by from the out-
★ door deck or upstairs dining room of Shirttail Charlie's. Boats glide up and down the New River. Sunday–Thursday diners may take a free 45-minute after-dinner cruise on the 24-passenger launch *Cavalier*, which chugs upriver past an alleged Al Capone speakeasy. Charlie's itself is built to look old, with 1920s blue-and-white five-sided tile on a floor that leans toward the water. The menu reflects Caribbean cuisine. Specialties include an alligator-tail appetizer served with Tortuga sauce (a béarnaise with turtle broth and sherry); conch served four ways; crab balls; shark bites; blackened tuna with Dijon mustard sauce; crunchy coconut shrimp with a not-too-sweet piña colada sauce; and a superbly tart Key-lime pie with graham-cracker-crust. *400 S.W. 3rd Ave., tel. 305/463–3474. Jacket preferred upstairs, casual downstairs. Reservations advised upstairs. AE, MC, V. Moderate.*

Seafood **Renaissance Seafood Grill.** This gourmet restaurant, in the Bonaventure Resort and Spa, 5-star-rated by the Confrerie de la Chaine des Rotisseurs, features mesquite-grilled seafood and California cuisine with Florida adaptations. You dine in a rain forest, with views of a waterfall surrounded by palm and fiscus trees, ferns and blooming flowers, and a pond with variegated foot-long carp. Specialties include chilled cream of avocado and cucumber soup; hot cream of popleno pepper soup with chunks of brie cheese; a spinach-and-beansprout salad with pickled eggs and rosemary vinaigrette dressing; wholewheat fettuccine sautéed with chunks of Maine lobster, scallops, and chives in a lobster sauce; mako shark in a lime-parsley-butter sauce. *250 Racquet Club Rd., tel. 305/389–3300 or 800/327–8090. Jacket preferred. Dinner only. Reservations required. AE, DC, MC, V. Expensive.*

Lodging

In Fort Lauderdale, Pompano Beach, and the Hollywood-Hallandale area, dozens of hotels line the Atlantic Ocean beaches. You can find a full spectrum of accommodations, from economy motels to opulent luxury hotels with posh, pricey suites.

Inland, the major chain hotels along I–95 north and south of the airport cater primarily to business travelers and overnight visitors en route to somewhere else.

Wherever you plan to stay in Broward County, reservations are a good idea throughout the year. Tourists from the northern United States and Canada fill up the hotels from Thanksgiving through Easter. In summer, southerners and Europeans create a second season that's almost as busy.

The list below is a representative selection of hotels and motels, organized geographically. The rate categories in the list are based on the all-year or peak-season price; off-peak rates may be a category or two lower.

The most highly recommended hotels are indicated by a star ★.

Category	Cost*
Very Expensive	over $120
Expensive	$90–$120
Moderate	$50–$90
Inexpensive	under $50

All prices are for a standard double room, excluding 6% state sales tax and nominal tourist tax.

The following credit card abbreviations are used: AE, American Express; CB, Carte Blanche; DC, Diners Club; MC, MasterCard; V, Visa.

Bahia Mar Resort & Yachting Center (a Clarion hotel). Naval architect J. H. Phillpot designed the Bahia Mar marina in 1949; it was the first in Fort Lauderdale to accommodate boats longer than 30 feet. Travis McGee, fictional hero of mystery author John McDonald, "lived" at Bahia Mar aboard a boat called *The Busted Flush.* Two months after McDonald died in December 1986, the Literary Landmark Association dedicated a plaque at slip F-18 in memory of McDonald and McGee. Ironically, McDonald never stayed on the premises. Marina wing rooms are furnished in tropical decor; tower rooms have a soft blue-white color scheme. Upper floors of the 16-story tower provide spectacular views of the ocean and Intracoastal Waterway. *801 Seabreeze Blvd., Fort Lauderdale 33316, tel. 305/764-2233 or 800/327-8154. 298 rooms with bath, including 9 suites, 30 non-smokers rooms, 3 rooms for handicapped guests. Facilities: outdoor freshwater swimming pool, 350-slip marina where 15 deep-sea-fishing charter boats dock, power-boating and sailing instruction, dive boat and shop, 4 tennis courts, conference center, shopping arcade, restaurants. AE, CB, DC, MC, V. Expensive.*

Bonaventure Resort and Spa. Mid-rise resort with spa and conference center on 1,250 acres, 17 miles west of Fort Lauderdale. The hotel lobby is light and airy, with colorful angelfish and a cuddly-looking sand shark in a large aquarium just inside the front entrance. All guest rooms are in nine four-story buildings. Room views look out on the pools, lake, and golf courses. Bathroom amenities include bidets in many rooms, heat lamps, and full-size bath towels. *250 Racquet Club Rd., Fort Lauderdale 33326, tel. 305/389-3300 or 800/327-8090. 504 rooms include 8 suites. Facilities: 5 outdoor solar-heated freshwater swimming pools; 2 18-hole golf courses; 24 tennis courts, 43,000-square-foot spa with separate facilities for men and women (see* Participant Sports*); canoes, paddleboats, and a small sailboat on a half-mile-long lake which winds through the resort; bicycles and bicycle paths, saddle club, bowling alley, roller-skating rink, 4 restaurants, 2 lounges. AE, DC, MC, V. Expensive.*

★ **Casa Alhambra Bed & Breakfast Inn.** Victoria Feaman, co-owner and manager of this guest house, lives on the premises and treats customers as honored guests in her home. In fact, Casa Alhambra was a private home, built in 1932-36 and restored in 1986-87. The white-stucco dwelling retains such charming touches as a red-tile roof, stained-glass windows, hardwood floors, and a working brick fireplace. Vicky serves a complimentary Continental breakfast each morning. The large upstairs bedroom has a medium-firm king-size bed overlooking the tile roof and deck; two smaller bedrooms upstairs share a bath, an arrangement ideal for a foursome. *3029 Alhambra St., Fort Lauderdale 33304, tel. 305/467-2262. 5 rooms with bath. Facilities: outdoor freshwater hot tub with Jacuzzi, bicycles, piano, library, refrigerator privileges. No children under 10. AE. Moderate.*

Di Vito By the Sea. This eccentric low-rise beachfront hotel was built by Anthony Di Vito to express his love for his wife and exalt their Italian origins. Its architecture incorporates a reproduction of the Leaning Tower of Pisa with sea-horses, mermaids, and friezes with mythological heroes. Most guests rent by the week. There is no lobby, just an office and a patio facing the boardwalk in front of the building. *3500 N. Boardwalk, Hollywood 33019, tel. 305/929-7227. 20 rooms with bath, 4 yearly-rental apartments in an adjoining building. Facilities: 200 feet of beach frontage, efficiency kitchens in some rooms. No credit cards. Moderate.*

Fort Lauderdale Marriott Hotel & Marina. This hotel's 13-story tower beside the Intracoastal Waterway commands a striking view of the beach and the entrance to Port Everglades. Most rooms have balconies overlooking the water and standard Marriott furnishings in natural dark woods with pink, mauve, and green fabrics and wall coverings. *1881 S.E. 17th St., Fort Lauderdale 33316, tel. 305/463–4000 or 800/228–9290. 583 rooms with bath, including 19 suites, 26 nonsmokers rooms, 17 rooms for handicapped guests. Facilities: outdoor freshwater swimming pool and whirlpool, free shuttle to beach, 32-slip marina for yachts up to 200 feet long, 4 tennis courts, fitness center, game room, in-room minibars and safes, pay-TV movies, AE, CB, DC, MC, V. Very Expensive.*

Marriott's Harbor Beach Resort. Fort Lauderdale's only AAA-rated 5-diamond hotel is a 14-story tower on 16 acres of oceanfront. Built in 1984, its guest rooms were renovated in 1989. The free-form pool has a cascading waterfall. Room furnishings are light wood with mauve, pink, blue, and green hues; each room has a balcony facing either the ocean or the Intracoastal Waterway. *3030 Holiday Dr., Fort Lauderdale 33316, tel. 305/525–4000 or 800/228–9290. 645 rooms with bath, including 36 suites, 45 nonsmokers rooms, 7 rooms for handicapped guests. Facilities: 1,100 ft of beach frontage, cabanas, windsurfing, Hobie cats, 65-foot catamaran, parasailing, outdoor heated freshwater swimming pool and whirlpool, 5 tennis courts, fitness center, men's and women's saunas, masseuse, 3 boutiques, 5 restaurants, 3 lounges, in-room minibars, HBO, TV movies. AE, DC, MC, V. Very Expensive.*

Palm-Aire Spa Resort. This mid-rise resort with spa and conference center on 1,500 acres 15 miles north of Fort Lauderdale is lushly landscaped, and planters on each terrace make the four-story main building resemble a hanging garden. The rooms have big closets, a separate dressing alcove, and choice of soft or firm pillows. *2501 Palm-Aire Dr. N, Pompano Beach 33069. tel. 305/972–3300 or 800/327–4960. 192 rooms with bath and private terrace, 4 outdoor freshwater swimming pools, 5 golf courses, half-mile jogging trail with exercise stations, 37 tennis courts, Continental and spa restaurants, boutique. AE, DC, MC, V. Very Expensive.*

★ **Pier 66 Resort and Marina.** Phillips Petroleum built Fort Lauderdale's original high-rise luxury hotel on the eastern bank of the Intracoastal Waterway. An octagonal rooftop cocktail lounge rotates slowly, offering patrons a spectacular view. Rooms are attractively furnished in tropical pastels. *2301 S.E. 17th St., Fort Lauderdale 33316, tel. 305/525–6666, in FL 800/432–1956, rest of USA 800/327–3796. 388 rooms, including 8 suites. Facilities: water taxi and van shuttle to beach, outdoor heated freshwater swimming pool, full-service marina with 142 wet slips for boats up to 200 ft long, scuba diving, snorkling, parasailing, small boat rentals, waterskiing, fishing and sailing yacht charters, 2 hard-surface tennis courts, indoor and outdoor health clubs with saunas and exercise equipment, men's and women's saunas, massage therapy. AE, CB, DC, MC, V. Very Expensive.*

Plaza Beach Resort. Built in 1966, this nine-story former Royce hotel came under new management in 1989. All rooms have balconies, air-conditioners, and triple dressers. In some, the color scheme is off-white and pastels; others have burgundy carpeting with mauve curtains and matching bedspreads. *4060 Galt Ocean Mile, Fort Lauderdale Beach 33308, tel. 305/565–6611 or 800/678–9022. 220 rooms with bath, including 14 suites, 4 rooms for handicapped guests. Facilities: 225 ft of beach front-*

age on Atlantic Ocean, outdoor heated freshwater swimming pool, complete water sports program, 2 restaurants, nightclub, ice cream shop, free cable TV, pay-TV movies. AE, DC, MC, V. Expensive.

★ **Riverside Hotel.** This six-story hotel, on For Lauderdale's most fashionable shopping thoroughfare, was built in 1936, and was extensively remodeled in 1987. An attentive staff includes many veterans of two decades or more. Each room is unique, with antique oak furnishings, framed French prints on the walls, in-room refrigerators, and European-style baths. Best rooms face south, overlooking the New River; worst rooms, where you can hear the elevator, are the 36 series. *620 E. Las Olas Blvd., Fort Lauderdale 33301, tel. 305/467–0671, in USA 800/325–3280, in FL 800/421–7666. 117 rooms with bath, including 5 suites, 15 nonsmokers rooms. Facilities: kidney-shaped heated outdoor freshwater swimming pool beside the New River, 540 ft of dock with mooring space available by advance reservation, volleyball court, two restaurants, poolside bar. AE, DC, MC. Expensive.*

Sheraton Design Center Hotel. This high-rise business hotel is near the airport, across a landscaped plaza from the interior-design showrooms in Design Center of the Americas. The hotel's color theme is mauve, with variations of peach, wine, and pink. In the two-story atrium lobby, art deco-style hanging chandeliers with double-round diffusers hang from a skylight; pale beige, peach, and gray fabrics predominate. *1825 Griffin Rd., Dania 33004, tel. 305/920–3500 or 800/325–3535. 250 rooms with bath, including 5 suites, 20 nonsmokers rooms, 20 rooms for handicapped guests. Facilities: outdoor heated freshwater swimming pool and whirlpool, 2 lighted tennis courts, fitness center, men's and women's saunas, 2 racquetball courts, 2 restaurants, 2 lounges, complimentary shuttle to airport, AE, CB, DC, MC, V. Very Expensive.*

Westin Cypress Creek. Built in 1986, this high-rise business hotel is in Radice Corporate Park, a suburban office complex surrounding a lagoon with a fountain in the center. The hotel's three-story atrium lobby was inspired by the Great Temple at Karnak, Egypt; eight weathered-looking concrete columns with a rough pink-stucco finish rise to a skylight through which you can see the building's facade. Best rooms are on the 14th and 15th floors, where concierge service includes a Continental breakfast and a cocktail hour. *400 Corporate Dr., Fort Lauderdale 33334, tel. 305/772–1331 or 800/228–3000. 294 rooms with bath, including 25 suites, 34 nonsmokers rooms, 19 rooms for handicapped guests. Facilities: outdoor heated freshwater swimming pool and Jacuzzi, poolside bar with lunchtime barbecue, health club with Nautilus equipment, men's and women's saunas, jogging trail, volleyball, basketball, 2 restaurants, 2 lounges, in-room minibars. AE, CB, DC, V. Very Expensive.*

The Arts and Nightlife

For the most complete weekly listing of events, read the "Showtime!" entertainment insert and events calendar in the Friday *Fort Lauderdale News/Sun Sentinel.*

Tickets are sold at individual box offices and through Ticketmaster, a computerized statewide sales system (tel. 305/

523–3309 in Broward County or 800/446–3939 statewide). Broward also has a concert information line (tel. 305/493–8811).

The Arts **Sunrise Musical Theatre** (5555 N.W. 95th Ave., Sunrise, tel.
Theater 305/741–7300) stages Broadway musicals, some dramatic plays with name stars, and concerts by well-known singers throughout the year. The theater is 14 miles west of Fort Lauderdale Beach via Commercial Boulevard.

Concerts **Bailey Concert Hall** is a popular place for classical music concerts, dance, drama, and other performing arts activities, especially October–April. *On the Central Campus of Broward Community College, 3501 S.W. Davie Rd., tel. 305/475–6500 for reservations.*

The Philharmonic Orchestra of Florida, South Florida's only fully professional orchestra, is Broward-based but performs in eight locations in Broward, Dade, and Palm Beach counties. It offers a variety of series and individual-performance tickets; write for schedule. *1430 N. Federal Hwy., Ft. Lauderdale 33304, tel. 305/561–2997 (Dade County), 305/945–5180 (Broward County), 407/392–5443 (Boca Raton), 407/659–0331 (Palm Beach), 800/446–3939 (Ticketmaster statewide). Office open weekdays 9–5. AE, MC, V.*

The Fort Lauderdale Opera Guild presents the current production of the Greater Miami Opera in War Memorial Auditorium (800 N.E. 8th st., Fort Lauderdale). For tickets, contact the Guild office. *333 S.W. 2nd St., Fort Lauderdale 33312, tel. 305/728–9700. Office open weekdays 9–5.*

Nightlife **Musician Exchange Downtown Cafe.** This 200-seat club fea-
Bars and tures an eclectic mix of blues, jazz, and rock-and-roll, with
Nightclubs reggae on Sundays. Performers include local bands as well as leading musicians like Woodie Herman, Buddy Rich, Carmen McCrae, and Stan Getz. *729 W. Sunrise Blvd., Fort Lauderdale, 305/764–1912. Admission price varies with show. National big-name acts Fri. and Sat. Call for schedule and reservations.*

Shirttail Charlie's Downstairs Bar. A scenic place to have a beer or snack and watch boat traffic on the New River through downtown Fort Lauderdale. No entertainment. Informal. *400 S.W. 3rd Ave., Fort Lauderdale, tel. 305/463–3474. Open Mon.–Fri. 11:30–10, Sat. 11:30–10, Sun. 11:30–9.*

Peppers. High-energy nightclub with art-deco decor in Westin Cypress Creek Hotel. Features rock-and-roll DJs most weekend nights, with videos produced in-house; occasional live jazz. Wood dance floor, pool table. *400 Corporate Dr., Fort Lauderdale, tel. 305/772–1331. Open Mon.–Thurs. 5 PM–1:30 AM with complimentary buffet 5–7 PM, Fri.–Sat. 7 PM–1:30 AM. No cover or minimum.*

Comedy Clubs **The Comic Strip.** Stand-up comedians from New York work surrounded by framed old newspaper funnies—Katzenjammer Kids, Superman, Prince Valiant, L'il Orphan Annie, Hubert, etc. Full restaurant menu, two-drink minimum, alcoholic and nonalcoholic beverages. Amateur night Sunday and Monday, phone ahead to sign up. *1432 N. Federal Hwy., Fort Lauderdale, tel. 305/565–8887. Showtime Sun.–Thurs. 9:30, Fri. 10, Sat. 8:30 and 11:30.*

Country/Western **Do-Da's Country Music Emporium.** The Frontier Room seats 800 at buckboard tables and has a 2,100-square-foot wood dance floor; the smaller pecky-board Tennessee Room seats 100.

Glass-and-brick arches enclose the Tex-Mex dining area, Rosa's Cantina. The shoot-'em-down corral bar in the Frontier Room has an old-fashioned barber chair. Free international buffet during happy hour, weekdays 5–8 PM. *700 S. U.S. 441, Plantation, tel. 305/791–1477. Open 11 AM–4 AM. Live country/ western music, with name bands on weekends 8 PM–3 AM.*

6 Palm Beach

Introduction

Wealth has its privileges. That's the continuing reality of Palm Beach. Those privileges include the finest homes, cars, food, wine, furniture, jewelry, art, clothing, and toys that money can buy—and the right to stare back at the tourists who visit this elegant barrier-island enclave 70 miles north of Miami.

Henry Morrison Flagler created Palm Beach in 1894. He helped John D. Rockefeller establish the Standard Oil Company, then retired and put his money into Florida railroads and real estate. He bought a small railroad between Jacksonville and St. Augustine, renamed it the Florida East Coast Railroad, and extended it southward. Along the rail line he built hotels to generate traffic, including a huge wooden structure, the 2,000-room Royal Poinciana, beside a tidal bay called Lake Worth.

Flagler created an international high-society resort at Palm Beach, attracting the affluent for the Season, December 15 to Washington's Birthday (Feb. 22). Then they departed for Europe, extolling Palm Beach's virtues and collecting great art to ship back to the mansions they were building on the island.

A workman told Flagler that people liked to picnic along the beach "down by the breakers," so he built a second hotel there in 1896. It burned, was rebuilt, and burned again. The third structure to bear the name The Breakers rose in 1926 and stands today as the grande dame of Palm Beach hostelries.

Socialites and celebrities still flock to The Breakers for charity galas. They browse in the stores along Worth Avenue, regarded as one of the world's classiest shopping districts. They swim on secluded beaches that are nominally public but lack convenient parking and access points. They pedal the world's most beautiful bicycle path beside Lake Worth. And what they do, *you* can do—if you can afford it.

Despite its prominence and affluence, the Town of Palm Beach occupies far less than 1% of the land area of Palm Beach County, which is 521 square miles larger than the state of Delaware and is a remarkably diverse political jurisdiction.

West Palm Beach, on the mainland across Lake Worth from Palm Beach, is the city Flagler built to house Palm Beach's servants; today it's the county seat and commercial center of Palm Beach County, with a population of about 70,000.

Lantana, to the south, has a large Finnish population and is the headquarters of the *National Enquirer*. Delray Beach began as an artists' retreat and a small settlement of Japanese farmers, including George Morikami, who donated the land for the beautiful Morikami Museum of Japanese Culture to the county park system (4000 Morikami Park Rd., Delray Beach 33446. tel. 407/499–0631. Open Tues.–Sun. 10–5. Donation). Boca Raton, an upscale community developed by pioneer architect Addison Mizner as a showcase for his Spanish Revival style, retains much of its 1920s ambience through strict zoning.

To the north, Palm Beach Gardens is a golf center, home of the Professional Golfer's Association. Jupiter boasts the Burt Reynolds Jupiter Theater and a dune-fringed beach that remains largely free of intrusive development.

Many visitors to Palm Beach County don't realize that it extends 50 miles inland to encompass the southeastern quadrant of 448,000-acre Lake Okeechobee, the fourth-largest natural lake in the United States. Its bass and perch attract fishermen; catfish devotees prize the hearty flavor of succulent Okeechobee "sharpies."

Marinas at Pahokee and Belle Glade provide lake access. Pahokee has a 125-foot tower, which you can climb for a view of the lake. In Lake Harbor, about as far west as you can go in Palm Beach County, the state is restoring a lock and lockmaster's house built early in the 20th century on the Miami Canal.

Palm Beach County is also the main gateway to the Treasure Coast, consisting of Martin, St. Lucie, and Indian River counties along the Atlantic coast to the north.

Arriving and Departing by Plane

Airport **Palm Beach International Airport (PBIA)** (Congress Ave. and Belvedere Rd., West Palm Beach) expanded to 24 gates in 1988 and handled just over 5 million passengers. It will add up to 24 more gates by 1993.

Between the Airport and City Center Route No. 10 of **Tri-Rail Commuter Bus Service** joins PBIA and Tri-Rail's Palm Beach Airport station during weekday rush hours only. For schedule, call 800/TRI–RAIL. For connections with CoTran (Palm Beach County Transportation Authority) routes, call 407/686–4560 or 407/686–4555 in Palm Beach, 407/272–6350 in Boca Raton–Delray Beach.

Palm Beach Transportation (tel. 407/689–4222) provides taxi and limousine service from PBIA. Reserve at least a day in advance for a limousine.

Arriving and Departing by Train and Car

By Train **Amtrak** (201 S. Tamarind Ave., West Palm Beach, tel. 800/872–7245 or 407/832–6169) connects West Palm Beach with cities along Florida's east coast daily.

Tri-Rail has six stations in Palm Beach County. For details, tel. 800/TRI–RAIL or tel. 305/728–8445.

By Car Most visitors explore Palm Beach County by car. I–95 runs north-south, to link West Palm Beach with Miami and Fort Lauderdale to the south. To get to central Palm Beach, exit at Belvedere Road or Okeechobee Boulevard. Southern Boulevard (U.S. 98) runs east-west. From West Palm Beach, take I–95 south to Boca Raton and Delray Beach, north to Palm Beach Gardens and Jupiter.

Getting Around

By Bus CoTran buses require exact change (80 cents, plus 15 cents for a transfer). Service is provided from 6 AM to 9 PM. For details, tel. 407/686–4560 or 407/686–4555 (Palm Beach), 407/272–6350 (Boca Raton-Delray Beach).

By Taxi **Palm Beach Transportation** (tel. 407/689–4222). Cab meters start at $1.25. Each mile is $1.50. Some cabs may charge more.

Important Addresses and Numbers

Tourist Information **Palm Beach County Convention & Visitors Bureau** (1555 Palm Beach Lakes Blvd., Suite 204, West Palm Beach 33401, tel. 407/471–3995) is open weekdays 8:30–5.

Chamber of Commerce of the Palm Beaches (501 N. Flagler Dr., West Palm Beach, tel. 407/833–3711) is open weekdays 8:30–5.

Deaf Service Center of Palm Beach County (5730 Corporate Way, Suite 210, West Palm Beach 33407, TDD tel. 407/478–3904, voice tel. 407/478–3903) is open weekdays 8:30–5.

Tickets Call **Ticketmaster** to order tickets for performing arts and sports events. *Tel. 800/446–3939 or 407/588–3309. MC, V.*

Emergencies Dial 911 for **police** and **ambulance** in an emergency.

Hospitals Two hospitals in West Palm Beach with 24-hour emergency rooms are **Good Samaritan Hospital** (Flagler Dr. and Palm Beach Lakes Blvd., tel. 407/655–5511; doctor-referral, tel. 407/650–6240) and **St. Mary's Hospital** (901 45th St., tel. 407/844–6300; doctor-referral, tel. 407/881–2929).

24-Hour Pharmacy **Eckerd Drugs** (3343 S. Congress Ave., Palm Springs, southwest of West Palm Beach, tel. 407/965–3367). **Walgreen Drugs** (1688 Congress Ave., Palm Springs, tel. 407/968–8211).

Exploring Palm Beach and West Palm Beach

Numbers in the margin correspond with points of interest on the Palm Beach and West Palm Beach map.

Palm Beach is an island community 12 miles long and no more than a quarter-mile across at its widest point. Three bridges connect Palm Beach to West Palm Beach and the rest of the world. This tour takes you through both communities.

❶ Begin at Royal Palm Way and County Road in the center of Palm Beach. Go north on County Road past **Bethesda-by-the-Sea Church,** built in 1927 by the first Protestant congregation in southeast Florida. Inspiring stained-glass windows and a lofty, vaulted sanctuary grace its Spanish-Gothic design. A stone bridge with an ornamental tile border spans the pond; bubbling fountains feed it. *141 South County Rd., Palm Beach, tel. 407/655–4554. Gardens open 8–5. Services Sun. 8, 9, and 11 AM in winter, 8 and 10 June–Aug.; phone for weekday schedule.*

❷ Continue north on County Road past **The Breakers** (1 S. County Rd., Palm Beach), an ornate Italian Renaissance hotel built in 1926 by railroad magnate Henry M. Flagler's widow to replace an earlier hotel, which burned (*see* Lodging). Explore the elegant public spaces—especially on a Sunday morning, when you can enjoy the largest champagne brunch in Florida at The Beach Club.

❸ Continue north on County Road to Royal Poinciana Way. Go inside the **Palm Beach Post Office** to see the murals depicting Seminole Indians in the Everglades and royal and coconut palms. *95 N. County Rd., Palm Beach, tel. 407/832–0633 or 1867. Open weekdays 8:30–5.*

❹ Continue north on County Road to the north end of the island, past the very-private **Palm Beach Country Club** and a neighborhood of expansive (and expensive) estates.

❺ You must turn around at **E. Inlet Drive,** the northern tip of the island, where a dock offers a view of Lake Worth Inlet, the U.S. Coast Guard Reservation on Peanut Island, and the Port of Palm Beach across Lake Worth on the mainland. Observe the no-parking signs; Palm Beach police will issue tickets.

❻ Turn south and make the first right onto Indian Road, then the first left onto Lake Way. You'll return to the center of town through an area of newer mansions, past the posh, private Sailfish Club. Lake Way parallels the **Palm Beach Bicycle Trail** along the shoreline of Lake Worth, a palm-fringed path through the backyards of some of the world's priciest homes. Watch on your right for metal posts topped with a swatch of white paint, marking narrow public-access walkways between houses from the street to the bike path.

❼ Lake Way runs into Country Club Road, which takes you through the **Canyon of Palm Beach,** a road cut about 25 feet deep through a ridge of sandstone and oolite limestone.

❽ As you emerge from the canyon, turn right onto Lake Way and continue south. Lake Way becomes Bradley Place. You'll pass the **Palm Beach Biltmore Hotel,** now a condominium. Another flamboyant landmark of the Florida boom, it cost $7 million to build and opened in 1927 with 543 rooms.

❾ As you cross Royal Poinciana Way, Bradley Place becomes Coconut Row. Stop at **Whitehall,** the palatial 73-room mansion that Henry M. Flagler built in 1901 for his third wife, Mary Lily Kenan. After the couple died, the mansion was turned into a hotel. In 1960, Flagler's granddaughter, Jean Flagler Matthews, bought the building. She turned it into a museum, with many of the original furnishings on display. The art collection includes a Gainsborough portrait of a girl with a pink sash, displayed in the music room near a 1,200-pipe organ. Exhibits also depict the history of the Florida East Coast Railway. Flagler's personal railroad car, "The Rambler," is parked behind the building. A tour by well-informed guides takes about an hour; afterwards, you may browse on your own. *Coconut Row at Whitehall Way, Palm Beach, tel. 407/655–2833. Open Tues.–Sat. 10–5, Sun. noon–5; closed Mon. Admission: $3.50 adults, $1.25 children.*

❿ Turn left on leaving Whitehall. Take Coconut Row back north to Royal Poinciana Way, turn left, and cross the **Flagler Memorial Bridge** into West Palm Beach. On the mainland side of the bridge, turn left onto Flagler Drive, which runs along the west **⓫** shore of Lake Worth. A half-mile south of the **Royal Palm Bridge,** turn right onto Acteon Street, which is the north edge **⓬** of a sloping mall leading up to the **Norton Gallery of Art**.

Founded in 1941 by steel magnate Ralph H. Norton, the Norton Gallery boasts an extensive permanent collection of French impressionist and 20th-century American paintings, Chinese bronze and jade sculptures, a sublime outdoor patio with sculptures on display in a tropical garden, and a library housing more than 3,000 art books and periodicals. The Norton also secures many of the best traveling exhibits to reach south

Palm Beach and West Palm Beach

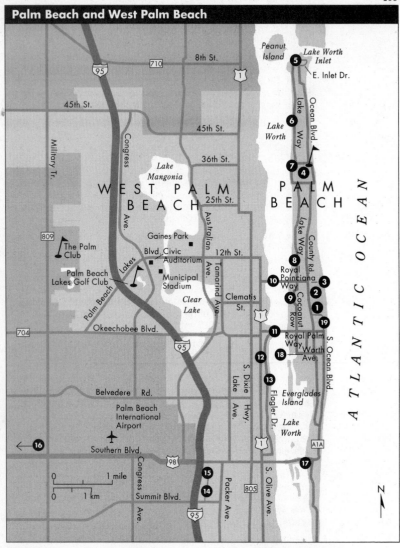

Florida. 1451 S. Olive Ave., West Palm Beach, tel. 407/832–5194. Open Tues.–Sat. 10–5, Sun. 1–5. Admission free; donations requested.

Return to Flagler Drive down Diana Street at the south edge of the mall, turn right, go a half-mile south to Barcelona Road, and turn right again. You're at the entrance to the **Ann Norton Sculpture Gardens,** a monument to the late American sculptor Ann Weaver Norton, second wife of Norton Gallery founder Ralph H. Norton. The gardens display, in a tropical jungle, seven granite figures and six brick megaliths. The brick forms reflect their creator's girlhood in Selma, Alabama, in a pre-World War I southern landscape dotted with the brick chimneys of burned-out farmhouses and haunted by memories of General Sherman's Civil War march to the sea. The garden also contains native plants and 132 different kinds of palms. Other sculptures in bronze, marble, and wood are on display in Norton's studio. *253 Barcelona Rd., West Palm Beach, tel. 407/832–5328. Open Tues.–Sat. noon–4 or by appointment. Admission: $2 adults, children under 12 free.*

Return again to Flagler Drive and continue south to Southern Boulevard (U.S. 98). Turn left and go west almost a mile, turn left onto Parker Avenue, and go south about a mile. Turn right onto Summit Boulevard, and right again at the next stoplight into the parking lot at the **Dreher Park Zoo.** The 32-acre zoo has nearly 100 different species of animals, including an endangered Florida panther. Of special interest are the reptile collection and the petting zoo. *1301 Summit Blvd., West Palm Beach, tel. 407/585–2197 (recording) or 407/533–0887. Open daily 9–5. Admission: $4 adults, $2 children 3–12 and seniors over 60, under 3 free.*

As you leave the zoo parking lot, turn left and follow a winding road for about a quarter-mile to the **South Florida Science Museum.** Here you'll find hands-on exhibits, aquarium displays with touch-tank demonstrations and feedings daily at 4 PM, planetarium shows, and a chance to observe the heavens Friday nights through the most powerful telescope in south Florida. *4801 Dreher Trail N, West Palm Beach, tel. 407/832–1988. Open Tues.–Sun. 10–5, Fri. 6:30–10 PM. Admission: $3 adults, $2.50 seniors over 62, $1.50 children 4–12, $8 family. Planetarium admission: $1 extra.*

Leaving the science museum, retrace your path on Summit Boulevard and Parker Avenue to Southern Boulevard (SR 80), turn left, and go about 16 miles west to **Lion Country Safari,** where you drive (with car windows closed) on eight miles of paved roads through a 500-acre cageless zoo where 1,000 wild animals roam free. Lions, elephants, white rhinoceroses, giraffes, zebras, antelopes, chimpanzees, and ostriches are among the species in residence. Try to go early in the day, before the park gets crowded. If you have a convertible or a new car on which you don't want animals to climb, the park will rent you a zebra-stripe, air-conditioned sedan. An adjacent KOA campground offers campers a park discount. *Box 16066, West Palm Beach 33416, tel. 407/793–1084. Open daily 9:30–5:30. Admission: $12.14 adults, $10.45 children 3–16, $8.55 seniors over 65, under 3 free, car rental $5 per hour.*

Returning to town on Southern Boulevard, look for the Italianate towers of **Mar-A-Lago** (1100 S. Ocean Blvd., Palm Beach) silhouetted against the sky as you cross the bridge to Palm Beach. Mar-A-Lago, the former estate of breakfast-food heiress Marjorie Meriweather Post, is now owned by real estate magnate Donald Trump. It's closed to the public, but you can catch a glimpse as you drive past.

Turn north on Ocean Boulevard, one of Florida's most scenic drives. The road follows the dune top, with the beach falling away to surging surf on your right, and some of Palm Beach's most opulent mansions on your left. You will pass the east end **⑱** of **Worth Avenue,** regarded by many as the world's classiest shopping street (*see* Shopping).

⑲ As you approach Worth Avenue, the **public beach** begins. Parking meters along Ocean Drive between Worth Avenue and Royal Palm Way signify the only stretch of beach in Palm Beach with convenient public access.

This concludes the tour. To return to its starting point, turn left on Royal Palm Way and go one block west to County Road.

What to See and Do with Children

Gumbo Limbo Nature Center. At this unusual nature center, you can stroll a 1,628-foot boardwalk through a dense tropical forest and climb a 50-foot tower to overlook the tree canopy. The forest is a coastal hammock, with tropical species growing north of the tropics. One tree species you're sure to see is the gumbo-limbo, often called "the tourist tree" because of its red, peeling bark. Ask for a guide to the hammock's flora, with photos and brief text keyed to numbered posts along the trail. In the nature center building, a diorama depicts the nest of a loggerhead sea turtle along the nearby beach. The center's staff leads guided turtle walks to the beach to see nesting mothers come ashore and lay their eggs. *1801 N. Ocean Blvd., Boca Raton, tel. 407/338–1473. Open Mon.–Sat. 9–4, fall–spring; weekdays 4–8 PM in summer. Admission free. Turtle walks early June–late July Mon.–Thurs. 9 PM–12:30 AM. Admission: $2. Reservations required.*

Off the Beaten Track

Arthur R. Marshall Loxahatchee National Wildlife Refuge Loxahatchee Refuge is 221 square miles of saw-grass marshes, wet prairies, sloughs, and tree islands. You go there to stroll the nature trails, see alligators and birds (including the rare snail kite). You can also fish for bass and panfish, ride an airboat, or paddle your own canoe through this watery wilderness.

Loxahatchee refuge recently was renamed in memory of Art Marshall, a Florida environmental scientist instrumental in Everglades preservation efforts.

Refuge entrance fee: $3 per car, $1 per pedestrian. Open ½ hr before sunrise–½ hr after sunset.

The refuge has three access points, each with its own facilities and services:

Headquarters The ranger at the visitor center will show a seven-minute slide presentation on request. Walk both nature trails—a boardwalk through a dense cypress swamp, and a marsh nature trail to a 20-foot-tall observation tower overlooking a pond. A seven-mile canoe trail starts at the boat-launching ramp here. *Entrance off U.S. 441 between Boynton Blvd. (Rte. 804) and Atlantic Ave. (Rte. 806), west of Boynton Beach. Mailing address: Rte. 1, Box 278, Boynton Beach, tel. 407/732–3684 or 407/734–8303.*

Hillsboro Recreation Area A concessionaire offers airboat rides, boat rentals, guide services, and a store with snacks, fishing tackle, and bait. The airboat ride lasts a half hour, in a 20-passenger craft with a Cadillac engine. The driver will take you into the middle of the Everglades, then shut off the engine and explain the unique ecosystem around you. *Entrance off U.S. 441 on Lox Rd. (Rte. 827), 12 mi south of Headquarters and west of Boca Raton. Loxahatchee Recreation, Inc., Rte. 1, Box 642–S, Pompano Beach 33060, tel. 305/426–2474. Concessionaire open 6 AM–30 min before park closing. Airboat rides 9–4:30, $7.50 adults, $4 children under 12, under 3 free. Rental for 14-ft. boat with outboard engine $27.50 for 5 hours, $13.75 evening special for last 3 daylight hours; for rowboat, $10 for 5 hours. Fishing and hunting guide $150 per half-day, $200 per day. MC, V.*

20-Mile Bend Recreation Area Boat ramp and fishing area at north end of refuge. *Entrance off U.S. 98 and 441, due west of West Palm Beach. No services.*

Shopping

Worth Avenue One of the world's last strongholds for quality shopping, Worth Avenue runs a quarter-mile east–west across Palm Beach, from the beach to Lake Worth.

The street has more than 250 shops. The 300 block, with a maze of Italianate villas designed by Addison Mizner, retains a quaint charm. The 100 and 200 blocks are more overtly commercial. Most merchants open at 9:30 or 10 AM, and close at 5:30 or 6 PM. Summer hours may be shorter.

Parking on and around Worth Avenue is quite limited. On-street parking has a one- or two-hour limit, strictly enforced. An alternative is Apollo Valet Parking at Hibiscus and Peruvian avenues, a block off Worth Avenue. Merchants will stamp your parking ticket if you buy something (or if you look like a prospective customer); each stamp is good for an hour of free parking.

Apollo's parking deal is just one reason to look presentable when you tour Worth Avenue. Come dressed to feel comfortable, blend in, and indulge your fantasies.

The Worth Avenue Association has strict rules to keep the street classy: no renovations are allowed from October to May, and special sales are limited to 21 consecutive days anytime between April and October.

Many "name" stores associated with fine shopping have a presence on Worth Avenue, including Bonwit Teller, Brooks Brothers, Cartier, Elizabeth Arden, Gucci, Pierre Deux, Saks Fifth Avenue, and Van Cleef & Arpels. No other street in the world has such a dense concentration of these upscale firms—and they tend to send their best merchandise to Worth Avenue to appeal to the discerning tastes of their Palm Beach clientele.

Beaches

The best beaches in Palm Beach County are in the Jupiter area, on Singer Island, and in Boca Raton. Surfing isn't a major draw for this portion of the Atlantic, but wading and surf diving into the shallow waves are.

Participant Sports

Biking Because of traffic, bicycle with caution while on city and county roads. A nice bike path is in *John D. MacArthur Park* (alongside PGA Blvd.) as it runs east toward Singer Island. Rentals are available at **Palm Beach Bicycle Trail Shop.** *223 Sunrise Ave., Palm Beach, tel. 407/659–4583. Open 9–5. AE, MC, V.*

Diving You can drift-dive or anchor-dive along Palm Beach County's 47-mile Atlantic coast. Drift divers take advantage of the Gulf Stream's strong currents and proximity to shore—sometimes less than a mile. A group of divers joined by nylon line may drift across coral reefs with the current; one member of the group carries a large, orange float which the charter-boat captain can follow. Drift diving works best from Boynton Beach north. South of Boynton Beach, where the Gulf Stream is farther from shore, diving from an anchored boat is more popular.

Dive Boats and Instruction The following **Force E** stores rent scuba and snorkeling equipment and have PADI affiliation. Instruction available at all skill levels. Dive-boat charters are also available.

1399 N. Military Trail, West Palm Beach, tel. 407/471–2676 or 800/527–8660. Open winter weekdays 10–9, summer weekdays 8–9, Sat. 8–7, Sun. 8–4.

155 E. Blue Heron Blvd., Riviera Beach, tel. 407/845–2333. Open weekdays year-round 8–7, Sat. 6:30–7, Sun. 6:30–5.

39 S. Ocean Blvd., Delray Beach, tel. 407/272–0311. Open Nov.– May. Contact store for hours.

877 E. Palmetto Park Rd., Boca Raton, tel. 407/368–0555. Hours same as West Palm Beach store.

7166 Beracasa Way, Boca Raton, tel. 407/395–4407. Hours same as West Palm Beach store.

Golf There are more than 130 public, private, and semiprivate golf courses in the Palm Beach County area. The **PGA Sheraton Resort** west of the city, has one of the most famous golf courses in the area (*see* Lodging, below).

Hunting **J. W. Corbett Wildlife Management Area.** You can hunt deer, wild hog, squirrel, and quail in season on this 57,892-acre state preserve. Access off Indiantown Road and Beeline Highway, west of Jupiter. For information on licensing, call the Florida Game and Fresh Water Fish Commission (tel. 407/683–0748).

Spas **Hippocrates Health Institute** (1443 Palmdale Ct., West Palm Beach, tel. 407/471–8876), was founded in Boston in 1963 by Ann Wigmore and moved to its present 10-acre site in 1987. Guests receive complete examinations by traditional and alternative health-care professionals. Personalized programs include juice fasts and the eating of raw foods.

Spectator Sports

The *Palm Beach Post*'s weekly "TGIF" section on Fridays carries information on sports activities.

Baseball The **Atlanta Braves** and the **Montreal Expos** both conduct spring training in West Palm Beach's Municipal Stadium, which is also home to the Palm Beach Expos, a Class-A team in the Florida State League. *1610 Palm Beach Lakes Blvd., Box 3087, West Palm Beach 33402, stadium tel. 407/683–6012. Expos tickets: Box 3566, West Palm Beach 33402, tel. 407/689– 9121, AE, MC. Braves tickets: Box 2619, West Palm Beach 33402, tel. 407/683–6100. No credit cards.*

Greyhound Racing **Palm Beach Kennel Club** opened in 1932 and has 3,000 free seats. Dine in the Paddock Dining Room or watch and eat on the Terrace. Call for schedule. *1111 Congress Ave., 33409, tel. 407/ 683–2222. Admission: 50 cents general admission, $2 dining rooms. Free parking.*

Jai Alai **Palm Beach Jai Alai.** This jai alai fronton is the site of two world records: for the largest payoff ever, $988,325; and for the fastest ball ever thrown, 188 mph. *1415 45th St., West Palm Beach, ¼ mi east of I–95 off exit 54, tel. 407/844–2444 or 407/427–0009 (toll-free south to Pompano Beach. Admission: 50 cents to $5. Free parking. Sala Del Toro Restaurant. Open: Sept. to July. Schedule changes seasonally. No cameras.*

Equestrian Sports and Polo Many Olympic riders will come to Palm Beach county in 1990 to compete in world-class show-jumping events at the 12th annual **Winter Equestrian Festival.** It will take place in a new 125-acre equestrian complex at the Palm Beach Polo and Country Club (*see* Lodging).

Palm Beach county is the home of three major polo organizations. Seventy miles north in Vero Beach, the **Windsor Polo and Beach Club** held its first polo match in February 1989. Although only the affluent can support a four-member polo team, admission is free for some games and priced reasonably for others. If you like horses and want to rub elbows with the rich and famous, dress like the locals in tweeds or a good golf shirt and khakis and spend an afternoon watching some of the world's best professional polo players.

Polo teams play under a handicap system in which the U.S. Polo Association ranks each player's skills; a team's total handicap reflects its members' individual handicaps. The best players have a 10-goal handicap. The average polo game lasts about 90 minutes. Each game consists of 6 periods or *chukkers* of 7½ minutes each.

Gulf Stream Polo Club, the oldest club in Palm Beach, began in the 1920s and plays medium-goal polo (for teams with handicaps of 8–16 goals). It has six polo fields. *4550 Polo Rd., Lake Worth 33467, tel. 407/965–2057. Play Dec.–April. Games Fri. 3 PM and Sun. 1 PM. Admission free.*

Royal Palm Polo, founded in 1959 by Oklahoma oilman John T. Oxley, has a total sports complex open to the public. It includes seven polo fields with two stadiums, a fitness center with 13 clay tennis courts, racquetball courts, a swimming pool and three restaurants. The complex is home to the $100,000 International Gold Cup Tournament. *6300 Clint Moore Rd., Boca Raton 33496, tel. 407/994–1876. Winter season Jan.–Apr. Summer season June–Oct. Games Sun. 1 and 3 PM. General admission $5, box seats $15, $3 children and students.*

Palm Beach Polo and Country Club. Started in 1979, this is the site each April of the $100,000 Cadillac World Cup competition *(see* Lodging). *Stadium address: 13240 Southshore Blvd., West Palm Beach, 33414, tel. 407/798–7605. Games Sun. 3 PM. General admission reserve $10, lower level $14, upper level $17. AE, MC, V.*

Rugby   **Boca Raton Rugby Club** practices on Tuesday and Thursday nights. Home games are played Saturday 2 PM at Boca Raton's Lake Wyman Park. *For information, contact Allerton "Bing" Towne, president, Florida Rugby Football Clubs, 1580 S.W. 6th Ave., Boca Raton 33432, tel. 407/395–3800 weekdays or 407/395–4259 weekends and nights.*

Dining

The list below is a representative selection of independent restaurants in Palm Beach County, organized geographically, and by type of cuisine within each region of the county. Unless otherwise noted, they serve lunch and dinner.

The most highly recommended restaurants are indicated by a star ★.

Category	Cost*
Very Expensive	over $55
Expensive	$35–$55
Moderate	$15–$35
Inexpensive	under $15

*per person, excluding drinks, service, and 6% state sales tax

The following credit card abbreviations are used: AE, American Express; CB, Carte Blanche; DC, Diners Club; MC, MasterCard; V, Visa.

Boca Raton   **Gazebo Cafe.** The locals who patronize this popular restaurant
Continental   know where it is, even though there is no sign. You'll probably circle the block three times. Look for the Barnett Bank in Sun Plaza, a block north of Spanish River Drive. Once you find the place, await your table in the open kitchen where Greek-born owner-chef William Sellas and his staff perform a gastronomic ballet. The main dining room has a high noise level. You may be happier in the smaller back dining room. Specialties include lump crabmeat with an excellent glaze of Mornay sauce on a marinated artichoke bottom; smoked spinach salad with *fresh* heart of palm, egg white, bacon, croutons, mushrooms, fruit garnish, and a dressing of olive oil and poupon mustard; Paul Sellas's (the chef's young son) "classic" bouillabaisse with Maine lobster, shrimp, scallops, clams, and mussel topped with julienne vegetables in a robust broth flavored with garlic, saffron, and tomatoes; and raspberries with a Grand Marnier-Sabayon sauce. The staff can accommodate travelers in seven languages. *4199 N. Federal Hwy., Boca Raton, tel. 407/395–6033. Jacket preferred. Reservations advised. Closed Sun. and Aug.–mid-Sept. AE, DC, MC, V. Moderate.*

French   **La Vieille Maison.** This elegant French restaurant occupies a
★   two-story dwelling, which architect Addison Mizner may have designed. The structure dates from the 1920s, hence the name, which means old house. It has been renovated repeatedly, but it retains features typical of Mizner's work. Closets and cubby-

holes have become intimate private dining rooms. You may order from a fixed-price or an à la carte menu throughout the year; in summer, a separate fixed-price menu available Sunday through Thursday offers a sampling of the other two at a more modest price. Specialties include saucisson chaud (pork-and-duck sausage with pistachios, baked in a phyllo pastry and served with a truffle sauce), *l'endive Cyrille* (smoked salmon, onions, and Belgian endive with light vinaigrette), and fresh pompano sauteed with buttered pecans and deglazed with white wine. Dessert specialties include crepe soufflé au citron and a chocolate tart. *770 E. Palmetto Park Rd., tel. 407/391–6701 in Boca Raton, 407/737–5677 in Delray Beach and Palm Beach, 305/421–7370 in Ft. Lauderdale. Jackets required. Reservations required. Closed Memorial Day, Labor Day, July 4th. AE, CB, MC, V. Expensive.*

Jupiter
American
Sinclair's Grill. This 140-seat restaurant in the Jupiter Beach Hilton overlooks the ocean and hotel pool. It has a relaxed Key West atmosphere, with louvered shutters, paddle fans, ceramic banana-tree table lamps, light wood furnishings, and hanging plants. Most of the cooking takes place in an open theater kitchen with a French rotisserie. The menu favors Florida seafood and tropical fruits and vegetables in season. Seafood specialties include Florida seafood chowder, grilled Florida swordfish with pineapple and cilantro salsa, and yellowfin tuna grilled with tomato vinaigrette, tapenade, and artichoke aiolio. Nonseafood specialties include rack of lamb with an herb crust served with rosemary sauce; Ponchartrain pie (ice cream, crème de menthe, meringue, and chocolate sauce in a graham cracker crust); and Key-lime mousse. For grazers, half-portions are available at half the menu price plus $1. *Indiantown Rd. and Rte. A1A, Jupiter, tel. 407/746–2511, in FL 800/432–1420, elsewhere 800/821–8791. Dress: informal, jacket preferred. Reservations advised. AE, CB, DC, MC, V. Moderate.*

Seafood
Charley's Crab. A sister restaurant to the Palm Beach Charley's Crab, this one opened in March 1988, in a lofty tin-roofed Florida Cracker-style structure. Its high ceilings—with beams and air-conditioning ducts exposed and painted pale hues of blue, gray, and beige—evoke feelings of sea, sky, and sand. The restaurant's centerpiece—a gilded nude statue, *Women Bathing,* by Edward Kasprowicz—stands on a six-foot-high pedestal in the main dining room. Menus change daily. Specialties include chilled crab bisque; swordfish *picatta* (sautéed in a lemon and sherry sauce); seafood paella with salmon, swordfish, littleneck clams, mussels, sausage, chicken, and rice with saffron; a pungently spiced seviche; a tangy Key-lime pie rich with extra egg yolks; and a French apple tart with cinnamon ice cream. *1000 N. Federal Hwy., Jupiter, tel. 407/744–4710. (Also in Stuart at 423 S. Federal Hwy., tel. 407/288–6800.) Dress: informal in cafe; jackets preferred at night in restaurant. Reservations suggested. AE, CB, DC, MC, V. Moderate.*

Palm Beach
American
Chuck & Harold's. Boxer Larry Holmes and thespians Brooke Shields and Burt Reynolds are among the celebrities who frequent this combination power-lunch bar, celebrity sidewalk cafe, and nocturnal big-band/jazz garden restaurant. A blue-and-yellow tent on pulleys rolls back in good weather to expose the garden to the elements. Local business people wheel and deal at lunch in the bar area while quaffing Bass Ale and Harp

Lager on tap. Locals who want to be part of the scenery frequent the front-porch area, next to pots of red and white begonias mounted along the sidewalk rail. Specialties include a mildly spiced conch chowder with a rich flavor and a liberal supply of conch; an onion-crunchy gazpacho with croutons, cucumber spear, and a dollop of sour cream; an outrageous charcoal-grilled pizza topped with sun-dried tomato, smoked turkey, and grilled red onions; and a tangy Key-lime pie with a graham-cracker crust and a squeezable lime slice for even more tartness. *207 Royal Poinciana Way, Palm Beach, tel. 407/659–1440. Dress: casual. Reservations suggested. AE, CB, DC, MC, V. Moderate.*

Doherty's. This local restaurant-pub feels like an old shoe, comfortable and unpretentious. Specialties include chicken hash Doherty with a secret cream sauce and sherry or currant jelly, eggs Benedict, a creamy oyster stew, and fish and chips (Wed.–Fri. only). *288 County Rd., Palm Beach 33480, tel. 407/655–6200. Dress: Informal. Reservations not accepted. AE, MC, V. Moderate.*

Continental **The Breakers.** The main hotel dining area at The Breakers consists of the elegant Florentine Dining Room, decorated with fine 15th-century Flemish tapestries; the adjoining Celebrity Aisle where the maître d' seats his most honored guests; and the Circle Dining Room, with a huge circular skylight framing a bronze-and-crystal Venetian chandelier. Specialties include rack of lamb Dijonnaise; salmon *en croute* with spinach, herbs and sauce Véronique (a grape sauce); *vacherin glacé* (praline-flavored ice cream encased in fresh whipped cream and frozen in a baked meringue base); and Key-lime pie. The Breakers also serves less formally at its Beach Club, where locals flock for the most sumptuous Sunday champagne brunch in Florida, and at the Fairway Cafe in the golf-course clubhouse. *1 S. County Rd., Palm Beach, tel. 407/655–6611 or 800/833–3141. Jacket and tie required. Reservations required. AE, CB, DC, MC, V. Expensive.*

International ★ **The Dining Room.** Since it opened in 1925, this formal hotel dining room in the Brazilian Court has been a favorite with the Palm Beach elite. The 94-seat dining room, with Romanesque arches and a sunny yellow color scheme, opens onto the outdoor Fountain Court. David Woodward, executive chef, uses only fresh ingredients and prepares all sauces from scratch. Specialties include Brazilian black-bean soup, a hotel standard throughout its history; ragout of Maine lobster with mousseline of scallops; and baked escalope of salmon with a smoked-salmon crust served with a mint and parsley sauce; roast rack of baby lamb with a timbale of spinach and sweet roasted garlic; and kiwi, mango, and raspberry sorbet on a bed of cantalope puree. *301 Australian Ave., Palm Beach, tel. 407/655–7740 or 800/351–5656. Jacket and tie required. Reservations required. AE, CB, DC, MC, V. Very Expensive.*

Seafood **Charley's Crab.** Audubon bird prints, fresh flowers, and French posters accent the walls of this restaurant across the street from the beach. During the season, the dinner line forms early. The raw bar in front is noisy and crowded, the back dining rooms more relaxed. Menus change daily. Specialties include 8–10 daily fresh fish specials. *456 S. Ocean Blvd., Palm Beach, tel. 407/659–1500. Dress: informal. Reservations suggested. AE, DC, MC, V. Expensive.*

Palm Beach Gardens
Continental

The Explorers. You sit in red leather hobnail chairs at tables lit with small brass and glass lanterns. The à la carte menu includes a variety of international and American regional preparations. Specialties include a fresh sushi appetizer with soy, wasabi, and pickled ginger; loin of axis deer with lingonberry conserve; and almond snow eggs, an egg-shaped meringue poached in almond cream, plated between three-fruit coulees (boysenberry, mango, and tamarillo) and garnished with a nest of butter caramel. The Explorers Wine Club meets monthly for wine and food tastings and is open to the public for a one-time $5 membership. Contact the club for a schedule of events. *400 Ave. of the Champions, Palm Beach Gardens, tel. 407/627–2000. Jacket required. Reservations advised. Closed Sun.–Mon. May–Sept. AE, MC, V. Expensive.*

Lodging

The list below is a representative selection of hotels and motels in Palm Beach County. The rate categories in the list are based on the all-year or peak-season price; off-peak rates may be a category or two lower.

The most highly recommended hotels are indicated by a star ★.

Category	Cost*
Very Expensive	over $120
Expensive	$90–$120
Moderate	$50–$90
Inexpensive	under $50

*All prices are for a standard double room, excluding 6% state sales tax and nominal tourist tax

The following credit card abbreviations are used: AE, American Express; CB, Carte Blanche; DC, Diners Club; MC, MasterCard; V, Visa.

Very Expensive

Boca Raton Resort & Club. Architect and socialite Addison Mizner designed and built the original. The tower was added in 1961, the ultramodern Boca Beach Club, in 1981. Room rates during the winter season are based on the modified American plan (including breakfast and dinner). The rooms in the older buildings tend to be smaller and cozily traditional; those in the newer buildings are light, airy and contemporary in color schemes and furnishings. *501 E. Camino Real, Boca Raton 33432, tel. 407/395–3000 or 800/327–0101. 1,000 rooms: 100 in the original 1926 Cloister Inn, 333 in the 1931 addition, 235 in the 27-story Tower Building, 212 in the Boca Beach Club, 120 in the Golf Villas. Facilities: 1½ mi of Atlantic Ocean beach, 4 outdoor freshwater swimming pools, 22 tennis courts (2 lighted), health spa, 23-slip marina, fishing and sailing charters, 7 restaurants, 3 lounges, in-room safes. AE, DC, MC, V.*
Brazilian Court. Built in 1925, the Brazilian Court received new owners and an extensive renovation in 1984–85. The yellow Mediterranean-style buildings still surround a pair of courtyards, where much of the original landscaping survives today.

An open loggia with ceiling beams of exposed pecky cypress was enclosed to provide a gracious European-style lobby. A concierge at an antique desk greets you for check-in. All guest rooms feature gold-plated plumbing fixtures, firm mattresses, and valances above the beds and windows. However, no two rooms are alike. *301 Australian Ave., Palm Beach 33480, tel. 407/655–7740 or 800/351–5656. 134 rooms with bath, including 6 suites, rooms for nonsmokers and handicapped guests. Facilities: outdoor heated freshwater swimming pool, cable TV, two restaurants, lounge, 24-hr room service. AE, CB, DC, MC, V.*

The Breakers. This historic seven-story oceanfront resort hotel, built in 1926 and enlarged in 1968, is currently undergoing renovation. At this palatial Italian Renaissance structure, cupids wrestle alligators in the Florentine fountain in front of the main entrance. Inside the lofty lobby, your eyes rise to majestic ceiling vaults and frescoes. The hotel's proud tradition of formality remains. After 7 PM, men and boys must wear jackets and ties in the public areas. (Ties are optional in summer.) The new room decor comes in two color schemes: cool greens and soft pinks in an orchid-patterned English cotton chintz fabric; the other is in blue, with a floral and ribbon chintz. Both designs include white plantation shutters and wall coverings, Chinese porcelain table lamps, and original 1920s furniture restored to its period appearance. The original building has 15 different sizes and shapes of rooms, many a bit cramped by today's standards. If you like a lot of space, ask to be placed in the newer addition. *1 S. County Rd., Palm Beach 33480, tel. 407/655–6611 or 800/833–3141. 528 rooms with bath, including 40 suites. Facilities: ½ mi of Atlantic Ocean beachfront, outdoor heated freshwater swimming pool, 19 tennis courts, 2 golf courses, health club with Keiser and Nautilus equipment, men's and women's saunas, lawn bowling, croquet, shuffleboard, shopping arcade with upscale boutiques, 3 restaurants, lounge. AE, CB, DC, MC, V.*

The Colony. Located a block off Worth Avenue, this mid-rise luxury city hotel caters to an older, upscale clientele. The Duke and Duchess of Windsor stayed here. John Lennon once was turned away from the dining room because he arrived tieless. Hotel built in 1947, restored in 1987–88; low-rise maisonettes built in mid-1950s, apartments built in 1960s. A striking lobby mural by Phil Brinkman depicts turn-of-the-century Palm Beach. Room decor is tropical chic, with rattan furnishings and pink, blue, and tropical green pastel fabrics in floral patterns. *155 Hammon Ave., Palm Beach 33480, tel. 407/655–5430, fax 407/659–1793. 106 rooms, including 36 suites and apartments. Facilities: outdoor heated freshwater swimming pool, restaurant serves 3 meals daily, dancing nightly with live band, beauty parlor. AE, MC, V.*

PGA Sheraton Resort. This sportsperson's mecca at PGA National Golf Club underwent a $1.8-million renovation in 1987–88 by an interior designer who likes mauve, peach, and aqua. The resort is headquarters for the Professional Golfer's Association and the U.S. Croquet Association, and hosts many major golf, tennis, and croquet tournaments. *400 Ave. of the Champions, Palm Beach Gardens 33418, tel. 407/627–2000 or 800/325–3535. 413 rooms with bath, including 25 suites, 36 nonsmokers rooms, 14 handicapped rooms, 80 2-bedroom, 2-bath cottages with fully equipped kitchen. Facilities: 5 golf courses, 19 tennis courts (10 lighted), 5 croquet courts, 6 indoor racquetball* *courts, outdoor freshwater swimming pool, sand beach on 26-acre lake, sailboats and aquacycles for rent, fitness center, sauna, whirlpool, aerobic dance studio, 4 restaurants, 2 lounges, in-room minibars and safes. AE, DC, MC, V.*

Palm Beach Polo and Country Club. Individual villas and condominiums are available in this exclusive 2,200-acre resort where Britain's Prince Charles comes to play polo. Arrange to rent a dwelling closest to the sports activity which interests you: polo, tennis, or golf. Each residence is uniquely designed and furnished by its owner according to standards of quality set by the resort. *13198 Forest Hill Blvd., West Palm Beach 33414, tel. 407/798-7000 or 800/327-4204. 140 privately owned villas and condominiums available for rental when the owners are away. Facilities: 10 outdoor freshwater swimming pools, 24 tennis courts, 2 18-hole golf courses and 1 9-hole course, men's and women's saunas, 10 polo fields, equestrian trails through a nature preserve, 5 stable barns, 2 lighted croquet lawns, squash and racquetball courts, sculling equipment and instruction, 5 dining rooms. AE, DC, MC, V.*

The Palm Court. A 66-room city hotel built in 1926, The Palm Court was restored by new owners in 1986 and reopened in November 1988. *363 Coconut Row, Palm Beach 33480, tel. 407/659-5800 or 800/233-8277. Facilities: outdoor swimming pool, restaurant, library. AE, MC, V.*

Expensive
★

The Jupiter Beach Hilton. This high-rise oceanfront resort hotel is frequented by celebrities and sea turtles. The sea turtles come ashore each summer to lay their eggs in the sand along this stretch of unspoiled beach. The Jupiter Beach Hilton's beach director leads turtle walks at night to look for nesting mothers. In the morning, he collects the eggs in a holding pen by the beach hut to protect them from predators. When the eggs hatch, he helps the baby turtles dig out and guards them as they scramble into the surf. Human guests are at least as well-pampered by a friendly and efficient staff. The nine-story hotel has interior decor of sophisticated informality. The lobby suggests Singapore, with wicker and bamboo furniture, whitewashed wood floors, white ceiling fans, and a plethora of palms, orchids, and other tropical plants. *Indiantown Rd. and Rte. A1A, Jupiter 33477, tel. 407/746-2511, in FL 800/432-1420, elsewhere in the USA 800/821-8791, in Canada 800/228-8810. 197 rooms with bath, including 4 suites, 26 nonsmokers rooms, 2 rooms for handicapped guests. Facilities: outdoor heated freshwater swimming pool, 400 ft of beachfront, 60 cabanas, snorkeling, windsurfing, lighted tennis court, poolside snack bar, boutique, fitness center, restaurant, lounge, cable TV, in-room minibars. AE, CB, DC, MC, V.*

The Arts

The *Palm Beach Post*, in its "TGIF" entertainment insert on Fridays, lists all events for the weekend, including concerts. Admission to some cultural events is free or by donation.

Performing Arts Center

Mizner Park (Box 1695, Boca Raton 33429), a cultural center between Federal Highway and Mizner Boulevard, is scheduled to open in 1990. It will house a performing arts complex; art, science, and children's museums; and a specialty shopping center.

Theater **Caldwell Theatre Company.** This professional equity regional theater, part of the Florida State Theater system, moved to a temporary site in 1989 while awaiting completion of permanent quarters in the new Mizner Center. *7887 N. Federal Hwy., Boca Raton 33487, tel. 407/368–7509 (Boca Raton), 407/832– 2989 (Palm Beach), 305/462–5433 (Broward County).*

Royal Palm Dinner Theater. Equity cast performs five or six contemporary musicals each year. *303 Golfview Dr., Royal Palm Plaza, Boca Raton 33432, tel. 407/426–2211 or in FL, 800/841–6725. Tues.–Sat. 8 PM, Sun. 6 PM, Wed. & Sat. matinees 2 PM. AE, MC, V.*

Excursion: Treasure Coast

Numbers in the margin correspond with points of interest on the Treasure Coast map.

This excursion north from **Palm Beach** through the Treasure Coast counties of Martin, St. Lucie, and Indian River traverses an area that was remote and sparsely populated as recently as the late 1970s. Resort and leisure-oriented residential development has swollen its population. If you plan to stay overnight or dine at a good restaurant, reservations are a must.

The interior of all three counties is largely devoted to citrus production, and also cattle ranching in rangelands of pine-and-palmetto scrub. St. Lucie and Indian River counties also contain the upper reaches of the vast St. Johns Marsh, headwaters of the largest northward-flowing river in the United States. If you take Florida's Turnpike from Palm Beach north to the Orlando—Disney World area, you will dip into the edge of St. Johns Marsh about eight miles north of the Fort Pierce exit. Along the coast, the broad expanse of the Indian River (actually a tidal lagoon) separates the barrier islands from the mainland. It's a sheltered route for boaters on the Intracoastal Waterway, a nursery for the young of many saltwater game fish species, and a natural radiator keeping frost away from the tender orange and grapefruit trees that grow near its banks.

Completion of I–95's missing link from Palm Beach Gardens to Fort Pierce in 1987 eliminated the Treasure Coast's last vestiges of relative seclusion. Hotels, restaurants, and shopping malls already crowd the corridor from I–95 to the beach throughout the 70-mile stretch from Palm Beach north to Vero Beach. The Treasure Coast has become another link in the chain of municipalities that some Floridians call "the city of U.S. 1."

Of special interest in this area are the sea turtles that come ashore at night from April to August to lay their eggs on the beaches. Conservation groups, chambers of commerce, and resorts organize turtle-watches, which you may join.

Exploring Treasure Coast

❶ This tour takes you north from **Palm Beach** along the coast as far as Vero Beach, but you can break away at any intermediate point and return to Palm Beach on I–95.

❷ From downtown **West Palm Beach,** take U.S. 1 about five miles north to Blue Heron Boulevard (Rte. A1A) in Riviera Beach,

Treasure Coast

turn right, and cross the **Jerry Thomas Bridge** onto Singer Island. Sightseeing boats depart from **Phil Foster Park** on the island side of the bridge.

Continue on Rte. A1A as it turns north onto Ocean Boulevard, past hotels and high-rise condominiums to **Ocean Reef Park** (3900 N. Ocean Dr., Riviera Beach, tel. 407/964–4420), a snorkeling spot where the reefs are close to shore in shallow water. You may see angelfish, sergeant-majors, rays, robin fish, and occasionally a Florida lobster (actually a species of saltwater crayfish). Wear canvas sneakers and cloth gloves.

Go north on Rte. A1A to **John D. MacArthur State Park** (10900 Rte. A1A, North Palm Beach, tel. 407/964–4420), which offers more good snorkeling along almost two miles of beach, and access to the mangrove swamps in the upper reaches of Lake Worth.

North of MacArthur State Park, Rte. A1A rejoins U.S. 1, then veers east again 1½ miles north at Juno Beach. Take Rte. A1A ❸ north to the **Children's Museum of Juno Beach**, established by Eleanor N. Fletcher, "the turtle lady of Juno Beach." Museum displays interpret the sea turtles' natural history; hatchlings are raised in saltwater tanks, tagged and released into the surf. The museum conducts guided turtle watches June 1–July 15, at the height of the nesting season. *1111 Ocean Dr., Juno Beach, tel. 407/627–8280. Admission free. Open Tues.–Sat. 10–3, Sun. 1–3.*

❹ From Juno Beach north to **Jupiter**, Rte. A1A runs for almost four miles atop the beachfront dunes. West of the road, about half the land is undeveloped, with endangered native plant communities. The road veers away from the dunes at **Carlin Park** (400 Rte. A1A, Jupiter, tel. 407/964–4420), which provides beach frontage, covered picnic pavilions, hiking trails, two tennis courts, and fishing sites.

At the northwest corner of Indiantown Road and Rte. A1A is **Burt Reynolds Jupiter Theater.** Reynolds grew up in Jupiter; his father was Palm Beach County sheriff. More than 150 Broadway and Hollywood stars have performed here since the theater opened in 1979. In 1989 Reynolds gave the theater to Palm Beach Community College, which will run it as a not-for-profit regional theater. At press time it was scheduled to reopen early in 1990. *1001 E. Indiantown Rd., Jupiter, tel. 407/746–5566.*

Leave the theater grounds on Indiantown Road, go west to U.S. 1, and turn right. About a mile north of Jupiter Island, turn right into Burt Reynolds Park to visit the **Loxahatchee Historical Society Museum.** Permanent exhibits in preparation will emphasize Seminole Indians, the steamboat era, pioneer life on the Loxahatchee River, shipwrecks, railroads and modern-day development. A pioneer dwelling at the mouth of the river, the Dubois Home, is open Sunday 1–3:30 PM; ask for directions at the museum. *805 N. U.S. 1, Box 1506, Jupiter, tel. 407/747–6639. Open Tues.–Fri. 10–3, weekends noon–3, closed Mon. Admission by donation.*

Continue north on U.S. 1 across the Loxahatchee River. The 105-foot-tall **Jupiter Lighthouse,** east of the bridge, is the oldest structure in Palm Beach County, built 1855–59. To reach the lighthouse and a small museum of local history on the ground floor, turn east on Route 707, then take the first right into Lighthouse Park. *No phone. Admission by donation. Open Sun. noon–2:30.*

⑤ Take Rte. 707 north from the lighthouse onto **Jupiter Island.** Just north of the Martin County line, stop at the Nature Conservancy's 113-acre **Blowing Rocks Preserve,** with plant communities native to beachfront dune, strand (the landward side of the dunes), marsh, and hammock (tropical hardwood forest). Sea grape, cabbage palms, saw palmetto, and sea oats help to anchor the dunes. The floral beauty of Indian blanket, dune sunflower, and goldenrod carpets the ground. You may see pelicans, seagulls, ospreys, redbellied and pileated woodpeckers, and a profusion of warblers in spring and fall. A trail takes you over the dune to the beach. At high tide, spray shoots up through holes in the largest Anastasia limestone outcropping on the Atlantic coast. At dead low tide, you can walk on the seaward side of the rocks and peer into caves and solution holes. Best time to go is early morning, before the crowds. The parking lot holds just 18 cars, with room for three cars to wait; Jupiter Island police will ticket cars parked along the road shoulder. *Box 3795, Tequesta, tel. 407/575–2297. Open 6–5. Admission by donation. No food, drink, ice chests, pets, or spearfishing allowed. No rest rooms.*

Continue north through the town of Jupiter Island, a posh community where President Bush's mother and many other notables dwell in estates screened from the road by dense vegetation. At the north end of Jupiter Island, **Hobe Sound National Wildlife Refuge** has a 3½-mile beach where turtles nest and shells wash ashore in abundance. On the mainland at refuge headquarters, visit the **Elizabeth W. Kirby Interpretive Center.** Take Rte. 707 and County Road 708 through the town of Hobe Sound to U.S. 1, then turn left and go about two miles south. The center is on the left (east) side of the highway. An adjacent ½-mile trail winds through a forest of sand pine and scrub oak —one of Florida's most unusual and endangered plant communities. *13640 S.E. Federal Hwy., Hobe Sound 33455, refuge tel. 407/546–6141, nature center tel. 407/546–2067. Trail always open. Nature center open weekdays 9–11 and 1–3, group tours by appointment.*

From the interpretive center, go south 2½ miles to the entrance to **Jonathon Dickinson State Park.** Follow signs to Hobe Mountain, an ancient dune topped with a tower where you'll have a panoramic view across the park's 10,284 acres of varied terrain. It encompasses sand pine, slash pine and palmetto flatwoods, mangrove river swamp, and the winding upper northwest fork of the Loxahatchee River, which is part of the federal government's wild and scenic rivers program and populated by manatees in winter and alligators all year. *14800 S.E. Federal Hwy., Hobe Sound, tel. 407/546–2771. Open daily 8–sundown. Admission: $1 driver, 50 cents per passenger. Facilities: bicycle and hiking trails, campground, snack bar. Contact State Vending Corp., 16450 S.E. Federal Hwy., Hobe Sound 33455, tel. 407/746–1466 for information and reservations on cabins, rental canoes and rowboats. 2-hr narrated river cruise: $9 adults, $4 children under 12.*

⑥ Turn north and take U.S. 1 through some unavoidable commercial development to **Stuart,** then rejoin Rte. A1A northbound to Hutchinson Island. Stop at the pastel-pink **Elliott Museum,**

built in 1961 in honor of inventor Sterling Elliott. On display is an early model of his Elliott Addressing Machine, forerunner of today's Addressograph machines. Elliott also invented a four-wheel bicycle, the quadricycle; the mechanism that makes its wheels turn is the basis of the automobile differential. In addition to Elliott's inventions, the museum features antique automobiles, dolls and toys, and fixtures from an early general store, blacksmith shop, and apothecary shop. Children enjoy feeding coins to a voracious collection of 19th-century mechanical banks. *825 N.E. Ocean Blvd., Stuart, tel. 407/225–1961. Open daily 1–4. Admission: $2.50 adults, 50 cents children 6–13, under 6 free.*

A mile south of the Elliott Museum stands the **House of Refuge Museum,** built in 1875 and now restored to its original appearance. It's one of 10 such structures erected by the U.S. Life Saving Service (an ancestor of the Coast Guard) to aid stranded sailors along Florida's then-remote Atlantic Coast. The keeper here patrolled the beach looking for shipwreck victims whose vessels foundered on Gilbert's Bar, an offshore reef. Exhibits include antique lifesaving equipment, maps, ships' logs, artifacts from nearby wrecks, boatmaking tools, and six tanks of local fish from the ocean and the Indian River. A 35-foot watchtower in the front yard was used during World War II by submarine spotters. *301 S.E. MacArthur Blvd., Stuart, tel. 407/225–1875. Open Tues.–Sun. 1–4, closed Mon. and holidays. Admission: $1 adults, 50 cents children 6–13, under 6 free.*

Driving north on Rte. A1A, you will pass Florida Power & Light Company's St. Lucie nuclear power plant. As you approach the South Beach Causeway Bridge into **Fort Pierce,** stop at the **St. Lucie County Historical Museum** to see more artifacts of the region's history. Exhibits include treasure from a Spanish fleet wrecked in a 1715 hurricane and a diorama depicting a Seminole Indian encampment with a *chickee* (palm-thatched shelter) and dugout canoe. On the grounds is the Gardner House, a restored and furnished Cracker-style pioneer dwelling built in 1907. *414 Seaway Dr., Fort Pierce, tel. 407/464–6635. Open Tues.–Sat. 10–4, Sun. noon–4. Admission: $1 adults, 50 cents children 6–12, under 6 free.*

Cross the bridge into Fort Pierce for a mile on U.S. 1, bypassing Fort Pierce Inlet (which divides Hutchinson Island), then veer east on Rte. A1A across North Beach Causeway. About a mile east, as you approach the ocean, Rte. A1A turns left. Go right instead to visit **Fort Pierce Inlet State Recreation Area,** where a sand bottom creates the Treasure Coast's safest surfing conditions and a nature trail winds through a coastal hammock.

North on Rte. A1A at Pepper Park is the **UDT-Seal Museum,** beside the beach where more than 3,000 Navy frogmen trained during World War II. The museum traces the exploits of Navy divers from the 1944 Normandy invasion through Korea, Vietnam, and astronaut landings at sea. *Box 1117, Ft. Pierce, tel. 407/464–FROG (3764). Open Wed.–Sun. 10–4. Admission: $1 adults, 50¢ children 6–11, under 6 free.*

Within a mile north of Pepper Beach, turn left to the parking lot for the **Jack Island wildlife refuge,** accessible only by footbridge. The one-mile Marsh Rabbit Trail across the island traverses a mangrove swamp to a 30-foot observation tower overlooking the Indian River. You'll see ospreys, brown pelicans, great blue herons, ibis, and other water birds.

8 Return to Rte. A1A and go north to **Vero Beach,** an affluent city of about 30,000; retirees comprise half the winter population. In the exclusive Riomar Bay section, north of the 17th Street Bridge, "canopy roads" shaded by massive live oaks cross the barrier island between Rte. A1A and Ocean Drive. **Painted Bunting Lane,** a typical canopy road, is lined with elegant homes—many dating from the 1920s.

The city provides beach-access parks with boardwalks and steps bridging the foredune. (Open daily 7 AM–10 PM, admission free.) From shore, snorkelers and divers can swim out to explore reefs 100–300 ft. off the beach. Summer offers the best diving conditions. At low tide you can see the boiler and other remains of an iron-screw steamer, *Breconshire*, which foundered in 1894 on a reef just south of Beachland Boulevard.

Along Ocean Drive near Beachland Boulevard, a specialty shopping area includes art galleries, antique stores, and upscale clothing stores. Also in this area is **The Driftwood Inn Resort** (3150 Ocean Dr., Vero Beach, tel. 407/231–0550), a unique beachfront hotel and restaurant built in the 1930s by Waldo Sexton, an eccentric plow salesman from Indiana. He used driftwood and other scavenged lumber as well as art treasures salvaged from Palm Beach mansions torn down during the Depression. Return to the mainland from Beachland Boulevard across the Merrill Barber Bridge or go 1½ miles south to the new high-rise 17th Street Bridge, which offers a sweeping view over the Indian River. At this point you can take Rte. 60 west through Vero Beach to I-95 for the return to Palm Beach.

Spectator Sports

Baseball The **Los Angeles Dodgers** train each March in the 6,000-seat Holman Dodgertown Stadium near the Municipal Airport. *Box 2887, Vero Beach 32961, tel. 800/334–PLAY or 407/569–4900.*

The **New York Mets** hold spring training in the 7,400-seat St. Lucie County Sport Complex, home stadium for the Florida League's St. Lucie Mets. *North Peacock Blvd., Box 8808, Port St. Lucie 34985, tel. 407/879–7378.*

Polo **Windsor Polo and Beach Club.** Geoffrey and Jorie Kent's new polo club featured England's Prince Charles in a special charity game, the Prince of Wales Cup, when it opened in February of 1989. For 1990 the Club plans an abbreviated season; the first complete season will be in 1991. *9300 North A1A, Suite 201, Vero Beach 32963, tel. 407/589–9800 or 800/233–POLO.*

Dining

The list below is a representative selection of restaurants on the Treasure Coast, organized geographically, and by type of cuisine within each community. Unless otherwise noted, they serve lunch and dinner.

Highly recommended restaurants in each price category are indicated by a star ★.

Category	Cost*
Very Expensive	over $55
Expensive	$35–$55
Moderate	$15–$35
Inexpensive	under $15

Average cost of a 3-course dinner, per person, excluding drinks, service, and 6% sales tax.

The following credit card abbreviations are used: AE, American Express; CB, Carte Blanche; DC, Diners Club; MC, MasterCard; and V, Visa.

Stuart
American

The Emporium. Indian River Plantation's coffee shop is an old-fashioned soda fountain and grill that also serves hearty breakfasts. Specialties include eggs Benedict, omelets, and fresh-baked pastries. *555 N.E. Ocean Blvd., Hutchinson Island, tel. 407/225-3700. Dress: informal. No reservations. AE, DC, MC, V. Inexpensive.*

The Porch. This casual indoor/outdoor restaurant overlooks the tennis courts at Indian River Plantation. Specialties include hearty clam chowder, a daily quiche, fried calamari, and two daily selections of fresh fish. *555 N.E. Ocean Blvd., Hutchinson Island, tel. 407/225-3700. Dress: informal. No reservations. AE, DC, MC, V. Inexpensive.*

Continental
★

The Inlet. This intimate 60-seat restaurant in the heart of Indian River Plantation features fine dining on gold-rimmed plates in a setting of ethereal pinks and earth tones. Specialties include oysters Rockefeller, creamy lobster bisque with cognac, steak Diane, and fresh snapper. *555 N.E. Ocean Blvd., Hutchinson Island, tel. 407/225-3700. Jacket and tie required. Reservations required. AE, DC, MC, V. No lunch. Closed Sun. Open July–Sept. Fri. and Sat. only. Expensive.*

★

Scalawags. Part of Indian River Plantation's new hotel complex, Scalawags can seat you on a terrace overlooking the marina, in a dining room decorated with original paintings of Florida birds, or in a private 20-seat wine room. Specialties include Caribbean conch soup, sea scallops with fresh dill sauce, seafood ravioli, and rack of lamb. The Sunday champagne brunch is superb. *555 N.E. Ocean Blvd., Hutchinson Island, tel. 407/225-3700. Jacket required. Reservations required. AE, DC, MC, V. Dinner only May–Sept. Expensive.*

Ft. Pierce
Seafood

Theo Thudpucker's Raw Bar. Businessmen in suits and ties mingle here with people off the beach in bathing suits. Specialties include oyster stew, smoked fish spread, conch salad and fritters, soft-shell crabs, fresh catfish, and alligator tail. *2025 Seaway Dr. (South Jetty), tel. 407/465-1078. Dress: informal. No reservations. No credit cards. Closed Christmas, New Year's Day, Easter, Mother's Day, and Thanksgiving. Inexpensive.*

Vero Beach
Continental
★

The Black Pearl. This small, intimate restaurant (19 tables) with red, pink, and green Art Deco furnishings offers entrées that combine fresh local ingredients with the best of the Continental tradition. Specialties include chilled leek-and-watercress soup, hearty conch-and-crab chowder, feta cheese and spinach fritters, mesquite-grilled swordfish, and dolphin brushed with lime juice and olive oil. *1409 Hwy. A1A, tel. 407/ 234-4426. Reservations advised. AE, MC, V. Dinner only. Closed Christmas, New Year's Day, and July 4th. Moderate.*

Seafood **Ocean Grill.** Opened as a hamburger shack in 1938, the Ocean Grill has since been refurbished and outfitted with antiques— Tiffany lamps, wrought-iron chandeliers, and Beanie Backus paintings of pirates and Seminole Indians. The menu has also changed with the times and now includes black bean soup, crisp onion rings, Indian River crab cakes, jumbo lump crabmeat salad, at least three kinds of fresh fish every day, prime rib, and a tart Key-lime pie. *Sexton Plaza (Beachland Blvd. east of Ocean Dr.), tel. 407/231-5409. Reservations accepted for parties of 5 or more. AE, MC, V. Closed 2 wks. after Labor Day. Moderate.*

Lodging

The list below is a representative selection of hotels and motels on the Treasure Coast. The rate categories in the list are based on the all-year or peak-season price; off-peak rates may be a category or two lower.

Highly recommended lodgings in each price category are indicated by a star ★.

Category	Cost*
Very Expensive	over $120
Expensive	$90–$120
Moderate	$50–$90
Inexpensive	under $50

*All prices are for a standard double room; excluding 6% state sales tax and nominal tourist tax.

The following credit card abbreviations are used: AE, American Express; CB, Carte Blanche; DC, Diners Club; MC, MasterCard; and V, Visa.

Stuart **Indian River Plantation.** Situated on a 192-acre tract of land on
★ Hutchinson Island, this resort includes a three-story luxury hotel that is an architectural gem in the Victorian Beach Revival style, with tin roofs, shaded verandas, pink stucco, and much latticework. Some 70 new condos are scheduled to open in spring 1990. *555 N.E. Ocean Blvd., Hutchinson Island, 34996, tel. 407/225-3700 or 800/444-1432. 200 hotel rooms with bath, including 10 rooms for handicapped guests; 54 1- and 2-bedroom oceanfront condominium apartments with full kitchens. Facilities: 3 swimming pools, outdoor spa, 13 tennis courts, golf course, 77-slip marina, power boat and jet-ski rentals, 5 restaurants. AE, DC, MC, V. Very Expensive.*

Vero Beach **The Pickett Suite Resort.** Built in 1986, this five-story rose stucco hotel on Ocean Drive provides easy access to Vero Beach's specialty shops and boutiques. First-floor rooms have patios opening onto the pool. *3500 Ocean Dr., 32963, tel. 800/742-5388 or 407/231-5666. 55 1- and 2-bedroom suites with bath. Facilities: swimming pool, outdoor pool bar/restaurant, TV. AE, DC, MC, V. Very Expensive.*

The Flori a
Keys

Introduction

by George and Rosalie Leposky

The Florida Keys are a wilderness of flowering jungles and shimmering seas, a jade pendant of mangrove-fringed islands dangling toward the tropics. The Florida Keys are also a 110-mile traffic jam lined with garish billboards, hamburger stands, shopping centers, motels, and trailer courts. Unfortunately, you can't have one without the other. A river of tourist dollars gushes southward along the only highway—U.S. 1—to Key West. Many residents of Monroe County live by diverting some of that river's green flow to their own pockets, in ways that have in spots blighted the Keys' fragile beauty—at least on the 31 islands linked to the mainland by the 42 bridges of the Overseas Highway.

As you drive down U.S. 1 through the islands, the silvery blue and green Atlantic, with its great living reef, are on your left, and Florida Bay, the Gulf of Mexico and the back country are on your right. At points the ocean and the gulf are ten miles apart; on the narrowest landfill islands, they are separated only by the road.

The Overseas Highway varies from a frustrating traffic-clogged trap to a mystical pathway skimming across the sea. There are more islands than you will be able to remember. Follow the little green mile markers by the side of U.S. 1, and even if you lose track of the names of the islands, you won't get lost.

There are many things to do along the way, but first you have to remind yourself to get off the highway, which is lined with junk and has the seductive power of keeping you to itself. Once you leave this road, you can rent a boat and find a secluded anchorage at which to fish, swim, and marvel at the sun, sea, and sky. To the south in the Atlantic, you can dive to spectacular coral reefs or pursue dolphin, blue marlin, and other deep-water game fish. Along the Florida Bay coastline you can seek out the bonefish, snapper, snook, and tarpon that lurk in the grass flats and in the shallow, winding channels of the back country.

Along the reefs and among the islands are over 600 kinds of fish. Diminutive deer and pale raccoons, related to but distinct from their mainland cousins, inhabit the Lower Keys. And throughout the islands you'll find such exotic West Indian plants as Jamaica dogwood, pigeon plum, poisonwood, satinwood, and silver and thatch palms, as well as tropical birds like the great white heron, mangrove cuckoo, roseate spoonbill, and white-crowned pigeon.

Another Keys attraction is the weather: in the winter it's typically 10 degrees warmer in the Keys than on the mainland; in the summer it's usually 10 degrees cooler. The Keys also get substantially less rain, around 30 inches annually compared to 55–60 inches in Miami and the Everglades. Most of the rain falls in brief, vigorous thunderstorms on summer afternoons. In winter, continental cold fronts occasionally stall over the Keys, dragging temperatures down to the 40s.

The Keys were only sparsely populated until the early 20th century. In 1905, however, railroad magnate Henry Flagler began building the overseas extension of his Florida East Coast Railroad south from Homestead to Key West. His goal was to establish a rail link to the steamships that sailed between Key West and Havana, just 90 miles away across the Straits of Florida. The railroad arrived at Key West in 1912 and remained a lifeline of commerce until the Labor Day hurricane of 1935 washed out much of its roadbed. For three years thereafter, the only way in and out of Key West was by boat. The Overseas Highway, built over the railroad's old roadbeds and bridges, was completed in 1938.

Although the Keys on the surface seem homogenous to most mainlanders, they are actually quite varied in terms of population and ambience. Most of the residents of the Upper Keys, which extend from Key Largo to Long Key Channel, moved to Florida from the Northeast and Midwest; many are retirees. Most of the work force is employed by the tourism and service industries. Key Largo, the largest of the keys and the one closest to the mainland, is becoming a bedroom community for Homestead, South Dade, and even the southern reaches of Miami. In the Middle Keys, from Long Key Channel through Marathon to Seven-Mile Bridge, fishing and related services dominate the economy. Most residents are the children and grandchildren of migrants from other Southern states. The Lower Keys from Seven Mile Bridge down to Key West have a diverse population: native "Conchs" (white Key Westers, many of whom trace their ancestry to the Bahamas), freshwater Conchs (longtime residents who migrated from somewhere else years ago), gays (who now make up at least 20 percent of Key West's citizenry), black Bahamians, Hispanics (primarily Cubans), recent refugees from the urban sprawl of Miami and Fort Lauderdale, transient Navy and Air Force personnel, students waiting tables, and a miscellaneous assortment of vagabonds, drifters, and dropouts in search of refuge at the end of the road.

Important Addresses and Numbers

Tourist Information
Florida Keys & Key West Visitors Bureau (Box 1147, Key West 33041, tel. 305/296–3811 or 800/FLA–KEYS). Ask for their free accommodations guide.

Local chambers of commerce in Key Largo, Islamorada, Marathon, and Key West have visitor centers with information on accommodations, recreation, restaurants, and special events:

Key Largo Chamber of Commerce (MM 103.4, BS, 103400 Overseas Hwy., Key Largo 33037, tel. 305/451–1414 or 800/822–1088).

Islamorada Chamber of Commerce (MM 82.6, BS, Box 915, Islamorada 33036, tel. 305/664–5603 or 800/FAB–KEYS).

Greater Marathon Chamber of Commerce (MM 49, BS, 330 Overseas Hwy., Marathon 33050, tel. 305/743–5417 or 800/842–9580).

Lower Keys Chamber of Commerce (MM 30.5, OS, Box 511, Big Pine Key 33043, tel. 305/872–2411).

Greater Key West Chamber of Commerce (402 Wall St., Key West 33041, tel. 305/294–2587).

Emergencies
Dial 911 for ambulance and police.

Hospitals
The following hospitals have 24-hour emergency rooms: **Mariners Hospital** (MM 88.5, BS, 50 High Point Rd., Tavernier, Plantation Key 33070; physician-referral service, tel. 305/852–9222), **Fishermen's Hospital** (MM 48.7, OS, 3301 Overseas Hwy., Marathon, tel. 305/743–5533), **De Poo Hospital** (1200 Kennedy Dr., Key West 33040, tel. 305/294–4692 or 294–5183),

and **Florida Keys Memorial Hospital** (MM5, BS, 5900 Junior College Rd., Stock Island, tel. 305/294–5531).

Late-Night The Keys have no 24-hour pharmacies. Hospital pharmacists
Pharmacies will help with emergencies after regular retail business hours.

Arriving and Departing

By Plane Shuttle and connecting flights go to **Key West International Airport** (S. Roosevelt Blvd., tel. 305/296–5439) from the Miami and Orlando International airports. From Miami, you can fly direct to Key West on Piedmont Airlines, Eastern Express, and Delta Airlines. From Orlando, you must change planes in Miami if you fly on Piedmont or Eastern Express; Delta provides nonstop service.

Eastern Express also flies direct to the **Marathon Airport** (MM 52, BS, 9000 Overseas Hwy., tel. 305/743–2996) from the Miami and Ft. Lauderdale–Hollywood International airports.

Between Miami **The Airporter.** Scheduled van and bus service is available from
and the Keys the lower level of MIA's Concourse E to major hotels in Key Largo and Islamorada. *701 S. Homestead Blvd., Homestead 33030, tel. 305/247–8874 (Miami) or 305/247–8876 (Keys). Reservations required.*

Island Taxi meets arriving flights at MIA. Reservations are required 24 hours in advance for arrivals, one hour for departures. Accompanied children ride free. *Tel. 305/852–9700 (Upper Keys), 305/743–0077 (Middle Keys), 305/872–4404 (Lower Keys). Fare: $4 for first 2 mi, then $1.50/mi.*

By Car If you want to avoid Miami traffic on the way to the Keys, take the Homestead Extension of Florida's Turnpike; although it's a toll road that carries a lot of commuter traffic, it's still the fastest way to go. From MIA, take LeJeune Road (SW 42nd Avenue) south, turn west on the Dolphin Expressway (Route 836) to the turnpike, then go south to the turnpike's southern end. If you prefer traffic to tolls, take LeJeune Road south to U.S. 1 and turn right.

Just south of Florida City, the turnpike joins U.S. 1 and the Overseas Highway begins. Once you cross the Jewfish Creek bridge at the north end of Key Largo, you're officially in the Keys.

From Florida City, you can also reach Key Largo on Card Sound Road. Go 13 miles south to the Card Sound Bridge (toll: $1), which offers a spectacular view of blue water and mangrove-fringed bays (and of Florida Power & Light Company's hulking Turkey Point nuclear power plant in the distance to your left). At low tide, flocks of herons, ibis, and other birds frequent the mud flats on the margin of the sound. Beyond the bridge, on north Key Largo, the road traverses a mangrove swamp with ponds and inlets harboring the exceedingly rare Florida crocodile. At the only stop sign, turn right onto Route 905, which cuts through some of the Keys' few remaining large tracts of tropical hardwood jungle. You'll rejoin U.S. 1 in north Key Largo 31 miles from Florida City.

Car Rentals All six of the rental-car firms with booths inside Miami International Airport also have outlets in Key West, which means you can drive into the Keys and fly out. Don't fly into Key West and drive out; the rental firms have substantial drop charges to leave a Key West car in Miami. Avis, Budget and Hertz also serve Marathon Airport.

Enterprise Rent-A-Car has offices at MIA, several Keys locations, and participating hotels in the Keys where you can pick up and drop off cars when the offices are closed. You can rent a car from Enterprise at MIA and return it there, or leave it in the Keys for a drop charge. *Tel. 305/576–1300 (Miami), 305/451–3998 (Key Largo), 305/664–2344 (Islamorada), or 800/325–8007. Key West and Marathon offices planned for 1990. Open weekdays 8–6, Sat. 9–noon. AE, DC, MC, V.*

By Bus **Greyhound/Trailways.** Buses traveling between Miami and Key West make 10 scheduled stops, but you can flag down a bus anywhere along the route. *Tel. 305/374–7222 (Miami) for schedule; 24-hr Miami Greyhound Station, tel. 305/871–1810; Big Pine Key, tel. 305/872–4022; Key West, 615½ Duval St., tel. 305/296–9072. No reservations.*

By Boat Boaters can travel to Key West either along the Intracoastal Waterway through Florida Bay, or along the Atlantic Coast. The Keys are full of marinas that welcome transient visitors, but they don't have enough slips for everyone who wants to visit the area. Make reservations in advance, and ask about channel and dockage depth—many Keys marinas are quite shallow.

Florida Marine Patrol (Marathon, tel. 305/743–6542).

Coast Guard Group Key West provides 24-hour monitoring of VHF-FM Channel 16. Safety and weather information is broadcast at 7 AM and 5 PM Eastern Standard time on VHF-FM Channel 16 and 22A. *Key West 33040, tel. 305/292–8727. 3 stations in the Keys: Islamorada, tel. 305/664–4404; Marathon, tel. 305/743–6778; Key West, tel. 305/292–8856.*

Getting Around

Directions and Maps The only address many people have is a mile marker (MM) number. The markers themselves are small green rectangular signs along the side of the Overseas Highway (U.S. 1). They begin with MM 126 a mile south of Florida City and end with MM 0 on the corner of Fleming and Whitehead streets in Key West. Keys residents also use the abbreviation BS for the Bay Side of U.S. 1, and OS for the Atlantic Ocean Side of the highway.

Florida Visitor Centers and the Florida Department of Commerce distribute *Florida's Official Transportation Map* free. Write to Florida Department of Commerce (Collins Bldg., Tallahassee 32304).

The best road map for the Florida Keys is published by the Homestead/Florida City Chamber of Commerce. You can obtain a copy at the Tropical Everglades Visitor Center in Florida City, or by mail. *160 U.S. Highway 1, Florida City 33034, tel. 305/245–9180. Open daily 8–6. Map costs $1.50; by mail add 25¢ in U.S., 75¢ elsewhere.*

Throughout the Keys, the local chambers of commerce, marinas, and dive shops will offer you the local **Teall's Guide**—a land and nautical map—for 50¢, which goes to build mooring buoys to protect living coral reefs from boat anchors. Separate guides in the *Teall's Miami and Keys Guides* series cover Miami to Key Largo, John Pennekamp Coral Reef State Park and Key

Largo National Marine Sanctuary, the Middle Keys, and Marathon–Key West. To order the entire series by mail, send $6.95 and your street address (not post office box) to Teall's Florida Keys Guides (111 Saguaro Ln., Marathon 33050, tel. 305/743–3942).

By Car The 18-mile stretch of U.S. 1 from Florida City to Key Largo is a hazardous two-lane road with heavy traffic (especially on weekends) and only two passing zones. Try to drive it in daylight, and be patient day or night. The Overseas Highway is four lanes wide in Key Largo and Marathon, but narrow and crowded elsewhere. Expect delays behind large tractor-trailer trucks, cars towing boats, and rubbernecking tourists. Allow at least five hours from Florida City to Key West on a good day. After midnight, you can make the trip in three hours—but then you miss the scenery.

In Key West's Old Town, parking is scarce and costly ($1.25/hour, $6 maximum at Mallory Square). Use a taxicab, bicycle, moped, or your feet to get around. Elsewhere in the Keys, however, having a car is crucial. Gas prices are higher in the Keys than on the mainland. Fill your tank in Miami and top it off in Florida City.

By Bus The **City of Key West Port and Transit Authority** operates three bus lines: Mallory Square (counterclockwise around the island), Old Town (clockwise around the island), and a free Shopping Center Shuttle (Key Plaza to Searstown). *Tel. 305/292–8165 or 292–8164. Exact fare: 75¢; monthly pass, $20.*

By Taxi **Island Taxi** offers 24-hour service from Key Largo to Boca Chica Key. Accompanied children ride free. There is no service to downtown Key West. *Tel. 305/852–9700 (Upper Keys), 305/743–0077 (Middle Keys), 305/872–4404 (Lower Keys). Fare: $4 for first 2 mi, then $1.50/mi.*
Maxi-Taxi (tel. 305/294–2222 or 296–2222) and **Sun Cab** (tel. 305/296–7777) offer 24-hour service in Key West. *Airport service: Maxi-Taxi $4/person, Sun Cab $4.50/person. Local service: Maxi-Taxi has zone rates and $7 group rate for 6 or more people. Sun Cab has meters, $1.40 first ½-mi, 35¢ each additional ¼-mi.*
Carriage Trade Limousine Service offers island tours in a 1980 stretch Cadillac. *tel. 305/296–0000. $40/hour, minimum 3 hrs.*

Guided Tours

Orientation Tours **The Conch Tour Train.** This 105-minute narrated tour of Key West travels 14 miles through Old Town and around the island. The driver pauses frequently to discuss points of historical interest and to chat with friends. *Boarding Locations: Mallory Sq. Depot on the half hr, Roosevelt Blvd. Depot on the hour, tel. 305/294–5161. Runs daily 9–4. Fare: $10 adults, $3 children. MC, V.*
Old Town Trolley. Key West has 11 trackless trolley-style buses that run every 30 minutes. The trolleys are smaller than the Conch Tour Train and go places the train won't fit. The narrated trolley tour lasts 90 minutes, passes more than 100 points of interest, and makes 16 stops all around the island. You may disembark at any stop and reboard a later trolley. *1910 N. Roosevelt Blvd., Key West 33040, tel. 305/296–6688. Runs 9 AM–4:30 PM. Admission: $10 adults, $4 children. MC, V.*

Special-Interest **Canoeing Nature Tours.** Stan Becker leads a full-day 5-mile ca-
Tours noe and hiking trip in the Key Deer National Wildlife Refuge.
Canoe Tours The trip includes three hours in canoes and four hours explor-
ing Watson Hammock on Big Pine Key. *MM 28, BS, Box 62, Big
Pine Key 33043, tel. 305/872–2620. Reservation required. Chil-
dren welcome; no pets. Box lunch provided. 9 AM–4 PM. Fee:
$60/person.*

Sunset and Harbor Residents and tourists alike flock to west-facing restaurants,
Boat Tours hotel docks, and bars to watch the glowing orb sink into the sea.
Hundreds of people gather on Key West's Mallory Square
Dock, where street performers and food vendors vie with the
sunset for your attention. Throughout the keys, many motor
yacht and sailboat captains take paying passengers on sunset
cruises. Contact local chambers of commerce and hotels for information.

M/V *Miss Key West* offers a one-hour narrated cruise that explores Key West's harbor up to a half-mile from shore. The 45-
passenger, 45-foot motor yacht passes Trumbo Point Navy
Base, home of all six of the Navy's hydrofoil guided-missile de-
stroyers. The sundown cruise includes live music. A morning
cruise seeks dolphins, sea turtles, and birds. *Zero Duval St.
(booth in front of Ocean Key House), tel. 305/296–8865, 800/328–
9815 (USA), or 800/231–9864 (FL). Open 8 AM–11 PM. Tours: 10
AM, noon, 2 PM, 4 PM, and sundown. Admission: harbor and
sunset cruise $8 adults, children under 12 free; dolphin watch
and nature trip, $10 adults, children under 12 free. AE, MC, V.*

Walking Tours **Pelican Path** is a free walking guide to Key West published by
the **Old Island Restoration Foundation.** The tour discusses the
history and architecture of 43 structures along 25 blocks of 12
Old Town streets. Pick up a copy at the Key West Chamber of
Commerce.

Solares Hill's Walking and Biking Guide to Old Key West, by local historian Sharon Wells, contains eight walking tours of the
city and a short tour of the Key West cemetery. Free copies are
available from Key West Chamber of Commerce, many hotels
and stores.

Exploring the Florida Keys

Attractions are listed by island or by mile marker (MM) number.

*Numbers in the margin correspond with points of interest on
the Florida Keys map.*

The Upper Keys

This tour begins on Key Largo, the northeasternmost of the
Florida Keys accessible by road. The tour assumes that you
have come south from Florida City on **Card Sound Road** (Rte.
5). If you take the Overseas Highway (U.S. 1) south from Florida City, you can begin the tour with John Pennekamp Coral
Reef State Park.

Cross the **Card Sound Bridge** onto **North Key Largo,** where
Card Sound Road forms the eastern boundary of **Crocodile
Lakes National Wildlife Refuge.** In the refuge dwell some 300 to
500 crocodiles, the largest single concentration of these shy,
elusive reptiles in North America. There's no visitor center

here—just 6,800 acres of mangrove swamp and adjoining upland jungle. For your best chance to see a crocodile, park on the shoulder of Card Sound Road and scan the ponds along the road with binoculars. In winter, crocodiles often haul out and sun themselves on the banks farthest from the road. Don't leave the road shoulder; you could disturb tern nests on the nearby spoil banks or aggravate the rattlesnakes.

Take Card Sound Road to Route 905, turn right, and drive for 10 miles through **Key Largo Hammock,** the largest remaining stand of the vast West Indian tropical hardwood forest that once covered most of the upland areas in the Florida Keys. The state and federal governments are busy acquiring as much of the hammock as they can to protect it from further development, and they hope to establish visitor centers and nature trails. For now, it's best to admire this wilderness from the road. According to law-enforcement officials, this may be the most dangerous place in the United States, a haven for modern-day pirates and witches. The "pirates" are drug smugglers who land their cargo along the ocean shore or drop it into the forest from low-flying planes. The "witches" are practitioners of voodoo, *santeria*, and other occult rituals. What's more, this jungle is full of poisonous plants. The most dangerous, the manchineel or "devil tree," has a toxin so potent that rainwater falling on its leaves and then onto a person's skin can cause sores that resist healing. Florida's first tourist, explorer Juan Ponce de León, died in 1521 from a superficial wound inflicted by an Indian arrowhead dipped in manchineel sap.

Time Out Pause for a drink at the **Caribbean Club,** a friendly neighborhood bar on a historic site. Scenes from *Key Largo*, the 1948 Bogart-Bacall movie, were filmed in the original Caribbean Club, which burned down in the 1950s. *MM 104, BS, Key Largo, tel. 305/451–9970. Open daily 7 AM–4 AM. No credit cards.*

Continue on U.S. 1 to Transylvania Avenue (MM 103.2) and turn left to visit the **Marine Resources Development Foundation.** The foundation expects by mid-1990 to have a 1-acre visitor center beside the Overseas Highway and to provide a minibus to transport visitors to its oceanside campus. There you'll find a museum devoted to the history of man and the sea, tanks for growing sea sprouts (a species of edible red algae), a 13-minute multimedia slide show, and a 280-foot moving sidewalk through a clear tube beneath the surface of a 30-foot-deep lagoon teeming with tropical fish. Also in the lagoon is **Jules' Undersea Lodge,** a two-room hotel for divers (*see* Participant Sports). *51 Shoreland Dr., Box 787, Key Largo, tel. 305/451–1139 or 800/858–7119 in FL. Phone for opening date, admission fees, and hours.*

❶ Return to U.S. 1, turn left, and left again into **John Pennekamp Coral Reef State Park.** The primary attraction here is diving on the offshore coral reefs (*see* Sports and Outdoor Activities), but even a landlubber can appreciate the superb interpretive aquarium in the park's visitor center. A huge central tank holds angelfish, stingrays, and Florida spiny lobsters. There's also a touch tank where you can fondle starfish, sponges, and various species of bivalves. A concessionaire rents canoes and sailboats and offers boat trips to the reef. The park also includes a nature trail through a mangrove forest, a swimming beach, picnic shelters, a snack bar, a gift shop, and a campground. *MM*

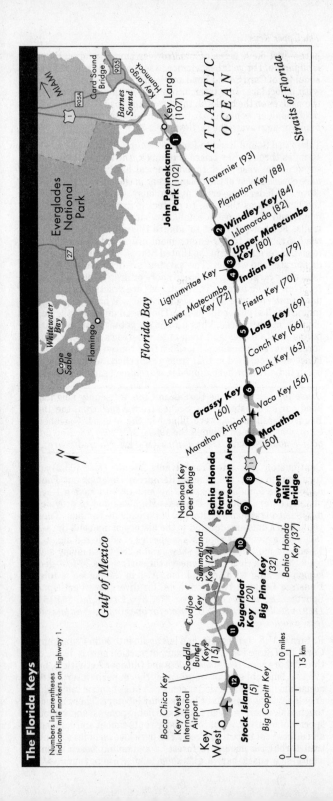

The Florida Keys

Numbers in parentheses indicate mile markers on Highway 1.

102.5, OS, Key Largo, tel. 305/451–1202. Admission: Florida residents $1.50/car and driver, $1/passenger; out-of-state visitors $2.50/car and driver, $1.50/passenger; children under 6 free. Open daily 8AM–sunset.

Return to U.S. 1 and turn left. At MM 100, turn left again into the parking lot of the Holiday Inn Key Largo Resort. In the adjoining Key Largo Harbor Canal you'll find the *African Queen*, the steam-powered workboat on which Katherine Hepburn and Humphrey Bogart rode in their movie of the same name. The 30-foot craft was built in England in 1912. James W. Hendricks, an attorney from Kentucky who owns the resort, bought the boat in 1982 and lovingly restored her. Hendricks also owns and displays at the resort the *Thayer IV*, a 22-foot mahogany Chris Craft built in 1951 and used by Ms. Hepburn and Henry Fonda in Fonda's last film, *On Golden Pond*.

Continuing south on U.S. 1 you'll cross **Plantation Key** (MM 93–87), named for the plantings of limes, pineapples, and tomatoes cultivated here at the turn of the century. Next comes **Windley Key,** notable for **Theater of the Sea,** where seven dolphins, two sea lions, and an extensive collection of tropical fish swim in the pits of a 1907 railroad quarry. Allow at least two hours to attend the dolphin and sea lion shows and visit all the exhibits, which include a "bottomless" boat ride, touch tank, shark-feeding pool, and a 300-gallon "living reef" aquarium with invertebrates and small reef fishes. *MM 84.5, OS, Box 407, Islamorada, tel. 305/664–2431. Admission: $9.50 adults, $5.50 children 4–12. Open daily 9:30 AM–4 PM. Swim with dolphins (30-min orientation and 30 min in the water): $50. Reservations required with 50% deposit, minimum age 13, mask and swim fins recommended, life vests optional. Video or still photos: $49.95 additional.*

Time Out   Stop at **Green Turtle Seafood Market & Cannery** on Upper Matecumbe Key. Owner Henry Rosenthal, who also operates the nearby **Green Turtle Inn** (*see* Dining), cans five kinds of chowder—turtle, conch, Manhattan clam, New England clam, and New England fish—plus turtle consomme and Key-lime pie filling. If the cannery is running when you visit, he'll show you the operation. Most of the fresh seafood on sale is local, right off the boats that dock behind the building, but the market also sells Key West shrimp, blue crabs from Maryland and Argentina, and oysters from Apalachicola Bay in North Florida. *MM 81.5, OS, Islamorada, tel. 305/664–4918. Open Tues.–Sun. 8–6.*

Just below the cannery, watch for the **Hurricane Memorial** (MM 81) beside the highway. It marks the mass grave of 423 victims of the 1935 Labor Day hurricane. Many of those who perished were veterans who had been working on the Overseas Highway; they died when a tidal surge overturned a train sent to evacuate them. The Art Deco–style monument depicts wind-driven waves and palms bowing before the storm's fury.

At the lower tip of **Upper Matecumbe Key** , stop at the **International Fishing Museum** in Bud n' Mary's Marina. The museum contains a collection of antique fishing tackle and a video library with information on fishing activities, fishery conservation, and the natural history of various species of local fishes. The videos don't circulate, but you can watch them in the museum. The museum staff can also help you find a charter captain for deep-sea or back-country fishing. *MM 79.5, OS. For information, contact Bob Epstein, 124 Gardenia St., Tavernier 33070, tel. 305/664–2767 (office), 852–8813 (home). Admission free. Open Mon.–Sat. 10–4.*

4 The dock on **Indian Key Fill** at MM 78, BS, is the closest point on the Overseas Highway to three unusual state parks accessible only by water. The newest of these parks, dedicated in 1989, is **San Pedro Underwater Archaeological Preserve** (*see* Sports and Outdoor Activities). State-operated boat tours aboard the M. V. *Monroe* will take you to the other two, **Indian Key State Historic Site** (OS) and **Lignumvitae Key State Botanical Site** (BS). Indian Key was a county seat town and shipwrecker's station until an Indian attack wiped out the settlement in 1840. Dr. Henry Perrine, a noted botanist, was killed in the raid. Today you'll see his plants overgrowing the town's ruins. A virgin hardwood forest still cloaks Lignumvitae Key, punctuated only by the home and gardens that chemical magnate William Matheson built as a private retreat in 1919. *MM 78. For information and tour boat reservations, contact Long Key State Recreation Area, Box 776, Long Key, tel. 305/664–4815. Indian Key open daily 8 AM–sunset; Lignumvitae Key open Thurs.– Mon. with 1-hr guided tour (admission: $1 adults, children under 6 free) at 10:30 AM, 1 and 2:30 PM for visitors from private boats. State tour boat admission: $6 adults, $3 children under 12, for 3-hr tours Thurs.–Mon. to Indian Key, 8:30 AM, to Lignumvitae Key, 1:30 PM.*

5 Return to U.S. 1 and turn right. Continue down to **Long Key** (MM 69), where you'll pass a tract of undisturbed forest on the right (BS) just below MM 67. Watch for a historical marker partially obscured by foliage. Pull off the road here and explore **Layton Trail,** named after Del Layton, who incorporated the city of Layton in 1963 and served as its mayor until his death in 1987. The marker relates the history of the Long Key Viaduct, the first major bridge on the rail line, and the Long Key Fishing Club that Henry Flagler established nearby in 1906. Zane Grey, the noted western novelist, was president of the club. It consisted of a lodge, guest cottages, and storehouses—all obliterated by the 1935 hurricane. The clearly marked trail leads through the tropical hardwood forest to a rocky Florida Bay shoreline overlooking shallow grass flats offshore.

Less than a mile below Layton Trail, turn left into **Long Key State Recreation Area,** then left again to the parking area for the **Golden Orb Trail.** This trail leads onto a boardwalk through a mangrove swamp alongside a lagoon where many herons and other water birds congregate in winter. The park also has a campground, a picnic area, a canoe trail through a tidal lagoon, and a not-very-sandy beach fronting on a broad expanse of shallow grass flats. Instead of a pail and shovel, bring a mask and snorkel here to observe the marine life in this rich nursery area. *Box 776, Long Key, tel. 305/664–4815. Admission: Florida residents $1.50/car and driver, $1/passenger; out-of-state visitors $2.50/car and driver, $1.50/passenger. Open daily 8 AM–sunset.*

The Middle Keys

Below Long Key, the Overseas Highway crosses Long Key Channel on a new highway bridge beside the railroad's **Long**

Key Viaduct. The second-longest bridge on the rail line, this two-mile-long structure has 222 reinforced-concrete arches. It ends at **Conch Key** (MM 63), a tiny fishing and retirement community. Below Conch Key, the causeway on your left at MM 61 leads to **Duck Key,** an upscale residential community where **Hawk's Cay Resort** (*see* Lodging) offers hotel guests a swim-with-the-dolphins experience at its Zoovet Dolphin Center.

6 Next comes **Grassy Key** (MM 59). Watch on the right for the **Dolphin Research Center** and the 35-foot-long concrete sculpture of the dolphin Theresa and her son Nat outside the former home of Milton Santini, creator of the original *Flipper* movie. The 17 dolphins here today are free to leave and return to the fenced area that protects them from boaters and predators. *MM 59, BS, Box Dolphin, Marathon Shores, tel. 305/289-0002. Admission: $5 donation. Visitor center open Wed.–Sun. 9 AM–3 PM, closed Christmas, New Year, and Thanksgiving. Walking tours at 9:30 and 11 AM, 1 and 3 PM. Swim with dolphins (20 min) $50. Children 5–12 swim with an accompanying swimming adult. Reserve for dolphin swim on the first day of the month before you plan to be in the Keys.*

7 Continuing down U.S. 1, you'll pass the road to **Key Colony Beach** (MM 54, OS), an incorporated city developed in the 1950s as a retirement community. It has a beach, golf course, and boating facilities. Soon after, you'll cross a bridge onto **Vaca Key** and enter **Marathon** (MM 53–47), the commercial hub of the Middle Keys. Marathon is notorious for perpetual road construction along U.S. 1, which has resulted in the disappearance of mile markers beside the road. You must navigate here by means of numbered cross streets.

On your right (BS) at 55th Street is **Crane Point Hammock,** a 63-acre tract that includes the world's last undisturbed thatch-palm hammock. The Florida Keys Land Trust, a private, non-profit conservation group, paid $1.2 million to acquire the property in 1988. At least part of it should be open to the public in 1990. The tract also includes an exotic plant arboretum, an archaeological site, a Bahamian village with the oldest surviving example of Conch-style architecture outside Key West, and a children's museum in a historic 1925 house. Future plans include the opening of a marine science education center, interpretive tram rides, and nature trails. *For current information, contact Dr. Chuck Olson, Florida Keys Land Trust, Box 1432, Key West 33041, tel. 305/745-1110.*

Across the Overseas Highway from **Crane Point Hammock,** between the K-Mart and the Marine Bank, Sombrero Beach Road (55th Street) leads two miles south past Marathon High School to a free county beach on the ocean. **Sombrero Beach** has a modest stretch of sand, some limestone rock ledges at the water's edge, and picnic tables in covered shelters for sun and rain protection. Just offshore is the world's first underwater county park, **Marathon Marine Sanctuary** (*see* Sports and Outdoor Activities).

As you approach the new Seven Mile Bridge, turn right at MM 47 to the entrance to the **Old Seven Mile Bridge.** An engineering marvel in its day, the bridge rested on 546 concrete piers spanning the broad expanse of water that separates the Middle and Lower Keys. Monroe County maintains a two-mile stretch of the old bridge to provide access to **Pigeon Key** (MM 45), where the county's public schools and community college run marine-science classes in a railroad work camp built around 1908. The county has applied to place Pigeon Key on the National Register of Historic Places, a status the Old Seven Mile Bridge already enjoys. Other plans for Pigeon Key include restoration of its six wood buildings (four dormitories, an office, and a laboratory), a railroad museum with historic photos not previously on public display, and a tram to bring visitors from Marathon across the old bridge to Pigeon Key. *For information, contact James Lewis, Chairman, Pigeon Key Advisory Authority, 2945 Overseas Hwy., Marathon 33050, tel. 305/743-6040.*

⑧ Return to U.S. 1 and proceed across the new **Seven Mile Bridge** (actually only 6.79 miles long!). Built between 1980 and 1982 at a cost of $45 million, the new Seven Mile Bridge is the world's longest segmental bridge, with 39 expansion joints separating its cement sections. Each April marathon runners gather in Marathon for the annual Seven Mile Bridge Run.

The Lower Keys

⑨ At **Bahia Honda State Recreation Area** (MM 37) on Bahia Honda Key, you'll find a sandy beach most of the time. Lateral drift builds up the beach in summer; winter storms whisk away much of the sand. The park's Silver Palm Trail leads you through a dense tropical forest where you can see rare West Indian plants, including the Geiger tree, sea lavendar, Key spider lily, bay cedar, thatch and silver palms, and several species found nowhere else in the Florida Keys: the West Indies satinwood, Catesbaea, Jamaica morning glory, and wild dilly. The park also includes a campground, cabins, gift shop, snack bar, marina, and dive shop offering snorkel trips to offshore reefs. *MM 37, OS, Rte. 1, Box 782, Big Pine Key, tel. 305/872-2353. Admission: Florida residents $1.50/car and driver, $1/passenger; out-of-state visitors $2.50/car and driver, $1.50/passenger; children under 6 free. Open daily 8 **AM**–sunset.*

⑩ Cross the Bahia Honda Bridge and continue past Spanish Harbor Key and Spanish Harbor Channel onto **Big Pine Key** (MM 32–30), where prominent signs warn drivers to be on the lookout for Key deer. Every year cars kill 50 to 60 of the delicate creatures. A subspecies of the Virginia white-tailed deer, Key deer once ranged throughout the Lower and Middle Keys, but hunting and habitat destruction reduced the population to fewer than 50 in 1947. Under protection in the **National Key Deer Refuge** since 1954, the deer herd grew to about 750 by the early 1970s. The government owns only about a third of Big Pine Key, however, and as the human population on the remaining land grew during the 1980s, the deer herd declined again until today only 250 to 300 remain.

To visit the refuge, turn right at the stoplight, then bear left at the fork onto Key Deer Boulevard (Rte. 940). Pass Road Prison No. 426 and a fire tower on the way to Watson Boulevard, then turn left and go about a mile to the **Refuge Headquarters** to see interpretive displays and obtain brochures.

The best place to see Key deer is on **No Name Key,** a sparsely populated island just east of Big Pine Key. To get there, take Watson Boulevard east to Wilder Road, and turn left. You'll go two miles from Key Deer Boulevard to the middle of the Bogie

Channel Bridge, which links Big Pine and No Name Keys, and 1½ miles from there across No Name Key. If you get out of your car at the end of the road to walk around, close all doors and windows to keep raccoons from wandering in. Deer may turn up along this road at any time of day—especially in early morning and late afternoon. Admire their beauty, but don't try to feed them—it's against the law. To resume your journey, take Wilder Road back to Key Deer Boulevard at the fork just before the stoplight on U.S. 1. Turn right at the stoplight, and continue on down the keys across **Big Torch, Middle Torch,** and **Little Torch Keys** (named for the torchwood tree, which settlers used for kindling because it burns easily even when green). Next comes **Ramrod Key** (MM 27.5), a base for divers in **Looe Key National Marine Sanctuary** five miles offshore (*see* Sports and Outdoor Activities).

⓫ On **Sugarloaf Key** (MM 20), you'll find the Sugar Loaf Lodge (MM 17, BS), an attractive motel known for its performing dolphin named Sugar, who lives in a lagoon behind the restaurant (*see* Lodging). Follow the paved road northwest from the motel for a half mile past an airstrip, and keep going on an unpaved spur. There, in bleak, gravel-strewn surroundings, you'll find a reconstruction of R. C. Perky's **bat tower.** Perky, an early real estate promoter, built the tower in 1929 to attract mosquito-eating bats, but no bats ever roosted in it.

Continue on through the Saddlebunch Keys and Big Coppitt Key to **Boca Chica Key** (MM 10), site of the Key West Naval Air Station. You may hear the roar of jet fighter planes in this vicinity.

⓬ At last you reach **Stock Island** (MM 5), the gateway to Key West. Pass the 18-hole **Key West Resort Golf Course,** then turn right onto Country Club Drive and pause at the **Key West Botanical Garden,** where the Key West Garden Club has labeled an extensive assortment of native and exotic tropical trees.

Key West

Numbers in the margin correspond with points of interest on the Key West map.

In April 1982, the U.S. Border Patrol threw a roadblock across the Overseas Highway just south of Florida City to catch drug runners and illegal aliens. Traffic backed up for miles as Border Patrol agents searched vehicles and demanded that the occupants prove U.S. citizenship. City officials in Key West, outraged at being treated like foreigners by the federal government, staged a mock secession and formed their own "nation," the so-called Conch Republic. They hoisted a flag and distributed mock border passes, visas, and Conch currency. The embarrassed Border Patrol dismantled its roadblock, and now an annual festival recalls the secessionists' victorious exploits.

The episode exemplifies Key West's odd station in life. Situated 150 miles from Miami and just 90 miles from Havana, this tropical island city has always maintained its strong sense of detachment, even after it was connected to the rest of the United States—by the railroad in 1912 and by the Overseas Highway in 1938. The U.S. government acquired Key West from Spain in 1818 along with the rest of Florida. The Spanish had named the island Cayo Hueso (Bone Key) in honor of Indian skeletons they found on its shores. In 1822, Uncle Sam sent Commodore David S. Porter to the Keys to chase pirates away.

For three decades, the primary industry in Key West was "wrecking"—rescuing people and salvaging cargo from ships that foundered on the nearby reefs. (According to some reports, when business was slow, the wreckers hung out lights to lure ships aground). Their business declined after 1852, when the federal government began building lighthouses along the reefs.

In 1845 the Army started to construct Fort Taylor, which held Key West for the Union during the Civil War. After the war, an influx of Cuban dissidents unhappy with Spain's rule brought the cigar industry to Key West. Fishing, shrimping, and sponge-gathering became important industries, and a pineapple-canning factory opened. Major military installations were established during the Spanish-American War and World War I. Through much of the 19th century and into the second decade of the 20th, Key West was Florida's wealthiest city in per-capita terms.

In the 1920s the local economy began to unravel. Modern ships no longer needed to stop in Key West for provisions, the cigar industry moved to Tampa, Hawaii dominated the pineapple industry, and the sponges succumbed to a blight. Then the depression hit, and even the military moved out. By 1934 half the population was on relief. The city defaulted on its bond payments, and the Federal Emergency Relief Administration took over the city and county governments.

Federal officials began promoting Key West as a tourist destination. They attracted 40,000 visitors during the 1934–35 winter season. Then the 1935 Labor Day hurricane struck the Middle Keys, sparing Key West but wiping out the railroad and the tourist trade. For three years, until the Overseas Highway opened, the only way in and out of town was by boat.

Ever since, Key West's fortunes have waxed and waned with the vagaries of world affairs. An important naval center during World War II and the Korean conflict, the island remains a strategic listening post on the doorstep of Fidel Castro's Cuba. Although the Navy shut down its submarine base at Truman Annex and sold the property to a real-estate developer, the nearby Boca Chica Naval Air Station and other military installations remain active.

As the military scaled back, city officials looked to tourism again to take up the slack. Even before it tried, Key West had much to sell—superb frost-free weather with an average temperature of 79°F, quaint 19th-century architecture, and a laid-back lifestyle. Promoters have fostered fine restaurants, galleries and shops, and new museums to interpret the city's intriguing past. There's also a growing calendar of artistic and cultural events and a lengthening list of annual festivals—including the Conch Republic celebration in April, Hemingway Days in July, and a Halloween Fantasy Fest rivaling the New Orleans Mardi Gras.

This tour begins at Front and Duval streets, near the Pier House hotel and Ocean Key House. Start by going west on ❶ Front Street to **Mallory Square,** named for Stephen Mallory, secretary of the Confederate Navy, who later owned the Mallory Steamship Line. On the nearby **Mallory Dock,** a nightly sunset celebration draws street performers, food vendors, and thousands of onlookers.

❷ Facing Mallory Square is the **Key West Aquarium,** which features hundreds of brightly colored tropical fish and other fascinating sea creatures from the waters around Key West. A touch tank enables visitors to handle starfish, sea cucumbers, horseshoe and hermit crabs, even horse and queen conchs—living totems of the Conch Republic. Built in 1934 by the Works Progress Administration as the world's first open-air aquarium, the building has been enclosed for all-weather viewing. *1 Whitehead St., tel. 305/296-2051. Admission: $5 adults, $2.50 children 8-15. Open daily, 10-6 (10-7 in winter). Guided tours 11 AM, 1 PM, 3 PM, 4:30 PM; shark feeding 3 PM.*

Return to Front Street and turn right to **Clinton Place,** where a Civil War memorial to Union soldiers stands in a triangle formed by the intersection of Front, Greene, and Whitehead streets. On your right is the **U.S. Post Office and Customs House,** a Romanesque Revival structure designed by prominent local architect William Kerr and completed in 1891. Tour guides claim that federal bureaucrats required the roof to have a steep pitch so it wouldn't collect snow.

❸ On your left is the **Mel Fisher Maritime Heritage Society Museum,** which displays gold and silver bars, coins, jewelry, and other artifacts recovered in 1985 from the Spanish treasure ships *Nuestra Señora de Atocha* and *Santa Margarita.* The two galleons foundered in a hurricane in 1622 near the Marquesas Keys, 40 miles west of Key West. In the museum you can lift a gold bar weighing 6.3 Troy pounds and see a 77.76-carat natural emerald crystal worth almost $250,000. One display replicates the hold of the *Atocha,* with smooth ballast stones, silver bars, and copper ingots for casting cannons and balls. A 20-minute video shows treasure being recovered from the wrecks. *200 Greene St., tel. 305/296-9936. Museum admission: $5 adults; $4 seniors, military, and Conch Train and trolley passengers with ticket stub; $1 children. Open daily 10-6; Christmas and New Year's Day 10-2; last video showing 4:30, last ticket sold 5:15.*

❹ Mel Fisher's museum occupies a former navy storehouse that he bought from Pritam Singh, the developer of **Truman Annex** (Key West 33040, tel. 305/296-5601), a decommissioned navy base. An American who embraced the Sikh religion, Singh speaks gently of his hope to "engender different forms of interaction" on the 103 acres the government sold him in 1986 for $17.25 million. Singh says people of modest means will be able to rub elbows with the wealthy in his planned development because 162 housing units will be sold at below-market rates, and restrictions will be imposed to prevent speculation and to foster a permanent community. Singh will keep 16 original structures (including six Victorian-style officers' houses) and several warehouses with 30,000 square feet of rentable space for art studios. The 1891 Customs House will become a yacht club. New construction will also include 93 condominiums in two waterfront complexes adjoining the deep-water harbor where submarines docked during World War II, 63 condominium town houses in four compounds, 60 single-family homes, a shopping village, and a 285-room Ritz-Carlton hotel. The Little

194

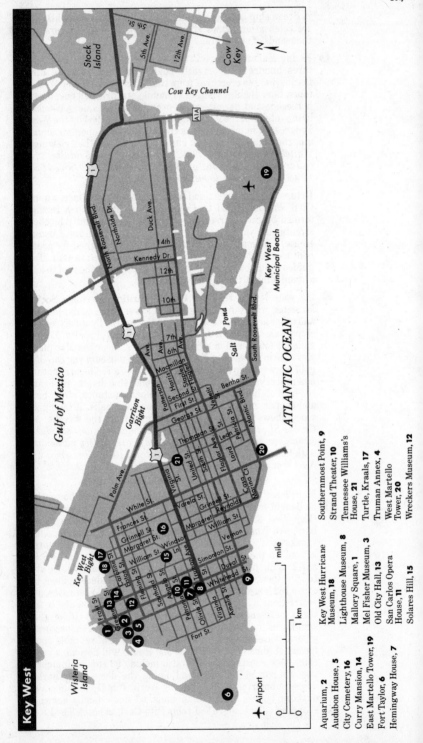

Key West

Aquarium, **2**
Audubon House, **5**
City Cemetery, **16**
Curry Mansion, **14**
East Martello Tower, **19**
Fort Taylor, **6**
Hemingway House, **7**

Key West Hurricane
Museum, **18**
Lighthouse Museum, **8**
Mallory Square, **1**
Mel Fisher Museum, **3**
Old City Hall, **13**
San Carlos Opera
House, **11**
Solares Hill, **15**

Southernmost Point, **9**
Strand Theater, **10**
Tennessee Williams's
House, **21**
Turtle, Kraals, **17**
Truman Annex, **4**
West Martello
Tower, **20**
Wreckers Museum, **12**

White House where President Harry Truman spent his vacations will become a museum, except for two presidential suites upstairs which the hotel will rent out to guests. Vehicular traffic in Truman Annex will be limited, but Singh intends to open the development to bicycle and pedestrian traffic daily from 8 AM to 9 PM. He also bought nearby **Tank Island,** where he plans to build 25 luxurious houses and 82 boat slips and 40 moorings. A ferry service will provide access from the mainland. Part of the island will be open to the public for a fee as a high-quality recreation area, with a beach, tennis center, concert pavilion, and perhaps an environmental center and aviary.

From Mel Fisher's museum, cross Whitehead Street to visit ⑤ the **Audubon House and Gardens.** A museum in this two-story dwelling built in the mid-1840s commemorates ornithologist John James Audubon's 1832 visit to Key West. On display are several rooms of period antiques and a large collection of Audubon lithographs. A 12-minute video in the upstairs gallery describes Audubon's travels, and an exquisite collection of porcelains of American birds and foliage by Dorothy Doughty is on display in the upstairs sitting room off the front porch. *205 Whitehead St., tel. 305/294–2116. Admission: $4.50 adults, $1 children 6–12. Open daily 9:30–5.*

Continue up Whitehead Street past **Pigeonhouse Patio Restaurant & Bar** (301 Whitehead St., tel. 305/296–9600). This building was the first headquarters of Pan American World Airways, the first U.S. airline to operate scheduled international air service. The inaugural flight took off from Key West International Airport on Oct. 28, 1927. Passengers paid $9.95 for the 90-mile, 80-minute flight from Key West to Havana aboard *The General Machado,* a Fokker F-7 trimotor.

Turn right onto Southard Street and follow the signs to the ⑥ **Fort Zachary Taylor State Historic Site.** Built between 1845 and 1866, the fort served as a base for the Union blockade of Confederate shipping during the Civil War. More than 1,500 Confederate vessels captured while trying to run the blockade were brought to Key West's harbor and detained under the fort's guns. What you will see at Fort Taylor today is a fort within a fort. In 1898 the army built poured-concrete gun emplacements for the Spanish-American War atop remnants of the original brick structure, burying the largest collection of Civil War cannons in the U.S. They are now being excavated and preserved for display. The concrete has been painted black as it was 90 years ago to absorb the muzzle flash and avoid disclosing the position of hideaway cannons that rolled forward to fire and then withdrew inside the walls. In 1989, the officers' kitchen became a 1,700-square-foot museum. Rangers give guided tours of the fort, including the museum and armament-preservation lab. *Box 289, tel. 305/292–6713. Admission: Florida residents $1.50/car and driver, $1/passenger; out-of-state visitors $2.50/car and driver, $1.50/passenger; children under 6 free. Park open daily 8–sunset, fort open 8–5. Free 90-min tour daily at 2 PM.*

Time Out Pause for a libation at the **Green Parrot Bar.** Built in 1890, the bar is Key West's oldest, a sometimes-rowdy saloon where locals outnumber the tourists. *601 Whitehead St. (corner of Southard St.), tel. 305/294–6133. Open daily 10 AM–4 AM. No credit cards.*

Return to Whitehead Street, turn right, and go three blocks to
7 the **Hemingway House,** now a museum dedicated to the novelist's life and work. Built in 1851, this two-story Spanish
Colonial dwelling was the first house in Key West to have running water and a fireplace. Hemingway bought the house in
1931 and wrote about 70% of his life's work here, including *A
Farewell to Arms* and *For Whom the Bell Tolls.* Three months
after Hemingway died in 1961, local jeweler Bernice Dickson
bought the house and its contents from Hemingway's estate
and two years later opened it as a museum. Of special interest
are the huge bed with a headboard made from a 17th-century
Spanish monastery gate, a ceramic cat by Pablo Picasso (a gift
to Hemingway from the artist), the handblown Venetian glass
chandelier in the dining room, and the swimming pool. The museum staff gives guided tours rich with anecdotes about
Hemingway and his family and feeds the 42 feline inhabitants
(for the 42 bridges in the Keys), descendents of Hemingway's
own 50 cats. Kitten adoptions are possible (for a fee), but
there's a four-year waiting list. Tours begin every 10 minutes
and take 35–40 minutes; then you're free to explore on your
own. *907 Whitehead St., tel. 305/294–1575. Admission: $5
adults, $1 children. Open daily 9–5.*

Down the block and across the street from Hemingway House
8 is the **Lighthouse Museum,** a 92-foot lighthouse built in 1847
and an adjacent 1887 clapboard house where the keeper lived.
Both underwent extensive restoration in 1989. You can climb 88
steps to the top of the lighthouse for a spectacular view. On display in the keeper's quarters are vintage photographs, ship
models, nautical charts, military uniforms, and a working submarine periscope. Note especially the old photos of the Key
West Naval Air Station and the relics from the battleship
U.S.S. *Maine,* which was blown up in Havana Harbor on February 15, 1898, precipitating the Spanish-American War. *938
Whitehead St., tel. 305/294–0012. Admission: $3 adults, $1
children 6–12. Open daily 9:30–5.*

Continue to the foot of Whitehead Street, where a huge con-
9 crete marker proclaims this spot to be the **Southernmost Point**
in the United States. Most tourists snapping pictures of each
other in front of the marker are oblivious to Key West's real
southernmost point, on a nearby navy base off limits to civilians
but visible through the fence to your right. Bahamian vendors
of shells and straw hats line the sidewalk and blow a conch horn
at passing Conch Tour Trains and Old Town Trolleys.

Turn left on South Street. To your right are two dwellings that
both claim to be the **Southernmost House**—the Spanish-style
home built in the 1940s at 400 South Street by Thelma Strabel,
author of *Reap the Wild Wind,* a novel about the wreckers who
salvaged ships aground on the reef in Key West's early days,
and the adjoining cream-brick Queen Anne mansion at Duval
and South streets. Neither is open to the public. Take the next
right onto Duval Street, which ends at the Atlantic Ocean and
the **Southernmost Beach.** *Admission free. Open daily 7 AM–11
PM.*

Time Out **The Eatery,** adjoining the Southernmost Beach, serves
carryouts and buffets for breakfast, lunch, and dinner. *Open
daily 6 AM–9 PM. MC, V.*

Now go north on Duval Street towards downtown Key West. Pause at the **Cuban Club** (1108 Duval St., tel. 305/296–8997). The original building—a social club for the Cuban community —burned in 1983 and was replaced by shops and luxury condominiums; some of the original facade was retained. Continuing on Duval Street, you'll pass several art galleries from the 1100 block through the 800 block.

⑩ Pause to admire the colorful marquee and ornamental facade of the **Strand Theater,** built in 1918 by Cuban craftsmen. After a career as a movie theater, it now offers a variety of live entertainment: reggae, rock-and-roll, etc. *527 Duval St., tel. 305/ 294–6700 (recording).*

⑪ Continue on to the **San Carlos Opera House,** a Cuban-American heritage center, which houses a museum and research library focusing on the history of Key West and of 19th- and 20th-century Cuban exiles. The building is owned by the San Carlos Institute, which was founded in 1871 by Cuban immigrants who wanted to preserve their language, customs, and heritage while organizing the struggle for Cuba's independence from Spain. Cuban patriot Jose Martí delivered many famous speeches in Key West under the institute's auspices. Opera star Enrico Caruso sang in the 400-seat auditorium of the Opera House, which reportedly has the best acoustics of any concert hall in the South. After Cuba and the United States broke off diplomatic relations in 1961, the building deteriorated. It was saved from demolition when Miami attorney Rafael A. Penalver, Jr., secured a $1.7 million state grant for its restoration. At press time, the opera house was scheduled to be reopened in October 1989. A regular schedule of evening performances by internationally acclaimed artists is planned. *516 Duval St., Key West 33040. For information, contact Mr. Penalver at 1101 Brickell Ave., Suite 1700, Miami 33131, tel. 305/579–9000 (Miami) or call Key West Directory Assistance for local phone number. Admission: $3 adults, $1.50 children. Open daily 9–5. Guided tour, concluding with 30-min film.*

⑫ Continue north on Duval Street to the **Wreckers Museum,** which is alleged to be the oldest house in Key West. It was built in 1829 as the home of Francis Watlington, a sea captain and wrecker. He was also a Florida state senator, but resigned to serve in the Confederate Navy during the Civil War. Six of the home's eight rooms are now a museum furnished with 18th- and 19th-century antiques. In an upstairs bedroom is an eight-room miniature dollhouse of Conch architectural design, outfitted with tiny Victorian furniture. *322 Duval St., tel. 305/294–9502. Admission: $2 adults, 50¢ children 3–12. Open daily 10–4; closed Christmas.*

⑬ Take Duval Street to Front Street, turn right, go two blocks to Simonton Street, turn right again and go one block to Greene Street to see the **Old City Hall,** which has recently been restored. Designed by William Kerr, the architect also responsible for the Customs House, the Old City Hall opened in 1891. It has a rectangular tower with four clock faces and a fire bell. The ground floor, used as a city market for many years, now houses the **Historic Key West Shipwreck Museum.** Among the displays are relics from the *Isaac Allerton,* built at Portsmouth, New Hampshire, in 1838 and sunk off Key West in 1856. The second floor houses the city commission's meeting room and offices of the city government and the Historic Florida

Keys Preservation Board. *516 Greene St., tel. 305/292–9740. Museum admission: $4 adults, $2 children 10–16. Open daily 9–6.*

⑭ Return to Simonton Street, go one block south to Caroline Street, and turn right to the **Curry Mansion.** Built in 1899 for Milton Curry, the son of Florida's first millionaire, this 22-room Victorian mansion is an adaptation of a Parisian town house. It has the only widow's walk open to the public in Key West. The owners have restored and redecorated most of the house. Take an unhurried self-guided tour with a comprehensive brochure, which includes floor plans, full of detailed information about the history and contents of the house. *511 Caroline St., tel. 305/294–5349. Admission: $5 adults, $1 children under 12. Open daily 10–5.*

⑮ Return to Simonton Street, go south to Angela Street, and turn left. Before you rises **Solares Hill,** the steepest natural grade in Key West. Its summit, the island's loftiest elevation, is 18 feet above sea level.

⑯ Now cross Elizabeth Street and bear right onto Windsor Lane to the **City Cemetery.** Turn left onto Passover Lane to the entrance at Margaret Street. Clustered near a flagpole resembling a ship's mast are the graves of 22 sailors killed in the sinking of the battleship U.S.S. *Maine. Admission free. Open sunrise–sunset. Guided tours weekends 10 AM and 4 PM. Tour donation: $5.*

⑰ Go up Margaret Street to the harbor docks and visit the **Turtle Kraals,** where the Florida Marine Conservancy runs a hospital for sea creatures. Biologist Linda Bohl maintains a touch tank with horseshoe crabs, sea anemones, sea urchins, and other benign beasts you can fondle—but keep your fingers away from Hawkeye and Gonzo, a churlish pair of 150-pound, 30-year-old hawksbill turtles. A fishpond on the premises gives you a good look at live denizens of local waters, including barracuda, bluefish, lemon and nurse sharks, and yellowtail snapper. *1 Land's End Village, tel. 305/294–2640. Admission free; donations accepted. Open 11 AM–1 AM weekdays, weekends noon–1 AM.*

⑱ Half a block from the Turtle Kraals is the **Key West Hurricane Museum,** which opened in 1989 in the former Singleton Shrimp warehouse. Displays explain the origins and life cycle of hurricanes and the differences between regular storms, tornadoes, and hurricanes. A treasure map shows where Spanish galleons were sunk by hurricanes in the Florida Keys. A chart tracks the 10 hurricanes that have hit the Florida Keys since 1846, including the great hurricane of 1906, the Labor Day hurricane of 1935 (which destroyed the Overseas Railroad), Donna in 1960, Betsy in 1965, and Floyd in 1987. Additional displays, including a wind tunnel, are scheduled to open in late 1989. *201 William St., tel. 305/294–7522. Admission: $3.50 adults, children under 12 free. Open daily 10–6.*

Go one block south on Margaret Street or William Street to Eaton Street, turn left and continue east past White Street, where Eaton Street doglegs to the right into Palm Avenue. You'll cross a causeway and bridge across a corner of **Garrison Bight Yacht Basin,** where many charter-fishing boats dock.

Turn left onto North Roosevelt Boulevard (U.S. 1) and go east. Past the turnoff to Stock Island at the east end of Key West,

North Roosevelt Boulevard becomes South Roosevelt Boulevard and turns west. On your left is a small community of houseboats. On your right, just past the entrance to Key West ⑲ International Airport, stands **East Martello Tower,** one of two Civil War forts of similar design overlooking the Atlantic Ocean. The **Key West Art and Historical Society** operates a museum in East Martello's vaulted casemates. The collection includes Stanley Papio's "junk art" sculptures, Cuban primitive artist Mario Sanchez's chiseled and painted wood carvings of historic Key West street scenes, memorabilia from movies shot on location in the Keys, and a display of books by many of the 55 famous writers (including seven Pulitzer Prize winners) who live in Key West. In 1989, new historical exhibits were being developed to present a chronological history of the Florida Keys. A circular 48-step staircase in the central tower leads to a platform overlooking the airport and surrounding waters. *3501 S. Roosevelt Blvd., tel. 305/296-6206. Admission: $3 adults, $1 children. Open daily 9:30-5.*

Continue west on South Roosevelt Boulevard past Smathers Beach on your left. To your right are the **salt ponds,** where early residents evaporated seawater to collect salt. The area is now a wildlife sanctuary. Turn right where South Roosevelt Boulevard ends at Bertha Street, then make the first left onto Atlantic Avenue. Near White Street are **Higgs Memorial** ⑳ **Beach** (a Monroe County park) and **West Martello Tower,** a fort built in 1861 and used as a lookout post during the Spanish-American War. Within its walls the Key West Garden Club maintains an art gallery and tropical garden. *Tel. 305/294-3210. Donations accepted. Open Wed.-Sun. 10 AM-noon and 1-4 PM.*

Take White Street nine blocks north to Duncan Street, turn ㉑ right, and go three blocks to **Tennessee Williams' House** (1431 Duncan St., at the corner of Duncan and Leon Sts.), a modest Bahamian-style cottage where the playwright lived from 1949 until his death in 1983.

Shopping

Throughout the Keys many strip shopping centers cater to the basic needs of locals and visitors alike. In season, supermarkets and roadside stands sell tropical fruits. Look for Key limes (Apr.-Jan.), guavas (Aug.-Oct.), lychee nuts (June), and sapodillas (Feb.-Mar.).

Key West In Key West's Old Town, you'll find specialty shops with international reputations:

Greenpeace. Opened in 1983, this is the only storefront in Florida operated by Greenpeace, an international conservation organization known for its efforts to prevent the killing of whales and seals. The store sells conservation-oriented educational materials, gift items, and T-shirts. The store planned to move to a new location on Duval Street in Key West late in 1989; phone for details. *Tel. 305/296-4442. Open Mon.-Sat. 10-9, Sun. 10-6. AE, MC, V.*

Key West Aloe. A company founded in a garage in 1971, Key West Aloe today produces some 300 perfume, sunscreen, and skin-care products for men and women. When you visit the factory store, you can watch the staff measure and blend ingredients, then fill and seal the containers. *Main store: 524 Front St., tel. 305/294-5592, 800/433-2563 (FL), 800/445-2563 (U.S.). Open Mon.-Sat. 9-8, Sun. 9-6. Factory store: Greene and Simonton Sts. Open 9-5, production weekdays 9-5. Free self-guided tour. AE, DC, MC, V.*

Key West Hand Print Fabrics. In the 1960s, Lilly Pulitzer's designs made Key West Hand Print Fabrics famous. Shoppers can watch workers making handprinted fabric on five 50-yard-long tables in the Curry Warehouse, a brick building erected in 1878 to store tobacco. *201 Simonton St., tel. 305/294-9535. Open daily 10-6. AE, MC.*

Key West Island Bookstore. You'll find a good selection of books on South Florida here and a rare book room to which you must request admittance. *513 Fleming St., tel. 305/294-2904. Open daily 10-6. AE, MC, V.*

Duval Books and Cards. Owned by the proprietors of Key West Island Bookstore, this shop specializes in new books and greeting cards. *817 Duval St., tel. 305/296-3508. Open Mon.-Sat. 9-9, Sun. 10-5. AE, MC, V.*

Tikal Trading Co. Since 1975, owners George and Barbara Webb have designed, produced, and sold double-stitched women's clothing of hand-woven Guatemalan cotton. *129 Duval St., tel. 305/294-6883. Open daily 10-9. AE, MC, V.*

The former Singleton Seafood, Inc., shrimp docks and warehouse along Key West Bight have been reincarnated as a row of marinas. One of these, **Key West Seaport,** a nautically oriented shopping area where boat builders work and charter-boat captains have booths to sign up customers. Merchants you might visit include the following:

Lazy Jake's Hammocks. Run by a man who describes himself as Key West's oldest beach bum, this establishment makes and sells hammocks of all shapes and sizes. *205 Elizabeth St., no phone. Open daily 8-5.*

Seafarers Heritage Library and Nautique. A storefront operated by the National Center for Shipwreck Research, Ltd., this shop sells maritime books and gift items. Its staff arranges archaeology dives, seminars, training programs, and other educational activities. *Seaport La., tel. 305/292-1301. Open daily 9 AM-8 PM. MC, V.*

Just east of Key West Seaport is Key West Bight. Popular stores there include the following:

Waterfront Baits & Tackle. This store sells bait and fishing gear. *201 William St., tel. 305/292-1961.*

Waterfront Fish Market, Inc. Fresh seafood is the draw here. *201 William St., tel. 305/294-8046.*

Waterfront Market. This store sells health and gourmet foods, deli items, fresh produce, and salads. *201 William St., tel. 305/ 294-8418.*

Ever since John James Audubon came to Key West in 1832, artists have flocked to the Florida Keys. Today's flourishing art community provides a rich array of merchandise for galleries throughout the Keys.

The Rain Barrel in Islamorada represents 300 local and national artists and has eight resident artists. *MM 86.7, BS, 86700 Overseas Hwy., Islamorada, tel. 305/852-3084. Open daily 9-5; closed Christmas. MC, V.*

Lane Gallery specializes in lesser-known local artists. *1000 Duval St., Key West, tel. 305/294–0067. Open winter, daily 10–6, in summer, daily noon–6. AE, MC, V.*

Gingerbread Square Gallery, owned by Key West Mayor Richard Heyman, represents Keys artists who have attained national prominence. *901 Duval St., Key West, tel. 305/296–8900. Open winter, daily 11–6; summer, Thurs.–Mon. AE, MC, V.*

Haitian Art Center sells the works of 175 Haitian artists. *600 Frances St., Key West, tel. 305/296–8932. Open daily 10–6. AE, CB, DC, MC, V.*

Sports and Outdoor Activities

Biking A bike path parallels the Overseas Highway from Key Largo through Tavernier and onto Plantation Key, from MM 106 (at the Route 905 junction) to MM 86 (near the Monroe County Sheriff's Substation). The **Marathon** area is popular with bikers. Some of the best areas include the paths along Aviation Boulevard on the bay side of Marathon Airport; the new four-lane section of the Overseas Highway through Marathon; Sadowski Causeway to Key Colony Beach; Sombrero Beach Road from the Overseas Highway to the Marathon public beach; the roads on Boot Key (across a bridge from Vaca Key on 20th Street, OS); and a two-mile section of the old Seven Mile Bridge that remains open to Pigeon Key, where locals like to ride to watch the sunset.

Key West is a cycling town, but many tourists aren't accustomed to driving with so many bikes around, so ride carefully. Some hotels rent bikes to their guests; others will refer you to a nearby bike shop and reserve a bike for you.

Key Largo Bikes stocks adult, children's and tandem bikes, all single-speed with coaster brakes. *MM 101.5 (RR 2, Box 19 C), Key Largo, tel. 305/451–1910. Open Mon.–Sat. 9:30–5:30. MC, V.*

KCB Bike Shop rents single-speed adult and children's bikes. *MM 53 (11518 Overseas Hwy.), Marathon, tel. 305/289–1670. Open weekdays 8:30–5, Sat. 8:30–2; closed Sun. MC, V.*

Holiday Rentals has moped and bicycle rentals for adults and children. *512 Greene St., Key West, tel. 305/296–1745. Open daily 8–6. No credit cards.*

Camping The State of Florida operates recreational-vehicle and tent campgrounds in **John Pennekamp Coral Reef State Park,** MM 102.5 (Box 487, Key Largo 33037, tel. 305/451–1202); **Long Key State Recreation Area,** MM 67.5 (Box 776, Long Key 33001, tel. 305/664–4815); and **Bahia Honda State Recreation Area,** MM 37 (Rte. 1, Box 782, Big Pine Key 33043, tel. 305/872–2353). Bahia Honda also has rental cabins.

The **Florida Campground Association** (1638 N. Plaza Dr., Tallahassee 32308, tel. 904/658–8878) publishes a free annual directory of over 200 member campgrounds in 11 regions. The Keys are in Region L, which lists 12 commercial campgrounds from Key Largo to Key West. The guide is available at Florida Welcome Centers or by mail.

Diving Although there are reefs and wrecks all along the east coast of Florida, the state's most extensive diving grounds are in the Keys. Divers come for the quantity and quality of living coral reefs within six or seven miles of shore, the kaleidoscopic beauty of 650 species of tropical fish, and the adventure of probing wrecked ships that foundered in these seemingly tranquil seas during almost four centuries of exploration and commerce. A popular dive destination is the nine-foot **Christ of the Deep** statue, a gift to the Underwater Society of America from an Italian dive equipment manufacturer. The statue is about six miles east-northeast of Key Largo's South Cut in about 25 feet of water. It's a smaller copy of the 50-foot Christ of the Abysses off Genoa, Italy.

Much of the Keys' expanse of coral reefs is protected in federal, state, and county parks and sanctuaries. From Key Biscayne south almost to Key Largo, **Biscayne National Park** (*see* The Everglades) encompasses most of Biscayne Bay, its barrier islands, and the patch reefs eastward to a depth of 60 feet. Biscayne National Park's southern boundary is the northern boundary of John Pennekamp Coral Reef State Park and Key Largo National Marine Sanctuary.

John Pennekamp Coral Reef State Park encompasses 78 square miles of coral reefs, seagrass beds, and mangrove swamps on the Atlantic Ocean side of Key Largo. The park is 21 miles long and extends to the seaward limit of state jurisdiction three miles offshore. Its reefs contain 40 of the 52 species of coral in the Atlantic Reef System. *MM 102.5, OS. Park admission: Florida residents $1.50/car and driver, $1/passenger; out-of-state residents $2.50/car and driver, $1.50/passenger. Park open daily 8 AM–sunset. Coral Reef Park Co., a concessionaire, offers glass-bottom boat, scuba, sailing, and snorkeling tours: Box 1560, Key Largo 33037, tel. 305/451–1621 or 800/432–2871. Concession open daily 8–5:30. AE, MC, V.*

The **Key Largo National Marine Sanctuary** (Box 1083, Key Largo 33037, tel. 305/451–1644) covers 103 square miles of coral reefs from the boundary of John Pennekamp Coral Reef State Park, three miles off Key Largo, to a depth of 300 feet some eight miles offshore. Managed by the National Oceanic and Atmospheric Administration (NOAA), the sanctuary includes Elbow, French, and Molasses reefs; the 1852 Carysford Lighthouse and its surrounding reefs; Christ of the Deep; Grecian Rocks, Key Largo Rocks, and the torpedoed WW II freighter *Benwood*.

San Pedro Underwater Archaeological Preserve. The state recently established this underwater park in 18 feet of water about a mile off the western tip of Indian Key. The *San Pedro* was part of a Spanish treasure fleet wrecked by a hurricane in 1733. You can get there on the *Coral Sea*, a 40-passenger glass-bottom dive and snorkel boat, from the dive shop at Bud 'n' Mary's Fishing Marina. *MM 78, OS, Box 1126, Islamorada, tel. 305/664–2211. 3-hr trips at 9 AM and 1 PM. Call for reservations. Cost: $13 adults, $7.50 children under 12. AE, MC, V.*

Marathon Marine Sanctuary. Monroe County recently established its first underwater park off the Middle Keys in Hawk Channel opposite MM 50, OS. It runs from Washerwoman Shoal on the west to navigation marker 48 on the east. The two-square-mile park contains a dozen patch reefs ranging from the size of a house to about an acre. *Greater Marathon Chamber of Commerce, MM 49, BS, 330 Overseas Hwy., Marathon, tel. 305/743–5417 or 800/842–9580.*

National Key Deer Refuge (Box 510, Big Pine Key 33043, tel. 305/872–2239) and **Great White Heron National Wildlife Refuge.** Reefs where the Keys' northern margin drops off into the Gulf of Mexico attract fewer divers than the better-known Atlantic Ocean reefs. A favorite Gulf spot for local divers is the Content Keys, off Big Pine Key (MM 30).

Looe Key National Marine Sanctuary (Rte. 1, Box 782, Big Pine Key, tel. 305/872–4039). Many divers say Looe Key Reef, five miles off Ramrod Key (MM 27.5), is the most beautiful and diverse coral community in the entire region. It has large stands of elkhorn coral on its eastern margin, large purple sea fans, and ample populations of sponges and sea urchins. On its seaward side, it has an almost-vertical dropoff to a depth of 50–90 feet. The reef is named for H.M.S. *Looe*, a British warship wrecked there in 1744.

From shore or from a boat, snorklers can easily explore grass flats, mangrove roots, and rocks in shallow water, almost anywhere in the Keys. You may see occasional small clusters of coral and fish, mollusks, and other sea creatures. Ask dive shops for snorkeling information and directions. Diving and snorkeling are prohibited around bridges and near certain keys.

Dive shops all over the state organize Keys dives and offer diving instruction. South Florida residents fill dive boats on weekends, so plan to dive Monday through Thursday, when the boats and reefs are less crowded.

Jules Undersea Lodge, the world's first underwater hotel, takes reservations a year in advance from divers who want to stay in its two-room lodge in 30 feet of water. A resort course for new divers is offered. PADI affiliation. *MM 103.2, OS, Box 3330, Key Largo 33037, tel. 305/451–2353. AE, MC, V.*

Dive Shops　All of the dive shops listed below organize dives, fill air tanks, and sell or rent all necessary diving equipment. All have NAUI and/or PADI affiliation.

Quiescence Diving Service, Inc. Six people per boat. *MM 103.5, BS, 103680 Overseas Hwy., Key Largo, tel. 305/451–2440. Open daily 8–6; closed Thanksgiving and Christmas. MC, V.*
Capt. Corky's Diver's World of Key Largo. A reef and wreck diving package is available. Reservations accepted for wreck diving of the *Benwood*, Coast Guard cutters *Bibb* and *Duane*, and French and Molasses reefs. *MM 99.5, OS, Box 1663, Key Largo 33037, tel. 305/451–3200 or 800/445–8231. Open 8–5; closed Thanksgiving and Christmas. MC, V.*
Florida Keys Dive Center organizes dives from just south of John Pennekamp Coral Reef State Park to Alligator Light. This center has two Coast Guard–approved dive boats and offers training from introductory scuba through instructor course. Full-day "scuba safari" dives include complimentary on-board box lunch and barbecue afterward at the store. *MM 90.5, OS, 90500 Overseas Hwy., Box 391, Tavernier, tel. 305/ 842–4599 or 800/433–8946. Open 8–5. AE, MC, V.*
Treasure Divers, Inc., a full-service dive shop with instructors, arranges dives to reefs, Spanish galleons, and other wrecks. *MM 85.5, BS, 85500 Overseas Hwy., Islamorada, tel. 305/661– 5111 or 800/356–9887. Open 8–5. AM, MC, V.*
Hall's Dive Center and Career Institute offers trips to Looe Key, Sombero Reef, Delta Shoal, Content Key, and Coffins Patch.

MM 48.5, BS, 1994 Overseas Hwy., Marathon, tel. 305/743–5929 or 800/331–4255. Open 9–6. AE, MC, V.

Looe Key Dive Center. This is the dive shop closest to Looe Key National Marine Sanctuary. *MM 27.5, OS, Box 509, Ramrod Key, tel. 305/872–2215. Open 7–6. AE, MC, V.*

Captain's Corner. Seven full-time instructors provide dive classes in English, French, German, and Italian. All captains are licensed divemasters. Reservations are accepted for regular reef and wreck diving, spear and lobster fishing, and archaeological and treasure hunting. Also has fishing charters. *Store at 201 William St., Key West, tel. 305/296–8918. Open 8–5. Booth at Zero Duval St., Key West, tel. 800/328–9815, 800/231–9864 (FL), or 305/296–8865. Booth open daily 8 AM–11 PM. AE, MC, V.*

Fishing and Boating Fishing is popular throughout the Keys. You have a choice of deep-sea fishing on the ocean or the gulf or flat-water fishing in the mangrove-fringed shallows of the backcountry. Each of the areas protected by the state or federal government has its own set of rigorously enforced regulations. Check with your hotel or a local chamber of commerce office to find out what the rules are in the area you're staying. The same sources can refer you to a reliable charter-boat or party-boat captain who will take you where the right kind of fish are biting.

Glass-bottom boats, which depart daily (weather permitting) from docks throughout the Keys, are popular with visitors who want to admire the reefs without getting wet. If you're prone to seasickness, don't try to look through the glass bottom in rough seas.

Motor yachts, sailboats, Hobie Cats, Windsurfers, canoes, and other water-sports equipment are all available for rent by the day or on a long-term basis. Some hotels have their own rental services; others will refer you to a separate vendor.

Treasure Harbor Charter Yachts on Plantation Key rents bare sailboats, from 25-foot Watkins to 44-foot CSY. Captains and provisions available. No pets are allowed. *MM 86.5, OS, 200 Treasure Harbor Dr., Islamorada, tel. 305/852–9440 or 800/ FLA–BOATS. Open 9–5. Reservations and advance deposit required; minimum 3-day rental; $100/day captain fee for boats returned elsewhere. No credit cards.*

Island Breeze Yacht Charters rents bare power boats from 32-foot Ranger Blaylinders to 42-foot Grand Banks. Captains and provisions available. No pets are allowed. *MM 103.5, OS, 51 Shoreland Dr., Box 815, Key Largo, tel. 305/451–4766 or 800/ FLA–BOATS. Open 9–5. Reservations and advance deposit required; weekly charters; $100/day captain fee for boats returned elsewhere. No credit cards.*

Golf Two of the five golf courses in the Keys are open to the public:

Key Colony Beach Par 3. Eight-hole course near Marathon. *MM 53.5, 8th St., Key Colony Beach, tel. 305/289–1533.*

Key West Resort Golf Course. Eighteen-hole course on the bay side of Stock Island. *6450 E. Junior College Rd., Key West, tel. 305/294–5232.*

The other three courses, open only to members and their guests, are the 18-hole **Ocean Reef Club** on Key Largo, the eight-hole executive course at **Cheeca Lodge** in Islamorada, and the 18-hole **Sombrero Country Club** course in Marathon.

Beaches

Keys shorelines are either mangrove-fringed marshes or rock outcrops that fall away to mucky grass flats. Most pleasure beaches in the Keys are manmade, with sand imported from the U.S. mainland or the Bahamas. There are public beaches in **John Pennekamp Coral Reef State Park** (MM 102.5), **Long Key State Recreation Area** (MM 67.5), **Sombrero Beach** in Marathon (MM 50), **Bahia Honda State Recreation Area** (MM 37), and at many roadside turnouts along the Overseas Highway. Many hotels and motels also have their own small shallow-water beach areas.

When you swim in the Keys, wear an old pair of tennis shoes to protect your feet from rocks, sea-urchin spines, and other potential hazards.

Key West   **Smathers Beach** features almost two miles of sand beside South Roosevelt Boulevard. Trucks along the road will rent you rafts, Windsurfers, and other beach "toys."
Higgs Memorial Beach. Near the end of White Street, this is a popular sunbathing spot. A nearby grove of Australian pines provides shade and the **West Martello Tower** provides shelter should a storm suddenly sweep in.
Dog Beach. At Vernon and Waddell streets, this is the only beach in Key West where dogs are allowed.
Southernmost Beach. On the Atlantic Ocean at the foot of Duval Street, this spot is popular with tourists at nearby motels. It has limited parking and a nearby buffet-type restaurant.
Fort Zachary Taylor State Historic Site. The beach here, several hundred yards of shoreline near the western end of Key West, adjoins a picnic area with barbecue grills in a stand of Australian pines. In 1989, the beach was badly eroded and a renourishment program was planned. This beach is relatively uncrowded and attracts more locals than tourists.
Simonton Street Beach. At the north end of Simonton Street, facing the Gulf of Mexico, this is a great place to watch boat traffic in the harbor, but parking here is difficult.
Two hotels in Key West have notable beaches:
Marriott's Casa Marina Resort (1500 Reynolds St.) grants access to its 1,000-foot Atlantic Ocean beach to nonguests who rent a cabana for $10/day.
Pier House (1 Duval St.) has a beach club for locals and patrons of certain nearby guest houses.
Several hotels allow varying degrees of undress on their beaches. Pier House permits female guests on its beach to go topless, and nude bathing is acceptable at the **Atlantic Shores Motel** (510 South St.). Contrary to popular belief, the rangers at Fort Taylor beach do *not* allow nude bathing.

Dining

by Rosalie Leposky   Don't be misled by the expression *Key-easy*. Denizens of the Florida Keys may be relaxed and wear tropical-casual clothes, but these folks take food seriously. A number of young, talented chefs have settled here in the last few years to enjoy the climate and contribute to the Keys' growing image as a fine-dining center. Best-known among them is Norman Van Aken, who oversees the cuisine at two Key West restaurants, Louie's

Backyard and Mira. Van Aken's book, *Feast of the Sunlight* (Random House, 1988) describes the delights of Key West's "fusion cuisine," a blend of Florida citrus, seafood, and tropical fruits with Southwestern chilis, herbs, and spices.

The restaurant menus, the rum-based fruit beverages, and even the music reflect the Keys' tropical climate and their proximity to Cuba and other Caribbean islands. The better American and Cuban restaurants serve imaginative and tantalizing dishes that incorporate tropical fruits and vegetables, including avocado, carambola (star fruit), mango, and papaya.

Freshly caught local fish have been on every Keys menu in the past, but that is starting to change. The Keys' growing population has degraded the environment, disrupting the fishery and pricing fishermen out of the local housing market. Because many venerable commercial fish houses have abandoned the business in the past decade, there's a good chance the fish you order in a Keys restaurant may have been caught somewhere else. Since 1985, the U.S. government has protected the queen conch as an endangered species, so any conch you order in the Keys has come fresh-frozen from the Bahamas, Belize, or the Caribbean. Florida lobster and stone crab should be local and fresh from August through March.

Purists will find few examples of authentic Key-lime pie: a yellow lime custard in a Graham-cracker crust with a meringue top. Many restaurants now serve a version made with white-pastry crust and whipped cream, which is easy to prepare and hold for sale. The Pier House's **Market Bistro** and **Pier House Restaurant** serve the real thing with an extra-high meringue, almost as tangy and puckery as the truly homemade version at **Island Jim's** on Big Pine Key.

The list below is a representative selection of independent restaurants in the Keys, organized by mile marker (MM) number in descending order, as you would encounter them when driving down from the mainland. Small restaurants may not follow the hours listed here. Sometimes they close for a day or a week, or cancel lunch for a month or two, just by posting a note on the door.

The most highly recommended restaurants are indicated by a star ★.

Category	Cost*
Very Expensive	over $55
Expensive	$35–$55
Moderate	$15–$35
Inexpensive	under $15

per person, excluding service, drinks, tip, 6% state sales tax, and local tourist tax

Florida City   **Alabama Jack's.** In 1953 Alabama Jack Stratham opened his restaurant on two barges at the end of Card Sound Road, 13 miles south of Homestead in an old fishing community between Card and Barnes sounds. The spot, something of a no-man's-land, belongs to the Keys in spirit thanks to the Card Sound toll bridge, which joined the mainland to upper Key Largo in 1969. Regular customers include Keys fixtures such as balladeer Jimmy Buffett, Sunday bikers, local retirees, boaters who tie up at the restaurant's dock, and anyone else fond of dancing to country-western music and clapping for cloggers. You can also admire the tropical birds cavorting in the nearby mangroves and the occasional crocodile swimming up the canal. Specialties include peppery homemade crab cakes; light, fluffy conch fritters; crunchy breaded shrimp; homemade tartar sauce; and a tangy cocktail sauce with horseradish. *58000 Card Sound Rd., Florida City, tel. 305/248–8741 (Miami). Open 8:30–7. Live band Sat.–Sun. 2–7. Dress: casual. No reservations. No credit cards. Moderate.*

Key Largo **Crack'd Conch.** Foreign money and patrons' business cards festoon the main dining room, where vertical bamboo stakes support the bar. There's also a screened outdoor porch. Specialties include conch (cracked and in chowder, fritters, and salad), fried alligator, smoked chicken, and 88 kinds of beer. *MM 105, OS, Rte. 1, 105045 Overseas Hwy., tel. 305/451–0732. Open Mon., Tues., Thurs., Fri. 5–10; weekends noon–10; closed Wed. No credit cards. Inexpensive.*

Italian Fisherman. White plaster statues of a fisherman, Columbus, and a nude goddess welcome you to the Italian Fisherman. You can dine indoors, but the best seating is on a deck overlooking Florida Bay where an audience of seagulls awaits any morsel you may hurl in their direction. Chef Joseph Rotonda is particularly adept at pasta and rich tangy marinara sauce. Specialties include hearty minestrone soup with lots of vegetables and fresh garlic bread; linguine marechiaro with shrimp, scallops, and clams; and the catch of the day blackened New Orleans–style. *MM104, BS, tel. 305/451–4471. Dress: casual. Reservations accepted for parties of 10 or more. Closed Christmas and Thanksgiving. AE, M, V. Moderate.*

★ **Mrs. Mac's Kitchen.** Hundreds of beer cans, beer bottles, and expired auto license plates from all over the world decorate the walls of this wood-paneled, open-air restaurant. At lunchtime, the counter and booths fill up early with locals. Regular nightly specials are worth the stop: meatloaf on Monday, Mexican on Tuesday, Italian on Wednesday, and seafood Thursday through Saturday. The chili is always good, and the imported beer of the month is $1 a bottle or can. *MM 99.4, Rte. 1, tel. 305/451–3722. Dress: casual. No reservations. No credit cards. Closed Sun. Inexpensive.*

Islamorada **Marker 88.** The best seats in chef/owner Andre Mueller's main
★ dining room catch the last glimmers of sunset. Hostesses recite a lengthy list of daily specials and offer you a wine list with over 200 entries. You can get a good steak or veal chop here, but 75% of the food served is seafood. Specialties include a robust conch chowder; banana blueberry bisque; Salad Trevisana, made with radicchio, leaf lettuce, Belgium endive, watercress, and sweet-and-sour dill dressing (President Bush's favorite); sautéed conch or alligator steak meuniere; grouper Rangoon, served with chunks of papaya, banana, and pineapple in a cinnamon and currant jelly sauce; and Key-lime pie. *MM 88 on Overseas Hwy., BS, Plantation Key, tel. 305/852–9315. Dress: informal. Reservations advised. AE, DC, MC, V. Expensive.*

Whale Harbor Inn. This coral rock building has oyster shells cemented onto the walls and a water mark at the seven-foot mark as a reminder of Hurricane Donna's fury in 1960. Several restaurant employees rode out the storm in the building's lighthouse tower. The main attraction is a 50-foot-long all-you-can-eat buffet, which includes a stir-fry area for wok cookery and a plentiful supply of shrimp, rock shrimp, crayfish, and snowcrab legs. Special on Sunday are black beans and ham and Belgian waffles. The adjoining Dockside Restaurant and Lounge has a raw bar and grill and a catwalk overlooking a marina. *MM 83.5, OS, Upper Matecumbe Key, tel. 305/664–4959. Dress: casual. No reservations. AE, CB, DC, MC, V. Moderate.*

Green Turtle Inn. Photographs of locals and famous visitors dating from 1947 line the walls and stuffed turtle dolls dangle from the ceiling over the bar. Harry Rosenthal, the restaurant's third owner, retains the original menu cover and some of the original dishes. Specialties include a rich, spicy turtle chowder; conch fritters, nicely browned outside, light and fluffy inside; conch salad with vinegar, lime juice, pimento, and pepper; alligator steak (tail meat) sautéed in an egg batter; and Key-lime pie. Whole pies are available for carry-out. *MM 81.5, OS, tel. 305/664–9031. Dress: casual. No reservations. AE, CB, DC, MC, V. Closed Mon. and Thanksgiving Day. Moderate.*

Marathon **Ship's Pub and Galley.** The collection of historic photos on the restaurant walls depict the railroad era in the Keys, the development of Duck Key, and many of the notables who have visited here. Dinners include soup and a 40-item salad bar with all the steamed shrimp you can eat. Specialties include homemade garlic bread, Swiss onion soup, certified New York Angus beef, at least two fish specials, Florida stone crab claws (in season), and mile-high shoofly mudpie, a six-inch-high coffee ice cream pie with a whipped cream topping. The adjoining lounge has live entertainment and a dance floor. *MM 61, OS, tel. 305/743–7000, ext. 3627. Dress: casual. Reservations accepted. Early bird specials. AE, CB, DC, MC, V. Moderate.*

Grassy Key Dairy Bar. Look for the Dairy Queen–style concrete ice-cream cones near the road. Locals and construction workers stop here for quick lunches. Owner/chefs George and Johnny Eigner are proud of their fresh-daily homemade bread, soups and chowders, fresh seafood, and fresh-cut beef. *MM 58.5, OS, Grassy Key, tel. 305/743–3816. Dress: casual. Reservations accepted. No credit cards. Closed Sun. and Mon. Moderate.*

Herbie's Bar. A local favorite for lunch and dinner since the 1940s, Herbie's has three small rooms with two bars. Indoor diners sit at wood picnic tables or the bar; those in the screened outdoor room use concrete tables. Specialties include spicy conch chowder with chunks of tomato and crisp conch fritters with homemade horseradish sauce. Nightly specials. *MM 50.5, BS, 6350 Overseas Hwy., tel. 305/743–6373. Dress: casual. No reservations. No credit cards. Closed Sun. and Mon. Inexpensive.*

Kelsey's. The walls in this restaurant at the Faro Blanco Marine Resort are hung with boat paddles inscribed by the regulars. All entrees here are served with fresh-made yeast rolls brushed with drawn butter and Florida orange honey. Chef David Leeper serves only fresh local seafood and lobster. Specialties include broiled swordfish with dill sauce and grouper gourmet (lightly floured, dipped in egg batter, sautéed in white wine and fresh lemon, and topped with artichoke hearts, mushrooms, and toasted almonds). You can bring your own cleaned and filleted catch for the chef to prepare. Dessert offerings change nightly and may include German chocolate cake, Mrs. Kelsey's original macadamia pie, and Key-lime cheesecake. *MM 48, BS, 1996 Overseas Hwy., tel. 305/743–9018. Dress: casual. Reservations accepted. AE, MC, V. Dinner only. Closed Mon. Expensive.*

Mile 7 Grill. This open-air diner built in 1954 at the Marathon end of Seven Mile Bridge has walls festooned with mounted fish, sponges, and signs describing individual menu items. Specialties include grouper chowder, fresh fish sandwich of the day, and a foot-long chili dog on a toasted sesame roll. *MM 47.5, BS, 1240 Overseas Hwy., tel. 305/743–4481. No credit cards. Closed Wed.–Thurs. and when they want to in Aug.–Sept. Inexpensive.*

Big Pine Key   **Island Jim's.** Good food comes out of this old 60-seat Conch-style building with screened windows, oilcloth-covered tables, and aerial photos of the Keys over the bar. The decor hasn't changed for decades, but the menu changes nightly, depending on what kind of fresh seafood is available. Specialties may include blacktip shark, conch, dolphin, shrimp, and tile fish, and steaks of midwestern beef. Owner Rita Ballard is especially proud of her meringue-topped Key-lime pie and Angel Strada pie (a semi-sweet cinnamon chocolate cream concoction), both made fresh daily by one of her waitresses. To order a whole pie, call a day ahead. *MM 31¼, BS, tel. 305/872–2017. Open lunch 11:30 AM–2 PM Mon.–Sat., dinner 5–9 PM, Sunday brunch 8 AM–1 PM. No reservations. Dress: casual. No credit cards. Inexpensive.*

Key West   **Louie's Backyard.** This place is really two restaurants and a
American   bar. The upstairs Cafe at Louie's has a coffered ceiling, an
★   open-theater kitchen, louvered transom windows, and a balcony. Downstairs in Louie's Backyard, the walls are decorated with abstract art and old Key West paintings. Menus in both restaurants change regularly. The cafe serves what chef Norman Van Aken calls "nouveau Cuban." The menu may include pan-charred grouper with a dash of soy sauce, Myer's dark rum, and cracked black pepper; chicken livers pan-fried in olive oil with Spanish sherry vinegar, sweet peppers, red onion, chilies, and celery; and marinated roast pork served with black bean sauce, plantains, slices of red onion, sour cream, and lime. At Louie's Backyard, innovative selections include Bahamian conch chowder with bird-pepper hot sauce and grilled catch of the day with tomato-butter and red-onion marmalade and roasted peppers. *700 Waddell Ave., tel. 305/294–1061. Jackets required. Reservations advised. Dinner only at the Cafe. AE, DC, MC, V. Very Expensive.*

Pepe's Cafe and Steak House. Judges, policemen, carpenters, and fishermen rub elbows every morning in their habitual breakfast seats, at three tables and four pine booths under a huge paddle fan. Outdoors are more tables and an open-air bar under a canvas tarp. Pepe's was established downtown in 1919 and moved to the current site in 1962. The specials change nightly: barbecue chicken, pork tenderloin, ribs, potato salad, red or black beans, and corn bread on Sunday; meatloaf on Monday; seafood Tuesday and Wednesday; a full traditional Thanksgiving dinner every Thursday; filet mignon on Friday;

and prime rib on Saturday. *806 Caroline St., tel. 305/294–7192. Dress: casual. No reservations. MC, V. Inexpensive.*

★ **Pier House Restaurant.** Steamships from Havana once docked at this pier jutting out into the Gulf of Mexico. Now it's an elegant place to dine, indoors or out, and to watch boats gliding by in the harbor. At night the restaurant shines lights into the water, attracting schools of brightly colored parrot fish. The menu emphasizes tropical fruits, spices, and fish. Specialties include a peppery, cream-based conch chowder; fresh homemade conch ravioli on a bed of radicchio leaves; the daily gulf catch sautéed and served with fresh avocado and papaya in Key-lime sauce; and rack of lamb with apple jalapeño chutney and goat-cheese polenta. The dessert menu always includes a medium-tart Key-lime pie with a five-inch meringue topping. *1 Duval St., tel. 305/296–4600, 800/327–8340 (U.S.), or 800/432–3414 (FL). Jacket required. Reservations advised. AE, MC, V. Very Expensive.*

Cuban **El Siboney.** This family-style restaurant serves traditional Cuban food. Specials include chicken and rice every Friday, oxtail stew with rice and beans on Saturday. Always available are roast pork with *morros* (black beans and white rice) and cassava, paella, and *palomilla* steak. *900 Catherine St., tel. 305/296–4184. Dress: casual. No reservations. No credit cards. Closed Thanksgiving, Christmas, New Year's Day, 2 wks in June. Inexpensive.*

Delicatessen **Market Bistro.** The Pier House's deli and fine-dining snack shop sells the hotel's classic Key-lime pie by the slice. A cooler holds a respectable selection of fine wines, champagnes, and beers. Specialties include tropical fruit drinks, sandwiches, salads, and gourmet cheeses and pates. *1 Duval St. in the Pier House, tel. 305/296–4600. Dress: casual. No reservations. AE, MC, V. Moderate.*

French **Cafe des Artistes.** This intimate 75-seat restaurant occupies part of a hotel building constructed in 1935 by C. E. Alfeld, Al Capone's bookkeeper. Haitian paintings and Keys scenes by local artists decorate the walls. Skylights in one of the five rooms are open in good weather, and some seating is available in a secluded courtyard. Executive chef Frederic Debiasio presents a French interpretation of tropical cuisine, using fresh local seafood and produce and light, flour-free sauces. Specialties include sautéed scallops served with almond-curry-rum sauce, salade "Jessica" (avocado, hearts of palm, strawberries, and orange/ginger vinaigrette dressing), pear and Champagne cream soup with bits of fresh pear, a very light raspberry Cointreau cheesecake, and pear tart with passion fruit ice cream. *1007 Simonton St., tel. 305/294–7100. Jacket required. Reservations advised. No lunch. AE, MC, V. Very Expensive.*

Seafood **The Buttery.** The Buttery's waiters have come to be known as
★ buttercups, a nickname they share with the house's special drink, a blended frozen concoction of vodka, Kahlua, amaretto, coconut milk, and cream. Each of the restaurant's six rooms has its own character. The back room with the bar has wood paneling and skylights; a small private dining room in front has green-painted woodwork and floral wallpaper. The front rooms have green carpets and swag lamps, candles in large glass hurricane chimneys, and many plants. Specialties include yellowtail snapper baked with sliced bananas, walnuts, and banana liqueur; steak "Ricardo" (fillets of tenderloin sautéed

with mushrooms in Madeira-wine sauce), and chilled Senegalese cream-of-celery soup made with curry, heavy cream, and mango chutney, and, for dessert, Poor Richard's Super Rich, a creamy blend of Godiva and three other kinds of chocolate in a chocolate pie crust topped with fresh whipped cream, and crushed English walnuts. *1208 Simonton St., tel. 305/294–0717. Jacket required. Reservations advised. AE, CB, DC, MC, V. Closed 2–3 wks in Sept. No lunch. Expensive.*

Dockside Bar and Raw Bar. When the crowds get too thick on the Mallory Dock at sunset, you can come up here, have a piña colada and a snack, and watch the action from afar. This establishment, on a 200-foot dock behind Ocean Key House, has a limited but flavorful menu: freshly smoked fish, crunchy conch salad, crispy conch fritters, and fresh clams, oysters, and shrimp. Live island music is featured nightly. *Ocean Key House, Zero Duval St., tel. 305/296–7701. Dress: casual. No reservations. AE, CB, DC, MC, V. Inexpensive.*

Lodging

Some hotels in the Keys are historic structures with a charming patina of age; others are just plain old. Salty winds and soil play havoc with anything manmade in the Keys. Constant maintenance is a must, and some hotels and motels don't get it. Inspect your accommodations before checking in. The best rooms in the Keys have a clear bay or ocean view and a deep setback from the Overseas Highway.

The city of Key West offers the greatest variety of lodgings, from large resorts to bed-and-breakfast rooms in private homes. Altogether there are about 4,000 units (including about 1,500 rooms in close to 60 guest houses) as well as approximately 1,800 condominium apartments that are available for daily or weekly rental through their homeowners associations.

Accommodations in the Keys are more expensive than elsewhere in South Florida. In part this is due to the Keys' popularity and ability to command top dollar, but primarily it's because everything used to build and operate a hotel costs more in the Keys. All materials and supplies must be trucked in, and electric and water rates are among the steepest in the nation.

The Florida Keys and Key West Visitors Bureau provides a free accommodations guide (*see* Important Addresses and Numbers). The list below is a representative selection of hotels, motels, resorts, and guest houses. In the Upper, Middle, and Lower Keys outside Key West, we've listed hotels, motels, and resorts by mile marker (MM) number in descending order, as you would encounter them when driving down from the mainland.

Category	Cost*
Very Expensive	over $175
Expensive	$110–$175
Moderate	$75–$110
Inexpensive	under $75

All prices are for a standard double room, excluding 6% state sales tax and local tourist tax.

Key Largo **Largo Lodge.** No two rooms are the same in this vintage 1950s resort. A tropical garden with palm trees, sea grapes, and orchids surrounds the guest cottages. Late in the day, wild ducks, pelicans, herons, and other birds come looking for a handout. *MM 101.5, BS, 101740 Overseas Hwy., 33037, tel. 305/ 451–0424 or 800/IN–THE–SUN. 7 rooms with bath, including 1 efficiency. Facilities: 200 feet of bay frontage, public phone, boat ramp and 3 slips. No children under 16 or pets. AE, MC, V. Moderate.*

★ **Holiday Inn Key Largo Resort.** James W. Hendricks, the Kentucky attorney who restored the *African Queen* (*see* Exploring the Keys), completed renovations and new landscaping at this resort at the Key Largo Harbor Canal in 1989. The hotel was built in 1971, and a new wing was added in 1981. Decor includes blonde wood furniture and pink and green bedspreads. Provides onshore accommodations for guests coming to Jules Undersea Lodge and pickup service from Marathon Airport. *MM 100, OS, Box 708, U.S. 1, 33037, tel. 305/451–2121, 800/ HOLIDAY, 800/THE KEYS, or 800/247–2345 (FL). 132 rooms with bath, including 13 nonsmoker rooms and 2 rooms for handicapped guests. Facilities: 2 swimming pools (1 with waterfall), marina with 35 transient spaces, gift shop, dive and glass-bottom tour boats, boat rentals. AE, MC, V. Expensive.*

★ **Marina Del Mar Resort and Marina.** This resort beside the Key Largo Harbor Canal caters to sailors and divers. Two buildings opened in 1986, a third in 1988. All rooms contain original art by local artists Sue and Zita. The best rooms are suites 502, 503 and 504, each of which has a full kitchen and plenty of room for large families and dive groups. The fourth-floor observation deck offers spectacular sunrise and sunset views. Advance reservations are required for boat slips. To find the hotel, turn OS on U.S. 1 by the Texaco station at Laguna Avenue, and left at the first intersection onto Caribbean Boulevard. Marina Del Mar is about 100 yards on the left. *MM 100, OS, Box 1050, 33037, tel. 800/451–3483 (U.S.), 800/253–3483 (FL), 800/638– 3483 (Canada), or 305/451–4107. 76 rooms with bath, including 16 suites, 16 nonsmoker rooms and 3 rooms for handicapped guests. Facilities: in-room refrigerators, 46-slip full-service marina, showers and washing machines for live-aboards, swimming pool, 2 lighted tennis courts, weight room, washers and dryers on all floors, diver lockers, picnic tables, free Continental breakfast in lobby, restaurant and bar, dive packages, diving and snorkeling charters, fishing charters. No pets. AE, CB, DC, MC, V. Moderate.*

Sunset Cove Motel. Each room has one hard and one soft mattress plus a sleeper sofa, tile floors, and original hand-painted murals. Special discounts are offered to senior citizens and members of conservation groups. *MM 99.5, BS, Box 99, 33037, tel. 305/451–0705. 10 units with bath and a dormitory group house with kitchen for up to 15 people. Facilities: free watersports equipment (canoes, glass-bottom and regular paddle boat, sailboats, trimaran, and Windsurfers), 115-foot fishing pier, boat ramp. No children under 16. No pets. MC, V. Moderate.*

Bay Harbor Lodge. Owner Laszlo Simoga speaks German, Hungarian, and Russian and caters to an international clientele. Situated on two heavily landscaped acres, this resort has a rustic wood lodge and several concrete-block structures. Unit 14, a large efficiency apartment with a deck, has a wood ceiling, original oil paintings, and a dining table made from the hatch cover of a World War II Liberty Ship. *MM 97.5, BS, Rte. 1, Box 35, 33037, tel. 305/852–5695. 12 rooms with bath. Facilities: Jacuzzi, saltwater shower, Olympic weightlifting equipment, individual outdoor barbecues, paddleboat, rowboats, canoes, 2 docks, cable TV, boat and trailer parking. No pets. MC, V. Inexpensive.*

Sheraton Key Largo Resort. This four-story hotel is nestled in 12½ acres of coastal hardwood hammock and mangrove swamp. A modern interpretation of traditional Conch architecture, the resort's three-story atrium lobby features a multitude of small glass windowpanes separated by prominent mullions, a Mexican-tile floor, coral-rock walls, and rattan furniture. *MM 97, BS, 97000 Overseas Hwy., 33037, tel. 305/852–5553, 800/325–3535 (U.S.), 800/268–9393 (Eastern Canada), or 800/268–9330 (Western Canada). 200 rooms with bath, including 10 suites. Facilities: minibars, 2 heated swimming pools, 2 lighted tennis courts, 2,000-foot labeled nature trail, sailboat and Windsurfer rental, fishing and dive charters, dive shop, 21-slip dock for hotel guests, 2 restaurants, 3 lounges, beauty shop. AE, CB, DC, MC, V. Expensive.*

Islamorada   **Holiday Isle Resorts and Marina.** Situated near Theater of the Sea, this is actually four separate resort motels under common ownership and management—the original Holiday Isle Resorts and Marina, El Capitan, Harbor Lights, and Howard Johnson's. All except El Capitan were renovated in 1988. Each motel in the complex offers variety in price and location. On weekends, the resort is popular with the under-30 set. Harbor Lights, off on its own a half mile up the road, is quieter than the rest. *MM 84.5, OS, Windley Key, 84001 Overseas Hwy., Box 588, 33036, tel. 305/664–2321. 800/432–2875 (FL), or 800/327–7070 (U.S. and Canada). 171 rooms with bath, including 18 suites and 21 efficiencies, 3 nonsmoker rooms in Howard Johnson's. Facilities: 3 swimming pools, 18-slip marina, 5 restaurants, Wave Runners charter fishing boats, Holiday Princess glass-bottom sightseeing boat; Caribbean Watersports, a concessionaire, rents Hobie 14s, jet skis, and sailboats and offers parasailing. No pets. AE, CB, DC, MC, V. Inexpensive–Very Expensive.*

Cheeca Lodge. Reminiscent of Miami Beach in the 1950s, this 27-acre resort on Upper Matecumbe Key appeals to affluent northeasterners who appreciate ostentatious informality. It reopened in 1989 after being closed for 17 months for a $30 million total renovation and expansion. Lobby decor includes cypress beams and Florida keystone floors. Two color schemes were used for the guest rooms and suites: periwinkle blue and strawberry, and hot orange and green. All guest units have British Colonial–style furniture with bamboo and wicker headboards and chairs. Ocean Suite 102 features a cathedral ceiling and a screened porch. Fourth-floor rooms in the main lodge open onto a terrace with either an ocean or bay view. *MM 82, Upper Matecumbe Key, Box 527, 33036, tel. 305/664–4651 (Islamorada), or 305/245–3755 (Miami), or 800/327–2888 (U.S. and FL). 203 rooms, including 64 suites, 160 nonsmoker rooms, and 5 rooms for handicapped guests. Facilities: in-room minibar, free golf-cart shuttle service around the resort, 9-hole par-3 executive golf course designed by Jack Nicklaus, 6 lighted tennis courts, 2 heated swimming pools and one saltwater tidal pool, 525-foot fishing pier, 2 restaurants, lounge. Sun. brunch served in the Atlantic's Edge Dining Room.*

Beach Hut rents Hobie Cats, rafts, snorkeling and fishing gear, parasailing equipment, and power boats. All-year children's program. AE, CB, DC, MC, V. Very Expensive.

Long Key **Lime Tree Bay Resort** Four new rooms with cathedral ceiling were added in 1986 to this 2.5-acre resort built in 1972. Each room is decorated differently. A palm tree grows through the floor of "The Treehouse," a two-bedroom unit with kitchen that is popular with larger families. You can swim and snorkel in the shallow grass flats just offshore. *MM 68.5, BS, Box 839, Layton, 33001, tel. 305/664-4740. 28 rooms with bath. Facilities: outdoor swimming pool and Jacuzzi, tennis court, power and sailboat rentals, 2 restaurants. No pets. AE, MC, V. Moderate.*

Marathon **Hawk's Cay.** Morris Lapidus, architect of the Fontainebleau
★ Hilton hotel in Miami Beach, designed this rambling West Indies–style resort, which opened in 1959 as the Indies Inn and Marina. Over the years it has entertained a steady stream of politicians (including Harry Truman, Dwight Eisenhower, and Lyndon Johnson) and film stars who come to relax and be pampered by a friendly, low-key staff. Hawk's Cay retains the comfortable ambience it has always had, even after an $8 million renovation of rooms, public areas, meeting space, and landscaping completed in 1989. The new decor features wickerwork rattan, a sea-green and salmon color scheme, and original contemporary artwork in guest rooms and public areas. Most rooms face the water. New in 1990 will be 86 two-bedroom marina villas available to hotel guests; a new health club is scheduled to open in 1991. *MM 61, OS, 33050, tel. 305/743-7000, 800/432-2242 (FL) or 800/327-7775. 177 rooms with bath, including 16 suites, 4 rooms for handicapped guests. Facilities: heated swimming pool, 2 whirlpool spas, 1-mi fitness trail, 8 tennis courts, Tim Farwell's Tennis School, use of Sombrero Golf Course in Marathon, 70-slip full-service marina, PADI-certified dive boats, Club Nautico boat rentals, fishing and sailing charter boats, Zoovet Dolphin Center (where guests can swim with the dolphins), 4 restaurants, complimentary full-breakfast buffet, nightclub, 4 boutique and specialty shops, billiard room, video game room. Free summer children's program. AE, DC, MC, V. Very Expensive.*

Rainbow Bend Fishing Resort. First you notice the shocking-pink exterior, then the well-kept appearance of this 2.7-acre resort built in the late 1950s as a lumberyard and CIA base. Every room is different. The Main House has a series of interconnecting rooms that can accommodate up to 14 people. A restaurant offering complimentary breakfast overlooks an ample manmade beach, good bonefish flats just a few yards offshore, and a dock with boats available free to guests. *MM 58, OS, Grassy Key, Route 1, Box 159, 33050, tel. 305/289-1505. 21 rooms with bath, including 18 suites. Facilities: heated swimming pool and Jacuzzi, small fishing pier, 4 hrs free use of 15-foot Boston Whaler, free use of sailboards and canoe, complete bait and tackle shop, 2 charter boats, restaurant. Quarterly newsletter for guests. AE, MC, V. Expensive.*

Valhalla Beach Resort Motel. Watch for this resort's large sign along the Overseas Highway. The resort itself is a half mile off the road, surrounded by water on three sides. It's a 1950s motel that has been run by the same family for over 20 years. *MM 56.5, OS, Crawl Key, Rte. 1, Box 115, 33050, tel. 305/289-0616.*

12 rooms with bath, including 8 efficiencies. Facilities: boat ramp and dock, private beach. No credit cards. Inexpensive.

Sombrero Resort & Lighthouse Marina. You can choose from marina or pool views in this complex of buildings ranging in height from one to three stories. The original structure built in 1960 was renovated in 1985, and new rooms were opened in 1988 and 1989. Turn OS off the Overseas Highway by the K-Mart onto Sombrero Beach Road, then right at the first corner onto Sombrero Boulevard. The resort is to your left, across from the Sombrero Country Club. *MM 50, OS, 19 Sombrero Blvd., 33050, tel. 305/743–2250 or 800/433–8660. 154 rooms with bath, including 102 suites. Facilities: pool, sauna, 4 tennis courts, tennis pro, marine store, boat ramp, 54-slip marina, restaurant, bar. AE, MC, V. Moderate.*

Boot Key Seaport Resort. Opened in 1989, this houseboat resort consists of permanently anchored barges that move in the wind. By prior arrangement, yachtsmen with boats under 25 feet can tie their craft alongside their houseboat unit. The proprietor also operates Faro Blanco Marine Resort in Marathon. *MM 47.8, OS, 1000 15th St., 33050, tel. 305/743–4200 or 800/343–9091. 31 suites with bath on 19 houseboats, 1 room for handicapped guests. Facilities: ship's store, gift shop, raw bar and grill, full-service marina with 100 slips, boat rentals. Pets welcome with $18 fee and advance reservation. Dockage fee for guests' boats $7/night. AE, MC, V. Expensive.*

Little Torch Key ★ **Little Palm Island.** The lobby is just off the Overseas Highway on Little Torch Key, but the resort itself is a three-mile boat ride away on a palm-fringed island at the western end of the Newfound Harbor Keys. There you'll find 14 thatch-roof villas, each with two suites, and two additional suites in the Great House, a concrete fishing lodge built in 1928. Each suite has a Mexican-tile bath and dressing area, beds draped with mosquito netting, and Mexican and Guatemalan wicker and rattan furniture. Built on stilts nine feet above mean high tide, all villas afford good views of the water. The island is in the middle of Coupon Bight Aquatic Preserve and is the closest point of land to the Looe Key National Marine Sanctuary. *MM 28.5, Overseas Highway, Route 4, Box 1036, 33042, tel. 305/872–2524 or 800/343–8567. 30 suites, 1 for handicapped guests. Facilities: air conditioners, wet bars and stocked refrigerators, room safes, heated lagoon-style swimming pool, sauna, tiki bar, gift shop, restaurant, 12-slip marina for hotel and restaurant guests. Free launch service 7 **AM**–11 **PM**. Pickup from Marathon Airport and Key West International Airport. Guided tours and excursions. Full American plan—breakfast, lunch, dinner, Sun. brunch. No children under 9 or pets. Very Expensive.*

Ramrod Key **Looe Key Reef Resort and Dive Center.** The rooms in this two-story divers' motel were refurnished in 1987. In the tiny lobby, the front desk doubles as a package liquor store. Rooms are spartan but comfortable, with firm mattresses and ocean-blue bedspreads and carpets. The least desirable rooms are the three singles without a canal view. Guests can make an appointment for free pickup from the private airstrip on Summerland Key. *MM 27.5, US 1, OS, Box 509, 33042, tel. 305/872–2215. 23 rooms with bath, 1 for handicapped guests. Facilities: air conditioners, cable TV, outdoor swimming pool, dive shop, 400 feet of boat dockage, two Coast Guard–certified dive* *boats, restaurant, poolside tiki bar and raw bar. AE, MC, V. Inexpensive.*

Sugarloaf Key   **Sugar Loaf Lodge.** This well-landscaped older motel overlooking mangrove islands and Upper Sugarloaf Sound has one building with soft beds and an eclectic assortment of furniture and another with high ceilings, wall murals, and balconies on the second floor. A friendly dolphin named Sugar inhabits a lagoon just outside the restaurant; diners can watch her perform through a picture window. *MM 17, BS, Box 148, 33044, tel. 305/ 745–3211. 55 rooms with bath. Facilities: swimming pool, tennis court, 18-hole miniature golf course, restaurant, lounge, free dolphin performances at 9 AM, 1 PM, and 5 PM. AE, CB, DC, MC, V. Moderate.*

Key West   **Key West Reservation Service** makes hotel reservations and *House and*   helps visitors locate rental properties (condominiums and pri- *Condominium*   vate homes). *628 Fleming St., Drawer 1689, 33040, tel. 305/294– Rentals*   7713, 800/356–3567 (FL), 800/327–4813 (U.S.), 716/823–1061 (Canada). AE, MC, V.*

     Property Management of Key West, Inc., offers lease and rental service for condominiums, town houses, and private homes, including renovated Conch homes. *1213 Truman Ave., 33040, tel. 305/296–7744. AE, MC, V.*

Hotels and Motels   **The Banyan Resort.** A time-share resort across the street from ★   the Truman Annex, the Banyan Resort includes five Victorian houses, a former cigar factory listed on the National Registry of Historic Places, and two modern buildings in the Victorian style. The award-winning gardens are a tropical cornucopia of avocado, Barbados cherry, eggfruit, papaya, Persian lime, and sapodilla. The rooms have a gray, maroon, and mauve color scheme and rattan and wicker furniture. *323 Whitehead St., 33040, tel. 305/294–9573 or 800/225–0639. 38 suites with bath. Facilities: 2 swimming pools (1 heated), 2 Jacuzzis, bar. No children under 16 or pets. AE, MC, V. Very Expensive.*

     Hyatt Key West. A first for Hyatt, this "baby grand" resort consists of three four-story buildings surrounding a tropical piazza. The lobby has a Mexican terra-cotta tile floor and cherry wood fixtures; the room decor employs mint, lilac, peach, and teal blue hues with light-wood dressers and wicker chairs. All rooms except 2209 and 2110 have water views. *601 Front St., 33040, tel. 305/296–9900, 800/228–9000, or 800/233–1234. 120 rooms with bath, including 16 suites, 16 nonsmoker rooms, and 6 rooms for handicapped guests. Facilities: honor bar, in-room safe, swimming pool and Jacuzzi, hot tub, fitness room, small private manmade beach, bicycle and motor scooter rental, 6-slip marina. AE, CB, DC, MC, V. Very Expensive.*

     Marriott's Casa Marina Resort. Henry Morrison Flagler built La Casa Marina in 1921 at the end of the Florida East Coast Railroad line. New wings were added in 1978 and 1986. The entire 13-acre resort revolves around an outdoor patio and lawn facing the ocean. The lobby has an elegant beamed ceiling, polished wood floor of Dade County pine, and wicker furniture. Rooms are decorated in purple, mauve, and green pastels and prints of fish and Key West scenes. Among the best rooms are the two-bedroom loft suites with balconies facing the ocean, and the lanai rooms on the ground floor of the main building with French doors opening directly onto the lawn. *1500 Reynolds St., 33040, tel. 305/296–3535, 800/235–4837 (FL), or 800/*

228–9290 (U.S.). 314 rooms with bath, including 63 suites, 16 nonsmoker rooms, 4 rooms for handicapped guests. Facilities: heated swimming pool, whirlpool, 600-ft. fishing pier, health club, massage studio and sauna, 3 tennis courts, 2 gift shops, activity center for children, game room, restaurant, poolside bar. Key West Water Sports, a concessionaire, offers deep-sea charter boats, light-tackle fishing, party-boat fishing, Hobie Cats, Sunfish, jet skis, scuba and snorkel trips, bicycle and moped rentals. AE, DC, MC, V. Very Expensive.

Ocean Key House. This newly refurbished five-story city resort hotel has large and comfortable rooms decorated in tasteful pastel colors and art-deco reproductions. The best rooms, penthouse suites 511 and 512, overlook the Gulf of Mexico. Ocean Key House is the closest hotel to Mallory Square. From its pool deck you can watch the sunset show while quaffing a piña colada from the outdoor bar. *Zero Duval St., 33040, tel. 305/296–7701, 800/231–9864 (FL), or 800/328–9815 (U.S.). 100 units with bath, including 52 1-bedroom suites and 16 2-bedroom suites. Suites have fully equipped kitchen, private Jacuzzi, full-size living room/dining room, minibar. Facilities: heated swimming pool, 6 boat slips, restaurant, pool bar, dive shop. AE, CB, DC, MC, V. Expensive.*

★ **Pier House.** This is the catbird seat for touring Key West—just off the intersection of Duval and Front streets and within easy walking distance of Mallory Square and downtown. Yet within the hotel grounds you feel the tranquility of a remote tropical island. Weathered-gray buildings flank a courtyard filled with tall coconut palms and hibiscus blossoms. Locals gather around a thatch-roof shelter at the Beach Club, a tiki bar. The complex's eclectic architecture includes an original Conch house. The entire hotel was renovated in 1989 and decorated in rich pastels. In an atrium just off the lobby, a trilevel waterfall plunges through a tropical rain forest. *1 Duval St., 33040, tel. 305/296–4600, 800/432–3414 (FL), or 800/327–8340 (U.S.). 120 rooms with bath, including 11 suites in 4 separate low-rise buildings. Facilities: heated swimming pool, 8 bars and restaurants. AE, MC, V. Expensive.*

Econo Lodge. Half the rooms of this six-story motel face the Gulf of Mexico, the rest face the pool. The sixth-floor penthouses have the best view of the Gulf's mangrove islands, grass flats, the nightly sunset, and Mount Trashmore on Stock Island. The rooms are decorated with Key West prints, floral-print bedspreads, and blonde-wood furniture. The trackless trolley stops in front of the main entrance. *3820 N. Roosevelt Blvd., 33040, tel. 305/294–5511, 800/533–9378 (FL), or 800/446–6900 (U.S.). 143 rooms with bath, including 4 1-bedroom suites with kitchenette and 4 penthouses with 2 bedrooms and 1½ baths. Facilities: swimming pool, restaurant, lounge, poolside tiki bar. AE, DC, MC, V. Inexpensive.*

★ **La Concha Holiday Inn.** This seven-story art-deco hotel in the heart of downtown Key West is the city's tallest building. It opened in 1926, was totally renovated and enlarged in 1986, and in 1987 was added to the National Register of Historic Places. Novelist Ernest Hemingway and playwright Tennessee Williams both stayed here. The lobby has a polished floor of pink, mauve, and green marble and a conversation pit with comfortable chairs. Rooms are large and furnished with 1920s-era antiques, lace curtains, and big closets. The restorers kept the old building's original louvered room doors, light globes, and floral trim on the archways. You can enjoy the sunset from "The Top," a restaurant and lounge that overlooks the entire island. *430 Duval St., 33040, tel. 305/296–2991 or 800/227–6151 (FL). 160 rooms with bath, including 8 suites, 18 nonsmoker rooms, and 8 rooms for handicapped guests. Facilities: pool and sun deck, whirlpool spa, fitness room, 2 restaurants, 3 bars, bicycle and motor scooter rentals. AE, CB, DC, MC, V. Moderate.*

★ **The Marquesa Hotel.** Key West architect Thomas Pope supervised the restoration of this four-story 1884 home and added onto it in a compatible style. The lobby resembles a Victorian parlor, with antique furniture, Audubon prints, fresh flowers, and a bowl of apples for nibbles. Rooms have French Provincial furnishings and dotted Swiss curtains. There are marble vanities in some baths, marble floors in others. Continental breakfast prepared by the Mira restaurant's pastry chef is served poolside ($5 extra). *600 Fleming St., Key West 33040, tel. 305/292–1919. 15 rooms with private bath. Facilities: solar-heated swimming pool, room service, 24-hr staff, in-room safe. AE, MC, V. Very Expensive.*

Guest Houses **The Curry Mansion Inn.** Careful dedication to detail by Key
★ West architect Thomas Pope and owners Al and Edith Amsterdam have produced a near-perfect match between the Victorian Curry Mansion (1899) and its modern bed-and-breakfast addition. Each room has a different color scheme of tropical pastels; all rooms have carpeted floors, wicker headboards and furnishings, and quilts from the Cotton Gin Store at MM 94.5 in Tavernier. Rooms 1 and 8 are honeymoon suites with canopy beds and balconies. *511 Caroline St., Key West 33040, tel. 305/294–5349. 15 rooms with bath, 4 rooms for handicapped guests. Facilities: wheelchair lift, swimming pool, in-room safes, wet bars. Guests have privileges at Pier House Beach Club. AE, CB, DC, MC, V. Expensive.*

★ **Eaton Lodge.** Built just after the great fire of 1886, the lodge has eight rooms in the main house and four in the adjoining coach house. The common parlor and guest rooms are furnished with fine antiques. The upstairs Jonquil Springfield suite (two rooms with a connecting bath and adjoining veranda) has white metal hospital-style beds, rag and sissal rugs, and London underground wall posters from the 1930s. A peahen named Matilda struts along brick walks in the tropical garden in search of cocktail peanuts. *511 Eaton St., Key West 33040, tel. 305/294–3800. 12 rooms with bath. Facilities: refrigerators in bathroom, whirlpool spa. Airport pickup service in London taxi. AE, MC, V. Expensive.*

Island City House. This guest house is actually three separate buildings: the vintage-1880s Island City House and Arch House (a former carriage house) and a 1970s reconstruction of an old cigar factory that once stood on the site. Guests share a private tropical garden. *422 William St., Key West 33040, tel. 305/294–5702 or 800/634–8230. 24 parlor suites with bath and kitchen. Facilities: swimming pool and Jacuzzi, bike rental. AE, MC, V. Expensive.*

Authors of Key West. This complex is made up of two turn-of-the-century Conch cottages and seven rooms in a 1940s main house. Each unit is named for a writer linked to Key West and decorated with appropriate posters and furnishings. *725 White St. (at Petronia St.), Key West 33040, 305/294–7381. 9 rooms with bath. No children under 18 or pets. AE, MC, V. Moderate.*

The Mermaid & The Alligator. This is a homey bed-and-breakfast convenient to the center of town. The original 1904 structure of Dade County pine recently underwent extensive restoration. The Garden Room, the only downstairs room, has Japanese wall hangings, a white paddle fan, and a private doorway to the garden. Upstairs, the Blue Room (also known as the honeymoon suite) has a canopied Charleston four-poster bed with a rice pattern, a Roman-style tub, and a balcony overlooking St. Mary's by the Sea Catholic Church. The South West Suite, under the eaves on the third floor, has the only air conditioner in the house. *729 Truman Ave., Key West 33040, tel. 305/294–1894. 5 rooms with bath. Facilities: heated Jacuzzi. No children under 16. MC, V. Moderate.*

The Arts and Nightlife

The Arts
The Keys are more than warm weather and luminous scenery—a vigorous and sophisticated artistic community flourishes here. Key West alone currently claims among its residents 55 full-time writers and 500 painters and craftsmen. Arts organizations in the Keys sponsor many special events, some lasting only a weekend, others spanning an entire season.

The monthly *Island Navigator,* Monroe County's only countywide general-interest newspaper, is free at banks, campgrounds, and convenience stores. Its monthly community calendar lists cultural and sports events.

Three free publications covering Key West arts, music, and literature are available at hotels and other high-traffic areas:

The weekly *Island Life,* the most current and complete, is published by Ocean Gulf Corp. *517 Duval St., Suite 200, Key West 33040, tel. 305/294–1616. Subscription by mail: $12/year.*
Entertainment Key West, a biweekly, and *Solares Hill,* a monthly community newspaper, are published by Solares Hill Co., Inc. (4 Key Lime Sq., Key West 33040, tel. 305/294–3602). In the Upper and Middle Keys, the weekly *Free Press* is available at hotels, motels, and retail outlets. *Box 469, Islamorada 33036, tel. 305/664–2266. Subscription by mail: $3/month.*

Theater
Jan McArt's Cabaret Theater at Mallory Square. In a brick wrecker's warehouse built in 1879 and restored in 1986, Jan McArt has established a 300-seat theater for equity and nonequity musical productions. (McArt also operates Jan McArt's Royal Palm Dinner Theater in Boca Raton.) *410 Wall St., Box 4866, Key West, tel. 305/296–2120, 800/346–3240 (FL), or 800/356–8217 (US). Closed Mon. AE, MC, V.*
Red Barn Theater. This nonequity, 95-seat theater in its 10th year performs dramas and musical comedies, including plays by new playwrights. *319 Duval St., Key West, tel. 305/296–9511. Closed Mon. and sometimes Tues. No credit cards.*
Waterfront Playhouse. This mid-1850s wrecker's warehouse was converted into an 185-seat nonequity community theater that specializes in comedy and drama. *Mallory Sq., Key West, tel. 305/294–5015. Open Dec.–May. No credit cards.*
Tennessee Williams Fine Arts Center. A 490-seat theater built in 1980 on Stock Island, BS, the center presents chamber music, dance, jazz concerts, plays (dramatic and musical) with national and international stars, and other performing-arts events. *Florida Keys Community College, 5901 Junior College Rd., Key West, tel. 305/294–6232. Open Nov.–Apr. MC, V.*

Nightlife
Key Largo

Coconuts Restaurant and Bar. The soft island music during dinner changes to top 40 after 10 PM. The outdoor bar at the marina is popular with the under-30 crowd. To find Coconuts from U.S. 1, turn OS at the Texaco station at Laguna Avenue, then left at the first intersection onto Caribbean Boulevard and continue about 100 yards. *MM 100, OS, in the Marina Del Mar Resort and Marina, Key Largo, tel. 305/451–4107. Open noon–4 AM. AE, CB, DC, MC, V.*

Key West

Cafe Exile. When everyone else on Duval Street closes, Cafe Exile is still going strong. You can get an espresso or capuccino coffee here 24 hours a day. The menu is American as Key-lime pie, but the ambience is decidedly Continental—an outdoor courtyard with a white fence, brick sidewalk, banyan trees festooned with white Italian lights, and umbrellas sheltering the tables. The Rum Runner is the most popular drink. There is jazz nightly 8 PM–1 AM; local musicians join the group. An adjoining indoor nightclub, Backstreet at Exile, is open 10 PM–4 AM. *700 Duval St., Key West, tel. 305/296–0991. Food service 8 AM–5 AM, bar service 8 AM–4 AM. No credit cards.*

Capt. Tony's Saloon. While tourists flock to Sloppy Joe's, a predominantly local crowd enjoys old-style Key West nightlife at this bar a block away in an 1852 structure first used as a morgue and ice house. Later it was Key West's first telegraph station. Old business cards and T-shirts cover the walls and ceiling. Coral Reef, the house drink, contains a secret rum-based formula. Live country and rhythm-and-blues entertainment is featured nightly; Jimmy Buffet got his start here. *428 Greene St., tel. 305/294–1838. Open 11 AM–4 AM. No credit cards.*

Coconuts. This is the southernmost of the Florida Coconuts Clubs. The room is decorated with photos of nationally known comedians, including Chevy Chase, Bill Murray, and Eddie Murphy. Two veteran stand-up comics perform. *2407 N. Roosevelt Blvd., Key West, tel. 305/294–8882. Show time: 9 PM Tues.–Thurs., 8 and 10 PM. Fri.–Sat. Cover charge: $6 Tues.–Thurs and Fri.–Sat. late show (10 PM), $8 Fri.–Sat. early show (8 PM). Closed Mon. AE, MC, V.*

Havana Docks Lounge. A high-energy disco club popular with young locals and visitors, this lounge is in the old William R. Porter Docks Shipping Office, now part of the Pier House hotel. The Havana Docks deck is a good place to watch the sun set when Mallory Square gets too crowded. *1 Duval St., Key West, tel. 305/296–4600 or 800/432–3414 (FL). Open Sun.–Thurs. 4 PM–2 AM, Fri.–Sat. 4 PM–4 AM. AE, MC, V.*

Margaritaville Cafe. This place is owned by Key West resident and MCA recording star Jimmy Buffett, who performs here several times a year. The menu, which changes often, includes Jimmy's mother's recipes. The house special drink is, of course, a margarita. *500 Duval St., Key West, tel. 305/292–1435. Open 11 AM–4 AM; closed Sun. noon–4 AM. Live music Tues.–Sun. Cover charge for special events. AE, MC, V.*

Sloppy Joe's. Named for its founder, Capt. Joe Russell, Sloppy Joe's started as a speakeasy. Ernest Hemingway liked to gamble in a partitioned club room in back. After Hemingway's death, the original manuscript of *To Have and Have Not*, sections of *Death in the Afternoon*, *The Fifth Column*, and notes for *A Farewell to Arms* were found among personal papers he had stored at the bar. Decorated with Hemingway memorabilia and marine flags, the bar is popular with tourists and is full and noisy all the time. There is live entertainment from noon to 2 AM by local and touring groups. *201 Duval St., Key West, tel. 305/294-5717. Dress: shoes and shirt required. No reservations. All customers must show proof of age at night. Open 9 AM–4 AM. $1 cover charge after 8 PM. No credit cards.*

The Top Lounge. Located on the seventh floor of the La Concha Holiday Inn, Key West's tallest building, this is one of the best places from which to view the sunset. The Top serves deli-style lunch and complete dinners and features live entertainment. *430 Duval St., Key West, tel. 305/296-2991 or 800/227-6151 (FL). Open 11 AM–2 AM. AE, CB, DC, MC, V.*

8 Disney Worl and the Orlando Area

Introduction

by David Wilkening

A freelance writer who lives in Orlando, David Wilkening is a contributing editor of Orlando Magazine. *He writes for several local and national publications, including travel books and travel magazines.*

Orlando, a high-profile city of fast growth boosted by a robust business climate and thriving tourist trade, seems to be an area touched by pixie dust. A magical city. But it was not always that way.

A military outpost was established here in 1838, and the area became known as Fort Gatlin. In 1850, that name gave way to Jernigan, in deference to one of the region's most prosperous residents. It wasn't until 1875 that the one square-mile-wide city was incorporated as Orlando. There are various theories why the name was chosen, but the most popular is that the new city was named after Orlando Reeves, a soldier killed fighting the Seminole Indians.

Upon its incorporation, Orlando had less than 100 residents. The town had no seaport or major waterway. There was no railroad to spur its growth. In short, there was little to stimulate or sustain any prosperity. But Orlando had a sunny year-round climate. And it had something else, the importance of which would become evident much later—a location in the very center of what would become one of the fastest-growing states in the country.

Citrus and cattle were the dominant industries in Orlando's early years. The English arrived in the mid-1860s, bringing with them tennis, polo, and afternoon tea. The great freezes of 1884 and 1885 virtually ruined the citrus industry, and traditional farming returned. Orlando remained a clean, sleepy, handsome city, known for its lakes and for its sprawling oak trees planted by northerners who wanted to remember the world they had left behind.

In the 1950s, large corporations gave the area a solid business base on which to build. Today, in large part because of Walt Disney World, Orlando is known for its tourism. But it's also a growing center of national and international business activity.

In its graceful and quiet past Orlando enjoyed a small-town pace that earned it the title of "The City Beautiful." The city today is far more metropolitan, even cosmopolitan, but much of the original charm remains. Many residents have homes near the hundreds of clear spring-fed lakes, far from the south Orlando-based tourist corridor. The aroma here is often that of orange blossoms and citrus trees. The city has retained its parklike atmosphere.

The population of the greater metropolitan area that includes Orange, Seminole, and Osceola counties is now approaching one million. Various surveys cite the greater Orlando area as among the fastest growing in the country.

With all its business activity, however, Orlando is better known as the world's Number One tourist destination. Disneyland had long been a successful staple in California when Disney decided, in the early 1960s, to build another theme park in the eastern United States. By 1963, Florida was chosen as the best state. Orlando was chosen for a variety of reasons, including its transportation system and its large amounts of open, available land.

By 1964, property was quietly purchased. Eventually, a huge tract of 28,000 acres was bought. But, it wasn't until late 1965 that news reports leaked out that Disney was buying those parcels of land in anticipation of a large-scale theme park.

The accumulation of the land, often in small parcels purchased by agents working silently for Disney, was a dramatic story in itself. But seeing how the surrounding tourist areas around his California park had suffered rampant commercial sprawl, Disney was determined to buy enough land in Orlando to prevent that from happening again. This time, he would have **control** of the surrounding area.

On November 16, 1965, Walt Disney outlined his dream of an innovative working and living center that would provide a new way of life. He called it Experimental Prototype Community of Tomorrow (EPCOT). The first phase: the Magic Kingdom and a vacation complex. Walt Disney died the next year and never saw his dream come true. But construction began in 1969 on the park, which opened in 1971. New attractions were added continually, and, by the end of the fifth year, almost 11 million visitors annually were parading through the Magic Kingdom.

Plans were announced for another phase of the Disney master plan in 1975. That was EPCOT. On October 1, 1982, Epcot Center, as it is now called, opened its gates. It was not a quiet opening but included a month-long celebration that featured the West Point Glee Club, the 450-piece All American Marching Band, and World Showcase Festival performers representing 23 countries. The Epcot Center that emerged after Disney's death was not the one he envisioned—a living, working community set next to theme parks—apparently because it was later determined that the concept was not practical. But Epcot Center, standing on its own, was an immediate success. Almost 23 million visitors passed through its gates the very first year.

Walt Disney World is now the most-popular man-made attraction on Earth. A slow day brings in 25,000 visitors, while a busy day can bring 150,000. The attraction's vast, varied complex occupies 43 square miles. There's something for everyone.

The Magic Kingdom itself offers 98 acres of amusement. Disney's vision is everywhere as visitors encounter the nostalgia of Main Street, the good times at Adventureland, the down-home atmosphere of Frontierland, the dignity and history of Liberty Square, the magic of Fantasyland, and the world of the future in Tomorrowland.

Three miles south of the Magic Kingdom, and only a few minutes by monorail, is Epcot Center—a 260-acre complex of entertainment. The two distinct dimensions here are Future World, which features the latest ideas in everything from lifestyles to communications, and World Showcase, where nations display their cultures through films and other displays.

Arriving and Departing

By Plane   More than 33 scheduled airlines operate in and out of Orlando's airport, with direct service to more than 50 U.S. cities. At last count, Delta, the official airline of Disney World, had 56 flights to and from the airport every day! Travel packages to Disney World are offered by Delta (tel. 800/221–1212) and Pan Am (tel. 800/221–1111).

Major U.S. airlines that serve Orlando include American, Braniff, British Airways, Continental, Delta, Eastern, Icelandair, KLM, Midway, Northwest, Pan Am, Piedmont, TWA, United, and USAir.

Between the Airport and the Hotels

You can catch a public bus between the airport and downtown Orlando, which goes to and from the main terminal of **Tri-County Transit Authority** (438 Woods Ave., Orlando, tel. 407/841–8240). The cost is 75¢. The downtown area, however, is far from most hotels, so you might want to consider other options. **Airport Limousine Service of Orlando** (tel. 407/423–5566) sends 11-passenger vans to Disney World and along Rte. 192 every 30 minutes. Prices range from $11 one-way for adults and $6 for children 4–14 to $20 round-trip for adults and $10 for children 4–14. **Town & Country Limo** (tel. 407/828–3035) and **First Class Transportation** (tel. 407/351–5590) also offer limousine service between the airport and WDW. The trip takes about 35 minutes.

By Taxi Taxis are the fastest way to travel (25–30 minutes to hotels), but the ride won't be cheap. To Walt Disney World hotels or to hotels along West 192, a cab trip will cost about $35 plus tip. To the International Drive area, it will cost about $25 plus tip.

By Car When leaving the airport, a left turn onto the Beeline Expressway (Rte. 528) leads you past Sea World to I–4. A left turn on I–4 takes you to Walt Disney World Village and Epcot Center or to U.S. 192 and the Magic Kingdom entrance. A right turn on I–4 from the Beeline takes you past Hwy. 482 and into downtown Orlando.

By Train **Amtrak** (tel. 800/USA–RAIL) stops in Winter Park (150 Morse Blvd.), in Orlando (1400 Sligh Blvd.), and then, 20 minutes later, in Kissimmee (416 Pleasant St.).

By Bus Contact **Greyhound** (tel. 407/843–7720) or consult your phone book or directory assistance for a local number that will automatically connect you with the national Greyhound/Trailways Information Center.

Getting Around

By Car The most important artery in the Orlando area is **Interstate 4 (I–4)**, which many locals simply refer to as "the Expressway." This interstate ties everything together, and you'll invariably receive directions in reference to it. The problem is that I–4 is considered an east-west expressway in our national road system (the even numbers refer to an east-west orientation, the odd numbers to a north-south orientation). I–4 does run from east to west *if* you follow it from the Atlantic Coast to Florida's Gulf of Mexico. But in the Orlando area, I–4 actually runs north-south. Always remember, therefore, that when the signs say east, you are often going north, and when the signs say west, you are often going south. Think north-east and south-west. Another main drag is **International Drive,** which has several major hotels, restaurants, and shopping centers. You can get onto International Drive from I–4 Exits 28 and 29.

The other main road, Irlo Bronson Memorial Highway (U.S. 192), cuts across I–4 at Exits 25A and 25B. This highway goes through the Kissimmee area and crosses Walt Disney World property.

By Bus   If you are staying along International Drive in Kissimmee or in Orlando proper, you can take advantage of the limited public bus system, but only to get places locally. To find out which bus to take, ask your hotel clerk or call the Tri-County Transit Authority Information Office (tel. 407/841–8240) during business hours. A transfer will add 10¢ to the regular 75¢ fare.

By Taxi   Taxi fares start at $2.25 and cost $1.30 for each mile thereafter, with slightly higher rates during nighttime hours. Call **Yellow Cab Co.** (tel. 407/699–9999) or **Town and Country Cab** (tel. 407/828–3035).

Guided Tours

General-Interest   **Cosmos/Globus Gateway** (150 S. Los Robles Ave., Suite 860,
Tours   Pasadena, CA 91101, tel. 818/449–0919 or 800/556–5454) offers a comprehensive eight-day tour that includes entry to Disney World and Epcot Center. If you live on the East Coast of the country, **Domenico Tours** (751 Broadway, Bayonne, NJ 07002, tel. 800/554–TOUR) will take you to Orlando via coach tour or direct flight; from the west, it's air only.

Special-Interest   **Rivership Romance.** A 110-foot, triple-decker catamaran takes
Tours   visitors up the cypress-lined, densely forested St. John's River
Boat Tours   for either a few hours or a couple of days. The day trips take you through a peaceful, tropical landscape. You may see some interesting wildlife, such as manatees (the endangered sea cows), blue herons, and bald eagles, but most of the time you'll be listening to the silence. The cost ranges from $17.14 to $36.19 per person ($190 for the overnight trip), including some meals. *Monroe Harbour, 433 N. Palmetto Ave., Sanford (from I–4 take Exit 51 and drive east 4 mi), tel. 800/423–7401 or 407/321–5091. Dress: casual. Reservations required. MC, V. Moderate.*

Balloon Tours   **Balloon Flights of Florida** (129 W. Church St., Orlando, tel. 407/422–2434). This Church Street Station event is not cheap, but it's an experience you'll never forget. The flight, led by a balloonist who made the first trip across the Atlantic, is followed by brunch at Lili Marlene's. $140 per person. *129 W. Church St., Orlando, tel. 407/841–UPUP.*
Rise and Float Balloon Tours (*5767 Major Blvd.,* Orlando, tel. 407/352–8191). Depart at dawn and indulge yourself with an inflight champagne breakfast.

Helicopter Tours   **J.C. Helicopters.** Sign up for aerial tours of Walt Disney World, Sea World, and other attractions. The flights at dark are spectacular. Prices start at $22.50 for adults, $10 for children. *Orlando Hyatt Heliport at I–4 and U.S. 192 (next to Walt Disney World), tel. 407/847–7222.*

Important Addresses and Numbers

Visitors to **Mickey's Kingdom** can direct all inquiries to Walt Disney World (Box 10000, Lake Buena Vista, FL 32830, Attention: Guest letters, tel. 407/824–4321.) Request a free copy of the *Walt Disney World Vacation Guide.*

For information on the greater Orlando area, contact the **Tourist Information Center** (8445 International Drive, Orlando 32819, tel. 407/363–5800). Open 8-8. Ask for the free *Discover Orlando* guidebook.

Visitors to the Kissimmee area on U.S. 192 can get brochures from the **Kissimmee/St. Cloud Convention and Visitors' Bureau,** 1925 E. Spacecoast Hwy., E. U.S. 192, Kissimmee 32742, tel. 407/849–5000, in FL 800/432–9199, outside FL 800/327–9159.

Emergency   Dial 911 for **police** and **ambulance** in an emergency.

Doctors   Hospital emergency rooms are open 24 hours a day. The most accessible hospital, located in the International Drive area, is the **Orlando Regional Medical Center/Sand Lake Hospital** (9400 Turkey Lake Rd., tel. 407/351–8500).

For hotel-room visits by physicians for minor medical care, contact a mobile minor emergency service called **Housemed** (tel. 407/648–9234 or 407/846–2093 in Kissimmee).

24-Hour **Eckerd Drugs** (908 Lee Rd., Orlando, tel. 407/644-6908).
Pharmacies **Walgreen Drug Store** (2410 E. Colonial Dr., Orlando, tel. 407/894–6781).

Road Service **AAA Emergency Road Service** (tel. 800/824–4432 or 407/896–1166).

Disney World   Walt Disney World Information, tel. 407/824–4321
Accommodations Reservations, tel. 407/W–DISNEY.
Dinner Show Reservations, tel. 407/W–DISNEY.
Walt Disney World Resort Dining/Recreation Information, tel. 407/824–3737
Tours (Magic Kingdom and Epcot Center), tel. 407/827–8233

Magic Kingdom Lost and Found, tel. 407/824–4521.
Epcot Center Lost and Found, tel. 407/827–8236
Car Care Center, tel. 407/824–4813
Western Union at Walt Disney World, tel. 407/824–3456
Banking Information (Sun Bank), tel. 407/824–5767
Time and Weather, tel. 407/422–1611
Walt Disney World Shopping Village Information, tel. 407/828–3058
KinderCare Child Care, tel. 407/827–5444

Exploring Walt Disney World and the Orlando Area

Walt Disney World has its own complete transportation system to get you wherever you want to go. Yet because the property is so extensive—28,000 acres, 98 of them for the Magic Kingdom and another 260 for Epcot—the system can be a bit confusing, even for an experienced visitor. Best-known is the elevated monorail, which connects Walt Disney World's biggest resorts and attractions. There are also extensive bus, motor-launch, and ferry systems. If you are staying at an on-site resort or a Walt Disney World Village hotel or if you hold a combination Magic Kingdom-Epcot Center ticket, transportation is free. If not, you can buy unlimited transportation within Walt Disney World for $2.50 a day.

By Monorail   This elevated train of the future operates daily 7:30 AM–11 PM (or until 1 hour after the Magic Kingdom closes). It does not go everywhere. The central connecting station for the monorail is called the **Transportation and Ticket Center** (TTC). One mono-

Orlando Area

3 miles

3 km

0

N

50

528

Narcoossee Rd.

Goldenrod Rd.

Forsyth Rd.

AZALEA PARK

Semoran Blvd.

WINTER PARK

Novel Training Center

Orlando Science Center

Lou Gardens

Colonial Dr.

Loch Haven Art Center

East-West Expwy.

Gore Ave.

Curry Ford Rd.

Conway Rd.

Bumby Rd.

Hoffner Rd.

CONWAY

Lake Conway

Bee Line Expwy.

Orlando International Airport

4

Lake Fairview

Orlando Stadium

O R L A N D O

Orange Ave.

Kaley St.

Michigan St.

EDGEWOOD

BELLE ISLE

PINE CASTLE

Land St.

527

TAFT

Dowden Rd.

Maury Rd.

Pine Hills Rd.

Clear Lake

Orange Blossom Trail

Tropical Dr.

Oak Ridge Rd.

Orlando Central Park

Sand Lake

Rd.

Vineland Rd.

4

Kirkman Rd.

Wet 'N Wild

Fun 'N Wheels

TANGELO PARK

Bee Line Connector

PINE HILLS

Hiawassee Rd.

Powers Dr.

Florida's Tnpk.

Conroy Rd.

Wallace Rd.

LAKE CAIN HILLS

Turkey Lake Rd.

Good Homes Rd.

Colonial Dr.

Old Winter Garden Rd.

Appco-Vineland Rd.

Windermere Rd.

Lake Down

Lake Windermere

Chase Rd.

Lake Tibet

rail line goes from the TTC to the Magic Kingdom and back in a loop around Seven Seas Lagoon. This line is primarily for visitors who are not guests at the on-site resorts. Another line connects the TTC with the Contemporary Resort, the Magic Kingdom, the Grand Floridian, and the Polynesian. A third line goes directly from the TTC to Epcot Center. The TTC is where you can transfer between the Disney bus system and the monorail. When you get to a monorail station, ask an attendant if you can sit in the conductor's cabin, called "the nose" by the crew.

By Bus Each bus carries a small color-coded or letter-coded pennant on the front and sides. Here's where the buses take you:

Green—Connects Disney Inn and Polynesian Village Resort with the TTC. This line operates every 15 minutes 7 AM–2 AM.

Blue—Connects Fort Wilderness Resort Area with the TTC. These buses operate every eight minutes 7 AM–2 AM.

Green and **Gold**—If the pennant has the letters EC/V on it, the bus connects Epcot, the Resort Villas, Disney Village Clubhouse, and Disney Village Marketplace. If the bus has the letters MK on it, it travels only between the TTC and the villas. These lines operate every 20 minutes 7 AM–2 AM.

Silver and **Red Stripe**—Connects Walt Disney World Village Hotel Plaza, and Epcot Center. This bus operates every 20 minutes from 8 AM until two hours after Epcot closes.

Red and **White**—Connects Walt Disney World Village Hotel Plaza and the TTC. This line operates every 20 minutes, 8 AM until about two hours after the Magic Kingdom closes.

Red—Connects TTC and Disney Village Marketplace with Epcot. This line operates at 15- to 25-minute intervals from 8 AM to 2 AM.

Gold—Connects the Grand Floridian, Polynesian Resort, and Contemporary Resort with the TTC at 15- to 25-minute intervals from 7 AM to 2 AM.

Orange-and-White Stripe—If the pennant has the letters MK on it, the bus connects Caribbean Beach Resort with the TTC from 7 AM until 2 AM. If the bus has the letters EC on it, it connects Epcot and Caribbean Beach Resort from 8 AM to two hours after Epcot closes. Both lines run at 15- to 25-minute intervals.

Brown—A Fort Wilderness Transportation Circle line. It connects the Trading Post, Trail Blaze Corral, the Outpost, Loops 600–1300, Loops 2100–2800, and the Meadow Recreation Complex from 7 AM to 2 AM at 15- to 25-minute intervals.

Silver—Another Fort Wilderness Transportation Circle line. It connects Creekside Meadow Group Camping with Loops 300–500 and Loops 1400–2300 from 7 AM to 2 AM at 15- to 25-minute intervals.

Orange—The Caribbean Beach Resort internal transportation line, operates from 7 AM to 2 AM about every 20 minutes.

By Motor Launch These boats depart about every 20 minutes and use color-coded flags to identify their route. They are for the use of Disney resort guests only, with the exception of day guests with special activity tickets to such places as Discovery Island and River Country.

Blue—Connects the Contemporary Resort with the Fort Wilderness Resort Area and Discovery Island every 15 minutes 10 AM–10 PM.

Gold—Connects the Grand Floridian, Magic Kingdom, and Polynesian Resort at 15- to 25-minute intervals from half an hour before the Magic Kingdom opens until it closes, with pick-up only from the Magic Kingdom until the park clears.

Green—Connects the Magic Kingdom, Fort Wilderness Resort Area, and Discovery Island (when it is open) every 20–25 minutes from half an hour before opening until closing time.

By Ferry   A ferry service runs across Seven Seas Lagoon connecting the TTC with the Magic Kingdom. They depart from each side of the lagoon about every 12 minutes when the Magic Kingdom is open. They often get you to the Magic Kingdom faster than does the monorail. It is a comfortable ride, gliding over the lagoon's silky waters. Most people heading for the Magic Kingdom opt for the monorail and then take the ferry back at day's end, so if you want to avoid the worst of the lines for both the monorail and ferry, take the opposite tack.

By Car   If you arrive at either the Magic Kingdom or Epcot Center by car, there is a $3 parking charge. If you're staying at a Disney World hotel, show your guest ID for free parking. Remember or write down *exactly* where you park; you'll have a long wait before the sea of automobiles has departed and yours is the only one left. Trams make frequent trips between the parking areas and the front gate.

Car Care: If your car won't start or it breaks down in Disney World, the **Car Care Center** near the Toll Plaza to the Magic Kingdom offers emergency road service. Open weekdays 7 AM–6 PM, tel. 407/824–4813.

Admission   Visiting Walt Disney World is not cheap, especially if you have a child or two along. There are no discounted family tickets. Seven different types of admission tickets are sold in one of two categories—adult, meaning everyone aged 10 and older, and children aged 3–9. Children under age 3 get in free.

The word "ticket" is used by Disney World only to mean a single day's admission to either the Magic Kingdom or Epcot Center. The price is $28 for adults and $22 for children. If you want to spend two days visiting either or both attractions, you have to buy a separate ticket each day. For more than two days, Disney World offers what it calls the Passport, which admits you to both the Magic Kingdom and Epcot Center, along with unlimited use of the internal transportation system.

Here is a list of prices. They are subject to change, so call for confirmation.

One-day ticket	$29 adults, $23 children
Four-day passport	$97 adults, $77 children; *$94/$75**
Five-day passport	$112 adults, $90 children; *$107/$85**
River Country, one day	$11.75 adults, $9.25 children; *$10.75/$8.25**
River Country, two days	$17.75 adults, $13.75 children; *$16.75/$12.75**

Discovery Island, one day	$7.50 adults, $4 children
Combined River Country/Discovery Island, one day	$15 adults, $11 children *$14/$10**
Annual pass	$180 adults, $155 children

**visitors staying in a Disney World Resort or in a resort in the
WDW Village Hotel Plaza*

Passports are available for four or five days. They can save you
a great deal of money and may be advisable even if you're staying in the area for only two days. Each time you use a Passport,
the entry date is stamped on it; the remaining days may be used
any time in the future. If you buy a one-day ticket and later decide to extend your visit, you can get full credit for it toward the
purchase of any Passport. Exchanges can be made at City Hall
in the Magic Kingdom or at Earth Station in Epcot Center. Do
this before leaving the park; once you've left, the ticket is
worthless.

Tickets and Passports to Walt Disney World and Epcot Center
may be purchased at admission booths at the TTC, in on-site or
Hotel Plaza resorts (if you're a registered guest), or at the Walt
Disney World kiosk on the second floor of the main terminal at
Orlando International Airport. If you want to buy tickets be-
fore you arrive in Orlando, send a check or money order to
Admissions, Walt Disney World, Box 10000, Lake Buena Vista,
FL 32830. Remember, it usually takes four to six weeks for the
order to be processed, so write well in advance.

If you want to leave the Magic Kingdom or Epcot Center and
return on the same day, be sure to have your hand stamped on
the way out. You'll need your ticket *and* the hand stamp to be
readmitted.

Operating Hours Hours vary widely throughout the year and change for school
and legal holidays. In general, the longest hours are during the
summer months, when the Magic Kingdom is open until midnight and Epcot Center is open to 11 PM. At other times of year,
Epcot Center is open until 8 PM, and the Magic Kingdom to 6 PM,
with Main Street remaining open until 7. Though both parks usually open at 9 AM, visitors can enter the grounds up to an hour
earlier and get a significant head start on the crowds. A good bet
for breakfast before 9 AM is the **Crystal Palace** (turn left at the
end of Main St.). For current hours, tel. 407/824–4321.

When to Go The busiest days of the week are Monday, Tuesday, and
Wednesday. You would think the weekend would be busiest,
but it's not. Perhaps everyone tries to beat the crowds by going
in the early part of the week, or perhaps vacationers leave on
Friday, travel over the weekend, and begin their visits on Monday. Whatever the reason, Friday and Sunday are the slowest
days, and Thursdays and Saturdays are only moderately busy.

The best time of the day to be at the parks is in the late afternoon and evening—especially during the summer months and
holidays, when the attractions stay open late. It also helps to
arrive as soon as the gates open, up to an hour before the "official" opening time. The most crowded time of the year is from
Christmas through New Year's Day. The parks are also packed
around Easter.

Walt Disney World

Lake Tibet

Lake Reams

Lake Mabel

Lake Sheen

Reams Rd.

535

Cast Dr.

The Magic Kingdom

Bay Lake

South Lake

Discovery Island

Zoological Park

River Country

Bay Lake

Fort Wilderness Campground

West Wilderness Rd.

Bonnet Creek

Winter Garden - Vineland Rd.

Monorail

Fort Wilderness Tr.

Floridian Way

World Dr.

Monorail

Vista Blvd.

Vista Blvd.

535

Bonnett Creek Rd.

Buena Vista Dr.

Cyprus Creek

Main Entrance

Reedy Creek

Epcot Center Dr.

Main Entrance

Epcot Center

Community Dr.

World Dr.

Buena Vista Dr.

Buena Vista Dr.

Reedy Creek

Buena Vista Dr.

Epcot Center Dr.

EXIT 26

Disney-MGM Studios

4

0   1 mile

0   1 km

World Dr.

192

EXIT 25

Memorial Day weekend is not only crowded, but hot. Other busy times of the year are mid-June–mid-August, Thanksgiving weekend, the week of Washington's Birthday in mid-February, and the weeks of college spring break in late March. The rest of the year is generally hassle-free, particularly from early September until just before Thanksgiving. The best time of all is from just after Thanksgiving weekend until the beginning of the Christmas holidays. Another excellent time is from early January through the first week of February. If you must go during summer, late August is best.

Magic Kingdom

You'll first see Town Square. City Hall is on your left. The railroad station is directly behind you.

Sprawling before you is Main Street—a shop-filled boulevard with Victorian-style stores, and dining spots. Walk two blocks along Main Street and you'll enter Central Plaza, with **Cinderella's Castle** rising directly in front of you. This is the hub of the Kingdom; all the "lands" radiate out from it.

This is as good a place as any to see the daily parade at 3 PM. All Disney's characters are featured in the 20-minute show. In summer and during holidays, there's also an Electrical Parade of giant floats at 9 and 11 PM.

City Hall is a good place to pick up the *Magic Kingdom Guide Book* and a schedule of daily events. It is also the lost-and-found point for property and people. Nearby, beneath the railroad, are lockers where bags and gifts may be stored.

A great way to get an overview of the Kingdom is to hop aboard the railroad and take a 14-minute, 1½-mile ride around the perimeter of the park. You can board at the Victorian-style station you pass beneath to enter Town Square. The only other station is at Frontierland. The Magic Kingdom is the home of Mickey and Minnie Mouse, Goofy, Pluto, and dozens of other Disney characters. Seen on the streets, they're a child's delight, and even adults beam with pleasure as they shake hands with the fantasies they've grown up with. Characters are always willing to pose for photos. They're most often found next to City Hall.

The Magic Kingdom is divided into six lands. Stories are told of tourists who spend an entire day in one land, thinking they have seen all the park; don't let that happen to you. The following is a selected list of Magic Kingdom attractions.

Adventureland These soft adventures to far-off lands are among the most crowded in the Kingdom. Visit as late in the afternoon as possible or, better yet, in the evening. Adventureland is the worst place to be in the morning, because other travel guides recommend it as a first stop.

Swiss Family Robinson Treehouse (popular; all ages) is a good way to get some exercise and a panoramic view of the park. Visitors walk up the many-staired tree in single file, a trip that can take up to a half hour.

Jungle Cruise (popular; all ages) takes visitors along the Nile, across an Amazon jungle, and so on. The tour guide's narration is corny but nevertheless brings laughs. The ride itself takes only 10 minutes, but the line can take as long as an hour. Go during the parade time at 3 PM or after 5 PM. Avoid 10 AM–noon.

Pirates of the Caribbean (very popular; all ages) is a journey through a world of pirate strongholds and treasure-filled dungeons. The Audio-Animatronics pirates are first rate.

Tropical Serenade-Enchanted Tiki Birds (not very popular; for children) was one of the first Audio-Animatronic creations. The show's talking birds are somewhat charming, but the show itself can be confusing because it's difficult to tell what bird is speaking at any time. If you're in a hurry, you can safely skip this one.

Fantasyland This is a land in which storybook dreams come true and children are very much in their element.

There are a few traditional amusement-park rides with Disney themes, such as the Mad Tea Party, where teacups spin around a large teapot. Other favorites are Dumbo the Flying Elephant and a spectacular merry-go-round. There are also several indoor rides that spook and enchant children as they pass through a cartoon world filled with many familiar fairy-tale characters.

20,000 Leagues Under the Sea (very popular; all ages) is an underwater cruise inspired by the Jules Verne novel. Lines move slowly, but how often do you get to ride in a submarine and explore the world beneath the sea?

Frontierland "Frontier Fun" is the theme of this gold-rush town of the Southwest.

Big Thunder Mountain (very popular) is a scream-inducing roller coaster. Children must be at least 4'2". For real rollercoaster fans, the ride is somewhat tame, but it's one of two fast rides in Walt Disney World (Space Mountain is the other one). Try to go in the evenings when the mountain is lit up and lines are relatively short.

Country Bear Jamboree (moderately popular; for children) is a somewhat dated show with furry bears who sing and dance. A better show is put on at **Diamond Horseshow Jamboree** (popular; all ages)—a live stage show with singing, dancing, and innocently rowdy entertainment. You must make reservations early in the morning at the Hospitality House on Main Street, because there are only five shows daily. The strongest demand is usually for the noon and 1:30 shows. Other performances are at 3, 4:30, and 6 PM.

Tom Sawyer's Island (not very popular; all ages) has little to see but offers a happy respite from the crowds on the mainland. Adults can relax at **Aunt Polly's Porch** with lemonade and lunch while the kids scramble up Harper's Mill (a working windmill) or explore the caves and bridges.

Liberty Square This is a small land adjoining and blending into Frontierland. It's theme is Colonial history and it has a few decent but tame attractions.

Haunted Mansion (very popular; all ages) is the most popular attraction here. The spine-tingling effects, with ghosts, goblins, and graveyards, are realistic and may be too intense for the very young. The best time to go is in the morning when the lines are short. Avoid the noon–4 PM rush.

Liberty Square Riverboats (moderately popular; all ages) take visitors on a quiet, half-mile cruise through the rivers of America, passing Wild West scenes. It's not great entertainment, but it can be a comfortable escape from the crowds and the sun.

Hall of Presidents (moderately popular; adults or mature children) was a sensation when it first opened, but now it seems a bit slow and unexciting. Still, visitors of all ages find it interesting to see the Audio-Animatronics presidents in action. Adults find it educational; young children find it boring.

Tomorrowland "Fun in the Future" is the motto of this land. Save it for the future if your time is limited because, except for Space Mountain, its rides are lackluster compared to others in the park. One major problem is that most attractions are sponsored by major corporations, and audiences are bombarded by commercial advertising.

Space Mountain (very popular; children must be at least age 3) is the main attraction, though children under 7 must be accompanied by an adult. The space-age roller coaster may never go over 20 miles an hour, but the experience in the dark, with everyone screaming, is thrilling, even for hardcore roller-coaster fans.

American Journey, including **CircleVision, Carousel of Progress,** and **Mission to Mars** (unpopular; all ages), is a series of 20-minute attractions that may be 20 minutes too long. Circlevision's patriotic look at the landscape of America on nine movie screens is perhaps the best bet.

Grand Prix Raceway (popular) takes children in mini race cars to speeds up to seven miles per hour. The ride is confining with little room to maneuver your vehicle. Children must be at least age 7 to ride alone, and there are usually long lines.

Epcot Center

Epcot Center is divided almost equally into two distinct areas separated by the 40-acre World Showcase Lagoon. The northern half, which is where the admission gates are, is filled with the Future World pavilions, sponsored by major American corporations. The southern half is World Showcase. If you want to minimize the time spent waiting in line, do the opposite of what most people do. In the morning, visitors head for what's closest, which is Future World, so you should begin at World Showcase. In the afternoon, come back and explore Future World when the crowds have shifted to World Showcase. Evening hours, of course, are the best times for visiting either area.

Visitors who are familiar with the Magic Kingdom find something entirely different at Epcot Center. For one thing, Epcot is twice as large. For another, Epcot's attractions all have an educational dimension. **Future World** explores technological concepts, such as energy and communications, in entertaining ways. **World Showcase** is a series of pavilions in which various nations portray their cultures through a combination of films, exhibits, and seemingly endless shops. Bring a hearty appetite, because ethnic cuisines are featured in each foreign pavilion.

As you enter Epcot Center, you'll pass beneath **Spaceship Earth,** a 17-story sphere that marks the start of Future World. World Showcase is behind Future World. Stop first at Earth Station to pick up a guidebook and entertainment schedule. Also, make reservations for the busy, full-service restaurants here. Remember that it's not unusual for most restaurants to be fully reserved by 10 AM in the peak season. Remember also that guests who are staying in on-site properties can make their reservations ahead of time.

Future World   The subjects explored at Future World include the ocean, agriculture, communications, energy, imagination, and transportation.

Communicore East and West (popular; all ages). These two buildings house exhibits by the various sponsoring companies of Epcot Center. The educational computer games are very popular with children.

Horizons (popular; all ages). A journey into the lifestyles of the next century, with robotic-staffed farms, ocean colonies, and space cities.

Journey Into Imagination (popular; for children). Two of the most popular characters, Dreamfinder and Figment, are your guides on a tour of the creative process that depicts how literature and art come from the sparks of ideas. Particularly popular with teenagers is **Captain EO,** a $17 million, 3-D film starring singer Michael Jackson. The experience here is well worth the wait in line, but try to go in the late afternoon when there are fewer people. Also be sure to see the "dancing waters" display in front of the entrance to Captain EO.

Listen to the Land (popular; for adults and mature children). The main event here is a boat ride through the experimental greenhouse that demonstrates how plants may be grown in the future, not only on Earth but in outer space. It's provocative for adults but somewhat dull for children. Those who are interested can arrange to join one of several walking tours. Reservations can be made in the morning on the lower floor, in the corner opposite the boat ride, behind the *Broccoli and Company* kiosk.

The Living Seas (popular; all ages). This is a new attraction and one of the most popular. It's the largest facility ever dedicated to the relationship of humans with the ocean and is sometimes known as the "eighth sea." Visitors take a gondola ride beneath the sea for a dynamic close-up look at marine life in a six-million-gallon aquarium more than four fathoms deep. There are more than 200 varieties of sea life among the 5,000 inhabitants. You can easily spend a half day here.

Spaceship Earth (very popular; all ages). This million-pound silver geosphere is so large that on clear days airline passengers on both coasts of Florida can see it. Inside the dome, visitors take a highly praised journey through the dramatic history of communications, from cave drawings to space-age technology. Visitors see the dome when they first get to Epcot Center and routinely make their way here. You would be well advised to wait until the late afternoon when the crowds have left **Universe of Energy** (very popular; all ages). This is a fast-paced exploration of the forces that fuel our lives and the universe. You'll ride on theater seats through a display on the

Earth's beginnings, past battling dinosaurs, through earth-quakes, and beneath volcanoes.

World Showcase

World Showcase offers an adventure that is very different from what you will experience in either the world of the future in Epcot Center or the world of fairy tales in the Magic Kingdom. The Showcase presents an ideal image—a Disney version—of life in 10 countries. Native food, entertainment, and wares are on display in each of the pavilions. Most of the nations have done an imaginative and painstaking job of re-creating scale models of their best-known monuments, such as the Eiffel Tower in France, a Mayan temple in Mexico, and a majestic pagoda in Japan. During the day, these structures are impressive enough, but at night, when the darkness inhibits one's ability to judge their size, you get the sense that you are seeing the real thing. It's a wonderful illusion, indeed.

Unlike Future World and the Magic Kingdom, the Showcase doesn't offer amusement-park-type rides (except in Mexico and Norway). Instead, it features breathtaking films, ethnic art, cultural entertainment, Audio-Animatronics presentations, and dozens of fine shops and restaurants featuring national specialties. The most enjoyable diversions in World Showcase are not inside the national pavilions but in front of them. At various times of the day, each pavilion offers some sort of live street show, featuring comedy, song, or dance routines and demonstrations of folk arts and crafts. Don't be shy about trying to improve your foreign-language skills!

The only unfortunate note in this cultural smorgasbord is that with so many shops and restaurants, there seems to be more of an emphasis on commercialism than on education or entertainment. Know in advance that a taste of a nation may mean a bite out of your bank account.

The focal point of World Showcase, on the opposite side of the lagoon from the entrance area, is the host pavilion, the **American Adventure.** The pavilions of the other countries fan out from the right and left of American Adventure, encircling the lagoon. Going clockwise from the left as you enter World Showcase are the pavilions of Mexico, Norway, People's Republic of China, Germany, Italy, the United States, Japan, Morocco, France, United Kingdom, and Canada.

Mexico: This tame "boat ride" inside the pavilion is much like rides you have seen in the Magic Kingdom. The major tourist attractions of Mexico are its theme. Windows and doorways are filled with colorful video images, and rooms are full of dancing, costumed puppets, and Audio-Animatronics landscapes that roar, storm, and light up as you journey from the jungles of the Yucatan to the skyline of Mexico City. In front of the pavilion is **Cantina de San Angel**—a fast-food joint and bar that's good for burritos, margaritas, and, at night, a great view of the laser show.

Norway: Visitors take a ride in small Viking vessels through the landscape and history of this Scandinavian country. You can tour a 10th-century Viking Village, sail through a fjord, and experience a storm and the midnight sun. The main spectacle of this pavilion is a re-creation of a 14th-century coastal fortress in Oslo called Akershus.

China: The much-talked about film should not be missed. It is a Circle Vision presentation on the landscape of China, taking viewers on a fantastic journey from inner Mongolia to the Tibetan mountains, along the Great Wall, into Beijing, and through some of the most glorious landscape on Earth. The Chinese pavilion also has an art gallery with treasures never before displayed in the West and a wonderful shopping gallery with ivory goods, jade jewelry, hand-painted fans, opulent carpets, and inlaid furniture.

Germany: The main event in this replica of a small Bavarian village is the restaurant's oompah band show, with singers, dancers, and musicians. The indoor village is worth a quick look. There are four shows daily. You'll also find plenty of German wines, sweets, glassware, and porcelain for sale.

Italy: The main attraction is the architecture—a reproduction of St. Mark's Square in Venice, with the Campanile (bell tower) di San Marco as its centerpiece, and, behind it, the elegant and elaborately decorated Doges Palace. Complementing these buildings are Venetian bridges, gondolas, colorful barber poles, and the sculpture of the Lion of St. Mark atop a column. In the plaza of this pavilion, you can watch and participate in a comedy show put on by an Italian theater troupe. The show can be amusing, but only if there is a full, lively audience.

American Adventure: This is a 30-minute Audio-Animatronics show about the development of the United States. The huge, colonial-style theater features the most sophisticated and realistic animatronics characters in Disney World. The show takes visitors from the arrival of the Pilgrims through the revolutionary war, the Civil War, the taming of the West, the two world wars; and so on. The voyage is hosted by Benjamin Franklin and Mark Twain. Some will find the presentation a bit long, even though 30 minutes is not much time to cover 200 years of history. Many people find it inspiringly patriotic, but children may take this opportunity to catch a few winks—the dramatic music often puts them right to sleep.

Directly opposite the American Adventure pavilion, on the lagoon, is the open-air **American Gardens Theater by the Shore,** where live, high-energy, all-American shows are performed about four times a day. Show times vary but are posted each day on boards in front of the theater's entrances.

Japan: Elegant landscaping of rocks, streams, trees, and shrubs combines with traditional architecture to create this peaceful and charming pavilion. Inside the *torii* gates are monumental bronze sculptures and a pagoda. Of special interest are the Mitsukoshi Department Store, where lacquered dinnerware, teapots, vases, bonzai trees, and Japanese dolls and toys are for sale, and the Bijutsu-kan Gallery, featuring temporary exhibits of traditional Japanese crafts. The Yakitori House serves inexpensive Japanese fast food in a pleasant garden—a good bet for lunch.

Morocco: This is one of the more spectacular-looking of the pavilions. It has a replica of the Koutoubia Minaret from a famous prayer house in Marrakesh; a gallery of Moroccan art, tapestries, and traditional costumes; and a street with shops selling basketry, leather goods, samovars, and exquisite jewelry. Dancers move to the exotic rhythms of North Africa.

France: This 18-minute film is projected on a five-panel semi-circular screen and takes viewers on a romantic tour of France —through the countryside, into the Alps, along the coast, and, of course, into Paris. It is a sophisticated visual adventure with little narration but much lyrical poetry and classical music.

The pavilion itself resembles a French boulevard, lined with shops and cafes. Of special interest are **Tout Pour le Gourmet** and **Les Vins de France,** two shops featuring French culinary specialties, such as wines, cheeses, mustards, herbs, and pâtés. A little patisserie/boulangerie prepares all kinds of baked goods. Two restaurants, **Bistro de Paris** and **Au Petit Cafe,** are ideal for lunch. Also in this pavilion is an impressive model of the Eiffel Tower that was constructed using Alexandre-Gustave Eiffel's original blueprints.

United Kingdom: On this street from Old London are a variety of architectural styles, from thatched-roof cottages to Tudor and ornate Victorian homes. The city square and rural streets are filled with numerous food, toy, and souvenir shops. The very British **Rose and Crown** pub serves Stilton cheese, ales, and simple English fare. Street artists and a minstrel troupe perform throughout the day.

Canada: A Circle Vision film takes its audience into Canada's great outdoors, from the magnificent snow-peaked Rockies, down sprawling Arctic glaciers, and across the plains to Montreal. Peaceful gardens, a rocky gorge, an emporium selling everything from sheepskins to lumberjack shirts and maple syrup, and a cafeteria-style restaurant called **Le Cellier** are other highlights of this quaint pavilion.

Other Attractions in Disney World

Typhoon Lagoon At press time, this 50-acre aquatic entertainment complex was scheduled to open in summer 1989. It will feature the largest water-slide mountain in the world and a huge wave-making lagoon for swimming and surfing. The water park will include a Swiss Family Robinson-type tropical island, covered with lush greenery, where guests may play at being shipwrecked. A saltwater pool will contain a coral reef, where snorkelers can come mask to face with all sorts of Caribbean sea creatures, such as groupers, parrotfish, and even baby sharks.

Disney-MGM Studio Tour The biggest new addition to Disney World is the Disney-MGM studios, a complete working film-production facility that consists of an animation complex, four massive sound stages, a back lot of streets and sets, and numerous film and television postproduction facilities, including some of the most technologically advanced special-effects studios in the business. Guests can visit the Animation Building and get a firsthand view of Disney artists at work in the many stages of creating a Disney animated feature.

River Country In the backwoods setting of the Fort Wilderness Campground Resort, kids can slide, splash, and swim about in an aquatic playground, complete with whitewater inner-tubing channels and corkscrew water slides that splash down into a 300,000 gallon pond. The pool is heated during the winter, so kids can take a dip here year-round. During the summer, River Country can get very congested, so it's best to come late in the afternoon. *Fort Wilderness Resort, tel. 407/824-3737. Admission: adults*

1 day $11.75, 2 days $17.75; children aged 3–9, 1 day $9.25, 2 days $13.75.

Discovery Island Covered with exotic flora; small, furry animals; and colorful birdlife, this little island makes a great escape from the man-made tourist attractions of Walt Disney World. Visitors listen to nature as they stroll along winding pathways and across footbridges. Disney did not create these creatures—he just brought them here. Keep an eye out for the Galapagos tortoises, trumpeter swans, scarlet ibis, and bald eagles. Tickets are sold at Fort Wilderness's River Country, at the TTC, at guest service desks in the Disney resorts, and on the island itself. You can get there by watercraft from the Magic Kingdom, Contemporary Resorts, Polynesian Village, Grand Floridian, and River Country in Fort Wilderness. *Discovery Island: $7.50 adults, $4 children aged 3–9. River Country/Discovery Island combination ticket: $15 adults, $11 children aged 3–9.*

The Orlando Area

Numbers in the margin correspond with points of interest on the Orlando Area Attractions map.

① **Alligatorland Safaro Zoo.** More than 1,600 exotic animals and birds in a natural setting. *U.S. 192 between Kissimmee and Walt Disney World, tel. 407/396–1012. Admission: $4.20 adults, $3.15 children 4–11. Open daily 8:30–8.*

② **Boardwalk and Baseball.** Live entertainment, shows, and some 30 rides in a 135-acre theme park. The highlight is the largest wooden roller coaster in the southeast. *U.S. 27 near I–4 interchange. Box 800, Orlando, FL 32802, tel. 407/422–0643. Admission: $16.95 adults, $12.95 children under 46".*

③ **Bok Tower Gardens.** A 128-acre garden with pine forests, shady paths, and a bell tower that rings daily at 3 PM. *Between Haines City and Lake Wales off U.S. 27, tel. 813/676–1408. Admission: $2 per person; children under 12 free. Open daily 8–5.*

④ **Central Florida Zoological Park.** A 110-acre zoo. *U.S. 17–92, 1 mi east of I–4 and 4 mi west of Sanford, tel. 407/323–6471. Admission: $3.50 adults, $1.50 children 3–12. Open daily, 9–5.*

⑤ **Cypress Gardens.** Central Florida's original theme park features exotic flowers, waterskiing shows, and bird and alligator shows. *East of Winter Haven off Rte. 540, tel. 407/351–6606. Admission: $14.95 adults, $9.95 children 3–11. Open daily 9 AM–6 PM.*

⑥ **Fun 'n Wheels.** An expensive but active family theme park with go-cart tracks, rides, minigolf course, bumper boats, and cars. No general admission charge. *6739 Sand Lake Rd. at International Dr., Orlando, tel. 407/351–5651. Open daily 10 AM–midnight.*

⑦ **Gatorland Zoo.** Thousands of alligators and crocodiles sleeping in the sun are viewed from a walkway. Also snakes, flamingos, monkeys, and other Florida critters. *South of Orlando on U.S. 17–92 near Kissimmee, tel. 407/855–5496. Admission: $5.40 adults, $3.95 children aged 3–11. Open daily 8 AM–6 PM.*

⑧ **Mystery Fun House.** Magic mirrors, moving floors, laughing doors, barrels that roll, a shooting arcade—all are favorites with children, though the price is high for not much more than few minutes' entertainment. *5767 Major Blvd., off Kirkman Rd. near International Dr., tel. 407/351-3355. Admission: $5.95 adults, $4.95 children. Open daily 10-9.*

9 **Places of Learning.** Great selection of children's books and educational games. Recommended for the non-bookish, too. *6825 Academic Dr., Orlando, tel. 407/345-1038. Admission free. Open daily 9-6.*

10 **Sea World.** A major theme park celebrating sea life, including popular Baby Shamu and the awesome Shark Encounter. Marine animals perform in seven major shows. The park also has tropical fish, otter habitats, walrus training exhibits, botanical gardens, and other educational diversions in a setting more tranquil than that of most theme parks. *Located 10 mi south of Orlando at the intersection of I-4 and the Beeline Expressway, 7007 Sea World Dr., Orlando, tel. 407/351-3600 or 800/327-2420. Admission: $23.95 adults, $19.95 children aged 3-11. Open daily 8:30 AM-9:30 PM, with extended summer and holiday hours.*

11 **Wet 'n Wild.** Water slides, flumes, lazy rivers, and other water-related activities for swimmers and sunbathers. *6200 International Dr., Orlando, tel. 407/351-3200. Admission: $14.95 adults, $12.95 children aged 3-12, under age 2 free. Open daily 10-5, except in winter.*

12 **Xanadu.** A dome-shaped home showcasing technological and electronic devices. Guided tours daily. *Located at the intersection of U.S. 192 and Rte. 535, Kissimmee, tel. 407/396-1992. Admission: $4.75 adults, $3.50 children aged 4-17, under age 3 free.*

Orlando for Free

Citrus World, Inc. Free film showing citrus processing from tree to grocer; free samples. The film is shown every 40 minutes. *U.S. 27S, Lake Wales, about 1 hr south of Orlando, tel. 813/676-1411. Open Nov.-June, weekdays 9-4:30.*

Florida Cactus. Self-guided tours through a cactus nursery in Plymouth, 30 minutes north of Orlando. *Tel. 407/886-1833. Open weekdays 7:30-4:30, Sat. 7:30-11:30.*

Kissimmee Livestock Market, Inc. Going, going, gone in a real cattle auction, one of the oldest in Florida. *Box 2329, Kissimmee, FL 32742, tel. 407/847-3521. Open Wed. at 1 PM.*

Lake Wales Museum. Railroad memorabilia and area history. *325 S. Scenic Hwy., Lake Wales, tel. 813/676-5443. Open weekdays 9-5, Sat. 10-4.*

Monument of the States. A 50-foot-tall step pyramid built in the 1940s from concrete and stones donated by every state in the union. *Monument St., Lake Front Park, Kissimmee, tel. 407/847-3174.*

Orange County Historical Museum. Local memorabilia. *Loch Haven Park, 812 E. Rollins St., Orlando, tel. 407/898-8320. Open Tues.-Fri. 10-4, weekends 2-5. Closed Mon.*

Slocum Water Gardens. An extensive display of water plants. *1101 Cypress Gardens, Winter Haven, FL 33880, tel. 813/293-7151. Open weekdays 8-noon and 1-4, Sat. 8-noon.*

Alligatorland Safari Zoo, **1**
Boardwalk & Baseball, **2**
Bok Tower Gardens, **3**
Central Florida Zoological Park, **4**
Cypress Gardens, **5**
Fun 'n Wheels, **6**
Gatorland Zoo, **7**
Mystery Fun House, **8**
Places of Learning, **9**
Sea World, **10**
Wet 'n Wild, **11**
Xanadu, **12**

Orlando Area Attractions

Tupperware World Headquarters. Narrated tours and displays depicting the evolution of food storage since the days of the ancient Egyptians. *U.S. 441 south of Orlando near Kissimmee, tel. 417/847-3111. Open weekdays 9–4.*

Water Ski Museum and Hall of Fame. Waterskiing fans will love what is probably the world's largest collection of equipment and memorabilia. *799 Overlook Dr., Winter Haven, tel. 813/ 324-2472. Open weekdays 10–5.*

Off the Beaten Track

Big Tree Park. One of the oldest and largest bald cypress trees in the country in a moss-draped park with picnic tables. *U.S. 17–92 on General Hutchinson Pkwy., Longwood, tel. 407/323-2500. Admission free. Open daily from 9 AM.*

Cassadaga. The mystic's mecca, an eerily tree-shaded village started by Spiritualists. Many of the residents read palms, peer into the future, and relay messages from the world beyond. When the psychics meet from January to March, many of the lectures and seminars are open to the public. Visit anytime. *Located off I–4, 7 miles south of DeLand. First Spiritualist Church of Cassadaga, Box 152, Cassadaga, FL 32706, tel. 904/ 228-2880.*

Hontoon Island State Park. Take a ferry-boat ride to a 1,650-acre park and campground with six rustic cabins, 22 campsites, a floating marina with slips for 54 boats, and an 80-foot observation tower. The park is off Rte. 44 on Hontoon Rd. *Hontoon Island, 2309 Riverride Rd., DeLand, FL 32720, tel. 904/736-5309. Open daily 8 AM–sunset. The ferry operates from 9 AM until an hour before the park closes.*

Navy Graduation. Recruit graduation parade every Friday at 9:45 AM. *Orlando Naval Training Center, General Rees Rd., entrance off Corrine Dr., Orlando, tel. 407/646-5054. Admission free.*

Pioneer Settlement for the Creative Arts. Folk museum with demonstrations of day-to-day pioneer lifestyles, a turn-of-the-century country store, and a train depot. *Intersection of U.S. 40 and 17 in DeLand, about 40 miles from Orlando, tel. 904/ 749-2959. Admission: $2.50 adults, $1 children under age 16. Open weekdays 9–4, weekends by appointment.*

Shopping

Altamonte Mall. Of the many regional retail centers, this is the largest and best known. The 30-acre, two-level, totally enclosed and air-conditioned mall has some 165 stores, including a huge Burdines, Jordan Marsh, Maison Blanche, and Sears. *A half mile east of I–4 on Rte. 436 in Altamonte Springs. Open Mon.–Sat. 10 AM–9 PM, Sun. noon–5:50 (except holidays).*

Florida Mall. This is a newer, large-scale center in Orlando, closer to the Walt Disney World tourism corridor. More than 160 stores in an enclosed mall that has three distinctive shopping areas—Victorian, Mediterranean, and Art Deco. *On the corner of Sand Lake Rd. (Rte. 482) and S. Orange Blossom Trail and near International Dr. Open Mon.–Sat. 10–9, Sun. noon–5:30.*

Flea World. Flea markets are scattered across the Orlando area, but this is the largest and most popular. Well over 1,000 booths, some air-conditioned, offer arts and crafts, auto parts, citrus produce, and so on. *Highway 17-92 between Orlando and Sanford. Admission free. Open Fri., Sat., and Sun. 8–5.*

Park Avenue. This is the place to go for fashionable, upscale shopping in Winter Park. Most stores are open weekdays 9–5, but you can window-browse anytime and enjoy the many restaurants and ice cream shops along the avenue. The shops range from the Ralph Lauren Polo Shop to small antique shops.

Mercado. The latest trend in Orlando is "festive retail," where shopping is combined with entertainment. At Mercado, visitors wander along brick streets and browse through more than 50 specialty shops in the atmosphere of a Mediterranean village. Free entertainment nightly includes the animated "Mugsy's Merry Medley." Exotic foods are all under one roof at the International Food Pavilion. *8445 International Dr. Open 10–10 daily.*

Old Town. Also in the tourist corridor is this collection of more than 70 specialty shops and restaurants along pedestrian walks. Tethered balloon rides are available. *5770 Spacecoast Pkwy., Kissimmee. Open daily 10–10.*

Walt Disney World. For unusual and sophisticated shopping, try World Showcase, where each country offers unique native merchandise. Walt Disney World Village in Lake Buena Vista, only two miles from Epcot Center and six miles from the Magic Kingdom, is a collection of some 20 shops that offer everything from Christmas tree ornaments to Disney memorabilia.

Participant Sports

Many resort hotels let nonguests use their golf and tennis facilities. Some hotels are affiliated with a particular country club and offer preferred rates. If you are staying near a resort with facilities you want to use, call and inquire about its policies. Be sure to call in advance to reserve courts and tee times. What follows is a list of the best places that are open to the public.

Bicycling The most scenic bike riding in Orlando is on the property of Walt Disney World, along roads that take you past forests, lakes, golf courses, and Disney's wooded resort villas and campgrounds. Bikes are available for rent at **Fort Wilderness Bike Barn** (tel. 407/824–2742). Bike rental $3 per hour, $7 per day.

Fishing **Fort Wilderness Campground** (tel. 407/W–DISNEY) is the starting point for two-hour fishing trips, departing at 8 AM and 3 PM. Boats, equipment, and guide for up to five anglers cost $110.

Bass Challenger Guide (726 Ashley Ct., Orlando, tel. 407/273–8045) rents Ranger boats equipped with drinks and tackle. Transportation can be arranged to and from their location. Half day (1 or 2 persons) from $110, full day from $160.

Bass Bustin' Guide (5935 Swoffield Dr., Orlando, tel. 407/281–0845) provides boat, tackle, transportation, and amenities for bass fishing on local lakes. And it guarantees fish! Half day from $125, full day from $160.

Golf   **Golfpac** (Box 484, Maitland, FL 32751, tel. 407/660–8559) packages golf vacations and prearranges tee times at over 25 courses around Orlando.

Poinciana Golf & Racquet Club (500 Cypress Pkwy., tel. 407/933–5300) has a par-72 course about 18 miles southeast of Walt Disney World.

Walt Disney World's three championship courses—all played by the PGA Tour—are among the busiest and most expensive in the region. Greens fees are $45 for guests staying in Disney World properties; $55 for nonguests; $25 after 3 PM.

Golf lessons are given in small groups at the Disney Inn courses, the Magnolia and the Palm. Private lessons are available both at these courses and at the Lake Buena Vista Club. There is also a nine-hole, 1,115-yard course on artificial turf with natural turf greens for children ($7) and adults ($9). For private lessons at the Lake Buena Vista Club, phone 407/828–3741. For all other information, phone the starter's number 407/824–2270.

Horseback Riding   **Grand Cypress Resort Equestrian Center** (tel. 407/239–1234) offers hunter/jumper private lessons and riding trails for guided outings. Private lesson $35 an hour, trailside $20 an hour.

Fort Wilderness Campground (tel. 407/W–DISNEY) in Walt Disney World offers tame trail rides through the backwoods and along lakesides. Open to the general public. Call in advance to arrange an outing. Rides at 9, 10:30, noon and 2. Cost: $10 per person for 45–60 minutes. Children must be over age 9.

Ice Skating   **Orlando Ice Skating Palace** (3123 W. Colonial Dr., Parkwood Shopping Plaza Orlando, tel. 407/299–5440) isn't the most attractive rink, but if you are homesick for a winter chill, this should do the trick. Open Wed.–Sun. 7:30–10:30 PM. Call for daytime hours.

Jogging   Walt Disney World has several scenic jogging trails. Pick up jogging maps at any Disney resort. **Fort Wilderness** (tel. 407/824–2900) has a 2.3-mile jogging course, with plenty of fresh air and woods, as well as numerous exercise stations along the way.

Tennis   **Disney Inn** has two courts, **Lake Buena Vista Club** has three, and the **Contemporary Resort Hotel** has six. Private and group lessons are available at the Contemporary (tel. 407/824–3578). Racquets may be rented by the hour.

Orange Lake Country Club (tel. 407/239–1050) offers golf, inexpensive tennis, and a variety of water sports. Greens fee $48, tennis $4 per hour.

The Orlando Vacation Resort (west of I–4 on U.S. 27, tel. 407/394–6171) has 17 asphalt courts open only to guests.

Water Sports   Marinas at **Caribbean Beach Resort, Contemporary Resort, Fort Wilderness, Polynesian Village,** and **Walt Disney World Village** rent Sunfish, catamarans, motor-powered pontoon boats, pedal boats, and Water Sprites for the 450-acre Bay Lake, the adjoining 200-acres of the Seven Seas Lagoon, Club Lake, Lake Buena Vista, and Buena Vista Lagoon. The Polynesian Village marina rents out-rigger canoes. Fort Wilderness rents canoes. For waterskiing ($65 per hour) reservations, phone 407/824–2222, ext. 2757.

Airboat Rentals (4266 Vine St., Kissimmee, tel. 407/845–3672) rents airboats ($15.99 per hour) and canoes for use on Shingle Creek, with views of giant cypress trees and Spanish moss.

Ski Holidays (tel. 407/239–4444) has waterskiing, jetskiing, and parasailing on a private lake next to Walt Disney World. Boats $50 per hour, $180 for four hours. Parasailing $30. To get there take I–4 to the Lake Buena Vista exit, turn east on Rte. 535 toward Kissimmee, and, about 200 yards east, you will see a sign to Lake Bryan.

Rent a powerful seven-seater ski boat at **Sanford Boat Rentals** (tel. 407/321–5906, in Florida 800/237–5105, outside Florida 800/692–3414) up the St. John's river. Bring your own equipment for bass fishing or rent waterski equipment. Very good rates for whole-day outings. Houseboats and pontoons are available for day, overnight, weekend, or weeklong trips. Pontoon and ski boats $60 for 4 hours; 44-foot houseboat $350 per day, $560 for 2 days, $450 weekends, $900 weekly. Rates vary seasonally.

Three Buoys Houseboat Rentals (2280 Hontoon Dr., DeLand, tel. 800/262–3454 or 904/736–9422) rents luxury houseboats on the St. Johns River. Among the packages is a $695 weekend deal and a weekly price of $1,195. Rates vary seasonally.

Spectator Sports

Jai Alai **Orlando-Seminole Jai-Alai.** The sport is fun to watch even if you don't bet. *Admission: $1 general, $2 reserved seating. Open May–mid-Jan. at 7:20 nightly except Sun. with noon matinees Mon., Thurs., and Sat., tel. 407/331–9191.*

Dog Racing **Sanford Orlando Kennel Club** (301 Dog Track Rd., Longwood, tel. 407/831–1600) has dog racing and betting nightly except Sun. at 7:45. Matinees Mon., Wed., and Sat. at 1. *Admission: $1. Open Nov.–May.*

Seminole Greyhound Park (2000 Seminola Blvd., Casselberry, tel. 407/699–4510) is a newer track with racing nightly at 7:45 except Sunday. *Admission: $1 general, clubhouse $2, children half price. Open May–Oct.*

Basketball **Orlando Magic** (Box 76, Orlando, FL 32802 tel. 407/89–MAGIC) joined the National Basketball Association in the 1989–90 season. The team plays in the new, 16,000-seat Orlando Arena. *Admission: $8–$17. Off I–4 at Amelia, the arena is 2 blocks west of the interstate.*

Baseball The **Orlando Twins** are Minnesota's Class AA Southern League affiliate. They play baseball at Tinker Field. *Get off I–4 at Colonial Ave. (Hwy. 50), go west to Tampa Ave. and south on Tampa to the stadium. Tel. 407/849–6346.*

The **Osceola Astros** are Houston's Class A team in the Florida State League. They play at Osceola County Stadium in Kissimmee. (tel. 407/933–5500).

The **Baseball City Royals** are Kansas City's Class-A team in the Florida State League. They play at Boardwalk and Baseball (tel. 407/648–5151), where you can get combination tickets for the park and game.

Soccer **Orlando Lions** play in the Americal Soccer League Games April through August at Orlando Stadium weekends at 7:30 PM. *Ad-*

mission: $6. The stadium is adjacent to Tinker Field (see Orlando Twins, above).

Dining

If you want to try some local specialties, consider stone crabs, pompano (a mild white fish), Apalachiocola oysters, small but tasty Florida lobsters, and conch chowder. Fresh hearts of palm are a treat, too.

The most highly recommended restaurants in each price category are indicated by a star ★.

Category	Cost*
Very Expensive	over $49
Expensive	$30–$40
Moderate	$20–$30
Inexpensive	under $20

per person without tax, service, or drinks

Credit card abbreviations: AE, American Express; DC, Diners Club; MC, MasterCard; V, Visa.

In Epcot Center World Showcase offers some of the finest dining not only in Walt Disney World but in the entire Orlando area. The problem is that the restaurants are often crowded and difficult to book. Many of them are operated by the same people who own internationally famous restaurants in their home countries. The top-of-the-line places, such as those in the French, Italian, and Japanese pavilions, can be expensive, but they are not as pricey as comparable restaurants in large, cosmopolitan cities such as Paris or New York. One good thing about Epcot's restaurants, besides the food, is that most of them have limited-selection children's menus with drastically lower prices, so bringing the kids along to dinner won't break the bank.

Visitors are not expected to go all the way back to their hotels to change and clean up and then return for dinner, so casual dress is expected in all the restaurants, even the finest.

If you want to eat in one of the more popular restaurants, it will be much easier to get a reservation for lunch than for dinner. It won't be quite the same experience, but it will be cheaper. Another way to get a table is to have lunch before noon and dinner before 6 or after 8.

Both lunch and dinner reservations are strongly recommended at all the finer restaurants in Epcot. Unless you are staying at one of the Walt Disney World hotels, you cannot reserve in advance of the day on which you wish to eat, and you can't book by phone. Instead, you must reserve in person at each restaurant or head for Earth Station at the base of Spaceship Earth as soon as you get to Epcot Center. There you will find a bank of computer screens called WorldKey Information. You need to stand in line to get to one of these screens and place the reservation, and the lines form very early. On busy days, most top restaurants are filled within an hour of Epcot's opening time, so you may have to line up at the Epcot admissions booth before opening time and then, once you're through the gate, make a mad dash for the WorldKey computer terminals. If there is a long line when you get to Earth Station, remember that on the far side of Future World, just before the bridge to World Show-case, is an outdoor kiosk with five WorldKey terminals that few people notice. There is also another WorldKey kiosk on the far side of the Port of Entry gift shop, near the boat dock for the water taxi to the Moroccan pavilion. Having made the reserva-tions, you can begin to enjoy your day at Epcot.

If you are a guest at an on-site Walt Disney World resort or at one of the Walt Disney World Village hotels, avoid the battle of the WorldKey by booking a table by phone (tel. 407/824–4000). Remember that if you are staying at one of these resorts, you cannot make a same-day reservation by phone but must book either one or two days in advance between noon and 9 PM. The restaurant will ask to see your resort identification card, so don't leave it in your hotel room. No matter how you book, try to show up at the restaurant a bit early to be sure of getting your table. You can pay with American Express, Visa, MasterCard, or, of course, cash. If you're a guest of a Disney hotel, you can charge the tab to your room.

British **Rose and Crown.** This is a very popular, friendly British pub, where visitors and Disney employees come at the end of the day to knock off a pint of crisp Bass Ale or blood-thickening Guinness Stout with a few morsels of Stilton cheese. "Wenches" serve up simple pub fare, such as steak-and-kidney pie, beef tenderloin, and fish and chips. The Rose and Crown sits on the shore of the lagoon, so on warm days it's nice to lunch on the patio at the water's edge and enjoy the soft breezes and the homiest atmosphere in Epcot Center. *Moderate.*

French **Bistro de Paris.** Located on the second floor of the French pavil-ion, above Chefs de France (*see* below), this is a relatively quiet and charming spot for lunch or dinner. The bistro specializes in regional cooking from southern France. A favorite is steamed filet of fresh grouper with tomato, mushrooms, fresh herbs, and white wine sauce, served with rice pilaf. Wines are moder-ately priced and available by the glass. *Moderate.*

★ **Chefs de France.** Three of France's most famous culinary art-ists came together to create this French restaurant. The most renowned of the three, Paul Bocuse, operates one restaurant north of Lyon and two in Tokyo and has published several fa-mous books on French cuisine. Another, Gaston Lenôtre, has gained eminence for his pastries and ice creams. The third of this culinary triumvirate, Roger Vergé, operates one of France's most highly rated restaurants, near Cannes. The three don't actually prepare each meal, but they were the ones who created the menu and carefully trained the chefs. Some of their most popular classic dishes are roast duck with prunes and wine sauce; beef filet with fresh ground pepper, raisins, and Armagnac sauce; and filet of grouper topped with salmon-vegetable mousse and baked in puff pastry. *Moderate.*

German **Biergarten.** This popular spot boasts Oktoberfest 365 days a year. Visitors sit at long communal tables and are served by waitresses in typical Bavarian garb. The cheerful—some would say raucous—atmosphere is what one would expect from a place where performers yodel, sing, and dance to the rhythms of an oompah band. The crowd, pounding pitchers of beer or wine while consuming hot pretzels and hearty German fare, is usually pretty active when audience participation is called for and just as active when it is not. *Moderate.*

Italian **L'Originale Alfredo de Roma Ristorante.** This is a World Show-case hot spot, with some of the finest food in Walt Disney World. During dinner, waiters skip around singing Italian songs and bellowing arias. The restaurant is named for the man who invented the now-classic fettuccine Alfredo, a pasta served with a sauce of cream, butter, and loads of freshly grated Parmesan cheese. Another popular dish is *lo Chef Consiglia* (the chef's selections), which consists of an appetizer of spaghetti or fettuccine, a mixed green salad, and a chicken or veal entree. The most popular veal dish is *piccata di Vitello*—veal thinly sliced and panfried with lemon and white wine. *Moderate.*

Japanese **Mitsukoshi.** This isn't just a restaurant, it's a complex of dining areas on the second floor above the Mitsukoski Department Store. Each of the five dining rooms (on your left as you enter) has four tables, which seat eight and are equipped with a grill on which chefs prepare meats and fish with acrobatic precision. It's an American's idea of the real Japan, but fun nonetheless. *Moderate.*

Mexican **San Angel Inn.** The lush, tropical surroundings—cool, dark, al-most surreal—make this one of the most exotic restaurants in Disney World. The ambience is at once romantic and lively. Tables are candlelit, but close together, and the restaurant is open to the pavilion, where folk singers perform and musicians play guitars or marimbas. One of the specialties is *Langosta Baja California*—Baja lobster meat, sautéed with tomatoes, onions, olives, Mexican peppers, and white wine, and baked in its shell. Try the margaritas, and, for dessert, don't miss the chocolate Kahlúa mousse pie. *Moderate.*

Moroccan **Marakesh.** Belly dancers and a three-piece Moroccan band set the mood in this exotic restaurant, where you may feel as though you have stumbled onto the set of *Casablanca*. The food is mildly spicy and relatively inexpensive. At lunch, you may want to try the national dish of Morocco, *couscous*, served with garden vegetables. For dinner, try the *bastila*, an appetizer of sweet and spicy pork between many layers of thin pastry, with almonds, saffron, and cinnamon. *Moderate.*

Restaurant Akershus. Norway's tradition of seafood and cold-meat dishes is highlighted at the restaurant's *koldtbord*, or Norwegian buffet. Hosts and hostesses explain the dishes to guests and suggest which ones go together. It is traditional to make several trips to the koldtbord, so there is no need to shovel everything you see onto your plate at one time. The first trip is for appetizers, usually herring prepared in a number of ways. On your next trip choose cold seafood items—try gravlaks, salmon cured with salt, sugar, and dill. Pick up cold salads and meats on your next trip, and then you fill up with hot dishes on your fourth trip, usually a choice of lamb, veal, and venison. Desserts are offered à la carte, including cloudberries, delicate, seasonal fruits that grow on the tundra. There are four dining rooms, seating 220 in an impressive copy of Oslo's famous Akershus Castle. *Moderate.*

The Walt Disney World Area These are restaurants close to Disney World, situated along International Drive or near Kissimmee, Disney Maingate, or Lake Buena Vista.

American **Empress Lilly.** Disney's 220-foot, 19th-century Mississippi-style riverboat is a popular tourist dining spot at the far end of Walt Disney World Shopping Village, right on Buena Vista Lagoon. Though the boat is permanently moored, it looks like an elegant old-fashioned Victorian showboat, complete with brass lamps, burgundy velvet love seats, and mahogany wood. The boat has several restaurants and lounges. Beef is served in the *Steerman's Quarters* and seafood in *Fisherman's Deck*. Only 5% of the tables are open for reservations, two days in advance. Visitors without reservations should arrive early, add their names to the list, then go and listen to banjo music in the *Baton Rouge Lounge*. The food is as predictable as it is expensive, but dining here can be an enjoyable experience for large families or groups who want a decent meal but do not want to feel inhibited by a stuffy atmosphere. The third restaurant on the showboat is the *Empress Room*, a plush, Victorian dining room filled with gilded reminders of another age. It is a luxurious (if gaudy) setting that might bring out the Rhett Butler or Scarlett O'Hara in you, but you will wish that the food were more palatable, especially at these prices. The menu reads elegantly, featuring such specialties as duck, pheasant, venison, and various seafood dishes, but the food is unlikely to live up to your elegant expectations. *Steerman's Quarters and Fisherman's Deck: Walt Disney World Shopping Village, tel. 407/828–3900. Dress: casual. Only a few reservations accepted. AE, CB, DC, MC, V. Moderate. Empress Room: Jacket required. Reservations required, up to a month in advance. AE, CB, DC, MC, V. Expensive.*

Australian **The Outback.** A glass elevator descends into this huge restaurant beside a waterfall and pool, located behind the Buena Vista Palace Hotel. In the middle of the room are the grills and barbecue pits, where the chefs cook up surf-and-turf Aussie specialties such as rack of lamb and lobster tail. Ninety-nine brands of beer are served in this fun, relaxed, family restaurant, where waiters serve you in outback safari outfits and the kids don't have to sit on their hands. *Buena Vista Palace, WDW Village, Lake Buena Vista, tel. 407/827–3430. Dress: casual. Reservations accepted. AE, DC, MC, V. Moderate.*

Cajun/Creole **Royal Orleans.** Some of the most authentic Louisiana cooking outside New Orleans is prepared under the direction of the award-winning Cajun chef, "Beany" MacGregor. Specialties include sherried turtle soup and *la truite roulee* (small slivers of trout fillet, shrimp, Louisiana blue crab, and fresh artichoke hearts wrapped in spinach leaves and topped with béarnaise sauce). Fresh seafood and crawfish are flown in daily from Louisiana. Royal Orleans is located in the back left corner as you drive into the Mercado Shopping Village on International Drive. *8445 International Dr., Orlando, tel. 407/352–8200. Jacket required. Reservations advised. AE, CB, DC, MC, V. Moderate.*

Continental **Arthur's 27.** Situated on the top floor of the Buena Vista Palace
★ Hotel, Arthur's 27 offers visitors elegant meals and one of the best views of the Magic Kingdom and Epcot Center. The fixed-price, seven-course Continental dinner costs $55 per person, *without* drinks; if you order à la carte, expect to pay more. Service and quality are first class, though bordering on the pretentious. The wine list is formidable, featuring everything from reasonable California wines to some vintage Bordeaux

that could be sold at auction. Specialties include venison and sautéed breast of duck with honey-ginger sauce. There is only one seating per night, so reservations are at a premium and should be made at the same time that you reserve your room. *Buena Vista Palace Hotel, Walt Disney World Village, tel. 407/ 827-3450. Jacket required. Reservations strongly recommended. AE, CB, DC, MC, V. Very Expensive.*

Atlantis. Those who associate Stouffer with frozen dinners will be happily surprised by the tasteful and art nouveau surroundings, the subdued atmosphere, and the sophisticated French menu. The waiters, even the busboys, are formally attired and very helpful. For an appetizer, try the warm duck salad. For entrees, the specialties are rack of lamb, blackened with Cajun spices and served with an avocado cream sauce, and swordfish grilled to perfection (though you may want to order it with the port-wine sauce on the side). The rich desserts border on divinity. *Stouffer Resort, 6677 Harbor Dr., Orlando, tel. 407/351-5555. Jacket required. Reservations recommended. AE, CB, DC, MC, V. Expensive.*

Dux. In the Peabody Hotel's gourmet restaurant, some creations are innovative, such as the grilled quail with poached quail eggs, served with wild rice in a carrot turrine nest. Others are a trifle self-conscious, like the avocado with sautéed salmon, artichoke chips, and champagne caviar sauce. For an entree, consider the baked Florida lobster with chanterelle mushrooms, spinach, and champagne sauce. The selection of California wines is outstanding. *Peabody Hotel, 9801 International Dr., Orlando, tel. 407/352-4000. Jacket required. Reservations strongly recommended. AE, CB, DC, MC, V. Expensive.*

La Coquina. This is a hotel restaurant with an emphasis on seafood and serious sauces. One popular meat specialty is loin of lamb with eggplant and goat cheese in grape leaves, served with grilled *polenta* (a type of cornmeal). The best bet here is Sunday brunch—a cornucopia of fruits, vegetables, pastries, pâtés, smoked fish, and a number of dishes cooked before your eyes. The $27 brunch is served with Domain Chandon champagne; the $52 brunch, with all the Dom Perignon champagne you can consume. If you're hungry and thirsty enough, you just might be able to put them out of business. *Hyatt Regency at Grand Cypress Resort, tel. 407/239-1234. Jacket required. Reservations suggested. AE, CB, DC, MC, V. Expensive.*

Indian **Darbar.** This lavishly decorated dining room features northern Indian cuisine. In addition to curries and pilafs, Darbar specializes in tandoori cooking—barbecuing with mesquite charcoal in a clay oven. Meats and vegetables are marinated in special sauces overnight and cooked to perfection. If you're not familiar with Indian cuisine, this is a good place to begin. The best bet is the tandoori dinner for two, with different types of lamb and chicken. *7600 Dr. Phillips Blvd., Orlando, tel. 407/345-8128. To get there, take Sand Lake Blvd. (exit 29 off I-4) and head west on to the Marketplace Shopping Center (right after the 2nd stop light). The restaurant is in the shopping center. Dress: casual. Reservations advised on weekends. AE, CB, DC, MC, V. Moderate.*

Italian **Christini's.** For traditional Italian cuisine, this is Orlando's fin-
★ est. The restaurant is not about to win any awards for decor, but the food couldn't be fresher and the service couldn't be

more efficient. The restaurant makes its own pastas daily and serves them with herbs, vegetables, and freshly grated Parmesan. Specialties include fresh fish; a fish soup with lobster, shrimp, and clams; and veal chops with fresh sage. *Intersection of Sand Lake Rd. and Dr. Phillips Blvd., in the Marketplace Shopping Center, tel. 407/345–8770. Jacket required. Reservations recommended. AE, CB, DC, MC, V. Expensive.*

Cappriccio. This is a smart-looking, California-chic Italian eaterie, slickly decorated with granite and marble tiles. The menu features traditional and innovative pasta dishes, such as spinach fettuccine with smoked salmon and mushrooms in a cream sauce. Also special are the exotic pizzas, cooked in old-fashioned wood-burning brick ovens. Try the *pizza al Cinque Formaggi* (pizza made with sun-dried tomatoes, five cheeses, fresh herbs, and tons of garlic). It's a far cry from the Pizza Hut, so be prepared for deep-dish prices. *Peabody Hotel, 9801 International Dr., Orlando, tel. 407/352–4000. Dress: casual. Reservations recommended. AE, CB, DC, MC, V. Moderate.*

Japanese **Ran-Getsu.** The best Japanese food in town is served in this palatial setting. The atmosphere may seem a bit self-conscious—an American's idea of the Orient—but the food is fresh and carefully prepared. Sit at the curved, dragon's tail-shaped sushi bar for the Matsu platter—an assortment of *nigiri-* and *maki*-style sushis—or, if you are with a group, sit Japanese style at tables overlooking a carp-filled pond and decorative gardens. Specialties are sukiyaki and *shab-shabu* (thinly sliced beef in a boiling seasoned broth, served with vegetables and prepared at your table). If you feel more adventurous, try the deep-fried alligator tail. *8400 International Dr., Orlando, tel. 407/345–0044. Dress: casual. Reservations accepted. AE, CB, DC, MC, V. Moderate.*

Kosher **Palm Terrace.** This is a kosher restaurant supervised by Rabbi Jakobs of the Orthodox Union. Diners who are not guests at the Hyatt Orlando pay a fixed price of just under $30 (half price, half portions for children) for Shabbos meals. Meals must be prepaid on Friday, and reservations are required one-half hour before candle lighting. Kosher breakfast and lunch items are available next door at the Marketplace Deli from 6 AM to midnight (the Hyatt also has a shul, with services held twice daily.) *Hyatt Orlando. 6375 Irlo Bronson Memorial Hwy., Kissimmee, tel. 407/396–1234. Dress: informal. Reservations required. AE, CB, DC, MC, V. Moderate.*

Seafood **Hemingway's.** Located by the pool at the Hyatt Regency Grand Cypress, this restaurant serves all sorts of sea creatures, from conch, scallops, and squid to grouper, pompano, and monkfish. In addition to the regular menu, Hemingway's also has what is called a "Cuisine Naturelle" menu, featuring dishes that are low in fat, calories, sodium, and cholesterol—recipes that are approved by the American Heart Association and Weight Watchers. What more could you want other than a big hot-fudge sundae for dessert? *Hyatt Regency Grand Cypress Resort, tel. 407/239–1234. Dress: casual. Reservations suggested. AE, CB, DC, MC, V. Moderate–Expensive.*

24 Hours **Beeline Diner.** This is a slick 1950s-style diner that's always open. It is in the Peabody Hotel, so it's not exactly cheap, but the salads, sandwiches, and griddle foods are tops. A good bet for breakfast or a late-night snack. And for just a little silver, you get to play a lot of old tunes on the jukebox. *Peabody Hotel, 9801 International Dr., Orlando, tel. 407/352–4000. Dress casual. Reservations not necessary. AE, CB, DC, MC, V. Moderate.*

The Orlando Area The following restaurants are in or near the city of Orlando and cater mostly to a local clientele.

American **The Bubble Room.** Some visitors will get a real kick out of this upbeat, nostalgia-themed restaurant with its big-band-era music and wacky wall-to-wall decor from the 1930s, '40s, and '50s. Every inch of space is covered with bric-a-brac, framed movie stills, and magazine covers of bygone luminaries. Not only is the place fun and crazy, but the food is pretty wild as well. The menu is a hodgepodge of the Bubble Room's interpretations of recipes from around the world, from Asian to Cajun. Seafood is shipped daily from the Gulf Coast. The specialty of the house, "The Eddie Fisherman," is a fillet of local black grouper covered with a light nut-crumb topping and then poached in a brown paper bag. *1351 S. Orlando Ave. (on Rte. 17–92), Maitland, tel. 407/628–3331. Dress: very casual. Reservations recommended. AE, CB, DC, MC, V. Moderate.*

Chinese **4, 5, 6.** Pedestrian surroundings don't hide well-prepared and
★ well-served traditional dishes, such as steamed sea bass and chicken with snow peas. Served in Chinatown fashion by cart-pushing waiters. *657 N. Primrose Dr., Orlando, tel. 407/898–1899. Dress: very informal. Reservations: Recommended on weekends. AE, CB, DC, MC, V. Open weekends to 2 AM. Inexpensive.*

Continental **Chalet Suzanne.** If you like to drive or are returning from a day
★ at Cypress Gardens, consider dining at this award-winning family-owned country inn and restaurant. It has been expanded bit by bit since it opened in the 1930s. Today, it looks like a small Swiss village—right in the middle of Florida's orange groves. The place settings, china, glasses, chairs, and even the tables are of different sizes, shapes, and origins. Strangely, however, it all works together as the expression of a single sensibility. For an appetizer, try broiled grapefruit. Recommended among the seven entrees are chicken Suzanne, shrimp curry, lobster Newburg, shad roe, and filet mignon. Crepes Suzanne are a good bet for dessert. The seven-course meals begin at $40. This unlikely back-road country inn should provide one of the most memorable dining experiences one can have in Orlando. *U.S. 27 north of Lake Wales, about 10 mi past Cypress Gardens turnoff, tel. 813/676–6011. Jackets requested. Reservations suggested. AE, CB, DC, MC, V. Closed Mon. during summer. Expensive.*

★ **Park Plaza Gardens.** This popular spot is a see-and-be-seen experience for the locals of beautiful old Winter Park. At lunch, the society grand dames enjoy fabulous salads and quiches among an assortment of local secretaries and yuppies on business lunches. In the evening, the area's well-heeled families come here to dine. The dinner menu emphasizes seafood and veal. For dessert, the baked Alaska is a must. During the day, the restaurant is a bright greenhouse filled with plants; at night it is candle lit and romantic. On Sunday, there is a good champagne brunch at bargain prices. *319 Park Ave. S., Winter Park; tel. 407/645–2475. Jackets usually worn but not required. Reservations advised. AE, CB, DC, MC, V. Moderate.*

Cuban **Numero Uno.** Long regarded by food critics as the best in town.
★ Ambience is casual plastic. Cuban roast pork with rice and
black beans is one of the specialties. *2499 S. Orange Ave., tel.
407/841–3840. Dress: informal. Reservations unnecessary.
AE, CB, DC, MC, V. Inexpensive.*

French **La Belle Verrière.** Dine among plants and fresh flowers in the
glow of Tiffany stained glass. Specialties include leg of lamb
and fresh fish dishes in delicate sauces. Save room for the crème
caramel or chocolate mousse. *142 S. Park Ave., Winter Park,
tel. 407/645–3377. Dress: upscale informal. Reservations recommended. AE, CB, DC, MC, V. Closed Sun. Moderate.*

Coq au Vin. The atmosphere here is Mobile Home Modern, but
the traditional French fare is first class, and you can pride
yourself on discovering a place few tourists know about but that
is nearly always filled with a friendly Orlando clientele. Owners Louis Perrotte (the chef) and his wife, Magdalena (the
hostess), are a charming couple who give the place its warmth
and personality. The specialties include homemade chicken liver pâté, fresh rainbow trout with champagne, and roast Long
Island duckling with green peppercorn sauce. For dessert, try
the crème brûlée. *4800 S. Orange Ave., Orlando, tel. 407/851–
6980. Dress: informal. Reservations suggested. AE, CB, DC,
MC, V. Moderate.*

Mexican **Bee Line Mexican Restaurant.** It looks like another hole-in-the-
★ wall eatery, but the burritos, taco salads, meat chalupas, and
chili rellenos are among the best in the area. *4542 Hoffner Rd.,
Orlando (near the airport), tel. 407/857–0566. Dress: casual.
No reservations. No credit cards, but checks are accepted. Inexpensive.*

★ **Paco's.** Good Mexican food in a cheerful but cramped little
house. Guacomole is hand mashed from avocados on the premises; so are the refried beans. *1801 W. Fairbanks Ave., Winter
Park, tel. 407/629–0149. No reservations or credit cards. Inexpensive.*

Villa Las Palomas. The building itself is a relatively faithful
recreation of its parent restaurant, the San Angel Inn, built in
1692 near Mexico City. It is a shame that the restaurant's architectural charm is lost along a street lined with gas stations and
shopping malls, but on entering, you feel as though you have
crossed the border and stepped into an elegant Mexican inn.
The menu includes traditional fare such as burritos and enchiladas, but do try more ambitious dishes, such as mole *poblano*,
a roasted half chicken simmered in a sauce of more than 20 Mexican spices. The food can be a bit heavy, so you may want to
stick with seafood. The margaritas are first class. Mexican gui-
tarists will sing requests for you, and on weekends there is a
10-piece mariachi band. *3552 E. Colonial Dr., Orlando, tel.
407/894–2610. Dress: casual. Reservations accepted. AE, CB,
DC, MC, V. Moderate.*

Pizza **Johnny's Pizza Palace.** Red leather booths are the setting for
crisp pizza and a two-crust pie that Chicagoans call a stuffed
pizza. Pasta and sandwiches are also on the menu. *4909 Lake
Underhill Rd., tel. 407/277–3452. Dress: pizza-parlor modern.
Reservations not necessary. MC, V. Inexpensive.*

Rossi's. This is a local pizza joint—a garlic bread pepperoni pizza and a pitcher of Bud or root beer type of spot. The food is not
about to win any awards, but Rossi's is a good escape from the

tourist/hotel scene, and the price is right. *5919 S. Orange Blossom Trail, Orlando, tel. 407/855–5755. Dress: very informal. AE, MC, V. Inexpensive.*

Seafood **South Seas.** The only problem here is deciding which of the 70 seafood dishes to order. Whatever you choose, it's likely to be fresh, for the kitchen is supplied by the restaurant's own fish market. The large, modern dining room gets no points for ambience, but the prices are the best around. Sink your teeth into alligator or shark that won't bite back, crack open some lobster or oysters, or butter up some catfish or snapper. Steak and burgers are also served, but that would be like ordering a quarter-pounder with cheese from Colonel Sanders. *3001 Curry Ford Rd., Orlando, tel. 407/898–8331. Dress: casual. Reservations not accepted. AE, MC, V. Moderate.*

Wekiwa Marina Restaurant. Plenty of local color here as customers ranging from three-piece-suited bankers to overall-clad farmers eat catfish, frog legs, and cheese grits in a Cracker-style wooden building on the wharf. *1000 Miami Springs Rd., Longwood (off I–4, about 20 min north of Orlando), tel. 407/ 862–9640. Dress: blue-jean informal. Reservations only for large parties. AE, CB, DC, MC, V. Inexpensive.*

Gary's Duck Inn. This long-time Orlando favorite is known for its knotty-pine nautical motif and its fresh shrimp, crab, and fish dishes. This was the model for a seafood chain known as Red Lobster. *3974 S. Orange Blossom Trail, Orlando, tel. 407/ 843–0270. Dress: casual. Reservations not required. AE, CB, DC, MC, V. Inexpensive.*

Steak **Cattle Ranch.** If you're hungry and looking for a big, thick, juicy, down-home American steak, then steer for the Cattle Ranch. It's cheap and, if you're insanely hungry, it's free. Just take "The 6-pound Challenge," in which you're given 75 minutes to eat an entire six-pound steak dinner, including salad, potato, and bread. If you can do it, you won't have to pay a dime. If you can't, it will cost you just over $30. There is nothing fancy about this cowboy cafeteria except the steaks that come off the burning orangewood fire. And you won't see another tourist for miles around. *6129 Old Winter Garden Rd., Orlando (2½ blocks west of Kirkman Rd.); tel. 407/298–7334. Dress: very informal. Reservations not needed. AE, MC, V. Inexpensive.*

24 Hours **Skeeter's.** After Orlando's nightclubs close, both old and young stagger over to this popular diner to sober up or to prolong the party over some fried eggs, hash browns, and pancakes. A fun diner, with lots of local character; open around the clock. *1212 Lee Rd., Orlando, tel. 407/298–7973. Dress: informal. No credit cards. Inexpensive.*

Lodging

To stay within or outside Walt Disney World—that is the question. The law of inertia seems to keep most Walt Disney World guests within its realm. And if you are coming to Orlando for only a few days and are interested solely in the Magic Kingdom, Epcot Center, and the other Disney attractions, the resorts on Disney property may be right for you. But if you plan to visit other attractions, you should at least consider the alternatives.

Let's look at the pros and cons of staying in an on-site hotel. On the positive side, you won't need to drive, and transportation within Disney World will be free. None of the hotels is within the actual confines of the Magic Kingdom or Epcot Center, but transportation is usually quick and efficient. Remember, though, that the monorail serves just three on-site hotels: the Grand Floridian, Contemporary, and Polynesian Village Resorts. If you stay anywhere else you will have to take Disney's bus to the monorail.

If you have kids, they will be able to fend for themselves more easily and stay out of trouble within Walt Disney World. Built with families in mind, rooms in the on-site resorts are large and can as a rule accommodate up to five persons. They offer cable TV with the Disney Channel and a channel providing the latest updates on special daily events.

The thrill—especially for children—of knowing you are actually staying in Walt Disney World may be worth staying here. The hotels offer many of their own special events, such as theme dinner shows and breakfasts at which Disney cartoon characters come to entertain the kids.

As a Disney guest, you get first rights to tee-off times at the busy golf courses, and you are able to call up to two days in advance to make hard-to-get reservations at any of the fine restaurants in Disney World. Outsiders can make reservations only by calling while at the park on the day they wish to dine or they must wait on line.

As an on-site guest, you also get a guest identification card that allows you to charge anything at Walt Disney World (except in the Magic Kingdom) to your room.

On the negative side, hotels with comparable facilities tend to cost more on Disney property than off it. You may have heard that by staying at a Disney hotel you get discounts on multiple-day Passports. This is little more than an advertising ploy— unless you consider the savings of a few dollars on hundreds of dollars worth of Passports a significant discount. Whatever small savings you may realize will be undercut by the higher cost of staying in an on-site property.

Reservations All on-site accommodations may be booked through the Walt Disney World Central Reservations Office (Box 10100, Lake Buena Vista 32830, tel. 407/W–DISNEY). Reservations must often be made several months in advance and sometimes, for the best rooms during high season, a year in advance. There are always cancellations, of course, so it's worth trying even at the last minute. Keep in mind that Delta Airlines (tel. 800/221–1212) has many rooms allotted to it for its travel packages, so check with Delta, too. Visitors on a tight budget should be aware that many hotels (and attractions) offer discounts up to 40% from September to mid-December.

If the on-site resorts are full, central reservations will automatically try to book a place for you at one of the Walt Disney World Village hotels. Be sure to tell them exactly what you are looking for. You must give a deposit for your first night's stay within three weeks of making your reservation, and you can get a refund if you cancel at least five days before your scheduled stay.

Land packages, including admissions tickets, car rentals, and hotels either on or off Disney property, can be made through Walt Disney Travel Co. (1675 Buena Vista Dr., Lake Buena Vista 32830, tel. 407/828–3232).

Land/air packages, with accommodations both on and off Disney property, can be booked through **Disney Reservation Service** (tel. 800/828–0228).

Ratings The most highly recommended properties in each price category are indicated by a star ★. Rates usually include the price of two children under 18.

Category	Cost*
Very Expensive	over $150
Expensive	$120–$150
Moderate	$65–$120
Inexpensive	under $65

double room; add 9% taxes or service

The following credit card abbreviations are used: AE, American Express; CB, Carte Blanche; DC, Diners Club; MC, MasterCard; and V, Visa.

Walt Disney World Hotels Visitors have a choice of staying at (1) hotels that are owned and operated by Disney, (2) hotels that are privately owned but that are located on Disney property, and (3) hotels in the Orlando area.

Let's look at the Disney-run hotels first. In brief, the *Contemporary* is the biggest and busiest resort—the one that is most crowded with children and conventioneers. Yet it is also the center of action, with the most entertainment, shops, and restaurants.

The *Polynesian Village* is the most popular, particularly with families and couples. It has a relaxed environment with low, tropical buildings and walking paths along the Seven Seas Lagoon. It can be difficult to find a place to be alone, however. The charm of the *Grand Floridian* will survive the crowds. The waterfront location makes it particularly attractive.

The most relaxed and low-key of the hotels is the *Disney Inn*. It is the smallest, and, because it is between two golf courses, it is the quietest. The *Resort Villas* are especially attractive for families or groups of two or more couples. There are four different types of villas in relatively isolated woodland settings. Least formal are the trailer and camp sites that are in an even more wooded setting in the Fort Wilderness Resort area.

Reservations sometimes become available at the last minute. For same-day reservations, phone each Disney property directly. For advance reservations, tel. 407/W–DISNEY.

Contemporary Resort Hotel. This high rise in the heart of Walt Disney World has a slick, space-age impersonality. Shops, lounges, and restaurants bustle under the 15-story atrium, creating an urban atmosphere not found in other, more easygoing Disney facilities. The futuristic monorail running right through the lobby contributes to the stark, modernistic mood. Rooms in the front are at a premium because they look out toward the Magic Kingdom. *Central Reservations, Box 10100, Lake Buena Vista 32830, tel. 407/W–DISNEY or 407/824–1000 for same-day reservations. 1,052 rooms. AE, MC, V. Expensive–Very Expensive.*

Disney Inn. Golfers are "fore" it, of course, but anyone who wants to get away from the crowds will appreciate this hotel once known as the Golf Resort. It's the smallest and quietest resort among the on-site hotels. The golf is world class, but since its name change the inn has also been discovered by couples who want some quiet time (with or without children). The most expensive rooms overlook the pool. Rooms on the first floor have direct access to the pool but can be noisy at times. Rooms with a view of the golf fairways are particularly pleasant. One of the quietest places to eat within Walt Disney World is located here—a new restaurant called the Garden Gallery, serving American cuisine. *Central Reservations, Box 10100, Lake Buena Vista 32830, tel. 407/W–DISNEY. 855 rooms. AE, MC, V. Expensive–Very Expensive.*

★ **Grand Floridian Beach Resort.** This Palm Beach-style coastal hot spot offers old-fashioned character with all the conveniences of a modern hotel. The gabled red roof, brick chimneys, and long ambling verandahs were built with loving attention to detail. Small touches, such as crystal chandeliers and stained-glass domes, create the feeling of a more sedate and leisurely era. As might be expected from a beach resort, there are all sorts of water sports at the marina. The Floridian also has its own monorail stop that links it to the TTC. Even the resort's monorail station elegantly carries off the Victorian theme. *Central Reservations, Box 10100, Lake Buena Vista 32830, tel. 407/W–DISNEY. AE, MC, V. 900 rooms, including 69 concierge rooms and 12 suites. Expensive–Very Expensive.*

Polynesian Village Resort. You are supposed to get the feeling that you are on a tropical island when you come here, so everything at The Poly, as it's called, has a South Pacific slant to it. The focal point of the resort is the Great Ceremonial House, where visitors check in. The atrium sets the tone, with its lush tropical atmosphere complete with volcanic rock fountains, blooming orchids, and coconut palms—the whole bit. You might think you were at a resort in Fiji if you didn't notice all the kids running around wearing Mickey Mouse caps.

Stretching from the main building are 11 two- and three-story "longhouses," each of which carries the name of some exotic Pacific Island. All rooms offer two queen-size beds and a small sleeper sofa, and accommodate up to five people. Except for some second-floor rooms, all have a balcony or patio. If you don't like to walk too much and want to be near the main building, with its shops and entertainment, request a room in the Bora Bora or Maui longhouses. For the best view of the Magic Kingdom and the Seven Seas Lagoon, with its sandy palm-trimmed beaches, stay in the Samoa, Moorea, or Tonga.

The least expensive rooms look out at the other buildings, the monorail, and the parking lot across the street. Slightly more expensive are the garden- and pool-view rooms. Rooms overlooking the lagoon are the priciest, but they are also the most peaceful and include a host of upgraded amenities and services that make them among the most sought after in Disney World. Recreational activities center around the hotel's large sandy beach and marina, where you can rent boats for sailing, waterskiing, and fishing. If you can pull together a group of eight, you can even rent an outrigger canoe. The two swimming pools can be overrun by children; you may want to go to the beach for a dip instead. *Central Reservations, Box 10100, Lake Buena Vista 32830, tel. 407/W–DISNEY or 407/824–2000 for same-day reservations. AE, MC, V. 855 rooms. Expensive–Very Expensive.*

The Caribbean Beach Resort. Like the Polynesian Village Resort, the Caribbean Beach Resort is made up of villages—Aruba, Barbados, Jamaica, Martinique, and Trinidad—all two-story buildings on a 42-acre tropical lake. Each village has its own swimming pool, laundry facility, and stretch of white-sand beach. Bridges over the lake connect the mainland with Parrot Cay, a one-acre island featuring footpaths, bike paths, and children's play areas. There is a 500-seat food court and an adjoining 200-seat lounge. Check-in is at the Custom House, off Buena Vista Drive. *WDW Central Reservations, 10100 Lake Buena Vista 32830, tel. 407/W–DISNEY or 407/934–3400. 1,200 1-bedroom units. AE, MC, V. Moderate.*

The Resort Villas There are a few good reasons why you may prefer the Resort Villas to the resort hotels:

• You are visiting Walt Disney World with your family or with other couples, and you want to stay together and avoid the expense of separate rooms.
• You enjoy the convenience of having your own kitchen and would like to save money by preparing some of your own meals.
• You don't like big, busy hotels, but you appreciate the amenities of a resort.

There are five types of villas, each with its own character and ambience. Though they are not quite as plush as rooms in the resort hotels, they are more spacious. Since the villas are not on the monorail, transportation to the parks can be slow, and to get around within the village you may want to use your car or rented golf cart. On the positive side, you have immediate access to great golf, great fishing, shopping, and an active nightlife. Check-in for resort villas is at the entrance to Disney Village Resort. *Disney World Co., Central Reservations, 10100 Lake Buena Vista 32830, tel. 407/W–DISNEY or 407/827–1100 for same-day reservations.*

The Vacation Villas. They were originally built in 1971 but were refurbished in 1986. Each unit has complete living facilities with equipped kitchens and one or two bedrooms. The one-bedroom villas have a king-size bed in one room and a queen-size sofa bed in the living room (accommodating up to four). The two-bedroom units, accommodating up to six, have a king-size bed or two twin beds in each bedroom and a sofa bed in the living room (accommodating as many as six). There are two outdoor pools at the Vacation Villas. *139 1-bedroom units, 87 2-bedroom units. Expensive–Very Expensive.*

Club-Suite Villas. These are the smallest and the least memorable of the villas—and also the least expensive. Built of cedar, they each have one bedroom, a sofa bed, a wet bar, but no kitchen—the only villas that don't. Their size and ambience reflect the needs of business people attending meetings at the nearby Conference Center. Facilities include two outdoor pools, a small game room, a playground, and boat rentals. *61 units. Expensive.*

Two-Bedroom Villas. These villas are built of cedar, like those at Club-Suite, but they are more tastefully decorated and very spacious. All have two bedrooms, and a full loft accommodating up to six. They were formerly known as the Fairway Villas because the property is surrounded by several fairways of the Lake Buena Vista Golf Course. Guests may use pools at the Villa Recreation Center or Disney Village Clubhouse. *64 units. Expensive–Very Expensive.*

Three-Bedroom Villas. If you really want to get away from it all, this is the place to stay. Isolated within a peaceful, heavily wooded area, these curious villas stand on stilts. You won't exactly feel like Tarzan and Jane in these bungalows, but you may hear some howls late at night. Predictably, this out-of-the-way little forest retreat is popular among young couples.

All "tree houses" accommodate six and have two bedrooms with queen-size beds and a third bedroom with a double bed, kitchen and breakfast bar, living room, and two bathrooms. The third bedroom is on a lower level. There is also a utility room with a washer/dryer. Guests can use nearby pools at the Villa Recreation Center or Disney Village Clubhouse. *60 units. Expensive–Very Expensive.*

Fort Wilderness. If you want to rough it, stay among 730 acres of woodland, streams, small lakes, and plenty of water activities along the southeastern edge of Bay Lake, at the northern edge of Walt Disney World property.

You can rent a 42-foot-long trailer (accommodating up to six) or a 35-foot trailer (accommodating up to four). Both types have one bedroom, a bath, a full kitchen, air-conditioning, heat, and daily housekeeping services. The trailer sites are spread over 80 forested acres.

For those who are more serious about getting in touch with the great outdoors, there are campsites spread across 21 areas. Some are for visitors' own trailers, complete with electrical outlets, outdoor charcoal grills, private picnic tables, water, and waste disposal. For a real wilderness experience, full maid service is provided. There are also tent sites with water and electricity but not sewage. The most expensive sites (100–700) are nearest the lake. The least expensive (1600–1900) are far from the lake in denser vegetation. If there's a bargain, this is it. Each site accommodates up to 10 people. *Central Reservations, Box 10100, Lake Buena Vista 32830, tel. 407/824–8000, or same-day reservations 407/824–2900. Trailers, Moderate; campsites, Inexpensive.*

Lake Buena Vista Village The formal name of this area is Walt Disney World Village Hotel Plaza at Lake Buena Vista, but most people refer to it simply as Lake Buena Vista Village or World Village. Aside from the resorts that are actually inside Walt Disney World, these seven hotels are the most popular among visitors to Walt Disney World. This is because the properties publicize themselves as official Walt Disney World Hotels and offer many of the same incentives. Many people believe these hotels are owned by Disney. Not true. They were invited to establish themselves on Disney property, and they pay for the privilege with a percentage of their revenues. Disney does keep a close eye on them, however, to ensure that they maintain certain standards.

Because these hotels are "official," there is a premium on rooms, and rates are somewhat inflated compared with what you can find off the Disney property. Many Disney fans believe, however, that the benefits of staying in these hotels make it worthwhile. You decide.

● You can avoid box-office lines at Magic Kingdom and Epcot Center by buying tickets at your hotel. However, you can also send for these tickets before leaving home. For a three-day passport, you get less than a 2% discount—a savings of only $1.

● You get free rides on Disney World transportation, but so does anyone with a Magic Kingdom/Epcot pass. Though you are very close to Disney World, the bus takes 15–20 minutes just to reach the monorail and runs every 10–15 minutes. Transportation from nonofficial hotels off Disney property is often just as fast.

● You can make telephone reservations for restaurants and dinner shows in Disney World in advance of the general public.

● You can use the tennis and golf facilities at Lake Buena Vista Village. The Buena Vista hotels are all part of an attractively landscaped complex. Each has its own restaurants and lounges, and all are within walking distance of the popular, if touristy, Walt Disney World Shopping Village (a pleasant outdoor mall filled with gift shops and restaurants).

● Unlike Disney-owned and -operated hotels, rates do not fluctuate according to season.

● All seven hotels are comfortable and convenient, and each has a character of its own. But all are usually crowded with conventions, tour groups, or just a full house of guests.

You can call each hotel's toll-free number for reservations, or you can book rooms at any of them through the **Walt Disney World Central Reservations Office,** Box 10100, Lake Buena Vista, 32830.

Buena Vista Palace. This is the largest of the Lake Buena Vista hotels, with one of its towers soaring 27 stories high. When you enter its lobby, the hotel seems smaller and quieter than its bold, modern exterior and sprawling parking lots might suggest. Don't be fooled. You have entered on the third floor; when you head down to the ground level, you'll see just how large this place truly is. Facilities include a health club, swimming pools, four tennis courts, a beauty salon, a game room, two gift shops, and a host of bars and restaurants. Rooms are well-appointed and comfortable, each with a small patio and a push-button Mickey Mouse telephone. Rooms on the upper floors are more expensive; the best ones look out toward Epcot Center. Ask for a room in the main tower to avoid the late-night noise from the nightclub that reverberates through the atrium. *1900 Lake Buena Vista Dr., Lake Buena Vista 32830, tel. 407/827–2727 or 800/327–2990. 841 rooms. AE, CB, DC, MC, V. Expensive–Very Expensive.*

Grosvenor Resort. This attractive hotel is probably the best deal in the neighborhood, with a wealth of facilities and comfortable rooms for a fair price. The former Americana Dutch Resort, it was completely refurbished in British colonial-style and renamed the Grosvenor. Public areas are spacious, with high molded ceilings and columns, warm cheerful colors, and plenty of natural light.

Recreational facilities are geared toward the active life and include two heated pools; two lighted tennis courts; racquetball, shuffleboard, basketball, and volleyball courts; a children's playground; and a game room. Rooms are average in size, but colorfully decorated, with a refrigerator/bar and a videocassette player. In the lobby, you may rent movies for the VCR or cameras to make your own videos. *1850 Hotel Plaza Blvd., Lake Buena Vista 32830, tel. 407/828–4444 or 800/624–4109. 614 rooms. AE, CB, DC, MC, V. Moderate–Expensive.*

★ **Hilton at Walt Disney World Village.** The Hilton is generally considered the top hotel in the Village. It is also one of the most expensive. In contrast to the lackluster facade, the interiors are richly decorated with brass and glass and softened with tasteful carpets. Guest rooms sparkle. Rooms are not huge, but they are cozy and contemporary, with high-tech amenities. All are the same size, with a king-size bed, two double beds, or two queen-size beds. The most expensive rooms have views of the shopping village and lake. Rooms overlooking the pool are also desirable. Although all rooms are the same size, they vary dramatically in price by location and floor, as well as by season. The Hilton provides a service that many parents will consider indispensable—a **Youth Hotel** for children aged 3–12. The hotel has full-time supervisors for its playroom, a large-screen TV (with Disney Channel, of course), a six-bed dormitory, and scheduled meals. The Youth Hotel is open daily 4 PM–midnight. The cost is $4 per hour. Other facilities include two swimming pools, a health club, two lighted tennis courts, and several outdoor and indoor bars and restaurants, including the popular **American Vineyards,** serving New American cuisine. *1751 Hotel Plaza Blvd., Lake Buena Vista 32830, tel. 407/827–4000 or 800/445–8667. 814 rooms. AE, MC, V. Expensive–Very Expensive.*

Pickett Suite Resort. Walt Disney World is certainly not one to fall behind the current trends in the hotel industry, so it is not surprising that the most recent addition to the Lake Buena Vista neighborhood would be an all-suite hotel. Suites consist of a comfortable living room area and a separate bedroom with two double beds or a king-size bed. With a sofa bed in the living room, a suite can accommodate up to six people, but certainly not all comfortably. The arrangement is convenient for small families who want to avoid the hassle of cots and the expense of two separate rooms. Each unit has a TV in each room (including a small one in the bathroom!), a stocked refrigerator, a wet bar, a coffee maker and, on request, a microwave oven. The hotel attracts a quiet, family-oriented crowd and few of the noisy conventioneers one finds at the larger, splashier properties. Facilities include a whirlpool spa, heated swimming and wading pools, two tennis courts, a game room, and a children's play area. *2305 Hotel Plaza Blvd., Lake Buena Vista 32830, tel. 407/ 934–1000 or 800/742–5388. 229 units. AE, CB, DC, MC, V. Expensive–Very Expensive.*

Royal Plaza. From the lobby, this hotel seems a bit dated in comparison with the slick, modern hotels in the neighborhood. But the extremely casual, fun-loving atmosphere makes it popular with families who have young children and teenagers. The rooms are generous in size, the best ones overlooking the pool. If you have any interest in afternoon naps, make sure your room isn't too close to the ground floor. The hotel has several restaurants and bars, a few shops, a hair salon, four lighted tennis courts, a sauna, pool, and putting green. *1905 Hotel Pla-*

za Blvd., Lake Buena Vista 32830, tel. 407/828–2828 or 800/ 248–7890. 396 rooms. AE, CB, DC, MC, V. Expensive–Very Expensive.

Maingate Resorts *Maingate* refers to an area full of large hotels that are not affiliated with Walt Disney World but are clustered around its northernmost entrance, just off I–4. These hotels are mostly resort hotels on sprawling properties, catering to Disney World vacationers. All are good-quality hotels with a resort sameness one can find the world over. However, they vary in size and price. As a simple rule of thumb, the bigger the resort and the more extensive the facilities, the more you can expect to pay. If you're looking for a clean, modern room, you cannot go wrong with any of them. All are equally convenient to Walt Disney World, but one may emphasize a particular recreational activity over others. Where you stay may depend on how much time you plan to spend at your hotel or on which stroke—drive or backhand—you feel needs most improving.

★ **Grand Cypress Resort.** If you were to ask someone familiar with the Orlando area which resort is the most spectacular, few would hesitate to name the Grand Cypress. The resort property is so extensive—over 1,500 acres—that guests need a trolley system to get around. There is virtually every activity you can imagine at a resort: a dozen tennis courts, boats of all shapes and varieties, scenic bicycling and jogging trails, a full health club, dozens of horses, a 600,000-gallon, triple-level swimming pool fed by 12 cascading waterfalls, a 45-acre Audubon nature reserve, 45 holes of Jack Nicklaus–designed golf, and a golfing academy for a high-tech analysis of your game. This huge resort has just one drawback: the king-size conventions that it commonly attracts. *1 Grand Cypress Blvd., Orlando 32819, tel. 407/239–1234 or 800/228–9000. 750 rooms. AE, CB, DC, MC, V. Very Expensive.*

Hyatt Orlando Hotel. This is another very large hotel, but without the extensive resort facilities. Instead of a single towering building, the hotel consists of 40 two-story buildings in four clusters. Each cluster is a community with its own pool, Jacuzzi, park, and playground at its center. The rooms are spacious but otherwise unmemorable.

The lobby and convention center are in a building at the center of the clusters. The lobby is vast and mall-like, with numerous shops and restaurants. One of the restaurants, the **Palm Terrace,** features a full kosher menu supervised by the Orthodox Union. There is also a very good take-out deli, with great picnic snacks for those who are wise enough to avoid the lines and prices at amusement-park fast-food stands. There are a few tennis courts, but not much else in the way of recreation. However, for busy travelers who will be spending most of their time attacking Orlando's attractions, this is a convenient, not-too-expensive headquarters. *6375 W. Irlo Bronson Memorial Hwy., Kissimmee 32741, tel. 407/396–1234 or 800/228–9000. 946 rooms. AE, CB, DC, MC, V. Moderate.*

Knight's Inn Orlando Maingate West. There's a good selection of rooms here for a budget motel, including rooms with two double beds and efficiency apartments. Nonsmoking rooms are available. *7475 W. Irlo Bronson Hwy., Kissimmee 32741, tel. 407/396–4200. 120 units. AE, CB, DC, MC, V. Inexpensive.*

Buena Vista Palace, **10**
Caribbean Beach Resort, **9**
Casa Rosa Inn, **27**
Chalet Suzanne, **6**
Contemporary Resort Hotel, **7**
Disney Inn, **2**
Embassy Suites, **22**
Fort Wilderness, **8**
Grand Cypress Resort, **14**
Grand Floridian Beach Resort, **1**
Grosvenor Resort, **11**
Hilton at WDW Village, **18**
Hyatt Orlando, **13**
Knight's Inn Orlando Maingate West, **4**
Orlando Heritage Inn, **25**
Park Plaza, **28**
Peabody Orlando, **24**
Pickett Suite Resort, **16**
Polynesian Village Resort, **3**
Radisson Inn, **23**
Radisson Inn Maingate, **5**
Ramada Resort Maingate East, **20**
Residence Inn, **21**
Resort Villas, **12**
Royal Plaza, **17**
Sonesta Village, **15**
Stouffer Orlando Resort, **26**
Vistana, **19**

Orlando Area Lodging

Orlando Area Lodging (detail)

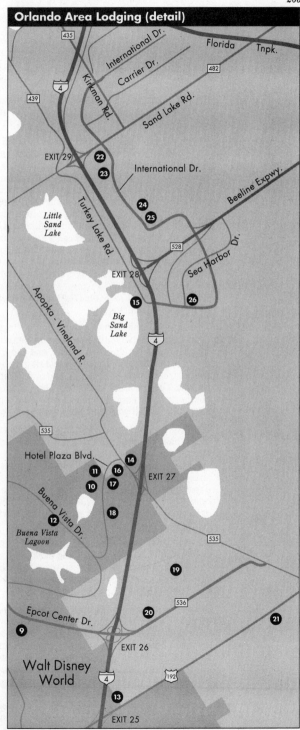

Ramada Resort Maingate East at the Park. The Ramada may offer the best deal in the neighborhood—a more attractive setting at more competitive prices. It has a few tennis courts, a swimming pool with a waterfall, a few shops and restaurants, and a delicatessen for picnickers. The rooms, like the rest of the hotel grounds, are spacious and bright, decked out in tropical and pastel colors. The best rooms, because of the view and light, face the pool. *2900 Parkway Blvd., Kissimmee 32741, tel. 407/396–7000 or 800/634–4774. 592 rooms. AE, CB, DC, MC, V. Moderate.*

Vistana Resort. Anyone interested in tennis should consider staying at this peaceful time-share resort spread over 50 beautifully landscaped acres. It is also popular with families or groups who are willing to share a spacious, tastefully decorated villa or town house, each with at least two bedrooms and all the facilities of home—a full kitchen, living room, a washer/dryer, and so on. The price may seem high, but considering the number of people each condominiumlike unit can accommodate (up to six or eight), the rates can be a bargain. The 14 clay and all-weather tennis courts can be used without charge. Private or semi-private lessons are available for every type of player. Other facilities include a huge, free-form swimming pool and a full health club. *13800 Vistana Dr., Lake Buena Vista 32830, tel. 407/239–3100 or 800/237–9152. 458 units. AE, CB, DC, MC, V. Very Expensive.*

Orlando Area
International Drive

The International Drive area, referred to by locals as "The Drive" and formally labeled "Florida Center," is a main drag for all sorts of hotels, restaurants, and shopping malls. As you head north along The Drive, the hotels get cheaper, the restaurants turn into fast-food joints, and malls translate into factory outlets. The southern end of The Drive is more classy, but the northern end may be more congenial to your budget—particularly if all you need is a place to put your head at night.

You will be hard pressed to find any structure around here older than you are, even if you are a teenager, because the area has been built up mostly in the past 10 years as an alternative to the Disney properties. For those who are not interested exclusively in Disney World, The Drive is a convenient point of departure for Orlando's countless other attractions. The Drive immediately parallels I–4 (at Exits 28 and 29), so a few minutes' drive north puts you in downtown Orlando, while a few minutes south on I–4 puts you in Disney World.

International Drive showcases such local attractions as Sea World, the labyrinth water-slide park, Wet 'n Wild, and many popular dinner shows. Many veteran Orlando visitors consider The Drive the territory's most comfortable home base, featuring some of the best hotels around.

Peabody Orlando. From afar, the Peabody looks like a high-rise office building. Don't let its austere exterior scare you away. Once inside, you will discover a very impressive, handsomely designed hotel. If you ignore the soaring numbers in the elevators and the sweeping view from your room, you will never know you are in a 27-story hotel. The Peabody's lobby has rich marble floors and fountains, and the entire hotel is decorated with modern art, giving it much color and flare. The rooms with the best views face Walt Disney World and a sea of orange trees that extends as far as the eye can see. If you want to be pampered, stay in the Peabody Club on the top three floors and enjoy special concierge service. The Peabody has a pool, a health club, and four lighted tennis courts. There are also two fine restaurants. *9801 International Dr., Orlando 32819, tel. 407/352-4000 or 800/262-6688. 891 rooms. AE, CB, DC, MC, V. Expensive–Very Expensive.*

★ **Sonesta Village Hotel.** The Sonesta, located off I-4 near International Drive, is a string of multiunit town houses on a lakefront. Following the lead of the all-suite hotels, the Sonesta "villas" consist of small apartments, some of which are bilevel with a fully equipped kitchenette, dining room/living room area, small patio, and bedroom. The units are comfortable and homey, each with its private, ground-floor entrance. One bonus of staying at the Sonesta is the outdoor facilities, including tennis courts, mini health club, swimming pool, and whirlpools convenient to each villa. Guests can sail and water-ski on the lake or offer themselves to the sun on a sandy beach. There is a restaurant and bar, but the only action is the nightly outdoor barbecue buffet. If you want to cook at "home" but are too busy to go shopping, the hotel offers a grocery delivery service. Laundry, however, is self-service. *10000 Turkey Lake Rd., Orlando 32819, tel. 407/352-8051 or 800/343-7170. 369 units. AE, CB, DC, MC, V. Expensive.*   800 766-3782 —

Stouffer Orlando Resort. This first-rate resort was originally the Wyndham Hotel Sea World, until it was sold to the Stouffer chain in 1987. Located directly across the street from Sea World, this bulky, 10-story building looks more like a Federal Reserve Bank than a comfortable hotel. When you enter, you step into what is billed as the largest atrium lobby in the world. Facilities include six lighted tennis courts, a swimming pool, a whirlpool, a child-care center, a game room, and access to an 18-hole golf course. On the second floor are a Nautilus-equipped fitness center and a beauty salon where you can work off or hide the effects of dinner.

Guest rooms are all large and spacious. The most expensive rooms face the atrium, but if you are a light sleeper, ask for an outside room to avoid the music and party sounds of conventioneers that rise through the atrium. *6677 Sea Harbor Dr., Orlando 32821, tel. 407/351-5555 or 800/327-6677. 778 rooms. AE, CB, DC, MC, V. Expensive.*

Embassy Suites Hotel at Plaza International. The concept of the all-suite hotel has become very popular in the Orlando area, and the Embassy Suites, a chain hotel, was the first to offer it. All suites have a bedroom and a full living room equipped with wet bar, refrigerator, desk, pull-out sofa, and two TVs. It is a comfortable and economical arrangement, somewhat less expensive than a single room in the top-notch hotels. Because the bedroom can be closed off, it is ideal for small families. The core of the hotel is a wide atrium. It is not nearly as large as the atrium at the Stouffer, but it is much cozier, with a relaxing lounge and a pianist as its centerpieces. The hotel has both an indoor and an outdoor pool, an exercise room with Jacuzzi, sauna, steam room, and game room, but with none of the other recreational facilities that the larger hotels have. *8250 Jamaica Court, Orlando 32819, tel. 407/345-8250 or 800/327-9797. 246 rooms. AE, CB, DC, MC, V. Moderate–Expensive.*

Orlando Heritage Inn. If you are looking for a simple, small hotel with reasonable rates but plenty of deliberate charm, the Heritage is the place to stay. Located next to the towering Peabody, this inn creates the atmosphere of Victorian-style Florida, complete with reproduction turn-of-the-century furnishings, rows of French windows and brass lamps, and a smattering of genuine 19th-century antiques. The guest rooms are decorated with a colonial accent—lace curtains on double French doors, folk-art prints on the walls, and quilted bed covers. The hotel has a small saloon-type lounge, and there is a dinner theater in the large Victorian rotunda several nights a week. With the exception of a swimming pool, there are few facilities. The whole place has a kitsch quaintness, in contrast to the area's other hotels, and a staff that is strong on southern hospitality. *9861 International Dr., Orlando 32819, tel. 407/ 352–0008 or in FL 800/282–1890 or outside FL 800/447–1890. 150 rooms. AE, CB, DC, MC, V. Moderate.*

Radisson Inn and Justus Aquatic Center. If you want to get in shape while visiting Orlando but want to avoid fancy resort prices, this is the place for you. Radisson is a big, modern, moderately priced hotel offering comfortable rooms (the best ones face the pool), but what makes it truly special are its outstanding athletic facilities. The hotel has a fine outdoor pool, but for those who are serious about swimming, there is also an indoor Aquatic Center with an Olympic-size swimming and diving pool. The center was built for competitive swimming and diving events and has a high-tech Human Performance Lab for personal health assessment. Other hotel facilities include a complete Nautilus center with weights and aerobicycles; tennis, raquetball, and handball courts; a jogging track; aerobics and swimmercise classes; and plenty more, including access to a local country club for golf. *8444 International Dr., Orlando 32819, tel. 407/345–0505 or 800/752–0003. 300 rooms. AE, CB, DC, MC, V. Moderate.*

U.S. 192 Area If you are looking for anything remotely quaint, charming, or sophisticated, head elsewhere. The U.S. 192 strip, formally called Irlo Bronson Memorial Highway and referred to as the Spacecoast Parkway, is generally known as Kissimmee, but whatever you call it, it is an avenue crammed with bargain-basement motels and hotels, inexpensive restaurants, fast-food chains, nickel-and-dime attractions, gas stations, and minimarts. If all you are looking for is a decent room with perhaps a few extras for a manageable price, this is your wonderland. The number of motels here is mind boggling. It is a buyer's market, and room rates start as low as $20 a night—or lower if it is the right time of year and you can cut the right deal. But most rooms will run about $30–$70 a night, depending on the hotel's facilities and its proximity to Disney World. Among the chain hotels are Travelodge, Econolodge, Comfort Inn, Holiday Inn, Radisson, Sheraton, and Best Western.

The Residence Inn. Of the all-suite hotels on U.S. 192, this one is probably the best. It consists of a row of four-unit town houses with private stairway entrances to each suite. One side of the unit faces the highway, the other overlooks an attractive lake, where visitors can sail, waterski, jet ski, and fish. Forty of the units are penthouses, with complete kitchens, small living rooms, loft bedrooms, and even fireplaces. The other units are set up like studio apartments, but they still contain full kitchens and fireplaces. Regular studio suites accommodate two people; double suites accommodate up to four. Both Continental breakfast and a grocery shopping service are complimentary. The price may seem expensive, considering the location, but there is no charge for additional guests, so you can squeeze in the whole family at no extra cost. *4786 W. Irlo Bronson Memorial Hwy., Kissimmee 32741, tel. 407/396–2056 or 800/468–3027. 160 units. AE, CB, DC, MC, V. Moderate–Expensive.*

Radisson Inn Maingate. This is one of the newest hotels on the strip, located just a few minutes from the Magic Kingdom's front door. It is a very sleek, modern building with cheerful guest rooms, large bathrooms, and plenty of extras for the price. Facilities include a swimming pool, a whirlpool, a few tennis courts, and a jogging trail. Not fancy, but sufficient. The best rooms are those with a view of the pool. One floor is reserved for nonsmokers. *7501 W. Irlo Bronson Memorial Hwy., Kissimmee 32741, tel. 407/396–1400 or 800/333–3333. 580 rooms. AE, CB, DC, MC, V. Moderate.*

★ **Casa Rosa Inn.** For simple motel living—no screaming kids or loud music, please—this is your place. The pink, Spanish-style motel does not have much in the way of facilities other than a little swimming pool and free in-room movies, but it is a good, serviceable place to hang your hat. *4600 W. Irlo Bronson Memorial Hwy., Kissimmee 32741, tel. 407/396–2020 or 800/874–1589. 50 rooms. AE, MC, V. Inexpensive.*

Off the Beaten Track Mention should be made of two hotels that are off the beaten track—close enough to be part of the immediate Orlando area, but not so close that they fit into one of our categories.

Winter Park
★ **Park Plaza Hotel.** Located in Orlando's very posh, established suburb of Winter Park, the Park Plaza is an old-fashioned, wood-and-wicker Southern hotel, built in 1922. If you are in need of recreational facilities or special amenities, look elsewhere, but if you are hoping to find real Southern charm and hospitality, this is perhaps the best place in the Orlando area to find it. You are as far from the world of tourism as you can get and still be within a short driving distance of all the major attractions. It is a small, intimate hotel that gives you the feeling that you are a guest in somebody's home. All rooms open up onto one long balcony, covered with ferns, flowers, and wicker furniture. *307 Park Ave. S, Winter Park 32789, tel. 407/647–1072 or 800/228–7220. To get there, drive east on I–4 and exit at Fairbanks Ave. Turn right for 1 mi until you reach Park Ave. The hotel is on your left. 27 rooms. AE, CB, DC, MC, V. Moderate–Expensive.*

Lake Wales **Chalet Suzanne.** You'll find this conversation piece of a hotel in orange-grove territory, in what seems the middle of nowhere. A homemade billboard directs you down a country road that turns into a palm-lined drive. Cobblestone paths lead to a row of chalet-style houses and cabins, complete with balconies and thatched roofing. The Chalet Suzanne has been built bit by unlikely bit over the years, and the furnishings range from the rare and valuable to the garage-sale special. Bathrooms are tiled and have old-fashioned tubs, and wash basins. The most charming rooms face the lake. *U.S. Highway 27S, Drawer AC, Lake Wales 33859, tel. 813/676–6011. To get there, either land your Cessna or Lear jet on their private airstrip, or drive. Go west on I–4 from Orlando to the Rte. 27 exit and head toward*

Cypress Gardens. The Chalet's billboard is past the Cypress Gardens turnoff, just after Lake Wales. 30 rooms. AE, CB, DC, MC, V. Moderate–Expensive.

Nightlife

Walt Disney World Dinner Shows

Top of the World. This is Disney's sophisticated nighttime entertainment spot, located on the top floor of the Contemporary Resort. A spirited show called "Broadway at the Top" runs for about an hour after the two nightly seatings for dinner. A cast of high-energy dancers and singers bring to life some of Broadway's greatest hits. A single price includes the show and dinner. Tax, gratuity, and alcoholic drinks are extra. *Contemporary Resort, tel. 407/W–DISNEY. Reservations necessary months in advance. Jackets required. Admission: $40 adults, $15 children 3–11. Seatings at 6 and 9:15.*

Polynesian Revue and Mickey's Tropical Revue. Put on some comfortable, casual clothes and head over to the Polynesian Village Resort for an outdoor barbecue and a tropical luau, complete with fire jugglers and hula drum dancers. It's a colorful, South Pacific setting and an easygoing evening that families find relaxing and trouble free. There are two shows nightly of the Polynesian Revue and an earlier show for children called Mickey's Tropical Revue, where Disney characters perform decked out in costumes befitting these South Seas surroundings. *Polynesian Village Resort, tel. 407/W–DISNEY. Dress: casual. Reservations necessary, usually months in advance. Polynesian Review: $28 adults, $23 juniors 12–20, and $15 children 3–11. Seatings at 6:45 and 9:30. Mickey's Tropical Revue: adults $24.50, juniors $19.50, children $11. Seating at 4:30.*

Hoop-Dee-Doo Revue. This family entertainment dinner show may be corny, but it is also the liveliest and most rollicking. A troupe of jokers called the Pioneer Hall Players stomp their feet, wisecrack, and make merry in this Western mess-hall setting. The chow consists of barbecued ribs, fried chicken, corn on the cob, strawberry shortcake, and all the fixins. There are three shows nightly at Pioneer Hall in the Fort Wilderness area —not the easiest place to get to. *Fort Wilderness Resort, tel. 407/W–DISNEY. Dress: informal. Reservations necessary, sometimes months in advance. Admission: $29 adults, $23 juniors 12–20, $15 children 3–11. Seatings at 5, 7:30, and 10 PM.*

Pleasure Island. There is a single admission charge to this nightlife entertainment complex, which features a comedy club, teenage dance center, rock-and-roller skating-rink disco, numerous restaurants, lounges, shops, and even a 10-screen theater complex. Six themed nightclubs offer everything from swinging jazz to foot-stompin' country and western to the latest pop video hits.

Laser Show. You won't want to miss Epcot Center's grand finale, a laser show that takes place along the shores of the World Showcase lagoon, every night just before Epcot closes. It is a show unlike any other. In the middle of the lagoon, laser projections of dancing images move across screens of spraying water. Orchestral music fills the air as multicolored neon lasers streak across the sky, pulsating to the rhythms of the music. Suddenly the night lights up with brilliant fireworks and the lagoon vibrates with the sounds of Tchaikovsky's 1812 Overture. Projections of the Earth's continents transform Spaceship

Earth into a luminescent, spinning globe. The lasers used to create these images are powerful enough to project an identical image on a golf ball up to five miles away. The projections are called Illuminations, and one of them creates a towering Mt. Fuji over the Japan pavilion. When the show is over, the crowds exit as Spaceship Earth continues to revolve. It is a stellar performance that you won't want to miss.

The Orlando Area Until a few years ago Orlando's nightlife was more like that of Oskaloosa, Iowa, than of a booming tourist haven. But slowly, an after-dark scene has developed, spreading farther and farther beyond the realm of Disney. Orlando entrepreneurs have now caught on that there is a fortune to be had by satisfying the fun-hungry night owls that flock to this city. New night spots open constantly, offering everything from flashy discos to ballroom dancing, country-and-western saloons, Broadway dinner theaters, and even medieval jousting tournaments.

The Arts If all the fantasyland hype starts to wear thin, and you feel the need for more sophisticated entertainment, check out the local fine arts scene in the "Happenings" and "Calendar" sections of *Orlando Magazine*, or *Center Stage*, available at any newsstand. The average price of a ticket to performing arts events in the Orlando area rarely exceeds $10–$12 and is often half that price.

Orlando has an active performing arts agenda of ballet, modern dance, classical music, opera, and theater, much of which takes place at the **Carr Performing Arts Centre** (401 Livingston St., Orlando, tel. 407/896–7365). This community auditorium presents a different play each month (Wed.–Sat., with Sun. matinees). The Broadway series features performances on the way to Broadway or current road shows.

During the school year, **Rollins College** (tel. 407/646–2233) in Winter Park has a choral and symphonic concert series that is open to the public and usually free. The first week of March, there is a **Bach Music Festival** (tel. 407/646–2182) that has been a Winter Park tradition for over 55 years. Also at the college is the **Annie Russell Theater** (tel. 407/646–2501), which has a regular series of productions.

Across the street from the Peabody Hotel on International Drive is the **Orange County Civic and Convention Center** (tel. 407/345–9898), which hosts many big-name performing artists.

Dinner Shows Dinner shows have become an immensely popular form of nighttime entertainment around Orlando. A set price usually buys a multiple-course dinner and a theatrical production—a totally escapist experience. The food tends to be predictable—but not the major attractions. Always make reservations in advance, especially on weekends. A lively crowd can be an asset; a show playing to a small audience can be a pathetic and embarrassing sight. What the shows lack in substance and depth, the audience makes up for in color and enthusiasm. The result is an evening of light entertainment, which kids in particular will enjoy.

Mardi Gras. This jazzy, New Orleans–style show is the best of Orlando's dinner attractions. The set menu consists of mixed vegetable soup, tossed salad, buckets of fried chicken, platters of roast beef, apple pie with ice cream, and all the beer, wine, or soda you can drink. It is not an elaborate meal, but it is as good as one can expect from a dinner theater. A New Orleans jazz band plays during dinner, followed by a one-hour cabaret with colorful song-and-dance routines to rhythms of the Caribbean, Latin America, and Dixieland jazz. Although the kids are more likely to vote for the Wild West or medieval shows, adults tend to prefer Mardi Gras because it is more of a restaurant night-club than a fantasyland. *At the Mercado Shopping Village, 8445 International Dr., Orlando, tel. 407/351–5151 or 800/641–5151. Dress: casual. Reservations necessary. AE, CB, DC, MC, V. Admission: $23.95 adults, $15.95 children 3–11.*

Fort Liberty. Run by the same company that operates Mardi Gras and King Henry's Feast, this dinner show whisks you out to the Wild West. The entertainment is a mixed bag of real Indian dances, foot-stompin' sing-alongs, and acrobatics. A British cowboy shows what he can do with bullwhips and lassos, and a musician plays the 1812 Overture on the tuba and "America the Beautiful" on an old saw (yes, the kind that cuts wood). The show is full of slapstick theatrics and country-western shindigging that children really enjoy. The chow is what you might expect to eat with John Wayne out on the prairie: beef soup, fried chicken, corn on the cob, and pork and beans. You are served by a rowdy chorus of cavalry recruits who keep the food coming and beverages freely pouring. All tables seat 12, so unless you are in a big party, expect to develop pass-the-ketchup relationships. Fort Liberty is a stockade filled with shops and stalls selling gifts and souvenirs with a Western theme. The ambience is set by the photographers snapping photos of visitors dressed in cowboy garb. Forever trying to attract tourists, the Fort Liberty entertainers perform in the courtyard during the day. If the kids are more intent on seeing Marlboro country than you are, go at lunch time (11–2), pick up some fast-food fried chicken for $2, and see many of the acts that are in the dinner show. *5260 Irlo Bronson Memorial Hwy. (U.S. 192), Kissimmee, tel. 407/351–5151 or 800/641–5151. Dress: casual. Reservations necessary. AE, CB, DC, MC, V. Admission: $23.95 adults, $15.95 children 3–11.*

King Henry's Feast. Driving along the strip of hotels and shopping malls on I–4 or International Drive, you may notice two Tudor-style buildings. One of them is the Econolodge; the other is the home of Orlando's King Henry VIII and his court of 16th-century jesters. The entertainment includes a corny but talented magician, a daring fire-swallowing acrobat, and much singing, dancing, and revelry as King Henry celebrates his birthday and begins his quest for his seventh bride. Saucy wenches, who refer to customers as "me lords" and "me ladies," serve potato-leek soup, salad, chicken and ribs, and all the beer, wine, and soft drinks you can guzzle. Bar drinks are extra. *8984 International Dr., Orlando, tel. 407/351–5151 or 800/641–5151. Dress: casual. Reservations necessary. AE, CB, DC, MC, V. Admission: $23.95 adults, $15.95 children 3–11.*

Medieval Times. In a huge, modern-medieval manor, visitors enjoy a four-course dinner while watching the struggle of good and evil in a tournament of games, sword fights, and jousting matches, including no less than 30 charging horses and a cast of 75 knights, nobles, and maidens. Sound silly? It is. Yet if you view it through the eyes of your children, this two-hour extravaganza of pageantry and meat-and-potatoes banquet fare can be amusing. Everyone faces forward along narrow banquet tables that are stepped auditorium-style above the tournament. If you and your family traveled the amusement-park route all day and are tired of looking and nagging at each other, you may get some respite, a bit of comic relief, and some vicarious pleasure from a night of crossing lances. $25 per person. *4510 W. Irlo Bronson Memorial Hwy. (U.S. 192), Kissimmee, tel. 407/239–0214 or 407/396–1518, in FL 800/432–0768, outside FL 800/327–4024. Dress: informal. Reservations necessary. AE, MC, V.*

Bavarian Schnitzel House. If you have any interest in German food, this fun-loving place serves the area's finest. The Red Baron would feel right at home in this kitschy Bavarian world, which none of the rowdy revelers seems to mind. The entertainment is a five-piece oompah band that shakes, rattles, and groans at its own corny jokes. They do a good job of getting the audience to sing, dance, and laugh the night away. Go on a crowded weekend night; if you're going to succumb, you may as well go all the way. There is no cover charge for the entertainment, and dinner is à la carte. Meals are hearty and not expensive. Goulash soup, Wiener schnitzel, and a few steins of German beer ought to set you up for a jovial evening. *6159 Westwood Blvd. (just off International Dr.), Orlando, tel. 407/352–8484. Dress: casual. Reservations suggested. AE, CB, DC, MC, V. Inexpensive–Moderate.*

Mark Two. This is the only true dinner theater in Orlando, with full Broadway musicals, such as *Oklahoma!*, *My Fair Lady*, *West Side Story* and *South Pacific*, staged through most of the year. During the Christmas holiday season, shorter Broadway musical revues are presented. A buffet and full-service cocktail bar open for business 90 minutes before the show. The food is nothing to write home about and should not be the reason to pay a visit. The buffet of seafood Newburg, baked whitefish, a variety of meats, and salad bar is only a few notches above cafeteria food. Best bets are the rich desserts that arrive during intermission. The shows are directed by the theater's owner, and the sets, costumes, music, and choreography are all done in-house. The actors are mostly from the Orlando area. It will not be the best performance you will ever see, but it can be a pleasure to hear the scores and see the routines of a favorite old musical while you sit comfortably at your table with a drink in hand. The cost of the show includes your meal. The buffet is served from 6:30 to 7:30. The performance starts at 8. *Edgewater Center, 3376 Edgewater Dr., Orlando (from I–4, take Exit 44 and go west), tel. 407/843–6275. Dress: casual. Reservations suggested. AE, MC, V. Closed Mon. Moderate.*

Church Street Station This downtown Orlando attraction is a complete entertainment experience. Widely popular among both tourists and locals, it single-handedly began Orlando's metamorphosis from a sleepy town to the nighttime hot spot it now boasts to be and is on its way to becoming. Unlike much of what you see in Walt Disney World, this place doesn't just look authentic—it *is* authentic. The train on the tracks is an actual 19th-century steam engine, and the whistling calliope was especially rebuilt to blow its original tunes. The buildings have been completely redecorated with collectibles and memorabilia from around the country. You can spend an evening in part of the complex, or you can wander from area to area, soaking up the peculiar characteristics of each. For a single admission price of $10, you're permitted to wander freely, stay as long as you wish, and do what you want, whether it's drinking, dancing, dining, or people-watching. Food and drink cost extra and are not cheap, but they add to the fun. Parts of the complex are open during the day, but the place is usually quiet then; the pace picks up at night, especially on weekends, with crowds thickets 10–11. *129 W. Church St., Orlando, tel. 305/422-2434. Reservations not necessary. Dress: casual. AE, MC, V.*

Rosie O'Grady's. This is a turn-of-the-century saloon with dark wood, brass trim, a full Dixieland band blaring out of a gazebo, and countertop cancan dancers, tap dancers, and vaudeville singers. Is this a set for *The Music Man* or an evening at the Moulin Rouge? It's difficult to tell at first. The 90-minute shows begin at 7 or 7:30 PM. The last show starts at 11:45. Multidecker sandwiches and hot dogs are sold in the Gay 90s Sandwich Parlour 4:30–11 PM.

Apple Annie's Courtyard. This is a relatively quiet nook that features continuous live folk and bluegrass music from about 8 PM to 2 AM. It's a good place to rest your feet, have a drink, and people-watch. Salads, fruit platters, and exotic drinks are served 11 AM–2 AM.

Lili Marlene's Aviator Pub. Here you have a relaxed, wood-paneled English-pub atmosphere and the finest dining on Church Street. Food is hearty, upscale, and very American—mostly steaks, ribs, and seafood. Prices are not cheap. The walls have biplane-era memorabilia, and a large-scale model aircraft hangs from the ceiling. Open for lunch and dinner until midnight.

Phileas Phogg's Balloon Works. This is a very popular disco filled with young singles over age 21 and a sprinkling of old-timers showing off their moves on the dance floor. It is a good-looking yuppie tourist crowd, leavened with locals. Contemporary dance tunes are played on a sound system that will blow your socks off. The place is jammed by midnight and open until 2 AM. Much of the young crowd feels it is worth the price of admission into the Church Street Station just to be able to come here.

Orchid Garden. Decorative lamps, iron latticework, arched ceilings, and stained-glass windows create a striking Victorian arcade where visitors sit, drink, and listen to first-rate bands pounding out popular tunes from the 1950s to the '80s. Open until 2 AM.

Cracker's Raw Bar. Located behind the Orchid Garden, Cracker's is a good place to get a quick gumbo or chowder and slam down a few oysters with a beer chaser. Open until midnight.

Cheyenne Saloon. This is the biggest, fanciest, rootin'-tootin' saloon you may ever see. The former triple-level opera house is covered with moose racks, steer horns, buffalo heads, and Remington rifles; a seven-piece country-and-western band darn near brings the house down. This is a fun crowd to watch, with all the pickin', strummin', fiddlin', hollerin', and do-see-doin'. Make sure you come equipped with your best stompin' shoes, cowboy hat, and catcalls. An upstairs restaurant serves chicken-and-ribs saloon fare. The shows start at 7:30 PM, 11 PM, and 12:45 AM.

Church Street Exchange. The newest addition to the complex, near Church Street Station, is a razzle-dazzle marketplace filled with all sorts of specialty shops and old-fashioned theme restaurants.

Bars and Clubs The bars and nightclubs have been divided into two sections. The first covers the tourist hotel districts in the Disney area, including Kissimmee, Lake Buena Vista, and International Drive. These places are usually filled with visitors to Disney

World. The other section covers the city of Orlando and Winter Park, both of which cater to a more local crowd. Remember that clubs on Disney property are allowed to stay open later than are bars elsewhere, and many of them don't have last call until 2:45 AM.

Disney Area **Little Darlin's Rock n' Roll Palace.** Shake, rattle, and roll the night away in this 1950s and '60s nostalgia nightclub. The interior looks like an opera house, with an orchestra-pit dance floor and a huge bandstand stage featuring famous old rock bands that still tour, such as The Drifters, Platters, and Bo Diddley. The crowd is a mix of young and old, singles and couples. The club features a very talented house band that serves up live music seven nights a week. The menu is vintage '50s: Philly hot dogs, cheese-steak sandwiches, banana splits, and, for some strange reason, escargots. *Old Town, 5770 Spacecoast Pkwy., Kissimmee 32741, tel. 407/396–6499. Dress: casual. AE, MC, V. Admission: $6.95 adults, $3.50 children under 8.*

Giraffe Lounge. Located inside the Hotel Royal Plaza, Lake Buena Vista (World Village), this flashy disco with spinning, colored lights is usually densely packed on weekends. It is a small place, and classy it ain't, but there's a lot going on, including live bands five nights a week. Happy hour runs daily 4–9:30 PM. Music plays and the bartender pours until 3 AM. *Hotel Royal Plaza, Walt Disney World Village, Lake Buena Vista, tel. 407/ 828–2828. Dress: casual. AE, CB, DC, MC, V. Open 4 PM–3 AM. No cover.*

The Laughing Kookaburra. A big hotel disco with live band music nightly and a serious singles crowd of all ages. The music is loud and the dance floor can get very crowded—a plus for some, a minus for others. The bar serves up 99 brands of beer, plus cocktails. Happy hour with free bar food runs daily 4–8 PM. The band plays six nights a week (off Mon.). *Buena Vista Palace Hotel, Walt Disney World Village, Lake Buena Vista, tel. 407/ 827–2727. Dress: casual. AE, CB, DC, MC, V. Open 4 PM–3 AM. No cover.*

La Cantina. This little bar in the Hotel Royal Plaza has guitar music seven nights a week and a happy hour, Sunday– Thursday, from midnight to 3 AM(!) It's a good thing most visitors are hotel guests—it's hard to get in an accident in an elevator! *Hotel Royal Plaza, tel. 407/828–2828. Open 11 AM– 3 AM.*

Top of the Tower. Listen to a comedian tell jokes and play country and rock-and-roll classics on the guitar while you check out a tremendous view of Disney World. A very comfy hotel bar with a nice tame bunch of people. *Viscount Hotel, tel. 407/828– 2424. Dress: casual. Open 8:30 PM–3 AM. No cover charge.*

Bennigan's. A young singles' spot that draws crowds in the early evening and during happy hours, from 4–7 PM and 11 PM–2 AM. It caters mostly to nontourists who work in the area. Food is served almost until closing. *6324 International Dr., Orlando, tel. 407/351–4436. Open 11 AM–2 AM.*

Orlando Area The nightclubs in Orlando have significantly more character than those in the Disney hotel area. If you have the energy to get in your car, you will probably find these spots more satisfying and less touristy—if you can find them.

J.J. Whispers. A classy, brassy singles crowd flocks to this trendy disco, which tries hard to maintain an image of cosmopolitan class. Expect to mingle with fashion-conscious locals in their tastefully outrageous attire. The club is equally popular with the over-30 set, who listen to music from the 1940s, '50s, and '60s in the Showroom. The young people do what young people do in a massive, multilevel, state-of-the-art disco. J.J.'s has one restaurant serving bar-food fare, and another, a deli, that is open for lunch. It sometimes features comedians, magicians, and other stage acts. Live entertainment (Tues.–Sun., 8 PM–2 AM) includes all-male and all-female revues and live bands. *5100 Adanson St., Orlando 32804, tel. 407/629–4779. To get there, take I–4 to the Lee Rd. exit and go west for about half a mile on Lee Rd. Watch for a sharp left-hand turn at Adanson St. J.J.'s is located at the end of the Lee Rd. Shopping Center. Dress: tasteful but outrageous—or just a jacket. AE, MC, V. Cover charge: $2 and up.*

Cheek-to-Cheek. Monday nights are a big deal here because of the many big-name performers—mostly contemporary jazz musicians in the Class Act Lounge, and rock and reggae in Cheek-to-Cheek. Past performers have included Al Stewart, Wynton Marsalis, Rita Coolidge, and even Tommy Dorsey. The place can get very crowded; tables are crammed so close together that you will become fast friends, or enemies, with your neighbors. Other nights of the week (Tues.–Sat.) are very popular with the 35–50-year-old crowd, who dance to Top 40s music played by Cheek-to-Cheek's house band. *839 N. Orlando Ave. (U.S. 17–92), tel. 407/644–2060. Open 8 PM–2 AM. Mon. cover charge up to $20. Tues.–Sat. cover charge $4. Closed some Sun.*

Crocodile Club. This bar, inside a restaurant called Bailey's in Winter Park, collects a young, well-dressed college crowd from neighboring Rollins College. The atmosphere is more sophisticated and yuppified than most Orlando bars. Expect to hear Motown and dance to pop. *Bailey's Restaurant, 118 W. Fairbanks Ave., Winter Park, tel. 407/647–8501.*

Sullivan's Trailways Lounge. A very popular place with much right-friendly charm, where people of all ages and many families come to strut their stuff on the largest dance floor in Florida. Even Yankees are welcome in this Southern country-and-western dance hall. Big name performers entertain on occasion; local bands play nightly, except Sunday. *1108 S. Orange Blossom Trail (U.S. 441), tel. 407/843–2934. Bands play 9 PM–2 AM. Cover charge: $2 and up.*

9 Central Florida

Introduction

by April Athey

Thick hardwood and pine wilderness, grassy rolling hills, spring-fed rivers, and hundreds of crystal-clear lakes are sandwiched here between the Gulf of Mexico wetlands and the beaches of Florida's mid-Atlantic coast. At least three distinct geographic areas are contained in this 60-mile-wide swath just north of Orlando that extends about 100 miles across the peninsula from coast to coast.

The Gulf of Mexico area lies west of I-75 between Crystal River and Weeki Wachee, a year-round manatee (sea cow) refuge.

The Daytona Beach area lies to the east (between I-95 and the Atlantic Ocean, from Ormond Beach to Melbourne) and includes the Kennedy Space Center. The area north of Orlando, between I-75 and U.S. 17/92, includes Ocala's horse farms, Marjorie Rawlings's Cross Creek country, and the St. Johns River.

Getting Around

By Plane
Tampa International Airport is nearest the first of our regions, west of Orlando (*see* Getting Around the Southwest Coast). One-way limousine service for two from the airport to the Homosassa Springs area runs $40–$48 and requires advance reservations. You can call *Friendship Limousine* (tel. 904/746–5233) or *Aire-Dale Limo Service* (tel. 904/628–7820). Orlando International Airport and Gainesville Regional provide service into the region north of Orlando. Limousine rates from either airport to Ocala run $45–$65. *Embassy Limo* (tel. 904/373–3280) and *Airport Passenger Express (tel. 904/622–2292)* are two available fleets. *Daytona/Orlando Transit Service* charges $18 per person one-way for its airport shuttle to the region east of Orlando (tel. 800/231–1965 in FL or 800/223–1965 in the rest of the USA).

By Car
U.S. 19/98 is the primary north-south route following the west coast; I-75 and U.S. 27 are the primary north-south routes through the center of the region; I-95, U.S. 1 and A1A are the primary north-south routes near the east coast; east-west routes, listed from north to south, include Rtes. 40, 42, 44, 46, and 50. It's useful to remember that most of the east-coast beaches are found on a series of barrier islands strung together by Rte. A1A.

By Train
Amtrak (tel. 800/USA–RAIL) serves Ocala, DeLand (near Daytona Beach), and Sanford.

By Bus
Greyhound/Trailways has stations in Crystal River (200 N.E. Hwy. 19, tel. 904/795–4445), Homosassa Springs (8666 W. Halls River Rd., tel. 904/628–4844), Brooksville (512 W. Broad St., tel. 904/796–3068), Ocala (512 N. Magnolia Ave., tel. 904/732–2677), DeLand (224 E. Ohio Ave., tel. 904/734–2747), Daytona Beach (910 Volusia Ave., tel. 904/253–5676), New Symrna Beach (502 N. Orange St., tel. 904/428–8211), Titusville (20 N. Washington Ave., tel. 407/267–8760), Cocoa Beach (302 Main St., tel. 407/636–6531), and Melbourne (460 S. Harbor City Blvd., tel. 407/723–4323).

Scenic Drives

Route 46 Views of natural Florida wilderness, marked by the distinctive clumps of cabbage palms that look like islands floating in a sea of waving marsh grasses, spread out in every direction along this route between U.S. 1 and Sanford.

Riverside Drive New Symrna Beach's grand old homes line the Intracoastal Waterway along this route, also a popular bicycle path.

Tropical Drive From the skinny southern tip of Merritt Island, which lies between the Indian and Bananna rivers south of Cocoa Beach, drive north past the foliage-shrouded waterfront homesteads for a look at tropical island living, Florida style.

Guided Tours

Bay Point Dive Center (Crystal River, tel. 904/563–1040) conducts hour-long guided boat tours of Kings Bay for viewing manatees. Cost: $10 per person (two-person minimum). The center also conducts guided scuba diving tours for viewing manatees underwater. Cost: $25 per person (two-person minimum).

Talley's Pro Dive (Crystal River, tel. 904/795–2776) conducts day-long guided diving tours, including snorkeling with manatees in Crystal River (Nov.–Mar.) and drift diving in the Rainbow River. Cost: $15 per person (two-person minimum).

Florida Thoroughbred Breeders' Association (tel. 904/629–2160) has opened the doors of horse farms throughout Ocala. Each day of the week a different farm is open for guided tours. Brochures are available from the association or the local chamber of commerce. Visitors are advised to call the farm in advance.

Weekend Safaris (tel. 904/867–7643) conducts guided tours via horseback, canoe, or a combination thereof through the wilderness areas bordering Ocala National Forest. Also available are overnight excursions that include stays at a country inn or under the stars. Trailside gourmet dining and hot-air balloon rides are optional.

Capt. Tom's Complete River Tours (tel. 904/236–0872) acquaint visitors with the rivers on which steamboats cruised in the 1800s. You can choose a three-, four-, or eight-hour river cruise on the Okalawaha and Silver rivers. Rates: $10–$24 per person. Two- and three-day trips with hotel accommodations along the route also are available. Cruises are by reservation only.

Gray Lines of Daytona Beach (tel. 904/761–6506) conducts sightseeing tours of Central Florida attractions: Disney-Epcot, Sea World, Cypress Gardens, and NASA Kennedy Space Center's Spaceport USA. Rates include round-trip transportation and admission.

Important Addresses and Numbers

Tourist Information Crystal River Chamber of Commerce (28 N. Highway 19, Crystal River, tel. 904/795–3149). Open weekdays, 9–4. **Homosassa Springs Chamber of Commerce** (N. Highway 19, Homosassa Springs, tel. 904/628–2666). Open weekdays 9–4. **Hernando County Chamber of Commerce** (101 E. Fort Dade Ave., Brooksville, tel. 904/796–2420). Open weekdays 9–5. **Ocala/**

Marion County Chamber of Commerce (Fort King Ave. and Broadway, Ocala, tel. 904/629–8051). Open weekdays 8:30–5. **DeLand Area Chamber of Commerce** (336 N. Woodland Blvd., DeLand, tel. 904/734–4331). Open weekdays 8:30–5. **Greater Sanford Chamber of Commerce** (400 E. First St., Sanford, tel. 407/322–2212). Open weekdays 9–5. **Destination Daytona** (126 E. Orange Ave., Daytona Beach, tel. 800/854–1234). Open weekdays 9–5; takes calls weekends 10–3. **New Symrna Beach Chamber of Commerce** (115 Canal St., New Symrna Beach, tel. 904/428–2449). Open weekdays 8:30–5. **Cocoa Beach Chamber of Commerce** (400 Fortenberry Rd., Merritt Island, tel. 407/452–4390). Open weekdays 8:30–5. **South Brevard Chamber of Commerce** (1005 E. Strawbridge Ave., Melbourne, tel. 407/724–5400). Open weekdays 9–5.

Emergencies Dial 911 for **police** or **ambulance** assistance.

Seven Rivers Community Hospital (6201 N. Suncoast Blvd., Crystal River, tel. 800/5–ACCESS). **Munroe Regional Medical Center** (131 S.W. 15th St., Ocala, tel. 904/351–7200 or 904/867–13 MD). **Halifax Medical Center** (303 N. Clyde Morris Blvd., Daytona Beach, tel. 904/254–4100). **Cape Canaveral Hospital** (on the 520 Causeway between Cocoa Beach and Merritt Island, tel. 407/799–7150).

Pharmacies **Wal-Mart Discount Pharmacies** are open daily in Homosassa Springs (tel. 904/628–4334), Ocala (tel. 904/237–7103), New Symrna Beach (tel. 904/427–6030), Cocoa Beach (tel. 407/452–4340), and Melbourne (tel. 407/773–0663).

Exploring Central Florida

Numbers in the margin correspond with points of interest on the Central Florida map.

The Gulf of Mexico Area

Touring the tropical wilderness and wetlands between Crystal River and Weeki Wachee will make one thing perfectly clear—this is manatee (sea cow) country. These shy vegetarian mammals, which early explorers mistook for mermaids when they rose from the water, once were plentiful. But their number has dwindled to less than 1,000, putting them on the state's endangered-species list. The spring-fed rivers and sheltered bays of the area are virtually a year-round sanctuary for them, and locals are taking advantage of the rising attention these creatures bring.

Whether your embarkation point is Tampa or Orlando, a good place to begin your tour is **Weeki Wachee,** with its spring of performing "mermaids." If sitting in a cool dark underground theater watching through thick glass as girls in mermaid suits perform underwater tricks (like peeling and eating a banana) doesn't interest you, the natural wilderness and wildlife at the attraction will. The jungle-boat cruise down the crystal-clear Weeki Wachee River is great for wildlife photography. Whatever you see peering back at you from the water or the trees is real. The "Birds of Prey" show makes you wonder if an eagle wouldn't make a fine pet, and the Animal Forest petting zoo is popular with children. *U.S. 19 South and Rte. 50, Weeki*

Wachee, tel. 904/596–2062. Admission: $10.95 adults, $6.95 children 3–11. Open daily 9–6.

On a hot day, the tower slides and natural springwater pools at Weeki Wachee's **Buccaneer Bay** are appealing. *U.S. 19 South and Rte. 50, Weeki Wachee, tel. 904/596–2062. Admission: $6.95 adults, $5.95 children 3–11. Open late Mar.–early Sept., 10–5.*

2 For a leisurely side trip, head east on Rte. 50 to **Brooksville** (*see* Off the Beaten Track). Farther north on U.S. 19 is **Chassahowitzka National Wildlife Refuge,** a 30,500-acre estuarine habitat that is home to bald eagles, manatees, marine turtles, and peregrine falcons. The refuge is accessible only by boat, and rentals are available at **Lyke's Chassahowitzka River Campground** (tel. 904/382–2200).

The closer you get to the town of Homosassa Springs, the heavier the traffic on U.S. 19 becomes. At the Hall's River Road traffic light, you'll see a large brown-and-white sign pointing
3 the way to **Homosassa Springs Nature World.** Turn left at the light (Rte. 490–A), then left again on Fish Bowl Drive. This narrow road winds through a tropical landscape to an attraction that hasn't changed much since it opened in the 1940s. Focal point is the giant Fish Bowl Spring, in which a 168-ton floating underwater observatory allows close-up views of the fresh- and saltwater fish that congregate at the spring. Other residents of the spring and adjacent lagoons are manatees, otters, alligators, and a 4,000-pound hippo named Lucifer. A nature trail threads through the wilderness surrounding the spring, where a variety of birds and small animals roam freely. From the boat docks on Fish Bowl Drive (across from the main entrance) a cruise on the tropical Homosassa River departs every half hour. *1 mi west of traffic light on U.S. 19, Homosassa Springs, tel. 904/628–2311. Admission: $6.95 adults, $3.95 children 3–11; 20% AARP discount with current card if presented prior to purchasing ticket. Open daily 9–5:30.*

Beyond the attraction, Fish Bowl Drive passes the historic **Yulee Sugar Mill Ruins** and an assortment of backwoods residences before it dead-ends at the Homosassa River, where fishing devotees frequent **The Riverside Villas and Yardarm Restaurant.** Across the river, you'll see a turn-of-the-century white-frame "Old Florida" homestead, **K.C. Crump's on the River** (*see* Dining).

To complete your tour of the Gulf Coast area, visit **Crystal River,** site of the Kings Bay manatee sanctuary (a holding of the Florida Nature Conservancy), and tiny **Yankeetown,** just north. Everywhere you look you'll see the distinctive red-and-white diver's flag. Diving with manatees is all the rage these days. But look, don't touch. Annoying a sea cow is against the law.

North of Orlando to Ocala

4 Dominated by **Ocala National Forest**— known to locals as the Big Scrub—this region is characterized by crystal-clear lakes, spring-fed rivers, thick hardwood forests, and grassy rolling hills that support more than 400 Thoroughbred horse farms. History recalls the days when steamboats cruised the region's St. Johns, Oklawaha, and Silver rivers. This is the Florida

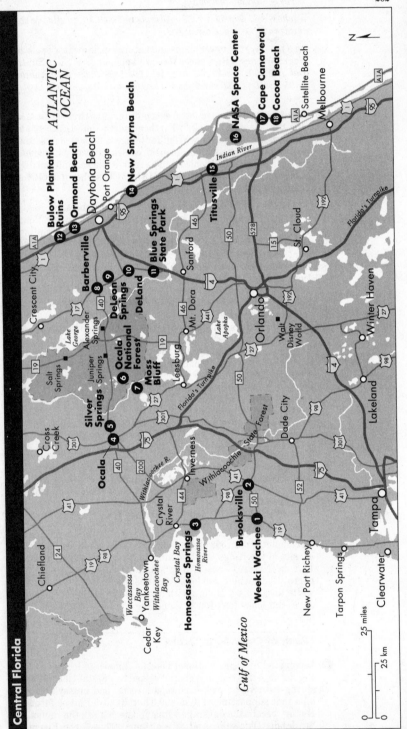

about which Marjorie K. Rawlings wrote so fondly, and it's the home of famed Silver Springs.

For a tour through the heart of Ocala's **horse farm country,** take the southwest segment of Rte. 200 between Ocala and Inverness. Several of the well-manicured farms are open for guided tours on a rotating basis (*see* Guided Tours).

South of Rte. 200 on I-75, take Exit 67 to Rte. 484 and visit the **Don Garlits Museum of Drag Racing.** Garlits, who was born in Florida, founded the nonprofit museum in 1976 and opened it to the public in 1984. The museum traces the history of drag racing, from its beginnings at California's Dry Lakes in the '40s to the present. On display is an array of unusual vehicles used by Garlits and other drag-racing greats, along with a collection of early-model Fords. *13700 S.W. 16th Ave., Ocala, tel. 904/245-8661. Admission: $6 adults, $3 children 3-12. Open daily 10-5.*

North of Rte. 200 on I-75, take Exit 70 to U.S. 27 and travel west 3½ miles to the new **Golden Ocala Golf Course,** worth a visit because it replicates nine famous holes. Duffers have the opportunity to play St. Andrews's 1 (the first hole played in golfing history), Baltusrol's 4, Augusta's 12 and 16, and Royal Troon's 8, among others. *7300 U.S. Hwy. 27, Ocala, tel. 904/622-0198. Starting times reserved up to 3 days in advance.*

Farther north on I-75 are the turn-of-the-century towns of **McIntosh** and **Micanopy,** pleasant stops on the way to Marjorie Kinnan Rawlings's Cross Creek country (*see* Off the Beaten Track).

The main street of **Ocala** is Silver Springs Boulevard, reached by taking Exit 69 off I-75 to Rte. 40 and heading east. The center of town is at N.E. 8th Avenue and Silver Springs Boulevard, where you can find the Chamber of Commerce and a pleasant town square park. To view the city's historic district, drive east on Fort King Avenue (a few blocks south of Silver Springs Boulevard).

Time Out   **Peter Dinkel's,** on Silver Springs Blvd. (look for the weird horse-and-rider metal sculpture guarding a brown-trimmed white Victorian house), is a popular lunch spot. Try the fried grouper and homemade honey or cinnamon ice cream. *725 E. Silver Springs Blvd., Ocala, tel. 904/732-8003. AE, CB, DC, V.*

On the way to Silver Springs, stop at **The Appleton Museum of Art.** The palatial pink travertine marble museum houses the collection of Arthur Appleton, retired president of the Appleton Electric Co. of Chicago and owner of Bridlewood Farm, an Ocala Thoroughbred operation. Sterling-silver thrones from India, ancient oriental vases, Peruvian pottery, 12th-century Persian earthenware, and a sword presented by Napoleon to one of his soldiers are among the more than 6,000 works displayed. *Silver Springs Blvd., Ocala, tel. 904/236-5050. Admission: $3 adults, $2 students; under 12 free with adult. Open Tues.-Sat. 10-4:30, Sun. 1-5.*

❺ **Silver Springs,** the state's oldest attraction (established 1890), is a National Landmark that centers on the world's largest collection of artesian springs. Today, the park features wild animal displays, glass-bottom boat tours on the Silver River, a jungle cruise on the Fort King Waterway, an antique and classic car museum, and walks through natural habitats. A multimillion-dollar project is recapturing the look and atmosphere of the 1890s. Now under new ownership, the attraction promises visitors a journey to the wild kingdom above and below the water. *Rte. 40, 1 mi east of Ocala, tel. 904/236–2121. Admission to all attractions: $14.95 adults, $9.95 children 3– 11. Open daily.*

Next door is Silver Springs's **Wild Waters,** a water theme park with a giant wave pool and seven water-flume rides. *Admission: $8.95 adults, $7.95 children 3–11. Open late Mar.–June 7, 10–5; June 8–Sept. 7, 10–8.*

❻ Farther east on Rte. 40 is the entrance to **Ocala National Forest,** a 366,000-acre wilderness with lakes, springs, rivers, hiking trails, campgrounds, and historic sites. Area residents recall the filming of *The Yearling* at several sites within the forest. The **Visitor Information Center,** on the left just over the bridge (tel. 904/625–7470), is the site of old-fashioned sugarcane grinding and cane-syrup making during the first two weeks of November each year. The syrup is bottled and sold on the premises.

Lake Waldena Resort & Campground (tel. 904/625–2851), several miles farther east into the national forest on Rte. 40, features a white-sand bathing beach and crystal-clear freshwater lake. Noncampers pay day-use fees for picnicking and access to the beach.

❼ South of Rte. 40 (via Rte. 314-A) is **Moss Bluff,** on the Oklawaha River, which forms the southern boundary of Ocala National Forest. Make reservations ahead to enjoy a day-long cruise on the Oklawaha and Silver Run rivers aboard the *Osprey II,* a comfortable modern riverboat based at Moss Bluff. Cruises depart Tuesday–Thursday at 9:30 AM. Rate includes lunch. *Oklawaha & Silver Run River Boat Co., Box 1301, Oklawaha, tel. 904/288–2470.*

Three major recreational areas are found in the national forest: **Juniper Springs,** off Rte. 40, featuring a picturesque stone waterwheel house, campground, natural-spring swimming pool, and hiking and canoe trails; **Salt Springs,** off Rte. 40 (via Rte. 19 North), featuring a natural saltwater spring, where Atlantic blue crabs come to spawn each summer; and **Alexander Springs,** off Rte. 40 (via Rte. 445 South), featuring a swimming lake and campground.

❽ Just outside the eastern boundary of the forest, at the crossroads of Rte. 40 and U.S. 17, are **Barberville** and the **Pioneer Settlement for the Creative Arts, Inc.** A bridge house, moved from the St. Johns River at Astor, forms the entrance to the museum. On the grounds are an old-time caboose, a railroad depot, the commissary store of a turpentine camp, and a newly constructed "post-and-beam" barn, built of wood milled on the premises. During the first weekend in May and November each year, the museum hosts a Country Jamboree, which features arts, crafts, folk music, and country cooking. *U.S. 17 and Rte. 40, Barberville, tel. 904/749–2959. Admission: $2.50 adults, $1 children 3–12. Open weekdays 9–4.*

North of Barberville on U.S. 17 is another 1800s steamboat stop, **Crescent City,** where the historic **Sprague House Inn** (125

Central Ave., Crescent City, tel. 904/698–2430) traces steamboat-era history through the inn's collection of stained-glass windows. The three-room bed-and-breakfast inn also features a full-service restaurant.

⑨ South on U.S. 17 is **DeLeon Springs State Recreation Area,** promoted as a fountain of youth to 1889 winter tourists. Today, visitors come to picnic, swim, fish, and hike the nature trails. *DeLeon Springs, tel. 904/985–4212. Admission: $2 per driver, $1 per passenger. Open daily, 8 AM–sundown.*

South of DeLeon Springs, at the crossroads of U.S. 17 and Rte. **⑩** 44, is **DeLand,** another St. Johns River steamboat stop. Founded in 1876 by Henry Addison Deland of New York, the town was incorporated in 1882, and its academy (now Stetson University, Florida's oldest private university) was established in 1883.

A drive down the city's scenic main street (U.S. 17/Woodland Blvd.) will acquaint you with the residential-style campus of Stetson University, home of the **Gillespie Museum of Minerals.** The display of more than 25,000 specimens includes meteorites, fluorescent minerals, and Florida corals. *Michigan and Amelia Aves., DeLand, tel. 904/734–4121, ext. 603. Admission free. Open fall, winter, and spring sessions Mon.–Sat. 9–4; summer session Mon.–Fri. 9–4.*

The museum is one of the first points of interest on the Chamber of Commerce's self-guided scenic tour of DeLand. Copies of the map/brochure outlining the route may be obtained from the chamber's offices on Woodland Boulevard.

For a scenic tour of the St. Johns River and its special points of interest, travel west of town on Rte. 40 to Old New York Avenue and turn left; drive two miles, then take the first right onto Hontoon Road and follow it to the river. Here, you'll find **Three Buoys** (2280 Hontoon Rd., DeLand, tel. 904/736–9422), formerly Sunshine Line, offering a fleet of 46-foot luxury houseboats, each with sleeping quarters for four couples. The fully equipped "floating villas" may be chartered for between $40 and $60 per couple per day.

Hontoon Landing Marina (2317 River Ridge Rd., DeLand, tel. 904/734–2474) rents less-luxurious houseboats. The craft that sleeps 10 may be chartered for between $30 and $50 per couple per day.

⑪ Once a steamboat landing in the 1880s, what is now **Blue Spring State Park** is still a popular landing for explorers on the St. Johns River. Standing as a memorial to the golden age of steamboat travel is the restored 100-year-old **Thursby House,** which may be toured Thursday–Sunday, 11 AM–4 PM. The park also has boardwalks that meander through the thick forest and provide views of the springhead, where manatees congregate during the winter. Camping, hiking, fishing, and swimming also may be enjoyed here. *2100 W. French Ave., Orange City, tel. 904/775–3663. Open daily 8 AM–sundown.*

Daytona Beach Area

Some people refer to this 100-mile stretch of mid-Atlantic beachfront—from Ormond and Daytona Beach south to Melbourne and Sebastian Inlet—as "Orlando's beach." But it has always been more than that. Cape Canaveral was a place-name that cartographers rarely failed to include on the earliest maps of the New World. Today, it is known as the spaceport to the stars.

A good place to begin touring is along a segment of Old Dixie Highway. From I-95 north of Ormond Beach, take Exit 90 and travel east.

The first left off Old Dixie Highway (Kings Hwy.) will take you **⑫** to the entrance of **Bulow Plantation Ruins State Historic Site,** built in 1821. From the entrance, a winding dirt road cuts through tangled vegetation and leads to a picnic area and dayuse facilities facing Bulow Creek. All that remains of the plantation are the massive ruins of the sugar mill, which may be reached either by auto or bicycle along a one-way loop road, or on foot via a scenic walking trail from the picnic area. *Tel. 904/ 439–2219. Open daily 9–5.*

Continue southeast on Old Dixie Highway through a tunnel of vine-laced oaks and cabbage palms. Next stop is **Tomoka State Park,** site of a Timucuan Indian settlement discovered in 1605 by Spanish explorer Alvaro Mexia. Wooded campsites, bicycle and walking paths, and guided canoe tours on the Tomoka and Halifax rivers are the main attractions. *North Beach St., Ormond Beach, tel. 904/677–3931. Open daily 8 AM–sundown.*

Time moves forward and the canopy thins east on Old Dixie **⑬** Highway to **Ormond Beach.** Auto racing was born on this hardpacked beach back in 1902, when R. E. Olds and Alexander Winton staged the first race. The Winter Speed Carnival became an annual event, attracting enthusiasts from across the nation. Sportsmen and socialites flocked to Ormond Beach each winter and made the massive Ormond Hotel their headquarters. The grand old wooden hotel (built in 1888 to pamper Flagler's East Coast Railroad passengers) still stands watch on the east bank of the Halifax, but it is now vacant and no longer entertains guests.

Across the street from the hotel is **The Casements,** the restored winter retreat of John D. Rockefeller, now serving as a cultural center and museum. The estate and its formal gardens, on the National Register of Historic Places, are the setting for an annual lineup of special events and exhibits. Tours of the estate also are offered. *25 Riverside Dr., Ormond Beach, tel. 904/673–4701. Open weekdays 9–5, Sat. 9–12.*

To reach the beach of Daytona Beach, where Ormond's Winter Speed Carnival now takes place, follow Rte. A1A south. During springbreak, race weeks, and summer holidays, expect heavy traffic along this strip of garishly painted beach motels and tacky souvenir shops. Rising above the strip is the new $45-million, 402-room Daytona Beach Marriott, which is part of a long-range downtown revitalization plan.

Several miles south of the new Marriott, on Rte. A1A, is **Ponce Inlet** beach, which is frequented by locals and visitors who are in the know. A manicured drive winds through low-growing shrubs and windblown scrub oaks to parking and picnic areas. Boardwalks traverse the delicate dunes and provide easy access to the wide beach. Marking this prime spot is a bright-red century-old lighthouse, now a historic monument and museum. *Open daily 10–5.*

Time Out **Lighthouse Landing,** only yards from the historic light, is a good place for sipping cocktails and watching the sunset (*see* Dining).

Sunset on the Halifax River may also be enjoyed aboard *The Dixie Queen.* The replica of an 1890s paddlewheeler is docked at the marina on the southwest side of the Seabreeze Bridge, north of Ponce Inlet. The 400-passenger, 65-foot vessel has a full-service galley and offers a variety of cruises.

From the marina, head south on Beach Street to Volusia Avenue (U.S. 92), drive two blocks west to U.S. 1 (Ridgewood Ave.), and head south to **New Smyrna Beach.** Across the Intracoastal Waterway via Rte. 44 is New Smyrna's beach, which, like the beaches north and south of it, lies along a barrier island.

South of New Smyrna Beach on U.S. 1 are **Titusville,** Merritt Island National Wildlife Refuge, and **NASA Kennedy Space Center's Spaceport USA.** To reach the space center, take Rte. 405 over the NASA Causeway, then follow the NASA Parkway to the entrance of Spaceport USA. Free museum exhibits and films are featured, as well as guided bus tours and an IMAX theater film presentation *(The Dream is Alive,* narrated by Walter Cronkite). *Visitors' Center TWA, Kennedy Space Center, tel. 407/452–2121. Bus tour admission: $4 adults, $1.75 children 3–12. IMAX Theater admission: $2.75 adults, $1.75 children 3–12. Open daily (except Christmas) 9–6.*

Port Canaveral, on the southern end of **Cape Canaveral,** is home to *SeaEscape* (tel. 407/784–3666), which departs on one-day cruises into the Atlantic and back from 10 to 10 every day except Friday, and **Premier Cruise Lines,** offering three- and four-night *Starcruise* experiences to the Bahamas, departing on Fridays and Mondays, respectively.

Port Canaveral also is the site of annual surfing championships, thanks to the well-formed Atlantic waves that wash the beaches between **Cocoa Beach** and **Sebastian Inlet. Ron Jon's Surf Shop** (4151 North Atlantic Ave., Cocoa Beach) is almost an attraction in itself, with its massive collection of swim wear, beach gear, and T-shirts. Beach-bike rentals are available.

To the south is Cocoa Beach. When looking for a place to park your beach umbrella, keep in mind that Cocoa Beach is more crowded than the beaches farther south, such as **Satellite Beach, Indialantic,** and **Melbourne Beach.**

A good way to become acquainted with the area's waterways is to take a sightseeing or dinner cruise on *The Little River Queen,* which departs daily from **Gatsby's Dockside** in Cocoa Beach. You'll see everything from elegant residential areas to native wildlife—dolphins, manatees, and wading birds. *480 W. Cocoa Beach Causeway, Cocoa Beach, tel. 407/783–2380. Reservations are suggested.*

Exploring **Olde Cocoa Village** (201 Michigan Ave., Cocoa, tel. 407/632–1830) may convince you that there was life in Cocoa before the space program. Cobblestone walkways thread through this landscaped cluster of restored 1890s buildings in downtown Cocoa, where specialty shops display pottery, macrame, leather and silvercraft, afghans, fine art, and fashions. The **Co-**

coa **Village Playhouse** community theater is based here and provides regular entertainment. Horse-drawn carriages can take you for a ride, and the **Brevard Museum** organizes village walking tours by appointment.

Sebastian Inlet marks the southern boundary of this region east of Orlando. Two recreational areas ensure the preservation of some great fishing grounds and beaches. If you like to camp, check out **Long Point Park** (tel. 407/732–3839) and **Sebastian Inlet State Recreation Area** (tel. 407/727–1752).

What to See and Do with Children

Buccaneer Bay (*see* The Gulf of Mexico Area).
Homosassa Springs (*see* The Gulf of Mexico Area).
Liberty Bell Memorial Museum. *Wells Park, west of Hickory St. and south of Hibiscus Blvd., Melbourne, tel. 407/727–1776. Open weekdays 10–4, Sat. 10–2.*
NASA Kennedy Space Center's Spaceport USA (*see* The Daytona Beach Area).
Sanford Zoo (*see* Off the Beaten Track).
Weeki Wachee (*see* The Gulf of Mexico Area).
Wild Waters (*see* The North of Orlando Area).

Off the Beaten Track

Brooksville Just east of Weeki Wachee at the intersection of Rte. 50 and U.S. 98 is **Brooksville**. This country hamlet looks like it hasn't quite caught up with the 20th century. Its quiet streets are lined with tidy cottages and an occasional imposing Victorian mansion. The town's **Heritage Museum** is housed in such a mansion. *601 S. May Ave., tel. 904/799–0129. Open Wed., Thurs., and Sat. noon–3.*

About two blocks south of the museum, off Liberty Street, is **Roger's Christmas House & Village,** a cluster of cottage shops, selling everything from tree decorations to linens, stuffed animals, and gourmet kitchen utensils. *103 Saxon Ave., Brooksville, tel. 904/796–2415. Open daily (except Christmas) 9:30–5.*

Cross Creek North of Ocala, via I–75 or U.S. 441, are the towns of **McIntosh**
Country and **Micanopy**—first stops on a tour of Marjorie K. Rawlings's Cross Creek country.

Fewer than 400 people reside in turn-of-the-century McIntosh, which didn't even bother putting up street signs until 1984. Each year in October or November (during a weekend when the Florida Gators aren't playing football at home), the townspeople dress in period clothing. Tours of Victorian homes, antique auto displays, horse-and-buggy rides, and a parade are featured. Overnight accommodations may be found at **Merrily Bed-and-Breakfast** (*see* Lodging).

Micanopy (on the National Register of Historic Districts) is home to at least 12 antique shops and **The Herlong Mansion** (built in 1875), another B&B (tel. 904/466–3322).

Just outside Micanopy on U.S. 441 is the entrance to **Paynes Prairie State Preserve** (Rte. 2, Box 41, Micanopy, tel. 904/466–3397), an 18,000-acre basinland, where Indian artifacts have been found dating back to 10,000 BC. The prairie supported the largest cattle ranch in Spanish Florida during the 1600s; it was visited and described by William Bartram in 1774. Each April park rangers take visitors on historical tours.

Within easy driving distance of Paynes Prairie is Cross Creek and the **Marjorie Kinnan Rawlings State Historic Site,** the Cracker farmhouse in which Rawlings lived and wrote *The Yearling, Cross Creek,* and other works. *Rte. 3, Box 92, Hawthorne, tel. 904/466–3672. Open Thurs.–Mon. 10–11:30 AM and 1–4:30 PM; closed Tues. and Wed.*

Sanford The last 1880s steamboat stop on the St. Johns River is **Sanford,** located between DeLand and Orlando on U.S. 17/92. Today, it's the celery capital of the United States, southern terminus for Amtrak's Auto Train, site of the annual Golden Age Olympic Games, and home of the **Central Florida Zoo.** *U.S. 17/ 92 at I-4, Lake Monroe, tel. 407/323–6471. Admission: $5 adults, $2 children 3–12. Open daily 9–5.*

Cruising the St. Johns River is still the reason why most people visit Sanford. The newest cruise operation is **St. Johns River Cruises, Inc.** (4359 Peninsula Point, Marine Park, tel. 407/330–1612), offering the only passenger tour boat that travels south of Lake Monroe on the scenic St. Johns.

The *Rivership Romance,* a 110-foot triple-deck catamaran, makes scheduled cruises on the St. Johns River from the city marina on Lake Monroe. Its most popular cruise is the 2½-hour Saturday morning Pancakes and Sausage Cruise. *433 N. Palmetto Ave., Sanford, tel. 407/321–5091. Reservations advised.*

The St. Johns may also be explored by houseboat. Contact **Sanford Boat Rentals** 4350 Orange Blvd., Sanford, tel. 407/321–5906), at the Hidden Harbour Marina.

Shopping

Gift Ideas When touring the Gulf of Mexico area, look for antiques and stuffed manatee dolls (proceeds usually support the "Save the Manatee" program). In the area north of Orlando, look for antiques at *Reeve & Howard* (105 W. Indiana Ave., DeLand; openMon.–Sat. 9–5) and outlet merchandise at *Flechbilt Handbags,Bass Shoes,* and *Manhattan Shirts,* all in Ocala. Country crafts and horse-farm souvenirs are sold throughout the area. When touring the Atlantic beaches, look for citrus products at *Harvey's Groves* (3811 N. Atlantic Ave., Cocoa Beach), and space-program memorabilia at the Spaceport USA gift shop.

Food and Flea **Flea World** has 1,200 booths under one roof selling everything
Markets from citrus fruits to jewelry and antiques. *U.S. 17–92, between Sanford and Orlando. Open Fri.–Sun. 8–5.*

Beaches

Don't expect to find sandy beaches along the Gulf coast between Crystal River and Weeki Wachee—it's more like marshland. But on the mid-Atlantic coast, between Ormond Beach and Sebastian Inlet, are about 100 miles of sandy beaches accessible to the public. The only beach area closed to the public borders the space center on Cape Canaveral. Choice beaches and parks are listed below.

The Boardwalk, at the center of Daytona Beach, is the place to see and be seen. The broad, hard-packed beach looks like a busy city sidewalk, complete with hawkers and pedestrians dodging vehicles—except everybody's wearing a bathing suit and a tan.

Ponce Inlet, about eight miles south of Daytona Beach, is a well-manicured beach park with tidy picnic pavilions, board-walks protecting the sand dunes, and a quiet assortment of locals escaping the crunch. There's lots of space to breathe here. When swimming, keep an eye out for surf fishermen and their lines.

Canaveral National Seashore (tel. 407/867–5069), just east of New Smyrna Beach on Rte. A1A, is a 57,000-acre park that is home to more than 250 kinds of birds and animals. The remote beach bordering the Atlantic is noted for its sand dunes and seashells. A self-guided hiking trail leads to the top of an Indian shell midden at Turtle Mound, where picnic tables are available. Free brochures and maps are available at the Visitor Center on Rte. A1A.

Paradise Beach (tel. 407/254–1764), a scenic 10-acre park north of Indialantic on Rte. A1A, has 1,600 feet of beach, picnic facilities, grills, showers, rest rooms, and a refreshment stand. A lifeguard is on duty during the summer. There is a fee for parking, and picnic tables must be reserved in advance.

Sebastian Inlet State Recreation Area (tel. 407/727–1752), about 12 miles south of Melbourne on Rte. A1A, offers three miles of beachfront for swimming, surfing, snorkeling, and scuba diving. The 576-acre park also features bathhouse facilities, campsites, a food concession, fishing jetty, and boat ramp (tel. 407/727–1752).

Participant Sports

Biking Serious cyclists tour central Florida's hilly countryside on their sleek racers; other prefer pedaling the coastal flatlands on a beach bike. In Daytona Beach, bicycle concessions set up shop along the beach year-round. Near New Smyrna Beach, try **Swift Cycles-Beach Concession** (1803 12th St., Edgewater, tel. 904/427–2413). In Cocoa Beach, visit **Ron Jon's Surf Shop** (4151 N. Atlantic Ave., tel. 407/799–8888).

Boardsailing The consistent ocean breezes, warm water, and sheltered waterways of Florida's mid-Atlantic coast make it a prime boardsailing site. Conditions are so good that the U.S. Boardsailing Team trains in Melbourne. *(See* Water Sports.)

Canoeing The gentle, spring-fed rivers that thread through this region pose no problems for beginners. Canoe trails begin upstream, so all you have to do is steer and enjoy the wildlife and wilderness. East of Brooksville, the **Withlacoochee River R.V. Park** (tel. 904/583–4778) on Rte. 575 provides livery for five river tours—including an overnight paddle to Nobleton. Janet and Tom Handley operate a canoe-rental concession at Juniper Springs Recreation Area in **Ocala National Forest** (tel. 904/625–2808 or 685–2194). The Juniper Creek trail is seven miles long and takes about three to four hours to paddle. Just outside the national park, **Katie's Wekiva River Landing** (tel. 407/322–4470) at 190 Katie's Cove in Sanford provides livery for four river tours.

Diving/Snorkeling You can scuba or snorkel with manatees in the clear spring water of Crystal River's Kings Bay *(see* Guided Tours) or snorkel the clear spring waters of DeLeon Springs State Recreation Area (Box 1338, DeLeon Springs, tel. 904/985–4212).

Fishing Both freshwater and saltwater fishing can be enjoyed here. Largemouth bass, bluegill, crappie, and other freshwater panfish are caught in the St. Johns River and its tributary lakes and streams. Fishing camps provide guides, bait, tackle, rental boats, and accommodations that range from efficiency cabins to campsites. A license, required for freshwater fishing, often can be purchased at the fishing camps. Saltwater fishing also requires a license. You can deep-sea troll in the Atlantic for blue and white marlin, sailfish, dolphin, king mackerel, tuna, and wahoo. Grouper, red snapper, and amberjack are deep-sea bottom-fishing prizes. Surf casting is popular for pompano, bluefish, flounder, and sea bass. From fishing piers, anglers hook sheepshead, mackerel, sea trout, weakfish, and tarpon. Most Atlantic beach communities have a lighted pier with a bait-and-tackle shop and rest rooms. Daytona Beach's charter fishing fleet departs from marinas near Ponce Inlet. Deep-sea charters also are found at Port Canaveral and on the gulf coast in Crystal River and Homosassa Springs.

Golf At the turn of the century, Florida boasted 14 golf courses; by 1988, it had more than 800. This region is home to at least 32, and one of them—designed by C. E. Clarke of Scotland in 1926 —was among the original 14. Guests of **Mission Inn Golf and Tennis Resort** in Howey-in-the-Hills play that course today. Other notables are **Plantation Golf Resort** in Crystal River; **Golden Ocala Golf & Country Club** (nine historic holes); **Indigo Lakes** off U.S. 92 in Daytona Beach; and **Spessard Holland Golf Course** (designed by Arnold Palmer), off Rte. A1A in Melbourne.

Horseback Riding Ocala's bluegrass horse country can be explored during trail rides organized by **Oakview Stable** (S.W. 27th Ave., behind the Paddock Mall, tel. 904/237–8844).

Hot Air Ballooning Contact **Weekend Safaris** near the Ocala National Forest (tel. 904/867–7643).

Skydiving Anybody who wants to jump out of an airplane when it's thousands of feet up in the air can do so with the help of **Skydive DeLand** (tel. 904/738–3539) or **Titusville Parachute Center** (tel. 407/267–0016). Open weekends 9 AM–sundown.

Water Sports Jet skiing, boardsailing, waterskiing, sailing, and power boating are popular pastimes on the Atlantic Intracoastal Waterway. Rental equipment is available at **The Water Works** (1891 E. Merritt Island Causeway, Rte. 520, Merritt Island, tel. 407/452–2007).

Spectator Sports

Auto Racing The massive **Daytona International Speedway** on U.S. 92 (Daytona Beach's major east–west artery) is home of year-round auto and motorcycle racing including the annual Daytona 500 in March and Firecracker 400 in July. Twenty-minute narrated tours of the historic track are offered daily 9–5 except on race days. For racing schedules, call 407/253–6711.

Greyhound Races During the summer, you can bet on the dogs every night but Sunday at the **Daytona Beach Kennel Club** (on U.S. 92 near the International Speedway, tel. 904/252–6484).

Jai Alai The world's fastest sport, jai alai, is played September–January at the **Sports Palace** (1100 N. Wickham Rd., Melbourne, tel. 407/259–9800), January–March and June–September at **Ocala Jai-Alai** (Rte. 318, Orange Lake, tel. 904/591–2345), and February–July at **Volusia Jai-Alai** (U.S. 92, across from the Daytona International Speedway, tel. 904/255–0222).

Dining

Fresh Florida seafood is on most menus, prepared in many ways. One of the most popular fish is grouper, because of its light, sweet taste, grillable white meat, and reasonable market price. Coconut shrimp is a favorite appetizer. Gator tail, cooter (soft-shell turtle), frogs' legs, "fingerling" catfish, and quail dishes are found on the menus of rustic backwoods diners. Family restaurants keep locals happy with simple country cooking, fresh-baked breads and cakes, and moderate prices.

The most highly recommended restaurants are indicated by a star ★.

Category	Cost*
Very Expensive	above $25
Expensive	$15–$25
Moderate	$10–$15
Inexpensive	under $10

* per person without 6% state sales tax, service, or drinks

The following credit card abbreviations are used: AE, American Express; CB, Carte Blanche; DC, Diners Club; MC, MasterCard; V, Visa.

Very Expensive **Bernard's Surf.** Don't come to Bernard's for the view; there are no windows in the two main dining rooms. Come for steaks and local fish and a few unusual dishes like alligator and buffalo. A specialty is Doc Stahl's Skillet, a combination of shrimp, crabmeat, mushrooms, and wild rice sautéed and served in the skillet. *2 S. Atlantic Ave., Cocoa Beach, tel. 407/783–2401. Dress: casual. Reservations advised. AE, DC, MC, V. Closed Christmas Day.*

★ **Churchill's.** The formal but intimate dining room at the Crown Hotel features classic French cuisine—beef, fish, and veal in a combination of sauces. Entrees are served hot from a cart that is wheeled from the kitchen to your table. A favorite is Grouper St. Pierre, featuring the light, sweet fish in a white wine and cream sauce, topped with strips of smoked Nova Scotia salmon. *109 N. Seminole Ave., Inverness, tel. 904/344–5555. Jacket and tie optional. Reservations required. AE, DC, MC, V.*

Izaak's Gourmet Restaurant. Set back in the woods by a river, Izaak Walton's Lodge (a 10-room fishing retreat built in 1924 and restored in 1987) has a 40-seat formal dining room with hunter-green wainscoting, formal black floral wallpaper, rosecolored tablecloths, and a fireplace. The chef's own favorite dish is Zuppa de Pesce: fresh lobster, crab, shrimp, scallops, and oysters in a seafood sauce, served over a bed of linguine. *1 63rd St. on Riverside Dr., Yankeetown, tel. 904/447–2311. Jacket and tie optional Reservations advised. MC, V.*

Mango Tree Restaurant. Candles, fresh flowers, white linen tablecloths, rattan basket chairs with fluffy cushions, and eggshell-color walls adorned with tropical watercolors by local artists set a romantic mood at the Mango Tree. The intimate dining room overlooks a garden aviary that is home to exotic doves and pheasants, and the menu is a blend of American and Continental. Try the grouper broiled and topped with scallops, shrimp, and hollandaise sauce. *Cottage Row, 118 N. Atlantic Ave., Cocoa Beach, tel. 407/799–0513. Dress: smart casual. Reservations advised. AE, MC, V.*

Expensive **Arthur's.** When the Ocala Hilton opened in 1987, its airy and intimate restaurant, Arthur's, garnered much attention. Light tropical colors, comfortable shellback chairs, floor-to-ceiling windows with tieback curtains, and fresh flowers complement the American/Florida regional cuisine. Special menu items include an alligator-tail appetizer, grilled swordfish, and veal split and stuffed with prosciutto and Swiss cheese, then coated with herbs and bread crumbs and panfried in peanut oil. *3600 S.W. 36th Ave., Ocala, tel. 904/854–1400. Jacket and tie at dinner, smart casual at lunch. Reservations accepted. AE, DC, MC, V.*

Gatsby's Restaurant and Lounge. This casual waterfront spot is part of a trio that includes Gatsby's Dockside and Jay Gatsby's Sports Emporium. Prime rib, steaks, and seafood are served American-style, and early-bird special dinner prices are in effect between 4:30 and 6:30. *480 W. Cocoa Beach Causeway, Cocoa Beach, tel. 407/783–2380. Dress: smart casual. Reservations advised. AE, CB, DC, MC, V.*

K.C. Crump on the River. This 1870 Old Florida residence on the Homosassa River was restored in 1986 and reopened as a restaurant in 1987. Lemon juice, butter, and garlic season most of the seafood, and rich cream or fruit sauces complement the meat dishes. There's a small marina on the river, as well as a riverfront lounge and outdoor dining. Indoors are several airy dining rooms, with large picture windows, rattan furniture, mauve cloth napkins, and thick cotton placemats. *3900 Hall River Rd., Homosassa Springs, tel. 904/628–1500. Dress: smart casual. Reservations advised. MC, V.*

★ **Pondo's.** American and nouvelle-cuisine dishes are served in this 1921 two-story house near the St. Johns River. It has the look of an old inn and offers a choice of three intimate dining rooms (white tablecloths, seating for 150) on the ground floor. Specialties include homemade pasta, veal, vegetarian dishes, duck, prime rib, and grilled steaks. An octogenarian jazz pianist entertains. *1715 W. Old New York Ave., DeLand, tel. 904/734–1995. Jacket and tie optional. Reservations advised. AE, MC, V.*

Moderate **Alma's Italian Restaurant.** Five crowded, noisy dining rooms
★ keep the waitresses busy. The specialties of the house are veal marsala and more than 200 imported and domestic wines. *306 N. Orlando Ave., Cocoa Beach, tel. 407/783–1981. Dress: casual. Reservations advised. AE, DC, MC, V.*

Aunt Catfish's. Down-home seafood is featured, along with cheese grits and baked beans. This wharfside restaurant is also known for its fresh cinnamon rolls. *550 Halifax Dr., Port Orange, tel. 904/767–4768. Dress: casual. Reservations accepted. AE, DC, MC, V.*

Original Holiday House. This popular buffet-style family restaurant opened in 1959 in an old two-story house. People come for home cooking at a reasonable price. The buffet features rare roast beef, baked fish, leg of lamb, tossed green salads, baked potatoes, carrot cake, and cobbler. *704 N. Boulevard, DeLand, tel. 904/734–6319. Dress: casual. Reservations not accepted. MC, V. Closed Christmas Eve.*

Lighthouse Landing. "If it smells like fish, eat it," is the philosophy of this funky waterfront eatery. The outdoor oak tree-shaded dining deck is popular for cocktails and sunset-watching. The menu is seafood only. *4940 S. Peninsula Dr., Ponce Inlet, tel. 904/761–9271. Dress: very casual. Reservations not required. MC, V. Closed Jan.*

Marko's Heritage Inn. Its bakery, gift shop, piano parlor lounge, and down-home American cooking draw crowds. Try the Kentucky Hot Brown—thinly shaved ham and sliced turkey, topped with cream sauce, cheese and bacon. Desserts are fresh baked goods. *900 S. Ridgewood Ave., Port Orange, tel. 904/767–3809. Dress: casual. Reservations accepted for 20 or more. AE, DC, MC, V. Closed Christmas Eve.*

Norwood's. Since 1946, this Old Florida seafood-oyster bar has served its popular seafood platters on glass-top tables filled with seashells. Some nights it serves all-you-can-eat crab claw dinners. Try the smoked mullet and broiled fish with cheese sauce. *400 2nd Ave., New Smyrna Beach, tel. 904/428–4621. Dress: casual. No reservations. AE, MC, V.*

★ **The Strawberry Mansion & Mister BeauJean's Restaurant.** A gingerbread-trimmed Victorian mansion with six dining rooms and a walled garden courtyard are the settings for reasonably priced California-style dishes. Try the tropical shrimp (fried in a coating of coconut and macadamia nuts) or Mrs. Brown's crab cakes (more crab than cake) for starters. Entrees include grouper with crab and scallops, homemade pasta, lamb, duck, veal, and steak. Mister BeauJean's serves breakfast and lunch in the courtyard or in its tropical-chic indoor dining room. Waffles, broccoli burritos, and Häagen-Dazs ice cream highlight the menu. *1218 E. New Haven Ave., Melbourne, tel. 407/724–8627. Dress: casual. Reservations accepted. MC, V.*

Inexpensive
★ **The Blueberry Patch Tea Room.** Though most entrees are less than $5, this cottage is the equal of many more expensive places, due to its homestyle cooking with a European flair. Crab soufflé and quiche lorraine are the chef's favorites. Dessert specials include banana silk pie and coconut sour-cream cake. Look for the white-and-cornflower-blue cottage. *414 E. Liberty St., Brooksville, tel. 904/796–6005. Dress: smart casual. Reservations advised. AE, DC, MC, V. Closed Christmas Day.*

Old Spanish Sugar Mill & Griddle House. Situated inside an old stone waterwheel house by the outflow of DeLeon Springs, this restaurant and country store features freshly milled flour and baked goods and provides patrons with ingredients for making their own hot cakes and side dishes (bacon, sausage, ham) on griddles that are built into every table. All you can eat. *DeLeon Springs, tel. 904/985–5644. Dress: casual. Reservations accepted for 10 or more. No credit cards.*

★ **The Oyster Bar.** This no-frills cinderblock seafood spot is popular with locals and features locally caught fish, oysters on the half shell, crab claws, and lobster. Beer and wine only. *224 N. U.S. 19, Crystal River, tel. 904/795–3949. Dress: very casual. Reservations not required. MC, V.*

Stavro's. This cafe is popular for its pizzas, Greek salads and desserts, pita-bread sandwiches, and baked Italian dishes. Try the Mostaccioli—ziti noodles, meat sauce, and three cheeses. *803 W. New York Ave., DeLand, tel. 904/734–5705. Dress: casual. Reservations not accepted. No credit cards.*

Lodging

Though the majority of hotels and motels in this region belong to national chains, there is an increasing number of country inns from which to choose. Turn-of-the-century homes are being restored and converted into bed-and-breakfast establishments. The B&B concept has crept into the marketing of national chain hotels as well. New luxury, suite-style properties are including breakfast and happy-hour cocktails in their regular room rates.

Category	Cost*
Very Expensive	over $100
Expensive	$60–$100
Moderate	$40–$60
Inexpensive	under $40

*per room, double occupancy, without 6% state sales tax and nominal tourist tax

The following credit card abbreviations are used: AE, American Express; CB, Carte Blanche; DC, Diners Club; MC, MasterCard; V, Visa.

Very Expensive **Daytona Beach Marriott.** This mammoth, pyramid-shape hotel, which celebrated its grand opening February 2, 1989, offers 402 luxury ocean-view rooms. Amenities include a heated indoor-outdoor pool with waterfall and tropical landscaping, a sauna, health-club exercise rooms, indoor and outdoor whirlpool spas, and a children's pool and beachside playground. Incorporated into the beachfront landscaping is the city's landmark, turn-of-the-century clock tower. Facilities include two restaurants, two lounges, and a poolside bar. *1401 N. Atlantic Ave., Daytona Beach 32018, tel. 904/254–8200. AE, DC, MC, V.*

Holiday Inn Cocoa Beach Resort. When two separate beach hotels were redesigned and a promenade park landscaped between them, the Holiday Inn Cocoa Beach Resort was born. It features plush modern public rooms, an Olympic-size heated pool, tennis courts, and private access to the beach. You can choose from a wide selection of accommodations—standard, king, and oceanfront suites; villas; and bilevel lofts—all with in-room movies. Free aerobics workouts are offered, as are planned activities for children. *1300 N. Atlantic Ave., Cocoa Beach 32931, tel. 407/783–2271. AE, DC, MC, V.*

Mission Inn Golf and Tennis Resort. Courtyard fountains, stucco walls, terra-cotta roofs, and columned breezeways reflect Florida's Spanish heritage at this lakeside sports complex. Amenities include a 1926 vintage 18-hole golf course, jogging trail, exercise room, six lighted tennis courts, an outdoor pool with Hydro-spa, a 52-slip marina, and a restored 1930s river yacht. *Howey-in-the-Hills 32737, tel. 904/324–3101. AE, DC, MC, V.*

Riverview Hotel. This restored 1886 bridge tender's house, at the foot of the Rte. 44 bridge, is only four blocks from the Atlantic. Its 18 rooms feature natural wicker, antiques, and vivid watercolor paintings. The third-floor Riverview Plaza Suite has the best view of the Intracoastal Waterway and displays the tongue-and-grove pine walls of the original structure. Amenities include complimentary continental breakfast, a courtyard swimming pool, seafood restaurant and lounge, and 10-slip marina. *103 Flagler Ave., New Smyrna Beach 32069, tel. 904/428-5858. AE, DC, MC, V.*

Seven Sisters Inn. Antique white wicker and potted red geraniums grace the wraparound veranda of this 1888 Victorian mansion. Restored in 1985, the three-story inn opened October 1987 and offers five plush rooms with private baths. Ralph Lauren linens, antiques, fresh flowers, and gourmet breakfasts pamper guests. Sylvia's Room—with its king-size bed, expansive windows, and antique chaise—is a favorite. *820 S.E. Fort King Ave., Ocala 32671, tel. 904/867-1170. AE, MC, V.*

Expensive   **Captain's Quarters Inn.** It may look like just another mid-rise hotel, but inside, it's like a home away from home. An antique desk, Victorian love seat, and tropical greenery greet guests in the lobby of this 25-suite beachfront inn. Fresh-baked goodies and coffee are served in The Galley, which overlooks the ocean and looks like grandma's kitchen with a few extra tables and chairs. Each guest suite features rich oak furnishings, a complete kitchen, and private balcony. There's a heated swimming pool and sunbathing deck facing the beach. *3711 S. Atlantic Ave., Daytona Beach Shores 32019, tel. 904/767-3119. AE, MC, V.*

The Crown Hotel. In the center of rural Inverness, occupying what once was a general store, is a cozy 34-room inn. Gilt-frame mirrors, polished woods and brass, and replicas of the British crown jewels adorn the lobby. Amenities include a small backyard pool, an English pub, and a Classic French gourmet restaurant. Guest rooms are small but comfortable, with large modern baths. *109 N. Seminole Ave., Inverness 32650, tel. 904/344-5555. AE, DC, MC, V.*

Ocala Hilton. A winding, tree-lined boulevard leads to this nine-story pink tower, which opened in 1987. Nestled in a forested patch of countryside just off I-75, the 200-room hotel features a marble-floor lobby with a piano bar, a restaurant featuring regional cuisine, an outdoor heated pool and Jacuzzi, two lighted tennis courts, and a pub with live entertainment. Pickled-pine armoires hide television sets in the spacious guest rooms, which are decorated in deep tropical hues. *3600 S.W. 36th Ave., Ocala 32674, tel. 904/854-1400. AE, DC, MC, V.*

Ritz—Ocala's Historic Inn. After an extensive interior redesign and renovation—completed in 1988—this pink stucco 1925 luxury apartment building is now a 32-suite luxury hotel on the National Register of Historic Places. Kilim rugs, 19th-century carved-stone Fu lion lamps with silk shades, arched French windows, and hand-painted trompe l'oeil murals bring Boca Raton's Mizner style to central Florida. There's a courtyard swimming pool and lobby/piano bar. Rates include a complimentary buffet breakfast and a nightly two-hour cocktail party. *1205 E. Silver Springs Blvd., Ocala 32670, tel. 904/867-7700. AE, DC, MC, V.*

Moderate   **Crossway Inn: A Cocoa Beach Resort.** This 94-unit resort motel is across the street from the Atlantic and within walking distance of a surf shop and at least 16 restaurants. You can choose from standard double rooms, minisuites, or fully equipped efficiencies—all are clean, comfortable, and decorated with light tropical colors. Amenities include a lighted volleyball court, a 15-foot "mallet pool" court (you sink the 8-ball with a croquet mallet), a children's playground, and an airy Key West-style lounge with rattan furnishings and hand-painted tropical murals. *3901 N. Atlantic Ave., Cocoa Beach 32931, tel. 407/ 783-2221. AE, DC, MC, V.*

EconoLodge Crystal Resort. A proximity to Kings Bay and the manatees that are drawing so much attention is what this two-story cinderblock roadside motel has to offer. Its 94 rooms are within a few steps of the marina, where dive boats depart for scuba and snorkeling excursions. The only rooms with a view of the water are 114 and 128. There's an outdoor pool and water-front restaurant, Cracker's, in a restored 1908 homestead. *U.S. 19, Crystal River 32629, tel. 904/795-3171. AE, CB, DC, MC, V.*

Pelican Landing Resort-On the Ocean. This tidy, two-story gray motel with royal-blue awnings features 11 efficiencies that were totally refurbished in 1987 with new appliances (including microwave ovens) and linoleum floors. Direct oceanfront views and screened porches are available in Units 1 and 6. A friendly family atmosphere, boardwalks to the beach, picnic tables, and a gas grill round out the amenities. *1201 S. Atlantic Ave., Cocoa Beach 32931, tel. 407/783-7197. MC, V.*

Inexpensive   **Izaak Walton Lodge.** This 1924 fishing retreat, the center supports of which are two huge trees, was completely restored in 1987. Stained black-cypress siding, white gingerbread trim, a gleaming tin roof, and red flower boxes brimming with geraniums greet those who venture off the main road to Yankeetown. There's a formal restaurant called Izaak's Gourmet and a casual seafood dining room overlooking the river. Upstairs are 10 lodge rooms with antique iron beds, carpeting, duck prints and shared baths. Out back are two very popular riverfront efficiencies decorated with natural wicker and rattan. *1 63rd Street on Riverside Dr., Yankeetown 32698, tel. 904/447-2311. MC, V.*

Merrily Bed & Breakfast. Margie Karow, one of the 400 residents of turn-of-the-century McIntosh, opened her 1888 Victorian home to guests in 1987. The pale-yellow house, with white trim and black shutters, shares an acre of land with spreading oak trees and has a screened back porch where Mrs. Karow likes to serve banana muffins for breakfast. Three guest rooms share two baths. *Ave. G and Sixth St., McIntosh 32664. tel. 904/591-1180. No credit cards.*

Sprague House Inn. Built in 1892, this Old Florida inn was used as a school for training domestics for area hotels. Renovated and reopened as a bed-and-breakfast inn in 1986, it features a full-service restaurant and three very clean rooms with private baths. Hundreds of books, stained-glass windows that depict the history of steamboat travel in Florida, and a hodgepodge of antiques and oddities decorate this unusual inn. *125 Central Ave., Crescent City 32012, tel. 904/698-2430. MC, V.*

The Arts

Oddly enough, the principal center for the arts is Daytona Beach. Side by side with pari-mutuel wagering and auto racing

is **Peabody Auditorium.** The 2,560-seat center hosts internationally known artists in theater, music, and dance. The
Daytona Beach Civic Ballet and the Daytona Symphony Society are also based here. *Peabody Auditorium, 600 Auditorium
Blvd., Daytona Beach, tel. 904/252–0821.*

South of Daytona, the Brevard Community College each year
sponsors the **Lyceum Series,** featuring a lineup of state, national, and international performing groups in the fields of music,
theater, and dance. *Dr. Rosemary Layne, Brevard Community College, 1519 Clearlake Rd., Cocoa, tel. 407/632–1111, ext.
3660.*

Theater   Community theater is popular throughout the region. Contact
the local chamber of commerce in each community for details
(see Important Addresses and Numbers).

Concerts   South Brevard County is home to the Brevard Symphony Orchestra, the Florida Spacecoast Philharmonic, the Civic Music
Association of South Brevard, and the Melbourne Chamber
Music Society. *1005 E. Strawbridge Ave., Melbourne, tel. 407/
724–5400.*

Nightlife

Bars and   **FiddlestiX Spirits & Such** (2286 Rte. A1A, Satellite Beach, tel.
Nightclubs   407/773–4135). Live entertainment by a band specializing in
'40s and '50s dance music.

Ocean Deck (127 S. Ocean Ave., Daytona Beach, tel. 904/253–
5224). Reggae bands, dancing.

Scallies Comedy Connection (131 Hibiscus Ave., Melbourne,
tel. 407/676–2260). A live band entertains with '50s dance music Tuesday–Thursday and comedy acts are scheduled Friday
and Saturday. Reservations are suggested.

Comedy Clubs   **Mac's Famous Bar** (2000 S. Atlantic Ave., Daytona Beach, tel.
904/258–5233). Formerly a rock-and-roll spot, it now features
comedy Wednesday–Sunday and live original pop-rock and
blues bands Monday and Tuesday.

Country Western   **Finky's** (640 N. Grandview, Daytona Beach, tel. 904/255–
5059). Top-name country entertainment all year, except during
spring break and race weeks, when it switches to rock and roll.

Stillwaters Saloon (1512 S.W. College Rd. [Rte. 200], Ocala,
tel. 904/629–6969). Music and dancing.

Discos   **Platters Lounge** (DeLand Hilton, 350 International Speedway
Blvd., DeLand, tel. 904/738–5200). Multilevel sound system,
flashing lights, and '60s, '70s, and '80s hits for dancing.

10 Southwest Florida

Introduction

*by Karen
Feldman Smith*

*A resident of
Florida for the
past decade,
Karen Feldman
Smith is the travel
and consumer
writer for the* Fort
Myers
News-Press, *a
contributing
writer for the
Gannett News
Service, and a
graduate of the
Columbia
University
Graduate School
of Journalism.*

Tourists and developers are fast discovering a region they formerly raced through in their haste to get to better-known Florida vacation destinations.

Southwest Florida spans some 200 miles and includes a host of diverse cities and towns. That variety satisfies the varied tastes of young singles, families, and older travelers. Sunning, shelling, sailing, and space to breathe characterize vacations on the Gulf coast.

Although the east coast of Florida may claim most of the state's historic sites there are lower-profile but equally worthy sites to enjoy on the Gulf coast. There are culturally rich ethnic neighborhoods, soothing natural sanctuaries harboring rare species, hotels from basic to deluxe, and some worthwhile tourist attractions. And, of course, there are the beaches, which stretch along the translucent waters of the Gulf of Mexico.

The sprawling region can be divided into three parts: the Tampa Bay area, encompassing Tampa, St. Petersburg, Tarpon Springs, and Clearwater; the Sarasota area, including Bradenton and Venice; and the Naples/Fort Myers region, from Port Charlotte south to the Everglades below Marco Island.

Getting Around

By Plane   Most major carriers fly into at least one of the area's three major airports, in Tampa, Sarasota, and Fort Myers.

Tampa International is six miles from downtown. It is served by Air Canada (tel. 800/422–6232), Air Jamaica (tel. 800/523–5585), American (tel. 800/433–7300), Braniff (tel. 800/272–6433), British Airways (tel. 800/247–9297), Cayman (tel. 800/422–9626), Continental (tel. 800/525–0280), Delta (tel. 800/221–1212), Eastern (tel. 800/EASTERN), Midway (tel. 800/621–5700), Northwest (tel. 800/225–2525), Pan Am (tel. 800/221–1111), Piedmont (tel. 800/251–5720), Transworld (tel. 800/221–2000), United (tel. 800/722–5243), and USAir (tel. 800/428–4322).

Sarasota's Airport is **Sarasota-Bradenton,** just north of the city. It is served by Air Sunshine (tel. 800/432–1744), American, Continental, Delta, Eastern, Florida Express (tel. 813/355–5323), Midway, Northwest, Transworld, and United.

The Fort Myers/Naples area's airport is **Southwest Florida Regional Airport,** about 12 miles south of Fort Myers, 25 miles north of Naples. It is served by American, Braniff, Continental, Delta, Eastern, Midway, Northwest, Piedmont, Transworld, United, and USAir.

Between the airports and the hotels: Major car-rental companies and taxi and limousine companies service all three airports. Many hotels also operate shuttles.

In Tampa, major transportation services include **Central Florida Limousine** (tel. 813/276–3730), serving Hillsborough and Polk counties; **The Limo** (tel. 813/822–3333 in St. Petersburg and Clearwater, serving Pinellas County; and **Florida Suncoast Limousines** (tel. 813/620–3597). Expect taxi fares to be about $9–$12 for most of Hillsborough County and about twice that for Pinellas County.

In Sarasota, transportation includes **Airport Limousine** (tel. 813/355–9645) and **Diplomat Taxi** (tel. 813/366–9822). Both deliver to most parts of the county. An average cab fare is $5–$10.

In Lee County, a taxi ride to downtown Fort Myers costs about $20 for the beaches, about twice that to Naples. Other transportation companies include **Airport Limousine** (tel. 813/489–1023), **Aristocat Super Mini-Van Service** (tel. 813/275–7228), **Boca Limousine Service** (tel. 813/936–5466), **Personal Touch Limousines** (tel. 813/549–3643), and **Sanibel Island Limousine** (tel. 813/472–8888).

By Car I-75 spans the region from north to south. Once you cross the border into Florida from Georgia, it should take about three hours to reach Tampa. Add an hour for Sarasota, two to Fort Myers, and three to Naples. Alligator Alley (Rte. 84) links up with I-75 at Naples and runs east to Fort Lauderdale. I-75 is being extended along the Alligator Alley right-of-way; expect construction delays.

U.S. 41 also runs the length of the region and serves as the business district in many communities. It's best to avoid all bridges and U.S. 41 during rush hours, 7–9 AM and 4–6 PM.

Rental car prices can vary dramatically, so it pays to shop around. Major companies serving Southwest Florida include **Alamo** (tel. 800/327–9633), **Avis** (tel. 800/331–1212), **Budget** (tel. 800/527–0700), **Dollar** (tel. 800/421–6868), **Enterprise** (tel. 800/325–8007), **Hertz** (tel. 800/654–3131), **Payless** (tel. 800/237–2804), **Sears** (tel. 800/527–0700), **Thrifty** (tel. 800/367–2277), and **Value** (tel. 800/327–2501).

By Train **Amtrak** (tel. 800/872–7245) connects the Northeast, Midwest, and much of the South to Tampa. From Tampa, Amtrak heads east, across the coast, then up to Jacksonville and points north. Amtrak's Autotrain runs from Lorton, Virginia (near Washington, DC), to Sanford, Florida (near Orlando). In Tampa, the Amtrak station is at 601 N. Nebraska Avenue (tel. 813/229–2473). Within Tampa, the PeopleMover rail line provides transportation between the business district and Harbour Island. Tokens cost 25 cents each way.

By Bus **Greyhound Lines/Trailways** provides service to and throughout the state. Call the nearest office for schedules and fares (Fort Myers, tel. 813/334–1011; St. Petersburg, tel. 813/898–1496; Sarasota, tel. 813/955–5735; and Tampa, tel. 813/229–2112).

Around Tampa, the **Hillsborough Area Regional Transit** (HART), (tel. 813/254–4278, 7 AM–6 PM) system serves most of the county.

In Sarasota, **Sarasota County Area Transit** (SCAT), (tel. 813/951–5850) is the public transit company. The **Lee County Transit System** (tel. 813/939–1303) serves Fort Myers and most of the county.

Scenic Drives **I-275 between St. Petersburg** and **Terra Ceia.** Motorists get a bird's-eye view of bustling Tampa Bay along the Sunshine Skyway and its bright-yellow suspension bridge.

Rte. 679 takes you along two of St. Petersburg's most pristine islands, Cabbage and Mullet keys.

Rte. 789 carries you over several of the coast's slender barrier islands, past miles of green-blue gulf waters, beaches, and waterfront homes. The road does not connect all the islands, however. It runs from Holmes Beach off the Bradenton coast south to Lido Beach in Sarasota, then begins again on Casey Key south of Osprey and runs south to Nokomis Beach.

Rte. 867 (McGregor Boulevard), Fort Myers's premier road, passes Thomas Edison's winter home and goes southwest toward the beaches. The road is lined with thousands of royal palm trees and many large old homes.

J.N. "Ding" Darling National Wildlife Refuge. Drive along the five-mile dirt road in Sanibel and, especially at low tide, you may see raccoons; alligators; and birds, such as roseate spoonbills, egrets, ospreys, herons, and anhingas.

Head west on **Mooringline Drive** in Naples for a drive past some of the cushiest coastline property in the state. Mooringline turns south and becomes Gulf Shore Boulevard. Condominiums, shops, hotels, and lots of beaches line this drive.

Just near the end of Gulf Shore Boulevard on Broad Avenue, you can pick up **2nd Street South,** which becomes Gordon Drive. It leads into Port Royale, where million-dollar homes are a dime a dozen. The architecture, landscaping, and statuary that are visible from the road make it a worthwhile expedition.

Guided Tours

Around the Town (tel. 813/932–7803) conducts tours for groups of 25 or more in the Tampa Bay area, plus Tarpon Springs and Sarasota, the dog tracks, and area theaters. Try to make reservations several weeks in advance.
Gulf Coast Gray Line (tel. 813/822–3577) makes daily trips from Tampa to Disney World, Epcot Center, Sea World, Busch Gardens, and other attractions.
Travel is Fun Tours of St. Petersburg (tel. 813/821–9479) offers day-long tours to area sights and attractions from St. Petersburg.
Trolley Tours (tel. 813/489–2339) of Fort Myers run during the winter tourist season. Drivers provide narrated, tours of various historic sites of interest, including the Edison Home, Fort Myers Historical Museum, and the downtown area. The trolleys also stop at area shopping malls. Passengers pay $5; the fare is good for unlimited travel all day.

Boat Tours *The Belle of St. Petersburg* (tel. 813/823–8171) is a double-decker boat offering lunch and dinner cruises from the Vinoy Basin, 401 Second Ave. NE, St. Petersburg.
Sea Escape Cruises (tel. 800/432–0900) are day-long excursions into the Gulf of Mexico on full-sized cruise ships departing from Tampa.
The *Captain Anderson* (tel. 813/367–7804) combines sightseeing and dinner cruises from the St. Petersburg Causeway, 3400 Pasadena Ave. It operates from October through May, St. Petersburg Beach.
The Admiral (tel. 813/462–2628) is docked at Clearwater Beach Marina. It runs dinner and sightseeing cruises all year, with lunch cruises for groups of 25 or more.
The *Starlite Princess* (tel. 813/595–1212) is a paddlewheel excursion boat offering three-hour, five-course meals from

Hamlin's Landing, Indian Rocks Beach. Old-fashioned boat adds to the fun.

The *Miss Cortez* (tel. 813/794–1223) departs from Cortez, just north of Bradenton, every Tuesday, Thursday, and Sunday for Egmont Key, a small abandoned island just north of Anna Maria Island.

Myakka Safari Tours (tel. 813/365–0100) is at Myakka River State Park, east of Sarasota on Rte. 72. *The Gator Gal*, a large airboat, conducts one-hour tours of the 29,000-acre wildlife and bird sanctuary. Three trips daily; closed Tuesday.

Epicurean Sailing Charters (tel. 813/964–0708) conducts half- and full-day cruises from Boca Grande to Useppa Island, Cabbage Key, and other area islands.

King Fisher Cruise Lines (tel. 813/639–0969) offers cruises and island sightseeing around Charlotte Harbor from Fishermen's Village, Punta Gorda.

Babcock Wilderness Adventures (tel. 813/639–4488) conducts guided swamp-buggy tours through the Telegraph Cypress Swamp on the 90,000-acre Crescent B Ranch, south of Punta Gorda. Reservations required.

Everglades Jungle Cruise (tel. 813/334–7474) explores the Caloosahatchee and Orange rivers of Lee County and makes day trips to Lake Okeechobee and two-day trips across the vast inland lake. Has lunch and dinner cruises as well. Trips last three hours to two days. They depart from the Fort Myers Yacht Basin. Rates: $8–$149.

The Norfolk Rover (tel. 813/463–SAIL) offers tall ship excursions in San Carlos Bay aboard the 72-foot sailboat departing from Gulf Star Marina.

The Capt. J.P. (tel. 813/334–7474) is a stern paddlewheeler that sails mid-November–mid-April, Tuesday–Sunday from the Fort Myers Yacht Basin. There are a variety of cruises, from three-hour excursions on the Caloosahatchee River to 12-hour trips to Lake Okeechobee. Brunch, lunch, and dinner-dance cruises also are offered.

Dalis Charter (tel. 813/262–4545) offers half-day fishing and sightseeing trips and sunset cruises. Also available for private cocktail cruises. It's docked at Old Marine Market Place at Tin City (1200 Fifth Ave. S, Naples.)

Tiki Islander Boat Tours (tel. 813/262–7577) conducts a variety of tours through the northern section of the Everglades' Ten Thousand Islands, including half-day fishing and shelling expeditions to Keewaydin Island and sightseeing along Naples Bay. Tours start at the dock behind Old Marine Market Place, Naples.

Wooten's Everglades (tel. 813/394–8080) runs a variety of airboat and swamp-buggy tours through the Everglades daily from Wooten's alligator farm, 35 miles east of Naples on U.S. 41.

Eden of the Everglades (tel. 813/695–2800) travels the wilderness wetlands of the Everglades' Ten Thousand Islands, departing from Everglades City in southern Collier County six times daily.

Florida Boat Tours (tel. 813/695–4400) depart from the Captain's Table Resort in Everglades City. The 80-minute tours of the Ten Thousand Islands set off three to five times daily.

By Plane Helicopter tours of the Tampa Bay area and the west coast of Florida are offered by Suncoast Helicopters (tel. 813/872–6625), based at Tampa International Airport; Topp of Tampa

Airport (6901 Rte. 54, Tampa, tel. 813/973–0056); and **West Florida Helicopters** (Albert Whitted Airport, tel. 813/823–5200). In the Charlotte Harbor area, sightseeing tours are offered by the **Boca Grande Seaplane Service** (tel. 813/964–0234), 4th and Bayou, Boca Grande.

Important Addresses and Numbers

Tourist Information All the following offices are open weekdays 9–5 and closed on holidays:

Charlotte County Chamber of Commerce (2702 Tamiami Trail, Port Charlotte, tel. 813/627–2222).

Greater Clearwater Chamber of Commerce (128 N. Osceola Ave., tel. 813/461–0011).

Greater Dunedin Chamber of Commerce (434 Main St., tel. 813/736–5066).

Gulf Beaches Chamber of Commerce (105 5th Ave., Indian Rocks Beach, tel. 813/595–4575).

Lee County Tourist Development Council (2180 W. First St., Fort Myers, tel. 813/335–2631 or 800/237–6444).

Madeira Beach Chamber of Commerce (501 150th Ave., tel. 813/391–7373).

Pinellas Suncoast Tourist Development Council (4625 E. Bay Dr., Suite 109, Clearwater, tel. 813/530–6452).

St. Petersburg Chamber of Commerce (100 2nd Ave. N, tel. 813/821–4069).

Sanibel-Captiva Chamber of Commerce (Causeway Rd., Sanibel, tel. 813/472–1080).

Tampa Bay Area **The Greater Tampa Chamber of Commerce** (801 E. Kennedy Blvd., tel. 813/228–7777). For information on current area events, call the **Visitors Information Department** (tel. 813/223–1111).

Tarpon Springs Chamber of Commerce (210 S. Pinellas Ave., Suite 120, tel. 813/937–6109).

Treasure Island Chamber of Commerce (152 108th Ave., tel. 813/367–4529).

Emergencies Dial 911 for **police** or **ambulance** in an emergency.

Hospitals Hospital emergency rooms are open around the clock. In Tampa: **University Community Hospital** (3100 E. Fletcher Ave.). In St. Petersburg: **Bayfront Medical Center** (701 6th St. S.). In Bradenton: **Manatee Memorial Hospital** (206 2nd St. E.). In Sarasota: **Sarasota Memorial Hospital** (1700 S. Tamiami Trail, U.S. 41). In Fort Myers: **Lee Memorial Hospital** (2776 Cleveland Ave.). In Naples: **Naples Community** (350 7th St. N.).

24-Hour Pharmacy **Eckerd Drugs** (11613 N. Nebraska, Tampa, tel. 813/978–0775).

Exploring Southwest Florida

Numbers in the margin correspond with points of interest on the Tampa-St. Petersburg-Sarasota Area map.

Exploring the Tampa Bay Area

Tampa boasts more business suits than any other part of the region. Its port is the country's seventh largest, with phosphate, shrimp, and bananas the primary cargo. The city's shrimp fleet, docked at Hooker's Point, is the state's largest. Industry flourishes as well, with millions of cigars rolled daily, phosphate mined from massive pits, and two major breweries—Busch and Schlitz—producing their wares here.

It's fitting that an area with a thriving international port should also be populated by a wealth of nationalities—Greeks, Scots, Hispanics, and Italians, to name only a few. American Indians were the sole inhabitants of the region for many years (Tampa is an Indian phrase meaning "sticks of fire"). The Spanish explorers Juan Ponce de Léon, Pánfilo de Narváez, and Hernando de Soto passed through in the mid-1500s. The U.S. Army and civilian settlers arrived in 1824; a military presence remains in the form of MacDill Air Force Base, where the U.S. Operations Command is located.

The Cubans brought their cigar-making industry to the area in 1866 and developed Ybor City. This east Tampa suburb is still primarily Cuban but contains a dwindling number of cigar makers.

Tampa does not have a gulf beach, and Tampa Bay, though lovely to look at, is too polluted for swimming. For that, visitors should head to neighboring St. Petersburg, which sits on a peninsula bordered on three sides by bays and the Gulf of Mexico, filled with pleasure and commercial craft.

North of Tampa, in Tarpon Springs, there has been a large Greek population for decades, since sponge divers from the Dodecanese Islands of Greece moved to the area at the turn of the century. This was the world's largest sponge center during the 1930s. Although a bacterial blight wiped out the sponge beds in the 1940s, the Greeks held on, and the sponge industry has returned, though in lesser force than during its heyday. Today, the Greek influence remains evident in the churches, the restaurants, and, often, in the language spoken on the streets.

The accent is Scottish in Dunedin, just south of Tarpon Springs. Two Scots were responsible for giving the town its Gaelic name in the 1880s. If the sound of bagpipes played by men in kilts appeals to you, head to Dunedin in March or April, when the Highland games and the Dunedin Heather and Thistle holidays pay tribute to the Celtic heritage.

Tampa Tampa is the business and commercial hub of this part of the state, as you'll quickly notice when driving by the busy port. The major north-south route is I-75; if you're heading from Orlando, you'll likely drive in on east-west I-4.

Let's begin a tour of Tampa along that I-4 corridor at Exit 5 (Orient Rd., east of the city). The water tower with an arrow sticking through it gives it away: this is the **Seminole Indian Village,** which contains a village and museum displaying artifacts of the Seminole Indians, who inhabited Florida long before white settlers arrived. You'll also be treated to alligator wrestling and snake shows. *5221 N. Orient Rd., tel. 813/ 621–2279. Open Mon.–Sat., 9–5. Sun. noon–5. Admission: $4.50 adults, $3.75 children under 12, $3.50 for senior citizens.*

Ybor City is Tampa's Cuban melting pot, which thrived on the cigar-making industry at the turn of the century. To get there, take I-4 west to Exit 1 (22nd St.) and go south five blocks to 7th Avenue. You're in the heart of Ybor City, where the smell of cigars—hand-rolled by Cuban refugees—mingles with old-world architecture. Take a stroll past the ornately tiled Columbia Restaurant and the stores lining the street, or step back to the past at **Ybor Square.** The restored cigar factory (1901 13th St.) now is a mall with boutiques, offices, and several restaurants. You can watch as artisans continue the local practice of hand rolling cigars.

For something a little more modern, head for the new skyscrapers downtown. From 7th Avenue, go west to Nebraska Avenue and turn left. That will take you to Kennedy Boulevard; turn right and drive a few blocks to the vicinity of Franklin Street. You are now in one of Tampa's booming growth areas, with a pedestrian mall down the center of Franklin Street.

A few more blocks to the east you'll find the **Tampa Museum of Art,** near Curtis Hixon Convention Center. Egyptian, Greek, and Roman artifacts are on display, as well as traveling exhibits. *601 Doyle Carlton Dr., tel. 813/223–8128. Open Tues. and Thurs.–Sat. 10–6, Wed. 10–9, Sun. 1–5. Donations accepted.*

On another day, enjoy a romp through **Busch Gardens.** A safari simulating a journey to the Dark Continent will let you watch free-roaming zebras, giraffes, rhinos, lions, and more—all from the comfort of a monorail. There are many other rides and attractions in this 300-acre park, so allow at least six hours here. *3000 Busch Blvd. (Rte. 580), 2 miles east of I-275, tel. 813/ 971–8282. Open daily 9:30–6. All-inclusive admission: $20.95, children under 2 free.*

St. Petersburg   St. Petersburg and the Pinellas Suncoast form the thumb of the hand jutting out of the west coast, holding in Tampa Bay. I-275 crosses the bay from Tampa through the heart of the city and then crosses the bay again at the Sunshine Skyway into Bradenton. U.S. 19 is the major north—south artery. Traffic can be heavy, and there are many lights, so U.S. 19 should be avoided on lengthy trips.

The bay and beaches offer two distinct communities to visit. Let's start with a trip over the **Sunshine Skyway.** A $1 toll will carry you across the causeway and to the top of a sparkling new suspension bridge for a bird's-eye view of the islands and of ocean freighters and sailboats plying Tampa Bay. You can also see what's left of the original twin span that collapsed and killed more than 30 people when a ship hit it in 1980. Across the

Tampa-St.Petersburg-Sarasota Area

St. John Sound

Oldsmar

Clearwater Beach

Dunedin

Hillsborough Ave.

TAMPA

Gulf-to-Bay Blvd.

Courtney Campbell Causeway

Old Tampa Bay

Howard Franklin Bridge

Riverview

Bay Dr.

Indian Shores

Largo

Pinellas Park

Ulmerton

Gandy Bridge

Gibsonton

Seminole

Lake Seminole

38th Ave.

5th Ave.

ST. PETERSBURG

Apollo Beach

Madeira Beach

22nd Ave. S.

Tampa Bay

Ruskin

Gulfport

Boca Ciega Bay

St. Petersburg Beach

Sun City

Mullet Key

Sunshine Skyway

Egmont Key

Gulf of Mexico

Anna Maria Key

Ellenton

River

Palmetto

Manatee

Holmes Beach

Bradenton

Cortez

Bradenton Beach

Oneco

Longboat Key

Longboat Key

Sarasota Bay

SARASOTA

N

0   10 miles

0   15 km

Ringling Causeway

bridge, you can picnic, toss in a fishing line, or turn around and mount the summit of the bridge again. This time, you'll get a view of a series of small islands that dot the bay, and you'll see St. Petersburg Beach as you head north.

When you reach the north end of the causeway, turn left on 54th Avenue South (Rt. 682), and follow it to Rt. 679. Turn left and cross the islands you saw from the Sunshine Skyway. You'll **⑥** end up eventually at **Fort Desoto Park** at the mouth of Tampa Bay. Here you can roam the fort that was built to protect gulf sea lanes during the Spanish-American War or wander the beaches of any of the islands that make up the park. *Mullet Key, 34th St. S. No admission, but tolls totaling 85 cents will be charged on the Bayway to the islands.*

Head back up the Bayway and turn left toward the beaches and then right on Gulf Boulevard (Rt. 699). The colossal pink Don CeSar Resort Hotel is off to the left. Head through St. Petersburg Beach and Treasure Island to Madeira Beach. Stop here **⑦** at **John's Pass Village and Boardwalk** (12901 Gulf Blvd.), a collection of shops in an old-style fishing village, where you can shop and eat at a variety of restaurants or pass the time watching the pelicans cavorting and dive-bombing for food.

When pelicans become entangled in fishing lines, locals some- **⑧** times carry them to the **Suncoast Seabird Sanctuary**, a nonprofit organization whose facilities are open to the public. Drive up Gulf Boulevard to Indian Shores. *18328 Gulf Blvd. Admission free, but donations welcome. Open daily 9– dark.*

⑨ Ready to get off the road and out on the water? **The Admiral** is the place to relax and enjoy dinner and a little dancing while sightseeing on Clearwater Harbor. *Up Gulf Blvd. to Clearwater Beach Marina, tel. 813/462–2628. Open Oct.–May. Fare is $9.50, dinner is extra. Boarding at 6:30 PM. Reservations required.*

For a second day in St. Petersburg, you'll enjoy a change of pace **⑩** along the cosmopolitan bayfront. Begin at the **Salvador Dali Museum.** To get there, take I-275 and then follow I-175 toward the bay. At 3rd Street South, turn right. The museum is on the left, about two blocks ahead. Inside you'll find a large collection of paintings of melting watches, colorful landscapes, and thought-provoking works of the late Spanish surrealist. *1000 3rd St. S., tel. 813/823–3767. Admission: $3 adults, $2 students and senior citizens. Open Tues.–Sat. 10–5, Sun. noon–5.*

Head up 3rd Street and turn right on 2nd Avenue. You're now **⑪** heading for the bayfront and **The Pier**, which looks as though a hurricane has turned it upside-down. The unusual building, a five-story inverted pyramid, was recently renovated and now contains a number of shops and eateries. *800 2nd Ave. NE. Admission free. Open daily 10–9.*

⑫ It's a short walk to the **Museum of Fine Arts,** the large building to your right along Beach Drive as you're returning from The Pier. French impressionists highlight the collection, but the museum also has outstanding examples of European, American, pre-Columbian, and Far Eastern art, as well as photography exhibits. *225 Beach Dr. NE., tel. 813/896–2667. Suggested donation: $2. Open Tues.–Sat. 10–5, Sun. 1–5.*

From here, it's a short drive to one of Florida's most colorful
⓭ spots, **Sunken Gardens**. To get there, take 4th Street North (a
right turn) to 18th Avenue North. Visitors can walk through an
aviary with tropical birds, stroll among more than 50,000 exotic
plants and flowers, and stop to smell the rare, fragrant orchids.
*Admission: $6.95 adults, $4 children. 1825 4th St. N., tel. 813/
896–3186. Open daily 9–5:30.*

To end the day, drive to U.S. 19, head north to Rte. 60, turn
⓮ right, and stop for dinner at the **Kapok Tree Restaurant.** *(see
Dining for details.)*

Exploring Sarasota and Bradenton

Sarasota is a city of two tales. Situated on the water, it is un-
questionably a beach resort. But it also has a thriving cultural
community, making it a suitable destination for those with a
taste for the arts. Much of the credit for the city's diversity is
due to the late John Ringling, founder of the now Ringling
Brothers Barnum & Bailey Circus, who chose to make Sarasota
the winter home of his circus and his family.

For those who like statistics, here are a few: Sarasota County
has 35 miles of Gulf beaches, 2 state parks, 22 municipal parks,
and 44 golf courses, many of them open to the public.

Nearby Bradenton maintains a lower profile, but also has its
share of sugar-sand beaches, golf courses, and historic sites
dating back to the mid-1800s.

To the south is Venice, with its multitudinous canals crisscross-
ing the city. Besides being the winter home of the circus, the
city contains the world's only clown college. And, though shell
collecting is quite good, the beaches of Venice are best known
for the wealth of shark teeth to be found.

Bradenton Bradenton is on a finger of land enclosing the southern end of
Tampa Bay; the Manatee River also borders the city's north
side. The barrier island, Anna Maria, lies off the mainland and
fronts the Gulf of Mexico. The combined U.S. 41 and 301 cuts
north-south through the center of the city. I-75 is to the east,
and Rte. 64 connects the interstate to Bradenton and Anna Maria Island.

Hernando DeSoto, one of the first Spanish explorers, set foot in
Florida in 1539 near what is now Bradenton. Take Rte. 64 to
⓯ 75th Street NW, turn north, and drive to **DeSoto National Memorial,** where park employees dressed in costumes of the
period demonstrate various 16th-century weapons and show
how the explorers who roamed the southeastern United States
prepared and preserved food for their journeys through the untamed land. Films, demonstrations, and a short nature trail are
on the grounds. *75th St. NW, tel. 813/792–0458. Admission: $1
per person. Open daily 8–5:30.*

Head back to the center of the city, to 10th Street West. A few
⓰ blocks from the river is the **South Florida Museum,** where you
can find artifacts on Florida's history, including displays of Indian culture and an excellent collection of Civil War
memorabilia. The museum is also home to "Snooty," the oldest
living manatee (or sea cow) in captivity. In the wild, manatees
are endangered, but here Snooty likes to shake hands and perform other tricks at feeding time. *201 10th St. W, tel. 813/746–*

4132. Admission: $4 adults, $3 children and students. Open Tues.–Fri. 10–5, weekends 1–5.

⑰ Also part of the museum is the **Bishop Planetarium**, where, inside a domed theater, you can see star shows and special-effects laser light displays. *Tel. 813/746–4131. Admission: $3 adults, $2 children and students; "Laser Fantasies" admission: $4 adults, $2 children. Star show Tues–Sat. at 1:30 and 3 PM. plus Fri. and Sat. at 7:30 PM.*

Time Out **The Pier Restaurant.** Take a lunch break on fresh-caught seafood and alligator and enjoy a view of the Manatee River in an old Spanish-style building. *At the foot of 12th St. on Memorial Pier, tel. 813/748–8087. Open daily from 11:30 AM.*

Cross the river on U.S. 41 and turn right when U.S. 301 splits off. On the left, three miles ahead, is the **Gamble Plantation State Historical Site.** The mansion, built in 1850, is the only pre-Civil War plantation house surviving in south Florida. This is where the Confederate secretary of state took refuge when the Confederacy fell to Union forces. Some of the original furnishings are on display in the mansion. *3708 Patten Ave., Ellenton, tel. 813/722–1017. Open 9–5 Thurs.–Mon., closed Tues. and Wed. Admission: $1. Tours of the house begin on the hour; no tours from noon to 1 PM.*

Sarasota The City of Sarasota sits on the eastern shore of Sarasota Bay. Across the water lie the barrier islands of Siesta Key, Longboat Key, and Lido Key, with myriad beaches, shops, hotels, condominiums, and houses. U.S. 41 is the main north-south thoroughfare in the city; further east, I-75 carries traffic past the city to Tampa or Fort Myers. Four state roads run west from the interstate highway into Sarasota.

Long ago, circus tycoon John Ringling found Sarasota an ideal spot to bring his clowns and performers to train and recuperate during the winter. Along the bay, Ringling also built himself a fancy home, patterned after the Palace of the Doges in Venice, **⑲** Italy. Today, the **Ringling Museums** include that mansion, as well as his art museum (with a world-renowned collection of Rubens paintings) and a museum of circus memorabilia. Also situated on the property is the Asolo State Theater, which was taken from an Italian castle and reassembled on-site. *Located a half mile south of the Sarasota-Bradenton Airport on U.S. 41, tel. 813/355–5101. Combined admission $6 ($1.75 for children 6–12) is good for the mansion and both museums. Open Mon.–Wed. and Fri.–Sun. 10–6, Thurs. 10–10.*

From the Ringling museums, head south on U.S. 41 about 1½ **⑳** miles to **Sarasota Jungle Gardens**. Here you can stroll through 10 acres of tropical plants and watch the bird and reptile shows. *3701 Bayshore Rd., tel. 813/355–5305. Admission: $5.95 adults, $2.95 children 3–12. Open daily 9–5.*

Time Out **St. Armand's Circle.** It's time to swing out across the bay. Continue south on U.S. 41 to Rte. 789. Turn right, and cross the Ringling Causeway to the small island of St. Armand's Key, where you'll find this chic little circle of shops and restaurants.

㉑ ㉒ Just up the road from **St. Armand's Key** is the **Mote Marine Science Center,** where marine biologists work to unlock the secrets of marine life. On display in the newly remodeled aquarium are sharks, rays, fish, and other marine creatures native to the area. A huge outdoor shark tank lets you see its inhabitants from above and below the water's surface. To get there from Harding Circle, turn north on Ringling Boulevard. Before you reach the bridge leading to Longboat Key, turn right at the sign for City Island and Mote Marine Lab. *1600 City Island Park, tel. 813/388–2451. Admission: $5 adults, $3 children 6–17. Open Tues.–Sun. 10–5.*

You now have an option. One choice is to either head back south, (23) past the public beach at Lido Key, to **South Lido Park**, where you can try your luck at fishing, take a dip in the waters of the bay or Gulf of Mexico, roam the paths of the 130-acre park, or picnic as the sun sets through the Australian pines into the gulf. *Open 8–sunset. Admission free.*

The alternative is to turn back east across Sarasota Bay and turn right into the Marina Plaza along U.S. 41. Here you can enjoy an evening on the water in style, with a sunset dinner (24) cruise on board a stern-wheel paddleboat, the *Marina Jack II*. *Marina Plaza, Island Park, tel. 813/366–9255. Cost: $4 plus dinner. Reservations.*

(25) Start out your second day of exploring Sarasota at **Marie Selby Botanical Gardens,** which are near the Island Park yacht basin. Here you can stroll through a world-class display of orchids and wander through 14 garden areas along Sarasota Bay. *800 S. Palm Ave., off U.S. 41, tel. 813/366–5730. Admission: $4 a-dults, free for children under 12 when accompanied by an adult. Open daily 10–5 except Christmas.*

(26) In the heart of Sarasota, you'll discover a **downtown art district**, with galleries such as Art Uptown (1367 Main St.), Adley Gallery (1620 Main St.), Corbino Galleries (69 S. Palm Ave.), Apple & Carpenter Gallery of Fine Arts (1280 N. Palm Ave.), and J. E. Voorhees Gallery (1359 Main St.).

(27) On the road to the airport (U.S. 41) is **Bellm's Cars & Music of Yesterday.** The display includes 130 classic cars, such as Pierce Arrows and Auburns, and 2,000 old-time music makers, such as hurdy-gurdies and calliopes. *5500 N. Tamiami Trail, tel. 813/ 355–6228. Admission: $5.50 adults, $3 children 6–16. Open Mon.–Sat. 8:30–6, Sun. 9:30–6.*

Exploring Fort Myers/Naples Region

Lee County has a split personality. Its inland communities— Fort Myers and Cape Coral—are primarily commercial and residential. Its gulf-front communities are beach resorts filled with people who are working mainly on relaxing and cultivating tans.

Fort Myers gets its nickname, the City of Palms, from the hundreds of towering royal palms that inventor Thomas Edison planted along a main residential street, McGregor Boulevard, on which his winter estate stood. Edison's idea caught on, and there are now more than 2,000 royal palms on McGregor Boulevard alone, with countless more throughout the city.

Along the county's western border are the resort islands of Estero, Sanibel, and Captiva. Estero contains Fort Myers Beach, a laid-back beach community favored by young singles and those who want to stay on the Gulf without paying the higher prices on Sanibel or Captiva. A few miles farther off the coast are Sanibel and Captiva, connected to the mainland by a mile-long causeway. In recent years development has threatened the charm of the islands. However, island dwellers have staunchly held the line on further development, keeping buildings low and somewhat farther apart than on the majority of Florida's barrier islands. Sanibel has long been a world-class shelling locale, with fine fishing, luxury hotels, and dozens of restaurants. You will not be able to see most of the houses, which are shielded by tall Australian pines, but the beaches and tranquil gulf waters are readily accessible.

Naples is often likened to Palm Beach for its ambience. Fifth and Third avenues south are lined with exclusive boutiques, shops, and restaurants. Here, first-time visitors and long-time members of the city's society mingle.

For those to whom beaches are important, Naples far outstrips Palm Beach with its abundance of public beach accesses—41 miles of beach are open to the public. The yen to go shelling, sunning, and fishing can be indulged to excess on the sun-drenched white shores.

South of Naples is yet another resort island, Marco. Here, high-rise condominiums and hotels line much of the waterfront, but many natural areas have been preserved, including the tiny fishing village of Goodland, where Old Florida lives on.

Fort Myers– Lee County *Numbers in the margin correspond with points of interest on the Fort Myers/Naples Region map.*

❶ **Fort Myers** is the heart of the county, but only a few major roads lead through it. I-75 runs north-south, as does the more commercial thoroughfare, U.S. 41 (called Cleveland Ave. in Fort Myers). McGregor Boulevard runs from downtown Fort Myers southwest to Sanibel-Captiva. Summerlin Road runs southwest from Colonial Boulevard in South Fort Myers to Sanibel-Captiva and Fort Myers Beach. Rte. 78 (Pine Island-Bayshore Rd.) leads from North Fort Myers through north Cape Coral onto Pine Island.

If you are headed downtown from the beaches, drive at least part of the way on palm-lined McGregor Boulevard (from College Parkway north into town is the most scenic).

Thomas Edison's Winter Home, containing a laboratory, botanical gardens, and a museum, is open for guided tours. The property straddles McGregor Boulevard (Rte. 867) about a mile west of U.S. 41 near downtown Fort Myers. The inventor spent his winters on the 14-acre estate, developing the phonograph and teletype, experimenting with rubber, and planting some 6,000 species of plants from those collected throughout the world. *2350 McGregor Blvd., Fort Myers, tel. 813/334–3614. Admission: $5 adults, $1 children 6–12. Open daily except Thanksgiving and Christmas. Tours 9–4 daily except Sun. 12:30–4.*

Just a few blocks east is the **Fort Myers Historical Museum,** which is housed in a restored railroad depot. Its displays depict the area's history dating back to 1200 BC. *2300 Peck St., Fort Myers, tel. 813/332–5955. Admission: $2 adults, 50 cents children 2–12. Open Tues.–Fri. 9–4:30, weekends 1–5.*

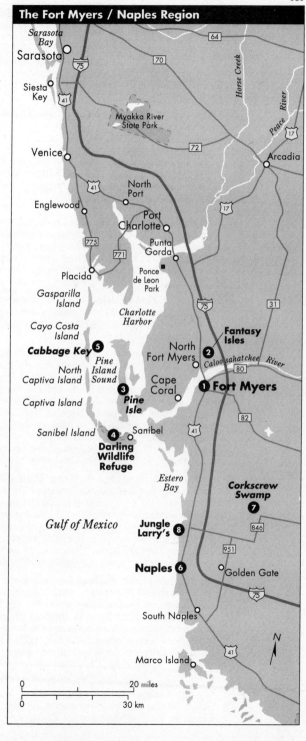

The Fort Myers / Naples Region

Sarasota Bay

Sarasota

75

64

70

Siesta Key

41

Myakka River State Park

72

Horse Creek

Peace River

17

Venice

41

North Port

Arcadia

17

Englewood

Port Charlotte

775

771

Punta Gorda

Placida

Ponce de Leon Park

Gasparilla Island

Charlotte Harbor

75

31

Cayo Costa Island

Cabbage Key ⑤

Pine Island

North Captiva Island

Pine Island Sound

Fantasy Isles

North Fort Myers

② Caloosahatchee River

Captiva Island

③ **Pine Isle**

Cape Coral

① **Fort Myers**

80

Sanibel Island

④ Sanibel

82

Darling Wildlife Refuge

41

Estero Bay

Corkscrew Swamp ⑦

Gulf of Mexico

Jungle Larry's ⑧

846

951

Naples ⑥

Golden Gate

75

South Naples

N

Marco Island

41

0 _____ 20 miles

0 _____ 30 km

Head northwest to Edwards Drive, which borders the Caloosahatchee River. The **City Yacht Basin** has tour boats that offer sightseeing and luncheon cruises on the river. Also on Edwards Drive, you can find a plethora of shuffleboard courts that weather heavy use on all but the hottest days. Adjacent to the courts is the **Hall of 50 States,** where the Fort Myers Chamber of Commerce dispenses information. *1365 Hendry St. Open weekdays, 9–4.*

Take U.S. 41 north across the Caloosahatchee Bridge into North Fort Myers.

Time Out **Mariner's Inn** (3448 Marinatown Lane, tel. 813/997–8300). Head north on U.S. 41 to the light at Hancock Bridge Parkway. Turn left, and the inn is less than half a mile ahead on the left. The dining room overlooks a busy marina, and the seafood is fresh, varied, and well prepared.

Heading north on U.S. 41 once again, you will find **The Shell Factory** two miles ahead on the right. If you can't find the shells you dreamed of on the beaches, you can buy them here. The Shell Factory is a long-standing tourist attraction that sells shells, shell crafts, and other gifts, souvenirs, and clothing. *Admission free. Open daily 9–6.*

2 Adjacent is **Fantasy Isles**, a small amusement park with a fairytale theme. *Tel. 813/997–4204. Admission free, rides 50 cents each. Open daily 10–5 during the winter, reduced hours other seasons.*

Backtracking south on U.S. 41 about two miles, you reach the intersection of Pine Island Road. A right takes you into the **3** heart of **Pine Island,** a classic Old Florida fishing community. Go right on Stringfellow Boulevard and wend your way past mango and citrus groves. Make a left on Pineland Road, a winding palm-lined road, past a Norman Rockwell–like post office and through the village of Pineland, where fishing is still a way of life. Continue north back to Stringfellow Boulevard. In **Bokeelia,** you will enjoy a sweeping view of Charlotte Harbor, one of the country's most pristine bodies of water.

4 On Sanibel, explore the **J. N. "Ding" Darling National Wildlife Refuge**—by car, foot, bicycle, or canoe. The 5,014-acre refuge is home to some 290 species of birds, 50 types of reptiles, and various mammals. A five-mile dirt road meanders through the sanctuary. An observation tower along the road is a prime bird-watching site, especially in the early morning and just before dusk. *Tel. 813/472–1100. Admission: $3 per car or $10 for a duck stamp (which covers all national wildlife refuges).*

5 Board a boat to visit **Cabbage Key**, which sits at Marker 60 on the Intracoastal Waterway. Atop an ancient Calusa Indian shell mound on Cabbage Key is the friendly inn that novelist and playwright Mary Roberts Rinehart built in 1938. Now the inn offers several guest rooms, a marina, and a dining room that is papered in thousands of dollar bills, signed and posted by patrons over the years. *Lunch and dinner tours available through Captiva's South Seas Plantation (tel. 813/472–5111), and Fishermen's Village in Punta Gorda (tel. 813/639–0969).*

Naples The city and surrounding suburbs are squeezed between the **6** Gulf of Mexico and the wilderness of the Big Cypress National Preserve, which stretches to the Everglades. I-75 and U.S. 41

lead from the north. Alligator Alley and U.S. 41 cut through the Everglades to bring travelers from the east coast.

To get a feel for what this part of Florida was like before humans began draining the swamps, take a drive out Rte. 846 to **7** the **Corkscrew Swamp Sanctuary**. The National Audubon Society manages the 11,000-acre tract to help protect 500-year-old trees and endangered birds, such as the wood storks that nest high in the bald cypress. Visitors taking the 1¾-mile self-guided tour along the boardwalk can glimpse alligators, graceful wading birds, and unusual "air" plants that cling to the sides of trees. *16 mi east of I-75 on Rte. 846, tel. 813/657-3771. Admission: $4 adults, $2 students, children under age 6 free. Open daily 9-5.*

8 If you want to monkey around, head for **Jungle Larry's African Safari Park**. Drive south on U.S. 41 past Mooringline Drive until you see the big sign for Jungle Larry's, then turn left. Here you can see a tiglon—a cross between a tiger and a lion—and other exotic wildlife in a junglelike park. The kids will also enjoy the petting zoo. *1590 Goodlette Rd., tel. 813/262-4053. Admission: $8.95 adults, $5.95 children 3-15. Open 9:30-5:30; shows at 11:30, 2, and 4. Closed Mon., May-Nov.*

Antique car enthusiasts should head to Naples' newest tourist attraction, the **Collier Automotive Museum,** where 75 antique and classic sports cars now enjoy a splendid retirement. *2500 S. Horseshoe Drive, Collier Park of Commerce, off Airport-Pulling Road, tel. 813/643-5252. Admission: $6 adults, $3 children under 12. Open Fri.-Sun., 10-6.*

Head back to U.S. 41 and go south to **Third Street South** or **Fifth Avenue South,** Naple's fashionable shopping areas.

Head south on U.S. 41 to the **Old Marine Market Place at Tin City** (1200 5th Ave. S). In a collection of former fishing shacks along Naples Bay, entrepreneurs and artisans have set up 40 boutiques, studios, and shops offering everything from scrimshaw to Haitian art.

Time Out   **Merriman's Wharf** (1200 5th Ave. S, tel. 813/261-1811), in the Old Marine Market Place, is a good bet for a drink or a seafood lunch—either along the dock or indoors in air-conditioned comfort.

What to See and Do with Children

Adventure Island is a water wonderland in the heart of Tampa, complete with water slides and pools with man-made waves. There are also changing rooms, snack stands, a gift shop, and a video arcade. *1 mi northeast of Busch Gardens. 4545 Bougainvillea Ave., tel. 813/971-7978. Admission: $13.95 per person, children under 2 free. Open daily; closed Jan. and Feb.*
Busch Gardens (*see* Exploring).
Great Explorations! is a museum where you will never be told, "Don't touch!" Everything is designed for a hands-on experience. The museum, which opened in late 1987, is divided into theme rooms, such as the Body Shop, which explores health; the Think Tank, which features mind-stretching puzzles and games; the Touch Tunnel, a 90-foot-long, pitch-black maze you crawl through; and Phenomenal Arts, which displays such

items as a Moog music synthesizer (which you can play) and neon-filled tubes that glow in vivid colors when touched. *1120 4th St. S, St. Petersburg just off I-275, tel. 813/821–8885. Admission: $4.75 adults, $4 senior citizens, $2.75 children under 8. Open daily 10–5.*

Sarasota Jungle Gardens *(see* Exploring).

Circus Galleries, Ringling Museum *(see* Exploring).

301 Raceway, go-cart rides and a video game room. *4050 N. Washington Blvd. (U.S. 301), Sarasota, tel. 813/355–5588. Open Sun.–Thurs. 11–10, Fri. and Sat. 11–11.*

Nature Center of Lee County and Planetarium offers frequently changing exhibits on wildlife, fossils, Florida Indians, and native habitats. An aviary is home to a variety of permanently disabled birds, including hawks, owls, and bald eagles. There are two miles of nature walks through the cypress swamps. The planetarium offers star and laser light shows and Cinema-360 films. *3840 Ortiz Ave., Fort Myers, tel. 813/275–3435. Nature Center admission. $2 adults, 50 cents children; Planetarium admission: $3.50 adults, $3 senior citizens, $2.50 children under 12. Open Mon–Sat. 9–4, Sun. 11–4:30.*

Waltzing Waters and Rainbow Golf. Fountains dance with lights and music indoors during the day, outdoors at night. Adjacent is an 18-hole miniature golf course. *18101 U.S. 41 SE (at San Carlos Park), Fort Myers, tel. 813/267–2533. Admission: $7.50 adults, $3.50 children 7–12. Golf $1 with show. Open daily 11–9.*

Everglades Wonder Gardens captures the flavor of untamed Florida with its exhibit of native wildlife and natural surroundings. *U.S. 41, tel. 813/992–2591. Admission: $5 adults, $3 children 5–15. Open daily 9–4.*

The DeSoto National Memorial. *(see* Exploring).

Southwest Florida for Free

Bradenton **Manatee Village Historical Park.** An 1860 courthouse, 1887 church, 1903 general store and museum, and 1912 settler's home are situated here, as is the Old Manatee Cemetery, which dates back to 1850 and contains the graves of early Manatee County settlers. (Appointments necessary to tour the cemetery.) *Rte. 64, 1 mi east of U.S. 41, tel. 813/749–7165. Open weekdays 9–5, Sun. 2–5 Sept.–June. Closed Sun. the rest of the year.*

Fort Myers Naples Area **Youth Museum of Charlotte County.** Mostly animal specimens from Africa and North America, plus dolls, shells, and a variety of programs, are displayed here. *260 W. Retta Esplanade, Punta Gorda. Open weekdays 10–5.*

St. Petersburg **Fort de Soto Park.** This 900-acre park is composed of six keys: Mullet, Bonne Fortune, Cunningham, Madeleine, St. Christopher, and St. Jean. Fort de Soto, begun during the Spanish-American War, is on the southern end of Mullet Key. *Reach it via 34th St. S., U.S. 19 and the Bayway. Open sunrise to sunset.*

Sarasota **Ringling Museum of Art.** This is one of three museums on the grounds of the John and Mable Ringling Estate. A stipulation in the wealthy circus owner's will requires the art museum to be open free every Saturday. *On U.S. 41, 3 mi north of downtown, tel. 813/355–5101. Open 9–6.*

Tampa   **Villazon and Co. cigar factory.** Free 30-minute guided tours are offered. You'll see the process from the selection of tobacco through the wrapping, banding, and packaging of the cigars. *3104 Armenia Ave., tel. 813/879–2291. Open weekdays 9:30–5. Closed holidays, late Dec.–mid-Jan., and late June–mid-July.*

Shrimp Docks. By late afternoon, the shrimp boats pull in at the 22nd Street causeway to unload their catches.

University of Tampa. Tour the administration building, built as a luxury hotel in 1890, which served as Theodore Roosevelt's headquarters during the Spanish-American War. *Tours Tues. and Thurs. at 1:30, Sept.–May. Closed holidays. Reservations required, tel. 813/253–6220.*

Tampa Bay Downs and Turf Club. Women are admitted free here on Thursdays. Rte. 580 (Hillsborough Ave.) in Oldsmar. *Races Dec.–mid-Mar.; post time 1 PM. PARKING $1. TEL. 813/855–4401.*

Tampa Jai Alai Fronton. This fast-paced and strenuous game is popular among Floridians, even those who don't like to bet. South Dale Mabry Highway and Gandy Boulevard (tel. 813/831 –1411). Men are admitted free to Wednesday noon matiness; women to Saturday noon matinees; senior citizens to Monday matinees. No one under age 18 admitted. Pari-mutuel betting.

The Suncoast Seabird Sanctuary. This refuge and rehabilitation center for injured birds houses brown pelicans, cormorants, white herons, ospreys, and many other species. Many are on exhibit for public viewing. *18328 Gulf Blvd., tel. 813/391–6211. Admission free, but the nonprofit center accepts donations. Open daily daylight hours.*

Tampa Bay Area   **Railroad Historical Museum.** Once a railroad station for the Orange Belt Railroad system, this place dates back to 1889. Drawings and relics from the Scottish community are on display. Maps for self-guided walking tours of historic areas are available. *341 Main St., Dunedin, tel. 813/733–4151. Open Wed. and Sat. 10–noon, Thurs. 9:30–11:30. Closed June 1–Oct. 1.*

Heritage Park and Museum. A collection of restored pioneer homes and buildings is spread on a 21-acre wooded site. The museum is the park's centerpiece, with exhibits depicting Pinellas County's pioneer lifestyle. Spinning, weaving, and other demonstrations are held regularly. *11909 125th St. N, Largo, tel. 813/462–3474. Open Tues.–Sat. 10–4, Sun. 1–4.*

Suncoast Botanical Gardens. Small by public botanical-garden standards, but all 60 acres are populated with cacti, eucalyptus trees, palms, crepe myrtle, and other flora of the Sunshine State. *10410 125th St., Largo, tel. 813/595–7218. Open daily daylight hours.*

Off the Beaten Track

Boca Grande   Before roads to southwest Florida were even talked about, the wealthy boarded trains to get to the Gasparilla Inn on **Boca Grande.** The small community continues to be a haven for the monied who seek to stay out of the limelight. The grand inn, built in 1912, remains in operation. From U.S. 41 in northern

Port Charlotte head southwest on Rte. 776, then south on Rte. 771 into Placida, where a causeway runs out to the island.

While condominiums and other forms of modern sprawl have begun to creep up on Gasparilla, much of Boca Grande looks as it has for a century or more. The mood is set by the old Florida homes, many made of wood, with wide, inviting verandas and wicker rocking chairs.

At the island's southern end is Old Lighthouse Beach, where a historic wooden lighthouse still stands and where there is ample parking and lots of gulf-front beach space. At mid-island is Banyan Street, so named for the huge trees that send down hundreds of shoots, shading the residential street, so that it appears to be twilight much of the day.

There is a generally sleepy ambience to the island, except in the spring, when the tarpon fishermen descend with a vengeance on Boca Grande Pass, considered among the best tarpon-fishing spots in the world.

Everglades City Nestled amidst the 10,000 Islands, this tiny fishing village is the western gateway to Everglades National Park. From here, you can get a close look at the Everglades, sometimes called the river of grass. **Wooten's** (tel. 813/394–8080) offers airboat and swamp buggy rides through the swamps. Some 200 alligators are on display at Wooten's, too. To get there, drive 35 miles east of Naples on U.S. 41. Rides depart about every 30 minutes.

North Fort Myers **ECHO** (Educational Concerns for Hunger Organization) is a small active group striving to solve the world's hunger problems. The group offers tours of its gardens that feature collections of tropical food plants, simulated rain forests, and fish farming. Tours are offered each Friday at 10 AM, or by appointment. *17430 Durrance Rd., tel. 813/543–3246.*

North Port An early-morning journey in a **hot-air balloon** gives the adventurous a bird's-eye view of a portion of southwest Florida (the portion depending on the prevailing winds). Rides commence (from North Port, south of Venice) early enough to watch the sunrise and are followed by leisurely breakfasts of quiche and champagne. *Contact Trans-America Balloons, North Port, tel. 813/426–7326. Cost: $89 per person, maximum of 3 people.*

Palmdale You aren't likely to happen upon Palmdale, a speck of a town about 40 minutes east of Punta Gorda, unless you make a point of visiting either of two singular attractions. You know you're approaching the **Cypress Knee Museum** when you see spindly hand-carved signs along Rte. 27 with sayings such as Lady, If He Won't Stop, Hit Him on Head with a Shoe. If you are younger than 6 or older than 80, you get in free; otherwise, you pay $2 for entry to Tom Gaskins's world of cypress knees. In the museum are thousands of cypress knees, the knotty, gnarled protuberances that sprout mysteriously from the bases of some cypress trees and grow to resemble all manner of persons and things. There are specimens resembling dogs, bears, ballet dancers' feet, an anteater, Joseph Stalin and Franklin D. Roosevelt. Many require Gaskins's handwritten explanations, such as Lady Hippopotamus Wearing a Carmen Miranda Hat.

After touring the museum, walk the narrow boardwalk through three-quarters of a mile of cypress swamp to see the knees and trees in an unspoiled setting. The diminutive, barefoot man wandering amid the cypress is apt to be the 79-year-old Gaskins, who has appeared twice on Johnny Carson's "Tonight" show to display—what else?—his cypress knees. *1 mi south of the U.S. 27 and U.S. 29 junction, tel. 813/675–2951. Open daily 8 AM—dusk. Admission: $2 adults, $1 children 6–12.*

Just two miles southeast on U.S. 27, **Gatorama's** 1,000 alligators and assorted crocodiles await visitors, smiling toothily. Visitors who want to take a good long gander at gators can get their fill here, where a variety of species and sizes cohabit. It's also a commercial gator farm, so you'll see how the "mink" of the leather trade is grown for profit. *Tel. 813/675–0623. Admission: $4.50 adults, $2.50 children 2–11.*

Shopping

Most visitors eventually get their quota of sun, sand, and surf and find themselves in need of something else to do. For many, that something is shopping.

Gift Ideas It is a rare vacationer who does not leave the state with at least one sack of oranges or grapefruit. Most produce stands are open during the citrus season (Dec.–Mar.). You cannot take citrus out of state without a USDA inspection sticker, so make sure you take only those sacks that are properly sealed.

In Tarpon Springs, natural sponges are plentiful and reasonably priced. Many shops along Dodecanese Boulevard, the town's main street, sell a variety of locally harvested sponges.

Tampa's Ybor City is a thriving Cuban community where the art of cigar making lives on. There are many small cigar shops in the area on Tampa's east side.

Shell items—jewelry, lamps, plant hangers, and such—are among the more kitschy commodities found in abundance in the region. Sanibel Island, one of the world's premier shelling grounds, has numerous shops that sell shell products (including two named She Sells Seashells, at 1983 and 1157 Periwinkle Way). **The Shell Factory** in North Fort Myers claims to have the world's largest display of seashells and coral. *2787 N. Tamiami Trail (U.S. 41). Open daily 9–6.*

Fine Shopping Those who gravitate toward exclusive boutiques have a wealth of them to explore in southwest Florida. In Sarasota, St. Armand's Key (just west of downtown Sarasota) has Harding Circle, a circular string of shops and restaurants that cater to consumers seeking out-of-the-ordinary items and willing to pay high prices for them.

In Fort Myers, there are two such centers—**Bell Tower** (U.S. 41 and Daniels Rd., South Fort Myers) and **Royal Palm Square** (Colonial Blvd., between McGregor Blvd. and U.S. 41). Both have about 36 shops and restaurants. Both are worth visiting if just to look at the elegant tropical landscaping, which includes ponds full of huge oriental carp and parrots that stand sentry from perches among the palms. Neither center is enclosed, but both have covered sidewalks. In Naples, 3rd and 5th streets south are lined with fine boutiques and restaurants.

Flea Markets **Wagonwheel** is 100-plus acres containing some 2,000 vendors and a variety of food concessions. Parking costs $1. There is a tram from the parking lot to the vendor area. *7801 Park Blvd., Pinellas Park, tel. 813/544–5319. Open weekends 8–4.*

Red Barn has the requisite big red barn, in which vendors operate daily except Mondays. The number of vendors increases to about 1,000 on weekends. *1707 1st St. E, Bradenton, tel. 813/ 747–3794. Open Wed., Sat., and Sun. 8–4.*

Dome has sheltered walkways under which can be found dozens of stalls selling new and recycled wares. *Rte. 775, west of U.S. 41, Venice, tel. 813/493–6773. Open Fri.–Sun. 9–4; closed Aug.*

Ortiz also features covered walkways and hundreds of vendors selling new and used items. *Ortiz and Anderson avenues, east of Fort Myers. Open weekends 8–4.*

Beaches

You can't drive on them like you can in Daytona. And the scantily attired college-age revelers who pack Fort Lauderdale each spring are not found in abundance here. But there are myriad reasons why a growing number of Florida-bound beach goers are heading to the southwest coast. For sun worshipers, there are beaches on which to bask in relative solitude; for singles, there are sands on which to see and be seen; for shell collectors, there is treasure to unearth. And not one beach offers less than a spectacular sunset.

Charlotte County (Punta Gorda Area) **Englewood Beach,** near the Charlotte-Sarasota county line, is popular with teenagers, although beach goers of all ages frequent it. In addition to a wide and shell-littered beach, there are barbecue grills, picnic facilities, and a playground.

Collier County (Naples Area) **Bonita Springs Public Beach** is 10 minutes from the I-75 exit at Bonita Beach Road, on the southern end of Bonita Beach. There are picnic tables, free parking, and nearby refreshment stands and shopping.

Delnor-Wiggins Pass State Recreation Area is at the gulf end of Bluebill Avenue, off Vanderbilt Drive in North Naples. The well-maintained park offers miles of sandy beaches, lifeguards, barbecue grills, picnic tables, a boat ramp, observation tower, rest rooms with wheelchair access, lots of parking space, bathhouses, and showers. Fishing is best in Wiggins Pass at the north end of the park. Admission: $1 for the operator of a vehicle, plus 50 cents per passenger. Boat launching costs $1. No alcoholic beverages allowed.

Lowdermilk Park stretches along Gulf Shore Boulevard in Naples. There are 1,000 feet of beach plus parking, rest rooms, showers, a pavilion, vending machines, and picnic tables. No alcoholic beverages or fires permitted.

Tigertail Beach is on Hernando Drive at the south end of Marco Island. Singles and families congregate here. Facilities: parking, concession stand, picnic area, sailboat rentals, volleyball, rest rooms, and showers.

Lee County (Fort Myers Area) **Estero Island,** otherwise known as **Fort Myers Beach,** is 18 miles from downtown Fort Myers. It has numerous public accesses to the beach, which is frequented by families and young singles. In most areas, you are never far from civilization, with houses, condominiums, and hotels nestled along the shore. The island's shores slope gradually into the usually tranquil and warm Gulf waters, affording a safe swimming area for children. From Fort Myers, it is reached via San Carlos Boulevard; from Naples and Bonita Springs, via Hickory Boulevard.

Lynn Hall Memorial Park is on Estero Boulevard, in the more commercial northern part of Fort Myers Beach. Singles can be found playing in the gentle surf or sunning and socializing on shore. A number of night spots and restaurants are within easy walking distance. A free fishing pier adjoins the public beach. Facilities: picnic tables, barbecue grills, playground equipment, and a bathhouse with rest rooms.

Carl E. Johnson Recreation Area is just south of Fort Myers Beach. The admission of $1 per adult, 50 cents per child includes a round-trip tram ride from the park entrance to Lovers Key, on which the park is situated. Shelling, bird-watching, fishing, canoeing, and nature walks in an unspoiled setting are the main attractions here. There are also rest rooms, picnic tables, a snack bar, and basic showers.

Sanibel

Sanibel and **Captiva** islands are about 23 miles from Fort Myers and are reached via a toll bridge on the Sanibel Causeway. Though the $3 round-trip toll may seem steep, avid shell collectors and nature enthusiasts are apt to get their money's worth. Sanibel beaches are rated among the best shelling grounds in the world. For the choicest pickings, get there as the tide is going out or just after a storm. Windsurfers need go only as far as the Sanibel causeway to find a suitable place to set sail.

Gulfside Park, off Casa Ybel Road, is a lesser-known and less-populated beach, ideal for those who seek solitude and do not require facilities.

Lighthouse Park, at Sanibel's southern end, attracts a mix of families, shellers, and singles. Rest rooms are available. One of the draws is a historic old lighthouse.

Bowman's Beach is mainly a family beach on Sanibel's northwest end, but nudists have been known to bathe unabashedly in more secluded areas of the beach.

Manatee County (Bradenton Area)

Anna Maria Island, just west of the Sunshine Skyway Bridge, boasts three public beaches. **Anna Maria Bayfront Park,** at the north end of the municipal pier, is a secluded beach fronting both the Intracoastal Waterway and the Gulf of Mexico. Facilities include picnic grounds, a playground, rest rooms, showers, and lifeguards. At mid-island, in the town of Holmes Beach, is **Manatee County Beach,** popular with all ages. It has picnic facilities, a snack bar, showers, rest rooms, and lifeguards. At the island's southern end is **Coquina Beach,** popular with singles and families. Facilities: picnic area, boat ramp, playground, refreshment stand, rest rooms, showers, and lifeguards.

Egmont Key lies just off the northern tip of Anna Maria Island. On it is Fort Dade, a military fort built in 1900 during the Spanish-American War, and Florida's sixth brightest lighthouse. The primary inhabitant of the two-mile-long island is the threatened gopher tortoise. The only way to get to the island is by boat. Shellers will find the trip rewarding. An excursion boat makes trips on Tuesday, Thursday, and Sunday. The *Miss Cortez* departs from Cortez, just west of Bradenton (tel. 813/794–1223).

Cortez Beach, on the mainland, just north of Coquina, is on Gulf Boulevard in the town of Bradenton Beach. This one's popular with those who like their beaches without facilities—nothing but sand, water, and trees. The Palma Sola Causeway takes Manatee Avenue on the mainland to Anna Maria Island and also offers beach goers a long, sandy beach fronting Palma Sola Bay. There are boat ramps, a dock, and picnic tables.

Greer Island Beach is at the northern tip of the next barrier island south on Longboat Key. It's accessible by boat or via North Shore Boulevard. The secluded peninsula has a wide beach and excellent shelling, but no facilities.

Pinellas County (Gulf Coast west of Tampa) Tarpon Springs has two public beaches: **Howard Park Beach,** where a lifeguard is on duty daily 8:30–6 Easter through Labor Day, and **Sunset Beach,** where there is similar lifeguard duty as well as rest rooms, picnic tables, grills, and a boat ramp.

Caladesi Island State Park lies three miles off Dunedin's coast, across Hurricane Pass. The 600-acre park is one of the state's few remaining undeveloped barrier islands. It's accessible only by boat. There is a beach on the gulf side and mangroves on the bay side. This is a good spot for swimming, fishing, shelling, boating, and nature study. A self-guided nature trail winds through the island's interior. Park rangers are available to answer questions. Facilities: boardwalks, picnic shelters, bathhouses, a ranger station, and concession stand. A ferry runs regularly between Caladesi Island and Honeymoon Island to the north but it runs in good weather only, 10–5. *Fee: $3.75 adults, $2.10 children 2–10. Park admission extra. Call for ferry information (tel. 813/734–5263).*

Clearwater Beach is another popular, more accessible island beach. It is south of Caladesi on a narrow island between Clearwater Harbor and the gulf. It is connected to downtown Clearwater by Memorial Causeway. Facilities: marina, concessions, showers, rest rooms, and lifeguards.

St. Petersburg Area The St. Petersburg beaches are numerous and wide-ranging in character.

Bay Beach (North Shore Dr. and 13th Ave. NE, on Tampa Bay) charges 10 cents admission. It has showers and shelters.

North Shore Beach (901 North Shore Dr. NE) charges $1 admission. Facilities: pool, beach umbrellas, cabanas, windbreaks, and lounges.

Maximo Park Beach (34 St. and Pinellas Point Dr. S) is on Boca Ciega Bay. There is no lifeguard. There is a picnic area with grills, tables, shelters, and a boat ramp.

St. Petersburg Municipal Beach (11260 Gulf Blvd.) is a free beach on Treasure Island. There are dressing rooms, metered parking, and a snack bar.

Pass-a-Grille Beach, on the gulf, has parking meters, a snack bar, rest rooms, and showers.

Fort DeSoto Park consists of the southernmost beaches of St. Petersburg, on five islands totaling some 900 acres. Facilities: two fishing piers, picnic sites overlooking lagoons, a waterskiing and boating area, and miles of beaches for swimming. Open daily until dark. To get there, take the Pinellas Bayway through three toll gates (cost: 65 cents).

Sarasota County The county contains 10 beaches, ranging from five to 113 acres. **South Lido,** at the southern tip of Lido Key, is among the largest and best beaches in the region. The sugar-sand beach offers little for shell collectors, but the interests of virtually all other beach lovers are served on its 100 acres, which probably accounts for the diverse mix of people it attracts. Facilities: fishing, nature trails, volleyball, playground, horseshoes, rest rooms, and picnic grounds.

Siesta Beach is on Beach Road on Siesta Key. The 40-acre park contains nature trails, a concession stand, soccer and softball fields, picnicking facilities, play equipment, rest rooms, and tennis and volleyball courts.

Turtle Beach is farther south on Siesta Key's Midnight Pass Road. Though only 14 acres, it includes boat ramps, horseshoe courts, picnic and play facilities, a recreation building, rest rooms, and a volleyball court.

North Jetty Park is at the south end of Casey Key, a slender barrier island. It's a favorite for family outings. Amenities include rest rooms, a concession stand, play and picnic equipment, fishing, horseshoes, and a volleyball court.

Nokomis Beach is just north of North Jetty on Albee Road. Its facilities are similar to those at North Jetty, except that it has two boat ramps and no horseshoe court.

Caspersen Beach, on Beach Drive in south Venice, is the county's largest park. It has a nature trail, fishing, picnicking, rest rooms, plus lots of beach for those who prefer space to a wealth of amenities. Along with a plentiful mix of shells, observant beachcombers are likely to find sharks' teeth on Venice beaches, washed up from the ancient shark burial grounds just offshore.

Manasota Key spans much of the county's southern coast, from south of Venice to Englewood. It has two choice beaches: *Manasota*, on Manasota Beach Road, with a boat ramp, picnic area and rest rooms; and *Blind Pass*, where you can fish and swim but will find no amenities.

Participant Sports

Biking Call the nearest chamber of commerce or bike store for the best bike paths. Two of the best are at Boca Grande and Sanibel Island.

Tampa Bay. There are many places to rent bikes, but not much in the way of bike paths. Rental stores include **St. Petersburg:** *The Beach Cyclist* (7517 Blindpass Rd., tel. 813/367–5001) and *Village Bike Shops* (7324 Central Ave., tel. 813/381–6667 and 2236 62nd Ave., tel. 813/867–6667); **Largo:** *D & S Bicycle Shop* (12073 Seminole Blvd., tel. 813/393–0300); and **Tarpon Springs:** *BiSick* (tel. 813/937–3030).

Sarasota/Bradenton. No bike paths. Rental shops include **Bradenton:** *Bicycle Center* (2610 Cortez Rd., tel. 813/756–5480); **Sarasota:** *Mr. CB's* (1249 Stickney Point Rd., tel. 813/349–4400), and *Pedal N Wheels* (Merchants Pointe Shopping Center, 2881 Clark Rd., tel. 813/922–0481); and **Venice:** *The Bike Doctor* (291 Trott Circle, tel. 813/426–4807); and *Bicycles International* (1744 Tamiami Trail S, [U.S. 41], tel. 813/497–1590).

Fort Myers/Naples. There are several bike paths in the area. **Boca Grande,** an hour's drive from Fort Myers or Sarasota, has good bike paths. Rentals are available at *Fun Rentals* (4th St., tel. 813/964–2070). **Fort Myers:** The best choice here is the path along Summerlin Road. For rental, try *Trikes & Bikes* (3224 Fowler St., tel. 813/936–4301). **Sanibel:** The island's extensive bike path is well used. It is in good condition and runs throughout the island, keeping bikers safely apart from the traffic and allowing them some time for reflection on the waterways and wildlife they will encounter. Rent bikes at *Finnimore's Cycle Shop* (1223 Periwinkle Way, Sanibel, tel. 813/472–5577) and *Jim's Bike & Scooter Rental* (11534 Andy Rossi La., Captiva, tel. 813/472–1296). **Naples:** *Pop's Bicycles* (4265 Bonita Beach Rd., Bonita Springs, tel. 813/947–4442) and *The Bicycle Shop* (813 Vanderbilt Beach Rd., Naples, tel. 813/566–3646); **Marco Island:** *Scooterville* (855 Bald Eagle Dr., tel. 813/394–8400).

Canoeing For those who like to travel slowly and under their own power, canoe rentals abound. Among them are **Art's Swap Shop** (Tampa, tel. 813/935–4011), canoe and car racks for rent; and **Myakka River State Park,** 15 miles south of Sarasota near Venice (tel. 813/924–1027), canoes, paddles, and life vests for rent. **Canoe Outpost** offers half-day, full-day, and overnight canoe-camping trips from a number of southwest Florida locations, including Little Manatee River (18001 U.S. 301 S, Wimauma, just south of Tampa, tel. 813/634–2228) and Peace River (Rte. 7, Box 301, Arcadia, 25 miles northeast of Port Charlotte, tel. 813/494–1215). **Lakes Park** in Fort Myers (tel. 813/481–7946) rents canoes on waterways where you can see the carp swimming, and, if you are quiet enough, some herons and osprey flying overhead; **Canoe Safari** (Arcadia, tel. 813/494–7865) has half- and full-day trips, plus overnighters including camping equipment; **Parkland Ventures** (Fort Myers, tel. 813/482–1328) has guided nature treks in canoes or kayaks; and **Tarpon Bay Marina** (Sanibel, tel. 813/472–8900) has canoes and equipment for exploring the waters of the J. N. "Ding" Darling National Wildlife Refuge.

Fishing Anglers flock to southwest Florida. You need very little to get started—a rod and reel will suffice. Just wander out to a bridge and cast off. Tampa Bay and its inlets are known for yielding tarpon, kingfish, and speckled trout. Snapper, grouper, sea trout, snook, sheephead, and shark are among the species to be found throughout the region. You can also charter your own boat or join a group on a party boat for full- or half-day outings.

Party boats in the area include **Flying Fish** (Marina Jack's, U.S. 41 and bay front, Sarasota, tel. 813/366–3373), **L-C Marine** (215 Tamiami Trail S., [U.S. 41], Venice, tel. 813/484–9044), **Kingfisher Charter** (Fishermen's Village, Punta Gorda, tel. 813/639–0969), **Deebold's Marina** (1071 San Carlos Blvd., Fort Myers, tel. 813/466–3525), **Gulf Star Marina** (708 Fisherman's Wharf, Fort Myers Beach, tel. 813/463–2219), **Lehman's Fishing Charters** (Bokeelia, tel. 813/283–2217), **Deep Sea Charter Fishing** (Old Marine Market Place, Naples, tel. 813/263–8171).

Golf Courses open to the public include **Apollo Beach Club** (Tampa, tel. 813/645–6212), **Babe Zaharias Golf Course** (Tampa, tel. 813/932–4401), **Rocky Point Golf Course** (Tampa, tel. 813/884–5141), **Clearwater Golf Park** (Clearwater, tel. 813/447–5272); **Dunedin Country Club** (Dunedin, tel. 813/733–7836), **Manatee**

County Golf Course (Bradenton, tel. 813/792–6773), **Bobby Jones Golf Course** (Sarasota, tel. 813/955–8097), **Forest Lake Golf Course** (Sarasota, tel. 813/922–1312), **Longboat Key Golf Course** (Longboat Key, tel. 813/383–8821), **Bird Bay Executive Golf Course** (Venice, tel. 813/485–9333), **North Port Golf Course** (North Port, tel. 813/426–2804), **Deep Creek Golf Club** (Charlotte Harbor, tel. 813/625–6911), **Bay Beach Club Executive Golf Course** (Fort Myers Beach, tel. 813/463–2064), **Cypress Pines Country Club** (Lehigh Acres, tel. 813/369–8216), **Fort Myers Country Club** (Fort Myers, tel. 813/936–2457), **Pelican's Nest Golf Course** (Bonita Springs, tel. 813/947–4600), and **Hibiscus Country Club** (Naples, tel. 813/774–3559).

Motorboating   Much of southwest Florida's charm lies beyond its shoreline. Fortunately, there are many concerns that rent boats of all sizes.

In Nokomis, **Don and Mike's Boat and Ski Rental** (tel. 813/485–7345) has water skis, jet skis, Windsurfers, wavejammers, and miniboats plus instruction in windsurfing and waterskiing.

Lakes Park Marina (7330 Gladiolus Drive, Fort Myers, tel. 813/481–6563) rents paddleboats, canoes, and fishing gear.

Boat House of Sanibel (Sanibel Marina, tel. 813/472–2531) rents power- or sailboats.

Getaway Bait and Boat Rental (1091 San Carlos Blvd., Fort Myers Beach, tel. 813/466–3200) rents powerboats and fishing equipment and sells bait.

Brookside Marina (2023 Davis Blvd., Naples, tel. 813/263–7250) rents 15- to 24-foot powerboats.

Sailing   Sailing schools and guided or bare-boat rentals are plentiful. Spend a week learning the ropes or a few hours luxuriating on a sunset cruise.

Gulfcoast Sailboat Charters (9600 W. Gulf Blvd., Treasure Island, tel. 813/367–4444); **O'Leary's Sarasota Sailing School** (near Marina Jack's, U.S. 41 and the bay front, Sarasota, tel. 813/953–7505); **Boat House of Sanibel** (Sanibel Marina, tel. 813/472–2531); **Southwest Florida Yachts** (3444 Marinatown La. NW, Fort Myers, tel. 813/656–1339); **CSA Charters** (110 Gulf Shore Blvd. N, Naples, tel. 813/649–0091); and **Marco Island Sea Excursions** (1281 Jamaica Rd., Marco Island, tel. 813/642–6400).

Scuba Diving   Dive shops are found all over the region. However, most make excursions to the Florida Keys or the east coast of Florida rather than dive in this area.

Tennis   Many hotels and motels in Florida have outdoor tennis courts, some lighted for night use. For those who are motivated to find other courts, a list of public ones follows:

City of Tampa Courts (59 Columbia Dr, Davis Islands, Tampa, tel. 813/253–3782), **Cedar Tennis Club** (Longboat Key, tel. 813/383–6461), **Port Charlotte Tennis Club** (22400 Gleneagles Terrace, Port Charlotte tel. 813/625–7222), **Bay Beach Racquet Club** (120 Lenell St., Fort Myers Beach, tel. 813/463–4473), **Lochmoor Country Club** (3911 Orange Grove Blvd., North Fort Myers, tel. 813/995–0511), **The Dunes** (949 Sand Castle Rd., Sanibel, tel. 813/472–3522), and **Forest Hills Racquet Club** (100 Forest Hills Blvd., Naples, tel. 813/774–2442).

Windsurfing **Watersports Inc.** (17624-312 San Carlos Blvd., Fort Myers Beach, tel. 813/466–SURF) offers Windsurfer rentals and lessons.

Spectator Sports

Baseball The season comes early to Florida with the annual convergence of the Grapefruit League—seventeen major league teams offer exhibitions in March and April. These teams hold their spring training in southwest Florida. For information on all the teams, tel. 904/488–0990. Home bases for area teams are Bradenton: **Pittsburgh Pirates** (McKechnie Field, 9th St. W and 16th Ave., tel. 813/748–4610); Clearwater: **Philadelphia Phillies** (Jack Russell Stadium, Seminole and Greenwood Ave., tel. 813/442–8496); Dunedin: **Toronto Blue Jays** (Grant Field, 311 Douglas Ave., North of Rte. 88, tel. 813/733–0429); Port Charlotte: **Texas Rangers** (Charlotte County Stadium, Rte. 776, tel. 813/625–9500); St. Petersburg: **St. Louis Cardinals** (Al Lang Stadium, 1st St. and 2nd Ave., tel. 813/822–3384); Sarasota: **Chicago White Sox** (Payne Park, U.S. 301 and Ringling Blvd., tel. 813/953–3388); and Tampa: **Cincinnati Reds** (Plant City Stadium, Park Road, Plant City, tel. 813/752–7337).

Football NFL football comes in the form of the **Tampa Bay Buccaneers**, who play at Tampa Stadium (4201 N. Dale Mabry Hwy.). For information, tel. 800/282–0683 or 813/461–2700.

Soccer The lone competitor in the area is the **Tampa Bay Rowdies** (tel. 813/877–7800). The team plays indoors at the Bayfront Center (400 1st St., St. Petersburg) and outside at Tampa Stadium in Tampa.

Gambling Casino gambling has yet to find its way into the state, but the odds are that there are more than enough alternatives to suit bettors. There is **horse racing** at Tampa Bay Downs (Race Track Rd. off Rte. 580, Oldsmar, tel. 813/855–4401, with Thoroughbred races Dec.–mid-April). **Dog racing** occurs somewhere in the region all year: Jan.—May at Derby Lane (10490 Gandy Blvd., St. Peterburg, tel. 813/576–1361); Sept.–Jan. at Tampa Greyhound Track. (8300 N. Nebraska Ave., Tampa, tel. 813/932–4313); May–Sept. at the Sarasota Kennel Club (5400 Bradenton Rd., Sarasota, tel. 813/355–7744); and Oct.–Aug. at the Naples–Fort Myers Kennel Club (10601 Bonita Beach Rd., Bonita Springs, tel. 813/334–6555). **Jai alai** is offered at the Tampa Jai-Alai Fronton (S. Dale Mabry Hwy. and Gandy Blvd., Tampa, tel. 813/831–1411) Jan.–Sept. Big-time **bingo** can be found at the singular Seminole Bingo Hall (5221 Orient Rd., Tampa, tel. 800/282–7016), run by the Seminole Indians. Jackpots regularly exceed $60,000.

Dining and Lodging

Dining As in most coastal regions, fresh seafood is plentiful. Raw bars, serving just-plucked-from-the-bay oysters, clams, and mussels, are everywhere. The region's ethnic diversity is also well represented. Tarpon Springs adds a hearty helping of classic Greek specialties such as moussaka, a ground meat and eggplant pie, and baklava, delicate layers of pastry and nuts soaked in honey. In Tampa, the cuisine is Cuban. Standard menu items include black beans and rice and paella, a seafood, chicken, and saffroned-rice casserole. In Sarasota, the accent is on the Continental, both in food and service. Heading toward Fort Myers and Naples, seafood reigns supreme, especially the succulent claw of the stone crab, in season October 15—May 15. It's usually served with drawn butter or a tangy mustard sauce. There are some people who proclaim its flavor superior to that of lobster.

The most highly recommended restaurants in each price category are indicated by a star ★.

Category	Cost*
Very Expensive	over $60
Expensive	$40–$60
Moderate	$20–$40
Inexpensive	under $20

per person without tax (6% in Florida), service, or drinks

The following credit card abbreviations are used: AE, American Express; CB, Carte Blanche; DC, Diners Club; MC, MasterCard; V, Visa.

Lodging There are old historic hotels and ultramodern chrome-and-glass high rises, sprawling resorts and cozy inns, luxurious waterfront lodges and just-off-the-highway budget motels. In general, inland rooms are considerably cheaper than those on the islands. The most expensive accommodations are those with waterfront views. Rates are highest mid-December–mid-April. The lowest prices are available May–November. Many apartment-motels are springing up in the area and can prove economical for families that wish to prepare some of their own meals or for groups who can share an apartment. Price categories listed below apply to winter rates. Many drop to a less expensive category at other times of the year.

Category	Cost*
Very Expensive	over $120
Expensive	$90–$120
Moderate	$50–$90
Inexpensive	under $50

per person, double occupancy, without 6% state sales tax and nominal (1%–3%) tourist tax.

Bradenton
Dining

High Seas. Choose the open deck or the wood-and-brass interior of this establishment that looks out on sparkling Palma Sola Bay. Continental cuisine is featured, with an emphasis on fresh seafood. *9915 Manatee Ave. W, tel. 813/792–4776. Dress: casual. Reservations suggested. AE, CB, DC, MC, V. Moderate.*
Charlie Brown's. Lots of antiques and collectibles here create a turn-of-the-century decor. A menu laden with steaks and fresh seafoods poses a difficult choice for diners. *7051 Manatee Ave. W, tel. 813/794–3138. Dress: casual. Reservations for parties of 10 or more. AE, CB, DC, MC, V. Moderate.*

Lodging **Holiday Inn Riverfront.** A Spanish Mediterranean-style motor inn near the Manatee River. *100 Riverfront Dr. W 34205, tel.*

813/747–3727. 153 rooms. Facilities: restaurant, lounge, pool, whirlpool. AE, CB, DC, MC, V. Moderate.

Cape Coral
Dining

Cape Crab House. Crabs are served Maryland-style—with mallet and pliers and heaped on a tablecloth of newspaper—or in the more refined atmosphere of a second dining room with linen tablecloths and a piano player. *Coralwood Mall, Del Prado Blvd., tel. 813/574–2722. Dress: casual. Reservations accepted. AE, MC, V. Moderate.*

Siam Hut. Thai music pings and twangs in the background while the dishes do the same to your tastebuds. Get it fiery hot or extra mild. Specialties: *Pad Thai* (a mixture of noodles, crushed peanuts, chicken, shrimp, egg, bean sprouts, and scallions) and crispy Siam rolls (spring rolls stuffed with ground chicken, bean thread, and vegetables). *1873 Del Prado Blvd. (Coral Pointe Shopping Center), tel. 813/772–3131. Dress: casual. No reservations. AE, MC, V. Closed Mon. Inexpensive.*

Venezia. A small, neighborhood restaurant serving straightforward Italian food including pastas, pizza, chicken, veal, and fresh seafood. *1515 SE 47th Terrace, tel. 813/542–0027. Dress: casual. No reservations. MC, V. Moderate.*

Lodging

Cape Coral Inn & Country Club. A resort for golf and tennis enthusiasts who also seek economy. Understated decor reflects the sporty atmosphere. *4003 Palm Tree Blvd. 33904, tel. 813/542–3191. 100 rooms. Facilities: restaurant, lounge, golf, driving range, tennis, pool, baby-sitting. AE, CB, DC, MC, V. Moderate.*

Quality Inn. Conveniently located in downtown Cape Coral. *1538 Cape Coral Pkwy. 33904, tel. 813/542–2121. 146 rooms. Facilities: pool; pets accepted. AE, CB, DC, MC, V. Moderate.*

Clearwater
Dining

The Kapok Tree. A cluster of dining rooms serving steak and seafood overlook tropical gardens. A strolling minstrel performs. *923 McMullen Booth Rd., tel. 813/726–0504. Dress: casual. Reservations suggested. AE, CB, DC, MC, V. Moderate.*

Bob Heilman's Beachcomber. Southern-fried chicken and mashed potatoes with gravy have long been the Sunday staple at this 40-year-old restaurant. Also known for its seafood, homemade desserts, and hearty portions. *447 Mandalay Ave., Clearwater Beach, tel. 813/442–4144. Dress: casual. Reservations suggested. AE, DC, MC, V. Moderate.*

Lodging

Belleview Biltmore Hotel & Spa. This large, historic resort on Clearwater Bay has extensive facilities and transportation to the beach. *25 Belleview Blvd. 34616, tel. 813/442–6171. 350 rooms. Facilities: restaurant, lounge, pools, whirlpools, saunas, golf, tennis, bicycles, playground, fishing, sailboats. AE, CB, DC, MC, V. Very Expensive.*

Adam's Mark Caribbean Gulf Resort. Situated on the gulf shore, this modern resort offers comfort. A taste of the islands is provided by the steel-drum band that plays poolside. *430 S. Gulfview Blvd. 34630, tel. 813/443–5714. 205 rooms. Facilities: restaurants, lounge, beach, pool, wading pool, whirlpool. AE, CB, DC, MC, V. Expensive.*

Sheraton Sand Key Resort. A resort for those who want lots of sun, sand, and surf. Balconies and patios overlook the gulf and well-manicured grounds. *1160 Gulf Blvd., Clearwater Beach 33515, tel. 813/595–1611. 390 rooms. Facilities: restaurant, lounge, pool, wading pool, beach, whirlpool, playground, ten-*

nis courts, windsurfing, sailboats. AE, CB, DC, MC, V. Expensive.

Radisson Inn. This is a comfortable, unpretentious motor inn near the airport and Tampa Bay. *3580 Ulmerton Rd. (Rte. 688) 34622, tel. 813/573–1171. 116 rooms. Facilities: restaurant, pool, whirlpool, fitness center. AE, CB, DC, MC, V. Moderate.*

Fort Myers
Dining

Peter's La Cuisine. The quiet elegance of this downtown restaurant blends perfectly with the fine Continental cuisine served within. The menu changes every few weeks but usually includes a fresh salmon dish, chateaubriand, and duck or some other exotic meat. *2224 Bay St., tel. 813/332–2228. Dress: semidressy. Reservations suggested. AE, DC, MC, V. Expensive.*

★ **The Prawnbroker.** Its ads urge you to scratch and sniff. There is no odor, says the ad, because fresh fish does not have one. What there is is an abundance of seafood seemingly just plucked from gulf waters, plus some selections for landlubbers. Almost always crowded. *6535 McGregor Blvd. tel. 813/489–2226. Dress: stylishly casual. Reservations accepted. AE, MC, V. Moderate.*

Smitty's Beef Room. An old and reliable local restaurant, offering an assortment of steaks, prime rib, and seafood. A great meat-and-potatoes place that is popular with locals and visitors. *2240 W. 1st St., tel. 813/334–4415. Dress: casual. AE, CB, DC, MC, V. Moderate.*

The Veranda. Within a sprawling turn-of-the-century home is served an imaginative assortment of American regional cuisine. This is a popular place for business and governmental bigwigs to rub elbows. *2122 2nd St., tel. 813/332–2065. Dress: stylishly casual. AE, CB, DC, MC, V. Moderate.*

Miami Connection. If you hunger for choice chopped liver, lean-but-tender corned beef, and a chewy bagel, this kosher-style deli can fill the bill. The sandwiches are huge. It is, as the local restaurant critic aptly said, "the real McCohen." *11506 Cleveland Ave. or 2112 2nd St., tel. 813/936–3811. Dress: casual. No reservations. No credit cards. Inexpensive.*

Woody's Bar-B-Q. A no-frills barbecue pit featuring chicken, ribs, and beef in copious amounts at bargain-basement prices. *6701 N. Tamiami Trail (U.S. 41), North Fort Myers, tel. 813/ 997–1424; 12961 S. Cleveland, Fort Myers, tel. 813/278–1300; and 17105 San Carlos Blvd., tel. 813/454–0454. Dress: casual. No reservations. MC, V. Inexpensive.*

Lodging

Sanibel Sonesta Harbour Resort. This high-rise apartment hotel sits on the east side of the Sanibel Causeway, not quite in Fort Myers, not quite on Sanibel. It overlooks San Carlos Bay and has a full complement of amenities. *17260 Harbour Pointe 33908, tel. 813/466–4000. 240 rooms, 100 condominiums. Facilities: restaurant, lounge, pools, health club, tennis, whirlpool. AE, DC, MC, V. Very Expensive.*

Sheraton Harbor Place. This modern high-rise hotel commands a dominant spot on the downtown Fort Myers skyline, rising above the Caloosahatchee River and Fort Myers Yacht Basin. *2500 Edwards Dr. 33901, tel. 813/337–0300. 437 rooms. Facilities: tennis, a game room, whirlpool, dock, exercise room. AE, DC, MC, V. Expensive.*

Best Western Robert E. Lee Motor Inn. Rooms are spacious, with patios or balconies overlooking the Caloosahatche River. *6611 U.S. 41N, North Fort Myers 33903, tel. 813/997–5511. 108* *rooms. Facilities: lounge, pool, dock. AE, CB, DC, MC, V. Moderate.*

Fort Myers Beach
Dining
★/

The Mucky Duck. Slightly more formal than its waterfront sister restaurant on Captiva, this restaurant concentrates on fresh, well-prepared seafood. A popular dish is the bacon-wrapped barbecue shrimp. *2500 Estero Blvd., tel. 813/463-5519. Dress: casual. Reservations for large parties only. AE, MC, V. Moderate.*

Snug Harbor. Casual, rustic atmosphere is evident at this seafood restaurant on the harbor at Fort Myers Beach. *645 San Carlos Blvd., tel. 813/463-4343. Dress: casual. No reservations. AE, MC, V. Moderate.*

Lodging

Seawatch-on-the-Beach. A modern seven-story hotel with two-bedroom suites. Each has a whirlpool, kitchen, and a view of the gulf. *6550 Estero Blvd. 33931, tel. 813/481-3636. 42 rooms. Facilities: beach, pool, tennis, baby-sitting. AE, MC, V. Very Expensive.*

The Boathouse Beach Resort. A nautical theme pervades this all-suite time-share resort, with lots of teak and brass throughout. *7630 Estero Blvd. 33931, tel. 813/481-3636 or 800/237-8906. 22 units. Facilities: kitchens, beach, pool, whirlpool, shuffleboard. AE, MC, V. Expensive.*

Sandpiper Gulf Resort. Gulf-front apartment-motel. *5550 Estero Blvd. 33931, tel. 813/463-5721. 63 rooms. Facilities: pools, beach, whirlpool, playground, shuffleboard. MC, V. Moderate.*

Marco Island
Dining

Marco Lodge Waterfront Restaurant & Lounge. Built in 1869, this is Marco's oldest landmark. Fresh local seafood and Cajun entrees are features, as is live Dixieland jazz Tuesday–Saturday. *1 Papaya St., Goodland, tel. 813/394-3302. Dress: casual. Reservations suggested. AE, DC, MC, V. Moderate.*

★ **European Cafe Restaurant.** A small and intimate European-style cafe specializing in seafood and Continental cuisine. Pompano is prepared in a multitude of ways. All fish comes from the family-owned fish market. Owned and operated by Kare DeMartino, a fifth-generation Marco Islander. *918 N. Collier Blvd., tel. 813/394-7578. Dress: casual. Reservations accepted. MC, V. Inexpensive.*

Lodging

Eagle's Nest Beach Resort. This time-share resort contains one- and two-bedroom villas (with French doors opening onto screened patios) clustered around a large tropical garden and a high rise with two-bedroom suites overlooking the gulf. *410 S. Collier Blvd. 33937, tel. 813/394-5167. 96 rooms. Facilities: kitchens, beach, pool, whirlpool, sauna, exercise room, tennis, racquetball, sailing, windsurfing. AE, MC, V. Very Expensive.*

Marco Bay Resort. An all-suite motor inn on Marco Bay. *1001 N. Barfield Dr. 33937, tel. 813/394-8881. 320 rooms. Facilities: restaurant, lounge, kitchens, pools, whirlpools, dock, fishing, putting green, transportation to beach, tennis. AE, CB, DC, MC, V. Very Expensive.*

Marriott's Marco Island Resort. Large rooms with balconies surrounded by lush, tropical grounds right next to the gulf. *400 S. Collier Blvd. 33937, tel. 813/394-2511. 736 rooms, 86 suites. Facilities: restaurants, lounge, pools, beach, whirlpool, waterskiing, sailboats, windsurfing, tennis, bicycles, golf, exercise room. AE, CB, DC, MC, V. Very Expensive.*

Radisson Suite Resort on Marco Island. All 214 one- and two-bedroom suites in this medium high-rise resort contain kitchens fully equipped with utensils to give a home-away-from-home touch. The casual decor of the suites contrasts sharply with the marble floors and chandelier in the lobby. Built in 1986, the resort faces a large beachfront. *600 S. Collier Blvd., Marco Island 33937, tel. 813/394–4100 or 800/333–3333. 214 rooms. Facilities: restaurant, lounge, pool, beach, whirlpool, exercise room, game room, water-sports equipment available. AE, CB, DC, MC, V. Very Expensive.*

Naples **The Chef's Garden.** A mixture of Continental, traditional, and
Dining California cuisines has consistently won this restaurant awards
★ over the past decade. Some daily specials include Scottish smoked salmon with avocado and caviar, roast rack of lamb, and spinach and fresh mango salad with toasted cashews and honey vinaigrette. *1300 3rd St. S, tel. 813/262–5500. Jackets during winter season. Reservations suggested. AE, CB, DC, MC, V. Expensive.*

Cafe La Playa. The soul is French, and from it comes classic offerings such as pâté de fois gras, veal in a Dijon mustard sauce, and vichyssoise. The view is of the gulf, either indoors or from the broad-screened patio. *9891 Gulfshore Dr., tel. 813/597–3123. Dress: semidressy. Reservations recommended. AE, MC, V. Moderate.*

★ **St. George and the Dragon.** A long-lived seafood-and-beef restaurant, with a decor reminiscent of an old-fashioned men's club—heavy on brass, dark woods, and deep-red tones. Among the specialties are conch chowder, various cuts of prime rib, and shrimp steamed in beer. *936 5th Ave. S, tel. 813/262–6546. Dress: dressy. No reservations. AE, CB, DC, MC, V. Closed Sun. and Christmas. Moderate.*

Truffles. The less-formal bistro upstairs from The Chef's Garden. A wealth of ethnic specialties appears on the frequently changing menu. Exceptional desserts such as chocolate-peanut butter pie, banana cream pie, and chocolate-mousse cake. *1300 3rd St. S, tel. 813/262–5500. Dress: casual. No reservations. AE, CB, DC, MC, V. Moderate.*

Lodging **Edgewater Beach Hotel.** An all-suite gulf-front hotel on fashionable Gulf Shore Drive, long an elegant address in Naples. Close to downtown. *1901 Gulf Shore Blvd. N 33940, tel. 813/262–6511. 124 rooms. Facilities: restaurant, beach, pool, exercise room. AE, CB, DC, MC, V. Very Expensive.*

The Registry Resort. This modern, luxurious high-rise resort is a half mile from the beach and offers a wealth of amenities, including a shuttle through the mangrove wetlands to the beach. *475 Seagate Dr. 33940, tel. 813/597–3232. 50 tennis villas, 29 suites, 395 rooms. Facilities: restaurants, lounge, pools, whirlpools, bicycles, tennis, health club. AE, CB, DC, MC, V. Very Expensive.*

Ritz-Carlton Hotel. Opulence reigns from its sweeping palm-lined driveway and through every inch of this Mediterranean-style resort on the gulf. *280 Vanderbilt Beach Rd. 33941, tel. 813/598–3300. 463 rooms. Facilities: restaurants, lounge, beach, pool, saunas, whirlpool, tennis, bicycles, exercise room, golf, children's program, windsurfing. AE, CB, DC, MC, V. Very Expensive.*

Comfort Inn. Modern motel on the banks of the Gordon River. *1221 5th Ave. S 33940, tel. 813/649–5800. 101 rooms. Facilities: pool. AE, CB, DC, MC, V. Moderate.*

Port Charlotte/   **Salty's Harborside.** Seafood is served from a dining room that
Punta Gorda   looks out on Burnt Store Marina and Charlotte Harbor. *Burnt*
Dining   *Store Marina, Burnt Store Rd. Punta Gorda, tel. 813/639–*
3650. Dress: casual. Reservations suggested. AE, CB, DC,
MC, V. Moderate.

Mexican Hacienda. Tex-Mex of a high order is presented in
humble surroundings. The building matches its well-worn
neighbors; inside are well-interpreted guacamole dip and tacos
made with tender shredded beef. *123 E. Retta Esplanade,*
Punta Gorda, tel. 813/639–7161. Dress: casual. Reservations:
parties of 6 or more. MC, V. Inexpensive.

★ **Ria's Ristorante.** This small, hard-to-find establishment serves
a range of pastas (lasagna, spaghetti, stuffed shells), seafoods,
and meats. *Olean Plaza, 21202 Olean Blvd., Port Charlotte,*
tel. 813/625–3145. Dress: casual. Reservations accepted. MC,
V. Inexpensive.

Lodging   **Burnt Store Marina Resort.** For golfing, boating, and getting
away from it all, Burnt Store can fill the bill. One- and two-
bedroom modern apartments are situated along a relatively undeveloped stretch of vast Charlotte Harbor. Two-bedroom
units available only on a weekly or monthly basis. *3150*
Matecumbe Key Rd., Punta Gorda, 33955, tel. 813/639–4151.
46 1-bedroom condominiums. Facilities: restaurant, lounge,
kitchens, pool, golf, marina, boats, tennis. Credit: AE, CB,
DC, MC, V. Expensive.

Days Inn of Port Charlotte. A modern mid-rise motel on Charlotte County's major business route. *1941 Tamiami Trail (U.S.*
41), Port Charlotte 33948, tel. 813/627–8900. 126 rooms. Facili-
ties: pool. AE, CB, DC, MC, V. Moderate.

St. Petersburg   **King Charles Room.** Quiet elegance, attentive service, and
Dining   soothing harp music are to be found in this restaurant on the
fifth floor of the Don CeSar Beach Resort. Continental specialties include beluga caviar on ice and smoked salmon stuffed
with crab mousse. *3400 Gulf Blvd., tel. 813/360–1881. Dress:*
dressy. Reservations recommended. AE, CB, DC, MC, V.
Very Expensive.

★ **Peter's Place-Cafe International.** Small, elegant dining rooms
with subdued lighting and fresh flowers atop crisp linen tablecloths offer Continental food that is seasoned and served with
flair and imagination. Specials change daily. Favorites include
breast of capon in a honey-lemon sauce and roast duckling with
brandied peaches and just a suggestion of Amaretto. *208 Beach*
Dr. NE, tel. 813/822–8436. Reservations advised. Jacket and
tie advised. AE, MC, V. Closed Sun. and Mon. Expensive.

The Wine Cellar Restaurant. The decor is Swiss chalet; the
food, classic French. This popular spot is usually crowded.
17307 Gulf Blvd., North Redington Beach, tel. 813/393–3491.
Jacket and tie advised. Reservations advised. AE, CB, DC,
MC, V. Closed Mon. Expensive.

★ **Ted Peters Famous Smoked Fish.** The menu is limited to mackerel and mullet, but both are smoked and seasoned to
perfection and served with heaping helpings of German potato
salad. All meals are served outdoors. *1350 Pasadena Ave. S,*
Pasadena, tel. 813/381–7931. Dress: casual. No reservations.
No credit cards. Closed Tues. Inexpensive.

Lodging   **Tradewinds on St. Petersburg Beach.** Old Florida ambience is
offered here, with white gazebos, gondolas gliding along canals, and hammocks swaying on 13 acres of beachfront

property. *5500 Gulf Blvd., St. Petersburg Beach 33706, tel. 813/ 367–6461. 365 rooms. Facilities: restaurant, lounge, kitchens, pools, wading pool, beach, sauna, whirlpools, boating, dock, fishing, tennis, racquetball, bicycles, playground, exercise room, scuba instruction, waterskiing, windsurfing. AE, CB, DC, MC, V. Very Expensive.*

Don CeSar Beach Resort. This palatial, pink-rococo resort sprawls along the gulf front. A favorite of author F. Scott Fitzgerald in the 1920s and '30s. *3400 Gulf Blvd., St. Petersburg Beach 33706, tel. 813/360–1881. 277 rooms. Facilities: restaurants, lounge, pool, whirlpool, beach, saunas, tennis, children's program, exercise room, sailboats, parasails, jet skis. AE, CB, DC, MC, V. Expensive.*

Colonial Gateway Resort Inn. This gulf-front hotel is family-oriented, with half of its 200 rooms equipped with kitchenettes. The resort was recently remodeled to give it a contemporary look for young families. *6300 Gulf Blvd., St. Petersburg Beach 33706, tel. 800/237–8918 outside FL, 800/282–5245 in FL. 200 rooms. Facilities: restaurants, lounge, beach bar, pool, water sports activities. AE, CB, DC, MC, V. Moderate.*

Sanibel/Captiva
Dining
★

The Bubble Room. It's hard to say which is more eclectic here, the atmosphere or the menu. Waiters and waitresses wearing Boy Scout uniforms race amid a dizzying array of Art Deco, while music from the 1940s sets the mood. The aged prime rib is ample enough to satisfy two hearty eaters—at least. Chances are you'll be too full for dessert, but it can be wrapped to go. *Captiva Rd., Captiva, tel. 813/472–5558. No reservations. AE, CB, DC, MC, V. Expensive.*

The Greenhouse. Though the kitchen is in full view of the diminutive dining area, all is calm and quiet as you wend your way through the day's specials. Chef-owner Danny Melman changes his Continental-style menu every four to six weeks. Each menu features fresh seafood and game among its selections. *Captiva Rd., Captiva, tel. 813/472–6066. Dress: stylishly casual. Reservations advised. No credit cards. Expensive.*

Jean Paul's French Corner. French food, finely seasoned with everything but the highfalutin attitude often dished up in French establishments. Salmon in a creamy dill sauce, sautéed soft-shell crabs, and roast duckling in fruit sauce are among the few but well-prepared choices on the menu. *Tarpon Bay Rd., tel. 813/472–1493. Dress: informal. Reservations suggested. MC, V. Expensive.*

McT's Shrimphouse and Tavern. Somewhat of a departure from most Sanibel establishments, McT's is lively and informal, featuring a host of fresh seafood specialties, including all-you-can-eat shrimp and crab. *1523 Periwinkle Way, Sanibel, tel. 813/ 472–3161. Dress: casual. No reservations. AE, CB, DC, MC, V. Moderate.*

Truffles at Thistle Lodge. A New Orleans–style mansion in the midst of the mangroves, it serves the same fine quality Continental fare as the Naples Truffles, including wondrous desserts. *Casa Ybel Resort, 2255 W. Gulf Dr., Sanibel, tel. 813/ 472–9200. Dress: stylishly casual. Reservations recommended. AE, MC, V. Moderate.*

Lodging

Casa Ybel Resort. This time-share property features recently redecorated one- and two-bedroom gulf-front condominium villas on 23 acres of tropical grounds, complete with palms, ponds, and a footbridge. *2255 W. Gulf Dr., Sanibel 33957, tel. 813/481– 3636 or 800/237–8906. 40 1-bedroom units, 74 2-bedroom units.*

Facilities: restaurant, lounge, kitchens, pool, whirlpool, biking, tennis, sailing, playground, shuffleboard, game room, baby-sitting. AE, CB, DC, MC, V. Very Expensive.

South Seas Plantation Resort and Yacht Harbour. Virtually an island unto itself, South Seas lies on the northernmost 330 acres of Captiva Island. There are villas and cottages clustered at various secluded spots throughout the grounds. *South Sea Plantation Rd., Captiva 33924, tel. 813/472–5111 or 800/237–1260 outside FL. 650 rooms. Facilities: restaurants, lounges, kitchens, boat docking, beauty parlor, baby-sitting, fishing, golf, game room, playground, pools, sailboats, sailing school, tennis, waterskiing, windsurfing, and a windsurfing school. AE, CB, DC, MC, V. Very Expensive.*

Sundial Beach & Tennis Resort. The largest all-suite resort on the island; many suites look out upon the Gulf of Mexico. *1246 Middle Gulf Dr., Sanibel 33957, tel. 813/472–4151 or 800/237–4184. 407 suites. Facilities: restaurants, lounge, kitchens, pools, beach, bicycles, tennis, sailboats, recreational program, children's program, baby-sitting, game room, shuffleboard. AE, CB, DC, MC, V. Very Expensive.*

Sarasota
Dining
★

Cafe L'Europe. Located on fashionable St. Armand's Key, this greenery- and art-filled cafe specializes in fresh veal and seafood. Menus change frequently, but might include fillet of sole Picasso, Dover sole served with a choice of fruits, Wiener schnitzel sautéed in butter and topped with anchovies, olives, and capers. *431 St. Armand's Circle, tel. 813/388–4415. Dress: semidressy. Reservations suggested. AE, CB, DC, MC, V. Expensive.*

Marina Jack. Have a dinner cruise on the *Marina Jack II* or eat fresh seafood overlooking Sarasota Bay. *2 Marina Plaza, tel. 813/365–4232. Dress: semidressy. Reservations suggested. No credit cards. Expensive.*

★ **The Bijou Cafe.** Wood, brass, and sumptuous green carpeting surround diners in this gas station turned restaurant. Chef Jean Pierre Knaggs's Continental specialties include crispy roast duckling with tangerine brandy sauce or cassis and blackberry sauce, rack of lamb for two, and *crème brûlée*, a custard with a carmelized brown-sugar topping. *Corner of 1st and Pineapple Sts., tel. 813/366–8111. Dress: semidressy. Reservations suggested. AE, MC, V. Moderate.*

Whisper Inn. Next to the K Mart in south Sarasota sits this small but choice Continental restaurant. The house specialty is charred prime rib. Other entrees include veal, fresh seafood, and rack of lamb. *8197 S. Tamiami Trail (U.S. 41), tel. 813/922–6400. Dress: informal. Reservations suggested. AE, MC, V. Moderate.*

Lodging

Hyatt Sarasota. Recently renovated, the Hyatt is contemporary in design and conveniently located in the heart of the city. Some rooms overlook Sarasota Bay. *1000 Blvd. of the Arts 34236, tel. 813/366–9000. 297 rooms. Facilities: restaurant, lounge, pool, sauna, sailing, health club, dock. AE, CB, DC, MC, V. Very Expensive.*

The Meadows VIP Program. This all-suite resort is a bit removed from downtown, but it is like a small city unto itself, including 54 holes of golf and 16 lighted tennis courts. *3101 Longmeadow Dr. 34235, tel. 813/378–6660. 12 1-bedroom suites. Facilities: restaurants, lounge, pool, sauna, golf, tennis, bicycles, children's program. AE, CB, DC, MC, V. Expensive.*

Days Inn Sarasota-Siesta Key. Modern, built in 1986, with earth-tone rooms, this inn is one mile from the beaches. *6600 S. Tamiami Trail (U.S. 41) 34231, tel. 813/924–4900. 132 rooms. Facilities: pool, whirlpool. AE, CB, DC, MC, V. Moderate.*

Hampton Inn Sarasota Airport. On the main drag, convenient to beaches and downtown. Budget prices. *5000 N. Tamiami Trail (U.S. 41) 34234, tel. 813/351–7734. 100 rooms. Facilities: pool, AE, CB, DC, MC, V. Moderate.*

Tampa
Dining
★

Bern's Steak House. Specialties include aged prime beef and an extensive wine list—some 6,000 choices, with selections ranging in price from $10 to $10,000 a bottle. The vegetables are grown on owner-chef Bern Lexer's organic farm. Upstairs are the dessert rooms: small, glass-enclosed rooms where sumptuous desserts are served. Each room is equipped with a control panel for TV, radio, or listening in to the live entertainment in the lounge. *1208 S. Howard Ave., tel. 813/251–2421. Dress: semidressy. Reservations advised. AE, CB, DC, MC, V. Expensive.*

Brothers Too. A gardenlike setting that blocks out bustling West Shore Boulevard complements the fine Continental cuisine served here. One recent specialty: baked shrimp stuffed with crabmeat, artichoke hearts, peppers, and Monterey Jack cheese. *1408 N. West Shore Blvd., tel. 813/879–1962. Dress: casual. Reservations suggested. AE, CB, DC, MC, V. Expensive.*

CK's. This revolving restaurant sits atop Tampa International Airport's Marriott Hotel. An eclectic Continental menu includes stir-fried shrimp and red snapper. Champagne brunch on Sunday. *Tel. 813/879–5151. Dress: stylishly casual. Reservations accepted. AE, CB, DC, MC, V. Moderate.*

Colonnade. The wharfside location of this popular restaurant is reflected in its nautical decor. Seafood—particularly grouper, red snapper, and lobster—is a specialty, but steak and chicken dishes are also served. *3401 Bayshore Blvd., tel. 813/839–7558. Dress: casual. No reservations. AE, CB, DC, MC, V. Moderate.*

★ **Columbia.** A Spanish fixture in Tampa's Ybor City for more than 80 years, this restaurant has several airy and spacious dining rooms and a sunny atrium with tile decor. Specialties include the Columbia 1905 salad—lettuce, ham, olives, cheese, and garlic; and paella—saffron rice with chicken, fish, and mussels. Flamenco dancing. *2117 E. 7th Ave., tel. 813/248–4961. Dress: casual weekdays, semidressy weekends. Reservations accepted. AE, CB, DC, MC, V. Moderate.*

Selena's. New Orleans Creole food served here with some Sicilian dishes as well, in antique-filled dining rooms. Shrimp scampi and other fresh seafood featured. *1623 Snow Ave., tel. 813/251–2116. Dress: casual. Reservations suggested. AE, CB, DC, MC, V. Moderate.*

★ **Bella Trattoria.** Brightly lit, slightly noisy, and filled with the smells of such Italian fare as *capelli di l'Angelo*—smoked salmon and caviar tossed with spinach and angel-hair pasta in a vodka and cream sauce—and *Bella! Bella!*, a truffle torte of bittersweet, semisweet, and white chocolates. Crayons and paper tablecloths afford a public outlet for frustrated artists. *1413 S. Howard Ave., tel. 813/254–3355. Dress: casual. No reservations. AE, MC, V. Inexpensive.*

Lodging **Wyndham Harbour Island Hotel.** Elegant ambience, with lots of dark wood paneling, substantial furniture, and attentive service. *725 S. Harbour Island Blvd. 33602, tel. 813/229–5000. 300 rooms. Facilities: restaurant, lounge, pool, dock, sailboats, tennis, health club. AE, CB, DC, MC, V. Very Expensive.*

Saddlebrook. This modern tennis and golf resort on sprawling, heavily wooded grounds is 15 miles north of Tampa. A variety of accommodations and amenities. *100 Saddlebrook Way, Wesley Chapel 34249, tel. 813/973–1111. 501 rooms. Facilities: restaurants, lounge, kitchenettes, pools, wading pools, whirlpools, saunas, fishing, golf, tennis, bicycles, health club. AE, CB, DC, MC, V. Very Expensive.*

Guest Quarters. Modern all-suite hotel midway between Tampa International Airport and downtown Tampa. *555 N. Westshore Blvd. 33609, tel. 813/875–1555. 221 rooms. Facilities: restaurant, lounge, pool, whirlpool, sauna, exercise room, transportation to airport; accepts pets. AE, CB, DC, MC, V. Expensive.*

Hyatt Regency-Downtown. A large, elegant high-rise hotel with a modern, mirrored ambience. *2 Tampa City Center 33602, tel. 813/225–1234. 517 rooms. Facilities: restaurant, lounge, pool, whirlpool, sauna, exercise room. AE, DC, MC, V. Expensive.*

Holiday Inn Busch Gardens. A family-oriented motor inn just one mile west of Busch Gardens. *2701 E. Fowler Ave. 33612, tel. 813/971–4710. 399 rooms. Facilities: restaurant, lounge, pool, sauna, exercise room, transportation to Busch Gardens. AE, CB, DC, MC, V. Moderate.*

Tahitian Inn. This family-run motel offers comfortable rooms at budget prices. *601 S. Dale Mabry Hwy. 33609, tel. 813/877–6721. 79 rooms. Facilities: pool. AE, CB, DC, MC, V. Inexpensive.*

Tarpon Springs
Dining
★

Louis Pappas' Riverside Restaurant. The decor consists mainly of wall-to-wall people who pour into this waterfront landmark for all manner of Greek fare, especially the Greek salad, made with lettuce, feta-cheese chunks, onions, and olive oil. *10 W. Dodecanese Blvd., tel. 813/937–5101. Dress: casual. Reservations advised. AE, CB, DC, MC, V. Moderate.*

Lodging

Innisbrook Resort. There are deluxe rooms and suites here, some with balconies or patios at this get-away-from-it-all resort on 1,000 wooded acres. *Box 1088, U.S. 19 34689, tel. 813/942–2000. 1,200 rooms. Facilities: dining rooms, nightclub, golf, tennis, racquetball, pools, health club, children's program (May-Sept.), miniature golf, saunas. AE, CB, DC, MC, V. Very Expensive.*

Venice
Dining
★

The Attic at Kissin' Cuzzins. The ambience is barnlike and the helpings of Pennsylvania Dutch fare are enough to feed a large and hungry horse. *1775 S. Tamiami Trail (U.S. 41), tel. 813/493–3666. Dress: casual. Reservations accepted. AE, MC, V. Moderate.*

Sharky's on the Pier. Gaze out on the beach and sparkling waters while dining on grilled fresh seafood. *1600 S. Harbor Dr., tel. 813/488–1456. Dress: casual. Reservations suggested. MC, V. Moderate.*

Lodging

Holiday House. Comfortable rooms in motor inn on the main business route through town. *1710 S. Tamiami Trail (U.S. 41) 34293, tel. 813/493–4558. 72 rooms. Facilities: restaurant, lounge, pool; accepts pets. AE, MC, V. Moderate.*

Veranda Inn–Venice. A landscaped pool is the focal point of this small but spacious inn. All rooms look out on the pool and courtyard. *625 S. Tamiami Trail (U.S. 41), tel. 813/484–9559. 37 rooms. Facilities: restaurant, pool. AE, DC, MC, V. Moderate.*

The Arts

Not too many years ago, southwest Florida was content to bask in the warmth of the sun and leave cultural matters to others. But as the population has boomed, a growing number of transplanted northerners have been unwilling to sacrifice the arts for nature. Hence, there are curtains going up at performing-arts centers throughout the region.

If you are interested in cultural events while staying in Florida, it's a good idea to purchase tickets before you arrive, especially during the busy winter tourist season. Most halls and theaters accept credit-card charges by phone. The area chambers of commerce (*see* Important Addresses and Numbers) can supply schedules of upcoming cultural events.

The **Tampa Performing Arts Center** (1010 W. C. MacInnes Pl., Box 2877, tel. 813/222–1010) occupies nine acres along the Hillsborough River and is said to be the largest such complex south of the Kennedy Center in Washington, DC. The festival hall, playhouse, and small theater accommodate opera, ballet, drama, and concerts.

Ruth Eckerd Hall (1111 McMullen Booth Rd., Clearwater, tel. 813/791–7400) also plays host to many national performers of pop, classical, and jazz music; ballet; and drama.

Sarasota's **Van Wezel Performing Arts Hall** (777 N. Tamiami Trail, tel. 813/953–3366) is easy to find. Just look for the purple shell rising along the bay front. It offers some 200 performances each year, including Broadway plays, ballet, jazz, rock concerts, symphonies, children's shows, and ice skating. For tickets and information, contact the box office.

Fort Myers's center for the arts is the **Barbara B. Mann Performing Arts Hall** (Edison Community College/University of South Florida campus, 8099 College Pkwy., tel. 813/489–3033), a 1,770-seat theater that opened in 1986. Plays, concerts, and ballets by local, national, and international companies perform here. For more information, contact the box office.

Theater The **Tampa Theater** (711 N. Franklin St., tel. 813/223–8981)
Tampa Bay presents shows, musical performances, and films. Area dinner theaters include the **Starlight Dinner Theatre** (Gateway Mall, 7951 9th St. N, St. Petersburg, tel. 813/577–5515), the **Encore Dinner-Theatre** (1850 Central Ave., St. Petersburg, tel. 813/821–6676), and the **Showboat Dinner Theatre** (3405 Ulmerton Rd., Clearwater, tel. 813/223–2545). All offer dinner and a variety of Broadway and off-Broadway shows throughout the year.

Sarasota/Bradenton The **Asolo State Theater** (Drawer E, tel. 813/355–5137) offers productions nearly year-round. Located in the new $10 million Asolo Performing Arts Center, this Sarasota theater is known for its well-rounded repertoire. The theater's company of actors performs about 10 plays per season (Dec.-Aug.). For tickets or information, contact the theater.

Florida Studio Theatre (1241 N. Palm Ave., Sarasota, tel. 813/366–9796) is a small professional theater that presents contemporary dramas, comedies, and musicals.

Golden Apple Dinner Theatre (25 N. Pineapple Ave., Sarasota, tel. 813/366–5454) combines a buffet dinner with musicals and comedies.

The **Players of Sarasota** (U.S. 41 and 9th St., tel. 813/365–2494), a long-lived troupe, provided opportunities for then-unknowns Pee-Wee Herman, Montgomery Clift, and Polly Holiday. The community theater features volunteer actors and technicians and performs comedies, thrillers, and musicals.

Theatre Works (1247 1st St., Venice, tel. 813/952–9170) presents professional, non-Equity productions at the Palm Tree Playhouse.

Venice Little Theatre (corner of Tampa and Nokomis Aves., Venice, tel. 813/488–1115) is a community theater offering comedies, musicals, and a few dramas during its October-May season.

Fort Myers/Naples **The Naples Dinner Theatre** (Immokalee Rd., halfway between U.S. 41 and the I-75 interchange, tel. 813/597–6031) is open October-August and features professional companies performing a variety of mostly musicals and comedies. Admission includes buffet.

The **Naples Playhouse** (Harbour Town Shopping Center, 399 Goodlette Rd., tel. 813/263–7990) has winter and summer seasons. The winter shows often sell out well in advance.

Concerts The **Florida Orchestra** (tel. 813/221–2365) performs throughout
Tampa Bay Area Tampa Bay each fall, at Clearwater's Eckerd Hall, St. Petersburg's Bayfront Center, and the Tampa Performing Arts Center.

The **Tampa Bay Chamber Orchestra** (tel. 813/251–2388) offers concerts throughout the region. Its 35 members perform works for chamber orchestras.

Sarasota/Bradenton The **Florida Symphonic Band** (Van Wezel Hall 709 N. Tamiami Trail [U.S. 41] Sarasota, tel. 813/955–6660) includes 50 players, many of whom are full-time musicians. The group performs monthly concerts.

Florida West Coast Music, Inc. (tel. 813/953–4252) consists of a number of area groups that perform in Manatee and Sarasota counties regularly. Included are the *Florida West Coast Symphony, The Florida String Quartet, Florida Brass Quintet, Florida Wind Quintet,* and *New Artists String Quartet.*

Opera **Florida Opera West** (tel. 813/381–2151) brings in guest soloists
Tampa Bay Area for its major operatic performances at Ruth Eckerd Hall in Clearwater and the Bayfront Center in St. Petersburg. The **St. Petersburg Opera Co.** and the **Florida Lyric Opera Company** perform at the Bayfront Center.

Sarasota The **Sarasota Opera** (61 N. Pineapple Ave., tel. 813/953–7030) operates from its home in a historic theater downtown at the corner of 1st and Pineapple streets. The company's season runs from February to March. Internationally known singing artists perform the principal roles, supported by a professional apprentice chorus—24 young singers studying with the company.

Dance The **St. Petersburg Concert Ballet** performs periodically
Tampa Bay Area throughout the year, mostly at the Bayfront Center in St. Petersburg.
The Tampa Ballet performs at the Tampa Bay Performing Arts Center.

Film   All areas have conveniently located commercial movie houses. Check the local newspapers for shows, times, and locations.

Sarasota   The **Ringling Fine Arts Film Series** brings classic, foreign, and second-run films to the Asolo State Theater on Mondays (5401 Bayshore Rd., tel. 813/355–5101). The **Sarasota Film Society** operates year-round, showing foreign and nonmainstream films on weekends at the Plaza Theatre (Crossroads Shopping Center, tel. 813/388–2441).

Nightlife

Bars and   **Harbour Island Hotel** (Harbour Island, Tampa, tel. 813/229–
Nightclubs   5000). Great view of the bay, large-screen television, and thickly padded, comfortable chairs.
Coliseum Ballroom (535 4th Ave. N, St. Petersburg, tel. 813/894–1812). Ballroom dancing Wednesday and Saturday night.
The Pier (Memorial Pier, Bradenton, tel. 813/748–8087). An incomparable view of the Bradenton waterfront.
The Patio (Columbia Restaurant, St. Armand's Key, tel. 813/388–3987). A casual lounge with live music nightly.
Marina 31 Restaurant and Lounge (17281 Rte. 31, Fort Myers, tel. 813/694–1331). Live bands playing top-40 hits.
'Tween Waters Inn (Captiva Rd., Captiva, tel. 813/472–5161). Live entertainment and large-screen TV catering to casual, over-30 crowd.
Harp & Thistle (650 Corey Ave., St. Petersburg Beach, tel. 813/360–4104). Live Irish music Wed.–Sat.

Jazz Clubs   Most offer jazz several nights a week. Call for details.
Baxters (714 S. Dale Mabry Hwy. Tampa, tel. 813/879–1161).
Brothers Lounge (Lincoln Center, 5401 W. Kennedy Blvd., Tampa, tel. 813/879–9378).
Brothers Too (1408 N. Westshore Blvd., Tampa, tel. 813/879–1962).
Maestro's (14727 N. Florida Ave., Tampa, tel. 813/961–5090).
The Beach Room (10650 Gulf Blvd., Treasure Island, tel. 813/360–5531).
Hurricane Lounge (807 Gulf Way, Pass-a-Grille Beach, tel. 813/360–9558).
Victoria Pier (2230 Edwards Dr., Fort Myers, tel. 813/334–4881).

Rock Clubs   **Volley Club** (1512 N. Nebraska Ave., Tampa, tel. 813/972–0176). Live rock-and-roll rings from the rafters Wednesday–Monday.
306th Bomb Group (8301 N. Tamiami Trail, Sarasota, tel. 813/355–8591). Amid World War II gear, a DJ spins top-40 tunes for a generally over-25 clientele.
Horsefeathers (1900 Main St., Sarasota, tel. 813/366–8088). A mainly professional crowd gathers at this lounge, where top-40 music spins nightly.
Club Yesterdays (2224 S. Tamiami Trail, Venice, tel. 813/493–2900). Top-40 is king every night at this club popular with the under-30 set.
Flashbacks (Metro Mall, Fort Myers, tel. 813/936–8545). Oldies from the '50s and '60s nightly, tea dances Sundays.
Edison's Electric Lounge (Holiday Inn, 13051 Bell Tower Dr., Fort Myers, tel. 813/482–2900). Top-40 tunes, usually live bands, rock nightly.

Country-Western	**Joyland Country Night Club** (11225 U.S. 19, St. Petersburg, tel. 813/573–1919).
	The Barn (13800 W. Hillsborough Ave., Tampa, tel. 813/855–9818).
	Dallas Bull (8222 N. Hwy. 301, Tampa, tel. 813/985–6877).
	Carlie's (5641 49th St., St. Petersburg, tel. 813/527–5214).
Comedy Clubs	**Comedy Corner** (3447 W. Kennedy Blvd., Tampa, tel. 813/875–9129).
	Coconuts Comedy Club at Barnacle Bill's (Howard Johnson's, 6110 Gulf Blvd., St. Petersburg, tel. 813/360–4575).
	Ron Bennington's Comedy Line (Rodeway Inn, 401 U.S. 19 S., Clearwater, tel. 813/799–1181).
	Bijou Comedy Club & Restaurant (McGregor Point Shopping Center, Fort Myers, tel. 813/481–6666).
Discos	**Club Paradise** (1927 Ringling Blvd., Sarasota, tel. 813/366–3830). A rock-and-roll palace, complete with extensive light show, music videos, a DJ, and several bars. Especially popular with the younger set.
	Norma Jean's (4797 U.S. 41, Fort Myers, tel. 813/275–9997) packs in the singles (21 and up) with such events as hot legs and lip-sync contests, hot-tub night, live bands and disc jockeys.

11 North Florida

Introduction

by Joice Veselka and Honey Naylor

A freelance writer, Honey Naylor has contributed to Travel & Leisure, USA Today, New Orleans Magazine, *and* Travel Today, *as well as other Fodor's guides. Joice Veselka, formerly publicity director for the Florida Division of Tourism, is regional travel editor for Chevrolet's* Friends Magazine.

If you think Florida is just one big beach, you're only partly right. And if, so thinking, you drive into the state from Alabama or Georgia, you'll probably figure you were totally wrong. In the northwestern part of Florida, called the Panhandle, gently undulating hills, natural swamplands, and thick forests of pine and oak trees cover the 40- or 50-mile interior before you reach the coastal resort strip, which does have incredibly white, fluffy sand. Tallahassee, the state capital, like Rome rolls over seven hills. As you move east the terrain levels out, and the Atlantic coastal plains are as flat as the proverbial pancake. Sandbars and islands protect much of the mainland from the Atlantic Ocean, but the waters sneak through the marshlands north of Jacksonville, creating a maze of rivers, inlets, and islands.

But north Florida is not without beaches—not by a long shot. The waters of the Gulf of Mexico nudge the coast of the Panhandle, where the modestly named Miracle Strip is a 100-mile stretch of lush white carpet dotted with hotels, condominiums, shops, shacks, and restaurants. The northeast coast is also awash, so to speak, with sun-kissed beaches, and the ocean is a fit place for surfing, snorkeling, scuba diving, and sailing.

In the 400-mile stretch between the Atlantic Ocean on the east and Pensacola in the Panhandle, you'll find ancient forts, deep caverns, and archaeological sites to explore; wineries to see (and wine to sip); historic districts with narrow old-brick streets; and a plethora of antique shops to poke around in. There are football games, fishing piers, canoeing and tubing, greyhound races, jai alai, lush hiking and biking trails, water sports of every sort, and a number of tennis courts and golf courses. And you'll never be far from a spot where you can just drop down and worship the sun for a spell.

Getting Around

By Plane The main airport for the region is **Jacksonville International.** It is served by American (tel. 800/433–7300), Continental (tel. 800/525–0280), Eastern (tel. 800/327–8376), Piedmont (tel. 800/251–5720), TWA (tel. 800/221–2000), United (tel. 800/241–6522), and USAir (tel. 800/428–4322). Vans from the airport to area hotels cost $15 per person. Taxi fare is about $17 to the downtown area, $32 to the beaches, and $38 to Amelia Island. Among the limousine services, which must be booked in advance, is *AAA Limousine Service* (tel. 904/751–4800 for Jacksonville and beaches, tel. 904/277–2359 for Amelia Island). The charge is $30 for one or two persons to downtown, $35 for one or $40 for two to the beaches, and $30 for one or $15 each for multiple passengers to Amelia Island.

Tallahassee Regional Airport is served by Delta (tel. 800/221–1212), Eastern, Piedmont, and Piedmont Regional (tel. 800/368–5425). Taxis (among them, *Yellow Cab*, tel. 904/222–3070) cost about $11 to area hotels. Some of the hotels provide free van service.

Both **Panama City-Bay County Airport** and **Fort Walton Beach/ Eglin AFB Airport** are served by Continental Express (tel. 800/

525–0280), Delta Connection (tel. 800/282–3424), Eastern Express (tel. 800/327–8376), and Northwest (tel. 800/225–2525). At the Panama City airport, *Deluxe Coach Limo Service* (tel. 904/763–0211) offers van service for $5–$8 to downtown Panama City and $10–$16.50 to Panama City Beach. Taxis *(Yellow Cab*, tel. 904/763–4691) charge about $14 to the beach area. The cost to hotels depends on location. At Fort Walton, taxis *(Yellow Cab*, tel. 904/244–3600) charge $10 to Fort Walton Beach, $18 to Destin. *Airport Limousine* (tel. 904/244–5638) charges $8–$10 to Fort Walton Beach, $13 to Destin.

Pensacola Regional Airport is served by Continental, Delta, Eastern, Northwest Airlink, Piedmont, and Piedmont Regional. Other than free van service provided by hotels, the only transportation from the airport is by taxi *(Yellow Cab*, tel. 904/433–1143). The cost is about $7 to downtown, $15 to Pensacola Beach.

By Car   Interstate 10 is the major east-west artery across the top of the state. U.S. 90 plays along with it for the most part, but cavorts off here and there. U.S. 98 is the scenic, coast-hugging route. North-south routes include I–75, U.S. 27, and U.S. 19/98 through the central area; and I–95, U.S. 1, and U.S. 17 on the east. U.S. 301 angles through Jacksonville, U.S. 319 through Tallahassee, and U.S. 331 and U.S. 231 dip into the Panhandle.

By Train   Jacksonville is Florida's entry city for *Amtrak* service (tel. 800/ USA-RAIL), with two southbound and two northbound trains daily. Other stations are at Waldo (in the Gainesville area) and Palatka. Schedules vary with the season.

By Bus   **Greyhound/Trailways Bus Line** has extensive service throughout the region, with stations in Jacksonville (tel. 904/356–5521), St. Augustine (tel. 904/829–6401), Gainesville (tel. 904/376–5252), Tallahassee (tel. 904/222–4240), Panama City (tel. 904/785–7861), Fort Walton Beach (tel. 904/243–1940), and Pensacola (tel. 904/476–4800).

Scenic Drives

Rte. 399 from Pensacola Beach to Navarre Beach takes you along Santa Rosa Island, a long white ribbon rolled out on blue-green waters. **U.S. 98** offers about 100 miles of soul-stirring views as it sweeps along the Gulf of Mexico eastward from Destin. The **Buccaneer Trail (Rte. A1A)** on the Atlantic Coast goes from Mayport (where a ferry is part of the state highway system) through marshlands laced with inlets and rivers, past unspoiled beaches, and into Fernandina Beach, a 300-year-old island seaport that was once a haven for freebooters. **Rte. 13** from Jacksonville to East Palatka winds along the banks of the north-flowing St. Johns River and drifts through sleepy hamlets, past citrus groves and Ravine Gardens State Park, which is awash with azaleas in the early spring.

Guided Tours

Right This Way, Pensacola (2875 W. Michigan Ave., tel. 904/944–1700) offers package tours personally tailored to your interests.
The **Capt. Anderson** and the **Capt. Anderson III** (Capt. Anderson's Pier, Panama City Beach, tel. 904/234–5940) offer a

variety of cruises during their June–August season. The original dinner cruise boat, *Capt. Anderson*, has replaced its seated
dining with a seafood buffet, $25. *Capt. Anderson III* offers
both dolphin-feeding trips and jaunts to Shell Island; either
trip is $6 adults, $3 children. (*Capt. Anderson II*, formerly sailing from Fort Walton Beach and Pensacola Beach, now operates
year-round in Clearwater Beach.)

Glass Bottom Boat (Panama City Beach, tel. 904/234–8944) offers outings year-round, on different seasonal schedules.
Prices range from $5 to $11.

Riverwalk Cruise Line (St. Johns River, Jacksonville, tel. 904/
398–0797) offers daily sightseeing cruises aboard the *First
Lady of Jacksonville* ($9.50 sightseeing, $13.50 luncheon/
sightseeing), as well as moonlight ($10.50)/ and dinner/dance
cruises ($28.50).

The **Annabelle Lee** (tel. 904/396–2333), Jacksonville's stern-
wheeler, does twice-monthly dinner cruises (more often in the
summer). Cost: $25.

St. Augustine Historical Tours (tel. 904/829–3800) has a trolley
you can take for a 7½-mile narrated city tour. The trolley operates daily 8:30–6, and tickets can be purchased at 167 San
Marco Avenue and at ticket booths throughout the city. A one-
time charge of $7 adults, $2 children is good for the duration of
your visit, and you can get off the trolley at the major sights and
reboard later.

St. Augustine Sightseeing Trains (170 San Marco Ave., tel. 904/
829–6545) offers tours that combine highlights of the historic
district with other points of interest. Tours range from a one-
hour orientation tour ($7) to special packages of three to 10
hours ($10–$25.50). All have one-time fees that are good for the
duration of your stay.

Colee Sightseeing Carriage Tours (St. Augustine, tel. 904/829–
2818) offers horse-drawn carriage tours through the narrow
streets of the historic district. Tours begin on Bayfront near
the entrance to Fort Castillo de San Marcos, 9–5 daily. Cost: $7
adults, $3 children.

Victory II Scenic Cruise (Municipal Yacht Pier, St. Augustine,
tel. 904/824–1806) offers a 1¼-hour tour of the waterfront and
Matanzas Bay. It operates seasonally, March–December.
Cost: $5 adults, $2.50 children.

Suwannee Country Tours (White Springs, tel. 904/397–2347)
has a variety of specialty tours at various prices, including bicycle tours, canoe trips on the Suwannee River, and a history
tour that combines biking and walking in St. Augustine with an
overnight stay in a country inn.

Important Addresses and Numbers

Tourist Information Amelia Island-Fernandina Beach Chamber of Commerce (102
Centre St., tel. 904/261–3248). Open weekdays 9–5.

Apalachicola Bay Chamber of Commerce (45 Market St., tel.
904/653–9419). Open weekdays 9–5.

Cedar Key Chamber of Commerce (2nd St., tel. 904/543–5600).
Open Monday, Wednesday, and Friday 10–2.

Destin Chamber of Commerce (Holiday Inn, Suite D, 1021 U.S.
98E, tel. 904/837–6241). Open weekdays 9–5.

Fort Walton Beach Chamber of Commerce (34 Miracle Strip
Pkwy., U.S. 98, tel. 904/244–8191). Open weekdays 8–5.

Convention & Visitors Bureau of Jacksonville and Its Beaches
(33 S. Hogan St., tel. 904/353–9736). Open weekdays 8:30–5.

Jacksonville Beaches Chamber of Commerce (413 Pablo Ave., tel. 904/249–3868). Open weekdays 8–5.
Panama City Beach Visitors & Convention Bureau (12015 W. U.S. 98 Alt. tel. 904/234–6575). Open weekdays 8–5.
Pensacola Visitor Information Center (1401 E. Gregory St., tel. 800/343–4321). Open daily 8:30–5.
St. Augustine Visitor Information Center (10 Castillo Dr., tel. 904/824–3334). Open daily 8:30–5:30.
Tallahassee Visitor & Convention Bureau (100 N. Duval St., tel. 904/224–8116). Open weekdays 8:30–5.

Emergencies Dial 911 for **police** and **ambulance** in a emergency.

Hospitals Emergency rooms are open 24 hours at the following: **White-Wilson Medical Center** (1000 Airport Rd., Destin, tel. 904/837–3848), **Shands Hospital** (1600 S.W. Archer Rd., Gainesville, tel. 904/395–0111), **University Hospital** (655 W. 8th St., Jacksonville, tel. 904/350–6988), **Beaches Hospital** (1430 16th Ave. S, Jacksonville Beach, tel. 904/246–6731), **Bay Medical Center** (615 N. Bonita Ave., Panama City, tel. 904/769–1511), **Baptist Hospital** (1000 W. Marina St., Pensacola, tel. 904/434–4011), **Flagler Hospital** (Health Park Blvd., off U.S. 1, St. Augustine, tel. 904/824–8411), **Tallahassee Memorial Regional Medical Center** (1300 Miccosukee Rd., Tallahassee, tel. 904/681–1155).

Pharmacies The only 24-hour pharmacy in the region is **Eckerd Drug** (4397 Roosevelt Blvd., Jacksonville, tel. 904/389–0314).

Exploring North Florida

Numbers in the margin correspond with points of interest on the Florida Panhandle and Northeast Florida maps.

Interstate 10 is the fastest way to get from Pensacola to St. Augustine. However, after our tour of Pensacola we'll head east on U.S. 98 and dawdle in the coastal resorts of Fort Walton Beach, Destin, and Panama City Beach. The beaches are almost irresistible; the pure white sands are 99% quartz—ancient sands from the ocean floor of the Caribbean, deposited by a maverick current that eddies offshore—and the blue-green waters are quite enticing. Having dried off, we'll visit Fort San Marcos de Apalache, whose history dates from 1528, and Wakulla Springs, where glass-bottom boats glide over the world's deepest freshwater spring. Next, we'll take in a bit of Tallahassee, the capital city, and continue eastward. Jacksonville, home of the Gator Bowl and site of the annual Georgia-Florida football game, sits on the banks of the north-flowing St. Johns River, while the Jacksonville Beaches bask on the Atlantic Coast. Our final destination is the nation's first city, St. Augustine, founded by the Spanish in 1565, where we'll wander ancient narrow streets and see the Oldest House, the Oldest Schoolhouse, and a whole raft of other "oldests."

1 Had it not been for a hurricane, **Pensacola** would be the nation's oldest city. In 1559, six years before the founding of St. Augustine, Don Tristan de Luna and 1,500 Spanish troops landed on Pensacola's shores. Shortly after their arrival the big wind blew through, taking with it not only de Luna's dreams of a Spanish settlement, but most of his fleet as well. It was not until the mid-18th century that a permanent Spanish settlement was established.

Northeast Florida

ATLANTIC OCEAN

Fernandina Beach

12 *Amelia Island*

Atlantic Beach
Jacksonville Beach

11 Jacksonville

St. Augustine
St. Augustine Beach

A1A

Flagler Beach

St. John's River

Palatka

Ocala National Forest

GEORGIA

N

St. Mary's River

Starke

Gainesville

Hawthorne

Cross Creek

Osceola National Forest

Lake City

High Springs

Santa Fe River

Live Oak

Suwannee River

Cross City

Suwannee National Wildlife Refuge

Horseshoe Beach

Suwannee

Madison

Perry

Steinhatchee

Greenville

Ochlockonee River

8 Tallahassee

9 *Natural Bridge*

10 *Wakulla Springs*

Gulf of Mexico

50 miles

75 km

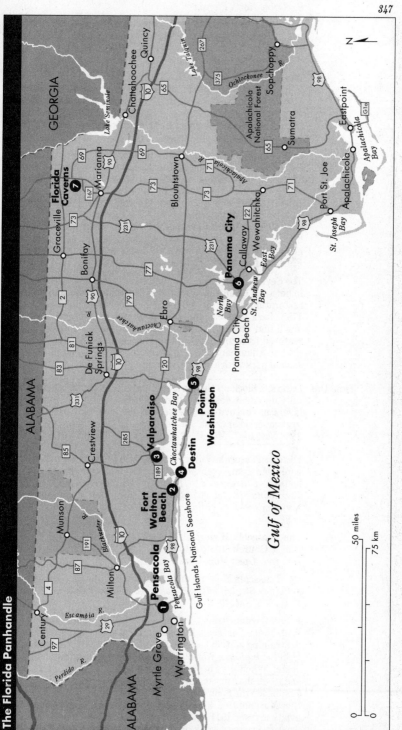

The Florida Panhandle

Be sure to stop first at the Visitor Information Center at the foot of the Pensacola Bay Bridge. You can pick up loads of brochures and maps, including self-guided walking tours of the city's two historic districts.

The North Hill Preservation District is bordered by Palafox, Reus, LaRua, and Blount streets. Driving through the 60-block district, you'll see fine turn-of-the-century southern homes with broad verandas, cupolas, turrets, and ornate gingerbread trim. The homes are private residences, so you'll have to do your admiring from the street.

Continuing down Palafox Street toward the Bay, you'll pass Palafox Place. Buildings in the three-block area from Garden Street to Government Street are decorated with handsome wrought-iron balconies that preserve the flavor of Old Pensacola. At Palafox and Garden streets you'll see the San Carlos Hotel, which dates from 1910. It's closed now, but for more than 50 years it was the center of the city's business and social life. At the corner of Palafox and Intendencia streets, a plaque marks the spot where Andrew Jackson lived when he was Florida's first territorial governor.

The Seville Square Historic District is just to the west, tucked in between Palafox, Cedar, Cervallos, and Chase streets. This restoration is near the site of the permanent Spanish colony of 1752. Park your car and wander along the old brick streets. You'll find shops, restaurants, and museums, most of them in restored 18th- and 19th-century homes. In the heart of the district at Adams and Zaragoza streets, Seville Square is a tree-shaded park with a lacy gazebo.

Time Out Dabo's, a block off the park on Zaragoza Street, has a wonderfully decadent dessert called Hello Dollies, which is made of layers of chocolate, butterscotch, coconut, and pecans on a graham-cracker crust. *Tel. 904/433–1133. Open Mon.–Fri. 10–2:30, Sat. 10–4. MC, V.*

Historic Pensacola Village is a five-site complex taking in **Hispanic Museum, Transportation Museum,** and three historic houses. *Entrance at Hispanic Museum, Zaragoza and Tarragona Sts., tel. 904/444–8905. Admission: $3 adults, $2.50 senior citizens, $2 children. Open Mon.–Sat. 10–4:30, Sun. 1–4:30.*

The **Pensacola Historical Museum** is housed in the 1830 Old Christ Church. *405 S. Adams St., tel. 904/433–1559. Admission free. Open Mon.–Sat. 9–4:30.*

The **Pensacola Museum of Art** utilizes the Old City Jail. *407 S. Jefferson St., tel. 904/432–5682. Admission free. Open Tues.–Fri. 10–5, Sat. 10–4.*

Follow Garden Street (U.S. 98) west to Navy Boulevard, which leads to the Pensacola Naval Air Station, the nation's first naval training station, established 1825. The NAS is home to the USS *Lexington,* a World War II veteran now used as a training vessel. When she's in port you can board the Lady Lex on weekends 9–3; she's docked in the port of Pensacola for public tours. Just inside the main gate of the NAS you'll find the Naval Aviation Museum (tel. 904/452–3604), which traces the history of aviation from 1911 to the space age. It's a huge structure, where you can see a Skylab Command Module, the NC-14 Flying Boat that made the first transatlantic air crossing, a replica of the Navy's first Curtiss biplane, and a variety of other exhibits. Just northeast of the Naval Museum, Sherman Field is home to the famed Blue Angels precision flying squadron. The Angels perform twice annually in the Pensacola area, in the summer and the fall. *Navy Blvd., tel. 904/452–2311. Admission free. Open daily 9–5.*

Retrace your route and follow U.S. 98 across both Pensacola Bay Bridge and the toll bridge from Gulf Breeze (35 cents) to **Santa Rosa Island,** where you enter **Gulf Islands National Seashore.** The park encompasses **Fort Pickens,** perched on the island's western end, which once held American Indian chief Geronimo captive. *(Entrance gate on Fort Pickens Rd., tel. 904/932–9994. Admission: $3 per car. Open daily 9–sunset.)*

Take Route 399 east to Navarre Beach for some splendid views. You're right on the Gulf of Mexico, passing, if you can resist them, miles and miles of white-sand beaches. To reach **Fort Walton Beach,** take the Navarre Bridge to U.S. 98 and head east.

②

Eglin Air Force Base covers 720 square miles of land northeast of Fort Walton Beach. Tours of the mammoth facility are offered January–March and June–August. *Main Gate is off Rte. 85, tel. 904/881–6668. Admission free.*

Just outside the main gate of Eglin, you'll find the **Air Force Armament Museum.** The museum has a vast collection of military weaponry, and there is a park with a display of aircraft and bombs. *Off Rte. 85, tel. 904/882–4062. Admission free. Open daily 9:30–4:30.*

The **Indian Temple Mound Museum** preserves an ancient Indian temple mound right in the heart of town. A reconstructed temple sits atop the mound, and a small museum displays artifacts recovered from this mound and from others long gone. *U.S. 98, downtown Fort Walton Beach, tel. 904/243–6521. Admission: 75 cents. Open Mon.–Sat. 9–4.*

③ A short detour north of Fort Walton Beach on Rte. 85 will bring you to the little town of **Valparaiso.** The **Valparaiso Historical Society Museum** displays the complete official records of the Union and Confederate armies, as well as a steam-powered cotton gin. *115 Westview Ave., tel. 904/678–2615. Admission free. Open Tues.–Sat. 11–4, Sun. 2:30–4:30.*

④ As you approach **Destin** on U.S. 98 you'll see yet another splendid view of white boats bobbing on turquoise waters. The Fort Walton Beach—Destin area is one of the most popular resort areas in the Panhandle. There are all sorts of water sports and places that cater to the beach crowd.

The **Village Art Gallery** is the Panhandle's oldest gallery, displaying the works of some 25 artists. *110 Melvin St., tel. 904/837–2228. Admission free. Open Mar.–Dec., Tues.–Sat. 11–4.*

The **Museum of the Sea and Indian** focuses on plant and animal life from the seven seas, and Indian artifacts from North and South America. *4801 Hwy. 98E (Old Hwy. 98), tel. 904/837–6625. Admission: $3.25 adults, $1.75 children. Open daily 8–5.*

⑤ Twenty-five miles east of Destin, **Eden State Gardens** border a graceful antebellum mansion that perches on the brink of Choctawhatchee Bay in **Point Washington.** The mansion, veiled in magnolias and moss-draped oaks, has a striking sleigh-bed among its period furnishings. In the spring, the gardens are ablaze with color. *Off U.S. 395N in Point Washington, tel. 904/ 231–4214. Admission: $1. Park open 8–sunset; mansion tours conducted on the hour Thurs.–Mon. 9–4. The mansion is closed Tues. and Wed.*

❻ Continuing on U.S. 98 you'll come to **Panama City Beach,** another hot ticket during the summer. U.S. 98 Alt. is the route to the beaches, and you should note that in the summer this alternate is jammed with traffic. This is the Miracle Strip, awash with hotels, motels, condominiums, amusement parks, bars, lounges.

Top of the Strip Tower, 203 feet above it all, goes in and out of business regularly, but it always manages to be in operation when summer rolls around to provide a gull's-eye view of the goings-on. *12001 W. Hwy. 98, no phone. Admission: 50 cents. Usually open Mar.–Labor Day only. Hours vary.*

Time Out **Pineapple Willie's** is a lighthearted bistro/restaurant that's always worth a stop because of its great beachside location and nice big deck from which to enjoy it. *On Beach Blvd. at Thomas Dr., tel. 904/235–0928. AE, MC, V.*

At the Treasure Island Marina, the **Treasure Ship** is a full-size replica of a schooner. It houses four levels of restaurants, snack bars, lounges and gift shops. The open-air observation decks offer a lovely view of Grand Lagoon.

If you continue east on Thomas Drive, you'll come to **St. Andrews State Recreation Area,** at the eastern tip of the peninsula, one of the state park system's most scenic facilities. Within its 1,063 acres you can swim, wander amid the dunes, stroll a nature trail, fish from either of two piers, or take a shuttle boat to offshore Shell Island.

Across the bay in **Panama City,** the **Junior Museum of Bay County** has science, art, and nature exhibits designed for children. There are concerts, puppet shows, and a pioneer village with a log cabin. Nature trails lead through a hardwood swamp, a pine island, and a hardwood hammock. *1731 Jenks Ave., tel. 904/769–6128. Admission free. Open Tues.–Sat. 9–4.*

Before heading east toward Tallahassee, we'll take a look at two other points of interest in the Panhandle.

Drive north on County Rte. 77A; in about an hour you'll reach **Falling Waters State Recreation Area.** There you'll find the Falling Waters Sink. It's a cylindrical, smoothwall pit, 100 feet deep and 15 feet in diameter, with a small stream flowing into it. *Rte. 77A, tel. 904/638–4030. Admission: $1 driver, 50 cents each passenger over age 6. Open daily 8 AM–sunset.*

From there, take I-10 east and exit on Rte. 167 to reach the ❼ **Florida Caverns State Park.** The 1,217 acres of the park contain a network of caves with unusual rock formations. Tours of the caves are conducted hourly. The park also offers camping, fishing, hiking, picnicking, swimming, and spelunking. *Rte. 167, tel. 904/482–3632. Admission to caverns: $2 adults, $1 children. Open daily 9–5.*

❽ I-10 rolls through thick pine forests. **Tallahassee,** the capital city, is noted for its lush canopies of trees.

Stop at the **Visitor and Convention Bureau** at 100 North Duval Street to pick up information about the capital and the surrounding area. The bureau is housed in The Columns, the city's oldest structure.

The **Museum of Florida History** houses hands-on exhibits that trace the state's history from prehistoric Indians to space shuttles. There is a skeleton of a mastodon, ancient gold doubloons, and a pre-Civil War dugout boat. *500 S. Bronough St., tel. 904/ 488–1484. Admission free. Open Mon.–Fri. 9–4:30, Sat. 10– 4:30, Sun. and holidays noon–4:30.*

The **Capitol Complex** encompasses both the New Capitol—a $50 million high-rise tower with an observation level on the 22nd floor—and the Old Capitol, a traditional domed structure restored to its 1902 appearance and now a museum. Each has guided and self-guided tours. *Monroe St. and Apalachee Pkwy., tel. 904/488–6167 for New Capitol, 487–1902 for Old Capitol. Admission free. Tours weekdays 8:30–4:30, weekends 11–4.*

St. John's Cemetery, at Call and Boulevard streets, holds the graves of Napoleon Bonaparte's nephew and his wife—the great-grandniece of George Washington.

North of town, the **Maclay State Ornamental Gardens** are ablaze in the spring with azaleas, dogwoods, and other showy plants and trees. There are reflecting pools, winding pathways, and a tiny walled garden. The 308-acre park also holds the Maclay residence, with period furnishings. *3450 Thomasville Rd. (U.S. 319), tel. 904/893–4455. Admission: $2 for house and gardens; for lakeside recreational area only, $1 driver, 50 cents per passenger May 1–Jan. 1; free rest of the year. Open daily 8 AM–sunset.*

9 To the south, the **Natural Bridge State Historic Site** is where a Confederate force of schoolboys and old men staved off Union troops in 1865, making Tallahassee the only southern capital east of the Mississippi to elude capture. Each March a colorful reenactment is staged. *On Natural Bridge Rd., Rte. 354, off U.S. 363 in Woodville, tel. 904/925–6216. Admission free. Open daily 8 AM–sunset.*

10 About 25 miles south of Tallahassee, **Wakulla Springs State Park** contains the world's deepest spring, the bottom of which has yet to be found. Glass-bottom boats take you over the springhead, which flows at 600,000 gallons per minute. The park also offers jungle cruises down the Wakulla River, a swimming area in the springs, and a 1930s Spanish-style lodge. *Off Rte. 61, tel. 904/224–5950. Admission: $1 driver, 50 cents per passenger; cruises: $3.75 adults, $1.75 children. Open daily 9– 5:30.*

San Marcos de Apalachee State Museum commemorates the site visited by Pánfilo de Narváez in 1527 and by Hernando de Soto in 1539. The crumbling ruins of a riverside fort attest to the presence of the Spanish in 1679, and there is a small interpretative museum. *Off Rte. 363, St. Marks, tel. 904/925–6216. Admission free. Open daily 9–5.*

Time Out   **Posey's,** "Home of the Topless Oyster," is a down-home place where the house specialty is half-shell oysters in hot sauce. *Old Fort Dr., off Rte. 363, tel. 904/925–6172. No credit cards. Open only during oyster season (Sept.–Apr.).*

⑪ From Tallahassee, I–10 is the direct route to **Jacksonville,** the hub of Florida's "First Coast."

Jacksonville is on the banks of the St. Johns River, one of the few rivers that flow from south to north. Most of the activity in the city takes place around the riverside developments. **Southbank Riverwalk** is a boardwalk that ties a string of hotels, restaurants, and kiosks to St. Johns River Park, whose Friendship Fountain, lighted at night, sprays as high as a ten-story building. On the opposite bank, accessible by water taxi, you'll find **Jacksonville Landing,** a glitzy festival marketplace, and the 23-acre **Metropolitan Park,** with a canopied pavilion where special events are held.

The **Cummer Gallery of Art** occupies the gardens of a former lumber baron's riverside mansion. Artworks, including a noted collection of Old Masters and early Meissen porcelain, fill 10 galleries. *829 Riverside Ave., tel. 904/356–6857. Admission free. Open Tues.–Fri. 10–4, Sat. noon–5, Sun. 2–5.*

The **Jacksonville Art Museum** displays the works of local and national artists. Its permanent exhibits include oriental porcelain and pre-Columbian artifacts. *4160 Boulevard Center Dr., tel. 904/398–8336. Admission free. Open Tues., Wed., and Fri. 10–4; Thurs. 10–10; weekends 1–5.*

⑫ Before heading south from Jacksonville, make a stop at **Amelia Island,** the vacation community in the Atlantic. Besides the resort facilities at Amelia Island Plantation and numerous condos throughout the lower part of the island, on the northern tip there's the salty little seaport of Fernandina Beach, with its restored Victorian buildings.

St. Augustine

Numbers in the margin correspond with points of interest on the St. Augustine map.

To reach **St. Augustine,** take U.S. 1 south and head straight for the **Visitor Information Center** (10 Castillo Dr.). The center has loads of brochures, maps, and information about the nation's oldest city.

① The massive **Castillo de San Marcos National Monument** hunkers over Matanzas Bay, looking every century of its 300 years. Park rangers provide an introductory narration, after which you're on your own. This is a wonderful fort to explore, complete with moat, turrets, and 16-foot-thick walls. The fort was constructed of coquina, a soft limestone made of broken shells and coral, and it took 25 years to build it. Garrison rooms depict the life of the era, and special artillery demonstrations are held periodically on the gun deck. *1 Castillo Dr., tel. 904/829–6506. Admission: $1 adults, children under 16 and senior citizens free. Open daily 8:30–5:15.*

② The **City Gate,** at the top of St. George Street, is a relic from the days when the Castillo's moat ran westward to the river and the Cubo Defense Line (defensive wall) protected the settlement against approaches from the north. Today it is the entrance to the popular restored area.

③ The **Museum Theatre** screens two 30-minute films several times daily. One tells the story of the founding of the city in 1565, and the other depicts life in St. Augustine in 1576. *5 Cordova St., tel. 904/824–0339. Admission: $2 adults, $1.50 children under 15; combination ticket for both films: $3 adults, $2.50 children. Open daily 9:30–5:30.*

The **Oldest Wooden Schoolhouse** (14 St. George St.) is a tiny 18th-century structure that, because it was the closest structure to the city gates, served as a guardhouse and sentry shelter during the Seminole Wars.

San Agustin Antiguo is a state-operated living-history village with eight sites. You can wander through the narrow streets at your own pace. Along your way you may see a Colonial soldier's wife cooking over an open fire; a blacksmith building his shop (a historic reconstruction); and craftsmen busy at candledipping, spinning, weaving, and cabinetmaking. They are all making reproductions that will be used within the restored area. *Entrance at Triay House, 29 St. George St., near the Old City Gate, tel. 904/824–6383. Admission: $3.50 adults, $2 students 6–18; $8 family ticket. Open daily 9–5.*

Time Out **Spanish Bakery,** behind Casa de Calcedo on St. George Street, has meat turnovers, cookies, and fresh-baked bread made from a Colonial recipe. *No credit cards.*

---

❹ **Basilica Cathedral of St. Augustine** has parish records dating back to 1594, the oldest written records in the country. Following a fire in 1887, extensive changes were made to the current structure, which dates from 1797. It was remodeled in the mid-1960s. *40 Cathedral Pl., tel. 904/824–2806. Admission free, but donations requested. Open weekdays 5:30–5, weekends 5:30 AM–7 PM.*

❺ **Plaza de la Constitución,** at St. George Street and Cathedral Place, is the central area of the original settlement. It was laid out in 1598 by decree of King Philip II, and little has changed since. At its center there is a monument to the Spanish constitution of 1812; at the east end is a public market dating from early American days. Just beyond is a statue of Juan Ponce de León, who discovered Florida in 1513.

❻ The **Ximenez-Fatio House** was built in 1797, and it became a boarding house for tourists in 1885. *20 Aviles St., tel. 904/829–3575. Admission free. Open Mar. 1–Aug. 31, Sun.–Thurs. 1–4.*

❼ The **Oldest Store Museum** re-creates a turn-of-the-century general store. There are high-button shoes, lace-up corsets, patent drugs, and confectionery specialties. *4 Artillery La., tel. 904/829–9729. Admission: $3 adults, $2.50 senior citizens, $1.50 children 6–12. Open Mon.–Sat. 9–5, Sun. noon–5.*

❽ The **Oldest House,** operated by the Historical Society, reflects much of the city's history through its changes and additions, from the coquina walls built soon after the town was burned in 1702 to the house's enlargement during the British occupation. *14 St. Francis St., tel. 904/824–2872. Admission: $3 adults, $2.75 senior citizens, $1.50 children. Open daily 9–5.*

❾ The **Lightner Museum** is housed in one of two posh hotels built in 1888 by railroad magnate Henry Flagler, who wanted to create an American Riviera. The museum contains a collection of ornate antique music boxes (ask about demonstrations!), and

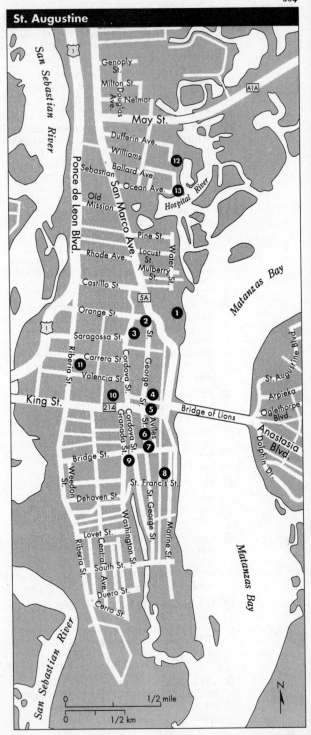

St. Augustine

the Lightner Antique Mall perches on three levels of what was the hotel's grandiose indoor swimming pool. *75 King St., tel. 904/824–2874. Admission to museum: $3 adults, $1 students, children under 12 free. Museum open daily 9–5; mall open Wed.–Sun. 9:30–5.*

⑩ Across from the Lightner Museum, **Flagler College** occupies the second of Flagler's hotels. It's a riveting structure replete with towers, turrets, and arcades and decorated by Louis Comfort Tiffany. The front courtyard is open to the public.

⑪ At Valencia and Sevilla streets, behind Flagler College, the **Flagler Memorial Presbyterian Church**, which Flagler built in 1889, is a splendid Venetian Renaissance structure. The dome towers more than 100 feet, and it is topped by a 20-foot Greek cross. The church is open Monday–Saturday 9–5.

⑫ The **Fountain of Youth** salutes Ponce de León. In the complex there is a springhouse, an explorer's globe, a planetarium, and an Indian village. *155 Magnolia Ave., tel. 904/829–3168. Admission: $3.50 adults, $2.50 senior citizens, $1.50 children 6–12, under 6 free. Open daily 9–4:45.*

⑬ The **Mission of Nombre de Dios** commemorates the site where America's first Christian mass was celebrated. A 208-foot stainless-steel cross marks the spot where the mission's first cross was planted. *San Marco Ave. and Old Mission Rd., tel. 904/824–2809. Admission free, but donations requested. Open daily 7 AM–8 PM summer; 8–6 winter.*

What to See and Do with Children

Wild Water Kingdom has water slides, miniature golf, go-carts, and an arcade with electronics games. *2 Via de Luna, Pensacola, tel. 904/934–3205. Admission: $4 per hour, $9 all day. Open daily June–Labor Day; weekends only Apr.–May. Closed Sept.–Mar.; arcade open weekends in Mar.; hours vary; call for current schedule.*

Big Kahuna features a water park with everything from speed slides to an underground tube ride, plus 56 holes of miniature golf and a 4,000-seat amphitheater with changing entertainment. *U.S. 98, Destin, tel. 904/837–4061. Water park admission: $9 adults, $4.50 children all day, $4.50 per person after 6 PM. Miniature golf: $5 for 18 holes, $6 for 36 holes. (Prices may be higher after planned expansion in 1990.) Open spring-summer 10–10 daily.*

Coconut Creek Mini-Golf and Gran Maze offers two 18-hole miniature golf courses plus a walking maze—clocks record the time it takes to thread your way through. *9807 W. Hwy. 98, Panama City Beach, tel. 904/234–2625. Golf: $5 one course, $8 both; Gran Maze: $5 per person. Open March–Labor Day, daily 9 AM–11 PM; hours vary rest of year.*

Gulf World is a tropical garden with flamingos and peacocks, a parrot show, dancing dolphins, sea lions, penguins, and a shark channel. *15412 W. Hwy. 98A, Panama City Beach, tel. 904/234–5271. Admission: $9.95 adults, $6.95 children. Open daily Mar.–Labor Day, 9–3 early in the season, 9–5 in the summer.*

Miracle Strip Amusement Park has among its rides a roller coaster with a 65-foot drop, a miniature train, and a hair-raising critter called the Sea Dragon. There are several snack bars, a game arcade, and a gift shop. *12000 W. Hwy. 98A, Panama City Beach, tel. 904/234–9873. Gate admission only: 75 cents adults, children under 4 free. Gate admission, including all rides: $12 adults, $10 children under 10. Open mid-March–June 1, Fri. 6–11 PM, Sat. 1–11; June 2–Aug. 31, weekdays 5–11:30 PM, Sat. 1–11:30, Sun. 3–11:30; closed Labor Day–early March.*

Shipwreck Island, adjoining the Miracle Strip Amusement Park, is a splashy place with a Zoom Flume, a wave pool, a Lazy River for old-folk tubing, a Tadpole Pond for the little tads, and a 300-foot racing slide. *12000 W. Hwy. 98A, Panama City Beach, tel. 904/234–9873. Admission: $13 adults, $11 children 5–10, free for children under 5 and senior citizens. Operating hours vary; call for current schedule.*

Snake-A-Torium features reptile shows and exhibits. *9008 W. Hwy. 98A, Panama City Beach, tel. 904/234–3311. Admission: $3.80 adults, $2.80 children. Open daily 10–4.*

Museum of Man and the Sea focuses on the history of diving. *17314 Hutchinson Rd., Panama City Beach, tel. 904/235–4101. Admission: $3.50 adults, $1.50 children. Open Dec.–Sept., daily 9–5; Oct. and Nov. Tues.–Sun. 9–5.*

Tallahassee Junior Museum covers a vast outdoor area that contains a log cabin, exhibits of wagons and buggies, a snake house, picnic grounds, a turn-of-the-century farm, an array of Florida wildlife, nature trails, and a restored plantation home. *3945 Museum Dr., Tallahassee, tel. 904/576–1636. Admission: $4 adults, $2 children. Open Tues.–Sat. 9–5, Sun. 12:30–5.*

Jacksonville Zoo is home to 700 animals, including a herd of rare white rhinos and an outstanding collection of rare waterfowl. There are elevated walkways and observatories, elephant rides, and a miniature train for zoo touring. *On Heckscher Dr., a half mi east of I–95, Jacksonville, tel. 904/757–4462. Admission: $3 adults, $1.50 children, $1.25 senior citizens. Open daily 9–4:45.*

The Museum of Science/Alexander Brest Planetarium's exhibits range from antique dolls to live snakes and treasures of the Spanish fleet. The planetarium produces multimedia sky shows and light shows to classical or rock music. *1025 Gulf Life Dr., Jacksonville, tel. 904/396–7062. Admission: $3 adults, $2 children 5–18, children under 4 free. Open Mon.–Thurs. 10–5, Fri. and Sat. 10–11, Sun. noon–5.*

The Old Jail displays early weapons and methods of incarceration. *167 San Marco Ave., St. Augustine, tel. 904/829–3800. Admission: $3.25 adults, $2.25 children 6–12, children under 6 free. Open daily 8:30–5.*

St. Augustine Alligator Farm, in operation since 1893, features gators, gators, and more gators. There are hourly wildlife shows, plus alligator wrestling demonstrations and a petting zoo. *Rte. A1A south, tel. 904/824–3337. Admission: $6.95 adults, $6.25 senior citizens, $3.95 handicapped, $4.95 children 3–11, children under 3 free. Open daily 9–5.*

Marineland has more than 300 windows for observing sea creatures on their own turf, so to speak, plus a stadium for watching the acrobatic feats of dolphins. *Rte. A1A south, St. Augustine, tel. 904/471–1111. Admission: $12 adults, $7 children 3–11, children under 3 free. Open daily 9–6.*

Off the Beaten Track

The space is meager but the surprises are many in **De Funiak Springs'** tiny **public library.** The one-room library, measuring only 17 feet by 24 feet, was built in 1887 and is Florida's oldest continuously operating public library. It houses about 14,000 volumes, some of them rare books as old as the library itself. There is also an impressive collection of European armor, with some pieces dating back to the Crusades (1100–1300). The Crusades? In De Funiak Springs? Therein lies one of the pleasures of this little place: tracing the history of the collection and learning how it came here. *Walton-De Funiak Public Library, 100 Circle Dr., De Funiak Springs, about 30 mi north of Destin, tel. 904/892–3624. Open Mon. 9–7, Tues.–Fri. 9–6, Sat. 9–3.*

If you hanker for some fresh seafood—the kind you pull in yourself and cook right there on the beach—join the locals who gather at **Indian Pass.** (On road maps it's shown as McNeills, which is the name of the family who first settled here.) This is serious oystering/shrimping/fishing country, where the locally owned Indian Pass Seafood Co. has its commercial oyster farms. The oysters in Indian Lagoon's shallow waters are up for grabs, and the place is also popular for castnetters going after the plentiful mullet. On the gulf side of the narrow spit of land, blue crabs are so plentiful in late summer that most crabbers dispense with nets and lines and use a garden rake to drag them onto the sand. *Public access area on Rte. 30, about 10 mi south of Port St. Joe.*

Beaches

Pensacola Beach. Pensacola's liveliest beach is located on Santa Rosa Island, five miles south of Pensacola. You'll have to cross two bridges to reach it—one to Gulf Breeze and the other to Santa Rosa Island. This is the center of the action, with a concentration of beachfront hotels, a fishing pier, bars, and a new water park. Beach-seekers will find a central parking lot, changing facilities, and lifeguards during the season.
Gulf Islands National Seashore. This 150-mile stretch of islands and keys between Ocean Springs, Mississippi, and Fort Walton Beach is rich with beaches and recreational areas. The **Fort Pickens area,** nine miles west of Pensacola Beach at the tip of Santa Rosa Island, is popular with families for its swimming beach, the Dunes Nature Trail, picnic areas and campgrounds, a fishing pier, jetties, parking facilities, outdoor showers, and lifeguards during the season. Ten miles east of Pensacola Beach, the **Santa Rosa Day Use Area** has undeveloped and uncluttered beaches, where there are parking and picnic areas, restrooms, and lifeguards in season. This section of the national seashore draws an almost equal mix of young singles and families. About 20 miles northwest of downtown Pensacola, **Johnson's Beach** on Perdido Key has miles and miles of quiet, white-sand beaches; there are outdoor showers, restrooms, parking and picnic facilities, and lifeguards in the summer.
John C. Beasley County Park is Fort Walton's showplace. It's across the bridge from Fort Walton Beach on Okaloosa Island and is especially popular with families. There is a boardwalk to the beach, covered picnic tables, a playground, changing

rooms, freshwater showers, and lifeguards during the summer
season.

Eglin Reservation Beach, about three miles west of the bridge
from Fort Walton, is a five-mile stretch of undeveloped military
land open to the public (restricted areas are clearly posted) and
is popular with the younger crowd of beachcombers.

Crystal Beach Wayside Park, five miles east of Destin, commands the most beautiful sweep of beach, buffered for an
additional five miles on each side by undeveloped state-owned
property. It draws singles and families, the young and the old,
and even passing motorists who stop to dig their toes into the
sand. Its facilities include picnic tables, shelters, changing
rooms, restrooms, and summer lifeguards.

Grayton Beach State Recreation Area, about 30 miles east of
Destin, is tucked away on Rte. 30A near the little communities
of Santa Rosa Beach and Grayton Beach. It's a quiet hideaway
for dawdling and daydreaming amid the dunes, and there are
changing rooms and restrooms, swimming, snorkeling, and a
scuba-diving area. It's open daily 8–sunset, and because it's a
state park, there is an admission charge: $1 driver, 50 cents per
passenger.

St. Andrews State Park, at the eastern end of the Panama City
Beach area, is the resort strip's most scenic and popular public
facility, with a swimming and snorkeling area on the gulf and in
a protected area behind the jetty. There are bathhouses and
picnic areas, as well as other park facilities.

Panama City Beach's public beach areas, near the county pier
across from the amusement area, are aswarm with singles and
families during the summer. There is a profusion of beachside
shops, bars, eateries, arcades, and places to rent everything
from floats to catamarans. You can also expect bumper-to-
bumper traffic in the summer.

Jacksonville Beach is the liveliest of the long line of Jacksonville
Beaches. Young people flock to the beach, where there are all
sorts of games to play and also beach concessions, rental shops,
and a fishing pier.

Neptune Beach, adjoining Jacksonville Beach to the north, is
more residential and offers easy access to quieter beaches.
Surfers take to the waves, and consider it one of the area's two
best surfing sites.

Atlantic Beach, north of Neptune Beach, is the other favored
surfing area. Around the popular Sea Turtle Inn, you'll find
catamaran rentals and instruction. Five areas have lifeguards
on duty in the summer 10–6.

Kathryn Abbey Hanna Park, near Mayport, is the Jacksonville
area's showplace park, drawing families and singles alike. It offers beaches, showers, and snack bars that operate April–
Labor Day.

Fort Clinch State Park, on Amelia Island's northern tip, includes a municipal beach and pier. That's where Fernandina
Beach's city beaches are, meaning you pay a state-park entrance fee to reach them. But the beaches are broad and lovely,
and there is parking right on the beach, bathhouses, picnic areas, and all the facilities of the park itself, including the fort.

Amelia Island's lower half is mostly covered by the Amelia Island Plantation resort. However, on the island's extreme
southern tip you can go horseback riding along the wide, almost deserted beaches.

St. Augustine has 43 miles of wide, white, level beaches. The
young gravitate toward the public beaches at St. Augustine

Beach and Vilano Beach, while families prefer the Anastasia State Recreation Area. All three are accessible via Rte. A1A: Vilano Beach is to the north, across North River, and Anastasia State Park and St. Augustine Beach are both on Anastasia Island, across the Bridge of Lions.

Participant Sports

Boating   North Florida's watery playgrounds range from small bays, sounds, and freshwater rivers to the Gulf of Mexico and the Atlantic Ocean. Powerboats for fishing, snorkeling, and water-skiing can be rented at **Dolphin Marine Service** (600 Barracks St., Harbor Village at Pitt Slip, Pensacola, tel. 904/438–6637) and at **Merc Charter** (3024 Harbor Dr., Cove Yacht Harbor, Camachee Island, St. Augustine, tel. 904/825–0100). Paddle boats can be rented at **Blue Surf, Inc.** (Navarre Beach, tel. 904/939–2741).

Canoeing   You don't have to be an experienced canoeist to enjoy north Florida's rivers, streams, creeks, and spring runoffs—though if you are, you can find some challenging waters with shoals and rapids. The Blackwater River, dotted with white sandbars, flows through the lush Blackwater River State Forest. You can rent canoes at **Blackwater River Canoe Rental** (Rte. 16, Box 72, Milton, tel. 904/623–0235) and at **Adventures Unlimited** (12 mi north of Milton off Hwy. 87, tel. 904/626–1669). The Adventures Unlimited outlet near Pensacola (River Annex Rd., Cantonment, tel. 904/968–5529) can set you up for a day or overnight trip on the Coldwater and Perdido rivers. For a trip on the Wakulla River, near Tallahassee, contact **TNT Hideaway** (Hwy. 98, St. Marks, tel. 904/925–6412). For a jaunt down Econfina Creek, north of Panama City, contact **Econfina Creek Canoe Livery** (Hwy. 20, Strickland Rd., tel. 904/722–9032).

Diving   A World War II British tanker and a jet airplane are among the sunken vessels in the Gulf of Mexico, and diving to the wrecks is a popular sport. In the Panama City area, wreck dives are offered by **Panama City Dive Center** (4823 Thomas Dr., by St. Andrews State Park, tel. 904/235–3390) and **Hydroplane Dive Shop** (3605 Thomas Dr., next to Treasure Ship, tel. 800/874–3483 or 904/243–3063). In the Destin-Fort Walton Beach area, divers favor the natural reefs about two miles offshore, where there is a wealth of sponges, coral, sea fans, and sea whips. Area firms offering outings are **Fantasea** (1 U.S. 98, Destin, tel. 904/837–6943) and **Scuba Shop** (230 N. Eglin Pkwy., Fort Walton Beach, tel. 904/863–1341).

Fishing   Your options range from fishing piers to luxury charters. If you opt for the former, you can stroll out and drop a line on the **Old Pensacola Bay Bridge,** called the world's longest fishing pier, and at the 3,000-foot **Destin Catwalk** along the East Pass Bridge. The **Jacksonville Beach Fishing Pier** extends 1,200 feet into the Atlantic, and the cost for fishing is $3 for adults, $1.50 for children and senior citizens, or 50 cents for watching. **Okaloosa Island Pier,** 1,216 feet, is $3.50 to fish, 75 cents to observe. **Panama City Beach's** 1,642-foot city pier is $2 adults, $1.50 children for fishing, $1 for watching. Fishing from the county pier is free. You can get bait and tackle at **Soundside Bait & Tackle** (¼ mi north of Navarre Beach on Hwy. 87, tel. 904/939–1804), **Penny's Sporting Goods** (1800 N. Pace Blvd., Pensacola, tel. 904/438–9633), and at **Hook, Line & Sinker**

(Camachee Cove Yacht Harbor, St. Augustine, tel. 904/829–6073). Boat rentals, bait, and tackle are available at **North Beach Camp Resort** (2300 Coastal Hwy., 4 mi north of St. Augustine on Rte. A1A, tel. 904/824–1806) and **Riverside Fishing Camp** (1 mi north of St. Augustine on Rte. A1A, tel. 904/829–8314).

Among the charter options (about $350 for half day, $550 for full day), there are **Barbi-Anne Charter Boats** (off U.S. 98 in Destin, at the docks next to Bayou Bill's, tel. 904/837–6059), **The Moorings** (655 Pensacola Beach Blvd., Pensacola Beach, tel. 904/932–0305), **The Duchess** (Treasure Island Marina, Panama City Beach, tel. 800/874–3483), **Monty's Marina** (Mayport, tel. 904/246–7575), and **Camachee Cove Charters** (Camachee Island, tel. 904/824–3328).

Party boats are more economical, carrying up to 100 anglers at a cost of $35–$40 per person (including tackle and bait). Contact *Capt. Anderson's* (Capt. Anderson's Pier, Panama City Beach, tel. 800/874–2415 or 904/234–3435), *Her Majesty II* (Destin, tel. 904/837–6313), or *Sea Love II* (St. Augustine, tel. 904/824–3328).

Golf North Florida boasts acres and acres of fairways. **Marriott at Sawgrass** at Ponte Vedra Beach (tel. 904/285–2261) is the area's top-ranked site, with 99 holes. There are 18-hole courses at the **Fort George Island Golf Club** (11241 E. Fort George Rd., Jacksonville, tel. 904/251–3132), **Hyde Park Golf & Country Club** (6439 Hyde Grove Ave., Jacksonville, tel. 904/786–5410), the **Jacksonville Beach Golf Club** (605 S. Penman Rd., tel. 904/249–8600), the **West Meadows Golf Club** (11400 W. Meadows Dr., Jacksonville, tel. 904/781–4834), and the **St. Augustine Shores Country Club** (295 Shores Blvd., tel. 904/794–0303). In the Pensacola area, there are two 18-hole courses at the **Tiger Point Golf & Country Club** (3455 Santa Rosa Dr., Gulf Breeze, tel. 904/932–1333) and one 18-hole course at the **Carriage Hills Golf Club** (2355 W. Michigan Ave., Pensacola, tel. 904/944–5497). The semipublic course at the **Sandestin Resort** has 36 holes with lots of water and bunkers (U.S. 98E, Destin, tel. 904/837–2121), and **Marriott's Bay Point** (100 Delwood Beach Rd., Panama City Beach, tel. 904/234–3307) has holes patterned after the top nine holes of golf in the world. Other 18-hole courses are the **Indian Golf Bayou & Country Club** (Airport Rd., Destin, tel. 904/837–6191), **Signal Hill Golf Course** (9615 N. Thomas Dr., Panama City Beach, tel. 904/234–3218), **Fort Walton Beach Municipal Golf Club** (Lewis Turner Blvd. and Mooney Rd., Fort Walton Beach, tel. 904/862–3314), and **Killearn Golf & Country Club** (100 Tyron Circle, Tallahassee, tel. 904/893–2186).

Sailing Hobie Cats can be rented at **The Hobie Shop** (12705 W. Hwy. 98, Panama City Beach, tel. 904/234–0023). Sailing instruction and bareboat rentals are offered by **Friend Ship Charter Sailing** (500 Hwy. 98, Destin, tel. 904/837–2694). Sailing lessons, rentals, and charters are available at **The Boat** (housed in a 1922 concrete-hull troopship at 32 Miracle Strip Pkwy., Fort Walton Beach, tel. 904/243–BOAT). Sunfish, catamarans, and lessons are available from **Key Sailing** (289 Pensacola Beach Blvd., Gulf Breeze, tel. 904/932–2000).

Tennis **Amelia Island Plantation** (Amelia Island, tel. 904/261–6161) has 19 clay courts, four artificial turf courts, and two hard courts in a world-class tennis center. **Sandestin Resort** (U.S.

98E, Destin, tel. 904/837–2121) boasts Florida's only public grass courts, and nearby **Seascape Resort** (Destin, tel. 904/837–9181) offers tennis clinics for the whole family. Courts are available in 30 locations in and around Pensacola, among them the **Pensacola Racquet Club** (3450 Wimbledon Dr., tel. 904/434–2434). There are 12 courts at the **Fort Walton Beach Tennis Center** and another 12 at various locations (contact Parks & Recreation Dept., 132 Jett Dr., Fort Walton Beach, tel. 904/243–3119). There are 10 courts at the **Destin Racquet Club** (Airport Rd., Destin, tel. 904/837–8548). In Jacksonville, there are eight courts at the **Whalen Tennis Center** (6009 Powers Ave., tel. 904/737–8800) and six at **Huguenot Park** at the beach (200 16th Ave. S, tel. 904/249–9407). There are 15 courts at the **Ponte Vedra Club** (Ponte Vedra Beach, tel. 904/285–6911), 13 at **Marriott at Sawgrass** (Ponte Vedra Beach, tel. 904/285–7777), 10 at the **St. Augustine Beach & Tennis Resort** (3960 Rte. A1A, tel. 904/471–9111), and six at the **Ponce de León Lodge & Country Club** (two mi north of St. Augustine on U.S. 1N, tel. 904/824–2821).

Windsurfing Windsurfers can be rented from **The Surf Station** (1002 Anastasia Blvd., St. Augustine Beach, tel. 904/471–9463), **The Boat** (32 Miracle Strip Pkwy., Fort Walton Beach, tel. 904/243–BOAT), and **Pensacola Beach Sailing Center** (Pensacola Beach Causeway, tel. 904/932–8585). Places offering parasailing include **Bonifay Water Sports** (460 Pensacola Beach Blvd., Pensacola Beach, tel. 904/932–0633) and **PBS Watersports** (1320 Hwy. 98E, Fort Walton Beach, tel. 904/244–2933). **The Surf Station** (St. Augustine Beach, tel. 904/471–9463) even rents "boogie boards," which you ride on your stomach.

Spectator Sports

Baseball The **Jacksonville Expos,** a Class A Southern League professional team, play home games in Wolfson Park, Gator Bowl complex (1400 E. Duval St., Jacksonville, tel. 904/358–2846).

Dog Racing Greyhounds race year-round in the Jacksonville area, with seasons split among three tracks: **Jacksonville Kennel Club,** May–September (1400 N. McDuff Ave., tel. 904/646–0001); **Orange Park Kennel Club,** November–April (U.S. 17 at I–295, tel. 904/264–9575); and **Bayard Raceway,** March and April (18 mi south on U.S. 1, tel. 904/268–5555). In the Panhandle, there is racing year-round at **Pensacola Greyhound Park** (U.S. 98W, tel. 904/455–8598) and March–October at **Jefferson County Kennel Club** (Monticello, tel. 904/997–2561).

Football The annual **Gator Bowl** (1400 E. Duval St., downtown, tel. 904/630–3900) and the annual grudge match between Florida and Georgia are played in Jacksonville.

Golf The Tournament Players Championship is a March event at the **Tournament Players Club** (near Sawgrass in Ponte Vedra Beach, tel. 904/285–7888), which is national headquarters of the PGA Tour. The annual Pensacola Open is held in October at the **Perdido Key Resort** (Perdido Key, tel. 904/456–8863).

Jai Alai This fast-paced Basque sport is presented October–May at **Big Bend Jai-Alai Fronton** (off I–10 south of Quincy, tel. 904/442–4111).

Tennis The top-rated Women's Tennis Association Championships is held in April, and the Men's All-American Tennis Champion-

ship in September, both at **Amelia Island Plantation** (Amelia
Island, tel. 904/387–5497).

Dining and Lodging

Dining   The state is embraced by the Atlantic Ocean and the Gulf of
Mexico and is laced with waterways, which means that seafood
is prominently featured. In coastal towns, the catches often
come straight from the restaurant's own fleet. Shrimp, oysters, snapper, and grouper are especially popular.

Category	Cost*
Very Expensive	over $60
Expensive	$40–$60
Moderate	$20–$40
Inexpensive	under $20

per person, exclusive of wine, service, or tax (6% in Florida)

Lodging   Accommodations range from splashy beachfront resorts and
glitzy condominiums to cozy inns and bed-and-breakfasts nestled in historic districts. As a general rule, the closer you are to
the center of activity in the coastal resorts, the more you'll pay.
You'll save a few dollars if you stay across from the beach rather
than on it, and you'll save even more if you select a place that's a
bit removed from the action.

Category	Cost*
Very Expensive	over $120
Expensive	$90–$120
Moderate	$50–$90
Inexpensive	under $50

*per double room, exclusive of 6% state sales tax and nominal
tourist tax*

The most highly recommended restaurants and lodgings are indicated by a star ★.

The following abbreviations are used for credit cards: AE,
American Express; CB, Carte Blanche; DC, Diners Club; MC,
MasterCard; and V, Visa.

Amelia Island   **Snug Harbor.** The New Orleans roots of the restaurant owner
Dining   show in the Mardi Gras masks and beads that decorate this cozy
★   place. The Cajun-inspired menu includes a blackened sampler
of fish, chicken, and prime rib. Appetizers include fried zucchini and boiled shrimp, and among the entrees are crabmeat
Norfolk (crabmeat sautéed in butter and spices), trout meu-
nière, and a seafood platter that comes in three sizes; petit,
regular, and pig-out. *N. 2nd and Alachua Sts., tel. 904/261–
8031. Dress: casual. No reservations. MC, V. Inexpensive.*

Lodging   **Amelia Island Plantation.** This 1,250-acre luxury sports resort
★   sprawls over about a third of the island and is so much a part of
the natural setting that you may be surprised when you round a
curve and encounter a building. There are rental villas with one

to four bedrooms (some with private indoor pools) and in the main building, rooms with balconies or terraces overlooking the Atlantic. *800 Amelia Pkwy, Amelia Island 32034, tel. 800/874-6878. 500 hotel rooms, 700 rental villas. Facilities: 17 pools, 5 restaurants, 2 lounges, 25-court tennis center with stadium, 45 holes of golf, beach club, health club, and numerous water sports and recreational activities. AE, CB, DC, MC, V. Expensive–Very Expensive.*

Shoney's Inn. The island's first chain facility, this modern motel is spic-and-span and has a helpful staff that sees to things. *2707 Sadler Rd., 32034, tel. 904/277-2300. 110 rooms. Facilities; pool, Jacuzzi, tennis courts, restaurant, lounge. AE, CB, DC, MC, V. Moderate.*

Cedar Key   **The Captain's Table.** This dockside seafood restaurant sits on
Dining   stilts and has a fine view of the anglers on the pier and the artists on the sea wall. Broiled seafood is the specialty, but there are fried dishes, and some chicken and steak offerings as well. The captain's platter includes lobster tail, deviled crab, shrimp, crab fingers, and scallops. The restaurant is particularly proud of its soft-shell crabs. You can get a side order of swamp-cabbage salad, which is lettuce and cabbage palm, sprinkled with dates and tropical fruit and topped with a house dressing. *On Dock St., tel. 904/543-5441. Dress: casual. Reservations recommended for Sat. dinner. MC, V. Inexpensive.*

Lodging   **Island Place.** One- and two-bedroom suites that sleep four are available in this small two-story condominium complex. The roof is tin, and the decks offer a view of the busy dock. *Box 687, Cedar Key 32625, tel. 904/543-5307. 25 suites. Facilities: pool, Jacuzzi, sauna, laundry room. MC, V. Moderate–Expensive.*

Destin   **Capt. Dave's.** This branch on the beach is a newer, quieter ver-
Dining   sion of Capt. Dave's on the harbor. The changing menu might include such specialties as grouper spectacular (grouper layered with celery, onions, bell peppers, tomatoes, and ripe olives, topped with mozzarella). *U.S. 98E, 5 mi east of Destin, tel. 904/837-2627. Dress: casual. No reservations. AE, MC, V. Inexpensive–Moderate.*

★   **Harbor Docks.** You can dine inside or on the deck of this dockside seafood eatery, and if you arrive as the sun sets you can watch the shrimp fleet come in. Sautéed red snapper with artichoke hearts is a specialty, and there is a taste of Thai in the stir-fried shrimp and chicken dishes. Live music nightly ranges from rock or reggae to jazz. *538 U.S. 98, tel. 904/837-2506. Dress: casual. No reservations. AE, MC, V. Inexpensive.*

Lodging   **Sandestin Beach Resort.** A sprawling (2,600-acre) luxury re-
★   sort that impresses without intimidating. Lodging sites include rooms in a bayside inn, cottages and villas amid lagoons or fairways, condominium units in a high rise, and waterside patio homes with large decks and tiny gazebo docks. *Emerald Coast Pkwy., Destin 32541, tel. 800/874-3950 outside FL or 904/267-8000 in FL. 175 rooms, 400 villas. Facilities: numerous pools and restaurants, 2 golf courses, 16 tennis courts, shopping mall, private beach, marina, water sports. AE, DC, MC, V. Expensive–Very Expensive.*

Summer Breeze. This small Victorian-style condominium has a white picket fence, overhanging tin roof, and gingerbread trim. Each one-bedroom suite has queen-size bed, sleeper sofa, and bunk beds, and each can accommodate six people. The traditional decor is done in mauve and aqua. It's located about half-way between Destin and Sandestin. *3885 U.S. 98E, Destin 32541, tel. 904/837–4853. 35 1-bedroom condominiums. Facilities: pool, Jacuzzi, laundry room. MC, V. Moderate.*

Village Inn. This two-story, family-oriented Best Western facility was built in 1983. Rooms are "modern motel," with either king-size beds or two queens. *215 U.S. 98E, Destin 32541, tel. 904/837–743. 100 rooms. Facilities: pool, cable TV, restaurant, lounge. AE, DC, MC. V. Moderate.*

Fort Walton Beach
Dining

Liollio's. Relax quietly here and enjoy some Greek-spiced sea-food or a steak, the specialties of the local restaurateur, who also owned the earlier restaurant on this site overlooking the sound. *14 Miracle Mile Strip Pkwy., tel. 904/243–5011. Dress: informal. Reservations accepted. AE, DC, MC, V. Inexpensive.*

★ **Seagull Restaurant.** At this restaurant on the sound, you'll find crisp white napery, broiled and sautéed seafood specialties, and, if you come early enough, a splendid sunset. Gourmet offerings include scallops St. Jacques (poached in white wine with Mornay sauce, scallions, and green onions, and topped with grated Parmesan cheese). Snapper *amandine* is a small tender fillet topped with a sour cream-based sauce with Dijon mustard and almonds. The menu also lists lobster tails and several steak offerings. This is a family-oriented place that caters to its local clientele. *1201 E. U.S. 98, tel. 904/243–3413. Dress: informal. Reservations recommended. AE, CBC, DC, MC, V. Inexpensive–Moderate.*

Lodging

Bluewater Bay Resort. This major resort property, 18 miles north of Fort Walton Beach, is a bit out of the way, but the setting is lovely. It spreads over 1,800 acres and is surrounded by thick forests, freshwater lakes, and the blue waters of the Choctawatche Bay. Accommodations are in motel-type rooms that overlook the 120-slip marina, or in three-room villas, some of which have fireplaces and fully equipped kitchens. *Rte. 20E, Box 247, Niceville 32578, tel. 904/897–3613 or 800/874–2128 outside FL. 134 units. Facilities: several pools, 3 9-hole golf courses, tennis stadium, private beach, marina, water sports, exercise rooms, bicycles, playground. AE, MC, V. Moderate–Very Expensive.*

Ramada Beach Resort. This property has changed hands a few times, but it is once more a Ramada after a short stint as the Regency Beach Resort. Its design and decor are less imaginative than the more recent of the chain's facilities, but its location and 800-foot beach more than offset its boxy exterior. It's located on Okaloosa Island, just beyond the bridge. *U.S. 98E, Fort Walton Beach 32548, tel. 800/874–8962 or in FL, 904/ 243–9161. 454 rooms. Facilities: several pools, outdoor Jacuzzi, complete spa facilities, exercise room, tennis courts, several restaurants and lounges, 5-story waterfall with grotto bar. AE, DC, MC, V. Moderate–Expensive.*

**Jacksonville/
Jacksonville Beach**
Dining
★

Homestead. A down-home place with several dining rooms, a huge fireplace, and country cooking, this restaurant specializes in skillet-fried chicken, which comes with rice and gravy. Chicken and dumplings, deep-fried chicken gizzards, buttermilk biscuits, and strawberry shortcake also draw in the locals. *1712 Beach Blvd., Jacksonville Beach, tel. 904/249–5240. Dress: informal. AE, DC, MC, V. Inexpensive.*

The Tree Steakhouse. You select your steak and watch the staff cook it over a charcoal fire. Charbroiled chicken is also on the list, and there are several seafood dishes, too. The atmosphere is low-key and casual. *942 Arlington Rd., in Arlington Plaza, Jacksonville, tel. 904/725–0066. Jacket required. AE, CB, DC, MC, V. Inexpensive.*

Lodging
★ **Jacksonville Omni Hotel.** The city's newest hotel is a 16-story, ultramodern facility with a splashy lobby atrium and large, stylish guest rooms. All rooms have either a king-size or two double beds. You'll feel pampered anywhere in the hotel, but the extra frills are to be found in the two floors of the concierge level. *245 Water St., Jacksonville 32202, tel. 904/355–6664. 354 rooms. Facilities: heated pool, restaurant, lounge, exercise room, nonsmokers rooms, cable TV. AE, DC, MC, V. Moderate–Very Expensive.*

Sheraton at St. Johns Place. This five-story luxury hotel, connected to the Riverwalk complex, has modern rooms with either a king-size or two double beds. It's located right in the center of things, and the hotel bustles with activity inside and out. Rooms overlooking the St. Johns River command the highest prices. *1515 Prudential Dr., Jacksonville 32207, tel. 904/ 396–5100. 350 rooms, 18 suites. Facilities: concierge, pool, 2 lighted tennis courts, 2 restaurants, lounge, shopping arcade, privileges at Downtown Athletic Club, nonsmokers rooms, facilities for handicapped persons. AE, CB, DC, MC, V. Expensive–Very Expensive.*

Holiday Inn Oceanfront. A $2.5-million refurbishment in 1988 brought a bright new look to this perennial favorite on the beachfront. The atmosphere remains light and friendly; beds come in king, queen, or double sizes. *1617 N. First St., Jacksonville Beach 32250, tel. 800/331–6151 outside FL or 800/331–2817 in FL. 149 rooms. Facilities: pool, sauna, exercise room, tennis courts. AE, DC, MC, V. Moderate–Expensive.*

Sea Turtle Inn. A long-time area favorite, this high-rise property fronts on a wide beach. It's a family-oriented hotel with a pleasant atmosphere. *1 Ocean Blvd., Atlantic Beach 32233, tel. 800/874–6000 outside FL or 800/831–6600 in FL. Facilities: pool, restaurant, lounge. AE, CB, DC, MC, V. Moderate.*

Panama City Beach
Dining
★ **Boar's Head.** This is a casually elegant eatery that features live Maine lobster, gulf sea critters, steaks, prime rib, duckling, veal, and baby back pork ribs. Starters include fried blue-crab fingers and oysters baked with artichoke hearts. One of the casserole dishes is lightly spiced shrimp baked with fresh tomatoes and studded with capers and chunks of feta cheese. *17290 W. Hwy. 98, tel. 904/234–6628. Tie and jacket required. Reservations recommended. AE, CB, DC, MC, V. Open daily for dinner. Inexpensive–Moderate.*

★ **Capt. Anderson's.** This is a landmark seafood restaurant, where a long wait is the name of the game. The 600-seat restaurant overlooks the Grand Lagoon and has tables made of hatch covers. Some of the recipes originated on the Greek island of Patmos, whence came the father of the present owners. Fried crab fingers open things up; entrees include stuffed gulf flounder, crab cakes, and "the world's finest seafood platter." *5551 N. Lagoon Dr., tel. 904/234–2225. Dress: casual. No reservations. AE, MC, V. Closed Sun. Inexpensive–Moderate.*

Mai Lin. This is the only place in Panama City Beach where you can satisfy your taste for *moo goo gai pan*, sweet and sour pork, cashew chicken, and lemon chicken. There are a few hot and spicy Szechuan dishes and four combination dinners. Several American seafood dishes and a children's menu round things out. *14662 W. Hwy. 98 in Open Sands Shopping Center, tel. 904/233–1311. Dress: casual. AE, DC, MC, V. Inexpensive.*

Lodging **Edgewater Beach Resort.** Luxurious condominium resort with modern one- to three-bedroom units in beachside towers or golf villas. Its sprawling, 11,500-square-foot lagoon pool is replete with *palapas*, islands, waterfalls, whirlpools, and a veritable forest of vegetation. *11212 Hwy. 98 Alt., Panama City Beach 32407, tel. 800/874–8686 outside FL or 904/235–4044 in FL. 400 villas. Facilities: golf, miniature golf, 12 lighted tennis courts, pool, private beach, lawn games, health club, game rooms. AE, MC, V. Expensive–Very Expensive.*

Marriott's Bay Point Resort. A glamorous and gracious Bermuda-style, pastel-colored resort on Grand Lagoon, this $40-million complex was originally a residential yacht and country club. There are vaulted ceilings, solid oak accents, and balconied guest rooms and suites with gulf, bay, or golf-course views. *100 Delwood Beach Rd., Panama City Beach 32407, tel. 800/874–7105 outside FL or 904/234–3307 in FL. 385 units. Facilities: 2 golf courses, 5 swimming pools, indoor heated pool and Jacuzzi, 12 lighted tennis courts, numerous restaurants and lounges, a 145-slip marina, sailing school, and water sports. AE, MC, V. Moderate–Expensive.*

Miracle Mile Resort. Multihotel complex (Sheraton, Sands, and Gulfside Inns) that covers one mile of beachfront. *9450 S. Thomas Dr., Panama City Beach, tel. 800/874–6613 or 800/342–8720. 763 units. Facilities: pools, restaurants and lounges, beach equipment, tennis, cabanas. AE, CB, DC, MC, V. Moderate.*

Pensacola **Jamie's.** An intimate French setting is evident in this Victorian
Dining house with soft candlelight and fireplaces in each of its four
★ rooms. For lunch you might start with escargots Bourguignonne and move on to tournedos with mushroom sauce or marinated chicken breasts served with steamed vegetables. The dinner menu features smoked salmon; sweetbreads layered with prosciutto in a mushroom with port-wine sauce; and shrimp sautéed in a cream sauce flavored with Pernod. There are more than 200 labels on the wine list. *424 E. Zaragoza St., tel. 904/434–2911. Jacket required for dinner. Reservations recommended for dinner. AE, MC, V. Inexpensive.*

Scotto's. Pat and Richard Scotto's eatery is in a pink gothic-style house in Seville Square. Recipes are those of Richard's grandfather, who came here from Capri. Among the appetizers are oysters Florentine and fried calamari. Fettuccine Scotto is crabmeat and shrimp sautéed in butter and covered with a light cream sauce. Chicken *bianco* is breast of chicken stuffed with prosciutto and provolone, simmered in a white cream sauce, and served with fresh mushrooms over fettuccine. For the *dolci*, cheesecake is the specialty, but the chocolate amaretto mousse is also memorable. *300 S. Alcaniz St., tel. 904/434–1932. Jacket required for dinner. Reservations recommended for dinner. AE, DC, MC, V. Closed Sun. Inexpensive.*

★ **The Hopkins House.** Dining in this North Hill Preservation District house is done family-style at long tables. The fare is southern, and bowl after bowl is passed around: fried chicken, chicken and dumpliings, roast beef, green beans, creamed corn, biscuits, and cornbread. *900 N. Spring St., tel. 904/438–*

3979. Dress: casual. No reservations. No credit cards. Inexpensive.

Perry's Seafood House & Gazebo Oyster Bar. This big red house near the Naval Air Station dates from 1858, and in the 1950s it was a fraternity house. There is an extensive menu of fried, boiled, broiled, and baked sea creatures. Perry's baked fish comes with a topping of Greek garlic sauce and lemon juice. "Tips and Tails" is lobster and broiled filet mignon. There are homemade pastries for dessert. *2140 S. Barrancas Ave., tel. 904/ 434–2995. Dress: casual. No reservations. AE, MC, V. Closed Tues. Inexpensive.*

Lodging **Holiday Inn/Pensacola Beach.** This is a landmark facility with 1,500 feet of beachfront, rooms with either king-size or two double beds, and an informal, friendly atmosphere. *165 Ft. Pickens Rd., Pensacola Beach 32561, tel. 904/932–5361 or 800/ HOLIDAY. 150 rooms and suites. Facilities: heated pool, tennis, golf, restaurant, lounge, courtesy airport transportation. AE, CB, DC, MC, V. Moderate–Very Expensive.*

Pensacola Hilton. A renovated railway depot dating from 1912 serves as the lobby for this glitzy hotel. Fresh flowers and turn-of-the-century accent pieces decorate the lobby, which connects with the high-rise hotel via a two-story glass-canopied galleria. Standard rooms are spacious and modern; bilevel penthouse suites have wet bars, whirlpool baths, and a spectacular view. The hotel is right in the center of things, near the Seville Square Historic District. *200 E. Gregory St., Pensacola 32590, tel. 904/433–3336. 212 rooms. Facilities: courtesy airport limo, heated pool, tennis, health club, restaurants, lounges, shopping arcade. AE, CB, DC, MC, V. Moderate–Very Expensive.*

Perdido Sun. Luxury condo hotel with one- to three-bedroom units in a high-rise facility on Perdido Key. *13753 Perdido Key Dr., Pensacola 32507, tel. 904/492–2390. 104 units. Facilities: domed heated pool, outdoor pool, health club, sauna, whirlpool, restaurant. AE, MC, V. Expensive–Very Expensive.*

New World Landing. You'd never know that this was once a waterfront warehouse. Public areas have wood paneling, parquet floors, and oriental rugs. Furnishings in the individually decorated guest rooms are Chippendale, Queen Anne, and Louis XV, with accent pieces collected from around the world. There are four-poster or canopied beds, ceiling fans, and baths with handsome brass fixtures. *600 S. Palafox St., Pensacola 32501, tel. 904/432–4111 or 800/258–1103 outside FL. 14 rooms, 2 suites. Facilities: complimentary Continental breakfast on weekends, cable TV, 3 dining rooms, lounge. AE, CB, DC, MC, V. Moderate–Expensive.*

Hospitality Inn. A new all-suites budget inn with modern furnishings, kitchenettes, and king- or queen-size beds. There is a giant-screen TV in the lobby where you can watch movies and eat popcorn. *6900 Pensacola Blvd., Pensacola 32503, tel. 800/ 321–0052 ouside FL, 800/821–2073 in FL. 126 units. Facilities: pool, kennels, laundry, in-room movies. AE, DC, MC, V. Inexpensive.*

Ponte Vedra Beach **Marriott at Sawgrass.** This luxury seven-story hotel is the cen-
Lodging ter for resort operations of the 4,800-acre Sawgrass complex.
★ The attention to detail shows everywhere, from the impressive public areas to the spacious, well-appointed hotel and villa rooms. *Box 600, Ponte Vedra Beach 32982, tel. 800/872–7248. 598 units. Facilities: 5 golf courses, 13-court tennis center, sev-*

eral pools, private beach, cabana club, marina, water sports, fishing, horseback riding, exercise rooms, bicycles, several restaurants and lounges, shopping village. *AE, CB, DC, MC, V. Expensive–Very Expensive.*

St. Augustine **Columbia.** This is a huge Spanish structure with courtyards,
Dining verandas, and 28 dining rooms where Latin fare is featured. Specialties are paella, snapper *alicante* served with shrimp and almonds, and *arroz con pollo*. There are old family recipes from 1905, such as the salad of yellow rice with herbs. *98 St. George St., tel. 904/824–3341 or 800/227–1905. Dress: casual. Reservations advised. AE, CB, DC, MC, V. Inexpensive.*

Fiddler's Green. A half mile east of the Vilano Beach Bridge, this cozy Continental eatery has a huge stone fireplace, wicker furniture, and big windows overlooking the beach. Begin with snails baked in butter with herbs and garlic or oysters Rockefeller, then you can contemplate the variety of seafood specialties. Offerings include fish Vilano, a fillet stuffed with Parmesan and ricotta, then layered with eggplant and mozzarella, topped with marinara sauce, and served over pasta. *50 Anahma Dr., Vilano Beach, tel. 904/824–8897. Dress: casual. No reservations. AE, MC, V. Inexpensive–Moderate.*

★ **Raintree.** You may enjoy tarrying over a mint julep on the front porch of this restored Victorian house. The menu includes Maine lobster, filet mignon béarnaise, and rainbow trout *amandine*. A specialty is the grouper fillets, which are stuffed with crab mousse and baked in puff pastry. Tender veal medallions are filled with ricotta and prosciutto and served with a mustard sauce. *102 San Marco Ave., tel. 904/829–5953. Jacket required. Reservations advised. AE, DC, MC, V. Inexpensive.*

Lodging **Ponce de León Resort & Convention Center.** This is the city's
★ most famous hotel, and it occupies a good-size piece of land north of town. Public rooms are spacious and airy, with massive wrought-iron chandeliers and Spanish/Moorish flourishes. Accommodations range from rooms to two-bedroom villas with kitchenettes. *Box 98, St. Augustine 32085, tel. 800/228–2821 in FL or 800/824–2821 in USA. 200 units. Facilities: pool, restaurants, lounge, 18-hole championship golf course, putting green, tennis courts, playground, shuttle to historic district. Moderate–Expensive.*

Holiday Inn St. Augustine Beach. Five-story beachfront property with casual atmosphere and real staff warmth. Oceanside rooms are best and command highest prices. *1601 A1A S, St. Augustine Beach, tel. 904/471–2555. 150 units. Facilities: pool, restaurant, lounge. AE, MC, V. Moderate–Expensive.*

★ **Westcott House.** This is another frilly Victorian house, dating from the late 1880s. The eight guest rooms are furnished with American and European antiques, oriental rugs, and queen- and king-size beds. Continental breakfast is served to you either in the courtyard or in your room. Amenities: complimentary bottle of wine upon arrival, turndown service with chocolates and snifter of brandy, terry-cloth robes, cable TV, central air-conditioning and heat, private phones, non-smokers rooms. *146 Avenida Menendez, St. Augustine 32084, tel. 904/824– 4301. 8 rooms. MC, V. Moderate–Very Expensive.*

Casa de la Paz. A three-story Mediterranean Revival house overlooking Matanzas Bay, the "house of peace" is a mere youngster by St. Augustinian standards. It was built between 1910 and 1917. The antique-filled rooms and suites have hardwood floors, ceiling fans, and tiled baths. Amenities include central air-conditioning and heat, cable TV, complimentary sherry or wine, non-smokers rooms, room service, Continental breakfast. *22 Avenida Menendez, St. Augustine 32084, tel. 904/ 829–2915, 5 units, including 2 suites. AE, MC, V. Moderate–Expensive.*

★ **Victorian House.** This gingerbread house is one of several bed-and-breakfasts in the heart of the Historic District. Here, you'll find pine floors with hand-hooked rugs, canopy beds with handwoven coverlets and quilts, stenciled walls, and 19th-century antiques. In the morning a full breakfast is served in the dining room. *11 Cadiz St., St. Augustine 32084, tel. 904/ 824–5214. 5 rooms and 1 suite. AE, MC, V. Moderate.*

St. Francis Inn. Señor Gaspar Garcia built this house in 1791, and it has been used as a boarding house or inn since 1845. Accommodations come in a variety of sizes and shapes, from rooms to apartments to a five-room, two-story cottage. Amenities: central air-conditioning and heat, cable TV, private parking lot, complimentary admission to the nearby Oldest House, Continental breakfast, pool. *279 St. George St., St. Augustine 32084, tel. 904/824–6068. 16 units including 7 suites. MC, V. Inexpensive–Moderate.*

Seaside Lodging
★ **Seaside.** Victorian cottages, graceful beach pavilions, gazebos, broad brick roads and every imaginable amenity make up this combination residential/resort community. The cottages sport white picket fences, gingerbread trim, and porches with rocking chairs. They have from two to five bedrooms, are furnished right down to vacuum cleaners, but have no air conditioning. The community is across the road from the gulf; there are two beach pavilions and miles of unspoiled beaches. More private and quiet than this there isn't. *County Rte. 30A, off U.S. 98 west of Panama City, Seaside 32454, tel. 904/231–4224. 38 fully equipped cottages, and development continues. Facilities: pool, tennis court, croquet and badminton, bicycles rentals, Hobie Cats, beach chairs and umbrellas, nearby restaurants and lounges. AE, MC, V. Moderate–Very Expensive.*

Tallahassee Dining
Andrew's Second Act. Below the street you'll find a small Continental eatery that's reminiscent of a European cafe. It's a casual place for noontime soups and salads, but things turn more formal after dark. The dinner menu includes tournedos St. Laurent (beef broiled with garlic, scallions, and parsley butter) and rack of lamb Dijonnaise. **Andrew's Upstairs** is a salad bar/hot bar with mesquite grill, and **Andrew's Adams St. Cafe** is a deli. *102 W. Jefferson St., tel. 904/222–2759. Jacket required. Reservations advised. MC, V. Inexpensive–Moderate.*

Silver Slipper. This is the city's landmark steak house, with numerous small private rooms surrounding the main dining room. *531 Scotty La., tel. 904/386–9366. Jacket required. Reservations advised. AE, CB, DC, MC, V. Inexpensive–Moderate.*

Lodging
★ **Governor's Inn.** There is a country ambience in this chic inn that sits in the shadow of the capitol. There are skylit hallways, brick floors, and warm wood paneling throughout. The suites, in an incorporated 100-year-old carriage house, are furnished with antique four-poster beds, rock maple armoires, and black-oak writing desks. Some have loft bedrooms, whirlpools, and wood-burning fireplaces. Amenities include Continental breakfast, newspapers, turndown, terry-coth robe, laundry/ valet, room service, and cable TV with HBO and ESPN. *209 S.*

Adams St., Tallahassee 32301, tel. 904/681–6855. 41 units. Facilities: restaurant, lounge. AE, DC, MC, V. Expensive–Very Expensive.

Ramada Inn North. Newest of the city's three Ramadas, this one has striking modern lines and above average facilities. It's at the intersection of I–10 and U.S. 27. Amenities include valet service, remote-control TVs, and baby-sitting service. *2900 N. Monroe St., Tallahassee 32303, tel. 904/386–1027. 198 rooms. Facilities: pool, restaurant, lounge, spa privileges. AE, DC, MC, V. Moderate–Expensive.*

Wakulla Springs **Wakulla Springs Lodge.** This Spanish-style lodge is surrounded
Lodging by 800,000 acres of national forest and wildlife refuge. In the lobby and public rooms there are Moorish arched doorways, and ceiling paintings trace the area's history from the Aztecs to the Spanish. There is a huge fireplace in the lobby, and walk-in closets are in the spacious rooms. Rooms are 1930s style with no TVs, but they do have private baths and phones. *Rte. 61 and Rte. 267, Wakulla Springs 32305, tel. 904/224–5950. 27 rooms. Facilities: restaurant, gift shop, boat rides, spring-fed swimming area. MC, V. Inexpensive–Moderate.*

The Arts and Nightlife

The Arts Broadway touring shows, top-name entertainers, and other major events are booked into the **Florida Theatre Performing Arts Center** (128 E. Forsyth St., Jacksonville, tel. 904/355–ARTS), the **Jacksonville Civic Auditorium** (300 Water St., tel. 904/633–2900), the **Saenger Theater** (118 S. Palafox St., Pensacola, tel. 904/438–2827), the **Tallahassee–Leon County Civic Center** (Box 10604, Tallahassee 32302, tel. 904/487–1691), and the **Marina Civic Center** (8 Harrison Ave., Panama City Beach, tel. 904/769–1217).

Concerts **Jacksonville Symphony Orchestra** (tel. 904/630–0701) presents classical, pops, and youth concerts at the Civic Auditorium (300 Water St.).

St. Johns River City Band (tel. 904/396–0200) is a professional brass band that performs free concerts during the fall, spring, and summer at Jacksonville's Metropolitan Park and at Jacksonville Landing.

Pensacola Symphony Orchestra (tel. 904/435–2533) performs a season of five concerts at the Saenger Theatre (118 S. Palafox St.).

Tallahassee Symphony Orchestra (tel. 904/224–0461) presents five performances annually during the winter and spring at Florida State University's Ruby Diamond Auditorium.

Dance **The Florida Ballet** (123 E. Forsyth St., Jacksonville, tel. 904/353–7518) performs classic and modern dance in the fall and winter and at Christmas.

Film **The Film Institute of Jacksonville** (tel. 904/743–5531) presents a series of films twice weekly at the Jacksonville Museum and Florida College Kent Campus.

Opera **The Lyric Opera Company** (tel. 904/264–5796) presents three operas each year in the Jacksonville Civic Auditorium.

Theater ***Cross and Sword*** (Box 1965, St. Augustine 32085, tel. 904/471–1965), Florida's official state play, is performed annually mid-June–mid-August at St. Augustine's Amphitheater.

The Pensacola Little Theatre (186 N. Palafox St., tel. 904/432–

8621) performs plays and musicals during its season, fall–spring.

The River City Playhouse (128 Park St., Jacksonville, tel. 904/355–6137) is a local professional group that stages musicals, dramas, comedies, and children's theater. Local playwrights are often showcased.

Theatre Jacksonville 2032 San Marco Blvd., Jacksonville, tel. 904/396–4425) is one of the nation's oldest community theaters.

Alhambra Dinner Theatre (12000 Beach Blvd., Jacksonville, tel. 904/641–1212) presents six major musicals each year. Performances are in a 388-seat Spanish-style castle.

Nightlife   North Florida nightlife ranges from free-wheeling beachfront bars to mellow piano bars. In the major cities, pick up a copy of the free *See* magazine to see what's doing in town. The *Panama City Beach Times*, also free, has a rundown of what to do when the sun goes down.

Bars and   **Spinnakers** (28 Thomas Dr., Panama City Beach, tel. 904/234–
Nightclubs   7882) has 19 bars in its beachside facility and draws a very lively young crowd (closed Oct.–Feb.). **Pineapple Willie's** (Beach Blvd. at Thomas Dr., Panama City Beach, tel. 904/235–0928) features live music of the 1960s, '70s, and '80s; it caters to an over-25 crowd. **McGuire's Irish Pub** (600 E. Gregory St., Pensacola, tel. 904/433–6789) attracts local politicos, aviators, and tourists who like live traditional Irish music. The Pensacola Hilton's **L&N Lobby Bar** (200 E. Gregory St., Pensacola, tel. 904/433–3336) is a favorite yuppie meeting place. An over-30 crowd dances nightly at the **Boar's Head** (17290 W. Hwy. 98A, Panama City Beach, tel. 904/234–6628) to live '60s–'80s music. A classy crowd dances to live hits at **Tickets** (Pensacola Hilton, tel. 904/433–3336). A crowd that remembers the '50s and '60s gathers at **Happy Days Again** (5061 Mobile Hwy., Pensacola, tel. 904/456–6819). **Jamaica Joe's** (790 Santa Rosa Blvd., Fort Walton Beach, tel. 904/243–8937), and **The Moon** (1020 E. Lafayette St., Tallahassee, tel. 904/222–6666) are popular hangouts for the young set.

Comedy Clubs **The Punch Line** (8535 Bay Meadows Rd., Jacksonville, tel. 904/737–9399) is on the coast-to-coast circuit of comic performers. Performances are Tuesday–Sunday evenings.

Discos   There's a hip crowd and lots of special activities at **Nightown** (Palmetto and Azalea, Destin, tel. 904/837–6448). Young people dance to discs and live bands at **La Vela Beach Club** (8813 Thomas Dr., Panama City Beach, tel. 904/234–3866). You can expect a young crowd also at **Mac's Disco** (623 Osceola St., Tallahassee, tel. 904/575–7365).

Index

Personal Itinerary

Departure *Date*

Time

Transportation

Arrival *Date* *Time*

Departure *Date* *Time*

Transportation

Accommodations

Arrival *Date* *Time*

Departure *Date* *Time*

Transportation

Accommodations

Arrival *Date* *Time*

Departure *Date* *Time*

Transportation

Accommodations

Personal Itinerary

Arrival *Date*   *Time*

Departure *Date*   *Time*

Transportation

Accommodations

Arrival *Date*   *Time*

Departure *Date*   *Time*

Transportation

Accommodations

Arrival *Date*   *Time*

Departure *Date*   *Time*

Transportation

Accommodations

Arrival *Date*   *Time*

Departure *Date*   *Time*

Transportation

Accommodations

Addresses

Name	Name
Address	Address
Telephone	Telephone
Name	Name
Address	Address
Telephone	Telephone
Name	Name
Address	Address
Telephone	Telephone
Name	Name
Address	Address
Telephone	Telephone
Name	Name
Address	Address
Telephone	Telephone
Name	Name
Address	Address
Telephone	Telephone
Name	Name
Address	Address
Telephone	Telephone
Name	Name
Address	Address
Telephone	Telephone

Fodor's Travel Guides

U.S. Guides

Alaska
Arizona
Atlantic City & the
  New Jersey Shore
Boston
California
Cape Cod
Carolinas & the
  Georgia Coast
The Chesapeake Region
Chicago
Colorado
Dallas & Fort
  Worth

Disney World & the
  Orlando Area
Florida
Hawaii
Houston &
  Galveston
Las Vegas
Los Angeles, Orange
  County, Palm Springs
Maui
Miami, Fort Lauderdale,
  Palm Beach
Michigan, Wisconsin,
  Minnesota

New England
New Mexico
New Orleans
New Orleans (Pocket
  Guide)
New York City
New York City (Pocket
  Guide)
New York State
Pacific North Coast
Philadelphia
The Rockies
San Diego
San Francisco

San Francisco (Pocket
  Guide)
The South
Texas
USA
Virgin Islands
Virginia
Waikiki
Washington, DC
Williamsburg

Foreign Guides

Acapulco
Amsterdam
Australia, New Zealand,
  The South Pacific
Austria
Bahamas
Bahamas (Pocket
  Guide)
Baja & the Pacific
  Coast Resorts
Barbados
Belgium & Luxembourg
Bermuda
Brazil
Britain (Great Travel
  Values)
Budget Europe
Canada
Canada (Great Travel
  Values)
Canada's Atlantic
  Provinces
Cancún, Cozumel,
  Mérida, the
  Yucatán
Caribbean

Caribbean (Great
  Travel Values)
Central America
China
China's Great Cities
Eastern Europe
Egypt
Europe
Europe's Great Cities
Florence & Venice
France
France (Great Travel
  Values)
Germany
Germany (Great Travel
  Values)
Great Britain
Greece
The Himalayan
  Countries
Holland
Hong Kong
Hungary
India, including Nepal
Ireland
Israel

Italy
Italy (Great Travel
  Values)
Jamaica
Japan
Japan (Great Travel
  Values)
Jordan & the Holy Land
Kenya, Tanzania,
  the Seychelles
Korea
Lisbon
Loire Valley
London
London (Great Travel
  Values)
London (Pocket Guide)
Madrid & Barcelona
Mexico
Mexico City
Montreal &
  Quebec City
Munich
New Zealand
North Africa
Paris

Paris (Pocket Guide)
Portugal
Rio de Janeiro
The Riviera (Fun on)
Rome
Saint Martin &
  Sint Maarten
Scandinavia
Scandinavian Cities
Scotland
Singapore
South America
South Pacific
Southeast Asia
Soviet Union
Spain
Spain (Great Travel
  Values)
Sweden
Switzerland
Sydney
Tokyo
Toronto
Turkey
Vienna
Yugoslavia

Special-Interest Guides

Bed & Breakfast
  Guide: North America
Health & Fitness
  Vacations

Royalty Watching
Selected Hotels of
  Europe

Selected Resorts
  and Hotels of the U.S.
Shopping in Europe

Skiing in North
  America
Sunday in New York

Help us evaluate hotels and restaurants for the next edition of this guide, and we will send you a free issue of Fodor's newsletter, TravelSense.

Title of this guide:

1 **Hotel** ❑ **Restaurant** ❑ *(check one)*

Name

Number/Street

City/State/Country

Comments

2 **Hotel** ❑ **Restaurant** ❑ *(check one)*

Name

Number/Street

City/State/Country

Comments

3 **Hotel** ❑ **Restaurant** ❑ *(check one)*

Name

Number/Street

City/State/Country

Comments

General Comments

Please complete for a free copy of TravelSense

Name

Number/Street

City/State/Zip

Business Reply Mail

First Class   Permit № 7775   New York, NY

Postage will be paid by addressee

Fodor's Travel Publications

201 East 50th Street

New York, NY 10022

Help us evaluate hotels and restaurants for the next edition of this guide, and we will send you a free issue of Fodor's newsletter, TravelSense.

Title of this guide:

1 Hotel ❏   Restaurant ❏   *(check one)*

Name

Number/Street

City/State/Country

Comments

2 Hotel ❏   Restaurant ❏   *(check one)*

Name

Number/Street

City/State/Country

Comments

3 Hotel ❏   Restaurant ❏   *(check one)*

Name

Number/Street

City/State/Country

Comments

General Comments

Please complete for a free copy of TravelSense

Name

Number/Street

City/State/Zip

Business Reply Mail

First Class   Permit No 7775   New York, NY

Postage will be paid by addressee

Fodor's Travel Publications

201 East 50th Street

New York, NY 10022